CONSUMER GUIDE™

AUTOMOBILE BOOK

ALL NEW 2000 EDITION

Publications International, Ltd.

CONTENTS

INTRODUCTION

USING THE BUYING GUIDE

SHOPPING TIPS

WARRANTIES AND SERVICE CONTRACTS

SAFETY

CONSUMER COMPLAINTS

INSURANCE

2000 BEST BUY AND RECOMMENDED

CONTENTS

INTRODUCTION

Buying a new car has always been a big decision, and it's not getting simpler. Different financing options, increasingly sophisticated technology, and a wider range of new models give shoppers a wealth of choices, but also more pitfalls to avoid.

Knowledge is the key to making an intelligent purchase. The more you know about the vehicle you're considering, the better. This edition of the *Automobile Book* gives you the information you need, including prices, specifications, ratings, and evaluations for more than 190 new cars, minivans, sport-utility vehicles, and pickup trucks.

To help you compare direct competitors, we divide vehicles into 14 model categories based on size, price, and market position. Ratings and Specifications, which appear at the back of the book, group vehicles by model category for easier comparison.

Each report contains a general description of the vehicle and its features based on information supplied by manufacturers. Evaluations and judgments are results of test drives conducted by the editors. Test vehicles are furnished by the manufacturers, and we use them as their owners would: commuting, shopping, vacations, highway travel, stop-and-go city driving.

Also included with each report are the latest available prices. In cases where 2000-model prices were not announced in time for publication, we include 1999 prices as a reference.

BEST BUY, RECOMMENDED, AND BUDGET BUYS

The Auto Editors of Consumer Guide™ have selected Best Buys as the best overall values in their respective model categories. This is our highest rating. Other models labeled Recommended also merit serious consideration. This is our second-highest rating. In some categories, Budget Buys have been chosen. These are good cars that are especially keenly priced against competitors.

RATINGS

In charts that begin on page 220, the editors rate each model's performance, room, comfort, and ergonomics, from a low of 1 to a high of 5. Each model also is rated for overall value based on its price. The ratings are derived from our road tests. Only one model in each model line is rated; usually the most popular one. For more details on our ratings, see the Ratings section.

SPECIFICATIONS

Engine specifications are included along with the vehicle report, but other specifications, such as wheelbase, overall length, and interior dimensions, are in charts that begin on page 213. All dimensions and capacities are supplied by the vehicle manufacturers and represent the base model in the line. Optional equipment usually increases curb weight, and such items as larger tires may increase overall height.

PRICE INFORMATION

We list these different prices for each vehicle:

• Retail price: the manufacturer's suggested retail price as set by the factory. "Suggested" is the key word here. The actual selling price is dictated by supply, demand, and competition.

• Invoice price: what the dealer pays to buy the car from the factory—the wholesale price.

• Destination charge: the cost of shipping the car to the dealership from the factory or port of entry.

Car companies are free to change their prices at any time, and may have done so after this issue was published. If a dealer claims our prices are incorrect, or the information in this book doesn't match what you see in showrooms, contact us and we'll do our best to help. Good luck in shopping for your next new vehicle!

Consumer Guide™
7373 N. Cicero Ave.
Lincolnwood, IL 60712

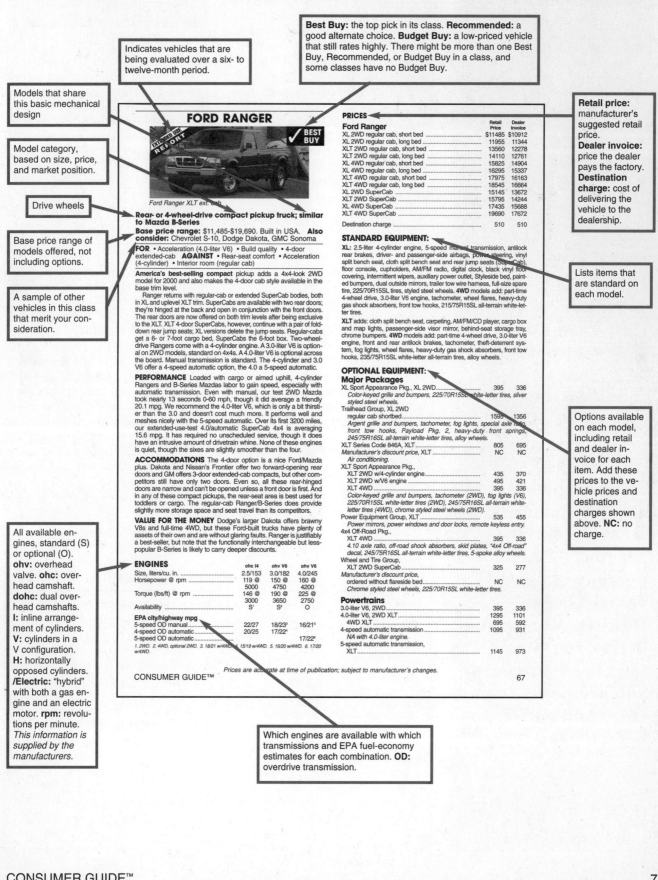

Indicates vehicles that are being evaluated over a six- to twelve-month period.

Best Buy: the top pick in its class. Recommended: a good alternate choice. Budget Buy: a low-priced vehicle that still rates highly. There might be more than one Best Buy, Recommended, or Budget Buy in a class, and some classes have no Budget Buy.

Models that share this basic mechanical design

Model category, based on size, price, and market position.

Drive wheels

Base price range of models offered, not including options.

A sample of other vehicles in this class that merit your consideration.

Retail price: manufacturer's suggested retail price. Dealer invoice: price the dealer pays the factory. Destination charge: cost of delivering the vehicle to the dealership.

Lists items that are standard on each model.

Options available on each model, including retail and dealer invoice for each item. Add these prices to the vehicle prices and destination charges shown above. NC: no charge.

All available engines, standard (S) or optional (O). ohv: overhead valve. ohc: overhead camshaft. dohc: dual overhead camshafts. I: inline arrangement of cylinders. V: cylinders in a V configuration. H: horizontally opposed cylinders. /Electric: "hybrid" with both a gas engine and an electric motor. rpm: revolutions per minute. *This information is supplied by the manufacturers.*

Which engines are available with which transmissions and EPA fuel-economy estimates for each combination. OD: overdrive transmission.

FORD RANGER

✓ BEST BUY

Ford Ranger XLT ext. cab

Rear- or 4-wheel-drive compact pickup truck; similar to Mazda B-Series
Base price range: $11,485–$19,690. Built in USA. **Also consider:** Chevrolet S-10, Dodge Dakota, GMC Sonoma

FOR • Acceleration (4.0-liter V6) • Build quality • 4-door extended-cab **AGAINST** • Rear-seat comfort • Acceleration (4-cylinder) • Interior room (regular cab)

America's best-selling compact pickup adds a 4x4-look 2WD model for 2000 and also makes the 4-door cab style available in the base trim level.

Ranger returns with regular-cab or extended SuperCab bodies, both in XL and uplevel XLT trim. SuperCabs are available with two rear doors; they're hinged at the back and open in conjunction with the front doors. The rear doors are now offered on both trim levels after being exclusive to the XLT 4-door SuperCabs, however, continue with a pair of fold-down rear jump seats; XL versions delete the jump seats. Regular-cabs get a 6- or 7-foot cargo bed, SuperCabs the 6-foot box. Two-wheel-drive Rangers come with a 4-cylinder engine. A 3.0-liter V6 is optional on 2WD models, standard on 4x4s. A 4.0-liter V6 is optional across the board. Manual transmission is standard. The 4-cylinder and 3.0 V6 offer a 4-speed automatic option, the 4.0 a 5-speed automatic.

PERFORMANCE Loaded with cargo or aimed uphill, 4-cylinder Rangers and B-Series Mazdas labor to gain speed, especially with automatic transmission. Even with manual, our test 2WD Mazda took nearly 13 seconds 0-60 mph, though it did average a friendly 20.1 mpg. We recommend the 4.0-liter V6, which is only a bit thirstier than the 3.0 and doesn't cost much more. It performs well and meshes nicely with the 5-speed automatic. Over its first 3200 miles, our extended-use-test 4.0/automatic SuperCab 4x4 is averaging 15.6 mpg. It has required no unscheduled service, though it does have an intrusive amount of drivetrain whine. None of these engines is quiet, though the sixes are slightly smoother than the four.

ACCOMMODATIONS The 4-door option is a nice Ford/Mazda plus. Dakota and Nissan's Frontier offer two forward-opening rear doors, and GM offers 3-door extended-cab compacts, but other competitors still have only two doors. Even so, all these rear-hinged doors are narrow and can't be opened unless a front door is first. And in any of these compact pickups, the rear-seat area is best used for toddlers or cargo. The regular-cab Ranger/B-Series does provide slightly more storage space and seat travel than its competitors.

VALUE FOR THE MONEY Dodge's larger Dakota offers brawny V8s and full-time 4WD, but these Ford-built trucks have plenty of assets of their own and are without glaring faults. Ranger is justifiably a best-seller, but note that the functionally interchangeable but less-popular B-Series is likely to carry deeper discounts.

ENGINES

	ohv I4	ohc V6	ohv V6
Size, liters/cu. in.	2.5/153	3.0/182	4.0/245
Horsepower @ rpm	119 @ 5000	150 @ 4750	160 @ 4200
Torque (lbs/ft) @ rpm	146 @ 3000	190 @ 3650	225 @ 2750
Availability	S[1]	S[2]	O

EPA city/highway mpg

5-speed OD manual	22/27	18/23[3]	16/21[5]
4-speed OD automatic	20/25	17/22[4]	
5-speed OD automatic			17/22[6]

1. 2WD. 2. 4WD, optional 2WD. 3. 18/21 w/4WD. 4. 15/19 w/4WD. 5. 16/20 w/4WD. 6. 17/20 w/4WD.

CONSUMER GUIDE™

PRICES

Ford Ranger

	Retail Price	Dealer Invoice
XL 2WD regular cab, short bed	$11485	$10912
XL 2WD regular cab, long bed	11955	11344
XLT 2WD regular cab, short bed	13560	12278
XLT 2WD regular cab, long bed	14110	12761
XL 4WD regular cab, short bed	15825	14904
XL 4WD regular cab, long bed	16295	15337
XLT 4WD regular cab, short bed	17975	16163
XLT 4WD regular cab, long bed	18545	16664
XL 2WD SuperCab	15145	13672
XLT 2WD SuperCab	15795	14244
XL 4WD SuperCab	17435	15688
XLT 4WD SuperCab	19690	17672
Destination charge	510	510

STANDARD EQUIPMENT:

XL: 2.5-liter 4-cylinder engine, 5-speed manual transmission, antilock rear brakes, driver- and passenger-side airbags, power steering, vinyl split bench seat, cloth split bench seat and rear jump seats (SuperCab), floor console, cupholders, AM/FM radio, digital clock, black vinyl floor covering, intermittent wipers, auxiliary power outlet, Styleside bed, painted bumpers, dual outside mirrors, trailer tow wire harness, full-size spare tire, 225/70R15SL tires, styled steel wheels. **4WD** models add: part-time 4-wheel drive, 3.0-liter V6 engine, tachometer, wheel flares, heavy-duty gas shock absorbers, front tow hooks, 215/75R15SL all-terrain white-letter tires.

XLT adds: cloth split bench seat, carpeting, AM/FM/CD player, cargo box and map lights, passenger-side visor mirror, behind-seat storage tray, chrome bumpers. **4WD** models add: part-time 4-wheel drive, 3.0-liter V6 engine, front and rear antilock brakes, tachometer, theft-deterrent system, fog lights, wheel flares, heavy-duty gas shock absorbers, front tow hooks, 235/75R15SL white-letter all-terrain tires, alloy wheels.

OPTIONAL EQUIPMENT:
Major Packages

	Retail	Dealer
XL Sport Appearance Pkg., XL 2WD	395	336
Color-keyed grille and bumpers, 225/70R15SL white-letter tires, silver styled steel wheels.		
Trailhead Group, XL 2WD regular cab shortbed	1595	1356
Argent grille and bumpers, tachometer, fog lights, special axle ratio, front tow hooks, Payload Pkg. 2, heavy-duty front springs, 245/75R16SL all-terrain white-letter tires, alloy wheels.		
XLT Series Code 846A, XLT	805	695
Manufacturer's discount price, XLT	NC	NC
Air conditioning.		
XLT Sport Appearance Pkg.,		
XLT 2WD w/4-cylinder engine	435	370
XLT 2WD w/V6 engine	495	421
XLT 4WD	395	336
Color-keyed grille and bumpers, tachometer (2WD), fog lights (V6), 225/70R15SL white-letter tires (2WD), 245/75R16SL all-terrain white-letter tires (4WD), chrome styled wheels (2WD).		
Power Equipment Group, XLT	535	455
Power mirrors, power windows and door locks, remote keyless entry.		
4x4 Off-Road Pkg.,		
XLT 4WD	395	336
4.10 axle ratio, off-road shock absorbers, skid plates, "4x4 Off-road" decal, 245/75R16SL all-terrain white-letter tires, 5-spoke alloy wheels.		
Wheel and Tire Group,		
XLT 2WD SuperCab	325	277
Manufacturer's discount price, ordered without flareside bed.	NC	NC
Chrome styled wheels, 225/70R15SL white-letter tires.		

Powertrains

3.0-liter V6, 2WD	395	336
4.0-liter V6, 2WD XLT	1295	1101
4WD XLT	695	592
4-speed automatic transmission	1095	931
NA with 4.0-liter engine.		
5-speed automatic transmission, XLT	1145	973

Prices are accurate at time of publication; subject to manufacturer's changes.

67

SHOPPING TIPS

Knowing what you want—or need—before you start making the rounds of dealerships can save time and money. It's human nature to go looking for a practical family vehicle like a minivan and be distracted in the showroom by a flashy red sedan that costs more. And more buyers than ever are climbing out of passenger cars and into trucks—sport-utility vehicles, minivans, and pickups—which account for 45 percent of new-vehicle sales. However, if emotion drives you to an impulsive purchase, you are likely to pay more and suffer regret later.

Car and light-truck sales have been on the fast track for five years, peaking at an estimated 17 million in 1999—the most ever. With so many brands and types of vehicles to choose from, consumers have more choices than ever.

This adds up to a buyer's market during a period of record sales. For the third year in a row, price increases have been modest, and several manufacturers are holding the line at 1999 price levels. Rebates, low-rate financing, and other incentives abounded last year, and those deal sweeteners should become more common this year because sales probably will cool down a bit.

Affordability remains a serious concern, however. The average transaction price for a new vehicle reached a record $23,600 last year, according to the National Automobile Dealers Association, as Americans showed greater appetite for higher-priced models.

Even in a buyer's market, it pays to explore your options and make informed, practical decisions about your next new vehicle.

GETTING STARTED

To get the right vehicle at the best price, it's more important than ever to do your homework before starting to shop. Begin with the basics.

• Decide how much you can afford and how much you are willing to pay before you shop for a vehicle. If, like most consumers, you have to borrow money, shop for a loan before you shop for a vehicle. The table at the bottom of this page can help you determine your monthly payments. It lists how much you'd have to pay for each $1000 borrowed based on the interest rate and term of the loan. For instance, if you borrow $10,000 for 4 years at 8 percent interest, your monthly payments would be $24.41 x 10, or 244.10. Also keep in mind you'll probably need a down payment of about 20 percent (in the example above, about $2000), unless your trade-in is worth that much. The total of your loan, down payment, and any trade-in would have to cover the price of the car, as well as fees and

Monthly payment per $1000 borrowed

Interest rate	2-Year	3-Year	4-Year	5-Year
0%	$41.67	$27.78	$20.83	$16.67
1%	42.10	28.21	21.26	17.09
2%	42.54	28.64	21.70	17.53
3%	42.98	29.08	22.13	17.97
4%	43.42	29.52	22.58	18.42
5%	43.87	29.97	23.03	18.87
6%	44.32	30.42	23.49	19.33
7%	44.77	30.88	23.95	19.80
8%	45.23	31.34	24.41	20.28
9%	45.68	31.80	24.89	20.76
10%	46.15	32.27	25.37	21.25
11%	46.61	32.74	25.85	21.75

sales tax. Your bank or credit union can discuss loan options to help you set a realistic price range that fits your budget.

You may need to look at insurance costs, too (see the Insurance section), as a new car might cost more to insure than your current vehicle. High-performance cars and some sport-utility vehicles cost more to insure than family sedans. Young drivers crave sporty cars, but high insurance premiums can put these cars out of reach.

Buying a new car is a financial stretch for many consumers and out of reach for some. Many have turned to used cars and others to leasing, hoping to avoid a hefty down payment and lower their monthly payment. (See "Lease or Buy?—Which Is Better?")

Your fuel costs are based not only on miles per gallon but whether the car requires expensive premium grade gas.

Maybe the right "car" for you is a "truck." Sport-utility vehicles, minivans, and pickups are "light trucks," and they account for nearly half of new-vehicle sales. However, some of these vehicles are tall and/or long, so make sure the one you want will fit in your garage. Specifications are listed in the back of this book. Whatever the case, it pays to do preliminary research before visiting dealerships.

Take the process in steps:
• Choose a model with options that suits your needs—not just your desires. The Buying Guide contains information and advice on each model and the latest prices.
• Once you've decided on a vehicle, compare prices from at least three dealers. But also look for dealers that appear to provide good service after the sale.

BE A SMART SHOPPER

Informed shoppers have an edge when negotiating price. To get the best deal, plan your moves and take your time.
• Know what you want, but be flexible. Narrow your list to two or three models that best suit your needs and pocketbook.
• Shop competing dealers to compare prices on the same car with the same equipment. That can be a tall order, as extra-cost options get more complex. Get written price quotes that are good next week, not just today.
• Never put a deposit on a car just to get a price quote. When a deposit is necessary to order or hold the car you intend to buy, keep it small: $100 is plenty.
• Manufacturers frequently group options in packages. This often reduces the cost of all the included items.
• Size up supply and demand for the car you want. A good deal on a slow selling model might be below dealer invoice, while a popular car can still command full suggested retail price. Dealer inventories often tell the story; if there are numerous examples of a model on the lot, it's probably not a hot seller.
• Consider resale value. How much will your car be worth when it's time to sell? Consult used-car price guides at the library to get an idea of which models hold their value best. A heavily-discounted car is no bargain down the road if it has low resale value.
• Test drive the exact car you decide on—before you buy. Think you want manual shift and a sport suspension? A 15-minute test drive might convince you to go with automatic and a softer suspension. A sunroof might sound enticing, but could be mounted so far back that it doesn't provide an "open air" feeling. Bottom line: Don't settle on major features until you've tried them.
• Establish the price of the new car before talking about the value of your trade-in. But if you've decided to trade in your old car, remember that the lowest "bottom line" figure is what you're after. One dealer may give you a lower price on the new car but also a lower price on your trade-in. In the end, you may decide to sell your old car yourself.

REBATES AND INCENTIVES

These are legitimate money-savers, and are likely to be available on more models this year.

Incentives are placed on specific models for a specified period. They come three ways: cash rebates direct to the customer, low interest rates on loans, and cash incentives to the dealer to sell a particular car. In each case, the manufacturer—not the dealer—is the source of this generosity. Remember, too, that rebates are designed to spur sales of specific models that are already on dealers' lots, so they won't apply to a car you have "built to order."

Cash rebates are usually advertised and consist of a check made out from the automaker to the buyer. As an alternative, you might get a low interest loan, often available instead of a cash rebate. Rates typically range from 2.9 percent to 7.9 percent APR and can be lower for shorter term loans. You have to do the math to determine which option is best: the low-interest loan, or receiving cash in hand.

Dealer incentives are trickier. It can be difficult to find out whether a manufacturer is offering dealers cash to sell certain cars, though the business or automotive sections of some newspapers run lists. But remember that incentives come out of the manufacturer's pocket, not the dealer's.

"BELOW INVOICE"—TOO GOOD TO BE TRUE?

Even if there are no rebates or incentives on a car, the dealer could probably sell it at invoice and still make a profit. However, few will do

Lease or Buy—Which Is Better?

More than one-third of consumers lease their vehicles instead of buying them. On vehicles costing $40,000 or more, about 60 percent are leased.

For most consumers, leasing a new vehicle every two or three years is more expensive than buying one and keeping it after the final payment. The greatest benefits of leasing are that you drive a newer vehicle that is always under warranty and seldom needs more than routine maintenance such as oil changes. Those benefits are likely to cost more, not less.

Some financial advisers argue that most advantages to owning a car have disappeared, making leasing more attractive. For example, the interest on car loans is not tax deductible (except for business use), and, as a depreciating asset, ownership is not a benefit.

Before you either embrace or reject leasing, having a better understanding of this alternative to buying should make it easier to decide which is better for you.

What You Should Know

Lease contracts were notorious for cryptic and incomplete language, but federal regulations that took effect two years ago require clearer language in lease contracts and advertising to remove some of the mystery.

Here are the key disclosures required in leasing contracts:
• Amount due at lease signing, with a separate list itemizing the charges. They include the down payment (or "capitalized cost reduction") and whether it is by trade-in, rebate, or cash, plus items such as a security deposit, "acquisition" or "bank fee," first monthly payment, and title and registration fees.
• Monthly payments, including when they are due and the total number of payments due over the term of the lease.
• Other charges, such as a "disposition fee" or "termination fee" if the consumer doesn't buy the vehicle at the end of the lease. This also covers items not included in the monthly payment, such as the annual state vehicle tax.
• Total of payments, including everything due up front, the monthly payments, and other charges.
• How the monthly payment is determined: This section must show the value of the vehicle ("gross capitalized cost"), the capitalized cost reduction (down payment, trade-in, etc.), the net amount remaining as the basis for the lease payments, and the residual value (how much the vehicle is worth at the end of the lease).

The contract also must show the depreciation and "rent charge"—the interest and other lease charges the consumer will pay. These two items add up to the base monthly payment.
• Purchase option at end: The contract must specify if there is an option to buy at lease end and name the price.

Read the Fine Print

Though consumers receive a lot of information in black-and-white, there are still some grey areas with leasing and potential costs to be aware of:

On most leases, you have to pay up front the first month's payment and a refundable security deposit.

Some leases require an up-front "acquisition fee" or "bank fee" to cover the cost of processing the credit application. Some add a "disposition" or "termination fee" at the end if you do not buy the car. Others may not charge these fees, which often are more than $500.

Ask about these fees because they can add $20 or more to your monthly payment. Because there is so much competition, some dealers and leasing companies may waive one or both, especially for repeat customers.
• Because they don't own their leased vehicle, some consumers don't take good care of it. However, when a leased vehicle is returned, it is inspected for excess wear that can lower its resale value. Damage such as ripped upholstery, dents, and broken accessories are obvious things you will be charged for. Some items you consider "normal"—parking lot dings and soft drink stains on the upholstery—may be "excessive" to the leasing company.

Because this area is still open to interpretation, consumers should treat leased vehicles with tender, loving care. If you're uncertain about what you will have to pay for, take the vehicle in a month or two before the lease expires for an estimate from the leasing company. This gives you the option of having the repairs done elsewhere at

so unless they're deserate for sales. It works like this: Many manufacturers refund to dealers a small percentage of the invoice price, such as 2 or 3 percent. These "holdbacks" are distributed to dealers as a lump sum several times a year.

Manufacturers might also offer dealers various cash incentives to sell specific cars, with the incentive increasing as they sell more cars. With these twin "safety nets," dealers can make a profit even if they sell the car at invoice price.

DEALING WITH DEALERS

Some dealers cling to traditional hard-sell methods. Others take a kinder, gentler approach. If a dealer makes you uncomfortable, look elsewhere. Buying a car should be a pleasant experience, so find a dealer who makes it one.

Even at dealerships where the atmosphere is congenial, however, the salesperson's job is to make as much money as possible on each sale. Your quest as a consumer is to get the lowest possible price on the car you want. You need to find a happy medium between getting a good deal and allowing the salesperson a reasonable profit.

When you're at the dealership, keep these tips in mind:
• Dealers make money not only from the sale itself but by selling financing, insurance, and add-ons. As profits from actual sales decline, dealers try harder to push

lower cost.

• Most leases prohibit customizing vehicles with aftermarket accessories such as vinyl tops, chrome exterior trim, even trailer hitches. Better to ask before you install them.

• All leases allow a certain number of miles per year, typically between 10,000 and 15,000. Exceed the limit and you will pay an excess mileage charge of 10 to 25 cents per mile when you return the car, a hefty addition to your total cost.

Does that mean leasing is a bad idea for those who rack up lots of miles? Not really. If you try to sell a car with high mileage, you'll pay a penalty in lower resale value, so ownership is no different.

Leasing companies usually allow buying additional miles at lower cost when the lease is signed, and some will refund your money if you don't use them. Be realistic about your mileage needs at the beginning and you're less likely to get burned at the end.

• Ask about "gap protection," which covers the full value of the vehicle if it is totaled in an accident or stolen. Most leases include gap ("guaranteed automobile protection") coverage, but some may still charge extra for it.

• The consumer typically pays for the sales tax, annual vehicle registration fees and taxes, maintenance, and insurance. All this should be spelled out in the contract, but find out which are included in your monthly payment and which you have to pay separately.

• Early termination fees: Before signing, ask whether you can terminate the lease early and how much of a penalty you must pay. It could cost thousands of dollars to get out of a lease.

Is Leasing for You?

Even if you master all the terms and facts of a particular lease, there is a bigger issue: Is leasing better than buying? Here are some guidelines:

• Leasing is most beneficial to those who claim their car as a business expense. Nearly all leasing expenses attributed to business purposes can be deducted.

If you buy a car for business, you can still write it off, but there are limits on depreciation. The maximum depreciation you can claim is $3160 the first year, $5000 the second year, $2950 the following year, and $1775 in subsequent years. Leasing has no such limits.

If you can deduct business use of your car, it is best to consult a tax adviser to find out which is better for you.

• A large down payment isn't required for most leases, and monthly lease payments also are generally lower than a loan payment for an equivalent car.

When you buy, banks usually want a down payment of 20 percent. With the average transaction price of a new car at nearly $24,000, that means $4800 in cash or trade-in value. If you don't have that much, a lease that requires only $500 down might be a better bet.

• While monthly payments may be lower on a lease, in the long run it is usually cheaper to buy and keep cars five years or longer.

• Lease now, buy later? To lease a car for a few years and then buy it at the end of the lease is probably more expensive than buying it in the first place. Most states charge sales tax on the cost of the lease, and then charge you again if you buy the car.

• Most leases are for two or three years. Avoid leases that run longer than the car's factory warranty, as you could be stuck paying for repairs on a vehicle you don't own.

Where to Look

Just as it pays to shop when you're buying, shop for a lease and have dealers compete for your business. One dealer might waive the down payment or cut the monthly payment to win your business. Make sure you compare costs for identical vehicles. A lease with low monthly payments and a hefty down payment might cost more overall than one with higher monthly payments but no money down. Do the math.

New-car dealers are a logical place to start your shopping, but there are alternatives. Leasing agents or brokers that lease several brands might beat the deal from the new-car franchise down the street. Some banks and credit unions also offer consumer leases.

If you lease from a dealer who uses an in-house finance company like Ford Credit or GMAC, at the end of the lease you generally can leave the car with any dealer who sells the same brand. This may not be the case if you lease from an agent or broker or if a dealer uses an independent leasing company. Be sure to ask.

these "back-end" items.

Popular moneymakers include rustproofing, "protection packages," burglar alarms, powerful audio systems, and extended-service contracts. Dealers pay little for these and mark them up sharply. You can usually buy them elsewhere for less money—and you might not need them at all. (See Warranties and Service Contracts section.)

• Because today's market is so competitive, try to get dealers to bid for your business through lower prices. As a rule, don't tell Dealer A how much Dealer B quoted you on the car you want. Just let each know that you will buy from the one who gives the best price and service.

• For a good deal, find a good dealer. Price is important, but it shouldn't be your only consideration. A dealership with a reputation for good service and giving customers the benefit of the doubt may deserve to charge more.

Ask friends and neighbors about their experiences with dealers. Your local Better Business Bureau can provide a Reliability Report, stating whether complaints have been filed against a specific dealership. Look for a pattern of complaints or for signs that problems remain unresolved.

• Notice how you're greeted when you arrive at a dealership, and whether the same salesperson stays with a customer through the entire transaction. Some pass cus-

tomers off to a "closer" who specializes in high-pressure tactics.
• Beware of dealers who slap a second price sticker onto every car, listing high-profit extras you may not want.
• Look for salespeople who exhibit real product knowledge, not just rattle off a set speech, and are neither pushy nor overly friendly. If you feel bulldozed or intimidated, shop elsewhere. You should expect—and get—professional treatment.
• Check out the service department of the dealership. Ask some people who are having their cars

serviced if they are happy with their buying experience and treatment after the sale.
• Many dealers continue to treat women and minorities differently from white males. Studies have found that women and minorities are less likely to be offered the lowest price on a car. Look for dealers and salespeople who treat every customer with an equally professional approach.
• Special-ordering the exact car and equipment you desire is usually possible only on domestic models. Dealers can search other dealers for the model you want

and can sometimes install options once the car arrives but seldom can order from the factory.

Even domestic dealers might be reluctant to order a car. Delivery can take six weeks or longer, though some manufacturers are speeding the process. The dealer may demand a deposit to order a car, which is fair because he has no guarantee you won't back out of the deal, leaving him with a car he might have trouble unloading.

The dealer has a financial interest in selling a car that is in stock. Storing the car on his lot is costing him money. Also, rebates and in-

Similar Models

It is common for manufacturers to use the same automotive platform—a car's basic architecture—for more than one vehicle. It is also typical for these "similar models" to share major mechanical components, including engines. However, they usually have individualized styling and are sold under different model names or even different brand names. Choosing the least-expensive member of the group might save you hundreds, even thousands, of dollars.

DaimlerChrysler

Plymouth	Dodge	Chrysler	Other Brand
—	Avenger	Sebring coupe	—
Breeze	Stratus	Cirrus, Sebring convertible	—
Neon	Neon	—	—
—	Intrepid	Concorde, LHS, 300M	—
Voyager	Caravan	Town & Country	—

Ford Motor Company

Ford	Mercury	Lincoln	Other Brand
Taurus	Sable	—	—
Crown Victoria	Grand Marquis	—	—
Contour	Cougar	—	—
—	Villager	—	Nissan Quest
Explorer	Mountaineer	—	—
Ranger	—	—	Mazda B-Series
Expedition	—	Navigator	—

American Honda Motor Co., Inc.

Honda	Acura
Accord	TL

American Isuzu Motors Inc.

Isuzu	Other Brand
Rodeo	Honda Passport

Nissan Motor Corporation USA

Nissan	Infiniti
Maxima	I30
Pathfinder	QX4

centives generally apply only to vehicles "in dealer stock."

NEW WAYS TO SHOP

Some people love to haggle, but others dread the prospect. Now, there are ways for you to minimize—or even skip—that part of the process.

If you're uneasy about negotiating with a dealer, shop for a "one-price" model, such as a Saturn. Or, pick dealers that advertise "no-haggle" sales practices. Major new players in the new-car business are changing the way cars are sold. CarMax and AutoNation started with used-car superstores, but both have obtained several franchises to sell new vehicles. Their plan is to become one-stop sources for everything automotive, providing a hassle free, uniform buying experience for several brands of vehicles.

There also are independent brokers, agents, and buying services that work in place of dealers or as "middlemen" who link consumers with dealers. Brokers typically receive payment from dealers for steering business their way. Some are dealers themselves, or they purchase cars from dealers for resale. Seven states ban brokers and 10 states license them.

One service we vouch for is the Consumer Guide Auto Buying Service (1-888-402-9182), which directs consumers to nearby dealers who offer vehicles at prearranged, nonnegotiable prices.

WEB SHOPPING

Technology is transforming the buying process, and many consumers now buy or shop for a car by computer to bypass all or some traditional routes.

Nearly two-thirds of the 19,600 new-car dealers have their own Web site, the National Automobile Dealers Association estimates. On over 50 percent of those dealer Web sites, consumers can browse new- and used-vehicle inventories.

Several on-line services transmit purchase requests to a participating dealer, who then responds with a price for that model. More dealers are getting involved in such programs, but the price you receive through the Internet may not be the lowest available, so it still pays to shop more than one location.

The trend toward a "virtual showroom" continues to grow. Nearly every automaker has established a site on the Internet to provide product information. Some are entertaining and informative, allowing you to "build" your vehicle of choice, obtain a complete retail price list, even apply for a loan and make an appointment with a dealership. Others are simply on-line sales brochures.

AutoNation, the largest dealership group with about 400 new-vehicle franchises, plans to sell vehicles over the Internet in the future. Ford Motor Company recently announced a venture with

Toyota Motors Sales, USA

Toyota	Lexus
Camry	ES 300
Land Cruiser	LX 470

General Motors

Chevrolet	Pontiac	Oldsmobile	Buick	Cadillac	Other Brand
—	—	—	Park Avenue	Seville	—
Impala, Monte Carlo	Grand Prix	Intrigue	Century, Regal	—	—
—	Bonneville	—	LeSabre	—	—
Camaro	Firebird	—	—	—	—
Cavalier	Sunfire	—	—	—	—
Metro	—	—	—	—	Suzuki Swift
—	Grand Am	Alero	—	—	—
Prizm	—	—	—	—	Toyota Corolla
Venture	Montana	Silhouette	—	—	—
Astro	—	—	—	—	GMC Safari
Blazer	—	Bravada	—	—	GMC Jimmy
Tahoe	—	—	—	—	GMC Yukon
Tahoe Limited, Z71	—	—	—	Escalade	GMC Denali
Silverado	—	—	—	—	Sierra
S-10 Pickup	—	—	—	—	GMC Sonoma, Isuzu Hombre
Suburban	—	—	—	—	GMC Yukon XL
Tracker	—	—	—	—	Suzuki Vitara

Volkswagen United States Inc.

Volkswagen	Audi
Golf, Jetta, New Beetle	A4, TT
Passat	A6

Every car sold in the U.S. must display in its window a "Monroney sticker" showing the manufacturer's suggested retail price for the vehicle and all of its options. Many dealers also affix a second price sticker containing items added at the dealership. See the "Window Stickers" section of the text for details.

Above: The federally mandated price sticker shows the manufacturer's suggested retail price for the vehicle and all of its options. **Right:** This is an example of what a second price sticker originated by the dealer might look like. These are items added at the dealership. They are often of dubious value and always generate huge profit margins for the dealer. Get a description of each item, then decide whether you wish to balk at paying the charge as listed.

XYZ MOTORS

PROTECTION PKG	$389
A.D.P.	225
RUSTPROOFING	226
ADVERTISING	200
DEALER PREP	121
SUBTOTAL	1161
XYZ MOTORS TOTAL PRICE	$23,981

Microsoft Corp. that will allow consumers to custom order vehicles over the Web and track its production and delivery. Consumers will still have to visit a dealer to sign a contract and take delivery.

The bottom line is that the retail end of the automobile business is changing rapidly—and mainly for the better.

Even with all of the options available, eventually you will probably have to go to a dealership to complete the deal. Besides, seeing, touching, and driving a vehicle is much more informative than a "virtual reality" display on a computer screen. A face-to-face meeting with a salesperson may also generate more answers than an on-line service can provide.

Our advice is to explore the new ways of shopping for a car, but don't abandon the traditional approaches.

WINDOW STICKERS

You can find out a lot about a particular vehicle just by "window shopping."

All cars sold in the U.S. must have posted on a side window what is called a "Monroney sticker" (named for the Congressman who introduced the legislation). This law does not apply to light trucks, including passenger vans and most sport-utility vehicles, but most car companies and dealers voluntarily put the price sticker on trucks. You decide if you want to do business with one that doesn't.

The Monroney sticker must show:
• The manufacturer's suggested retail price (MSRP) for the vehicle and all factory-installed options.
• A destination charge for shipping from final assembly point or port of importation to the dealer.
• EPA fuel economy estimates.

DEALER PRICE STICKERS

Many dealers add a second window sticker that lists accessories installed at the dealership, and/or other charges. Everything on this added sticker should be considered "optional"—and probably overpriced. If you don't want a particular item—say, pinstriping or rustproofing—don't pay for it. If the dealer insists it is already on the car, you can still refuse to pay.

Such add-on stickers typically include:
• Rustproofing: Most manufacturers advise against extra-cost rustproofing (see Warranties and Service Contracts).
• Protection packages: These usually consist of dealer-applied paint sealers and fabric protectors, often in addition to rustproofing. They are of little or no value or duplicate the substances applied at the factory or those you can apply yourself for far less cost.
• M.V.A., A.D.P., or another abbreviation or code: These are smoke screens for dealer-invented profit-generators. M.V.A. stands for "Market Value Adjustment," and A.D.P. is "Additional Dealer Profit." Both sound official but are created by dealers to squeeze more money out of you. Some dealers dream up dandy new names for old add-on charges, such as "Currency Valuation Fee" and "Import Tariff." Those that do are best avoided.

Rather than arguing over individual charges like dealer prep, take the "bottom line" approach. Simply ask for a final price—the total amount you'll have to pay—and compare it to the price offered by competing dealers.

ADVERTISING FEES

Dealers might add a separate charge for advertising. Challenge this extra fee.

Some manufacturers do levy an advertising fee on some or all cars. Dealers also join regional associations to advertise their vehicles—though not every dealer participates.

Dealers often post ad fees that are round numbers, like $200. However, the fees are usually assessed as a percentage of each car's invoice price: typically 1 to 1.5 percent for domestic models, as high as 3 percent for other manufacturers. How can 1.5 percent of the invoice price work out to $200 on every vehicle?

Businesses should factor in advertising costs when setting their prices. After all, how many others try to charge you separately for them?

GAS GUZZLER AND LUXURY TAXES

Special federal taxes apply to certain cars. A gas-guzzler tax is levied on cars that average less than 22.5 mpg in combined city/highway driving based on the EPA fuel economy estimates. This tax does not apply to light trucks, including SUVs and vans.

A federal luxury tax applies to all passenger vehicles with a gross vehicle weight of less than 6000 pounds. Pickup trucks and most SUVs are exempt from this tax, which for calendar 2000 is expected to be 5 percent of the transaction price over $36,000. The tax is levied on the purchase price before any trade-in value is deducted.

BEFORE YOU SIGN

Buying a new set of wheels is a big event. Rushing to complete a deal invites a dealer to take advantage of you.
• Before you sign anything, read the entire contract and be certain you understand exactly what

Study the Fine Print

Not all of the statements and numbers in retail car ads mean quite what they appear to.
This is a composite advertisement for fictional models, but it contains
examples of advertising techniques you should watch for in real ads.

Who declared this dealer #1? Even if true, compared to how many other dealers?

Every new-car dealer is a "factory outlet."

All sales of new cars are "factory authorized." And is this really a liquidation?

Does "new" mean it's a 2000 model, or a leftover 1999?

An attractive price, but you must surrender all rebates, put a minimum amount down, and pay additional fees. Plus, the deal is based on a 60-month loan to "qualified buyers." Are you one of them? Could you get better terms elsewhere? The dealer sets the value of your trade-in. Who determines whether you qualify for the rebates and the 7.95 percent loan rate? Note, too, that only cars in dealer stock are included.

Acknowledges that other factors contribute to dealer profit. And what is the source of the "invoice available for inspection"? Is it the true factory invoice?

Not everyone qualifies for 2.9 percent. Plus, a 10-percent down payment is often required.

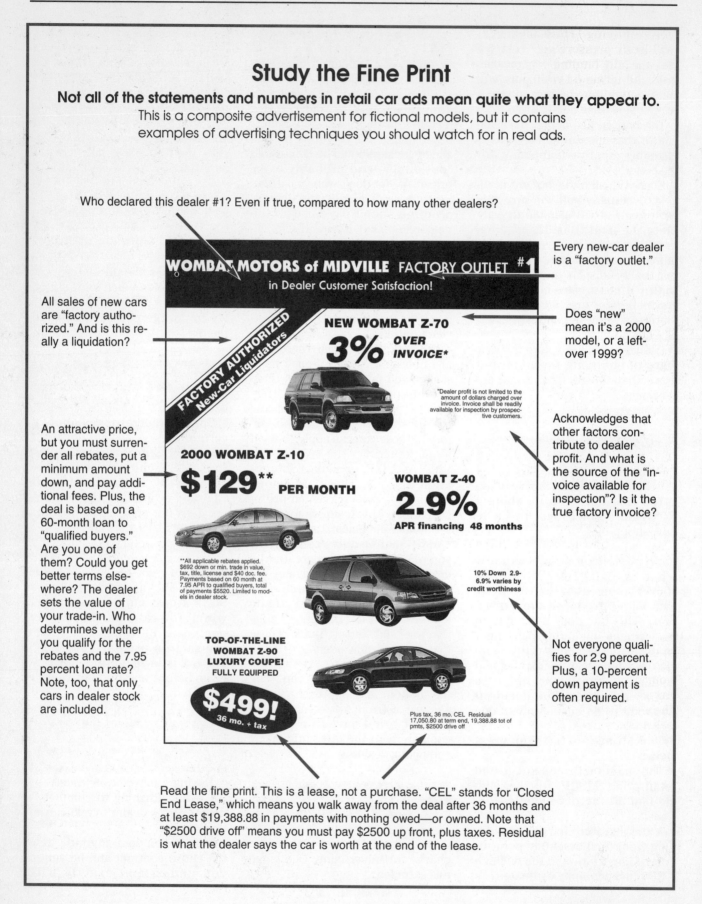

WOMBAT MOTORS of MIDVILLE FACTORY OUTLET #1
in Dealer Customer Satisfaction!

FACTORY AUTHORIZED
New-Car Liquidators

NEW WOMBAT Z-70
3% OVER INVOICE*

*Dealer profit is not limited to the amount of dollars charged over invoice. Invoice shall be readily available for inspection by prospective customers.

2000 WOMBAT Z-10
$129** PER MONTH

WOMBAT Z-40
2.9%
APR financing 48 months

**All applicable rebates applied. $692 down or min. trade in value, tax, title, license and $40 doc. fee. Payments based on 60 month at 7.95 APR to qualified buyers, total of payments $5520. Limited to models in dealer stock.

10% Down 2.9-6.9% varies by credit worthiness

TOP-OF-THE-LINE WOMBAT Z-90 LUXURY COUPE!
FULLY EQUIPPED

$499!
36 mo. + tax

Plus tax, 36 mo. CEL Residual 17,050.80 at term end, 19,388.88 tot of pmts, $2500 drive off

Read the fine print. This is a lease, not a purchase. "CEL" stands for "Closed End Lease," which means you walk away from the deal after 36 months and at least $19,388.88 in payments with nothing owed—or owned. Note that "$2500 drive off" means you must pay $2500 up front, plus taxes. Residual is what the dealer says the car is worth at the end of the lease.

you're buying. The salesperson will likely pressure you to sign to get a legally binding contract that sets the terms of your purchase. Worse, you may be in a hurry because you're eager to drive off in your new car. Once you sign that document, it's difficult, if not impossible, to get it changed.

• If in doubt, take the contract home. Go over it at your own pace, and contact the dealer if you have questions. If a dealer doesn't want you to take the contract home, get a written purchase agreement that spells out all the details. Once you're satisfied with that agreement, it can be written into a contract.

Here's what a contract should spell out:

• Sale price: The amount you've agreed to pay for the car and optional equipment, plus any dealer-installed accessories.

• Down payment: How much you have to pay immediately, either in cash or combined with a trade-in.

• Trade-in value: The amount you're getting for your old car.

• Destination charge: Sometimes called freight, this is the cost of shipping the car to the dealer. Many automakers advertise prices that include the destination charge, but it is still listed separately on the window sticker. Dealers get no discount; they pay the amount listed, and so will you. Just don't pay it twice.

• Sales tax: Check with your state or local government to determine how tax is assessed in your area. Most states levy sales tax on the full purchase price of the new vehicle. In some states, sales tax is calculated on the net price after trade-in value has been deducted.

• Total cost: Be sure the all-important "bottom line" is filled in, so you know your total price including options, accessories, destination charge, dealer prep, and taxes. If a dealer leaves this portion blank, you can end up paying more than you expected.

• Loans: Federal regulations require lenders to disclose all charges. Be sure you know how much you're borrowing, the interest rate, your monthly payment, the length of the loan (in months), and the total amount you will pay over the life of the loan.

Four-Wheel-Drive Systems and How They Differ

All sport-utility vehicles (SUVs) and pickup trucks are available with 4-wheel drive, and some cars and minivans are as well. But there are substantial differences in the types of 4WD systems offered. The most important determining factor is whether 4WD can be left engaged on dry pavement. Part-time 4WD systems must be "turned off" on dry pavement to avoid mechanical damage. Full-time 4WD and permanently engaged 4WD systems can be left engaged, a convenience that relieves the driver of deciding when 4WD is needed. Here is a more detailed description of each system. In some cases, more than one system is available for a given vehicle.

Part-time 4WD. The most basic system. Transfer case gives a choice of settings, usually 2WD, 4WD High, and 4WD Low. It can usually be shifted from 2WD to 4WD High "on the fly," which means while driving down the road, but 4WD must be disengaged when running on dry pavement. This is because there's no mechanical compensation for the differences in tire speeds that occur when rounding corners. Leaving 4WD engaged on dry pavement causes wear—and eventually failure—on the transfer case, which is expensive to fix. Part-time systems are inconvenient in a light rain or patchy snow, because the system must be switched back and forth while driving. To engage 4WD Low, which is typically used only in severe off-road driving, the vehicle must be brought to a stop.

Full-time 4WD. More advanced—and more convenient. The transfer case gives a choice of settings, usually 2WD, 4WD High, and 4WD Low, sometimes adding an Automatic 4WD or Full-Time 4WD setting. Full-Time systems can be left engaged even when running on dry pavement. To engage 4WD Low, which is typically used only in severe off-road driving, the vehicle must be brought to a stop.

Permanently engaged 4WD. Sometimes called "All-Wheel Drive." Transfer case is always in 4WD, so there is no switch for the driver to bother with. Some systems offer a 4WD Low for serious off-road work.

It is important to note that while 4WD helps you "go in the snow," it does little to aid cornering ability and virtually nothing for braking. Many drivers, finding they can accelerate in snow as quickly as on dry roads, assume they can corner and brake as well, also. This is untrue, and often leads to over-confidence, which in turn leads to accidents.

WARRANTIES AND SERVICE CONTRACTS

The warranties that come with your new vehicle are probably comprehensive enough to make extra-cost coverage and additional rustproofing a waste of money. A factory warranty is the manufacturer's pledge to absorb certain repair or replacement costs until a specified period of time elapses or the car has accumulated a stated number of miles—whichever comes first. It is expressed as number of years/number of miles, the most common being 3 years/36,000 miles. Here's an overview of how manufacturers' warranties work and what they generally cover.

The **Basic Warranty** is "bumper-to-bumper" coverage for the entire car. It generally excludes tires and the battery, which are warranted by their manufacturers. Typical exclusions of most basic warranties include:

• Normal wear and maintenance items (oil, filters, brake linings).
• Damage from the environment (hail, floods, "acts of God").
• Damage from improper maintenance, such as incorrect fuel.
• Damage caused by the owner or vehicle occupants.

A few manufacturers include a **Maintenance Warranty** that covers routine maintenance such as oil changes, wiper-blade replacement, and other items. Some last the duration of the basic warranty, but others are for a shorter period.

A separate **Powertrain Warranty** that extends beyond the basic warranty is offered by some manufacturers. It applies to such components as the engine, transmission, and drive shafts.

Also extending beyond the basic warranty is a **Corrosion Warranty** that covers "perforation" rust.

Roadside Assistance that offers on-the-road help is now included with most new vehicles.

If the factory warranty has not expired when the vehicle is sold, the warranty may be transferred to the new owner at no charge. Specific second-owner exclusions may apply to leased and fleet vehicles.

The federal government requires two other warranties. The **Exhaust Emission Warranty** extends for 8 years/80,000 miles on some items, such as the catalytic converter and on-board diagnostic device. The **Passenger Restraint Warranty** covers seatbelts and airbags for 5 years/50,000 miles.

SERVICE CONTRACTS

Service contracts are insurance policies, not real warranties, and are often loaded with loopholes. They are sold at dealerships but typically underwritten by independent agents.

These extra-cost contracts usually extend coverage of the car's powertrain and other major components beyond the duration of the manufacturer's warranty. If you expect to put a lot of miles on your vehicle, it could be worth the price.

Be careful, however. With most policies, it's the underwriter who determines which items will be covered, and the list might not be as complete as the factory's bumper-to-bumper or powertrain coverage. In some, all work must be approved beforehand, and there's a deductible of $25 to $100 per visit.

Many independent service-contract firms have gone bankrupt, stranding both the dealers and customers. A contract issued by the vehicle manufacturer may be better, as the automaker is more likely to remain in business.

Scrutinize any service contract at home. Get a copy of the actual contract, not a summarizing brochure.

RUSTPROOFING

With modern anti-corrosion techniques, aftermarket rustproofing is unnecessary—and may actually be harmful. Also, the plans are often loaded with loopholes. But dealers still push them due to their high profit margins.

Toyota's statement is typical: "Application of additional rust-inhibiting materials is not necessary." General Motors goes further, warning that "after-manufacture rustproofing products may create an environment which reduces the corrosion resistance built into your vehicle." Holes drilled into doors and fenders to apply rustproofing may actually promote rusting and void your factory anti-corrosion warranty.

2000 Manufacturers' Warranties

Make/Model	Bumper-To-Bumper Warranty (Years/miles)	Maintenance Warranty (Years/miles)	Powertrain Warranty (Years/miles)	Corrosion Warranty (Years/miles)	Roadside Assistance (Years/miles)
Acura	4/50,000	—	—	5/50,000	4/50,000
Audi	3/50,000	3/50,000	—	12/unlimited	3/50,000
BMW	4/50,000	3/36,000[1]	—	6/unlimited	4/50,000
Buick	3/36,000	—	—	6/100,000	3/36,000
Cadillac	4/50,000	—	—	6/100,000	4/50,000
Chevrolet	3/36,000	—	—	6/100,000	3/36,000
Chrysler	3/36,000	—	—	5/100,000	3/36,000
Daewoo	3/36,000	—	5/60,000	5/unlimited	3/36,000
Dodge	3/36,000	—	—	5/100,000	3/36,000
Ford	3/36,000	—	—	5/unlimited	3/36,000
GMC	3/36,000	—	—	6/100,000	3/36,000
Honda	3/36,000	—	—	5/50,000	Not Available
Hyundai	5/60,000	—	10/100,000	5/100,000	5/unlimited
Infiniti	4/60,000	—	6/70,000	7/unlimited	4/unlimited
Isuzu	3/50,000	1/12,000	10/120,000[2]	6/100,000	5/60,000
Jaguar	4/50,000	—	—	6/unlimited	4/50,000
Jeep	3/36,000	—	—	5/100,000	3/36,000
Kia	3/36,000	—	5/60,000	3/50,000	3/36,000
Land Rover	4/50,000	—	—	6/unlimited	4/50,000
Lexus	4/50,000	1/12,000[3]	6/70,000	6/unlimited	6/70,000
Lincoln	4/50,000	1/12,000[4]	—	5/unlimited	4/50,000
Mazda	3/50,000	—	—	5/unlimited	3/50,000
Mercedes-Benz	4/50,000	4/50,000	—	4/50,000	Unlimited
Mercury	3/36,000	—	—	5/unlimited	3/36,000
Mitsubishi	3/36,000	—	5/60,000	7/100,000	3/36,000
Nissan	3/36,000	—	5/60,000	5/unlimited	Extra Cost
Oldsmobile	3/36,000	—	—	6/100,000	3/36,000
Plymouth	3/36,000	—	—	5/100,000	3/36,000
Pontiac	3/36,000	—	—	6/100,000	3/36,000
Porsche	4/50,000	—	—	10/unlimited	4/50,000
Saab	4/50,000	1/12,000[4]	—	6/unlimited	4/50,000
Saturn	3/36,000	—	—	6/100,000	3/36,000
Subaru	3/36,000	—	5/60,000	5/unlimited	3/36,000
Suzuki	3/36,000[5]	—	—	3/unlimited	3/36,000
Toyota	3/36,000	—	5/60,000	12/unlimited	Not Available
Volkswagen	2/24,000	2/24,000	10/100,000[6]	12/unlimited[7]	2/24,000
Volvo	4/50,000	—	—	5/unlimited	4/unlimited

1. 4/50,000 on 750 models. 2. 6/60,000 on Hombre. 3. First and second scheduled maintenance. 4. First scheduled maintenance. 5. 2/24,000 on Vitara convertible. 6. 5/50,000 on Eurovan. 7. 6/unlimited on Cabrio and EuroVan.

SAFETY

Airbags have been the center of attention in automotive safety the past few years, as the federal government and auto industry search for an answer to a perplexing question: How do you make airbags safer for *everyone* without increasing the risks for *anyone*?

Federal regulations require that all 1999 model year and later passenger cars and light trucks (except those over 8500 pounds gross vehicle weight) have dual front airbags. More than 90 million vehicles on the road today have driver-side airbags, and more than 65 million have dual front airbags.

About the same time airbags became universal, it became apparent they didn't always work as intended. While there was no question airbags saved lives, there also was growing evidence that they *took* lives, especially the lives of small women and children, because they deployed too aggressively.

Airbags have saved an estimated 4650 lives, according to the National Highway Traffic Safety Administration, the federal agency that creates and enforces our motor vehicle safety regulations.

However, at least 145 people have died from airbag deployments since 1990, many in low-speed collisions. The number may rise after additional investigation of fatal accidents.

NHTSA says most of the deaths occurred because occupants were improperly restrained or not at all. Of the victims, 83 were children riding in the front passenger seat. Eighteen were infants in rear-facing child seats, which are not supposed to be placed in front, and 56 were unbelted or improperly belted, leaving them too close to the airbag when it deployed at maximum force.

Forty of the 56 drivers killed were improperly belted. Four of six adult passengers killed were unbelted.

Despite overwhelming evidence most victims were not properly restrained, accident investigations indicated airbags deployed with too much force. Children and women who are 5-foot 2-inches or shorter appeared most vulnerable.

That resulted in a short-term change to NHTSA's testing procedures to certify airbags (explained below under "Making Airbags Safer" and "Crash Tests.") and proposals for overhauling auto-safety regulation.

While airbags dominate the news, there is much more to automotive safety that consumers should consider when choosing a new vehicle. If you are concerned about the safety of you and your family, we recommend you study this entire section and explore other resources if necessary.

HOW AIRBAGS WORK

An airbag is an inflatable cushion that remains concealed in the steering-wheel hub or, with a passenger-side airbag, in the dashboard, until it is activated by a crash.

In a frontal impact of about 12 mph or more, sensors send an electrical signal to trigger the explosive release of a gas that inflates the fabric bag. All of this happens in less than one-tenth of a second, and the bags inflate at speeds of up to 200 mph.

The inflated bag creates a protective cushion between the person and the steering wheel, dashboard, and windshield. After a

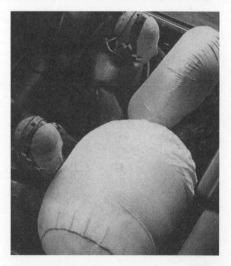

Since 1999, all new passenger cars and light trucks have been equipped with dual front airbags.

fraction of a second, the bag deflates, restoring visibility and allowing the driver to continue steering the car to a safe stop.

Airbags are designed to open only in frontal collisions, which account for 60 percent of occupant fatalities. Frontal airbags have no effect in side or rear impacts.

Many people incorrectly believe that an airbag is the only type of restraint needed. As NHTSA discovered in studying the deaths caused by airbags, people who aren't properly restrained by seatbelts can end up perilously close to an airbag, which deploys with tremendous force.

MAKING AIRBAGS SAFER

It is ironic that airbags, which were mandated by the federal government to save lives, had to be fixed so they would stop taking lives.

NHTSA responded to deaths from airbags by changing test procedures and allowing auto manufacturers to use lower-powered airbags starting with the 1998 model year. Though the federal requirements for occupant protection did not change, the force with which frontal airbags deploy could be reduced 20 to 35 percent. Safety officials and car companies also urged that children under 13 be seated in back, small adults should move as far back as possible from airbags—at least 10 inches—and everyone should buckle up.

Analysis by NHTSA, auto manufacturers, and the insurance industry of early crash and injury data on vehicles with depowered airbags indicates they provide ample protection while reducing the risks to those most vulnerable—small women and children.

Deaths and injuries have occurred in cars equipped with depowered airbags, but researchers don't think the airbags were at fault. Instead, the victims were unbelted and either too close to the airbag when it deployed or too out of position for it to be effective.

"As far as we know, there has never been a fatality because an airbag was not powerful enough," a spokesperson for the Insurance Institute for Highway Safety said of the depowered airbags.

If you are concerned about the dangers of airbags to your family, you should obtain information from the manufacturer about the type of airbag system that is installed on a particular vehicle you are considering.

SMARTER AIRBAGS

Advanced airbag systems that deploy with less force, or not at all, based on whether a child, small adult, or no one is sitting in a seat are coming soon, ahead of federal regulations that will require them.

NHTSA has proposed rules that would require—by the 2003 model year—smart airbags that will deploy based on the size, weight, and position of occupants, whether they are belted or unbelted, and the speed or severity of the crash.

Elements of smart airbag technology are available now, but the car companies say a truly smart system is a few years away.

NHTSA and the car companies prefer to call them "advanced" airbags because describing them as "smart" implies the current systems are "dumb." However, the new technology is, indeed, smarter than ordinary airbags, which deploy at maximum force when triggered by collision sensors.

The 2000 Ford Taurus and Mercury Sable have sensors that detect the driver's seat position and whether the seatbelts are buckled. The front airbags will deploy at one of two inflation levels depending on vehicle speed, crash severity, or whether the front occupants are belted. The airbags will not deploy at speeds below about 10 mph if front occupants are belted, and they will deploy with lower force in a minor collision if the driver's seat is all the way forward.

General Motors will introduce an airbag suppression system on the 2000 Cadillac Seville. The bag won't deploy if the front passenger seat is empty or occupied by a child weighing less than 66 pounds. GM uses a grid of wires in the seat cushion to measure weight distribution.

The Hyundai Sonata has a weight sensor that disables the front airbag if it detects less than 66 pounds in the passenger seat. If it detects less than 33 pounds, it disables the side airbag as well.

Several other manufacturers use dual-stage inflators that adjust deployment levels depending on crash speed. Among them are Acura, Audi, BMW, Mercedes-Benz, and Volvo. Though they differ in details, they generally work like this: If the front-seat occupants are unbelted, the airbags will deploy in a collision of about 12 mph. The bags will not deploy until about 15 mph if they are belted. On some, the passenger-side airbag will not deploy if a sensor detects less than roughly 25 pounds in the seat.

Mercedes also offers the BabySmart child seat recognition system. A sensor in the front passenger seat detects when a special child seat (sold by Mercedes and a company called Britax) is in use and automatically disables the airbag. Without the special child seat, a second sensor disables the airbag if there is less than 26 pounds in the passenger seat.

AIRBAG ON-OFF SWITCHES

NHTSA allows the installation of on-off switches that disable airbags for consumers with special needs, such as a medical condition that can make deployment dangerous, or the need to carry a child in the front seat.

Only pickup trucks, 2-seat passenger cars, and cars with back seats too small to hold a child safety seat can be equipped with on-off switches installed by the manufacturer at the factory. In these vehicles, children and infants have to ride in front, where they are exposed to the full force of the passenger-side airbag.

On other vehicles, NHTSA reviews requests from consumers to disable airbags on a case-by-case basis.

Through August 1999, NHTSA authorized 54,329 cutoff switches, but only 8748 switches were reported installed. NHTSA officials surmise that some consumers change their minds after getting approval, and others cannot find a dealer or repair shop willing to install the switch because of liability risks. The cost of installing a switch varies, but NHTSA says it averages $150.

NHTSA says 78 percent of the on-off switches approved for the driver's side are because the consumer is too close—less than 10 inches—to the airbag. Sixteen percent are for both proximity to the airbag and medical reasons, and six percent are for medical reasons. On the passenger side, 69 percent of approvals are to carry infants or children in the front seat; the rest are for medical reasons.

To apply for an on-off switch, consumers need to obtain a one-page form from NHTSA (the telephone number and address are listed in this section under "Auto Safety Hotline." Consumers must certify that they fit one of the high-risk categories described on the authorization form and submit the form to NHTSA for approval.

SIDE AIRBAGS

Despite continuing debate over front airbags, more manufacturers offer side airbags aimed at protecting occupants in side collisions.

Side airbags (at shoulder) and inflatable head restraints are being offered in an increasing number of vehicles. (BMW photo)

Side collisions account for 30 percent of passenger-vehicle deaths, the second highest after frontal collisions. Unlike front airbags, which are required on all passenger cars and light trucks, side airbags are not federally mandated. All vehicles must meet federal side-impact standards, but the rules do not specify side airbags.

Side airbags are mounted in the sides of seatbacks or in door panels. They usually are smaller than front airbags but deploy quicker because the crush zone is much narrower. Sensors must detect impact in 4-5 milliseconds, versus 15-20 milliseconds in a frontal crash. They must inflate within 20 milliseconds, versus the usual 60-75 milliseconds.

Most car companies first offered side airbags on luxury models that cost $30,000 and more, but now they are available on lower-priced vehicles such as the Chevrolet

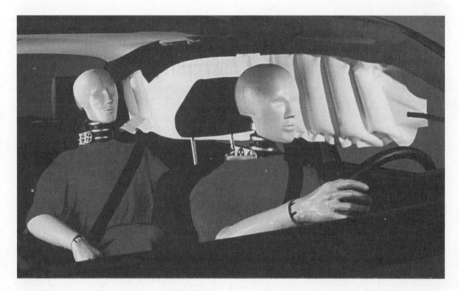

Some vehicles now come with side "curtain" airbags, full-length upper-body restraints that drop down from above the side windows in a side collision to protect front and rear passengers. (Mercedes-Benz photo)

Prizm, Ford Focus, and Volkswagen Jetta.

A handful of companies offer side airbags for the rear seat, and a few offer side head protection.

BMW has a feature called the Head Protection System (HPS), a cloth tube that inflates to prevent head injuries to front seat occupants in side impacts. Volvo's Inflatable Curtain is an airbag that drops down from above the side windows and inflates for three seconds to protect the heads and necks of occupants in side collisions and rollovers. Mercedes offers "curtain-like" side airbags that deploy from above the side windows and extend the length of the passenger compartment—more than six feet.

SEATBELTS: STILL THE MOST EFFECTIVE RESTRAINT

The car companies, the government, and the insurance industry are often at odds over safety matters. One thing they agree on is that all vehicle occupants should be securely buckled.

NHTSA says a combination of 3-point lap/shoulder belts and airbags offers the greatest chance of survival. Lap/shoulder belts are 45 percent effective in cars and 60 percent effective in light trucks in preventing occupant deaths. Airbags reduce driver fatalities 31 percent in cars and 27 percent in trucks.

Though most attention recently has been on the benefits and risks of airbags, seatbelts remain the most effective safety feature required by the government. Seatbelts are the primary restraints in motor vehicles, while airbags are supplementary restraints.

Indeed, the federal government estimates seatbelts have saved more than 112,000 lives since 1975—11,000 in 1998 alone. Airbags, which are newer and less common, are credited with saving

4650. Ironically, 72 percent of those saved by airbags were not wearing seatbelts.

Any discussion of auto safety should include the caveat that all vehicle occupants need to be buckled, not just those in front. Passengers who aren't buckled are tossed around inside a vehicle in a collision or rollover, exposing themselves and others to injury. Unbelted occupants can also be thrown from a vehicle, in which case they can be hit by other vehicles. Seventy-five percent of those ejected from vehicles die.

NHTSA estimates that 69 percent of Americans buckle up, a dramatic improvement in the last 10 years from about 40 percent. However, 56 percent of passenger-car occupants and 74 percent of light truck occupants killed last year were not belted. NHTSA says another 9300 lives could have been saved if everyone over the age of four wore seatbelts.

Seatbelt usage is still far lower in the U.S. than in countries such as Canada, Germany, and Australia, where more than 90 percent of vehicle occupants buckle up.

Part of the reason is that, unlike in those other countries, there is no national law in the U.S. that mandates seatbelt use or sets uniform penalties. Instead, each state sets its own laws and punishment, and most have weak laws with small fines.

All vehicles come with manual 3-point lap/shoulder belts for the outboard seating positions. Most also have 2-point lap belts for the inboard seats, though a growing number of passenger vehicles are using 3-point belts for the center seats.

Seatbelts should fit snugly. Shoulder belts should pass over the shoulder and across the chest, with no more than an inch or so of slack.

Belts can bother shorter people and children because they rest on the side of the neck or even across the face, and this is often used as an excuse for not wearing a belt.

To help solve this problem, NHTSA requires height adjustable shoulder belt anchors for the front seats. This allows adjusting the upper anchor points vertically to suit occupants of various heights. Some manufacturers also provide height adjustments for the rear seatbelts, and others provide "comfort guides," a small clip that routes the belt to a more comfortable position.

KEEPING CHILDREN SAFE

Putting kids in back and using new child seats are two good ways to protect youngsters.

Children may squawk about not riding in front, but safety experts strongly recommend that they stay in the back seat until age 13. Passenger-side airbags are hazardous to children 12 and younger—even if they are belted—in the front seat. They are too small and fragile to be so close to a deploying airbag. Children who weigh less than about 40 pounds and are under four feet tall should ride in a child safety seat—either the forward-facing type or, for infants, a rear-facing seat, again, mounted in the back seat. Bigger children can ride in back without a special seat if the shoulder belts fit. If the belts rub their neck or face, then a booster seat is recommended.

The risks are greatest for infants. Safety officials warn that a rear facing child seat should never be used in the front seat of a vehicle with a passenger-side airbag unless the bag can be disabled.

Putting children under the age of 13 in back reduces the risks of injury in frontal collisions—by far the most common—because they will be further from the impact.

All 50 states and the District of Columbia require infants and toddlers to be placed in a child safety seat when riding in a car. Many laws apply to children up to three or four years of age, but the cut-offs vary widely. A few state laws apply specifically to children weighing 40 pounds or less.

Despite these laws, NHTSA estimates that 68 percent of children under the age of five who die in crashes were not properly restrained. Child seats can reduce the death risk by 70 percent if correctly installed, yet NHTSA says as many as four out of five are improperly used.

NHTSA recently announced a new universal child-seat attachment system to make it easier to install the seats properly. Previously, child seat manufacturers devised their own mounting systems, some of which proved problematic for users. Now, they have to use a simpler standard system for securing the seats to the vehicle. Additionally, forward-facing child seats must now come with a tether strap that secures the back of the seat to the vehicle for better head protection.

The new regulations are being phased in. Child seats manufactured after Sept. 1, 1999, must have tether straps. Eighty percent of passenger cars built after Sept. 1, 1999, must have attachment points for the tethers, and all cars and light trucks must have them by Sept. 1, 2002. Most car manufacturers will offer free or low-cost installation of attachment points on older models, and some car-seat manufacturers plan to offer tether kits for older seats.

Safety experts recommend consulting the instructions from both the child seat and vehicle manufacturer to make sure you are installing the seat correctly. The owner's manual for new vehicles usually has ample information on installing child seats. The first step is to secure the seat so that it will not move excessively in a collision. The next step is to properly secure the child with the belts attached to the seat.

Built-in child safety seats are a factory option on some vehicles, particularly minivans, though some manufacturers have dropped them because of low demand.

This handy feature is integrated into the seatback and folds out when needed. Some automakers also offer approved child seats as accessories.

Built-in child safety seats are offered on some cars and minivans.

CRASH TESTS

All vehicles sold in the U.S. are required to pass a 30-mph crash test, but this test is not conducted by the federal government. The car companies themselves test their own vehicles and certify they meet the standards.

More consumers are familiar with the New Car Assessment Program, a 35-mph crash test conducted by the government on 40 to 50 vehicles per year as a public-information service.

Here are how the two programs operate:

• 30-mph crash: Every car and light truck must pass this test. The tests are done with both belted and unbelted dummies (they are male, about 5-feet 9-inches and 170 pounds) placed in the front seats.

In the belted test, a vehicle crashes head-on into a fixed barrier. Sensors transmit signals to electronic monitoring devices that detect the extent of the injuries people would have suffered to their head, chest, and upper legs.

Automakers currently do not have to conduct the unbelted test by crashing an actual vehicle into a barrier. Instead, they can simulate a crash with a "sled test." Dummies are placed in a mock vehicle mounted on a sled. Instead of crashing into a barrier, the sled travels a short distance on rails and comes to a sudden stop.

This rapid deceleration simulates the forces generated in a 30-mph crash but is not as severe as an actual crash. The sled test allows manufacturers to use less-powerful airbags and still meet federal safety requirements.

• 35-mph crash: This test is head-on into a concrete barrier, and it is conducted by NHTSA using production vehicles. Results of the 35-mph tests are released to the public periodically during the year and are popularly known as the "government crash test."

Vehicles are not required to pass this test, which NHTSA conducts on 40 to 50 vehicles each year as a "consumer information program." Results for other vehicles, tested in previous model years and not significantly changed in design, are presumed still valid.

Belted dummies are monitored for forces to the head, chest, and upper legs. Vehicles are crashed at 35 mph—a speed that generates 36 percent more energy (and potential for injury) than the required 30-mph test.

This test is intended to illustrate the differences between vehicles and is used by the government as a basis for evaluating the relative safety of the cars tested. Each tested vehicle gets a rating of one to five "stars," with the highest number of stars indicating the best protection against head and chest injury in a head-on collision.

NHTSA does not advise consumers to use its 35-mph crash results to choose one car over an-

NHTSA's 35-mph frontal crash test is the basis for the "star" ratings often quoted by auto manufacturers. Five stars is the highest rating.

The federal government also conducts side-impact tests. All cars must pass this test; some do so with the aid of side airbags.

other or to judge that a vehicle is safe or unsafe. The tests are intended only to compare vehicles of similar size and weight (within about 500 pounds).

The 35-mph test has been criticized for not reflecting real-world collisions because:

• Actual crashes are rarely head-on into flat barriers that involve the full width of the car. More often, frontal collisions occur at an angle. Many safety advocates argue that testing at an offset angle is more valid.

• Dummies represent an average-size male. A larger or smaller person might produce different results, and NHTSA has proposed adding smaller dummies representing women and children for the 2003 model year.

• Test results often differ from death and injury rates compiled by the insurance industry and even NHTSA itself.

A NHTSA spokesperson responds: "No matter what kind of test you do, you're only going to simulate one situation. The goal is to use a simulation that brings about improvements to the safety of the vehicles."

REAL-WORLD STATISTICS

Size matters. Fatality rates show that large, heavy vehicles offer better occupant protection than smaller, lighter vehicles. Large vehicles provide more crush space around occupants and more mass to absorb the energy of an impact instead of transmitting it to the occupants. Indeed, according to NHTSA and the insurance industry, death rates are higher in small SUVs than all other classes of vehicles. Small cars and small pickup

trucks have the second and third highest death rates.

The Insurance Institute for Highway Safety analyzed driver deaths in popular 1994-96 vehicles, and the ones with the highest (worst) driver death rates were small cars, small pickups, and mini sport-utility vehicles. Those with the lowest death rates were large cars, full-size pickups, and large and mid-size sport-utility vehicles.

This study's value is limited when choosing a current model. Some of the 1994-96 vehicles with the worst scores did not have airbags all those years, including the mini SUVs and most compact pickups. Most vehicles have been redesigned since 1996 and may have new features such as anti-lock brakes and traction control. They may also have greater structural integrity to make them safer.

The Highway Loss Data Institute (HLDI), an insurance information and lobbying group affiliated with the IIHS, ranks cars by the number of injury claims filed. Insurance-based data reflects only claims experience, and cannot prove design flaws. The HLDI ratings show that size alone doesn't guarantee how a car will fare in real-world driving: Some small cars have fewer injury claims than some mid-size cars, though in general large vehicles have fewer injury claims than small ones.

Death rates and injury claims are influenced not only by the size and type of vehicle but by who drives them and how they are driven.

Large, expensive cars most often are driven by older, more experienced drivers, and mini-vans are usually driven by adults who have children—people who tend to have fewer accidents than the population as a whole.

Small cars and mini SUVs, on the other hand, are used primarily by younger, less experienced drivers, who tend to have more accidents that involve death or injury.

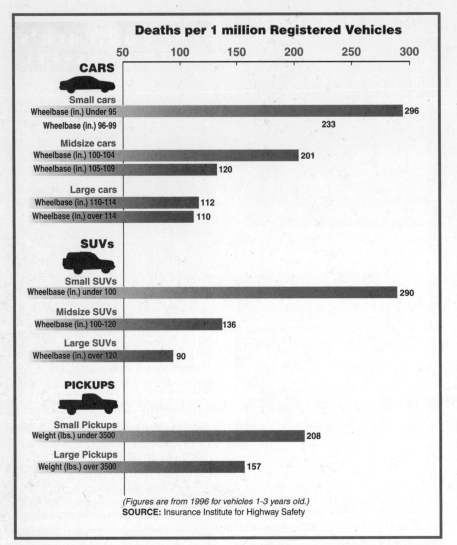

Deaths per 1 million Registered Vehicles

| | 50 | 100 | 150 | 200 | 250 | 300 |

CARS

Small cars
Wheelbase (in.) Under 95 — 296
Wheelbase (in.) 96-99 — 233

Midsize cars
Wheelbase (in.) 100-104 — 201
Wheelbase (in.) 105-109 — 120

Large cars
Wheelbase (in.) 110-114 — 112
Wheelbase (in.) over 114 — 110

SUVs

Small SUVs
Wheelbase (in.) under 100 — 290

Midsize SUVs
Wheelbase (in.) 100-120 — 136

Large SUVs
Wheelbase (in.) over 120 — 90

PICKUPS

Small Pickups
Weight (lbs.) under 3500 — 208

Large Pickups
Weight (lbs.) over 3500 — 157

(Figures are from 1996 for vehicles 1-3 years old.)
SOURCE: Insurance Institute for Highway Safety

Fatality rates are highest for smaller cars, SUVs, and pickups. Vehicle size, weight, and driver demographics all play a role in real-world safety.

Copies of the brochure "Injury, Collision & Theft Losses" are available from:

Highway Loss Data Institute
1005 N. Glebe Road
Arlington, VA 22201

LIGHT TRUCKS AND SAFETY

As trucks become more popular, they account for a larger portion of motor vehicle deaths. While annual fatalities in passenger cars dropped more than 2000 to 22,957 between 1987 and 1997, the number of deaths in sport-utilities and pick-ups climbed from 7127 to 8291.

Historically, trucks have had fewer safety requirements than cars, but starting with the 1999 model year, federal regulations require light trucks to meet the same major safety requirements as cars, including dual front airbags and identical side impact standards.

The only vehicles exempt are heavy-duty sport-utilities, pickups, and vans with gross-vehicle weights of more than 8500 pounds, such as the Ford Excursion and Chevrolet Suburban 2500 series.

Many drivers feel safer in a truck than in a car. They argue that trucks and vans weigh more than most cars, and weight provides more protection in a collision. You also sit higher in a truck or a van, so you can see trouble coming. This adds to a sense of security and is one of the key reasons women cite for buying sport-utility vehicles.

By far the deadliest risk facing truck occupants is an accident in which the vehicle rolls over. In 1998, the death rate from rollovers was more than twice as high in SUVs than in passenger cars, and considerably higher in pickups than in cars.

Rollovers are directly related to a vehicle's stability in turns. That stability is influenced by the relationship between the center of gravity and the track width (distance between left and right wheels). A high center of gravity and narrow track can make a vehicle unstable in fast turns or sharp changes of direction—increasing the odds it will tip over once it begins to skid sideways. The problem is most pronounced in 4-wheel-drive pickup trucks and sport-utility vehicles, which have higher ground clearance for off-road driving. Sport-utility vehicles must carry warnings that they handle and maneuver differently than passenger cars, both on and off the road.

Despite concerns that some SUVs—particularly small ones—tip too easily, NHTSA has found that rollovers are a problem common to all 4WD vehicles, due largely to the way they're driven. Most fatal 4WD rollovers are single-vehicle accidents that occur on weekend nights. The drivers are most frequently males under 25 years of age, and alcohol is usually involved.

In two out of three fatal rollovers, the victims were ejected from the vehicle, indicating they weren't wearing a seatbelt.

Neither cars nor trucks are subject to a federal rollover standard, though NHTSA is looking into this issue.

ACTIVE SAFETY FEATURES

While airbags and seatbelts are designed to protect you in the event of a collision, active safety features such as antilock brakes and traction control can help you avoid accidents.

More than a million vehicles on the road have an antilock brake system (ABS). It is standard on many new vehicles and well worth the extra expense when offered as optional equipment.

ABS is designed to help maintain steering control and prevent skids during braking in rain, snow, and even on dry pavement. A computer controls braking force to prevent the wheels from locking, which results in skidding and robs the driver of steering control.

When ABS brakes are applied, the computer senses when a wheel is about to lock up and then "pumps" the brakes many times per second—much faster than a human foot could. The wheels continue to rotate while slowing the car and the driver maintains steering control.

Stopping distances with ABS may not be any shorter—and on some surfaces may be longer—but the degree of control is dramatically higher. To let drivers know when ABS is activated, the brake pedal pulsates noticeably, sometimes accompanied by a clicking noise.

Many drivers do not understand how ABS works and in an emergency become alarmed by the pedal pulsations. Then, they mistakenly let up on the pedal or begin to "pump" it manually. The correct method, as recommended by NHTSA, is to "stomp and steer." Keep your foot hard on the pedal, and continue to steer the car around hazards.

Essentially working in the reverse of ABS is traction control, which uses the ABS sensors to detect wheel slip on acceleration. The system then applies the brakes to the driving wheels, cuts engine power, or does both, to retard wheel slip until traction is restored. Traction control is optional on many cars and standard on others. It is particularly worthwhile on rear-wheel-drive cars, which tend to lose traction more easily on slippery surfaces.

Some recent studies have questioned the value of antilock brakes (ABS) in preventing accidents, and some insurance companies have reduced or eliminated discounts for this feature based on their claims experience. Other studies, however, have concluded that vehicles equipped with ABS are involved in fewer accidents and have fewer injuries.

Consumer Guide™ supports antilock brakes enthusiastically and encourages shoppers to buy vehicles equipped this feature.

Auto Safety Hotline

The federal National Highway Traffic Safety Administration (NHTSA) operates a toll-free Auto Safety Hotline for information on government crash tests, safety recalls, and other safety-related questions. Consumers can also call this number to report safety problems with their vehicles. An answering system is available during non-business hours.

NHTSA Auto Safety Hotline
1-800-424-9393

Hearing-impaired persons
may call:
1-800-424-9153

Consumers can also write to:
National Highway Traffic Safety
Administration
400 7th Street, SW
Washington, DC 20590

Web Site: www.nhtsa.dot.gov

THE CONSUMER'S ROLE IN SAFETY

Though the government's regulations are often criticized, and the car companies are frequently chided for putting profits ahead of safety, motor vehicle safety has made significant strides since the forerunner of the NHTSA was created in 1966, launching the federal safety programs.

Motor vehicle deaths declined from 50,894 in 1966 to 41,471 in 1998. This reduction occurred even though Americans rack up millions more miles now and millions more vehicles are on the road. The death rate, which was 7.6 deaths per 100 million miles in 1950, declined from 5.5 in 1966 to 1.6 in 1998.

Pushed by federal safety rules, prodded by the insurance industry, and pressed by consumers, the auto industry has to build much safer vehicles today. Many car companies exceed the federal safety requirements on their own and, through their own research and innovation, find new ways to make vehicles safer. However, no matter what features the government requires or the car companies offer, motor vehicle safety to a large extent depends on who is behind the wheel and how they are driving.

Alcohol was involved in seven percent of all vehicle crashes in 1998 but 38 percent of traffic deaths. As a result, 15,935 people died because somebody had too much to drink. Speeding was a factor in 30 percent of fatal crashes last year. The blame for those deaths cannot be placed on the manufacturers of those vehicles or the lack of regulation.

Despite the best efforts of the government and auto industry, we continue to kill ourselves by ignoring traffic laws and common sense, refusing to wear seatbelts, and driving while impaired by drugs or alcohol.

CONSUMER COMPLAINTS

Auto complaints historically rank near the top of consumer grievances. The best time to resolve problems is before you take delivery of your new vehicle. If trouble develops, a good relationship with the dealer can eliminate the need for more serious action.

BEFORE YOU DRIVE AWAY

Take steps now to prevent problems early on. Vehicles and dealers keep improving, but problems can still occur, even if you buy a vehicle with a track record for reliability from a dealer with a reputation for good service. Good treatment during the sale doesn't guarantee the same reception when you return for service, though it's often a good predictor. Here are some tips on addressing problems before they become major hassles:

• Always test drive the vehicle before taking final delivery.

• Take delivery in the daytime. Artificial light can hide scratches or blemishes.

• Make sure it is the vehicle you paid for. Match the title and all other documents to the Vehicle Identification Number (VIN) atop the dashboard and the information on the window sticker.

• Is every option you purchased listed on the window sticker? Are they all on the vehicle and in working order?

• Inspect paint, trim, and body panels. Look for evidence of body repair, such as a color mismatch; glass fragments in the carpet; loose or missing pieces. Vehicles can be damaged in transit, and dealer prep work isn't always perfect.

• See that doors, hood, and trunk open and close easily. Examine upholstery and interior trim.

• Insist that all problems get fixed before you drive away. Why should you have to come back for something that is not your fault?

• Check for vital items such as the spare tire, jack, and owner's manual.

• Do you have copies of all documents, including the bill of sale, warranty papers, vehicle registration, etc.?

• Do you know where to go and whom to contact if service is needed?

• Do you have a copy of the recommended maintenance schedule?

• If a dealer-installed option isn't available at the time of delivery, get installation details in writing.

• Don't sign the contract until you're satisfied that everything you're paying for is accounted for and operating to your satisfaction.

• If the dealership doesn't volunteer to give you a "tour" of your new vehicle, ask them to do it. Be sure you know how to operate all controls and accessories before you leave.

SERVICE VISITS

A few simple steps can increase the chances your car or truck is fixed right the first time.

When you arrive for maintenance or repair work, be prepared to discuss the problem in detail. Make certain the service advisor writes a complete and correct description of each problem you've noticed—technicians rely on that service order.

No need to apologize if you can't make the problem appear during a test drive with the service advisor. It happens all the time. Just describe the symptoms and explain the circumstances under which they occur. Insist that service people examine the car under conditions in which the problem is likely to surface. That may require leaving the car overnight.

If parts must be ordered, the process might take a day or even a week, so don't expect miracles. Parts for low-volume models often take longer.

Letting the dealer conduct routine service, such as oil changes, may be wise. Regular customers tend to get prompt attention when a problem appears. Your vehicle also will be up to date in the dealer's records—a point in your favor if a serious flaw develops.

Don't leave the dealership until you're satisfied that all service work has been done correctly.

Keep a detailed record of service visits, including all receipts. Always be prepared to:

• Provide full vehicle data: mileage, date of purchase, and Vehicle Identification Number.

• Describe the problem and what's been done to correct it.

• If you are displeased with the service, explain why and the solution you're seeking.

RESOLVING DISPUTES

Third-party mediation and arbitration programs should be a last resort. They seldom produce miracles.

In a dispute over service or the performance of your new vehicle, we advise that you exhaust each rung up the ladder of solutions before considering bringing in a third party. That means starting with your dealer. This will strengthen your case, should you proceed to mediation or beyond.

If the dealer can't solve your problem, take it to the manufacturer's district or regional representative (your owner's manual should contain this address and phone number). The next avenue should be a mediation or arbitration program.

A few automakers mediate customer disputes internally, but most participate in a program that allows dissatisfied owners to seek resolution through an independent third party.

These programs usually involve the consumer and the manufacturer, not against the dealer. The consumer presents a complaint, supported by documentation (repair receipts, correspondence, etc.), to a mediator or arbitration panel. The manufacturer's representative presents its side of the story. Then, the panel issues a decision or a recommendation.

Some findings are binding on the manufacturer. Remedies could range from providing the consumer the repair they requested (such as repainting the car) to, in rare cases, providing the customer with a new vehicle. But when a panel sides with the manufacturer's position, pursuing the complaint grows difficult for the consumer.

Two mediation/arbitration services handle the bulk of cases:

• The Council of Better Business Bureaus operates the Auto Line program, which provides mediation and arbitration of disputes over manufacturing defects on vehicles still under warranty. Consumers should first contact the Better Business Bureau (BBB) headquarters at 1-800-955-5100. The BBB will refer the complaint to the appropriate automaker and try to arrange a resolution.

• Mediation is provided by the Automotive Consumer Action Program (AUTOCAP), a service directed by the National Automobile Dealers Association (NADA) but performed by state or local dealer associations. BMW, Honda/Acura, Isuzu, Jaguar, Mitsubishi, Nissan/Infiniti, and Volvo use the AUTOCAP mediation program.

Both programs first try to settle the dispute in an informal mediation stage that gets both sides of the story on the table and tries to find a solution. The vast majority of cases are resolved this way.

If you're dissatisfied with a mediator's recommendation, the next option is arbitration. With Auto Line, unsettled complaints are presented to an impartial volunteer who decides the outcome. With AUTOCAP, a panel of consumer volunteers and dealer representatives decides the outcome.

Some manufacturers, including Ford Motor Co. and Daimler Chrysler, run their own arbitration programs. Most others work through an outside group. Your owner' manual should tell you which program will be used.

In any program, you'll present your case orally and/or in writing. You'll need complete records, including work orders, letters, receipts, and notices. You must prove the vehicle has a problem, that both dealer and manufacturer have failed in several attempts to fix it, and that you've exhausted all other avenues. The manufacturer and/or dealer will then present its case through a representative familiar with repair problems.

Arbitration is similar to a court hearing, though less formal, and a lawyer is not required. The panel's decision is binding only on the company. The consumer can accept the verdict or go on to the next step: formal legal action.

Less than one-third of consumers have a dispute settled wholly their way. In most mediation and arbitration cases, however, the decision at least partially satisfies both sides.

LEMON LAWS

Every state now has some form of "lemon law," but the promise usually outweighs the results.

Manufacturers can be ordered to refund the purchase price of a new vehicle or replace a vehicle that is proven critically flawed. Such dramatic results are rare, however. In most states, you must exhaust all other possible remedies first. That means making a specified number of tries—typically three—at the dealership, then passing through arbitration without successful resolution.

You will have to retain a lawyer. To qualify for consideration, a car generally has to be inoperable for at least 30 days during its first 12 months or 12,000 miles. Details vary, so inquire at your state attorney general's office, a consumer protection agency, or the Center for Auto Safety.

Lemon laws typically stipulate that a manufacturer be given one last chance to remedy the complaint. Even if you "win," the automaker nearly always can deduct for the mileage you've put on the vehicle.

Government Agencies
and Consumer Groups

The arbitration programs, government agencies, and consumer groups listed below may be able to help with auto-related problems. Many states and some local governments have their own consumer protection agencies that may respond faster than a federal agency.

Better Business Bureau Auto Line
1-800-955-5100
Web Site: www.bbb.org
Provides reports on dealers and other businesses and operates the Auto Line mediation and arbitration service between consumers and auto companies regarding manufacturing defects. Check your local phone book for the nearest office or call 1-800-955-5100 for information.

Center for Auto Safety
1825 Connecticut Avenue, NW
Washington, DC 20009-5708
Web Site: www.autosafety.org
Non-profit group lobbies on behalf of consumer interests regarding vehicle safety and quality. Also provides information on vehicle defects and common problems and lemon laws and provides a lawyer referral service. Send a letter explaining your request with a self-addressed stamped envelope.

DaimlerChrysler Customer Assistance Center
P.O. Box 21-8004
Auburn Hills, MI 48321-8004
1-800-992-1997
Handles complaints not resolved at the dealer or zone-office level and provides information about Chrysler's customer arbitration boards. Also answers calls for roadside assistance and inquiries on recalls and other consumer issues.

Federal Trade Commission
Consumer Response Center
600 Pennsylvania Avenue, NW
Washington, DC 20580
1-877-382-4357
Web Site: www.ftc.gov
Provides information on arbitration and consumer complaints and publishes brochures with advice on loans, leasing, and other auto-related topics. Regional offices are in major cities.

Ford Motor Company
Customer Assistance Center
P.O. Box 43360
Detroit, MI 48243
1-800-392-3673 (Ford and Lincoln Mercury)
Handles complaints not resolved at the dealer or regional-office level and provides information on Ford's arbitration program. Also answers calls for roadside assistance and inquiries on recalls and other consumer issues.

Highway Loss Data Institute (HLDI) and Insurance Institute for Highway Safety (IIHS)
1005 N. Glebe Road
Arlington, VA 22201
(703) 247-1500
HLDI Web Site: www.carsafety.org
IIHS Web Site: www.highwaysafety.org
Insurance industry lobbying group compiles information on vehicle and highway safety.

National Automobile Dealers Association AUTOCAP
8400 Westpark Drive
McLean, VA 22102
(703) 821-7000
Web Site: www.nada.org/consumer/autocap.htm
NADA headquarters will refer you to a state or local office to answer questions on the AUTOCAP mediation service and inform you if your dealer is a member. Also provides information on recalls.

National Highway Traffic Safety Administration
400 7th Street, SW
Washington, DC 20590
Web Site: www.nhtsa.dot.gov
NHTSA investigates safety defects and enforces federal safety regulations. Call the toll-free consumer hotline for information on crash tests and safety recalls and to report safety problems: 1-800-424-9393.

U.S. Department of Energy
1-800-363-3732
Web Site: www.fueleconomy.gov
Distributes free single copies of the EPA Gas Mileage Guide, which is available in electronic form on the Web site. Copies of the guide also are supposed to be available at car dealers.

U.S. Department of Justice
Office of Consumer Litigation
P.O. Box 386
Washington, DC 20044
(202) 307-0092
This office enforces federal laws covering price labeling of new vehicles and odometer tampering.

INSURANCE

How much you pay for auto insurance depends on several factors, including your age, where you live, and what you drive. You can't do anything about your age, and few people will move just to lower their insurance premium. You can, however, choose a vehicle that costs less to insure.

TYPES OF COVERAGE

Six types of coverage are included in most insurance policies:

• Bodily injury liability: Covers injury and/or death claims against you and legal costs if your car injures or kills someone.

• Property damage liability: Covers claims for property that your car damages in an accident. Because liability coverage protects the other party, it is required in most states.

• Medical payments: Pays for injuries to yourself and to occupants of your car. It is optional in some states. In "no-fault" states, personal injury protection replaces medical payments as part of the basic coverage.

• Uninsured motorist protection: Covers injuries caused to you or the occupants of your car by uninsured or hit-and-run drivers. "Underinsured" coverage also is available to cover claims you may make against a driver who has inadequate insurance.

• Collision coverage: Covers damage to your car up to its book value. Collision coverage carries a deductible, which is the amount per claim you have to pay before the insurance takes effect. The lower the deductible, the higher the premium. While legally it is optional, a lending institution or leasing company usually requires it.

• Comprehensive (physical damage): Covers damage to your car from theft, vandalism, fire, wind, flood, and other non-accident causes. Comprehensive also carries a deductible.

WHY SOME CARS COST MORE

Insurance premiums are based partly on the price of the vehicle, which affects the replacement cost if it is stolen or "totaled" in an accident. How expensive the vehicle is to repair—including parts and labor—can also affect the cost.

In addition, surcharges may apply to vehicles that are frequently involved in accidents or stolen.

Industry-wide information on injury claims, collision repair costs, and theft rates by vehicle is available from the Highway Loss Data Institute (HLDI), 1005 North Glebe Road, Arlington, VA 22201 (www.carsafety.org). Also see the chart Costly-to-Insure Models in this section.

According to HLDI, the lowest injury claims are from large vehicles—cars, pickup trucks, and sport-utility vehicles. Small 2- and 4-door cars have the highest injury claims, and small cars also are among the highest in collision costs, along with sports cars. If you have your heart set on a sporty vehicle, you'll probably pay dearly; insuring a high-performance car can cost two or three times the amount for an ordinary model.

Sport-utility vehicles, the hottest market segment, tend to have higher insurance rates than mid- and full-size cars. SUVs are "hot" for other reasons: They are now among the most frequently stolen vehicles, and they are more expensive than most cars. SUVs also can cost more to fix after an accident if the 4-wheel-drive system is damaged.

However, insurance companies set rates based on their own experience. If Company *A* has more collision and theft claims for a particular vehicle than Company *B*, then *A* will charge more for the same coverage. It all boils down to a company's actual experience with a particular vehicle or category of drivers. That is why it pays to shop for insurance.

WHO YOU ARE, WHERE YOU LIVE

Your age, gender, and driving record are key factors that affect your insurance premium. Single males under the age of 25 pay the highest rates. Statistics show they are involved in the most accidents, so insurance companies charge young men higher premiums than women of the same age. Married men, who statistically have fewer accidents, pay less than single men. A handful of states do not allow rates based on sex or age, but that prohibition has tended to result in higher rates for women, not lower rates for men.

If you are convicted of moving traffic violations or cause accidents, your premiums will likely go up, no matter what your age. Drivers with clean records—no tickets, no accidents—pay the lowest rates.

Where you live also plays a big role in how much you pay. Urban areas, with their greater population density and heavier traffic, get higher rates than rural areas. Insurance premiums in mainly urban New Jersey—traditionally the most-expensive state—might run three times higher than those in North Dakota, a rural state with the lowest average premiums.

In most states, insurers set rates by zip codes. If you live in a major city like Chicago or Los Angeles, you will probably pay more than if you lived in a nearby suburb.

How Much Do You Need?

Without insurance, your property is put at risk in an accident that is your fault. The minimum amount of insurance required in your state is seldom enough.

State law may require as little liability coverage as $15,000 per person, $30,000 per accident, and $5000 property damage. If you can afford it, buy more than the minimum. After all, $10,000 for property damage may not be enough if you broadside a $100,000 Mercedes-Benz.

The more assets and income you have, the more insurance you need. Most insurers recommend liability coverage of at least $100,000 per person, $300,000 per accident, and $50,000 property damge for anyone with assets to protect, such as a house.

Some insurers also recommend a $1 million "personal liability umbrella" policy issued in conjunction with homeowner's coverage that costs $200 to $300 a year. It can protect a family from financial ruin in a major lawsuit.

Shop Around

Rates vary widely; surveys indicate you could pay anywhere from $500 to $2000 annually for the same coverage from different companies. Shop for insurance by consulting two or three of the largest insurers, such as State Farm and Allstate, and then contact one or two independent agents who can quote premiums from more than one company. In addition, there are direct-marketing companies, such as GEICO and Amica, which do business over the phone rather than through agents and offer some of the lowest rates. Ask for an itemized list of coverage and costs.

Everyone wants to save a buck—including insurance companies. One way they save is by not paying for

How to Cut Your Insurance Premiums

1. Buy a vehicle that qualifies for a discount or at least doesn't carry a surcharge. Ask your insurance agent about the cost of insuring vehicles you are interested in before you buy.

2. Most companies give a break to those who drive less than 7500 miles a year. If you take public transportation instead of driving to work, your premium will go down. Out of the question? Try car pooling.

3. Make sure you get all the discounts you are entitled to. You might qualify if your vehicle has an alarm, airbags, or antilock brakes. Discounts might also be available if you insure your vehicles and your home with the same company. People who pass a defensive-driving course or don't smoke or drink often get discounts.

Review the status of all the drivers in your family with your agent. Most discounts apply only to one portion of the policy, so don't expect dramatic savings.

4. Increase your deductible for collision and comprehensive. Switching from a $100 deductible to $500 can reduce your collision and comprehensive premiums by 25 percent. Going to a $1000 deductible might cut it in half. You're still covered for catastrophes, but you foot the bill for fender-benders. Also, think twice about filing small claims with your insurance: Why risk a premium increase?

5. Shop around. Instead of just renewing, study the fine print of your policy to see if its terms—or your situation—have changed. Another company might have better rates, but you won't know unless you shop. Most insurers give rates over the phone and many via on-line computer services, making it easy to compare premiums.

6. Drop collision coverage on older cars. Claims are limited to "book" value, so you're not likely to get much anyway if you car is more than, say, seven years old. A good rule of thumb is to drop collision when the annual premium reaches 10 percent of your car's value.

7. Be a good driver. Avoid accidents and traffic violations and you will be rewarded with good-driver discounts. Bad driving is expensive. The North Carolina Department of Insurance estimates a driver with a speeding conviction or one at-fault accident on their record pays 45 percent more for insurance than a good driver.

8. Drop coverage for such extras as towing costs or the expense of renting a car while yours is in the shop. The savings are probably small, but your new-car warranty's roadside assistance provision may provide them at no cost.

9. Have your teenager share the family car instead of owning his or her own. Be sure to tell your agent if your son or daughter makes the Honor Roll or moves away to college. Both qualify for discounts with most companies.

10. If your group health insurance provides generous coverage, consider dropping the medical-payments portion of your policy.

original-equipment replacement parts. Instead, insurance companies may recommend cheaper parts—or even used parts—that are not the same quality or durability. Ask for an explanation of an insurer's policy on this issue because you may have to pay the cost difference if you insist on getting original-equipment factory parts.

Most state insurance departments publish guidelines on the types of coverage required in your state, recommended amounts of coverage, and shopping advice.

More than half the states provide rate comparisons, using typical drivers as examples to compare premiums from several companies for the same coverage. They can give you an idea which companies offer lower premiums.

The best time to find out the cost of insuring the vehicle of your dreams is *before* you buy it, not after. Contact your present insurance company and some competitors for estimates on vehicles you are considering. Also, the Internet is a good source of

information. Your state insurance department may have a World Wide Web site, and many insurance companies have a home page that can direct you to an agent or let you type in personal information to generate a sample premium.

Among sources on the Web are the Insurance Information Institute (www.iii.org) and the Consumer Insurance Guide (www.insure.com). The Insurance Information Institute operates the National Insurance Consumer Helpline (800-942-4242) and produces a brochure.

Costly-to-Insure Models

All makes and models of vehicles are involved in accidents, but some are involved more often and cost more to repair. Insurance companies look at the history of collision and comprehensive claims (the latter includes theft losses) for each model when determining rates. Those that have more frequent and expensive claims cost more to insure. Collision and comprehensive coverage makes up a major chunk of your premium, often more than 50 percent of the total.

Insurance companies use their own data from claims made by their policyholders to decide how much to charge. Each insurer has its own list of vehicles that qualify for a discount from the standard rate and another for vehicles that warrant a surcharge based on their claims.

Listed below are the models in each category as determined by State Farm Insurance Company, the largest auto insurer. The lists are for 1999 models (the latest available) and may be different for 2000 models. State Farm says premiums can be 10 to 45 percent higher or lower depending on which category a vehicle falls into. Models not listed qualified for standard rates at State Farm.

Models With Lower-Than-Average Collision and Comprehensive Premiums

Acura CL, RL
Audi A4 sedan, A6
BMW Z3, 7-Series
Buick (all models)
Cadillac Catera, DeVille, Eldorado, Seville
Chevrolet Astro, Corvette, Lumina, Suburban, Tahoe, Venture
Chrysler Concorde, Town & Country
Dodge Caravan
Ford Crown Victoria, Expedition, Explorer, F-150, Taurus, Windstar
GMC Jimmy 4-door, Safari, Suburban, Yukon
Honda CR-V, Odyssey
Infiniti I30, Q45
Isuzu Oasis, Trooper
Jaguar XJ Sedan, XK8
Jeep Grand Cherokee
Lexus ES 300, LS 400

Lincoln Continental, Navigator, Town Car
Mercedes-Benz (all models except CLK430 and E55)
Mercury Grand Marquis, Mountaineer, Sable, Villager
Nissan Frontier, Quest
Oldsmobile Bravada, Cutlass, Eighty Eight/LSS, Intrigue, Silhouette
Plymouth Voyager
Pontiac Bonneville, Grand Prix, Montana
Porsche Boxster
Saab 9-3 4-door, convertible
Saturn wagon
Toyota Avalon, Sienna
Volkswagen Passat
Volvo S70/V7

Models With Higher-Than-Average Collision and Comprehensive Premiums

Acura Integra, NSX
Audi A8
BMW 3-Series
Chevrolet Blazer 2-door, Camaro, Cavalier, Metro, Prizm, S-10 2WD, Tracker
Chrysler Sebring
Dodge Avenger, Dakota 2WD, Neon, Ram 1500, Viper
Ford Escort/ZX2, Mustang, Ranger 2WD
GMC Jimmy 2-door, Sonoma 2WD
Honda Civic, Prelude
Hyundai (all models)
Jeep Wrangler
Kia Sephia
Lexus SC 400
Mazda B-Series, Millenia, Protege, 626
Mitsubishi (all models)
Nissan Altima, Maxima, Pathfinder, Sentra
Plymouth Neon
Pontiac Firebird, Sunfire
Porsche 911
Land Rover Range Rover 4.0 SE/4.6 HSE
Saturn coupe
Subaru Forester, Impreza
Suzuki (all models)
Toyota Corolla, Tacoma, 4Runner
Volkswagen Cabrio, Golf, Jetta

SOURCE: State Farm Insurance Company.

BEST BUY AND RECOMMENDED

The auto editors of Consumer Guide™ have selected Best Buy and Recommended vehicles in 14 categories of passenger cars, minivans, pickup trucks, and sport-utility vehicles. In some categories there are models designated Budget Buys.

At least one Best Buy has been chosen in each category as the vehicles the editors rank as the best overall choices. Those vehicles are pictured under their respective categories. Models labeled Recommended also are highly worthy of consideration, and are listed under their categories. Budget Buys are competent vehicles that sell for significantly less than the average for their category.

Vehicles are assigned to one of 14 categories based on their size, price, and market position. Thus, a $13,000 subcompact competes against other low-priced small cars, not against $45,000 luxury cars.

Only models that have been road tested by the editors are considered. Some new or redesigned models, such as the BMW X5 sport-utility vehicle, weren't available for testing in time to be considered for this issue.

SUBCOMPACT CARS

Honda Civic

RECOMMENDED
Chevrolet Cavalier and Prizm
Dodge/Plymouth Neon
Mazda Protege
Toyota Corolla
Volkswagen Jetta/Golf

BUDGET BUY
Ford Escort

COMPACT CARS

Mazda 626

RECOMMENDED
Mitsubishi Galant
Nissan Altima
Oldsmobile Alero
Volkswagen Passat

BUDGET BUY
Hyundai Sonata

MIDSIZE CARS

Honda Accord

Toyota Camry

RECOMMENDED
Buick Century
Chevrolet Malibu
Nissan Maxima
Oldsmobile Intrigue
Pontiac Grand Prix

BUDGET BUY
Chevrolet Impala
Plymouth Breeze

FULL-SIZE CARS

Chrysler Concorde

Dodge Intrepid

RECOMMENDED
Buick LeSabre   Toyota Avalon

BUDGET BUY
Ford Crown Victoria

NEAR-LUXURY CARS

Acura TL

RECOMMENDED
Audi A6   Infiniti I30
Buick Park Avenue   Lexus ES 300

LUXURY CARS

Acura RL

Lexus LS 400

Mercedes-Benz E-Class

RECOMMENDED
BMW 5-Series
Cadillac DeVille
Jaguar S-Type
Lexus GS 300
Mercedes-Benz CLK

SPORTS COUPES

Honda Prelude

Volkswagen New Beetle

RECOMMENDED
Acura CL
Chrysler Sebring

BUDGET BUY
Ford Escort ZX2

SPORTS & GT CARS

Chevrolet Corvette

Mazda Miata

RECOMMENDED
BMW Z3
Mercedes-Benz SLK230

BUDGET BUY
Chevrolet Camaro
Ford Mustang

MINIVANS

Dodge Caravan

Honda Odyssey

Plymouth Voyager

RECOMMENDED
Chevrolet Venture
Ford Windstar
Toyota Sienna

COMPACT SPORT-UTILITY VEHICLES

Honda CR-V

Subaru Forester

RECOMMENDED
Toyota RAV4

BUDGET BUY
Jeep Wrangler

MIDSIZE SUVs

Ford Explorer

Lexus RX 300

Mercedes-Benz M-Class

RECOMMENDED
Dodge Durango
Mercury Mountaineer
Nissan Xterra
Toyota 4Runner

BUDGET BUY
Jeep Cherokee

FULL-SIZE SUVs

Ford Expedition

RECOMMENDED
Toyota Land Cruiser

COMPACT PICKUP TRUCKS

Dodge Dakota

Ford Ranger

Mazda B-Series

RECOMMENDED
Chevrolet S-10
GMC Sonoma
Nissan Frontier
Toyota Tacoma

FULL-SIZE PICKUP TRUCKS

Chevrolet Silverado 1500

GMC Sierra 1500

FORD F-150

RECOMMENDED
Dodge Ram 1500
Toyota Tundra

ACURA INTEGRA

Acura Integra Type R

Front-wheel-drive sports coupe

Base price range: $19,300-$22,500. Built in Japan. **Also consider:** Honda Prelude, Mitsubishi Eclipse, Volkswagen New Beetle

FOR • Fuel economy • Steering/handling • Acceleration (with manual transmission) • Exterior finish **AGAINST** • Rear-seat room • Road noise • Acceleration (with automatic transmission)

Longer tune-up intervals and the return of the high-performance Type R coupe are among the few changes for the entry-level 2000 Acuras. Hatchback coupes and 4-door sedans return in LS, GS, and GS-R trim. All use 1.8-liter 4-cylinder engines. GS-Rs have 170 horsepower, LS and GS 140, the Type R 195. Manual transmission is standard, automatic is optionally available on LS and GS. The limited-edition Type R is back from its brief furlough with standard instead of optional air conditioning. For 2000, all Integras get a standard anti-theft engine immobilizer and 100,000-mile tune-up intervals.

EVALUATION Nimble and taut, Integras are high-revving fun to drive. But engine and tire noise intrude at highway speeds, and these 4-cylinders don't have enough low-speed torque to pull with much gusto when linked to the automatic transmission, which is none too smooth. Manual-shift models are quick and frugal. Our test LS did 0-60 mph in 8.3 seconds and averaged nearly 25 mpg, a GS-R did 0-60 in 7.6 seconds and averaged 28.3. Expect less with an automatic. The sedan's ride is controlled and comfortable. The shorter, lighter coupes react abruptly to some bumps, especially the tightly damped GS-Rs and the even stiffer Type R. Front-seat room is fine in both models, but rear-seat space is tight, especially in the coupes. Sedans have small trunks. The coupes' hatchback layout is a plus for cargo versatility, but it brings an awkwardly high liftover. Integra's driving position is low but comfortable, its dashboard simple and handy. Outward visibility is good, despite being slightly restricted to the rear in coupes. Detail finish is exemplary, though some interior plastics lack eye appeal. This Integra hasn't changed much since its debut for 1994, and it's due for a redesign, probably for 2002. Nonetheless, it's a premium small car that offsets relatively high prices with fine reliability, strong resale value, and loads of driving fun. And Acura has a longer warranty and more comprehensive customer service than many makes, Honda included. The Integra 2-door is far more popular than the sedan and rates as a solid, if aging, sports coupe choice.

ENGINES

	dohc I4	dohc I4	dohc I4
Size, liters/cu. in.	1.8/112	1.8/110	1.8/110
Horsepower @ rpm	140 @ 6300	170 @ 7600	195 @ 8000
Torque (lbs./ft.) @ rpm	124 @ 5200	128 @ 6200	130 @ 7500
Availability	S[1]	S[2]	S[3]
EPA city/highway mpg			
5-speed OD manual	25/32	25/31	25/31
4-speed OD automatic	24/32		

1. LS, GS. 2. GS-R. 3. Type R.

PRICES

Acura Integra

	Retail Price	Dealer Invoice
LS 2-door hatchback, 5-speed	$19300	$17403
LS 2-door hatchback, automatic	20100	18578
LS 4-door sedan, 5-speed	20100	—
LS 4-door sedan, automatic	20900	18843
GS 2-door hatchback, 5-speed	$20950	$18888
GS 2-door hatchback, automatic	21750	20064
GS 4-door sedan, 5-speed	21500	—
GS 4-door sedan, automatic	22300	20104
GS-R 2-door hatchback, 5-speed	22200	20014
GS-R 4-door sedan, 5-speed	22500	20284
Destination charge	455	455

LS sedan 5-speed and GS sedan 5-speed dealer invoice prices not available at time of publication. Type R prices and standard equipment not available at time of publication.

STANDARD EQUIPMENT:

LS: 1.8-liter dohc 140-horsepower 4-cylinder engine, 5-speed manual or 4-speed automatic transmission, driver- and passenger-side airbags, antilock 4-wheel disc brakes, air conditioning, variable-assist power steering, tilt steering wheel, leather-wrapped steering wheel and shift knob, cruise control, cloth upholstery, front bucket seats w/driver-side height and lumbar adjustment, center console w/armrest, split folding rear seat (hatchback), one-piece folding rear seat (sedan), cupholders, power sunroof, map lights, power mirrors, power windows, power door locks, tachometer, AM/FM/CD player w/six speakers, power antenna (hatchback), digital clock, remote fuel-door and decklid/hatch releases, rear defogger, rear wiper/washer (hatchback), intermittent wipers, visor mirrors, cargo cover (hatchback), theft-deterrent system, 195/55VR15 tires, alloy wheels.

GS adds: leather upholstery, rear spoiler (hatchback).

GS-R adds: 1.8-liter dohc VTEC 170-horsepower engine, woodgrain console (sedan).

Options are available as dealer-installed accessories.

ACURA NSX

Acura NSX

Rear-wheel-drive sports and GT car

Base price range: $84,000-$88,000. Built in Japan. **Also consider:** Chevrolet Corvette, Dodge Viper, Porsche 911

FOR • Acceleration • Steering/handling • Build quality • Exterior finish • Interior materials **AGAINST** • Fuel economy • Rear visibility • Ride

This mid-engine 2-seater comes as a fixed-roof coupe and as the NSX-T with a removable roof panel. With the 6-speed manual transmission, they get a 290-horsepower 3.2-liter V6. With the 4-speed automatic, they use a 252-hp 3.0-liter V6. The automatic is Acura's SportShift with manual gear-change capability via a small steering-column lever. For 2000, a new perforated leather trim is standard on seats, door panels, steering wheel, and hand brake handle. Acura also claims revisions that improve manual-shift action. And the NSX now meets low-emissions vehicle standards.

EVALUATION It's a high-performance "exotic," but the all-aluminum NSX is as reliable as any Honda product. It's relatively undemanding to drive, easy enough to get into and out of, and even has good outward visibility. Despite smallish engines, acceleration matches that of the Porsche 911 or V8 Chevrolet Corvette, and handling ranks among the world's best. Our most-recent 6-speed test coupe averaged a relatively frugal 22 mpg. Some may pine for more raw power, but the NSX offers most of the rewards of a true exotic with almost none of the usual drawbacks—except a sky-high price.

ENGINES

	dohc V6	dohc V6
Size, liters/cu. in.	3.0/181	3.2/194
Horsepower @ rpm	252 @ 6600	290 @ 7100

Ratings begin on page 213. Specifications begin on page 220.

CONSUMER GUIDE™

	dohc V6	dohc V6
Torque (lbs./ft.) @ rpm	210 @ 5300	224 @ 5500
Availability	S¹	S²
EPA city/highway mpg		
6-speed OD manual		17/24
4-speed OD automatic	18/24	

1. Automatic transmission. 2. Manual transmission.

PRICES

Acura NSX	Retail Price	Dealer Invoice
Base 2-door coupe	$84000	$73920
T 2-door coupe	88000	77439
Destination charge	745	745

STANDARD EQUIPMENT:

Base: 3.2-liter dohc V6 engine w/6-speed manual transmission or 3.0-liter dohc V6 engine w/4-speed automatic transmission w/manual-shift capability, traction control, limited-slip differential, driver- and passenger-side airbags, antilock 4-wheel disc brakes, air conditioning w/automatic climate control, variable-assist power steering, leather-wrapped tilt/telescopic steering wheel, cruise control, leather upholstery, 4-way power bucket seats, center console, cupholders, power mirrors, power windows, power door locks, Bose AM/FM/cassette, power antenna, digital clock, tachometer, variable intermittent wipers, rear defogger, remote fuel door and decklid releases, rear spoiler, theft-deterrent system, 215/45ZR16 front tires, 245/40ZR17 rear tires, alloy wheels.

T adds to Base: removable roof panel.

Options are available as dealer-installed accessories.

ACURA RL

✓ BEST BUY

Acura 3.5RL

Front-wheel-drive luxury car

Base price range: $42,000-$44,000. Built in Japan. **Also consider:** BMW 5-Series, Lexus GS 300/400, Mercedes-Benz E-Class

FOR • Acceleration • Steering/handling • Ride • Build quality • Exterior finish • Interior materials **AGAINST** • Navigation system controls • Steering feel

Addition of a standard antiskid system and a front side airbag that senses the passenger's size and position are the big changes for 2000. Honda's premium-brand flagship sedan. RL has a V6 engine and standard automatic transmission, heated front seats, front side airbags, antilock brakes, and traction control. Taking advantage of the last two is newly standard Vehicle Stability Assist, which Acura says is specially tuned for front-wheel-drive cars. Like other such systems, it's designed to apply individual brakes to keep the RL on course in changes of direction. In what Acura says is an exclusive feature, seven sensors in the RL's front passenger seat measure the size and position of the occupant to determine whether to deploy the side airbag. It's designed to reduce the potential of injury to a small child from the airbag itself. The RL's only factory option is an in-dash satellite-linked navigation system. For 2000, it gets a larger, 7-inch touch screen with matte finish designed for easier reading, plus a digital-video-disc (DVD) database.

EVALUATION Though it lacks the punch of most V8 rivals, the RL is no slouch at 8.0 seconds 0-60 mph by our stopwatch. It also gets slightly better fuel economy than the class norm—17.3 mpg in our tests on the required premium gas—despite having a 4-speed automatic to many competitors' 5-speed. The RL otherwise behaves as a luxury car should, exhibiting a firm yet supple ride, shudder-free solidity, and low noise levels. It's also one of the more agile big

sedans, though that's spoiled a bit by slightly numb steering. The new antiskid system is a welcome addition, as are the sophisticated side airbag sensors. RL offers plenty of room for four adults, comfortable seats, and an easily tailored driving position. Controls are simple and intuitive, although the navigation system requires study and practice. Its new, larger screen is easier to read, but still subject to fingerprint smuging. Acura keeps adding equipment without huge price increases, but RL sales remain sluggish, so you should be able to work a good deal on a fine car that's often overlooked.

ENGINES

	ohc V6
Size, liters/cu. in.	3.5/212
Horsepower @ rpm	210 @ 5200
Torque (lbs./ft.) @ rpm	224 @ 2800
Availability	S
EPA city/highway mpg	
4-speed OD automatic	19/24

PRICES

Acura RL	Retail Price	Dealer Invoice
Base 4-door sedan	$42000	$36972
Base w/Navigation System 4-door sedan	44000	38732
Destination charge	455	455

STANDARD EQUIPMENT:

Base: 3.5-liter V6 engine, 4-speed automatic transmission, traction control, driver- and passenger-side airbags, front side-impact airbags, antilock 4-wheel disc brakes, antiskid system, air conditioning w/front and rear automatic climate controls, interior air filter, variable-assist power steering, power tilt/telescopic steering wheel w/memory, leather-wrapped steering wheel and shifter, cruise control, leather upholstery, heated front seats, 8-way power driver seat w/memory and lumbar support, 4-way power passenger seat, center console, cupholders, rear-seat trunk pass-through, wood interior trim, power sunroof, heated power mirrors w/memory, power windows, power door locks, remote keyless entry, Bose AM/FM/cassette, 6-disc CD changer, digital clock, tachometer, rear defogger, automatic day/night rearview mirror, remote fuel-door and decklid releases, variable intermittent wipers, illuminated visor mirrors, map lights, auxiliary power outlets, universal garage door opener, theft-deterrent system, Xenon headlights, fog lights, 215/60VR16 tires, alloy wheels.

Base w/Navigation System adds: Global Positioning/Navigation System.

Options are available as dealer-installed accessories.

ACURA TL

✓ BEST BUY

Acura 3.2TL

Front-wheel-drive near-luxury car; similar to Honda Accord

Base price range: $28,400-$30,400. Built in USA. **Also consider:** Audi A4, BMW 3-Series, Infiniti I30, Lexus ES 300

FOR • Acceleration • Build quality • Exterior finish • Interior materials • Steering/handling **AGAINST** • Navigation System controls

A 5-speed automatic transmission and front side airbags are 2000 additions to this American-built sedan from Honda's upscale division. Acura's best-selling model, the TL shares its platform with Honda's Accord and the redesigned Acura CL coupe due later in the 2000 model year.

A 3.2-liter V6 and automatic transmission return, but the engine is tuned to deliver more low-speed power, and a 5-speed automatic replaces last year's 4-speed. The transmission retains Acura's SportShift manual gear-selection feature. Correcting another competitive deficit is the addition of standard front side airbags. Sensors

Prices are accurate at time of publication; subject to manufacturer's changes.

in the right front seat are designed to determine the size and positioning of the passenger and to prevent that side airbag from deploying if doing so would injury a small child. The right front dashboard airbag also gains a system that regulates the rate of its deployment based on the severity of the collision.

TLs come with leather upholstery, heated front seats, power moonroof, antilock 4-wheel disc brakes, and traction control. The sole major factory option is an in-dash navigation system. For 2000, its touch-screen gets a matte finish designed to make it easier to read, and the database is upgraded to use DVD (digital video disc) technology. There's also now lighting for all power-window switches, not just the driver's switch.

PERFORMANCE Quick, quiet, and composed, the TL is an uncommonly polished performer. The 5-speed automatic subtly improves acceleration, adding some zip off the line, enhancing throttle response at midrange speeds, and providing more relaxed cruising. In tandem with the revised V6, Acura says the 2000 TL is a half-second quicker 0-60 mph, which would mean about 7 seconds flat based on our 1999-model tests. And fuel economy should improve slightly from the 19.3 to 24.5 mpg we averaged in tests of '99 models. Premium fuel again is required.

Complementing the smooth powertrain is unerring high-speed stability allied to grippy, athletic cornering. The downside is a firmer ride than that of less dynamic rivals, such as the Lexus ES 300 and Infiniti I30. Tire rumble and slap are above the class norm, too, but not irksome. Engine and wind noise are low. "Panic" stops are swift and stable and pedal feel improves for 2000, but nosedive is heavier than expected.

ACCOMMODATIONS Sharing the Accord sedan's basic architecture, the TL offers the same ample adult-size room up front, plus good clearance for heads and toes behind. Aft leg space is only adequate, though, and the rear seat provides unexceptional thigh support. Trunk space is generous, though the trunklid hinges intrude into the cargo area.

The driving position is low and sporty but accommodating, gauges large and legible, outward vision unhindered. Climate controls are a fair reach away for the driver and, with the optional navigation system, too small and inadequately lit. The navigator itself can be useful, but like most of its kind, it can also be a driver distraction.

VALUE FOR THE MONEY Solidly built and impeccably finished, the TL equals or exceeds anything in the near-luxury class for quality and refinement. It also has a sporty nature that will please demanding drivers but may turn off buyers who expect Lexuslike isolation. Overall, the new 5-speed transmission and standard side airbags make the 2000 TL an even stronger Best Buy.

ENGINES

	ohc V6
Size, liters/cu. in.	3.2/196
Horsepower @ rpm	225 @ 5500
Torque (lbs./ft.) @ rpm	216 @ 4700
Availability	S
EPA city/highway mpg	
4-speed OD automatic	19/29

PRICES

Acura TL	Retail Price	Dealer Invoice
Base 4-door sedan	$28400	$25596
Base 4-door sedan w/Navigation System	30400	27397
Destination charge	455	455

STANDARD EQUIPMENT:

Base: 3.2-liter V6 engine, 5-speed automatic transmission w/manual-shift capability, traction control, driver- and passenger-side airbags, front side-impact airbags, antilock 4-wheel disc brakes, air conditioning w/automatic climate control, interior air filter, variable-assist power steering, leather-wrapped tilt steering wheel, cruise control, leather upholstery, heated front bucket seats, 8-way power driver seat w/manual lumbar adjustment, 4-way power passenger seat, console w/armrest, cupholders, trunk pass-through, wood interior trim, heated power mirrors, power windows, power door locks, remote keyless entry, power sunroof, Bose AM/FM/cassette/CD player, steering wheel mounted radio controls, rear defogger, automatic day/night rearview mirror, variable intermittent wipers, universal garage door opener, auxiliary power outlets, illuminated visor mirrors, automatic-off headlights, theft-deterrent system,

205/60VR16 tires, alloy wheels.

Base w/Navigation System adds: navigation system with global positioning system, LCD screen.

Options are available as dealer-installed accessories.

AUDI A4

Audi A4 1.8T 4-door

Front- or all-wheel-drive near-luxury car
Base price range: $23,990-$37,900. Built in Germany. **Also consider:** BMW 3-Series, Infiniti I30, Lexus ES 300, Mercedes-Benz C-Class

FOR • Cargo room (wagon) • Ride • Handling • Optional all-wheel drive • Build quality • Exterior finish • Interior materials
AGAINST • Rear-seat room • Ride (with Sport Pkg.)

Available "curtain" side airbags and a new performance model are year-2000 highlights for Audi's entry-level line. A4 sedans and Avant wagons come as turbocharged 4-cylinder 1.8T models with 150 horsepower and as V6 2.8 models with 190 hp. A 5-speed manual transmission is standard on these models and a 5-speed automatic is optional. Audi's Quattro all-wheel drive is included on Avants and optional on sedans in place of front drive. Traction control is standard on front-drive 2.8s but is no longer available on front-drive 1.8Ts. For 2000, these models get a mild restyle, reworked center console, and standard trip computer; the 2.8s also add a standard power front passenger's seat.

The new performance model, called S4, is a Quattro sedan with a 250-hp twin-turbocharged 2.7-liter V6 and the 5-speed automatic or a 6-speed manual transmission. S4s also have a sport suspension, 17-inch performance tires, and unique grille, bumpers, and leather-upholstered interior.

Newly optional for all models are Audi's Sideguard airbags designed to deploy from above the side windows as a head-protecting curtain against side impacts. Seat-mounted front side airbags are standard. Other new options include high-intensity headlamps and a satellite-based navigation system with audio and visual direction prompts but no video-type display screen.

PERFORMANCE The new S4 has outstanding acceleration, but other A4s are not impressively quick. We timed an automatic 2.8 Quattro sedan at 9.3 seconds 0-60 mph. The lighter front-drive versions are a tad faster, but still trail most class rivals. The 1.8 turbo is adequate with automatic but performs best with manual shift. Our test V6 Quattro sedans averaged 17.5-21.5 mpg, our test 1.8T Quattros around 23 mpg.

Quattro provides great traction in any situation, and any A4 is fun to drive. Steering is linear and communicative. A well-designed suspension checks undue cornering lean while smothering most bumps, though there's noticeable impact harshness with the available Sport package, which is comparable to the S4's chassis. Stops are short and straight. Wind noise is moderate, but the high-performance tires on some models thrum audibly on rough pavement. The V6s are smooth and quiet, but the turbo-4 growls at high rpm.

ACCOMMODATIONS A4s have good passenger room in front but not in back, where rear leg space all but vanishes without the front seats moved well forward. All-around head room is only adequate with the optional sunroof. Cargo space in sedans is okay, while the Avant is more casual hauler than big-load wagon.

This Audi caters nicely to drivers of all sizes. Gauges and most switchgear are clear and well-placed, though controls for the standard automatic climate system are too low and complex, and the new navigation system isn't easy to operate while driving. All A4s have a solid driving feel, exemplary detail finish, and attractive interior materials.

VALUE FOR THE MONEY Despite the tight rear seat, the A4 compares well with near-luxury competitors. It's also one of the few with a wagon, with all-wheel drive, and with a performer to rival the pricey but potent S4. Add in free scheduled maintenance for 3 years/50,000 miles and any A4 deserves a look.

ENGINES

	Turbocharged dohc I4	dohc V6	Turbocharged dohc V6
Size, liters/cu. in.	1.8/107	2.8/169	2.7/163
Horsepower @ rpm	150 @ 5700	190 @ 6000	250 @ 5800
Torque (lbs./ft.) @ rpm	155 @ 1750	207 @ 3200	258 @ 1850
Availability	S[1]	S[2]	S[3]
EPA city/highway mpg			
5-speed OD manual	23/32[4]	20/29[5]	
6-speed OD manual			17/24
5-speed OD automatic	21/31[4]	18/29[5]	17/24

1. 1.8T and 1.8T Avant. 2. 2.8 sedan and 2.8 Avant. 3. S4. 4. 21/29 and 18/27 w/Quattro. 5. 19/27 and 17/27 w/Quattro.

PRICES

Audi A4	Retail Price	Dealer Invoice
A4 1.8T 4-door sedan	$23990	$21356
A4 1.8T Avant 4-door wagon	26740	23986
A4 2.8 4-door sedan	28790	25580
A4 2.8 Avant 4-door wagon	31540	28210
S4 4-door sedan	37900	33908
Destination charge	525	525

STANDARD EQUIPMENT:

A4 1.8T: 1.8-liter dohc turbocharged 4-cylinder engine, 5-speed manual transmission, electronic limited-slip differential, driver- and passenger-side airbags, front side-impact airbags, antilock 4-wheel disc brakes, air conditioning w/automatic climate control, interior air filter, variable-assist power steering, tilt/telescoping steering wheel, leather-wrapped steering wheel and shifter, cruise control, cloth upholstery, front bucket seats with height and lumbar adjustment, center console, cupholders, split folding rear seat, tachometer, outside temperature indicator, AM/FMcassette/CD player, analog clock, trip computer, heated power mirrors, power windows, power door locks, remote keyless entry, rear defogger, remote decklid and fuel-door releases, variable intermittent wipers, illuminated visor mirrors, map lights, auxiliary power outlets, floormats, theft-deterrent system, first-aid kit, headlight washers, front and rear fog lights, 205/60R15 tires, alloy wheels.

A4 1.8T Avant adds: permanent all-wheel drive, electronic limited-slip front and rear differentials, ski sack, rear wiper/washer, cargo cover, roof rails.

A4 2.8 adds to A4 1.8T: 2.8-liter dohc V6 engine, traction control, 10-way power front seats, wood interior trim, 205/55HR16 tires.

A4 2.8 Avant adds: permanent all-wheel drive, electronic limited-slip front and rear differentials, ski sack, rear wiper/washer, cargo cover, roof rails, deletes traction control.

S4 adds to A4 1.8T: 2.7-liter dohc turbocharged V6 engine, 5-speed automatic w/manual-shift capability, permanent all-wheel drive, electronic limited-slip front and rear differentials, leather upholstery, front sport seats, steering wheel manual-shift controls (automatic transmission), Xenon headlights, sport suspension, 225/45R17 tires.

OPTIONAL EQUIPMENT:
Major Packages

Convenience Pkg.	1200	1056

Power sunroof, automatic day/night outside and rearview mirrors, universal garage door opener.

All-Weather Pkg., A4 sedans	600	506
S4	575	506
wagons	440	387

Includes heated driver-side door lock, heated front seats, ski sack (sedans).

Sport Pkg., 1.8T, 1.8T Avant	750	660
2.8, 2.8 Avant	400	352

Leather-wrapped sport steering wheel, steering wheel manual-shift controls (automatic transmission), sport suspension, 205/55WR16 tires, special alloy wheels.

Powertrains

5-speed automatic trans. w/manual-shift capability, A4	1075	1047

	Retail Price	Dealer Invoice
6-speed manual transmission, S4	NC	NC
Quattro IV all-wheel-drive system, sedans	$1750	$1750

Safety Features

Front and rear side-head-protection system	300	264

Comfort and Convenience

Navigation System	1280	1138
Bose sound system	650	572
6-disc CD changer	550	484
Front sport seats, A4	500	440
Leather upholstery, 2.8, 2.8 Avant	1320	1162
Sport Interior Pkg., S4	NC	NC

Alcantara suede seat trim, aluminum interior trim.

Sport steering wheel, A4	160	141

Includes manual-shift controls with automatic transmission.

Integrated mobile telephone	495	431

Appearance and Miscellaneous

Xenon headlights, A4	500	440

AUDI A6

RECOMMENDED

Audi A6 2.8 4-door

Front- or all-wheel-drive near-luxury car; similar to Volkswagen Passat

Base price range: $33,950-$48,900. Built in Germany. **Also consider:** Acura TL, Infiniti I30, Lexus ES 300

FOR • Steering/handling • Passenger and cargo room • Build quality • Exterior finish • Interior materials **AGAINST** • Rear visibility • Climate controls

Audi's midrange models offer "curtain" side airbags for 2000, plus two new performance sedans, one with the line's first V8 engine. A6 2.8 sedans and Avant wagons use a 200-horsepower 2.8-liter V6 and 5-speed automatic transmission with manual shift capability. The Avant comes only with Audi's Quattro all-wheel drive, the sedan with Quattro or front-wheel drive. The 2.8 Quattro sedans are now available with a 5-speed manual transmission. The new 2.7T is a Quattro sedan with a 250-hp twin-turbo V6 and 6-speed manual or the automatic. Topping the line is a new 4.2 Quattro sedan with a 300-hp V8, automatic transmission, and slightly different styling. Standard on the 4.2 and optional on other A6s are Audi's new Sideguard airbags, which drop down from above the side windows for head protection in a side impact. A new linewide option is a satellite-linked navigation system with audio and visual direction prompts but no video-type display.

EVALUATION Though not neck-snappers, A6 2.8s move well if you make liberal use of the automatic's manual shift capability and keep hard on the throttle. They average a decent 19.2-22.4 mpg in our tests. Audi says the new 2.7T and 4.2 hit 60 mph in under 7 seconds; both felt that strong on our brief preview drives and easily rank among the faster cars in the near-luxury class. All A6s offer no-sweat braking, agile handling, and a quiet, mostly supple ride, though tire thump and roar occur on rough, coarse pavement. A6s also boast more rear passenger room than the rival BMW 5-Series and Mercedes E-Class, plus ample, easily accessed cargo space, sophisticated interior decor, and intelligent switchgear—save fiddley, low-mounted climate controls. These Audis cost less than many rivals, yet deliver Teutonic solidity, high driving satisfaction, and top-drawer workmanship, plus free scheduled maintenance for 3 years/50,000 miles. We recommend them highly.

ENGINES

	dohc V6	Turbocharged dohc V6	dohc V8
Size, liters/cu. in.	2.8/169	2.7/163	4.2/255
Horsepower @ rpm	200 @	250 @	300 @

Prices are accurate at time of publication; subject to manufacturer's changes.

	dohc V6 6000	Turbocharged dohc V6 5800	dohc V8 6200
Torque (lbs./ft.) @ rpm	207 @ 3200	258 @ 1850	295 @ 3000
Availability	S[1]	S[2]	S[3]
EPA city/highway mpg			
6-speed OD manual............................		17/24	
5-speed OD automatic	17/27[4]	17/24	17/24

1. 2.8 models.. 2. 2.7T. 3. 4.2. 4. 17/26 w/Quattro

PRICES

Audi A6

	Retail Price	Dealer Invoice
2.8 4-door sedan	$33950	$30222
2.8 Avant 4-door wagon	36900	33028
2.7T 4-door sedan	38550	34480
4.2 4-door sedan	48900	43588
Destination charge	525	525

STANDARD EQUIPMENT:

2.8: 2.8-liter dohc V6 engine, 5-speed automatic transmission w/manual-shift capability, traction control, electronic limited-slip differential, driver- and passenger-side airbags, front side-impact airbags, antilock 4-wheel disc brakes, air conditioning w/dual-zone automatic climate controls, variable-assist power steering, tilt/telescoping steering wheel, leather-wrapped steering wheel, cruise control, cloth upholstery, 12-way power front bucket seats w/power lumbar adjustment, center console, cupholders, split folding rear seat, wood interior trim, outside-temperature indicator, trip computer, heated power mirrors, power windows, power door locks, remote keyless entry, remote fuel-door and decklid release, AM/FM/cassette/CD player, analog clock, tachometer, map lights, illuminated visor mirrors, rear defogger, variable intermittent wipers, auxiliary power outlets, floormats, theft-deterrent system, first-aid kit, headlight washers, front and rear fog lights, 205/55R16 tires, alloy wheels.

2.8 Avant adds: Quattro permanent all-wheel drive, electronic limited-slip front and rear differentials, rear wiper/washer, ski sack, remote tailgate release, manual rear window sunshade, cargo cover, roof rails.

2.7T adds to 2.8: 2.7-liter dohc turbocharged V6 engine, Quattro permanent all-wheel drive, electronic limited-slip front and rear differentials, full-size spare tire, 215/55R16 tires.

4.2 adds: 4.2-liter dohc V8 engine, front and rear side-head-protection system, power sunroof, power tilt/telescoping steering wheel, leather upholstery, driver seat and mirror memory, ski sack, Bose sound system, steering wheel radio controls, automatic day/night outside and rearview mirrors, universal garage door opener, 235/50R16 tires.

OPTIONAL EQUIPMENT:
Major Packages

Preferred Equipment Group,		
2.8, 2.8 Avant	1950	1716
Leather upholstery, power sunroof, universal garage door opener.		
Convenience Pkg., 2.8, 2.8 Avant, 2.7T	1650	1452
Memory driver seat and outside mirrors, steering wheel manual-shift and radio controls, automatic day/night rearview and outside mirrors, power sunroof, universal garage door opener.		
Sport Pkg., 2.7T	750	660
Sport steering wheel, front sport seats, 215/55R16 performance tires, special alloy wheels.		
Sport Pkg., 4.2	1500	1320
Front sport seats, 17-inch alloy wheels.		
Warm Weather Pkg., sedan	1000	880
wagon	800	704
Power rear sunshade (sedan), manual rear side shades, solar panel sunroof. Requires Convenience Pkg.		
Cold Weather Pkg., 2.8, 2.7T...................	625	550
2.8 Avant	475	418
Heated front and rear seats, ski sack (sedan).		

Powertrains

5-speed manual transmission, 2.8 sedan	NC	NC
Requires Quattro IV all-wheel-drive.		
6-speed manual transmission, 2.7T	NC	NC
Quattro IV permanent all-wheel-drive system,		
2.8 sedan	1750	1750

Safety Features

	Retail Price	Dealer Invoice
Front and rear side-head-protection system,		
2.8, 2.8 Avant, 2.7T..........................	$300	$264
Front and rear side head protection system		
w/rear side-impact air bags, 2.8, 2.8 Avant, 2.7T	500	440
4.2	350	308
Antiskid system, 4.2	550	484

Comfort and Convenience

Navigation system.............................	1280	1138
Leather upholstery, 2.8, 2.8 Avant, 2.7T.........	1550	1364
Cloth rear-facing seat, 2.8 Avant..............	700	616
Heated front and rear seats, 4.2	475	418
6-disc CD changer	550	484
Bose sound system, 2.8, 2.8 Avant, 2.7T........	750	660
Integrated mobile telephone....................	495	431
Rear acoustic parking assist	350	308

Appearance and Miscellaneous

Xenon headlights	500	440
Polished alloy wheels, 4.2	750	660

AUDI A8

Audi A8

All-wheel-drive luxury car

Base price: $62,000. Built in Germany. **Also consider:** BMW 7-Series, Jaguar XJ Sedan, Mercedes-Benz S-Class/CL500

FOR • Ride • Quietness • Acceleration • Build quality • Exterior finish • Interior materials **AGAINST** • Price • Fuel economy • Control layout

Audi's flagship sedan returns for 2000 with a minor restyle, "curtain" side air bags, and a $3000 base-price cut. The A8's 4.2-liter V8 gains 10 horsepower this year, to 310, mainly from a switch from two to five valves per cylinder. Audi's Quattro all-wheel drive and a 5-speed automatic transmission with manual-shift capability are standard. Matching a safety feature of high-end German rivals, the A8 gets Audi's Sideguard airbags that drop down from above the doors in a side impact. Also added are a 3-point rear center seatbelt, steering-wheel audio controls, and auto-dimming mirrors. There are also three new options: a satellite-linked navigation system, an "Acoustic" parking system that warns of obstacles when backing up, and an antiskid system. Audi also is reportedly readying a higher-priced long-wheelbase version with three extra inches of rear legroom.

EVALUATION The 2000 A8 feels much like earlier models, though Audi says it does 0-60 mph in 6.7 seconds, a full second quicker than before. A composed ride, powerful braking, impressive refinement, and adroit handling are still strong points. The unerring traction of Quattro is exclusive in this class and this year is enhanced by the new skid-control option. Although the A8 trails the largest Mercedes and BMWs for rear passenger room, it matches their high comfort levels, ample trunk space, ingot-solid driving feel, and now their head-protecting curtain airbags. The A8's all-aluminum construction contributes to its high price, but adds another dimension to a luxury sedan that deserves to be more popular.

ENGINES

	dohc V8
Size, liters/cu. in.	4.2/255
Horsepower @ rpm	310 @ 6200
Torque (lbs./ft.) @ rpm	302 @ 3000
Availability	S
EPA city/highway mpg	
5-speed OD automatic.........................	17/24

PRICES

Audi A8

	Retail Price	Dealer Invoice
Base 4-door sedan	$62000	$54805

	Retail Price	Dealer Invoice
Destination charge	$525	$525

STANDARD EQUIPMENT:

Base: 4.2-liter dohc V8 engine, 5-speed automatic transmission w/manual-shift capability, permanent all-wheel-drive system, electronic limited-slip front and rear differentials, traction control, driver- and passenger-side airbags, front and rear side-impact airbags, front and rear side-head-protection system, antilock 4-wheel disc brakes, air conditioning w/dual-zone automatic climate control, interior air filter, variable-assist power steering, power tilt/telescoping steering wheel, leather-wrapped steering wheel and shifter, cruise control, leather upholstery, 14-way power front bucket seats w/power lumbar adjustment and headrests, memory functions (driver seat, outside mirrors, steering wheel), center console, cupholders, rear seat power lumbar adjustment and headrests, wood interior trim, power sunroof, trip computer, outside-temperature indicator, heated power mirrors, power windows, power door locks, remote keyless entry, automatic day/night rearview mirror, remote fuel-door and decklid release, Bose AM/FM/cassette/CD player w/6-disc CD changer, digital clock, steering wheel radio controls, tachometer, map lights, auxiliary power outlets, illuminated visor mirrors, rear defogger, intermittent wipers, floormats, dual pane acoustic glass, theft-deterrent system, first-aid kit, heated washer nozzles, headlight washers, front and rear fog lights, full-size spare tire, 225/60HR16 tires, alloy wheels.

OPTIONAL EQUIPMENT:

Major Packages

	Retail Price	Dealer Invoice
Warm Weather Pkg.	$1200	$1056

Solar panel sunroof, manual rear-side-window sunshades, power rear sunshade.

Premium Comfort Pkg.	1500	1320

Heated front and rear seats, soft optic front and rear seats, heated steering wheel, ski sack.

Safety Features

Antiskid system	550	484

Comfort and Convenience

Navigation system..	1280	1138
Alcantara and Leather Trim Pkg.	3500	3080

Additional leather trim, alcantara suede door trim, alcantara suede headliner and rear parcel shelf. Requires Warm Weather Pkg. and Premium Comfort Pkg.

Integrated mobile telephone.............................	495	431
Acoustic rear parking system............................	700	616

Appearance and Miscellaneous

Xenon headlights	500	440
Polished alloy wheels and 225/55R17 tires	1000	880

AUDI TT

Audi TT coupe Quattro

Front- or all-wheel-drive sports and GT car

Base price: $30,500. Built in Germany. **Also consider:** BMW Z3 Series, Honda Prelude, Mazda Miata

FOR • Build quality • Handling/roadholding • Interior materials • Acceleration   **AGAINST** • Noise • Visibility • Rear-seat room

Audi's sports car bowed last spring as a front-wheel-drive hatchback coupe and has since made available optional Quattro all-wheel drive. The TT uses the same platform as the Audi A4 and sister division Volkswagen's New Beetle, Jetta, and Golf. It's shorter and lower than those cars, however, and has a firmer suspension. A 180-horsepower version of the 150-hp turbocharged 4-cylinder available in the

A4 and New Beetle is linked to a 5-speed manual transmission. Antilock 4-wheel disc brakes and front head/chest side airbags are standard. Front-drive models have traction control. Available later in calendar 2000: a 225-hp engine, 6-speed manual transmission, and a 2-seat convertible model.

EVALUATION Racy though it looks, the 180-hp TT isn't super quick—we clocked 8.2 seconds 0-60 mph with a front-drive coupe—and it needs lots of revs for fast takeoffs and brisk passing. Premium gas is required but fuel economy is great; our test cars averaged between 25.3 and 29 mpg. We haven't yet tested a 225-hp model or a convertible. Handling is sharp and balanced, though the steering wheel can wriggle as the optional performance tires "tramline" along deep grooves. Ride can be harsh on bad pavement and noise levels are on the high side, but the TT is civilized for a sports car. Seating is cozy in front and the coupe's rear seat suits parcels, not passengers. But the cabin delights with imaginative design and top-notch materials. Visibility is poor to the sides, but not that bad astern. Cargo space is good with the coupe's rear seatbacks up and terrific with them folded. In all, the TT offers practical sports-car fun with a style all its own.

ENGINES

	Turbocharged dohc I4
Size, liters/cu. in.	1.8/107
Horsepower @ rpm	180 @ 5500
Torque (lbs./ft.) @ rpm	173 @ 1950
Availability	S
EPA city/highway mpg	
5-speed OD manual..	22/31[1]

1. 20/29 w/Quattro.

PRICES

Audi TT	Retail Price	Dealer Invoice
Base 2-door coupe	$30500	$27085
Destination charge	525	525

STANDARD EQUIPMENT:

Base: 1.8-liter dohc turbocharged 4-cylinder engine, 5-speed manual transmission, traction control, driver- and passenger-side airbags, front side-impact airbags, antilock 4-wheel disc brakes, air conditioning w/automatic climate control, variable-assist power steering, tilt/telescoping leather-wrapped steering wheel, cruise control, leather upholstery, front bucket seats, center console, split folding rear seat, cupholders, heated power mirrors, power windows, power door locks, remote keyless entry, AM/FM/cassette, digital clock, tachometer, rear defogger, remote fuel door/decklid release, illuminated visor mirrors, variable-intermittent wipers, floormats, theft-deterrent system, front and rear fog lights, 205/55ZR16 tires, alloy wheels.

OPTIONAL EQUIPMENT:

Major Packages

Performance Pkg.	1000	880

Xenon headlights, 225/45YR17 tires, special cast-alloy wheels.

Comfort Pkg.	700	616

Heated front seats, driver's information center, trip computer.

Powertrains

Quattro IV System	1750	1750

Permanent all-wheel drive, electronic limited-slip front and rear differentials. Deletes traction control.

Comfort and Convenience

Audio Pkg.	1200	1056

Bose sound system, 6-disc CD changer.

Cellular telephone	495	431

BMW X5

4-wheel-drive midsize sport-utility vehicle

Base price: $49,400. Built in USA. **Also consider:** Lexus RX 300, Mercedes-Benz M-Class

For its first sport-utility vehicle, BMW chooses the new-age blend of carlike attributes and minivan-type styling typified by the Lexus RX 300 over the off-road wagon tradition exemplified by the Mercedes-Benz M-Class. The all-new X5 debuted this winter with seats for five,

---

Prices are accurate at time of publication; subject to manufacturer's changes.

BMW X5

a standard V8 engine, permanent all-wheel drive, and the German automaker's promise that it echoes the luxury and performance of a V8 BMW sedan.

Built at BMW's plant in South Carolina, the X5 does not share its platform with any other vehicle. It has unibody construction, all-independent suspension, four side doors, and a drop-down tailgate with separate liftglass. Though stylistically similar to the RX 300, the X5 is larger on the outside and slightly smaller on the inside than the Lexus. The BMW is 3.6 inches longer on an 8-inch longer wheelbase. It's 2.2 inches wider and taller, and about 900 pounds heavier than the 4-wheel-drive RX 300, which also seats five but comes only with a V6 engine. The X5 has between 1 and 1.4 inches less head room and leg room at all seating positions than the Lexus, and, with all seats folded, 54.8 cubic feet of cargo space to 75 cubic feet for the RX 300.

The X5 borrows from BMW's 5- and 7-Series cars its 4.4-liter V8 and 5-speed automatic transmission with a floor-mounted gear lever that has a separate gate for manual shifting. BMW acknowledges its new SUV is not intended for serious off-road duty and does not equip the permanently engaged 4WD system with low-range gearing. The X5 does come with traction and antiskid systems similar to those on BMW cars, while adding technology specifically designed for its role as an SUV. This includes a system that can automatically apply each wheel's brake selectively to limit slip in extreme low-grip conditions; the M-Class employs a similar capability, as does the Discovery from Britain's Land Rover, which is owned by BMW. Both the X5 and Discovery also have so-called hill descent control, which automatically applies the brakes to keep speeds below 6 mph when descending steep slopes. BMW says the X5's stanard antilock 4-wheel disc brakes provide the same stopping power as a 7-Series sedan.

Standard safety features include front side airbags and BMW's head protection system—tubular airbags that deploy from above the front side windows in a side impact. Rear lower-body side airbags are optional. A load-leveling suspension and 18-inch wheels and tires are standard; an optional Sport package includes 19-inch wheels and tires and a sport suspension. Leather upholstery, power tilt/telescope steering wheel, and a 60/40 split folding rear seat are standard. A heated steering wheel, navigation system, and a system that sounds a warning of obstacles when backing up are options.

According to BMW's preliminary figures, the X5 is among the fastest SUVs, with a 0-60 mph time of 7.5 seconds and, with the Sport package, a top speed of 143 mph. We have not tested an X5 and thus cannot provide an evaluation or ratings.

ENGINES

	dohc V8
Size, liters/cu. in.	4.4/268
Horsepower @ rpm	282 @ 5400
Torque (lbs./ft.) @ rpm	324 @ 3600
Availability	S
EPA city/highway mpg	
5-speed OD automatic	NA

PRICES

BMW X5	Retail Price	Dealer Invoice
Base 4-door wagon	$49400	$44620
Destination charge	570	570

STANDARD EQUIPMENT:

Base: 4.4-liter dohc V8 engine, 5-speed automatic transmission w/manual-shift capability, permanent 4-wheel drive, traction control, driver- and passenger-side airbags, front side-impact airbags, front side-head-protection system, antilock 4-wheel disc brakes, antiskid system, air conditioning w/dual-zone automatic climate control, interior air filter, variable-assist power steering, power tilt/telescoping leather-wrapped steering wheel, cruise control, leather upholstery, 8-way power front bucket seats, memory system (driver seat, mirrors, steering wheel), center console, cupholders, split folding rear seat, wood interior trim, heated power mirrors w/passenger-side tilt-down parking aid, power windows, power door locks, remote keyless entry, AM/FM/cassette, steering wheel radio controls, map lights, variable intermittent wipers, trip computer, outside temperature indicator, illuminated visor mirrors, rear defogger, intermittent rear wiper/washer, power tailgate release, cargo cover, theft-deterrent system, fog lights, roof rails, rear automatic-leveling suspension, 255/55HR18 all-terrain tires, alloy wheels.

OPTIONAL EQUIPMENT:

	Retail Price	Dealer Invoice
Major Packages		
Sport Pkg.	$2470	$2100

Sport seats, black headliner, titanium-colored grille insert, Shadowline trim, black chrome exhaust pipes, sport suspension, performance tires (255/50R19 front, 285/45R19 rear).

Activity Pkg.	850	725

Heated front seats, ski sack, rain-sensing wipers, headlight washers.

Safety Features		
Rear side-impact airbags	385	325

Comfort and Convenience		
Navigation system	1990	1690

Includes upgraded trip computer.

Power sunroof	1050	895
CD player	200	170

NA with navigation system.

Premium sound system	1200	1020
Upgraded trip computer	300	255
Heated steering wheel	150	—

Requires Activity Pkg.

Park distance control	350	300
Front lumbar support	400	340
Inside and outside automatic day/night mirrors	300	255
Rear side-window shades	180	155
Retractable load floor	380	325

Appearance and Miscellaneous		
Xenon headlights	500	425
Privacy glass	275	235

BMW Z3 SERIES

RECOMMENDED

BMW Z3 2.3

Rear-wheel-drive sports and GT car

Base price range: $31,300-$42,700. Built in USA. **Also consider:** Mazda Miata, Mercedes-Benz SLK230, Porsche Boxster

FOR • Steering/handling • Acceleration • Exterior finish
AGAINST • Noise • Cargo space

Convertible versions of BMW's American-built 6-cylinder 2-seaters got revised tail styling and some new standard features for a spring unveiling as 2000 models. The lineup again consists of the 2.5-liter Z3 2.3 convertible, the 2.8-liter Z3 2.8 convertible and hatchback coupe, and the high-performance 3.2-liter M Roadster and M Coupe. Convertibles also got an inner top liner and a new center console. All models get upgraded interior materials and a 3-spoke steering wheel. Standard side airbags and traction control are joined on 2.3 and 2.8 models by BMW's anti-skid Dynamic Stability Control, which counteracts skids by automatically applying individual brakes in a turn. Manual transmission is standard, automatic optional except on M models. A power top is standard on the M Roadster, optional on other convertibles.

EVALUATION These BMWs encourage exuberant driving. The M models are scorchers, and even the entry-level 2.3 convertible is quick, at least with manual shift. Fuel economy in our tests was between 20.2 and 22.3 mpg for all models. Noise levels are high and the ride can be choppy in the more stiffly sprung M, but all models are comfortable enough for sports cars. Handling is uniformly great, braking terrific. Wet-weather grip can be a problem, but standard traction control and the anti-skid system are proven safety assists. Gripes? Large drivers can feel cramped at the wheel, luggage space is meager (coupes have more than convertibles, but still not much), and convertibles suffer some body shake. In all, these are fine sports-car choices, with the base 2.3 convertible being the best value.

ENGINES

	dohc I6	dohc I6	dohc I6
Size, liters/cu. in.	2.5/152	2.8/170	3.2/192
Horsepower @ rpm	170 @ 5500	193 @ 5500	240 @ 6000
Torque (lbs./ft.) @ rpm	181 @ 3500	206 @ 3500	225 @ 3800
Availability	S[1]	S[2]	S[3]
EPA city/highway mpg			
5-speed manual	20/27	19/26	19/26
4-speed OD automatic	19/26	19/26	

1. Z3 2.3. 2. Z3 2.8. 3. M Roadster, M coupe.

PRICES

BMW Z3 Series	Retail Price	Dealer Invoice
2.3 2-door convertible	$31300	$28330
2.8 2-door convertible	36900	33370
2.8 2-door hatchback	36550	33055
M-Series 2-door convertible	42700	38590
M-Series 2-door hatchback	41800	37780
Destination charge	570	570

STANDARD EQUIPMENT:

2.3: 2.5-liter dohc 6-cylinder engine, 5-speed manual transmission, limited-slip differential, traction control, driver- and passenger-side airbags, side-impact airbags, anti-skid system, antilock 4-wheel disc brakes, roll bars (convertible), air conditioning, variable-assist power steering, leather-wrapped steering wheel/shifter/handbrake, vinyl upholstery, 4-way power driver seat, 2-way power passenger seat, center storage console, cupholders, 6-speaker AM/FM/weatherband/cassette, analog clock, power mirrors, power door locks, power windows, tachometer, visor mirrors, intermittent wipers, tool kit, 225/50ZR16 tires, alloy wheels.

2.8 adds: 2.8-liter dohc 6-cylinder engine, leather upholstery, sport seats (hatchback), wood interior trim (hatchback), cruise control, Harman/Kardon sound system, fog lights.

M-Series add: 3.2-liter dohc 6-cylinder engine, power convertible top (convertible), upgraded leather upholstery, heated sport seats, heated mirrors and washer jets, heated driver door lock, chrome interior trim, metallic paint, 225/50ZR17 front tires, 245/40ZR17 rear tires, deletes anti-skid system, wood interior trim, fog lights.

OPTIONAL EQUIPMENT:

Major Packages

Premium Pkg., 2.3	2000	1700
2.8	950	810

Power convertible top, leather upholstery (2.3), wood interior trim.

Powertrains

4-speed automatic transmission, 2.3, 2.8	975	925

Comfort and Convenience

Cruise control, 2.3	475	405
Leather upholstery, 2.3	1150	980
Extended leather upholstery, 2.8	1200	1020

Includes color-keyed leather steering wheel, instrument cluster hood, console sides, door upper ledges and pulls.

Chrome interior trim, 2.3, 2.8	150	130
Aluminum interior trim, 2.8 hatchback	150	130
Heated seats, 2.3, 2.8	500	425

Includes heated mirrors.

Sport seats, 2.3/2.8 convertible	400	340

Requires heated seats.

AM/FM/CD player	200	170

	Retail Price	Dealer Invoice
Harman/Kardon sound system, 2.3	$675	$575
Trip computer, 2.3, 2.8	300	255
Power convertible top, 2.3, 2.8 convertible	750	640
Power tilt-up roof panel, hatchback	300	255

Appearance and Miscellaneous

Fog lights, 2.3	260	220
Hardtop, convertibles	1900	1615
17-inch alloy wheels, 2.8	1125	955

Includes 225/45ZR17 front tires, 245/40ZR17 rear tires.

BMW 3-SERIES

BMW 323Ci

Rear-wheel-drive near-luxury car
Base price range: $26,990-$33,990. Built in Germany.
Also consider: Acura TL, Audi A4, Mercedes-Benz C-Class and CLK

FOR • Acceleration • Steering/handling • Build quality • Exterior finish **AGAINST** • Cargo room (coupe and convertible)

Redesigned for '99, BMW's entry-level sedans are joined this summer by a pair of similarly redesigned coupes. The new 323Ci and 328Ci 2-doors have the same 2.5- and 2.8-liter 6-cylinder engines as the respective 4-doors. They're a bit lower, longer, and wider than the sedans, and have different body panels. The 4-seat 323i and 328i convertibles will be similarly updated for sale in the first quarter of 2000, and will be joined by the first 3-Series wagons to be sold in America. A high-performance M3 coupe is due later in the year. Discontinued for 2000 is the 4-cylinder 318ti hatchback.

All 3-Series come with manual transmission and offer an optional 5-speed automatic with BMW's Steptronic manual-shift feature. Traction control and front side airbags are standard across the board. These coupes and sedans add BMW's front Head Protection System tubular airbags, plus Cornering Brake Control, designed to enhance stability under hard braking in turns. Anti-skid Dynamic Stability Control is standard for coupes and now sedans, and rear side airbags are optional for sedans.

PERFORMANCE Coupe or sedan, the latest 3-Series models shine for silky engines, solid on-road feel, modest noise levels, and athletic, top-of-the-class rear-drive handling. The Sport suspension that's standard on the new coupes and available for sedans sharpens cornering grip and steering response, but produces some ride jiggle on rough pavement. The coupe's Sport Package includes low-profile tires that amplify that, so try before you buy.

Acceleration is another plus of the newest models. The 323's 2.5-liter six is a model of smoothness and not much slower than the 2.8 version, which pushed a manual-shift sedan 0-60 mph in 7.5 seconds by our clock. Premium fuel is mandatory, but economy is laudable. We averaged 23.5 mpg with our test 328i.

ACCOMMODATIONS A one-inch wheelbase stretch helps increase rear leg room in the newer models by about a half-inch, and combines with new front seat frames for decent knee and toe clearance. The absence of rear cupholders and air ducts is conspicuous at these prices, however. Interior materials are sturdy and attractive, though leather and wood are optional instead of standard, as on many near-luxury rivals. A tilt/telescoping steering wheel is finally standard as part of the 1999-2000 makeover, as are first-time options like power memory seats, power lumbar adjusters, and in-dash CD player. The new dash improves an already good design, augmented by newly available steering-wheel audio and cruise controls. Outward vision is good. Trunk space in sedans is ordinary, and just a bit smaller in coupes, but what's there is usable and easily accessed. And there's an inside trunk release at last. Front seats in coupes automatically slide forward to ease entry to the rear.

Prices are accurate at time of publication; subject to manufacturer's changes.

VALUE FOR THE MONEY With more features included at little-changed prices, the newest 3-Series sedans and coupes really are more car for the money, though a few options can boost stickers well past $35,000. Some rivals deliver greater interior room and more standard amenities, but none is more refined or as sporty.

ENGINES

	dohc I6	dohc I6
Size, liters/cu. in.	2.5/152	2.8/170
Horsepower @ rpm	170 @ 5550	193 @ 5500
Torque (lbs./ft.) @ rpm	181 @ 3500	206 @ 3500
Availability	S[1]	S[2]

EPA city/highway mpg

5-speed manual	20/29	20/29
5-speed OD automatic	19/28	19/27

1. 323i, 323Ci. 2. 328i, 328Ci.

PRICES

BMW 3-Series

	Retail Price	Dealer Invoice
323i 4-door sedan	$26990	$24450
323Ci 2-door coupe	28990	26250
328i 4-door sedan	33400	30220
328Ci 2-door coupe	33990	30750
Destination charge	570	570

STANDARD EQUIPMENT:

323i: 2.5-liter dohc 6-cylinder engine, 5-speed manual transmission, traction control, driver- and passenger-side airbags, daytime running lights, front side-impact airbags, front side-head-protection, anti-skid system, antilock 4-wheel disc brakes, daytime running lights, air conditioning w/dual-zone automatic climate control, interior air filter, variable-assist power steering, tilt/telescoping steering wheel, vinyl upholstery, front bucket seats, cupholders, power mirrors, power windows, power door locks, remote keyless entry, AM/FM/cassette, digital clock, tachometer, outside temperature indicator, speed-sensitive intermittent wipers, rear defogger, Service Interval Indicator, theft-deterrent system, tool kit, 195/65R15 tires, alloy wheels.

323Ci adds: cruise control, leather-wrapped steering wheel w/radio and cruise controls, split folding rear seat, heated power mirrors, trip computer, fog lights, sport suspension, full-size spare tire, 205/55HR16 tires.

328 models add: 2.8-liter dohc 6-cylinder engine, power front seats w/driver memory, front center armrest, heated washers, illuminated visor mirrors (328i), 328i deletes split folding rear seat, sport suspension.

OPTIONAL EQUIPMENT:

Major Packages

Premium Pkg., 323i	3500	2975

Cruise control, leather-wrapped steering wheel w/radio and cruise controls, power front seats w/driver seat memory, power sunroof, automatic day/night rearview mirror, map and footwell lights, trip computer, illuminated visor mirrors, wood interior trim, 205/55HR16 tires.

Premium Pkg., 323Ci	2100	1785

Power front seats w/driver seat memory, power sunroof, automatic day/night rearview mirror, wood interior trim.

Premium Pkg., 328	2900	2465

Leather upholstery, power lumbar adjustment, wood interior trim, power sunroof, automatic day/night rearview mirror, rain-sensing wipers.

Sport Pkg., 323i	2000	1700

Cruise control, leather-wrapped steering wheel w/radio and cruise controls, sport bucket seats, fog lights, sport suspension, 225/50WR16 tires.

Sport Pkg., 323Ci	1000	850

Sport bucket seats, 225/45WR17 tires.

Sport Pkg., 328i	1350	1150

Sport bucket seats, sport suspension, 225/45WR17 tires, special alloy wheels.

Sport Pkg., 328Ci	1200	1020

Sport bucket seats, 225/45ZR17 front tires, 245/40ZR17 rear tires, special alloy wheels.

Sport Premium Pkg., 323i	4300	3655

Sport Pkg. plus power sunroof, power front seats w/driver seat memory, trip computer, automatic day/night rearview mirror, illuminated visor mirrors, map and footwell lights, wood interior trim, heated mirrors.

Powertrains

	Retail Price	Dealer Invoice
5-speed automatic trans. w/manual-shift capability	$1275	$1210

Safety Features

Rear side-impact airbags, sedans	385	325

Comfort and Convenience

Radio navigation system	1200	1020

NA with AM/FM/CD player. Requires trip computer.

Onboard navigation system	1800	1675

NA with AM/FM/CD player.

Cruise control, 323i	475	405

Includes leather-wrapped steering wheel w/radio and cruise controls.

Leather upholstery	1450	1235
Power front seats, 323	845	805

Includes driver seat memory.

Heated front seats	500	425
Harman/Kardon audio system	675	575
AM/FM/CD player	200	170
Trip computer, 323i	300	255
Power sunroof	1050	895
Parking distance control, 328	350	300

Appearance and Miscellaneous

Fog lights, 323i	260	220

Includes heated mirrors.

Xenon headlights	500	425

323i requires fog lights.

BMW 5-SERIES

RECOMMENDED

BMW 540i sedan

Rear-wheel-drive luxury car

Base price range: $38,900-$69,400. Built in Germany. **Also consider:** Acura RL, Lexus GS 300/400, Mercedes-Benz E-Class

FOR • Acceleration (540i, M5) • Steering/ handling • Ride • Cargo room (wagon) • Quietness • Build quality • Exterior finish • Interior materials **AGAINST** • Low-speed acceleration (528i) • Fuel economy (540i, M5)

Return of the high-performance M5 sedan highlights the latest changes to BMW's 5-Series line of rear-wheel-drive midsize luxury cars. The roster consists of sedans and wagons offered as 528i models with a 193-horsepower 6-cylinder engine and as 540i models with a 282-hp V8. Built in limited numbers, the M5 uses a 400-hp V8 and comes with a firmer suspension, 18-inch wheels, a mandatory 6-speed manual transmission, and exclusive interior trim. The 528i models are available with a 5-speed manual transmission and now share with the 540i models a 5-speed automatic with BMW's Steptronic manual-mode shifting. The 6-speed manual 540i sedan includes a firmer suspension and 17-inch wheels, which are part of a Sport option package for 528i and 540i models.

For 2000, rain-sensing windshield wipers and Xenon headlamps are standard instead of optional for the 540i and are newly available for 528i models. The 528i versions also gain the 540i models' standard antiskid system. And all models now have daytime running lights, a right outside mirror that tilts down when the car is put into reverse, and fog lamps. Every 5-Series has front side airbags, plus a head protection system with tubular airbags that deploy from the ceiling to cover front outboard passengers. Lower-body rear side airbags are standard on the M5 and optional for other models.

PERFORMANCE Road manners set the standard for like-priced sports-luxury cars. All 5-Series models are surefooted in corners despite fair body lean. Steering is quick and precise, if a bit sensitive at higher speeds. A stout structure assists the standard suspension in delivering a quiet, absorbent ride, though the firmer sport suspensions jiggle and thump more.

We haven't driven the new M5, but it's bound to be fast—and thirsty. At the other extreme, 528i models produce most of their power at higher engine speeds, and so are best with manual shift, though automatic models should be sprightlier with this year's upgrade to the 5-speed transmission. Any 540i has plenty of muscle for quick launches and spirited passing with either transmission, though the 6-speed manual has balky shift action and a heavy clutch. We averaged 20.9 mpg in a test of a manual 528i sedan and 18.8 mpg with an automatic. Our test automatic 540i sedan averaged 15.9 mpg; a 6-speed 19.3 mpg. Though not as quiet as a Lexus LS 400, 528s and 540s are nonetheless free of unpleasant noises, and tire roar is audible over only the coarsest surfaces.

ACCOMMODATIONS These sedans and wagons are more compact than most rivals, so four adults is the practical limit. The rear seat has acceptable head and leg room, but only because the seat cushion is fairly low and short. Some minor controls annoy, especially the complex audio/climate/trip computer display. The sedan's trunk isn't wide, but has a long, flat floor. Split folding rear seatbacks, optional on sedans and standard on wagons, enhance cargo space. Workmanship and interior materials are first-class, as they ought to be at these prices.

VALUE FOR THE MONEY The 5-Series is aimed at enthusiasts who demand premium engineering and superior road manners. We recommend any version that fits your budget. Although base prices are steep, they didn't increase for 2000, despite added standard equipment.

ENGINES

	dohc I6	dohc V8	dohc V8
Size, liters/cu. in.	2.8/170	4.4/268	4.9/303
Horsepower @ rpm	193 @ 5500	282 @ 5400	400 @ 6600
Torque (lbs./ft.) @ rpm	206 @ 3500	324 @ 3600	369 @ 3800
Availability	S[1]	S[2]	S[3]
EPA city/highway mpg			
5-speed manual	20/29		
6-speed OD manual		15/23	NA
5-speed OD automatic	NA	18/24	

1. 528i. 2. 540i. 3. M5.

PRICES

BMW 5-Series	Retail Price	Dealer Invoice
528i 4-door sedan, manual	$38900	$35170
528i 4-door wagon, manual	40700	36790
540i 4-door sedan, automatic	51100	46150
540i 4-door sedan, manual	53900	48670
540i 4-door wagon, automatic	53480	48290
M5 4-door sedan	69400	62620
Destination charge	570	570

540i w/6-speed manual transmission and 540i with automatic transmission and Sport Pkg. add $1300 Gas Guzzler Tax. M5 add $2100 Gas Guzzler Tax.

STANDARD EQUIPMENT:

528i: 2.8-liter dohc 6-cylinder engine, 5-speed manual transmission, traction control, driver- and passenger-side airbags, front side-impact airbags, front side-head-protection system, antilock 4-wheel disc brakes, antiskid system, daytime running lights, variable-assist power steering, power tilt/telescopic steering wheel, leather-wrapped steering wheel, shift knob and hand brake, steering-wheel-mounted radio and telephone controls, cruise control, air conditioning with dual-zone automatic climate controls, interior air filter, 10-way power vinyl front seats (with power head restraints and memory driver seat, steering wheel and outside mirrors), split folding rear seat (wagon), cupholders, AM/FM/cassette, diversity antenna, heated power mirrors w/passenger-side tilt-down parking aid, power windows, power door locks, remote keyless entry, tachometer, outside temperature display, trip computer, map lights, intermittent wipers, remote decklid release, rear defogger, Service Interval Indicator, Active Check Control system, illuminated visor mirrors, cargo cover (wagon), theft-deterrent system, fog lights, tool kit, roof rails (wagon), full-size spare tire, 225/60HR15 tires, alloy wheels.

540i automatic models add: 4.4-liter dohc V8 engine, 5-speed automatic transmission (sedan), 5-speed automatic transmission w/manual-shift capability (wagon), 14-way power front seats, leather upholstery, wood interior trim, power sunroof, automatic day/night rearview mirror, rain-sensing wipers, upgraded trip computer, self-leveling suspension (wagon), Xenon headlights, 225/55HR16 tires and deletes Active Check Control System.

540i manual adds: 6-speed manual transmission, front sport seats, multi-function M-Sport steering wheel, sport suspension, 235/45WR17 front tires, 255/40WR17 rear tires.

M5 adds: 4.9-liter dohc V8 engine, limited-slip differential, rear side-impact air bags, navigation system, upgraded audio system w/6-disc CD player, heated front seats, rear spoiler, 245/40ZR18 front tires, 275/35ZR18 rear tires, chrome alloy wheels.

OPTIONAL EQUIPMENT:

	Retail Price	Dealer Invoice
Major Packages		
Premium Pkg., 528i sedan	$3100	$2635
528i wagon	3250	2765
Leather upholstery, wood interior trim, automatic day/night rearview mirror, rain-sensing wipers, cargo net (wagon), cross-spoke alloy wheels.		
528i Sport Pkg., 528i sedan	1970	1675
528i wagon	2470	2100
Sport steering wheel, sport suspension, self-leveling suspension (wagon), cross-spoke alloy wheels, 235/45WR17 tires. NA with Cold Weather Pkg.		
528i Sport Premium Pkg., 528i sedan	4300	3655
528i wagon	4950	4210
Includes Premium Pkg. and Sport Pkg. NA with Cold Weather Pkg.		
540i Sport Pkg.,		
540i sedan automatic, 540i wagon	2800	2380
Automatic transmission w/manual-shift capability (sedan), performance axle ratio (sedan), front sport seats, Sport steering wheel, sport suspension, 235/45WR17 front tires (sedan), 255/40WR17 rear tires (sedan), 235/45WR17 tires (wagon).		
Cold Weather Pkg.	750	640
Heated front seat and steering wheel, heated headlight washers. NA 540i manual or M5.		
Powertrains		
4-speed automatic transmission, 528i (early production)	975	925
5-speed automatic trans. w/manual-shift capability, 528i (late production)	1275	—
Safety Features		
Rear side-impact airbags, 528i, 540i	385	325
Comfort and Convenience		
Power sunroof, 528i	1050	895
Navigation system, 528i	1990	1690
540i	1800	1530
528i requires Premium Pkg. or Sport Premium Pkg.		
Leather upholstery, 528i	1450	1235
Comfort 16-way power front seats, 528i, 540i automatic	1200	1020
Includes power lumbar support. NA with 540i Sport Pkg.		
Power lumbar support, 528i, 540i automatic	400	340
NA with 540i Sport Pkg. or sport seats.		
Sport seats, 528i	475	405
Requires Sport Pkg. and leather upholstery or Premium Pkg.		
Split folding rear seat, sedans	475	405
Includes ski sack. 528i requires Premium Pkg.		
Heated front seats, 528i, 540i	500	425
Premium sound system, 528i, 540i	1200	1020
Power rear and manual rear-door sunshades, sedans	575	490
Manual rear-door sunshades, wagons	180	155
Rear park distance control	350	300
Appearance and Miscellaneous		
Xenon headlights, 528i	500	425
Self-leveling suspension, 528i wagon	760	645
Mixed parallel spoke alloy wheels, 540i	300	255
540i automatic requires Sport Pkg.		

Prices are accurate at time of publication; subject to manufacturer's changes.

BMW 7-SERIES

BMW 740i

Rear-wheel-drive luxury car
Base price range: $62,400-$92,100. Built in Germany.
Also consider: Infiniti Q45, Lexus LS 400, Mercedes-Benz S-Class

FOR • Acceleration • Ride • Steering/handling • Passenger room/comfort • Build quality • Exterior finish • Interior materials
AGAINST • Fuel economy • Navigation system controls

Added features mark BMW's 2000-model flagships, which went on sale in April at base prices unchanged from 1999. The line again comprises the V8-powered 740i and longer-wheelbase 740iL, and the V12 750iL. All gain standard rain-sensing wipers, and V8 models add as standard an onboard navigation system, Xenon headlights, and premium audio with 6-disc CD changer like the 750. BMW says these additions represent a $4400 value increase for the V8 models. Also new for 740s is an optional Active Ride Package that borrows the V12 model's Electronic Damping Control shock absorbers and self-leveling rear suspension. Newly standard for the 750 and optional for 740s is BMW's Active Comfort driver's seat, with rollers in the cushion that move periodically in an effort to minimize fatigue. All 7s come with BMW's anti-skid Dynamic Stability Control, front side airbags, and BMW's front Head Protection System with side-window tubular airbags. Rear head protection airbags are now part of the rear side airbag option.

EVALUATION Every 7-series model is quiet, comfortable, and enjoyable to drive. The V8 is so strong and silky we see little need to pay so much more for the V12. The 740i doesn't lack for interior or cargo space, but few cars of any size have more rear seat room than the longer-wheelbase models. Seats in all are supportive and comfortable. Other pluses include clear gauges, strategically placed major controls, and a multitude of standard amenities. Unfortunately, lots of gizmos means lots of controls, not all of which are easy to use, the available in-dash navigation system in particular. The aging 7-Series models have a tough rival in the new 2000 Mercedes-Benz S-Class, but are impressive cars by any measure.

ENGINES

	dohc V8	ohc V12
Size, liters/cu. in.	4.4/268	5.4/328
Horsepower @ rpm	282 @ 5400	326 @ 5000
Torque (lbs./ft.) @ rpm	324 @ 3700	361 @ 3900
Availability	S[1]	S[2]
EPA city/highway mpg		
5-speed OD automatic	17/23	13/20

1. 740i, 740iL. 2. 750iL.

PRICES

BMW 7-Series	Retail Price	Dealer Invoice
740i 4-door sedan	$62400	$56320
740iL 4-door sedan	66400	59920
750iL 4-door sedan	92100	83050
Destination charge	570	570

750iL adds $2600 Gas Guzzler Tax.

STANDARD EQUIPMENT:

740i: 4.4-liter dohc V8 engine, 5-speed automatic transmission, traction control, driver- and passenger-side airbags, front side-impact airbags, front side-head-protection system, antilock 4-wheel disc brakes, anti-skid system, variable-assist power steering, power tilt/telescopic leather-wrapped steering wheel, cruise control, air conditioning w/dual automatic climate control, interior air filter, navigation system, memory system

(steering wheel, driver seat, outside mirrors), leather upholstery, 14-way power front seats, 4-way lumbar support adjustment, front storage console w/armrest, cupholders, wood interior trim, folding rear seat, heated power mirrors, power windows, power door locks, remote keyless entry, remote decklid release, rain-sensing variable intermittent wipers and heated windshield-washer jets, heated driver-side door lock, automatic day/night rearview mirror, front and rear reading lamps, illuminated visor mirrors, universal garage door opener, tachometer, Service Interval Indicator, Active Check Control system, trip computer, rear defogger, power sunroof, AM/FM/cassette w/6-disc CD changer, steering wheel radio controls, theft-deterrent system, Xenon headlights, fog lights, tool kit, 235/60R16 tires, alloy wheels.

740iL adds: 6-inch longer wheelbase.

750iL adds: 5.4-liter V12 engine, 5-speed automatic transmission w/manual-shift capability, Nappa leather upholstery, Active Comfort Seats, heated front and rear seats, heated steering wheel, power rear seats with power lumbar adjustment, power rear headrests, cellular telephone, power rear sunshade, parking distance control, ski sack, Electronic Damping Control, self-leveling rear suspension.

OPTIONAL EQUIPMENT:

	Retail Price	Dealer Invoice
Major Packages		
Cold Weather Pkg., 740i, 740iL	$1100	$935
Heated front and rear seats, heated steering wheel, ski sack.		
Sport Pkg., 740i, 740iL	2600	2210
Automatic transmission w/manual-shift capability, performance axle and torque converter, contour sport seats, Shadowline exterior trim, sport suspension, 235/50ZR18 front tires, 255/45ZR18 tires, M-parallel Spoke alloy wheels.		
Safety Features		
Rear side-impact air bags and rear side-head-protection system	550	470
Break-resistant security glass	2600	2210
Active Comfort Seats, 740i	1700	1445
740iL	500	425
Includes 2-way power upper backrest adjustment, power lumbar support.		
Parking distance control, 740i, 740iL	900	765
Power rear sunshade, 740i, 740iL	740	630
Appearance and Miscellaneous		
Active Ride Pkg., 740i, 740iL	1900	1615
Electronic Damping Control, self-leveling rear suspension.		
Special Purpose, Wheels and Tires		
M-Parallel Spoke alloy wheels	1450	1235
Includes 235/50ZR18 front tires, 255/45ZR18 rear tires.		

BUICK CENTURY

RECOMMENDED

Buick Century Custom

Front-wheel-drive midsize car; similar to Buick Regal, Chevrolet Impala, Oldsmobile Intrigue, and Pontiac Grand Prix
Base price range: $19,725-$21,860. Built in Canada. **Also consider:** Honda Accord, Mercury Sable, Toyota Camry

FOR • Passenger and cargo room **AGAINST** • Handling • Steering

The 2000 Century arrived last summer with more power, standard dual-zone climate control, and an available side airbag for the driver. Buick aims Century at mainstream midsize-sedan buyers, while the sportier Regal, which shares Century's basic platform, targets a younger audience.

Century's sole engine remains a 3.1-liter V6, but horsepower increases by 15, to 175. Automatic transmission, traction control, and a tire-inflation monitor remain standard, as does 6-passenger seating with a standard front bench seat; bucket seats aren't offered. General Motors' simplified 3-button OnStar assistance system is optional.

Custom and up-trim Limited models are offered. Exclusive to the Limited is standard leather upholstery and the side airbag for the driver. Among additions to both models are new Century 2000 Special Edition options packages that include a blacked-out grille and door moldings, body-colored exterior trim, alloy wheels, steering-wheel audio controls, and "Century 2000" emblems. The Limited's package also includes a split folding rear seatback.

PERFORMANCE Century isn't exciting, but it is a quiet, comfortable, economical sedan at an affordable price. The soft suspension absorbs most bumps easily, and although body lean in turns is pronounced, overall control is good. The low-effort steering furnishes little road feel, but makes for easy low-speed maneuverability. Acceleration and passing power are adequate, helped by smooth gear changes and rapid downshifts. It growls when furnishing passing power, but the V6 is otherwise a peaceful runner and nicely suited to this duty. The 1999 Century we tested averaged 19.4 mpg, about what we expect from the 2000. Wind and road noise are low.

ACCOMMODATIONS Four adults get plenty of room, but the softly padded standard cloth seats have subpar thigh and lower-back support. The optional leather seats are firmer and more comfortable. As for why there is a side airbag for the driver only, Buick says it's developing a side airbag for front passengers that deploys depending on their size and position. Instrumentation is confined to a speedometer and fuel and coolant gauges, but they're easy to read, and a dashboard light that warns of low tire pressure is a thoughtful touch. No control is obstructed or complex, although those for the climate system are mounted low in the center of the dashboard where they interfere with a center passenger's knees. Generous doorways make for easy entry and exit. Centurys are solidly built with interior materials that feel substantial for this price class. The trunk has a wide, flat floor, but loading and unloading requires stretching over a wide bumper-level shelf.

VALUE FOR THE MONEY Century is a modern, well-thought-out sedan with a no-surprises formula that's proved appealing to conservative buyers. It's worth a look.

ENGINES

	ohv V6
Size, liters/cu. in.	3.1/191
Horsepower @ rpm	175 @ 5200
Torque (lbs./ft.) @ rpm	195 @ 4000
Availability	S
EPA city/highway mpg	
4-speed OD automatic	20/30

PRICES

Buick Century	Retail Price	Dealer Invoice
Custom 4-door sedan	$19725	$18048
Limited 4-door sedan	21860	20002
Destination charge	560	560

STANDARD EQUIPMENT:

Custom: 3.1-liter V6 engine, 4-speed automatic transmission, traction control, driver- and passenger-side airbags, antilock brakes, daytime running lights, air conditioning w/dual-zone manual climate control, interior air filter, power steering, tilt steering wheel, cloth reclining front split bench seat, front storage armrest, cupholders, power mirrors, power windows, power door locks, remote keyless entry, AM/FM radio, digital clock, rear defogger, variable intermittent wipers, visor mirrors, automatic headlights, theft-deterrent system, cornering lights, tire-pressure monitor, 205/70R15 tires, wheel covers.

Limited adds: driver-side side-impact airbag, variable-assist power steering, leather-wrapped steering wheel, leather upholstery, 6-way power driver seat, heated power mirrors, illuminated visor mirrors, rear courtesy/reading lights, floormats.

OPTIONAL EQUIPMENT:
Major Packages

	Retail Price	Dealer Invoice
Popular Pkg. 1SB, Custom	310	267
Cruise control, cargo net, floormats.		

	Retail Price	Dealer Invoice
Premium Pkg. 1SC, Custom	$935	$804
Popular Pkg SB plus 6-way power driver seat, heated power mirrors, AM/FM/cassette, rear window antenna.		
Elite Pkg. 1SG, Custom	1085	933
Premium Pkg. 1SC plus upgraded AM/FM/cassette w/automatic tone control, steering wheel radio controls.		
Century 2000 Special Edition Pkg. 1SJ, Custom	1810	1557
Manufacturer's discount price	1310	1127
Elite Pkg. 1SG plus badging, special grille and body trim, special headrests and floormats, alloy wheels.		
Luxury Pkg. 1SE, Limited	460	396
Cruise control, AM/FM/cassette, cargo net.		
Elite Pkg. 1SH, Limited	845	727
Luxury Pkg. 1SE plus dual-zone automatic air conditioning, rear window antenna, upgraded AM/FM/cassette w/automatic tone control, steering wheel radio controls.		
Prestige Pkg. 1SF, Limited	1505	1294
Luxury Pkg. 1SH plus 6-way power passenger seat, Concert Sound III speakers, automatic day/night rearview and outside mirrors.		
Century 2000 Special Edition Pkg. 1SK, Limited	2608	2243
Manufacturer's discount price	2108	1813
Prestige Pkg. 1SF plus AM/FM/cassette/CD player, split folding rear seat, badging, special grille and body trim, special headrests and floormats, alloy wheels.		

Comfort and Convenience

	Retail Price	Dealer Invoice
OnStar System	695	—
Includes Global Positioning System, roadside assistance, emergency services. Requires annual service charge. Price may vary.		
6-way power driver seat, Custom	330	283
Split folding rear seat	275	237
Includes armrest, cupholders.		
Power sunroof	695	598
Custom requires Pkg. 1SC/1SG/1SJ, automatic day/night rearview mirror, and illuminated visor mirrors. Limited requires Pkg. 1SF/1SH/1SK.		
Automatic day/night rearview and outside mirrors	120	103
Custom requires illuminated visor mirrors, Pkg. 1SC/1SG/1SJ. Limited requires option pkg.		
Heated power mirrors, Custom	60	51
Illuminated visor mirrors, Custom	137	118
Requires Pkg. 1SC/1SG/1SJ.		
AM/FM/cassette	195	168
Upgraded AM/FM/cassette,		
Custom w/Pkg. 1SB, Limited	220	189
Custom w/Pkg. 1SC, Limited w/Pkg. 1SE	25	22
Includes automatic tone control.		
AM/FM/cassette/CD player,		
Custom w/Pkg. 1SB, Limited	420	361
Custom w/Pkg. 1SC, Limited w/Pkg. 1SE	225	194
Custom w/Pkg. 1SG, Limited w/Pkg. 1SF/1SH/1SJ	200	172
Includes automatic tone control.		
Concert Sound III speakers	250	215
Custom w/Pkg. 1SC/1SG/1SJ, Limited w/Pkg. 1SH	210	181
Requires upgraded AM/FM/cassette or AM/FM/cassette/CD player.		
Steering-wheel radio controls	125	108
Requires upgraded AM/FM/cassette, AM/FM/cassette/CD player. Requires cruise control. Custom requires option pkg.		
Alloy wheels	375	323

BUICK LeSABRE   `RECOMMENDED`
Front-wheel-drive full-size car; similar to Pontiac Bonneville

Base price range: $23,235-$27,340. Built in USA. **Also consider:** Chrysler Concorde, Mercury Grand Marquis, Toyota Avalon

FOR • Acceleration • Automatic transmission performance • Instruments/controls • Ride **AGAINST** • Fuel economy • Rear-seat comfort

America's best-selling full-size car was redesigned for a mid-1999 debut as Buick's first 2000 model. Slightly taller and wider on a longer wheelbase than before, LeSabre shares its structure with Buick's larger Park Avenue and with the Cadillac Seville and Pontiac

Buick LeSabre Custom

Bonneville. Among new features are standard front side airbags and independent rear suspension.

An unaltered 3.8-liter V6 and automatic transmission return as the sole powertrain. Traction control is optional and antilock brakes standard, with rear drum brakes replaced by standard 4-wheel discs. Custom and Limited models return, both available with a Gran Touring package offering firmer suspension and 16-inch wheels in place of 15s. A redesigned interior offers a split front bench seat or optional buckets with center console. Safety belts mount to the outboard front seats, which Buick says are shaped to reduce whiplash injury. The side airbag for the driver protects chest and head; the front passenger's covers chest only.

Remote keyless entry and automatic-leveling suspension are standard. A new Driver Confidence Package option includes self-sealing tires, head-up windshield display, and GM's StabiliTrak anti-skid system. Other new options include a trunk-mounted 12-disc CD changer, power sunroof, and rain-sensing windshield wipers. Added to the Limited's standard equipment this fall were heated front seats and mirrors.

PERFORMANCE LeSabre is a generally capable performer that makes few demands on its driver. It takes off smartly, has ample passing power, and enjoys smooth, fairly responsive gear changes. We averaged 17.9 mpg in our test. Handling is quite competent for a large family 4-door, with moderate lean in turns and good grip in steady-state cornering.

The base suspension provides a smooth ride marred by some body float over big humps and dips. The Gran Touring suspension does a poor job of absorbing most sharp bumps and ridges, but worse, it compromises control by feeling jittery over all but blemish-free pavement. There's good directional stability with either suspension, but the steering feels artificially heavy in changes of direction. The new disc brakes are easy to modulate, but stopping power isn't particularly impressive. Wind and road noise are well-muffled, but tires whine on grooved or pebbled surfaces. The engine is quiet at cruise and emits a muted growl in hard acceleration.

ACCOMMODATIONS LeSabre's cabin has a slightly closed-in feel, and this sedan isn't wide enough to seat three adults across without squeezing. But buckets or bench, the front seats are roomy and most test drivers find them comfortable; to some, the cushions too pillowy. A shorter steering column than in previous LeSabres enhances the driving position.

Rear-seat comfort is disappointing for a full-size family car. The cushion is low to the floor and its soft foam provides little thigh or back support. Legs and feet are a bit pinched without the front seats moved well up. Oddly, a rear center armrest is unavailable on the Custom model.

Gauges and controls are large, simple, and most are well-placed. Power-seat switches relocate from doors to seat bases and cruise controls make the logical move from the turn-signal stalk to steering wheel. Headlamp controls are now on the dashboard, not the door, but use an awkward pushbutton design. Demerits also to the Limited's automatic climate controls; they're too busy for easy adjustment while driving. In daylight, highly reflective plastic faceplates make it hard to read the transmission-position indicator, trip odometer, and audio and climate panels.

A large glovebox and an optional bucket-seat center console provide plenty of interior storage, though the console's large cupholder is awkward to deploy. Rear seatbacks don't fold, but the roomy trunk has a large opening. Our test cars were tight and rattle free, but the interior suffers an abundance of unsubstantial-feeling hard-plastic surfaces and budget-grade upholstery.

VALUE FOR THE MONEY LeSabre imparts a feeling of size and substance, and the standard-equipment list is well thought out. Subpar rear-seat accommodations and indifferent interior furnish-

ings are letdowns, but overall, this Buick should satisfy the expectations of its conservative core audience. Base prices are competitive, too, though options add up quickly and well-equipped Limiteds easily nudge $30,000.

ENGINES

	ohv V6
Size, liters/cu. in.	3.8/231
Horsepower @ rpm	205 @ 5200
Torque (lbs./ft.) @ rpm	230 @ 3700
Availability	S
EPA city/highway mpg	
4-speed OD automatic	19/30

PRICES

Buick LeSabre	Retail Price	Dealer Invoice
Custom 4-door sedan	$23235	$21260
Limited 4-door sedan	27340	25016
Destination charge	630	630

Custom requires Base Pkg. 1SA.

STANDARD EQUIPMENT:

Custom: 3.8-liter V6 engine, 4-speed automatic transmission, driver- and passenger-side airbags, front side-impact airbags, antilock 4-wheel disc brakes, daytime running lights, air conditioning, variable-assist power steering, tilt steering wheel w/radio controls, cruise control, cloth front split bench seat, cupholders, power mirrors, power windows, power door locks, remote keyless entry, overhead console, auxiliary power outlets, AM/FM radio, digital clock, intermittent wipers, rear defogger, visor mirrors, power decklid release, automatic headlights, floormats, theft-deterrent system, automatic level control, 215/70R15 tires, wheel covers.

Limited adds: front and rear automatic climate controls, interior air filter, heated 10-way power front seats, AM/FM/cassette w/Concert Sound II speakers, Driver Information Center (tachometer, oil pressure and voltmeter gauges, oil-life monitor, dual trip odometers), heated mirrors, automatic day/night driver-side and rearview mirrors, compass, illuminated visor mirrors, variable intermittent wipers, theft-deterrent system w/alarm, cornering lights, alloy wheels.

OPTIONAL EQUIPMENT:
Major Packages

Base Pkg. 1SA, Custom	100	86
Power front seat recliners.		
Premium Pkg. 1SC, Custom	1088	936
AM/FM/cassette, 6-way power driver seat, cargo net, bodyside stripes, alloy wheels.		
Luxury Pkg. 1SD, Custom	1593	1370
Luxury Pkg. 1SC plus Concert Sound II speakers, illuminated visor mirrors, automatic day/night rearview mirror, Driver Information Center (tachometer, oil pressure and voltmeter gauges, oil-life monitor, dual trip odometers).		
Prestige Pkg., Custom	2463	2118
Luxury Pkg. 1SD plus 6-way power passenger seat, universal garage opener, automatic day/night rearview mirror, compass, interior air filter, rain-sensing windshield wipers, theft-deterrent system w/alarm.		
Prestige Pkg., Limited	615	529
Traction control, AM/FM/cassette/CD player w/automatic tone control, universal garage door opener, rain-sensing wipers.		
Driver Confidence Pkg.	880	757
Ordered w/Gran Touring Pkg.	730	628
Antiskid system, head-up instrument display, self-sealing tires (deleted when ordered w/Gran Touring Pkg.). Requires Prestige Pkg. Requires Gran Touring Pkg. or cross lace alloy wheels. Custom requires traction control.		
Gran Touring Pkg.	185	159
Magnetic variable-assist power steering, leather-wrapped steering wheel, 3.05 axle ratio, sport suspension, 225/60R16 tires, polished alloy wheels. Custom requires Luxury Pkg. 1SD or Prestige Pkg., optional radio.		
Seating/Convenience Console Pkg.	70	60
Bucket seats, convenience console w/writing surface, additional cupholders and power outlets, provisions for cellular telephone and fax.		

Powertrains

Traction control	175	151
Custom requires Luxury or Prestige Pkg.		

Comfort and Convenience

	Retail Price	Dealer Invoice
Power sunroof, Custom	$1045	$899
Limited	995	856
Custom requires Prestige Pkg.		
Leather upholstery, Custom	695	598
Limited	735	632
Custom requires Luxury or Prestige Pkg.		
Power driver seat, Custom	423	364
Power passenger seat, Custom	330	284
Requires Luxury Pkg. 1SD.		
Driver seat memory, Limited	145	125
Includes memory mirrors. Requires Prestige Pkg.		
Illuminated visor mirrors, Custom	92	79
Requires Luxury Pkg. 1SD.		
Universal garage door opener, Limited	100	86
AM/FM/cassette w/automatic tone control, Custom	150	125
Custom Prestige Pkg.	NC	NC
Includes steering-wheel radio controls. Requires Luxury Pkg. or Prestige Pkg.		
AM/FM/CD player, Custom	250	215
Custom w/Prestige Pkg.	100	86
Includes automatic tone control and steering-wheel radio controls. Requires Luxury or Prestige Pkg.		
AM/FM/cassette/CD player, Custom	350	301
Custom w/Prestige Pkg., Limited	200	172
Includes automatic tone control and steering-wheel radio controls. Custom requires Luxury or Prestige Pkg.		
12-disc CD changer	595	512
Custom requires Prestige Pkg.		
Alloy wheels, Custom	325	280
Cross lace alloy wheels, Custom	375	323
Custom w/option pkg., Limited	50	43
Includes 225/60R16 tires.		

BUICK PARK AVENUE

RECOMMENDED

Buick Park Avenue

Front-wheel-drive near-luxury car

Base price range: $31,725-$36,800. Built in USA. **Also consider:** Chrysler LHS and 300M, Oldsmobile Aurora, Toyota Avalon

FOR • Acceleration • Passenger and cargo room • Steering/handling (Ultra) **AGAINST** • Fuel economy (supercharged V6) • Steering/handling (base suspension) • Rear visibility

Front side airbags are newly standard on Buick's flagship sedan for 2000. Park Avenue returns in base form with a 205-horsepower V6 and as the Ultra model with a 240-hp supercharged version of the V6. Both have automatic transmission, antilock brakes, and self-leveling rear suspension. Optional on both is a Gran Touring suspension package that includes firmer suspension settings and more-aggressive tire tread.

Newly standard on Ultra and optional on the base Park Avenue is General Motors' StabiliTrak system, designed to sense an impending skid in a turn and apply the brakes to an individual wheel to keep the car on its intended course. Both models also gain child-seat anchors on the rear package shelf. GM's OnStar assistance system has been temporarily dropped from the options list.

PERFORMANCE Both Park Avenues are quiet, substantial-feeling cars with ample power over a broad speed range. Ultra's supercharged performance is impressive, but premium gas is recommended. We averaged 15.3 mpg in mostly city driving with one test Ultra, 19.5 in a more even mix of city and highway work with another. Our test base model averaged 19.8 mpg on regular fuel.

The standard chassis is calibrated for comfort, so steering is light at freeway speeds and the body "floats" a bit over undulations. The optional Gran Touring suspension provides better ride control while reducing body lean and front-end plowing in corners. It includes magnetic variable-effort steering (standard on Ultra) that responds quickly but feels a tad numb. Braking is strong and stable, but panic stops induce marked nose-dive. We know StabiliTrak works well based on experience with recent Cadillacs, so we applaud its availability in the 2000 Park Avenue.

ACCOMMODATIONS Park Avenue has abundant head and leg room, but not quite enough shoulder width for three large adults front or back. Seats are comfortable, despite lacking good lateral support in turns. The outboard front safety belts anchor to the seat, so they're easy to reach and always fit comfortably. The dash layout is traditional but works well enough. However, sounding the horn demands a hefty shove on the steering-wheel hub, and the moisture-sensing wipers standard on Ultra and optional on the base model aren't that useful. Outward vision is good, and the roomy trunk has a low liftover.

OnStar and the tire-pressure monitor are worthwhile features, but the available EyeCue display, which projects speed and other readings onto the windshield, is dubious. Overall fit and finish have been good on Park Avenues we've tested, though sub-freezing weather brought out some suspension creaking in one Ultra.

VALUE FOR THE MONEY In a class dominated by imports, Park Avenue offers traditional American room, power, and amenities at a competitive price. If that appeals to you, it merits strong consideration.

ENGINES

	ohv V6	Supercharged ohv V6
Size, liters/cu. in.	3.8/231	3.8/231
Horsepower @ rpm	205 @ 5200	240 @ 5200
Torque (lbs./ft.) @ rpm	230 @ 4000	280 @ 3600
Availability	S[1]	S[2]
EPA city/highway mpg		
4-speed OD automatic	19/28	18/27

1. Base model. 2. Ultra.

PRICES

Buick Park Avenue	Retail Price	Dealer Invoice
Base 4-door sedan	$31725	$28711
Ultra 4-door sedan	36800	33304
Destination charge	695	695

STANDARD EQUIPMENT:

Base: 3.8-liter V6 engine, 4-speed automatic transmission, driver- and passenger-side airbags, front side-impact airbags, antilock 4-wheel disc brakes, daytime running lights, air conditioning w/dual-zone automatic climate control, rear-seat climate controls, interior air filter, power steering, tilt steering wheel, cruise control, cloth upholstery, front split bench seat w/driver- and passenger-side 10-way power, front storage armrest, cupholders, rear seat trunk pass-through, power mirrors, power windows, power door locks, remote keyless entry, overhead console, rear defogger, tachometer, AM/FM/cassette, digital clock, power remote decklid and fuel-door releases, front and rear reading lights, illuminated visor mirrors, variable intermittent wipers, automatic headlights, auxiliary power outlet, floormats, automatic level-control suspension, theft-deterrent system with starter interrupt, cornering lights, 225/60R16 tires, alloy wheels.

Ultra adds: supercharged 3.8-liter V6 engine, traction control, anti-skid system, magnetic variable-assist power steering, leather upholstery, leather-wrapped steering wheel w/radio and climate controls, memory driver seat and memory mirrors w/parallel park assist passenger-side mirror, memory climate control and radio presets, heated mirrors w/driver-side automatic day/night mirror, Seating Pkg. (power lumbar adjustment, heated front seats, power front and manual rear articulating headrests), rear-seat storage armrest, wood interior trim, automatic day/night rearview mirror w/compass, rain-sensing windshield wipers, driver information center (tire-pressure monitor, oil-life monitor, low-washer-fluid, dual trip odometers, additional warning lights, and trip computer), AM/FM/CD player with automatic tone control and upgraded sound system, rear illuminated vanity mirrors, universal garage door opener, 3-note horn.

OPTIONAL EQUIPMENT:
Major Packages

Gran Touring Pkg., Base w/1SE Pkg.	335	288
Base w/1SE Pkg. and leather upholstery	285	245

Prices are accurate at time of publication; subject to manufacturer's changes.

	Retail Price	Dealer Invoice
Ultra..	$200	$172

Includes Gran Touring suspension, magnetic variable-assist power steering (Base), leather-wrapped steering wheel (Base), 225/60R16 touring tires. Base requires traction control.

1SE Prestige Pkg., Base	1125	968

Memory driver seat and mirrors w/parallel park assist passenger-side mirror, front power lumbar adjustment, heated mirrors, automatic day/ night driver-side mirror, automatic day/night rearview mirror w/compass, universal garage door opener, UL0 audio system (AM/FM/cassette player w/automatic tone control, and steering-wheel radio controls), rain-sensing windshield wipers, driver information center (tire-pressure monitor, additional warning lights, oil-life monitor, and trip computer).

Powertrains

Traction control, Base w/1SE Pkg.	175	151

Safety Features

StabilTrac anti-skid system, Base	495	426

Comfort and Convenience

UL0 audio system, Base	150	129

Includes AM/FM/cassette with automatic tone control, and steering-wheel radio controls.

UN0 audio system, Base..	250	215
Base w/1SE Pkg.	100	86

Includes AM/FM/CD player with automatic tone control, and steering-wheel radio controls.

UP0 audio system, Base..	350	301
Base w/1SE Pkg.	200	172
Ultra..	100	86

AM/FM/cassette/CD player with automatic tone control and steering wheel radio controls.

12-disc CD changer..	595	512
Concert Sound III speakers, Base w/1SE Pkg.	280	241
Power sunroof...	1095	942

Base requires 1SE Pkg.

Heated front seats, Base w/1SE Pkg.	225	194

Power lumbar adjustment, heated front seats, and power front articulating headrests.

Convenience Console/Five Person Seating Pkg., Ultra	185	159

Bucket seats, console with writing surface and accommodations for phone and fax, cupholders, auxiliary power outlets.

Leather upholstery, Base w/1SE Pkg.	750	645
EyeCue head-up display	275	237

Base requires 1SE Pkg.

Chrome alloy wheels	695	598

BUICK REGAL

Buick Regal LS

Front-wheel-drive midsize car; similar to Buick Century, Chevrolet Impala, Oldsmobile Intrigue, and Pontiac Grand Prix

Base price range: $22,220-$25,065. Built in Canada. **Also consider:** Honda Accord, Mercury Sable, Nissan Maxima, Toyota Camry/Solara

FOR • Acceleration • Instruments/controls **AGAINST** • Fuel economy (supercharged V6)

A standard split folding rear seatback and an available side airbag for the driver are main additions to Buick's upscale midsize sedan for 2000.

Regal comes in LS trim with a 200-horsepower 3.8-liter V6 and in GS form with a 240-hp supercharged version of that engine. Both

have automatic transmission and antilock 4-wheel disc brakes. Traction control is standard on both, with the GS's setup upgraded for 2000 to use front-wheel braking as well as reduced engine power to limit tire slip.

The side airbag for the driver is standard on the GS and included with optional leather upholstery on the LS; leather upholstery is standard on the GS. A firmer Gran Touring suspension with 16-inch wheels in place of 15s is standard on the GS and optional on the LS. Optional both is GM's OnStar information and emergency assistance system. The GS also gets a body-color grille and new-look alloy wheels for 2000.

Regal shares its basic design with Buick's Century but is styled and equipped to appeal to younger, sport-oriented buyers. It's also similar under the skin to the Oldsmobile Intrigue and Pontiac Grand Prix.

PERFORMANCE Buick's 3.8-liter V6 is smooth, quiet, and strong, and is backed by a well-mannered automatic transmission. The supercharged GS is fast, clocking 0-60 mph in 6.9 seconds in our tests, about a second quicker than the LS. Unfortunately, the GS suffers some steering-wheel tug—called torque steer—in hard takeoffs. It also demands premium fuel, but is not much thirstier than the LS, averaging between 16.9 mpg and 20.1 in our tests.

The LS's base suspension rides and handles nearly as well as the GS's Gran Touring setup. Both are controlled and comfortable, though no Regal combines bump absorption and cornering balance as well as a European sport sedan. Wind and road noise are noticed but not intrusive at highway speeds.

ACCOMMODATIONS Like most midsize sedans, Regal carries four adults in comfort, five in a pinch. Front seats are supportive even in spirited driving, something encouraged by legible, well-placed gauges and controls. A dashboard light that warns of low tire pressure is a thoughtful addition. Minor lapses include a slightly complex climate panel, no interior trunk release (though there's one on the remote-entry key fob), and a console-bin cover that can pinch fingers. The trunklid opens 90 degrees on hinges that don't intrude on the ample luggage space, but there's a wide bumper shelf to stretch over. Workmanship is generally solid and satisfying, but interior ambiance is compromised by too many hard plastic surfaces.

VALUE FOR THE MONEY Regal is solid, competitively priced, and well-equipped, but falls just short of the cohesive feel that earns the Intrigue and Grand Prix our Recommended label.

ENGINES

	ohv V6	Supercharged ohv V6
Size, liters/cu. in.	3.8/231	3.8/231
Horsepower @ rpm	200 @ 5200	240 @ 5200
Torque (lbs./ft.) @ rpm	225 @ 4000	280 @ 3600
Availability	S[1]	S[2]
EPA city/highway mpg		
4-speed OD automatic	19/30	18/27

1. LS, LSE. 2. GS.

PRICES

Buick Regal	Retail Price	Dealer Invoice
LS 4-door sedan	$22220	$20331
GS 4-door sedan	25065	22934
Destination charge	560	560

STANDARD EQUIPMENT:

LS: 3.8-liter V6 engine, 4-speed automatic transmission, traction control, driver- and passenger-side airbags, antilock 4-wheel disc brakes, daytime running lights, variable-assist power steering, leather-wrapped tilt steering wheel, cruise control, air conditioning w/dual-zone manual climate control, interior air filter, cloth reclining front bucket seats, front console, cupholders, auxiliary power outlets, split folding rear seat, heated power mirrors, power windows, power door locks, remote keyless entry, tachometer, variable intermittent wipers, rear defogger, map lights, visor mirrors, AM/FM/cassette, digital clock, automatic headlights, theft-deterrent system, fog lights, tire pressure monitor, 215/70R15 tires, wheel covers.

GS adds: supercharged 3.8-liter V6 engine, full traction control, driver-side side-impact airbag, leather upholstery, 6-way power driver seat, illuminated visor mirrors, driver information center (supercharger boost gauge, oil-change monitor, additional warning lights, trip computer), floormats, Gran Touring Suspension, 225/60R16 tires, alloy wheels.

OPTIONAL EQUIPMENT:
Major Packages

	Retail Price	Dealer Invoice
Luxury Pkg. 1SB, LS	$542	$466

Includes map lights, illuminated visor mirrors, 6-way power driver seat, floormats, cargo net.

Prestige Pkg. 1SC, LS	1182	1017

Luxury Pkg. plus dual-zone automatic climate control, automatic day/night rearview mirror and driver-side mirror, AM/FM/cassette/CD player, steering-wheel-mounted radio controls.

Touring Pkg. 1SD, LS	2407	2070

Prestige Pkg. plus 6-way power passenger seat, Monsoon sound system, Gran Touring Pkg. (Gran Touring suspension, 225/60R16 tires, alloy wheels).

Luxury Pkg. 1SE, GS	640	550

Dual-zone automatic climate control, AM/FM/cassette/CD player w/automatic tone control, steering-wheel-mounted radio controls, automatic day/night rearview mirror and driver-side mirror.

Gran Touring Pkg., LS	600	516

Consists of Gran Touring suspension, 225/60R16 tires, alloy wheels. Requires option pkg.

Comfort and Convenience

Dual-zone automatic climate control	195	168

LS requires option pkg.

Driver information center, LS	75	65

Includes oil-change monitor, additional warning lights, trip computer. Requires Pkg. 1SC or 1SD.

AM/FM/cassette/CD player	200	172
Monsoon sound system	295	254

LS requires option pkg.

Power sunroof	695	597

Requires automatic day/night mirrors. LS requires option pkg.

Leather upholstery, LS	795	684

Includes driver-side side-impact airbag. Requires option pkg.

Heated front seats	225	194

LS requires leather seats.

6-way power passenger seat	330	283

Requires option pkg.

Automatic day/night mirrors	120	103

Includes rearview and driver-side mirrors. LS requires option pkg.

Alloy wheels, LS	350	301
16-inch chrome alloy wheels	650	559

LS requires Gran Touring Pkg.

CADILLAC CATERA

Cadillac Catera

Rear-wheel-drive near-luxury car

1999 base price: $34,180. Built in Germany. **Also consider:** Acura TL, BMW 3-Series, Infiniti I30, Lexus ES 300, Mercedes-Benz C-Class

FOR • Ride **AGAINST** • Control layout

Freshened styling, a revised interior, and suspension revisions highlight changes to this year's entry-level Cadillac. Built in Germany by General Motors' Opel subsidiary, Catera offers regular and Sport models with an Opel-designed V6, 4-speed automatic transmission, antilock 4-wheel disc brakes, traction control, and leather upholstery. The Sport adds a rear spoiler, high-intensity headlamps, and heated seats, plus a matte-chrome grille (versus black) and new 17-inch wheels in lieu of the base 16s. Both models now have standard front side airbags—only the Sport did before. Both also add new cupholders and upper child-seat anchors in the rear, a redesigned dashboard and door panels, ventilation filter, and GM's new three-button OnStar communications system. Last year's firmer Sport suspension is now fitted to the base Catera, while the Sport gets even tighter calibrations.

EVALUATION
We haven't yet driven the 2000 Cateras, but Cadillac's aim with the newly firmed-up chassis is to bring them in step with the dynamic abilities of most Euro-brand rivals without turning their ride uncomfortably harsh. The unchanged powertrain should again provide okay acceleration and decent fuel economy (19.1 mpg in our usual hard driving), but road noise and full-throttle engine drone have been high for the class. Catera does boast a solid feel, strong brakes, and decent room for four adults, but is only average for ergonomics, visibility, and entry/exit. So despite its updating, the baby Cadillac may well remain an also-ran in the near-luxury sales race.

ENGINES

	dohc V6
Size, liters/cu. in.	3.0/181
Horsepower @ rpm	200 @ 6000
Torque (lbs./ft.) @ rpm	192 @ 3600
Availability	S
EPA city/highway mpg	
4-speed OD automatic	18/24

PRICES

1999 Cadillac Catera	Retail Price	Dealer Invoice
Base 4-door sedan	$34180	$31772
Destination charge	640	640

STANDARD EQUIPMENT:

Base: 3.0-liter dohc V6 engine, 4-speed automatic transmission, traction control, driver- and passenger-side airbags, antilock 4-wheel disc brakes, daytime running lights, air conditioning w/dual-zone automatic climate control, back seat air conditioning vent, variable-assist steering, leather-wrapped tilt steering wheel, cruise control, leather upholstery, 8-way power front seats with power recliners, front console w/storage armrest, cupholders, split folding rear seat, memory driver seat and outside mirrors, heated power mirrors, power windows, power door locks, remote-keyless entry system, AM/FM/cassette with eight speakers, integrated rear window antenna, steering-wheel radio controls, variable intermittent wipers, Driver Information Center, auxiliary power outlets, tachometer, outside temperature display, remote fuel-door and decklid release, rear defogger, automatic day/night rearview mirror, universal garage door opener, illuminated visor mirrors, front and rear reading lights, automatic parking-brake release, automatic headlights, wiper-activated headlights, floormats, theft-deterrent system, cornering lights, fog lights, load-leveling suspension, full-size spare, 225/55HR16 tires, alloy wheels.

OPTIONAL EQUIPMENT:
Major Packages

Sport Pkg.	795	676

Includes front side-impact airbags, articulating sport seats w/adjustable thigh bolsters, heated front and rear seats, special grille, rear spoiler, rocker panel moldings, sport suspension, unique alloy wheels.

Comfort and Convenience

OnStar System	1300	—

Includes Global Positioning System, voice-activated cellular telephone, roadside assistance, emergency services. Requires monthly service charges. Dealer installed option, prices may vary.

Heated front and rear seats	425	361
Power sunroof	995	846
AM/FM/cassette/CD player	973	827

Includes weatherband, radio data system, Bose sound system.

Power rear sunshade	295	251

Appearance and Miscellaneous

Chrome alloy wheels	795	507

CADILLAC DeVILLE `RECOMMENDED`

Front-wheel-drive luxury car

Base price range: $39,500-$44,700. Built in USA. **Also consider:** Infiniti Q45, Lexus LS 400, Lincoln Town Car

FOR • Acceleration • Build quality • Entry/exit • Interior materials • Quietness • Passenger and cargo room **AGAINST** • Navigation system controls • Fuel economy • Rear visibility

Cadillac's biggest sedan is redesigned for 2000, with new styling

---

Prices are accurate at time of publication; subject to manufacturer's changes.

Cadillac DeVille DHS

and a host of high-tech features, including an infrared night-vision system. DeVille's new wheelbase is 1.5 inches longer but its body is 2 inches shorter and narrower. Base, DHS (DeVille High Luxury Sedan), and DTS (DeVille Touring Sedan) models are offered; the last two replace the D'Elegance and Concours, respectively.

Front-wheel drive, 4-speed automatic transmission, and Cadillac's Northstar V8 return; the DTS has 300 horsepower, the others 275. Traction control and antilock 4-wheel disc brakes are standard. Standard on DTS and optional elsewhere is Cadillac's StabiliTrak antiskid system, which selectively applies front brakes and varies steering effort to fight skids in turns. DTS models also get Cadillac's Continuously Variable Road Sensing Suspension. All DeVilles have front side airbags with a head/chest bag for the driver; rear side torso airbags are newly optional. New taillamps use light-emitting diode (LED) technology; Cadillac says they illuminate faster than incandescent bulbs.

Base and DHS have a front bench seat with column shift, the DTS has buckets and console shift. The base model has digital instrumentation. DHS and DTS have analog gauges, plus standard leather upholstery and lumbar-massaging front seats. Cadillac's continuously adjusting air-cell front seat cushions are DHS/DTS options. DHS also gets a power rear-seat lumbar adjustment, power rear-window sunshade, and manual rear side widow shades. New on all models are steering-wheel audio and climate controls and separate rear-seat temperature adjustment. GM's OnStar assistance system is standard, and a satellite navigation system with touch-screen display is a new DHS/DTS option.

DeVille's Night Vision is an industry first. Optional on DHS and DTS, it uses infrared technology to detect heat-generating objects beyond headlight range and projects a black-and-white image onto the windshield just above hood level. The new Ultrasonic parking assist option gives audio and visual warnings of obstacles when backing up.

PERFORMANCE Cadillac's desire to broaden DeVille's audience to people under 60 years of age shows in the 2000 models' dynamics. The poised DTS easily holds its own against other imported luxury sedans and while base and DHS models aren't quite so athletic, they're still a welcome improvement over their predecessors. All benefit from the stiffer new platform, as well as StabiliTrak and the reprogrammed variable suspension, which reduces body lean and dip in cornering and emergency maneuvers. DeVille's comfortable ride isn't compromised, it's just more controlled.

Acceleration is again strong at around 7 seconds 0-60 mph. Fuel economy should remain about 17 mpg overall, though premium gas is no longer required. A new engine intake system, extra sound-deadening, and the tighter new platform makes the well-bred Northstar powertrain feel more refined than ever. Wind and road nose are hushed, the automatic transmission smooth and responsive.

ACCOMMODATIONS Few sedans are more spacious or comfortable. Front seats provide fine support and while a middle rider on the base and DHS models' bench seat will feel squeezed, the outboard positions have stretch-out room. Even more impressive is the rear bench, which features limousinelike leg clearance, a generous cushion elevated to provide "theater" seating, and enough width for three adults. Rear temperature control and the DHS's sunshades and adjustable lumbar are useful amenities, and all doors open wide for exceptional entry and exit.

We prefer the analog gauges to the base model's dated digital array, but both are unobstructed and legible. There's an abundance of controls on dashboard and steering wheel; most are and clearly labeled and generously sized. Once programmed, the new navigation system is an aid, but we're leery of fingerprint build-up on its touch-screen display. Thick rear roof pillars compromise the driver's over-the-shoulder view despite larger new outside mirrors.

Night Vision really works and is likely to be of most benefit to those who frequently drive in rural areas. A moving image that resembles a photographic negative is projected onto the lower left windshield. It's alien at first, but doesn't interfere with normal vision and can be adjusted for brightness or switched off.

Cabin materials and workmanship are a step up from other domestic brands and competitive with those of imported luxury cars—except for some low-budget plastic trim in the center of the dashboad and the crude movement of the vent adjusters. Interior storage space is good, and the 4-golf-bag trunk opens at bumper level.

VALUE FOR THE MONEY They're spaciousness and powerful, brim with space-age gizmos, and are priced to undercut most V8 luxury rivals. Just as significant, these new DeVilles perform on par with some of the world's most prestigious luxury sedans.

ENGINES

	dohc V8	dohc V8
Size, liters/cu. in.	4.6/279	4.6/279
Horsepower @ rpm	275 @ 5600	300 @ 6000
Torque (lbs./ft.) @ rpm	300 @ 4000	295 @ 4400
Availability	S[1]	S[2]

EPA city/highway mpg

1. DeVille, DHS. 2. DTS.

PRICES

Cadillac DeVille	Retail Price	Dealer Invoice
Base 4-door sedan	$39500	$36298
DHS 4-door sedan	44700	41056
DTS 4-door sedan	44700	41056
Destination charge	670	670

STANDARD EQUIPMENT:

Base: 4.6-liter dohc V8 275-horsepower engine, 4-speed automatic transmission, traction control, driver- and passenger-side airbags, front side-impact airbags, antilock 4-wheel disc brakes, daytime running lights, OnStar System (Global Positioning System, roadside assistance, emergency services), air conditioning w/tri-zone automatic climate control, variable-assist power steering, tilt leather-wrapped steering wheel, cruise control, cloth upholstery, front split bench seat, 8-way power front seats, front storage armrest, cupholders, rear seat trunk pass-through, heated power mirrors w/driver-side automatic day/night, power windows, power door locks, remote keyless entry, AM/FM/cassette, steering wheel radio and climate controls, trip computer, outside temperature indicator, illuminated front visor mirrors, variable intermittent wipers, power decklid release and power pull-down, remote fuel door release, rear defogger, automatic day/night rearview mirror, compass, map lights, automatic headlights, automatic parking brake release, floormats, theft-deterrent system, cornering lights, load-leveling suspension, 225/60SR16 tires, alloy wheels.

DHS adds: leather upholstery, heated front and rear seats, 12-way power front seats w/lumbar massage, front and rear power lumbar adjustment, driver seat and mirror memory, power tilt and telescoping wood and leather-wrapped steering wheel, wood shift knob, Bose AM/FM/cassette/CD player, analog instruments, tachometer, wood interior trim, rear illuminated visor mirrors, rain-sensing automatic wipers, power rear window sunshade, manual rear side sunshades, chrome alloy wheels.

DTS adds: 4.6-liter dohc V8 300-horsepower engine, antiskid system, front bucket seats, center console, tilt leather-wrapped steering wheel, fog lights, Continuously Variable Road-Sensing Suspension, 235/55HR17 tires, alloy wheels, deletes driver seat and mirror memory, power tilt and telescoping wood and leather-wrapped steering wheel, wood shift knob, rear seat lumbar adjustment, rear illuminated visor mirrors, power rear window sunshade, manual rear side sunshades, chrome alloy wheels.

OPTIONAL EQUIPMENT:
Major Packages

Comfort and Convenience Pkg., Base	1095	931
DTS	695	591
Heated front and rear seats, front seat lumbar adjustment (Base), memory driver seat and mirror, power tilt and telescoping steering wheel (DTS), trunk mat.		
Safety and Security Pkg., Base, DHS	895	761

Ratings begin on page 213. Specifications begin on page 220.

	Retail Price	Dealer Invoice
DTS	$400	$340
StabliTrak anti-skid system (Base, DHS), ultrasonic rear parking assist, universal garage door opener.		
Trailer Towing Provisions	110	94
Trailer wiring harness, engine oil cooler.		

Safety Features
Rear side-impact airbags	295	251
Night Vision, DHS, DTS	1995	1696
Requires Safety and Security Pkg.		

Comfort and Convenience
Navigation System, DHS, DTS	1995	1696
Navigation system with Global Positioning System, LCD screen, 6-disc CD changer.		
Power sunroof	1550	1318
DHS deletes rear illuminated visor mirrors.		
Leather upholstery, Base	785	667
Adaptive front seats, DHS, DTS	995	846
DTS requires Comfort and Convenience Pkg.		
AM/FM/cassette/CD player, Base	300	255
Bose AM/FM/cassette/mini CD player, DHS, DTS	300	255
6-disc CD changer	595	506
Wood Trim Pkg., DTS	595	506
Wood and leather-wrapped steering wheel, wood shift knob.		
Chrome alloy wheels, Base, DTS	795	509

CADILLAC ELDORADO

Cadillac Eldorado ETC

Front-wheel-drive luxury car
Base price range: $39,120-$42,695. Built in USA. **Also consider:** Lexus SC 300/400, Mercedes-Benz CLK

FOR • Acceleration • Steering/handling • Interior materials
AGAINST • Fuel economy • Rear visibility • Climate controls (base model)

Despite slow sales, this big 2-door continues in base and sportier Eldorado Touring Coupe (ETC) models, with the former rebadged ESC for Eldorado Sport Coupe. Both get General Motors' OnStar communications system as standard equipment for 2000, and leather upholstery is now standard instead of optional for the base model. Returning as standard are automatic transmission, antilock 4-wheel disc brakes, and traction control. Eldorado's Northstar V8 now runs on regular instead of premium gas but continues to make 275 horsepower in the ESC and 300 in the ETC. The ETC also has Cadillac's Continuously Variable Road Sensing Suspension and StabiliTrak antiskid system; the latter is optional for the ESC. Massaging front seats remain an ETC option. Unlike other Cadillacs, Eldorados do not offer front side airbags.

EVALUATION Both Eldo versions average a mediocre 18 mpg or so in our tests but have strong acceleration and low overall noise levels. Road manners depend on model. The comfort-oriented ESC has an almost pillowy ride but leans a lot in corners. The ETC's firmer suspension offers better body control at the expense of some harshness over sharp bumps. StabiliTrak adds an extra measure of safety, especially on wet roads. Eldorado seats four in comfort and offers plenty of luggage room, but aft entry/exit demands the usual coupe contortions, and wide rear roof pillars impede visibility. Workmanship is good, but falls short of best-in-class brands like Lexus and BMW. Overall, Eldorado is worth considering for those few who still like big, heavy coupes, especially since meager demand should mean sizable discounts.

ENGINES
	dohc V8	dohc V8
Size, liters/cu. in.	4.6/279	4.6/279
Horsepower @ rpm	275 @ 5600	300 @ 6000
Torque (lbs./ft.) @ rpm	300 @ 4000	295 @ 4400
Availability	S[1]	S[2]
EPA city/highway mpg		
4-speed OD automatic	17/26	17/26

1. Sport Coupe. 2. Touring Coupe.

PRICES
Cadillac Eldorado	Retail Price	Dealer Invoice
ESC 2-door coupe	$39120	$35950
ETC 2-door coupe	42695	39221
Destination charge	695	695

STANDARD EQUIPMENT:
ESC: 4.6-liter dohc V8 275-horsepower engine, 4-speed automatic transmission, traction control, driver- and passenger-side airbags, antilock 4-wheel disc brakes, wiper-activated headlights, daytime running lamps, air conditioning w/dual-zone automatic climate control, OnStar System (Global Positioning System, roadside assistance, emergency services), variable-assist power steering, leather-wrapped steering wheel with controls for radio and climate, tilt steering wheel, cruise control, leather upholstery, 8-way power front bucket seats, center console, cupholders, overhead console, heated power mirrors w/driver-side automatic day/night, power windows, power door locks, remote keyless entry, rear defogger, automatic day/night rearview mirror, compass, outside temperature indicator, AM/FM/cassette, power antenna, digital clock, tachometer, remote fuel-door release, remote decklid release w/power pull-down, trip computer, wood interior trim, variable intermittent wipers, automatic parking-brake release, automatic headlights, map lights, illuminated visor mirrors, floormats, automatic level control suspension, theft-deterrent system, fog lights, cornering lights, 225/60R16 tires, alloy wheels.

ETC adds: 4.6-liter dohc V8 300-horsepower engine, antiskid system, Bose AM/FM/weatherband/cassette/CD player, Memory Pkg. (memory seats, mirrors, climate control, and radio presets), power lumbar adjustment, heated front seats, rear seat trunk pass-through, passenger-side mirror tilt-down parking aid, rain-sensing windshield wipers, Continuously Variable Road Sensing Suspension, 235/60HR16 tires.

OPTIONAL EQUIPMENT:
Major Packages
Comfort/Convenience Pkg., ESC	867	737
Memory Pkg. (memory seats, mirrors, climate control, and radio presets), power lumbar support, heated front seats.		

Safety Features
Antiskid system, ESC	495	421

Comfort and Convenience
Massaging lumbar front seats	200	170
Power sunroof	1550	1318
Bose AM/FM/cassette/CD player, ESC	1219	1036
12-disc CD player	595	506
Leather-wrapped and wood steering wheel	395	336
Universal garage door opener	107	91
235/60ZR16 tires, ETC	250	213
Chrome alloy wheels	795	507

CADILLAC ESCALADE

Cadillac Escalade

4-wheel-drive full-size sport-utility vehicle; similar to Chevrolet Tahoe Limited and Z71 and GMC Yukon Denali
Base price: $46,225. Built in USA.
Also consider: Land Rover Range Rover, Lexus LX 470,

Prices are accurate at time of publication; subject to manufacturer's changes.

Lincoln Navigator

FOR • Passenger and cargo room • Trailer towing capability
AGAINST • Ride/handling • Fuel economy • Entry/exit

Introduced for 1999 to answer Lincoln's hot-selling Navigator, Cadillac's first truck is a gussied-up GMC Yukon Denali. Escalade, Denali, and the Chevrolet Tahoe Z71 and Limited retain their basic 1999 design for the 2000 model year, while their redesigned Chevrolet Tahoe and GMC Yukon cousins get new platforms, styling, and engines. Escalade's main Cadillac cues are its grille and its interior trim, which uses real wood and the same leather as Cadillac cars. It also has an enhanced version of GM's OnStar assistance system with a "reminder service" that helps owners keep track of appointments, birthdays, etc. Escalade now offers a choice of rear liftgate/tailgate or no-cost center-opening full doors; the latter were unavailable on '99 models. Escalade continues with an unchanged 5.7-liter V8, automatic transmission, and Autotrac 4WD, which can be used on dry pavement. Maximum towing capacity is 6500 pounds.

PERFORMANCE GM claims Escalade and Denali do 0-60 mph in 10.5 seconds, which would put their acceleration about mid-pack among luxury SUVs. Still, these 5500-pound wagons feel sluggish, especially in highway passing situations. Weight also hurts fuel economy. We averaged just 13.6 mpg in a test Denali and 11.2 in an Escalade.

Neither Escalade nor Denali is as quiet or as comfortable as a luxury sedan—or even as refined as the 2000 Tahoe and Yukon. Worse, ride and handling are subpar by any measure, with mediocre suppression of harsh impacts and a ponderous feel in turns. Stopping power is good enough, but brake-pedal feel is mushy.

ACCOMMODATIONS Escalade's Cadillac-grade leather upholstery imparts an impressively rich feel, but most of our testers find the front buckets in both these vehicles to be too soft and flat for best comfort. And lack of a power backrest recliner and automatic climate control, even as options, are telling omissions at this lofty price level. At least the front cabin is spacious, and there's enough room in back for three adults without crowding, though rival Navigator and the 2000 Tahoe and Yukon offer seats for up to eight. A high interior step-up and surprisingly narrow rear-door bottoms make getting in and out of the back seat more trouble than it should be.

Cargo room is generous even with the rear seatback in use. And with Escalade joining Denali in offering a choice of horizontal or vertical rear doors, buyers get a choice unavailable elsewhere. Storage bins and cubbies abound inside. Still, an abundance of hard plastic interior panels and parts-bin switchgear give these cabins an ambiance that's more GM truck than luxury car.

VALUE FOR THE MONEY They're packed with standard goodies, but Escalade and Denali feel more like rushed-together collections of "luxury" SUV cues than intelligent, cohesive designs. Cadillac does promise superior customer service, but neither Escalade nor its GMC cousin warrants a place on our shopping list.

ENGINES

	ohv V8
Size, liters/cu. in.	5.7/350
Horsepower @ rpm	255 @ 4600
Torque (lbs./ft.) @ rpm	330 @ 2800
Availability	S
EPA city/highway mpg	
4-speed OD automatic........................	13/16

PRICES

Cadillac Escalade	Retail Price	Dealer Invoice
Base 4-door wagon	$46225	$42451
Destination charge	675	675

STANDARD EQUIPMENT:

Base: 5.7-liter V8 engine, 4-speed automatic transmission, full-time 4-wheel drive, electronic two-speed transfer case, limited-slip differential, driver- and passenger-side airbags, antilock brakes, daytime running lights, OnStar System (Global Positioning System, roadside assistance, emergency services), air conditioning w/automatic climate control, rear air conditioning controls, variable-assist power steering, leather-wrapped/wood tilt steering wheel, cruise control, leather upholstery, 10-way power front bucket seats, heated front and rear seats, split folding rear seat, center console, overhead console (universal garage door opener, rear audio controls, rear headphone jacks), wood interior trim, cupholders, heated power mirrors w/automatic day/night, power windows, power door locks, remote keyless entry, Bose AM/FM/cassette/CD player, 6-disc CD changer, digital clock, tachometer, automatic day/night rearview mirror, compass, outside temperature display, auxiliary power outlets, intermittent wipers, rear defogger, rear wiper/washer, illuminated visor mirrors, automatic headlights, cargo cover, floormats, theft-deterrent system, fog lights, running boards, roof rack, front tow hooks, 8-lead trailer wiring harness, trailer hitch, transmission oil cooler, full-size spare tire, 265/70R16 tires, chrome alloy wheels.

Options are available as dealer-installed accessories.

CADILLAC SEVILLE

Cadillac Seville STS

Front-wheel-drive luxury car

Base price range: $43,880-$48,480. Built in USA. **Also consider:** BMW 5-Series, Lexus LS 400, Mercedes-Benz E-Class

FOR • Acceleration • Automatic transmission performance • Handling/roadholding • Interior storage space • Interior materials
AGAINST • Fuel economy • Rear visibility

Cadillac's sportiest sedan returns in 275-horsepower SLS and 300-hp STS models with Northstar V8s that now run on regular instead of premium gas. Both also gain a revised version of General Motors' OnStar assistance system as standard. Also standard are automatic transmission, front side airbags, antilock 4-wheel disc brakes, traction control, and Cadillac's StabiliTrak antiskid system. Both models have Cadillac's Continuously Variable Road Sensing Suspension, which is designed to work with StabiliTrak to minimize body lean and front-end "plow" in turns. StabiliTrak can now also briefly raise steering effort when needed, and is recalibrated to apply the front brakes to recover from a 4-wheel-drift type skid. A newly standard front-seat sensor deactivates passenger airbags if no child or occupant is detected. New options include an onboard navigation system and Ultrasonic Rear Parking Assist, which warns of obstacles when backing up.

EVALUATION Both Sevilles are quick but thirsty—only 14.8 mpg in our tests—so it's good they no longer need pricey premium gas. This year's added chassis capabilities enhance safety, but these heavy front-wheel-drive sedans still aren't as nimble as most rear-drive rivals. The SLS has a quiet, absorbent ride. But the firmly damped STS thumps over bumps and its rumbly exhaust note is equally odd for a luxury 4-door. Plus points include comfortable room for four adults, a well-designed dashboard, and quality interior materials—though workmanship on our test Sevilles has been below that of leading luxury imports. Of the two models, the SLS offers the better blend of performance and comfort.

ENGINES

	dohc V8	dohc V8
Size, liters/cu. in.	4.6/279	4.6/279
Horsepower @ rpm	275 @ 5600	300 @ 6000
Torque (lbs./ft.) @ rpm	300 @ 4000	295 @ 4400
Availability	S[1]	S[2]
EPA city/highway mpg		
4-speed OD automatic	17/26	17/26

1. SLS. 2. STS.

PRICES

Cadillac Seville	Retail Price	Dealer Invoice
SLS 4-door sedan	$43880	$40305
STS 4-door sedan	48480	44514
Destination charge	695	695

STANDARD EQUIPMENT:

SLS: 4.6-liter dohc V8 275-horsepower engine, 4-speed automatic transmission, traction control, driver- and passenger-side airbags w/automatic child recognition system, front side-impact airbags, antilock 4-wheel disc brakes, antiskid system, wiper-activated headlights, daytime running lights, OnStar System (Global Positioning System, roadside assistance, emergency services), air conditioning w/dual zone automatic climate control, outside temperature display, interior air filter, rear heat/air conditioning outlet with fan, variable-assist power steering, leather-wrapped tilt steering wheel w/radio and climate controls, cruise control, leather upholstery, 10-way power front seats with power recliners, front and rear articulating headrests w/power height adjustment for front headrests, center storage console with armrest, cupholders, overhead console, trunk passthrough, wood interior trim, heated power mirrors w/driver-side automatic day/night, power windows, power door locks, remote keyless entry, automatic day/night rearview mirror, compass, AM/FM/cassette/CD player, map lights, illuminated visor mirrors, trip computer, tachometer, automatic parking brake release, remote fuel door and decklid releases, variable intermittent wipers, automatic headlights, rear defogger, floormats, cornering lights, theft-deterrent system, variable suspension, automatic level control suspension, 235/60R16 tires, alloy wheels.

STS adds: 4.6-liter dohc V8 300-horsepower engine, Performance Shift Algorithm 4-speed automatic transmission, Memory Pkg. (two-driver memory seats, mirrors, climate control and radio presets), 14-way power front seats w/power lumbar adjustment, power tilt and telescoping steering wheel, AM/FM/weatherband/cassette/CD player, w/Bose sound system, radio data system, and automatic volume control, Curb-View passenger-side mirror, rain-sensing automatic wipers, fog lights, STS suspension tuning, 235/60HR16 tires.

OPTIONAL EQUIPMENT:

Major Packages

	Retail Price	Dealer Invoice
Convenience Pkg., SLS	$598	$508
Includes power lumbar support for front seats, rain-sensing automatic wipers, universal garage door opener.		
Convenience Pkg., STS	632	537
Heated front and rear seats, universal garage door opener.		
Personalization Pkg., SLS	1698	1443
Convenience Pkg. plus Memory Pkg. (two-driver memory for seats, mirrors, climate control, and radio presets), heated front and rear seats, power tilt and telescoping steering wheel.		
Adaptive Seat Pkg., SLS	2401	2041
STS	1627	1383
Adaptive and heated front seats, heated rear seats, universal garage door opener, Personalization Pkg. (SLS).		

Comfort and Convenience

	Retail Price	Dealer Invoice
Navigation system, SLS	2945	2503
STS	1995	1696
Navigation system with Global Positioning System, LCD screen.		
UM5 Bose sound system, SLS	950	808
Includes AM/FM/weatherband/cassette/CD with radio data system, automatic volume control.		
UM9 Bose sound system, SLS	1250	1063
STS	300	255
Includes AM/FM/weatherband/cassette/mini CD player with radio data system, automatic volume control.		
6-disc CD player	595	506
Ultrasonic rear parking assist	295	251
Power sunroof	1550	1318
Wood Trim Pkg.	595	506
Wood trimmed steering wheel and shift knob.		
Chrome alloy wheels	795	507
235/60ZR16 tires, STS	250	213

CHEVROLET ASTRO

Rear- or all-wheel-drive minivan; similar to GMC Safari

Base price range: $20,040-$23,687. Built in USA. **Also consider:** Chevrolet Venture, Dodge Caravan, Ford Windstar

FOR • Passenger and cargo room • Trailer towing capability
AGAINST • Fuel economy • Entry/exit • Ride

Eight passenger seating is newly standard for 2000 as Chevrolet's truck-based minivan enters its 17th model year. Astro is also sold as

Chevrolet Astro

the near-identical GMC Safari. It continues in a single body length with a passenger-side sliding door and choice of base, LS, and LT trim levels. A no-frills 2-seat Cargo Van returns for commercial users. Passenger models discard 5-passenger seating in favor of the previously optional 8-passenger arrangement (two front buckets and two 3-place rear benches). A 7-passenger setup with two second-row buckets remains an option.

The sole powertrain is a 190-horsepower V6 and automatic transmission, but Chevy says internal changes make the engine quieter and smoother for 2000. And a Tow/Haul mode, as on Chevy's big Silverado pickups, has been added for more efficient shifting when carrying heavy loads. Antilock brakes remain standard, and an all-wheel-drive system returns at extra cost. Other new standard features include headlamps that switch on automatically in low-light conditions, a larger fuel tank made of plastic instead of metal, and retained accessory power that permits operating electrical accessories for up to 20 minutes after shutting off the ignition.

PERFORMANCE General Motors is the only automaker to offer a distinct choice in minivans, and the Astro and Safari are better suited to heavy-duty work than front-drive offerings like Chevy's own Venture. For example, Astro's 5500-pound towing capacity exceeds Venture's by a full ton. But the penalty for this trucky brawn is a rougher ride. Steering and handling aren't as nimble either, though Astro and Safari aren't as ponderous as full-size vans. They do suffer more road and wind noise than sleeker car-based minivans, however.

The torquey V6 and smooth-shifting transmission provide good acceleration and passing response, but don't expect to average more than 15 mpg overall—less with the heavier AWD models. At least the AWD requires no input from the driver, and is worth considering if you live in the snowbelt.

ACCOMMODATIONS Front entry/exit is hampered by a fairly tall step-up and narrow lower doorways. The front footwells are also uncomfortably narrow. Head room is abundant throughout, and there's good passenger space in the second and third rows, though getting to the third-row bench is difficult. Astro and Safari's seats aren't as easy to remove as the lighter modular seating in GM's front-drive minivans, but once out, there's plenty of cargo space. Unlike the swing-out rear doors, the optional Dutch doors allow an unobstructed rear view and include the convenience of a lift-up glass hatch and available defroster. An optional dual sound system allows front-seat passengers to listen to one audio source and rear-seaters another on headphones.

VALUE FOR THE MONEY Consider Astro or Safari if you're looking for a minivan to haul cargo and handle light-duty towing. For primarily passenger use, go with one of the many front-drive alternatives.

ENGINES

	ohv V6
Size, liters/cu. in.	4.3/262
Horsepower @ rpm	190 @ 4400
Torque (lbs./ft.) @ rpm	250 @ 2800
Availability	S

EPA city/highway mpg

4-speed OD automatic	16/20[1]

1. 15/19 w/AWD.

PRICES

Chevrolet Astro	Retail Price	Dealer Invoice
2WD 3-door Cargo van	$20040	$18136
AWD 3-door Cargo van	22440	20308
2WD 3-door Passenger van	21387	19355
AWD 3-door Passenger van	23687	21437

Prices are accurate at time of publication; subject to manufacturer's changes.

	Retail Price	Dealer Invoice
Destination charge	$620	$620

STANDARD EQUIPMENT:

Cargo: 4.3-liter V6 engine, 4-speed automatic transmission, driver- and passenger-side airbags, antilock brakes, daytime running lamps, front air conditioning, variable-assist power steering, black rubber floormats, reclining highback vinyl front bucket seats, cupholders, variable intermittent wipers, AM/FM radio, digital clock, remote fuel-door release, auxiliary power outlets, automatic headlights, theft-deterrent system, dual manual outside mirrors, 215/75R15 tires. **AWD** models add: permanent 4-wheel drive.

Passenger adds: 8-passenger seating with front bucket seats and two 3-passenger rear bench seats, carpeting, cloth door trim, visor mirrors, cloth headliner, rear heat ducts, swing-out rear side windows, rear storage compartments. **AWD** models add: permanent 4-wheel drive.

OPTIONAL EQUIPMENT:
Major Packages

LS Preferred Equipment Group 1SC, Passenger	3326	2860
Manufacturer's discount price,		
2WD Passenger..	1243	1069
AWD Passenger	743	639

LS Pkg. (tilt steering wheel, cruise control, power mirrors, power windows and door locks, illuminated visor mirrors, custom cloth upholstery, Seat Pkg. [front inboard and outboard armrests, adjustable lumbar supports, map pocket], map lights, cargo net, floormats, deep-tinted glass, swing-out rear door glass, lower bodyside cladding, chrome accent grille, chrome styled steel wheels), AM/FM/cassette, remote keyless entry, overhead storage console, front passenger seat storage compartment (ordered without 6-way power passenger seat), roof rack.

LT Preferred Equipment Group 3 1SE, Passenger	6683	5747
Manufacturer's discount price	5883	5059

LS Preferred Equipment Group 1SC plus LT Pkg. (upgraded upholstery, leather-wrapped steering wheel, overhead storage console w/ compass and outside temperature indicator, split folding center bench seat w/console and additional cupholders, alloy wheels), 6-way power driver seat, front and rear air conditioning, rear heater, rear Dutch doors.

Seat Pkg.	168	144
Front seat armrests, map pocket, manual lumbar supports. Requires cloth upholstery.		
ZQ3 Convenience Pkg.	383	329
Tilt steering wheel, cruise control.		
ZQ2 Convenience Group	474	408
Power windows and door locks.		
Trailering Special Equipment	309	266
Platform trailer hitch, 8-lead wiring harness.		

Powertrains

Locking rear differential..	252	217

Comfort and Convenience

Front and rear air conditioning, Passenger	523	450
Rear heater	205	176
Dutch doors	518	445
Cargo, Passenger w/LT Group	459	395
Includes rear wiper/washer and electric release.		
Overhead storage console, Passenger........................	83	71
Overhead storage console w/illuminated visor mirrors,		
Passenger	159	137
Overhead console w/electronics, Passenger...............	223	192
Includes storage, compass, outside temperature indicator.		
7-passenger seating, Passenger	574	494
Passenger w/LS Group	318	273
Passenger w/LT Group.......................................	NC	NC
Front- and second-row bucket seats, third-row bench seat, Seat Pkg.		
6-way power driver seat	240	206
Passenger requires LS Group.		
6-way power passenger seat.....................................	240	206
Requires 6-way power driver seat. Deletes front passenger seat storage compartment.		
Leather upholstery, Passenger	950	817
Requires LT Group.		
Cloth upholstery	NC	NC
Rear defogger	154	132
Requires Dutch doors.		

	Retail Price	Dealer Invoice
Leather-wrapped steering wheel,		
Passenger w/LS Group	$54	$46
Remote keyless entry	170	146
Requires power door locks.		
Power mirrors, Passenger	98	84
Requires ZQ2 Convenience Group.		
Universal garage-door opener, Passenger	115	99
Requires overhead console w/electronics or LT Group.		
AM/FM/cassette	147	126
AM/FM/cassette w/automatic tone control	307	264
Passenger w/LS or LT Group..............................	160	138
Cargo requires ZQ2 Convenience Group.		
AM/FM/CD player	407	350
Passenger w/LS or LT Group..............................	260	224
Includes automatic tone control. Cargo requires ZQ2 Convenience Group.		
AM/FM/cassette/CD player, Cargo	507	436
Passenger w/LS or LT Group..............................	360	310
Includes automatic tone control. Cargo requires ZQ2 Convenience Group.		
Rear radio controls, Passenger	125	108
Includes headphone jacks. Requires LS or LT Group, AM/FM/cassette w/automatic tone control or AM/FM/cassette/CD player.		

Appearance and Miscellaneous

Running boards..	400	344
Passenger requires alloy wheels.		
Deep-tinted glass, Passenger	290	249
Roof rack, Passenger	126	108
Alloy wheels, Passenger	365	314
Passenger w/LS Group	25	22
Chrome styled steel wheels	340	292
Painted styled steel wheels	92	79

CHEVROLET BLAZER

Chevrolet Blazer 4-door

Rear- or 4-wheel-drive midsize sport-utility vehicle; similar to GMC Jimmy/Envoy and Oldsmobile Bravada
Base price range: $18,970-$31,570. Built in USA. **Also consider:** Ford Explorer, Jeep Grand Cherokee, Toyota 4Runner

FOR • Acceleration • Cargo room **AGAINST** • Rear-seat comfort • Fuel economy

Chevrolet's midsize SUV gets detail updates and an altered lineup for 2000. Blazer drops its base-trim models, leaving 2-door wagons in LS form and 4-door versions in LS, LT, and top-line TrailBlazer models. The carried-over ZR2 package for 2-doors includes a high-riding off-road suspension. A 5-speed manual transmission is standard on 2-doors. Automatic is optional on 2-doors and standard on 4-doors. Blazer uses a 190-horsepower V6 that Chevy says is smoother and quieter this year thanks to internal changes.

All models offer rear-wheel drive or optional 4-wheel drive. LTs and TrailBlazers get General Motors' Autotrac system, which can be used on dry pavement and automatically engages the front axle only when needed. Other 4x4s have GM's Insta-Trac, which shifts on-the-fly into or out of 4WD but is for use only on slippery surfaces. Both systems provide high- and low-range 4WD gearing.

For 2000, the Premium Ride suspension with its gas-charged shock absorbers is standard on all models, while no-cost options now include the softer Smooth Ride setup for 4-doors and the tauter Solid Smooth Ride for 2-doors. And an in-dash CD player is added to uplevel audio options. GM's OnStar assistance system remains available. Blazer is built from the same design as the GMC Jimmy and the Oldsmobile Bravada.

Ratings begin on page 213. Specifications begin on page 220.
CONSUMER GUIDE™

PERFORMANCE GM's 4.3-liter V6 furnishes lively takeoffs and good midrange passing power, but can be rough and loud until it warms up. This year's modified engine may answer that criticism. Fuel economy is about par for midsize 6-cylinder SUVs—16-16.6 mpg in our recent tests—though a TrailBlazer averaged just 12.6 mpg in mostly city driving.

Autotrac puts Blazer and Jimmy in league with Ford Explorer, Jeep Grand Cherokee, Dodge Durango, and the top-line Toyota 4Runner, which also offer the convenience of 4WD that doesn't have to be disengaged on dry pavement. Note, however, that the Jimmy/Envoy has GM's "tow/haul" transmission mode that automatically provides more efficient shift points when pulling a trailer. Blazer does not have this feature.

Both Blazer and Jimmy offer an unmatched variety of suspension options. Our choice is Blazer's Premium Ride or Jimmy's Luxury Ride setup, which provide more comfortable going than an Explorer. Firm steering, adequate stopping ability, and good overall handling balance are present in most any model. Wind noise and road noise are moderate at highway speeds.

ACCOMMODATIONS GM's midsize SUVs aren't as roomy as an Explorer but have ample space for four adults. However, our testers find the driver's seat too soft for best support, and most of us can't find acceptable seat/steering wheel positioning. Jimmy/Envoy has a floor-mounted automatic-transmission shift lever; all automatic Chevys except TrailBlazer use a clumsier column shift.

Front passengers in any version must contend with an intrusive footwell hump, necessary to clear part of the exhaust system. And as on the Ford, a short rear seatback compromises comfort. A low step-in eases front entry/exit, but rear access is subpar even in 4-door models. Outward visibility is compromised by thick center and rear roof pillars and over-tinted rear windows.

The spare tire stows under the vehicle, so cargo room is good with the rear seatback up and generous with it folded. GM scores a point by offering two cargo-access choices, both with independent-opening upper glass. We prefer the liftgate because you don't have to stretch over a drop-down tailgate to get to the cargo hold.

VALUE FOR THE MONEY A capable engine is a Blazer/Jimmy asset, and with the right suspension, ride quality is quite comfortable. But Explorer, helped by its optional V8 and stouter overall feel, wins our Best Buy nod among direct competitors. Still, optioned thoughtfully, Blazer and Jimmy cost less than many rivals.

ENGINES

	ohv V6
Size, liters/cu. in.	4.3/262
Horsepower @ rpm	190 @ 4400
Torque (lbs./ft.) @ rpm	250 @ 2800
Availability	S

EPA city/highway mpg

5-speed OD manual..	17/23[1]
4-speed OD automatic..	16/21[2]

1. 15/18 w/4WD. 2. 16/20 w/4WD.

PRICES

Chevrolet Blazer

	Retail Price	Dealer Invoice
LS 2-door wagon, 2WD	$18970	$17168
LS 2-door wagon, 4WD	21970	19883
LS 4-door wagon, 2WD	24570	22236
LS 4-door wagon, 4WD	26570	24045
LT 4-door wagon, 2WD	26370	23865
LT 4-door wagon, 4WD	28570	25856
TrailBlazer 4-door wagon, 2WD	29570	26761
TrailBlazer 4-door wagon, 4WD	31570	28571
Destination charge	550	550

TrailBlazer requires a Preferred Equipment Group.

STANDARD EQUIPMENT:

LS 2-door: 4.3-liter V6 engine, 5-speed manual transmission (2-door), 4-speed automatic transmission w/column shift (4-door), driver- and passenger-side airbags, antilock 4-wheel disc brakes, daytime running lights, cloth split front bench seat with storage armrest (4-door), variable-assist power steering, air conditioning, cloth upholstery, front bucket seats w/manual lumbar adjustment (2-door), front console (2-door), split folding rear seat, cupholders, tachometer, visor mirrors, AM/FM/cassette,

digital clock, automatic headlights, variable intermittent wipers, floormats, theft-deterrent system, roof rack, dual outside mirrors, tailgate, 8-lead trailer wiring harness, Touring Suspension, full-size spare tire, 235/70R15 tires, alloy wheels. **4WD** adds: Insta-Trac part-time 4-wheel drive, electronic-shift transfer case, front tow hooks.

LT adds: cruise control, tilt leather-wrapped steering wheel, heated power mirrors, power windows, power door locks, remote keyless entry, front bucket seats, 8-way power driver seat, overhead console, compass, outside temperature indicator, illuminated visor mirrors, AM/FM/CD player, auxiliary power outlets, rear defogger, rear wiper/washer, power liftgate release, deep-tinted rear glass. **4WD** adds: Autotrac full-time 4-wheel drive, electronic-shift transfer case, front tow hooks.

TrailBlazer adds: leather upholstery, upgraded interior, floor shifter, automatic climate control, automatic day/night rearview and driver-side mirrors, liftgate/liftglass. **4WD** adds: Autotrac full-time 4-wheel drive, electronic-shift transfer case, front tow hooks.

OPTIONAL EQUIPMENT:

	Retail Price	Dealer Invoice
Major Packages		
1SB Preferred Equipment Group, LS 2-door................	$1200	$1032
LS 4-door...	1050	903

Tilt steering wheel, cruise control, heated power mirrors, power windows and door locks, AM/FM/cassette w/automatic tone control, rear defogger, rear wiper/washer, power tailgate window release, deep-tinted rear glass, bodyside moldings (4WD).

1SC Preferred Equipment Group, LS 2-door................	2300	1978

1SC Preferred Equipment Group plus remote keyless entry, AM/FM/CD player, 6-way power driver seat, overhead console, compass, outside temperature indicator.

1SC Preferred Equipment Group, LS 4-door................	1450	1247

1SB Preferred Equipment Group plus AM/FM/CD player, overhead console, compass, outside temperature indicator, front bucket seats.

1SE Preferred Equipment Group, LT	1000	860

Leather upholstery, automatic climate control, liftgate/liftglass.

1SF Preferred Equipment Group, LT............................	1900	1634

1SE Preferred Equipment Group plus driver seat memory, 8-way power passenger seat, automatic day/night rear and driver-side mirrors, trip computer, universal garage door opener, fog lights.

1SG Preferred Equipment Group, TrailBlazer	NC	NC

Two-tone leather upholstery, driver seat memory, 8-way power passenger seat, trip computer, universal garage door opener, fog lights, 235/75R15 on/off-road white-letter tires (4WD).

ZR2 Wide Stance Performance Pkg., 2-door 4WD	2000	1720

Heavy-duty wide stance chassis, heavy-duty suspension, Bilstein shock absorbers, Shield Pkg., heavy-duty differential gears and axles, fender flares, 31x10.5R15 tires. NA w/Trailering Special Equipment.

Trailering Special Equipment	210	181

Includes platform hitch, heavy-duty flasher. 2WD models require automatic transmission.

Powertrains

4-speed automatic transmission, LS 2-door	1000	860
Locking rear differential...	270	232
Autotrac transfer case, LS 4WD	225	194

Comfort and Convenience

OnStar System...	695	—

Includes Global Positioning System, roadside assistance, emergency services. Requires annual service charge. Price may vary.

Heated front seats, LT, TrailBlazer	250	215
Power sunroof..	750	645

LS requires Preferred Equipment Group.

Custom overhead console, LS 2-door..........................	147	126

Includes compass, outside temperature indicator.

Deluxe overhead console, LS w/1SB Group	277	238
LS w/1SC Group..	130	112

Includes trip computer, compass, outside temperature indicator, universal garage door opener.

AM/FM/CD player, LS..	100	86
AM/FM/cassette/CD player, LS w/1SB Group	200	172
LS w/1SC Group, LT..	100	86

Requires automatic transmission.

6-disc CD changer	395	340

Requires AM/FM/cassette, automatic transmission. LS requires 1SB Preferred Equipment Group.

	Retail	Dealer

Prices are accurate at time of publication; subject to manufacturer's changes.

	Price	Invoice
Bose sound system	$495	$426

NA with AM/FM/cassette/CD player. Requires automatic transmission. LS 4-door requires 1SC Preferred Equipment Group.

Steering-wheel radio controls	125	108

LS requires automatic transmission, Preferred Equipment Group.

Cargo cover, LS 4-door	69	59

Requires Preferred Equipment Group.

Appearance and Miscellaneous

Fog lights, LS 2-door 2WD, LS 4-door, LT	115	99

LS requires Preferred Equipment Group.

Rear liftgate/liftglass, LS 4-door	NC	NC

Requires a Preferred Equipment Group.

Tailgate, LT	NC	NC

Special Purpose, Wheels and Tires

Shield Pkg., 4WD	126	108

Includes transfer case and front differential skid plates, fuel tank and steering linkage shields.

Solid Smooth Ride Suspension, LS 2-door	NC	NC
Smooth Ride Suspension, LS 4-door, LT	NC	NC
235/75R15 on/off-road white-letter tires, 4WD LS 4-door	360	310

CHEVROLET CAMARO

BUDGET BUY

Chevrolet Camaro coupe

Rear-wheel-drive sports and GT car; similar to Pontiac Firebird

Base price range: $16,840-$28,365. Built in Canada. **Also consider:** Chevrolet Corvette, Ford Mustang

FOR • Acceleration (Z28) • Handling **AGAINST** • Fuel economy (Z28) • Ride (Z28) • Rear-seat room • Wet weather traction (without traction control) • Rear visibility

Sales keep slip-slidin' away, but Chevrolet's "ponycar" hangs on for 2000 with little change. Camaro continues as a convertible or hatchback coupe in base V6 and V8 Z28 form. All come with 4-wheel antilock disc brakes and offer optional traction control. Convertibles have a standard power top with glass rear window; a T-top remains optional for coupes. Base models use a 5-speed manual transmission or optional automatic; the Z28 offers automatic or a 6-speed manual at no price difference. Also back is the Z28-based SS package with high-power V8, functional hood scoop, larger tires, rear spoiler, and upgraded suspension. This year, all models get standard steering-wheel audio controls, engines are retuned to Low Emissions Vehicle (LEV) standards for states requiring it, Z28 coupes go from black to body-color door mirrors, and wheels are redesigned for both the SS option and the Performance and Handling package available on other Camaros. The Pontiac Firebird shares Camaro's mechanical components but has different styling.

PERFORMANCE V8 versions deliver torrid acceleration yet are relatively docile in traffic. Base Camaros and Firebirds have spirited acceleration and are cheaper to insure than V8 models. They use less fuel, too. In our tests, we averaged 18.6 mpg with a base 5-speed Camaro and 15.1 with an automatic Z28. A Camaro SS returned 14.7 mpg, a Ram-Air Formula Firebird 16.2, both with 6-speed manuals.

All these cars have sporty, responsive steering and handling, and even the high-power models aren't punishing over bumps, though the stiffly sprung tails can skip around on rough pavement, so the available traction control is a must on slippery surfaces. Brakes are strong, with good pedal modulation. We expect lots of mechanical ruckus in "muscle" cars, and V8 Camaros and Firebirds have a tiresome exhaust rumble, plus noisy high-performance tires.

ACCOMMODATIONS Camaro/Firebird's zoomy styling results in a wide but low cockpit that feels cramped even in front. Long, heavy doors aggravate entry/exit, and the "bathtub" seating combines with wide rear pillars to impede driver vision. As in most such cars, the back seat is fit only for kids. Instruments and controls are easy to locate and decipher, though Firebird's dashboard is unnecessarily over-styled. Cargo space is concentrated in a rectangular rear well big enough to swallow a set of golf clubs, and the rear seatback in coupes folds for extra versatility, but both body styles suffer high rear liftover. Only the Ram-Air Firebird among our recent test cars has suffered squeaks and rattles, though convertibles have more body flex over bumps than modern ragtops should.

VALUE FOR THE MONEY V8 models are among the world's best high-performance values, but Camaro and Firebird's '60s-think Detroit design is way out of step with today's tastes. Relatively speaking, Camaro gets our nod as the more sensible buy of the two, but Mustang outsells Camaro and Firebird combined, so if you take the GM plunge, demand a sizable discount from your Chevy or Pontiac dealer.

ENGINES

	ohv V6	ohv V8	ohv V8
Size, liters/cu. in.	3.8/231	5.7/346	5.7/346
Horsepower @ rpm	200 @ 5200	305 @ 5200	320 @ 5200
Torque (lbs./ft.) @ rpm	225 @ 4000	335 @ 4000	345 @ 4400
Availability	S[1]	S[2]	S[3]
EPA city/highway mpg			
5-speed OD manual	19/30		
6-speed OD manual		19/28	18/27
4-speed OD automatic	19/29	17/24	17/25

1. Base. 2. Z28. 3. SS.

PRICES

Chevrolet Camaro	Retail Price	Dealer Invoice
Base 2-door hatchback	$16840	$15409
Base 2-door convertible	24140	22088
Z28 2-door hatchback	21265	19457
Z28 2-door convertible	28365	25954
Destination charge	550	550

STANDARD EQUIPMENT:

Base hatchback: 3.8-liter V6 engine, 5-speed manual transmission, driver- and passenger-side airbags, antilock 4-wheel disc brakes, daytime running lights, air conditioning, power steering, tilt steering wheel, cloth upholstery, front bucket seats, center storage console, cupholders, auxiliary power outlet, folding rear seat, intermittent wipers, AM/FM/cassette, digital clock, map lights, tachometer, low-oil-level indicator, visor mirrors, automatic headlights, front floormats, left remote and right sport mirrors, theft-deterrent system, rear spoiler, 215/60R16 tires, wheel covers.

Base convertible adds: power mirrors, power windows, power door locks, remote keyless entry, rear defogger, Monsoon sound system, leather-wrapped steering w/radio controls, cruise control, rear floormats, fog lights, power folding top, 3-piece hard boot with storage bag.

Z28 adds to Base hatchback: 5.7-liter V8 305-horsepower engine, 6-speed manual or 4-speed automatic transmission, limited-slip differential, Monsoon sound system, low-coolant indicator system, performance ride and handling suspension, 235/55R16 tires, alloy wheels.

Z28 convertible adds: power mirrors, power windows, power door locks, remote keyless entry, rear defogger, leather-wrapped steering wheel w/radio controls, cruise control, 6-way power driver seat, rear floormats, fog lights, power folding top, 3-piece hard boot with storage bag.

OPTIONAL EQUIPMENT:
Major Packages

Preferred Equipment Group 1SB, Base hatchback	1170	1041

Cruise control, remote hatch release, power mirrors and windows, power door locks, remote keyless entry, theft-deterrent system w/alarm, fog lights.

Preferred Equipment Group 1SD, Z28 hatchback	1715	1526

Pkg. 1SB plus 6-way power driver seat, leather-wrapped steering wheel w/radio controls, rear floormats, bodyside moldings.

SS Performance/Appearance Pkg., Z28	3950	3516

Includes 320-horsepower engine, composite hood w/functional air scoop, forced-air induction system, low-restriction dual exhaust, power steering fluid cooler, special rear spoiler, Special High Performance Ride and Handling Pkg., 275/40ZR17 tires, special alloy wheels.

	Retail Price	Dealer Invoice
Sport Appearance Pkg., Base............................	$1755	$1562
Z28	1348	1200

Front and rear body moldings, 235/55R16 tires (Base), alloy wheels (Base).

Performance Handling Pkg., Base	275	245

Limited-slip differential, performance axle ratio (w/automatic transmission), dual exhaust, sport steering ratio. Requires Preferred Equipment Group 1SB., 235/55R16 tires, and alloy wheels.

Performance Pkg., Z28 hatchback	1200	1068

Larger stabilizer bars, stiffer springs and bushings, dual adjustable shock absorbers, power steering fluid cooler. Requires Preferred Equipment Group 1SD, 245/50ZR16 performance tires, performance axle ratio w/automatic transmission. NA w/removable roof panels.

Powertrains

4-speed automatic transmission, Base	815	725
Hurst shifter, Z28...	325	289
Requires 6-speed manual transmission.		
Traction control, Z28.......................................	450	401
Base...	250	223
Requires Preferred Equipment Group. Base requires Performance Handling Pkg.		
Performance axle ratio, Z28.................................	300	267
Requires automatic transmission and 245/50ZR16 tires.		

Comfort and Convenience

AM/FM/cassette w/Monsoon sound system, Base hatchback	350	312
AM/FM/CD player w/Monsoon sound system, Base hatchback	450	401
Base convertible, Z28....................................	100	89
12-disc CD changer	595	530
Requires AM/FM/cassette with Monsoon sound system.		
Leather-wrapped steering wheel, Base hatchback	170	151
Includes radio controls. Requires Preferred Group 1SB, optional radio.		
6-way power driver seat, Base	270	240
Leather bucket seats	500	445
Z28 hatchback requires preferred equipment group.		
Rear defogger, hatchback	170	151
Removable roof panels, hatchback	995	886
Includes locks, storage provisions, and sun shade. NA Performance Pkg.		
235/55R16 tires, Base	132	120
Requires alloy wheels.		
245/50ZR16 performance tires, Z28	225	200
245/50ZR16 all-season performance tires, Z28	225	200
Alloy wheels, Base	275	245
Requires 235/55R16 tires.		
Polished alloy wheels, Base..............................	750	668
Base w/Sport Appearance Pkg. or Performance Handling, Z28	500	445
Base requires 235/55R16 tires.		

CHEVROLET CAVALIER

Chevrolet Cavalier 2-door

Front-wheel-drive subcompact car; similar to Pontiac Sunfire

Base price range: $13,160-$19,830. Built in USA and Mexico.
Also consider: Chevrolet Prizm, Dodge/Plymouth Neon, Ford Focus

FOR • Fuel economy • Acceleration (2.4-liter engine) • Visibility
AGAINST • Rear-seat room • Interior materials

The 2000 version of General Motors' best-selling car arrived last summer with slightly revised styling inside and out, plus some new features. Cavalier is offered as a 2-door coupe in base and Z24 form, as a 4-door sedan in base and LS trim, and as a Z24 convertible with standard power top. All get minor front and rear appearance changes, with the Z24's exclusive exterior touches including a new rear spoiler. Inside, the dashboard and console are revamped, uplevel radios gain Radio Display System (RDS) capability, there are more cupholders, and child-seat top anchors are added for all three rear positions. Air conditioning becomes standard on all models, as does the previously optional rear defroster. Cavalier shares its basic design with the Pontiac Sunfire, which is similarly updated for 2000.

All Cavaliers have 4-cylinder engines. Base and LS come with 115 horsepower; a larger 150-hp unit is standard in Z24 and optional for LS. Manual transmission is standard on all but the LS sedan. A 3-speed automatic is optional on base models. A 4-speed automatic and traction control are standard on LS and optional elsewhere. Antilock brakes are standard.

PERFORMANCE The base 2.2-liter engine furnishes adequate acceleration, but has no power to spare with automatic transmission. The 2.4 is noticeably stronger and works better with automatic than do many twin-cam 4-cylinders. A new Getrag 5-speed provides somewhat slicker shifts for 2000, and both automatics are smooth, prompt operators. A test automatic '99 Sunfire GT convertible averaged 23 mpg, and we've logged 20.8-23.8 mpg with automatic base Cavalier sedans—not great for economy cars, though you can expect over 30 mpg on the highway. Engines are coarse and loud when pushed hard, but settle down at cruising. Highway wind and road noise are evident, but no more so than in most subcompacts.

Like counterpart Sunfire SEs, the base and LS Cavaliers corner with adequate grip and moderate body lean. Ride quality is above the subcompact-class average, though bumps and ruts trigger loud thumps. Z24s and Sunfire GTs ride more stiffly, but handling is above the class norm. Kudos to GM for giving these low-priced cars standard antilock brakes; they have good stopping power.

ACCOMMODATIONS Cavaliers and Sunfires are as roomy and accommodating as most any competitor, and the standard air conditioning and rear defroster are nice amenities. Low-to-the-floor front bucket seats create plenty of headroom and still allow shorter drivers to see easily over the dashboard. Rear room is adequate for two smaller adults or three children. Gauges and controls are unobstructed and clearly labeled, and the automatic transmission gear indicator is now illuminated for better visibility. Cabin storage includes a large glovebox and now four instead of two cupholders.

Despite lots of flimsy plastic trim, the padded dashtop is a nice feature in this price range. Both Cavalier and Sunfire have a trunk opening that's too small for easy loading of large objects, but cargo space is good. All rear seatbacks fold, though there's no lock to secure trunk from interior.

VALUE FOR THE MONEY They don't match the refinement of the Toyota Corolla or Honda Civic, but Cavalier and Sunfire include plenty of useful standard features and should be available with discounts to their already attractive list prices. Cavalier edges out Sunfire as the better overall value.

ENGINES

	ohv I4	dohc I4
Size, liters/cu. in.	2.2/134	2.4/146
Horsepower @ rpm	115 @ 5000	150 @ 5600
Torque (lbs./ft.) @ rpm	135 @ 3600	155 @ 4400
Availability	S[1]	S[2]
EPA city/highway mpg		
5-speed OD manual	24/34	23/33
3-speed automatic	23/29	
4-speed OD automatic	23/31	22/30

1. Base and LS. 2. Z24; optional, LS.

PRICES

Chevrolet Cavalier	Retail Price	Dealer Invoice
Base 2-door coupe	$13160	$12305
Base 4-door sedan	13260	11398
LS 4-door sedan	14805	13843
Z24 2-door coupe	16365	15301
Z24 2-door convertible	19830	18541
Destination charge	510	510

STANDARD EQUIPMENT:

Base: 2.2-liter 4-cylinder engine, 5-speed manual transmission, driver-

Prices are accurate at time of publication; subject to manufacturer's changes.

and passenger-side airbags, antilock brakes, daytime running lights, air conditioning, power steering, cloth and vinyl reclining front bucket seats, folding rear seat, center console, cupholders, AM/FM radio, digital clock, intermittent wipers, rear defogger, left remote and right manual mirrors, theft-deterrent system, 195/70R14 tires, wheel covers.

LS adds: 4-speed automatic transmission, traction control, tilt steering wheel, cruise control, cloth upholstery, tachometer, AM/FM/cassette, visor mirrors, reading lights, variable intermittent wipers, remote decklid release, floormats, 195/65R15 tires.

Z24 adds: 2.4-liter dohc 4-cylinder engine, 5-speed manual transmission, easy-entry front passenger seat, power mirrors, power windows, power door locks, remote keyless entry, AM/FM/CD player, power top (convertible), sport suspension, rear spoiler, fog lights, 205/55R16 tires, alloy wheels, deletes 4-speed automatic transmission, traction control.

OPTIONAL EQUIPMENT:
Major Packages

	Retail Price	Dealer Invoice
Preferred Equipment Group 1, Base coupe	$430	$387
Base sedan	413	372
AM/FM/cassette, remote decklid release, variable intermittent wipers, easy-entry front passenger seat (coupe), visor mirrors, bodyside moldings, mud guards, cargo net, floormats.		
Preferred Equipment Group 2, Base coupe	1000	900
Group 1 plus cruise control, tilt steering wheel, AM/FM/CD player, 195/65R16 tires, special wheel covers.		
Preferred Equipment Group 3, Base coupe	1714	1543
Group 2 plus power mirrors and windows, power door locks, remote keyless entry, power decklid release, theft-deterrent system w/alarm.		
Sport Pkg., Base coupe w/Group 1	185	167
Base coupe w/Group 2 or 3	135	122
AM/FM/CD player, tachometer, rear spoiler.		
Preferred Equipment Group 1, LS	880	792
Power mirrors, power windows and door locks, remote keyless entry, AM/FM/CD player, power decklid release, theft-deterrent system w/alarm.		

Powertrains

2.4-liter dohc 4-cylinder engine, LS	450	405
3-speed automatic transmission, Base	600	540
NA coupe w/Preferred Equipment Group 3.		
4-speed automatic transmission, Base coupe, Z24	780	702
Includes traction control. Base requires Preferred Equipment Group 2 or 3.		

Comfort and Convenience

Power sunroof, coupe	595	536
Includes map lights. Base requires Preferred Equipment Group.		
Remote keyless entry, Base coupe	370	333
Base sedan, LS	410	369
Includes power door locks, power decklid release, theft-deterrent system w/alarm.		
AM/FM/cassette, Base	165	149
AM/FM/CD player, Base	215	194
Base w/Group 1, LS	50	45
AM/FM/cassette/CD player, Base coupe w/Group 1, LS	230	207
Base coupe w/group 2 or 3, LS w/Group 1, Z24	180	162

Appearance and Miscellaneous

Rear spoiler, LS	150	135
Alloy wheels, Base coupe, LS	295	266

CHEVROLET CORVETTE

✓ **BEST BUY**

Chevrolet Corvette coupe

Rear-wheel-drive sports and GT car

Base price range: $38,320-$45,320. Built in USA. **Also consider:** Chevrolet Camaro, Dodge Viper, Porsche Boxster

FOR • Acceleration • Steering/handling • Instruments/controls

AGAINST • Fuel economy • Ride (Z51 suspension) • Rear visibility

The base hardtop adds some equipment as the only change of note to Chevrolet's fiberglass-body sports car for 2000. Corvette comes in fixed-roof hardtop, hatchback coupe, and convertible models. The hardtop comes only with a 6-speed manual transmission and Z51 sport suspension, which are optional for the others. All three have a 345-horsepower V8, "run-flat" tires, traction control, and an available Active Handling anti-skid system. The hatchback and convertible have standard automatic transmission and offer a base suspension or optional three-mode driver-adjustable suspension. The hardtop adds as standard visor mirrors and remote trunk release, and is now available with optional head-up instrument display, dual-zone climate control, fog lamps, and magnesium wheels.

EVALUATION The current "C5" series is the best 'Vette yet, but it's still a Corvette. That means fierce acceleration (about 5 seconds to 60 mph in our tests) and racer-sharp handling and braking. It also means lots of noise and a rugged ride that invites tail hop in bumpy turns; we prefer the base suspension as the best blend of ride and grip. Fuel economy depends on conditions and driving style: We've averaged 20 mpg with lots of highway driving and low as 12.9 in mostly city work. Entry/exit is crouch-and-crawl, but the 2-seat cabin is fairly spacious and operating well-planned, and operating the convertible's manual top is a breeze. Structures are solid, but detail finish and some materials disappoint. Corvettes aren't inexpensive, and they're still a bit crude for all their high-tech hardware. But if you like your high-performance sports cars big, bold, and brawny, there's no better all-around value.

ENGINES

	ohv V8
Size, liters/cu. in.	5.7/346
Horsepower @ rpm	345 @ 5600
Torque (lbs./ft.) @ rpm	350 @ 4400
Availability	S
EPA city/highway mpg	
6-speed OD manual	18/28
4-speed OD automatic	17/25

PRICES

Chevrolet Corvette	Retail Price	Dealer Invoice
Base 2-door hardtop	$38320	$33530
Base 2-door hatchback coupe	38895	34033
Base 2-door convertible	45320	39655
Destination charge	600	600

STANDARD EQUIPMENT:

Base hardtop: 5.7-liter V8 engine, 6-speed manual transmission, traction control, limited-slip differential, 3.42 axle ratio, driver- and passenger-side airbags, antilock 4-wheel disc brakes, low tire-pressure warning system, daytime running lights, air conditioning, variable-assist power steering, leather-wrapped tilt steering wheel, cruise control, leather bucket seats, center console, auxiliary power outlet, heated power mirrors, power windows, power door locks, remote keyless entry, tachometer, AM/FM/cassette, digital clock, intermittent wipers, rear defogger, visor mirrors, reading lights, remote decklid/hatch release, theft-deterrent system, Z51 Performance Handling Pkg., extended-mobility tires (245/45ZR17 front, 275/40ZR18 rear), alloy wheels.

Base coupe/convertible add: 4-speed automatic transmission, 2.73 axle ratio, 6-way power driver seat, Bose speakers, integrated antenna (coupe), power antenna (convertible), body-colored removable roof panel (coupe), manually folding convertible top (convertible), deletes Z51 Performance Handling Pkg.

OPTIONAL EQUIPMENT:
Major Packages

Memory Pkg., coupe, convertible	150	129
Memory for driver seat, outside mirrors, climate control, and radio presets.		
Continuous Variable Real Time Damping Suspension, coupe, convertible	1695	1458
Adjustable ride control.		
Z51 Performance Handling Pkg., coupe, conv.	350	301
Sport suspension (Bilstein shock absorbers, stiffer springs, stabilizer bars, and bushings) special alloy wheels. Automatic transmission requires performance axle ratio. NA w/Continuously Variable Real Time Damping Suspension.		

Powertrains

	Retail Price	Dealer Invoice
6-speed manual transmission, coupe, convertible	$815	$701
Includes performance axle ratio.		
Performance 3.15 axle ratio, coupe, convertible	100	86

Safety Features

Active handling system	500	430

Comfort and Convenience

Dual-zone climate controls	365	314
Perforated leather sport seats, coupe, convertible	700	602
6-way power driver seat, hardtop	305	262
6-way power passenger seat, coupe, convertible	305	262
AM/FM/CD player	100	86
Hardtop requires Bose speakers.		
12-disc CD changer	600	516
Bose speakers, hardtop	820	705
Head-up instrument display	375	323
Power telescoping steering column, coupe, convertible	350	301

Appearance and Miscellaneous

Transparent roof panel, coupe	650	559
Dual roof panels, coupe	1100	946
Standard removable roof panel and transparent roof panel.		
Fog lights	69	59
Magnesium wheels......................................	2000	1720
Polished alloy wheels	895	770

CHEVROLET IMPALA

BUDGET BUY

Chevrolet Impala LS

Front-wheel-drive midsize car; similar to Buick Century and Regal, Chevrolet Monte Carlo, Oldsmobile Intrigue, and Pontiac Grand Prix

Base price range: $18,705-$22,365. Built in Canada. **Also consider:** Ford Taurus, Honda Accord, Toyota Camry

FOR • Passenger and cargo room • Handling/roadholding • Instruments/controls **AGAINST** • Road noise

Chevrolet revives a famous big-car name for a new front-wheel-drive midsize sedan. Impala shares its basic understructure with the Buick Century and Regal, the Oldsmobile Intrigue, and Pontiac's Grand Prix. A 3.4-liter V6 is standard on the base Impala, while the upscale LS comes with a 3.8-liter that's optional on the base. Both models come with automatic transmission, 4-wheel-disc brakes, 16-inch wheels, air conditioning, and power windows and locks.

A side airbag for the driver is optional for the base Impala, standard on LS. The LS also includes antilock brakes, tire-inflation monitor, traction control, and a "firm ride" suspension, all of which are included in the base model's 3.8-liter option. The base Impala seats six via a front bench seat, but can be ordered with the LS's buckets and floor shift console. Leather upholstery is available for both and includes a split-fold rear seatback. And General Motors' OnStar assistance system is optional.

PERFORMANCE It's not the V8 Super Sport of yore, but the new Impala acquits itself well in most areas. The base engine provides adequate power, while the 3.8 delivers usefully stronger takeoffs and passing response. An alert, smooth-shifting transmission aids the cause, but neither engine sounds smooth or refined when pressed. The 3.8-liter LS we tested averaged a likable 20.1 mpg, though that reflects lots of highway miles. The 3.4 liter works a little harder in this sizable sedan, and our test 3.4 -liter base model averaged 19.8 mpg in an even mix of driving.

A good ride/handling balance makes this family 4-door pleasing to drive. Even the "Ride and Handling" suspension that goes with the

larger engine absorbs most bumps well, and it quells much of the float and wallow that can plague the base suspension over high-speed dips. The "Ride and Handling" setup also enhances control and reduces body lean in turns, but any Impala furnishes good grip and balance, plus authoritative steering feel. Braking brings assured stopping power, though some of our testers feel the need for firmer pedal action. We agree that ABS should be standard on the base model—as on Chevy's smaller Malibu. Wind noise is low, but tire roar intrudes some on coarse pavement.

ACCOMMODATIONS This is a roomy sedan, with enough cabin length for 6-footers to ride in tandem without cramping anyone's legs. There's not quite enough rear-seat width for three large adults, however, and the rear seat cushion is far too soft, short, and lacking in contour for best comfort. Head room is good all around, even with the optional moonroof, and entry/exit is big-car easy. The flat-floor trunk should swallow a family's vacation gear, and its opening is low and wide.

Drivers enjoy a standard manual tilt wheel, a convenient in-dash ignition switch, conveniently high-set stereo, and simple climate controls (with dual-zone temperature adjustment on LS). Quibbles include high-tail styling that hurts rearward vision and a puny in-dash glovebox, but there are roomy front-door map pockets and additional storage in either a front console or pull-down center armrest. Chevy says it's awaiting development of a "smart" front passenger-side airbag before offering one in its cars. Interior materials are nice, but not special. Early Impalas we tested displayed a tight assembly feel, but one car's heater fan emitted an annoying, high-pitched whistle.

VALUE FOR THE MONEY Impala is a clear alternative to the redesigned Ford Taurus, featuring a comfort-oriented American style to Taurus's import-influenced approach. Impala leads in powertrain response, Taurus in safety features and rear-seat comfort. Both offer more room and equipment for the price than do the Honda Accord and Toyota Camry, though those Japanese-brand rivals are still more polished all-around cars.

ENGINES

	ohv V6	ohv V6
Size, liters/cu. in.	3.4/205	3.8/231
Horsepower @ rpm	180 @ 5200	200@ 5200
Torque (lbs./ft.) @ rpm	205 @ 4000	225 @ 4000
Availability	S[1]	S[2]
EPA city/highway mpg		
4-speed OD automatic	20/32	20/29

1. Base. 2. LS; optional, Base.

PRICES

Chevrolet Impala	Retail Price	Dealer Invoice
Base 4-door sedan	$18705	$17115
LS 4-door sedan	22365	20464
Destination charge	560	560

STANDARD EQUIPMENT:

Base: 3.4-liter V6 engine, 4-speed automatic transmission, driver- and passenger-side airbags, 4-wheel disc brakes, daytime running lights, air conditioning, power steering, tilt steering wheel, cloth upholstery, front split bench seat, cupholders, overhead console, power mirrors, power windows, power door locks, AM/FM radio, digital clock, rear defogger, variable intermittent wipers, visor mirrors, power remote decklid release, floormats, theft-deterrent system, 225/60R16 tires, wheel covers.

LS adds: 3.8-liter V6 engine, traction control, driver-side side-impact airbag, antilock brakes, manual dual-zone climate controls, interior air filter, cruise control, leather-wrapped steering wheel, front bucket seats, 6-way power driver seat w/manual lumbar support, center console, split folding rear seat, overhead console w/storage, heated power mirrors, remote keyless entry, AM/FM/cassette, tachometer, automatic day/night rearview mirror, map lights, illuminated visor mirrors, rear spoiler, fog lights, Ride and Handling Suspension, tire inflation monitor, 225/60R16 touring tires, alloy wheels.

OPTIONAL EQUIPMENT:
Major Packages

Preferred Equipment Group 1, Base...........................	993	884
Cruise control, remote keyless entry, AM/FM/cassette, automatic day/night rearview mirror, map lights, overhead console w/storage, illuminated visor mirrors, cargo net.		

Prices are accurate at time of publication; subject to manufacturer's changes.

	Retail Price	Dealer Invoice
Preferred Equipment Group 2, Base	$1599	$1423

Preferred Equipment Group 1 plus manual dual-zone climate controls, steering-wheel radio controls, heated power mirrors, alloy wheels.

Preferred Equipment Group 1, LS	517	460

Steering-wheel radio controls, Driver Information/Convenience Center (trip computer, compass, outside temperature indicator, universal garage door opener, theft-deterrent system w/alarm).

Custom Cloth Trim, Base	765	681

Driver-side side-impact airbag, 6-way power driver seat, split folding rear seat. Requires Preferred Equipment Group.

Custom Cloth Seat Trim w/bucket seats, Base	815	725

Custom Cloth Seat Trim plus front bucket seats, center console, additional cupholder. Requires Preferred Equipment Group.

Leather Seat Trim, Base	1390	1237

Custom Cloth Seat Trim plus leather upholstery. Requires Preferred Equipment Group, steering-wheel radio controls. NA with front bucket seats.

Comfort Seating Pkg.	425	378

Heated front seats, 6-way power passenger seat. Requires Leather Seat Trim, Base requires Preferred Equipment Group.

Powertrains

3.8-liter V6 engine, Base	986	878

Includes traction control, antilock brakes, tire inflation monitor, Ride and Handling Suspension. Requires Preferred Equipment Group, 225/60R16 touring tires, alloy wheels.

Safety Features

Antilock brakes, Base	600	534

Includes tire inflation monitor.

Comfort and Convenience

OnStar System	695	—

Includes Global Positioning System, roadside assistance, emergency services. Requires annual service charge. Price may vary.

Power sunroof	700	623

Base requires Preferred Equipment Group.

Driver Information/Convenience Center, Base	275	245

Trip computer, compass, outside temperature indicator, universal garage door opener, theft-deterrent system w/alarm. Requires Preferred Equipment Group.

6-way power passenger seat, Base	305	271

Requires Preferred Equipment Group 1 and Custom Cloth Seat Trim.

Leather Seat Trim, LS	625	556
AM/FM/CD player, Base	405	360
Base w/Preferred Equipment Group, LS	123	109

Includes premium speakers.

AM/FM/cassette/CD player, Base	505	449
Base w/Preferred Equipment Group, LS	223	198

Includes premium speakers.

Steering-wheel radio controls, Base	171	152

Includes leather-wrapped steering wheel. Requires Preferred Equipment Group 1.

Alloy wheels, Base	300	267
225/60R16 touring tires, Base	45	40

CHEVROLET LUMINA

Chevrolet Lumina

Front-wheel-drive midsize car

Base price: $18,790. Built in Canada. **Also consider:** Ford Taurus, Honda Accord, Toyota Camry

FOR • Quietness • Passenger and cargo room • Ride • Instruments/controls **AGAINST** • Steering feel

Though the 2000 Impala was supposed to replace it, Lumina sur-

vives as a less expensive midsize Chevrolet sedan aimed mainly at the fleet market. It now comes in one model equipped between last year's base and LS. That means the 3.8-liter V6 is no longer offered. The standard equipment list now includes a 3.1-liter V6—newly retuned for 15 extra horsepower—plus automatic transmission, antilock brakes, air conditioning, power windows and mirrors, and cassette stereo. Front bucket seats are no longer available, leaving a standard 60/40 bench. GM's OnStar communications system also has been dropped from the options list. A new optional Appearance Package includes a CD player and 16-inch aluminum wheels with higher-performance touring tires.

EVALUATION The 3.1-liter V6 provides adequate acceleration and overall economy of about 20 mpg. Lumina is quieter than some competitors, and suspension tuning gives a comfortable family-sedan ride. Handling is competent if unexciting, marred by steering that's short on road feel and on-center precision. The antilock brakes provide adequately short stops with good control. There's ample room for four adults or, with the front bench, six with some crowding. The instrument panel is contemporary and convenient, outward visibility is fine. The roomy trunk has a flat floor that goes well forward. Chevy's newer Malibu is a roomier and better sedan, but Lumina is proficient enough and should be available at deep discounts.

ENGINES

	ohv V6
Size, liters/cu. in.	3.1/191
Horsepower @ rpm	175 @ 5200
Torque (lbs./ft.) @ rpm	190 @ 4000
Availability	S

EPA city/highway mpg
4-speed OD automatic	20/29

PRICES

Chevrolet Lumina	Retail Price	Dealer Invoice
Base 4-door sedan	$18790	$17193
Destination charge	560	560

STANDARD EQUIPMENT:

Base: 3.1-liter V6 engine, 4-speed automatic transmission, driver- and passenger-side airbags, daytime running lights, air conditioning, power steering, tilt steering wheel, cruise control, cloth reclining front split bench seat with center armrest and 4-way manual driver seat, cupholder, AM/FM/cassette, digital clock, power mirrors, power windows, power door locks, visor mirrors, variable intermittent wipers, rear defogger, theft-deterrent system, 205/70R15 tires, wheel covers.

OPTIONAL EQUIPMENT:
Major Packages

Preferred Equipment Group 1	320	285

Remote keyless entry, power decklid release, floormats.

Appearance Pkg.	718	639

AM/FM/CD player, custom cloth seat trim, 225/60R16 tires, alloy wheels.

Safety Features

Antilock brakes	575	512

Comfort and Convenience

OnStar System	695	—

Includes Global Positioning System, roadside assistance, emergency services. Requires annual service charge. Price may vary.

AM/FM/CD player	93	83
6-way power driver seat	305	271
Custom cloth upholstery	150	134

CHEVROLET MALIBU   RECOMMENDED

Front-wheel-drive midsize car

Base price range: $16,445-$19,215. Built in USA. **Also consider:** Dodge Stratus, Honda Accord, Toyota Camry

FOR • Passenger and cargo room • Ride • Build quality
AGAINST • Steering feel

This midsize sedan with a storied '60s name gets a mild facelift and loses its base 4-cylinder engine in favor of a standard V6 for 2000.

Slotting below the larger new Impala in price and market position,

Chevrolet Malibu

Malibu again offers base and upscale LS models, but the base version's 4-cylinder engine is dropped in favor of the same 3.1-liter V6 that powers the LS; it has 15 more horsepower for 2000. Both models get a fresh face with a faint resemblance to Impala's, and a rear spoiler is newly optional for the LS, as are gold exterior badges. Unlike Impala, which can seat six, Malibu has standard front bucket seats for 5-passenger capacity. Both Malibu models come with floorshift automatic transmission, antilock brakes, air conditioning, and tachometer. Leather upholstery is optional for the LS. Malibu had shared its design with the Oldsmobile Cutlass, which was discontinued in spring 1999.

PERFORMANCE We haven't yet tested a 2000 Malibu, but the V6's extra power should help performance in all situations. Last year, the V6 was quicker off the line than the 4-cylinder, but not much faster in highway passing situations. It didn't use much more fuel than the four, either, with the six averaging about 19 mpg and the four around 22 in our tests. The retuning won't make this engine the smoothest or quietest V6 around, but the 3.1 is adequate on both counts. The transmission is smooth, but doesn't always downshift quickly enough for passing.

In normal driving, Malibu is maneuverable and secure. Aggressive cornering brings tire scrubbing and substantial body lean and makes the steering feel slow and vague. Rough pavement is easily absorbed, though the suspension and tires thump loudly over ruts and potholes. Wind and road noise are high enough to keep Malibu from qualifying as a serene long-distance cruiser. Stopping power is adequate and pedal modulation good.

ACCOMMODATIONS Malibu is spacious for its size, with generous front head room and leg room that's more than adequate all around. Rear head room is sufficient for those under 6-feet tall. Front seats are firm and nicely contoured, but the rear bench is hard and flat. Instruments are unobstructed, stalks for wipers and headlamps convenient, audio and climate controls large and accessible. A tasteful blend of fabrics, plastics, and padded surfaces give Malibu the ambience of some costlier cars. Interior storage space is generous, and the large trunk has a flat floor, huge opening, and a near-bumper-level sill. Thin pillars and large outside mirrors provide good visibility, but the rear parcel shelf is high enough to impede vision directly astern.

VALUE FOR THE MONEY It's no cut-rate Camry, but Malibu delivers a fine blend of utility, driving satisfaction, and features at an attractive price. It's a strong Recommend pick.

ENGINES

	ohv V6
Size, liters/cu. in.	3.1/191
Horsepower @ rpm	170 @ 5200
Torque (lbs./ft.) @ rpm	190 @ 4000
Availability	S

EPA city/highway mpg

4-speed OD automatic	20/30

PRICES

Chevrolet Malibu	Retail Price	Dealer Invoice
Base 4-door sedan	$16445	$15047
LS 4-door sedan	19215	17582
Destination charge	550	550

STANDARD EQUIPMENT:

Base: 3.1-liter V6 engine, 4-speed automatic transmission, driver- and passenger-side airbags, antilock brakes, daytime running lights, air conditioning, power steering, tilt steering wheel, cloth upholstery, reclining front bucket seats, storage console w/armrest, cupholder, tachometer,

AM/FM radio, digital clock, variable intermittent wipers, visor mirrors, remote decklid release, auxiliary power outlet, automatic headlights, dual outside mirrors w/driver-side remote, theft-deterrent system, 215/60R15 tires, wheel covers.

LS adds: cruise control, 6-way power driver seat, split folding rear seat, power mirrors, power windows, power door locks, remote keyless entry, AM/FM/cassette/CD player, rear defogger, passenger-side illuminated visor mirror, dual reading lights, floormats, fog lights, alloy wheels.

OPTIONAL EQUIPMENT:	Retail Price	Dealer Invoice
Major Packages		
Preferred Equipment Group 1, Base	$1380	$1242
Power windows and door locks, power mirrors, cruise control, AM/FM/cassette, rear defogger, floormats.		
Preferred Equipment Group 1, LS	1320	1188
Leather upholstery, power sunroof, rear spoiler.		
Comfort and Convenience		
Cruise control, Base	225	203
Requires Preferred Equipment Group 1.		
Power sunroof, LS	650	585
Split folding rear seat, Base	195	176
Includes cargo net. Requires Preferred Equipment Group 1.		
Leather upholstery, LS	595	536
Includes leather-wrapped steering wheel.		
6-way power driver seat, Base	310	279
Requires Preferred Equipment Group 1.		
AM/FM/cassette, Base	220	198
AM/FM/CD player, Base	320	288
AM/FM/cassette/CD player, Base	420	378
Remote keyless entry, Base	150	135
Requires Preferred Equipment Group 1.		
Rear defogger, Base	180	162
Appearance and Miscellaneous		
Rear spoiler, LS	175	158
Alloy wheels, Base	310	279
Requires Preferred Equipment Group 1.		

CHEVROLET METRO

Chevrolet Metro 4-door

Front-wheel-drive subcompact car; similar to Suzuki Esteem/Swift

Base price range: $9,185-$10,610. Built in Canada. **Also consider:** Ford Escort/ZX2, Honda Civic, Nissan Sentra

FOR • Fuel economy • Maneuverability • Visibility **AGAINST** • Rear-seat room • Ride • Noise • Acceleration (3-cylinder) • Interior materials

A remote cargo-lid release for the uplevel LSi model is the only 2000 change to Chevrolet's smallest car. Metro shares its design with the Suzuki Swift and is offered as a 2-door hatchback and 4-door sedan. The base hatchback has a 3-cylinder engine; the LSi hatchback and sedan use a 4-cylinder. Manual transmission is standard. A 3-speed automatic is optional with the 4-cylinder, and antilock brakes are available on all models.

EVALUATION These are among the lightest cars sold in North America, which makes for outstanding fuel economy but also a tinny feel and high noise levels. Metros are also among the smallest cars around, so interior room is predictably tight. LSi models work hard to keep up with traffic; the 3-cylinder base hatchback struggles even more. Low prices and high mileage may tempt, but we think a more substantial car—even a used one—is a smarter choice than Metro.

Prices are accurate at time of publication; subject to manufacturer's changes.

ENGINES

	ohc I3	ohc I4
Size, liters/cu. in.	1.0/61	1.3/79
Horsepower @ rpm	55 @ 5700	79 @ 6000
Torque (lbs./ft.) @ rpm	58 @ 3300	75 @ 3000
Availability	S[1]	S[2]
EPA city/highway mpg		
5-speed OD manual	41/47	39/43
3-speed automatic		30/34

1. Base. 2. LSi.

PRICES

Chevrolet Metro	Retail Price	Dealer Invoice
Base 2-door hatchback	$9185	$8652
LSi 2-door hatchback	10035	9353
LSi 4-door sedan	10610	9889
Destination charge	400	400

STANDARD EQUIPMENT:

Base: 1.0-liter 3-cylinder engine, 5-speed manual transmission, driver- and passenger-side airbags, daytime running lights, cloth/vinyl reclining front bucket seats, folding rear seat, center console, cupholders, dual outside mirrors, 155/80R13 tires, wheel covers.

LSi adds: 1.3-liter 4-cylinder engine, upgraded cloth/vinyl upholstery, intermittent wipers, remote decklid/hatch release, floormats (2-door).

OPTIONAL EQUIPMENT:
Major Packages

Preferred Equipment Group 2, Base.............	115	102
Easy-entry passenger seat, bodyside moldings, floormats.		
Preferred Equipment Group 2, 4-door.............	1790	1593
Air conditioning, power steering, power door locks, AM/FM radio w/digital clock, split folding rear seat, remote decklid release, cargo area light, floormats, bodyside moldings, dual remote mirrors.		
Convenience Pkg., LSi 2-door	125	111
Easy-entry passenger seat, dual manual remote mirrors, cargo cover.		

Powertrains

3-speed automatic transmission, LSi............	595	530

Safety Features

Antilock brakes	565	503

Comfort and Convenience

Air conditioning..............................	785	699
Power steering, 4-door	290	258
AM/FM radio	330	294
Includes seek and scan, digital clock, four speakers.		
AM/FM/cassette	495	441
4-door w/Group 2	165	147
AM/FM/CD player	595	530
4-door w/Group 2	265	236
Rear defogger	160	142
Rear wiper/washer, LSi 2-door...............	125	111
Requires rear defogger.		
Tachometer..................................	70	62
Base includes trip odometer.		

CHEVROLET MONTE CARLO

Chevrolet Monte Carlo LS

Front-wheel-drive sports coupe; similar to Chevrolet Impala

Base price range: $19,290–$21,735. Built in USA. **Also consider:** Acura CL, Dodge Avenger, Toyota Solara

FOR • Acceleration (SS) • Steering/handling (SS)

• Instruments/controls **AGAINST** • Engine noise • Road noise

Chevrolet's midsize sports coupe is redesigned for 2000, switching from the platform of the Lumina sedan to that of the larger new 2000 Impala. It loses two inches of body length but gains three inches in wheelbase for an extra inch of rear leg room. Other interior dimensions change fractionally. The 2000 Monte comes only with front bucket seats for 5-passenger capacity. Side airbags aren't offered.

The LS model has a 180-horsepower 3.4-liter V6, the sporty SS a 200-hp 3.8-liter V6. Both come only with automatic transmission, although the SS has a firmer suspension than the LS, plus standard alloy wheels. Antilock 4-wheel disc brakes are standard on both, as are power windows, tilt steering column, and tire-inflation monitor. Leather upholstery is optional.

PERFORMANCE The LS version of this relatively large coupe has modest handling abilities, but feels reasonably balanced and secure in corners. The SS shines on twisty roads, showing little body lean and terrific grip. Both Montes have firm, accurate steering and a comfortable ride. They're also stable in freeway cruising, and even the SS is compliant enough on bumpy city streets.

A responsive automatic transmission works with the base V6 to provide adequate acceleration. The SS is no muscle car, but its bigger V6 provides brisk takeoffs and ready power for freeway merging or backroad passing. Alas, both engines in our test cars were loud and gruff in full-bore acceleration, and tire roar was prominent on coarse surfaces. We had no opportunity to measure fuel economy. Standard antilock disc brakes are a welcome feature; they feel strong and have good pedal modulation, but hard stops induce excessive nosedive.

ACCOMMODATIONS Monte Carlo has more interior space than other sports coupes, which are built off smaller platforms. Two adults can stretch out in front, and rear leg room is adequate for average-size adults. Head room gets tight with the optional sunroof, but there's far more clearance than in such rivals as the Mercury Cougar. The cabin also feels roomier than two other competing coupes, Honda's 2-door Accord and the Toyota Solara. Cargo room is another advantage, Monte's trunk being tall, wide, and deep with a convenient bumper-height liftover.

The driver gets a comfortable bucket seat with plenty of lateral bolstering, but thick rear roof pillars impede over-the-shoulder vision. Gauge groupings and graphics are excellent, controls fall easily to hand, and driver and front passenger have individual temperature controls.

VALUE FOR THE MONEY Monte Carlo trounces coupes like the Dodge Avenger in size, comfort, and performance, and beats Accord and Solara on a features-per-dollar basis. It isn't as polished as the Japanese-brand rivals and won't hold its value as well, but this new Chevy has its own American-car character.

ENGINES

	ohv V6	ohv V6
Size, liters/cu. in.	3.4/205	3.8/231
Horsepower @ rpm	180 @ 5200	200 @ 5200
Torque (lbs./ft.) @ rpm	205 @ 4000	225 @ 4000
Availability	S[1]	S[2]
EPA city/highway mpg		
4-speed OD automatic	20/32	19/29

1. LS. 2. SS.

PRICES

Chevrolet Monte Carlo	Retail Price	Dealer Invoice
LS 2-door coupe	$19290	$17650
SS 2-door coupe	21735	19888
Destination charge	560	560

STANDARD EQUIPMENT:

LS: 3.4-liter V6 engine, 4-speed automatic transmission, driver- and passenger-side airbags, antilock 4-wheel disc brakes, daytime running lights, air conditioning, power steering, tilt steering wheel, cloth upholstery, front bucket seats, center console, cupholders, split folding rear seat, overhead console, AM/FM/cassette, digital clock, tachometer, power mirrors, power windows, power door locks, auxiliary power outlet, rear defogger, variable intermittent wipers, power decklid release, automatic headlights, visor mirrors, floormats, theft-deterrent system, tire inflation monitor, 225/60R16 tires, wheel covers.

SS adds: 3.8-liter engine, traction control, dual-zone manual climate control, cruise control, leather-wrapped steering wheel w/radio controls, remote keyless entry, illuminated visor mirrors, fog lights, rear spoiler, sport suspension, 225/60SR16 tires, alloy wheels.

OPTIONAL EQUIPMENT:
Major Packages

	Retail Price	Dealer Invoice
Preferred Equipment Group 1, LS	$918	$817
Dual-zone manual climate control, cruise control, remote keyless entry, illuminated visor mirrors, cargo net, alloy wheels.		
Preferred Equipment 1, SS	736	655
Heated power mirrors, 6-way power driver seat, automatic day/night rearview mirror, universal garage door opener, Driver Information/Convenience Center (includes trip computer, compass, outside temperature indicator), theft-deterrent system w/alarm.		

Comfort and Convenience

OnStar System	695	—
Includes Global Positioning System, roadside assistance, emergency services. Requires annual service charge. Price may vary.		
Driver Information/Convenience Center	275	245
Trip computer, compass, outside temperature indicator, universal garage door opener, theft-deterrent system w/alarm. LS requires Preferred Equipment Group 1.		
AM/FM/CD player	123	109
Includes 6-speaker sound system, Radio Display System.		
AM/FM/cassette/CD player	223	198
Includes Radio Display System and 6-speaker sound system.		
6-speaker sound system	—	—
Steering wheel radio controls, LS	171	152
Includes leather-wrapped steering wheel.		
Leather upholstery	625	556
Requires power driver seat.		
Heated front seats, LS	120	107
Requires leather upholstery, power driver and passenger seats.		
6-way power driver seat	305	271
6-way power passenger seat	305	271
Requires leather upholstery and power driver seat.		
Power sunroof	700	623
LS requires Preferred Equipment Group 1.		
Automatic day/night rearview mirror, LS	121	108
Requires Preferred Equipment Group 1.		
Alloy wheels, LS	300	267

CHEVROLET PRIZM

RECOMMENDED

Chevrolet Prizm

Front-wheel-drive subcompact car; similar to Toyota Corolla

Base price range: $13,816-$15,842. Built in USA. **Also consider:** Honda Civic, Mazda Protege, Volkswagen Jetta/Golf

FOR • Fuel economy **AGAINST** • Rear-seat room • Automatic transmission performance

Chevrolet's version of the Toyota Corolla gets a little more power and added standard features for 2000. Prizm returns with base and uplevel LSi sedans powered by a Toyota-designed 1.8-liter 4-cylinder engine that now gains 5 horsepower with the addition of variable valve timing. Manual transmission is standard, 3- and 4-speed automatics optional. Front seatbelt pre-tensioners remain standard, too. Antilock brakes return at extra cost, as do front side airbags.

This year, the base Prizm gains standard air conditioning like the LSi, plus 4-speaker AM/FM stereo and full wheel covers. LSi standards expand to include slightly wider 185/65R14 tires, power windows, rear defroster, tilt steering wheel, and a tachometer with out-

side temperature gauge, all of which had been options. Despite their design similarity, Prizm is outsold by Corolla nearly 5-1. Prizm's performance and accommodations mirror those of comparable Corolla models.

The Toyota Corolla report includes an evaluation of the Prizm.

ENGINES

	dohc I4
Size, liters/cu. in.	1.8/110
Horsepower @ rpm	125 @ 5600
Torque (lbs./ft.) @ rpm	125 @ 4000
Availability	S
EPA city/highway mpg	
5-speed OD manual	31/37
3-speed automatic	28/33
4-speed OD automatic	29/37

PRICES

Chevrolet Prizm	Retail Price	Dealer Invoice
Base 4-door sedan	$13816	$13153
LSi 4-door sedan	15842	14606
Destination charge	440	440

STANDARD EQUIPMENT:

Base: 1.8-liter dohc engine, 5-speed manual transmission, driver- and passenger-side airbags, daytime running lights, air conditioning, power steering, cloth reclining front bucket seats, center console, cupholders, AM/FM radio, digital clock, variable intermittent wipers, automatic headlights, visor mirrors, remote fuel door and decklid release, floormats, dual outside mirrors, wheel covers, 175/65R14 tires.

LSi adds: cruise control, tilt steering wheel, power mirrors, power windows, power door locks, remote keyless entry, AM/FM/cassette, tachometer, outside temperature indicator, rear defogger, split folding rear seat w/trunk pass-through, 185/65R14 tires.

OPTIONAL EQUIPMENT:
Major Packages

Preferred Equipment Group 2, Base	570	490
Cruise control, power door locks, AM/FM/cassette.		

Powertrains

3-speed automatic transmission	495	426
4-speed automatic transmission	800	688

Safety Features

Antilock brakes	645	555
Front side-impact airbags	295	254
Integrated child safety seat, LSi	125	108

Comfort and Convenience

Tilt steering wheel, Base	80	69
Rear defogger, Base	180	155
Power windows, Base	300	258
Power sunroof	675	581
Tachometer, Base	70	60
Includes outside temperature indicator.		
AM/FM/cassette, Base	165	141
AM/FM/CD player, Base	215	185
Base w/Preferred Group 2, LSi	50	43

Appearance and Miscellaneous

Alloy wheels	283	243

CHEVROLET SILVERADO 1500 ✓ BEST BUY

Rear- or 4-wheel-drive full-size pickup truck; similar to GMC Sierra 1500

Base price range: $15,655-$31,720. Built in USA. **Also consider:** Dodge Ram 1500, Ford F-150, Toyota Tundra

FOR • Acceleration (V8s) • Instruments/controls **AGAINST** • Fuel economy • Ride

Chevrolet's full-size pickup returns from its 1999 redesign with an available fourth door and more V8 power. Silverado continues in half-ton 1500-series models and light-duty three-quarter-ton 2500s with choice of regular and extended cabs, 2- or 4-wheel drive, and

Prices are accurate at time of publication; subject to manufacturer's changes.

Chevrolet Silverado 1500 extended cab

base, LS, and LT trim. GMC's Sierra offers a parallel lineup with slightly different styling, features mix, and pricing. This report covers Silverado 1500s.

The new left-side rear door is optional for extended cabs to supplement a standard right-side door. Both cab styles offer flush-fender Fleetside cargo boxes of 6.5 or 8.1 feet; a 6.5-foot flare-fender Sportside box is available on certain LT models. All Silverados come with antilock 4-wheel disc brakes. A class exclusive shared with GMC is optional adjustable ride control offering two levels of shock absorber firmness to suit road or load.

A 4.3-liter V6 repeats as base power, while the available 4.8- and 5.3-liter V8s gain 15 horsepower each. All engines team with manual or automatic transmission; the latter features GM's Tow/Haul mode that adjusts shifting to maximize power under heavy loads. Silverado's AutoTrac is the only 4-wheel-drive system on a full-size pickup that can be left engaged on dry pavement. It can be locked in 4WD or allowed to automatically engage the front axle when rear-wheel slip is detected.

Among lesser changes for 2000 are a standard self-dimming inside mirror for LS and LT models. And power door locks on LS and LT models can now be programmed to lock and unlock according to individual driver preferences. New options include wheel flares for 4x4s and a factory-fit bed cover.

PERFORMANCE Silverado and Sierra have fine all-around performance and are an easy match for the top-selling Ford F-150. The V6 engine struggles under a heavy load or up long grades, but it's a smooth runner, as are the V8s. Our choice is the 5.3-liter engine, which has good power in all conditions, though it still trails the F-150's 5.4-liter V8 in torque. An alert, fuss-free automatic transmission helps get the most from both engines. Fuel economy is about par for this class. We averaged 13.7 mpg with extended-cab 4WD models equipped with the 5.3 V8 and automatic transmission; a 2WD 5.3 Sierra returned 12.6.

Among useful features are the Tow/Haul mode and adjustable suspension options, since 70 percent of big-pickup owners haul or tow at some point. Silverado and Sierra enjoy firm, progressive brake-pedal action and good stopping power from their standard ABS 4-wheel discs. Steering is accurate, but doesn't feel quite as firm as the Ford's. The GM twins have a more compliant ride than the F-150, however, though as in any pickups, the tail stutters over bumps with the bed empty. Road, wind, and engine noise levels are unobjectionable and slightly less than in comparable F-150s.

ACCOMMODATIONS Extended-cabs account for more than 60 percent of big-truck sales, so the belated fourth door option is a good thing for Silverado and Sierra, putting them abreast with the Dodge Ram Quad Cab and Ford F-Series SuperCab. SuperCab's second rear door is standard, though, and the new 2000 F-150 SuperCrew boasts four full-size, front-hinged doors. The Silverado/Sierra rear doors open wide and have robust exterior pull handles instead of slip-prone flippers.

GM's extended-cabs also offer a more accommodating rear cabin than conventional rivals, with more leg space and a seat whose contoured cushion and reclined backrest provide near sedanlike accommodations. The back seat folds for in-cab storage, as in the Ford and Dodge, but the carpeted load area is more vulnerable to gouging and marring than the F-Series' metal surfaces. Also, the GM trucks don't offer handy bins and nets like those available in extended-cab Rams.

Location of gauges and the placement and feel of switchgear is top-notch, though some of our testers think the wipers deserve their own control rather than being activated by twisting the turn-signal lever. GM is alone in offering an engine-hour meter to supplement the usual odometer. Front seats are roomy and supportive, with integrated safety belts that move comfortably with the seats themselves. Reaching the power seat controls with the door closed is a squeeze, but the power lower cushion adjusts independently from the backrest—a nice touch. A spare-tire lock is a thoughtful standard, but only Ford offers a locking tailgate.

VALUE FOR THE MONEY They're a step behind Ford in the race toward innovations such as a ½-ton crew cab, but in performance, comfort, design, and pricing, Silverado and Sierra are Best Buy values.

ENGINES

	ohv V6	ohv V8	ohv V8
Size, liters/cu. in.	4.3/262	4.8/292	5.3/325
Horsepower @ rpm	200 @	270 @	285 @
	4600	5200	5200
Torque (lbs./ft.) @ rpm	260 @	285 @	325 @
	2800	4000	4000
Availability	S	O	O[1]
EPA city/highway mpg			
5-speed OD manual	17/23[2]	16/20[3]	
4-speed OD automatic	16/20	16/21[2]	16/20[2]

1. Standard LT extended cab. 2. 15/18 w/4WD. 3. 15/19 w/4WD.

PRICES

Chevrolet Silverado 1500	Retail Price	Dealer Invoice
2WD Base Fleetside regular cab, short bed	$15655	$14168
2WD Base Fleetside regular cab, long bed	15955	14439
2WD LS Fleetside regular cab, short bed	19751	17282
2WD LS Fleetside regular cab, long bed	20051	17545
4WD Base Fleetside regular cab, short bed	18770	16987
4WD Base Fleetside regular cab, long bed	19070	17258
4WD LS Fleetside regular cab, short bed	22851	19995
4WD LS Fleetside regular cab, long bed	23151	20257
2WD Base Fleetside extended cab, short bed	19729	17263
2WD Base Fleetside extended cab, long bed	20724	18134
2WD LS Fleetside extended cab, short bed	22501	19688
2WD LS Fleetside extended cab, long bed	23496	20559
2WD LT Fleetside extended cab, short bed	28210	24684
2WD LT Fleetside extended cab, long bed	28510	24946
4WD Base Fleetside extended cab, short bed	23524	20584
4WD Base Fleetside extended cab, long bed	23824	20846
4WD LS Fleetside extended cab, short bed	26296	23009
4WD LS Fleetside extended cab, long bed	26596	23272
4WD LT Fleetside extended cab, short bed	31420	27493
4WD LT Fleetside extended cab, long bed	31720	27755
Destination charge	665	665

STANDARD EQUIPMENT:

Base: 4.3-liter V6 engine (regular cab, 2WD extended cab short bed), 4.8-liter V8 engine (4WD extended cab, 2WD extended cab long bed), 5-speed manual transmission, driver- and passenger-side airbags, antilock 4-wheel disc brakes, daytime running lights, variable-assist power steering, tilt steering wheel, third door (extended cab), vinyl split bench seat, rear bench seat (extended cab), cupholders, auxiliary power outlets, AM/FM radio, digital clock, tachometer, engine hour meter, passenger-side visor mirror, rear heat ducts (extended cab), cargo box light, intermittent wipers, automatic headlights, theft-deterrent system, dual outside mirrors, chrome front bumper, painted rear step bumper, 7-lead trailer harness, full-size spare tire, 235/75R16 tires. **4WD** models add: part-time 4-wheel drive, 2-speed transfer case, front tow hooks, 245/75R16 tires.

LS adds: air conditioning, cruise control, leather-wrapped steering wheel, AM/FM/CD player, reclining 40/20/40 cloth split bench seat, power mirrors, power windows, power door locks, remote keyless entry, overhead console, carpeting, floormats, chrome rear step bumper, chrome steel wheels. **4WD** models add: part-time 4-wheel drive, 2-speed transfer case, front tow hooks, 245/75R16 tires.

LT extended cab adds: 5.3-liter V8 engine, 4-speed automatic transmission, leather upholstery, heated dual 6-way power seats w/driver seat memory, AM/FM/cassette/CD player, automatic day/night rearview mirror w/compass, outside temperature indicator, rear defogger, heated power mirrors, fog lights, deep-tinted glass, 255/70R16 tires, alloy wheels. **4WD** models add: full-time 4-wheel drive, 2-speed transfer case, front tow hooks, 245/75R16 tires.

OPTIONAL EQUIPMENT:
Major Packages

Exterior Appearance Pkg., Base Fleetside	625	538
Base w/Sportside	525	452

Chrome grille, chrome rear step bumper (Fleetside), bodyside moldings, chrome steel wheels.

	Retail Price	Dealer Invoice
Off-Road Suspension Pkg., LS 4WD	$395	$340
Includes heavy-duty air cleaner, skid plates, stabilizer bars, off-road jounce bumpers.		
Snow Plow Prep Pkg., 4WD regular cab short bed	285	245
4WD regular short bed w/Trailering Pkg.	190	163
Includes heavy-duty cooling, heavy-duty alternator.		
Trailering Pkg.	285	245
Includes trailer hitch platform, transmission oil cooler. Requires V8 engine, automatic transmission.		

Powertrains

4.8-liter V8,		
regular cab, 2WD Base/LS extended cab short bed	695	598
5.3-liter V8,		
regular cab, 2WD extended cab short bed	1495	1286
4WD extended cab, 2WD extended cab long bed...	800	688
Std. LT.		
4-speed automatic transmission, Base, LS..................	1095	942
Locking differential	285	245
Autotrac full-time 4WD, 4WD LS	375	323
Requires automatic transmission.		

Comfort and Convenience

Fourth door, extended cab	330	289
Air conditioning, Base	825	710
AM/FM/cassette player, Base regular cab	170	146
Base extended cab	150	129
AM/FM/cassette/CD player, LS extended cab.............	100	86
Requires automatic transmission. 4WD requires bucket seats.		
Leather upholstery, LS extended cab.........................	1480	1273
Includes dual 6-way power seats. Requires automatic transmission.		
Bucket seats, LS	375	323
Dual 6-way power seats, LS	480	413
Rear defogger, Base, LS	175	151
NA with sliding rear window. Base requires air conditioning.		
Power door locks, Base...	162	139
Automatic day/night rearview mirror, LS....................	175	151
Includes compass and outside temperature indicator.		
Heated power mirrors, LS	42	36
Requires rear defogger.		
Cruise control, Base	240	206

Appearance and Miscellaneous

Sportside body, Base short bed..................................	895	770
LS short bed..	795	684
Base includes chrome rear step bumper.		
Tonneau cover, Fleetside	240	206
Fog lights, LS	140	120
Deep-tinted glass, Base/LS regular cab......................	50	43
Base/LS extended cab	107	92
Sliding rear window, Base, LS	125	108
Wheel flares, 4WD	180	155
Skid plates, 4WD	95	82
Firm ride suspension, Base, LS, 4WD LT	95	82
2WD LT..	NC	NC
Includes heavy-duty shock absorbers. 2WD requires 255/75R16 tires.		
Ride Control Suspension, 2WD LS	420	361
2WD LT..	325	280
Includes adjustable shock absorbers. Requires 255/75R16 tires.		
Alloy wheels, LS...	110	95
235/75R16 white-letter tires, Base, LS	125	108
245/75R16 all-terrain white-letter tires, 4WD	230	198
LT245/75R16 on/off-road white-letter tires, 4WD.........	286	246
Requires Firm Ride Suspension or Off-Road Pkg.		
255/75R16 white-letter tires,		
2WD Base, 2WD LS..	295	254
2WD LT..	125	108
Base and LS require Firm Ride Suspension or Ride Control Suspension.		
265/75R16 all-terrain white-letter tires,		
4WD LS, 4WD LT	365	314
Requires Firm Ride Suspension or Off-Road Pkg. LS requires alloy wheels.		
LT265/75R16 on/off-road white-letter tires, 4WD.........	286	246
Requires Firm Ride Suspension or Off-Road Pkg.		

CHEVROLET S-10

RECOMMENDED

Chevrolet S-10 regular cab

Rear- or 4-wheel-drive compact pickup truck; similar to GMC Sonoma and Isuzu Hombre

Base price range: $12,605-$20,081. Built in USA. **Also consider:** Dodge Dakota, Ford Ranger, Toyota Tacoma

FOR • Acceleration (V6) • Instruments/controls **AGAINST** • Ride • Rear-seat comfort (extended cab)

Extended-cab versions get a new base-trim model and 4x4s get standard bucket seats in the big changes to Chevy's compact pickup for 2000. GMC's Sonoma shares the S-10 design and powertrains, but differs in trim and some equipment. Isuzu also sells a version called Hombre with fewer model and equipment choices.

S-10 regular cabs come with a 6- or 7.3-foot cargo bed. Extended cabs get the shorter bed and offer an optional driver-side rear door. All can be had with base or uplevel LS trim; extended-cabs had come only in LS form. A flared-fender Sportside short-bed is again available with either cab in LS trim. Also back is the Xtreme package that gives a low-riding "custom truck" look to 2-wheel-drive models. The high-riding off-road-oriented ZR2 option also returns for LS 4WD models, but now it's offered only on extended-cab versions. Front bucket seats are now standard on all extended-cab 4WD S-10s. The 2WD models continue with a standard 3-place front bench seat and offer buckets as options. Extended-cabs have two standard rear jump seats, though 3-door versions get a right seat only.

A 2.2-liter 4-cylinder repeats as the base engine, and a 4.3-liter V6 returns with 180 horsepower in 2WD models and 190 hp with the Xtreme package or 4WD. Manual transmission is standard with either engine, automatic optional. The 4WD system offers high- and low-range gearing, but is for use on slippery surfaces only. All S-10s have standard antilock brakes and a deactivation switch for the passenger-side airbag.

PERFORMANCE Whether the truck wears a Chevy, GMC, or Isuzu badge, if it's equipped with the 4-cylinder engine, it'll perform best with manual transmission and provide adequate acceleration in light-duty chores. Want automatic or plan even occasional hauling? Get the V6, which has plenty of muscle, though even the 190-hp version doesn't feel as strong as its power rating implies. Fuel economy is competitive, at least with manual shift. We've averaged 19.8 mpg with a 4-cylinder, 18 mpg with a 4WD extended-cab, and 22.2 with a 2WD Xtreme.

The base suspension provides a relatively soft, controlled ride. The much firmer off-road and heavy-duty chassis give a harsh ride, so try before you buy. As in any light truck running without a load, the rear end tends to hop over sharp bumps and ridges. The S-10 Xtreme is no exception, but it's among the best handling pickups of any stripe and its ride quality is reasonable. Too bad the package can't be used for towing. Cornering lean is evident in any model, but these GM-built pickups feel balanced and poised, with a natural feel to the power steering and good resistance to gusty crosswinds. Brake-pedal action is mushy and stopping power only adequate despite the standard ABS.

ACCOMMODATIONS Front-seat comfort is good, and extended-cabs benefit from generous rearward seat travel. Predictably, the extended-cab's twin rear jump seats suit only children, and you lose the right jump seat to get the convenience of the available third door. Note that rival Ford Ranger/Mazda B-Series extended-cabs offer two rear doors and two rear jump seats, while Nissan's Frontier Crew Cab and the new Dodge Dakota Quad Cab boast independent forward-opening back doors.

Gauges are unobstructed and soft-touch rotary knobs for the climate system and large radio buttons enhance the simple control layout. The center console contains dual cupholders and several bins; door panels have map pockets. Some plastic panels and trim pieces

Prices are accurate at time of publication; subject to manufacturer's changes.

feel low-budget.

VALUE FOR THE MONEY Dakota and the Ranger/B-Series are our compact pickup Best Buys, with the S-10, Sonoma, and Hombre penalized by their age and the absence of two rear doors. But their prices, payloads, and power are competitive with most others in this class, and discounts are readily available.

ENGINES

	ohv I4	ohv V6	ohv V6
Size, liters/cu. in.	2.2/134	4.3/262	4.3/262
Horsepower @ rpm	120 @ 5000	180 @ 4400	190 @ 4400
Torque (lbs./ft.) @ rpm	140 @ 3600	245 @ 2800	250 @ 2800
Availability	S[1]	O[1]	S[2]
EPA city/highway mpg			
5-speed OD manual	23/29	17/23	17/23
4-speed OD automatic	19/26	17/22	17/22

1. 2WD. 2. 4WD; included in 2WD Xtreme option package.

PRICES

Chevrolet S-10

	Retail Price	Dealer Invoice
Base 2WD regular cab, Fleetside, short bed	$12605	$11912
Base 2WD regular cab, Fleetside, long bed	12956	12243
LS 2WD regular cab, Fleetside, short bed	13627	12332
LS 2WD regular cab, Fleetside, long bed	13978	12650
Base 4WD regular cab, Fleetside, short bed	16839	15913
LS 4WD regular cab, Fleetside, short bed	18031	16318
Base 2WD extended cab, Fleetside, short bed	15492	14020
LS 2WD extended cab, Fleetside, short bed	15928	14415
Base 4WD extended cab, Fleetside, short bed	18762	17730
LS 4WD extended cab, Fleetside, short bed	20081	18173
Destination charge	535	535

All models require a Preferred Equipment Group.

STANDARD EQUIPMENT:

Base: 2.2-liter 4-cylinder engine, 5-speed manual transmission, driver- and passenger-side airbags, antilock brakes, daytime running lights, variable-assist power steering, cloth or vinyl bench seat, cloth split bench seat (extended cab), vinyl rear jump seats (extended cab), cupholders, AM/FM radio, digital clock, variable intermittent wipers, automatic headlights, vinyl floor covering, theft-deterrent system, dual outside mirrors, rear step bumper, Solid Smooth Suspension (regular cab, short bed), Increased Capacity Suspension (long bed, extended cab), 205/75R15 tires. **4WD** models add: part-time 4-wheel drive, electronic-shift 2-speed transfer case, 4.3-liter V6 190-horsepower engine, 4-wheel disc brakes, bucket seats w/floor console (extended cab), tachometer, front tow hooks, Increased Capacity Suspension, 235/70R15 tires.

LS adds: cloth split bench seat with storage armrest, carpeting, map lights, auxiliary power outlets, Increased Capacity Suspension (long bed, extended cab), wheel trim rings. **4WD** models add: part-time 4-wheel drive, electronic-shift 2-speed transfer case, 4.3-liter V6 190-horsepower engine, 4-wheel disc brakes, bucket seats, floor console, tachometer, front tow hooks, Increased Capacity Suspension, 235/75R15 tires.

OPTIONAL EQUIPMENT:

Major Packages

	Retail Price	Dealer Invoice
YC5 Appearance Pkg., LS	295	254

Chrome grille and bumpers, bodyside and wheel opening moldings, argent alloy wheels (2WD), cast alloy wheels (4WD). NA with long bed, ZR2 Wide Stance Sport Performance Pkg., Xtreme Pkg.

ZQ6 Power Convenience Pkg., LS	795	684

Heated power mirrors, power windows and door locks, remote keyless entry, theft-deterrent system w/alarm.

ZQ3 Comfort Convenience Group	395	340

Tilt steering wheel, cruise control.

Preferred Equipment Group 1SA, Base	NC	NC
Manufacturer's discount price, (credit)	(450)	(387)

Standard equipment.

Preferred Equipment Group 1SB, LS short bed	1232	1060
Manufacturer's discount price	232	200

Air conditioning, AM/FM/cassette, floormats, alloy wheels.

Preferred Equipment Group 1SB, LS long bed	147	127
Manufacturer's discount price, (credit)	(853)	(734)

AM/FM/cassette, floormats.

	Retail Price	Dealer Invoice
Preferred Equipment Group 1SC (ZR2), LS 4WD extended cab	$5271	$4533
Manufacturer's discount price, manual transmission	4271	3673

ZR2 Wide Stance Suspension Pkg. (Bilstein shock absorbers, heavy-duty suspension, chassis enhancements for increased height and width, wheel opening flares, heavy-duty axles and front differential, Underbody Shield Pkg., full-size spare tire, dark gray grille, unique fenders), 3.73 axle ratio, limited-slip rear differential, third door, air conditioning, heated power mirrors, power windows and door locks, remote keyless entry, theft-deterrent system w/alarm, deep-tinted glass, sliding rear window, leather-wrapped tilt steering wheel, cruise control, AM/FM/cassette w/automatic tone control, floormats, 31x10.5R15 tires, alloy wheels. NA with Sportside bed, fog lights.

Preferred Equipment Group 1SD (Xtreme), Base 2WD regular cab short bed	3189	2743
Manufacturer's discount price	2189	1883

Xtreme Sport Appearance Pkg. (lowered sport suspension, monotube shock absorbers, air conditioning, color-keyed grille, bumpers and lower body cladding, tachometer, leather-wrapped steering wheel, fog lights, wheel flares, 235/55R16 tires, alloy wheels).

Preferred Equipment Group 1SE (Xtreme), LS 2WD regular cab short bed, LS 2WD extended cab	3336	2869
Manufacturer's discount price, manual transmission	2336	2009
automatic transmission	2011	1729

Preferred Equipment Group 1SD plus AM/FM/cassette, floormats.

Powertrains

4.3-liter V6 180-horsepower engine, 2WD	1295	1114

Includes tachometer, engine- and transmission-oil coolers. Requires limited slip differential with Preferred Equipment Group 1SE (Xtreme).

4-speed automatic transmission	1095	942
Locking differential	270	232

Requires V6 engine.

Comfort and Convenience

Third door, extended cab	315	270

Deletes driver-side jump seat.

Air conditioning	805	692
Bucket seats, LS 2WD regular cab, 2WD extended cab	341	293

Includes console.

AM/FM/cassette, Base	122	105
AM/FM/cassette w/automatic tone control, LS	80	69

Includes Enhanced Performance Speakers.

AM/FM/CD player, LS	180	155

Includes auto. tone control, Enhanced Performance Speakers.

AM/FM/cassette/CD player, LS	280	241

Includes automatic tone control, Enhanced Performance Speakers. Requires automatic transmission and bucket seats.

Tachometer	59	51
Leather-wrapped steering wheel, LS	54	46

Appearance and Miscellaneous

Sportside bed, LS short bed	475	409
Sliding rear window	120	103
Deep-tinted glass, regular cab	75	65
extended cab	115	99
Fog lights, LS	115	99

Special Purpose, Wheels and Tires

Shield Pkg., 4WD	126	108

Includes transfer-case and front-differential skid plates, fuel-tank and steering-linkage shields.

Increased Capacity Suspension, 2WD Base short bed	64	55

Includes heavy-duty shock absorbers.

Sport Suspension, 2WD LS short bed	785	675

Lowered suspension, monotube shock absorbers, color keyed bumpers, alloy wheels, 235/55R16 tires.

Alloy wheels, 2WD LS long bed	280	241
235/75R15 on/off-road white-letter tires, 4WD LS	143	123

CHEVROLET TAHOE LIMITED AND Z71

Chevrolet Tahoe Z71

Rear- or 4-wheel-drive full-size sport-utility vehicle; similar to Cadillac Escalade and GMC Yukon Denali

Base price range: $33,929-$38,894. Built in USA. **Also consider:** Ford Expedition, Toyota Land Cruiser

FOR • Acceleration • Passenger and cargo room • Trailer towing capability **AGAINST** • Fuel economy • Ride

Chevrolet sells these specialty versions of its 1995-1999 vintage Tahoe alongside the redesigned all-new 2000 models. The Tahoe Z71 and Limited also are labeled 2000s, but are available only through June. A similar strategy holds for the 2000 Cadillac Escalade and GMC Yukon Denali, which are retrimmed versions of this Tahoe. The Chevy models are 4-door wagons with a 5.7-liter V8 and automatic transmission. The Z71 features off-road-oriented equipment, including Autotrac 4-wheel drive, which can remain engaged on dry pavement, plus underbody skid plates, a grille brush guard, protective taillamp cages, and all-terrain tires. The style-conscious Limited comes only with rear-wheel drive and is built around police-package equipment, including heavy-duty suspension, brakes, and cooling and electrical systems. Limited deletes a roof rack and bodyside moldings, but gets body-colored bumpers and grille, special chrome wheels, integrated front foglamps, and ground-effects skirts. Both models come with two-tone leather seats, gas-charged shock absorbers, and a locking rear differential.

EVALUATION The Z71 and Limited represent niche models not yet available in the all-new 2000 Tahoe. The Z71 is a taut-riding back-trail-ready wagon, while the Limited emphasizes handling and, in the words of Chevy's press release, presents a "menacing appearance." Neither is as refined as their redesigned replacements, but do their jobs quite well nonetheless. And their robust V8 packs more low-speed punch than the more-sophisticated but smaller V8s in the new-design Tahoe. Note, however, that both holdovers seat only five passengers, versus the 9-seat arrangement available on the new versions.

ENGINES

	ohv V8
Size, liters/cu. in.	5.7/350
Horsepower @ rpm	255 @ 4600
Torque (lbs./ft.) @ rpm	330 @ 2800
Availability	S
EPA city/highway mpg	
4-speed OD automatic	14/18

PRICES

Chevrolet Tahoe Limited and Z71	Retail Price	Dealer Invoice
Limited 4-door wagon 2WD	$33929	$29688
Z71 4-door wagon 4WD	38894	34032
Destination charge	675	675

STANDARD EQUIPMENT:

Limited: 5.7-liter V8 engine, 4-speed automatic transmission, locking rear differential, driver- and passenger-side airbags, antilock brakes, daytime running lights, front and rear air conditioning w/manual dual-zone controls, variable-assist power steering, tilt leather-wrapped steering wheel, cruise control, leather upholstery, front bucket seats w/power lumbar adjustment, power driver seat, center console, cupholders, split folding rear seat, power mirrors, power windows, power door locks, remote keyless entry, AM/FM/cassette/CD player, digital clock, tachometer, aux-

iliary power outlets, overhead console, map lights, automatic day/night rearview mirror, compass, outside temperature indicator, illuminated visor mirrors, rear defogger, cargo cover, floormats, theft-deterrent system, rear panel doors, fog lights, roof rack, deep-tinted glass, trailer hitch, 8-lead trailer wiring harness, full-size spare tire, 255/70R16 tires, chrome alloy wheels.

Z71 adds: Autotrac full-time 4-wheel drive, brush and taillight guards, step rails, skid plates, front tow hooks, 265/75R16 all-terrain tires.

OPTIONAL EQUIPMENT:	Retail Price	Dealer Invoice
Major Packages		
Comfort and Security Pkg., Limited	$1047	$900
Z71	1597	1373
Heated front seats, power passenger seat, heated power mirrors w/automatic day/night, universal garage door opener.		
Appearance and Miscellaneous		
Tailgate w/lift glass	NC	NC
Includes rear wiper/washer, power release.		

CHEVROLET TAHOE AND SUBURBAN

Chevrolet Tahoe LT

Rear- or 4-wheel-drive full-size sport-utility vehicle; similar to GMC Yukon and Yukon XL

Base price range: NA. Built in USA . **Also consider:** Ford Expedition, Lincoln Navigator, Toyota Land Cruiser

FOR • Passenger and cargo room • Towing ability **AGAINST** • Fuel economy •

Chevrolet's full-size SUVs are redesigned for 2000, and include new V8 engines and standard front side airbags. And Tahoe's seating capacity grows from six to nine. Tahoe retains its GMC Yukon cousin, while GMC's version of the larger Chevy Suburban is renamed Yukon XL.

Tahoe loses its 2-door body style, so both it and Suburban come only as 4-door wagons. Both have standard swing-open tail doors, but a liftgate with separate-opening glass replaces a drop-down tailgate as a no-cost alternative. The 2000 Tahoe and Suburban ride a 1.5-inch shorter wheelbase than their predecessors, but their bodies are about two inches wider and up to two inches taller. Overall lengths change little. Suburban and Yukon XL are General Motors' largest SUVs. They're 14.7 inches longer than the Ford Expedition, but 7.4 inches shorter than the Ford Excursion.

Tahoe repeats in a half-ton payload series only, while Suburban is returns in half-ton 1500 and three-quarter-ton 2500 models. Both Tahoe and Suburban come in base, LS, and LT trim levels. All have V8 engines. The base Tahoe gets a 4.8 liter with 275 horsepower. Suburban 1500s and LS and LT Tahoes use a 5.3 liter with 285 hp. Standard on Suburban 2500s is a 300-hp 6.0. The previous base engine was a 255-hp 5.7-liter V8, with 2500-series Suburbans offering a 290-hp 7.4-liter V8, plus a turbocharged diesel V8.

All models have an automatic transmission with GM's Tow/Haul mode designed to optimize shifts under heavy loads. Four-wheel models use GM's Autotrac system that can be left engaged on dry surfaces. Traction control is a new option on 2WD models. Antilock brakes are again standard, but 4-wheel discs replace a disc/drum combination. Suspension changes include rear coil springs in place of leaf springs on Tahoes and on Suburban 1500s, and newly available rear load-leveling.

For 2000, Tahoe joins Suburban with available third-row seating, so both seat up to nine with the available front bench. New for Suburban is a pair of optional second-row bucket seats. Rear air

---

Prices are accurate at time of publication; subject to manufacturer's changes.

conditioning is standard on LS models, while LT versions add fog lamps, automatic climate control, and leather upholstery with heated front seats.

PERFORMANCE Advances are evolutionary not revolutionary, but the 2000s do erase some weak points of the previous generation Tahoe/Yukon and Suburban/Yukon XL.

The new V8s feel slightly smoother than the engines they replace, but aren't dramatically stronger. Aided by the transmission's smooth, astute shifting, acceleration is nonetheless adequate, even with a full complement of passengers and cargo. Maximum towing capacity is 9000 pounds on Tahoe/Yukon, 10,500 on Suburban/Yukon XL. We haven't had an opportunity to measure fuel economy, but GM says the new engines should be slightly more economical than the ones they replace. (A 1999 5.7-liter 4x4 Tahoe averaged 14.0 mpg in our tests.)

These big SUVs don't corner like cars, but handling is better than their size might imply. They feel balanced in changes of direction, and with a turning radius reduced by 7 inches on Tahoe/Yukon and by 2.4 feet on Suburban/Yukon XL, they're fairly easy to maneuver. Steering is reasonably precise and road feel adequate, but at lower speeds, the speed-variable assist makes the steering too light for some tastes.

The biggest improvements come in ride quality and brake feel. The redesigned suspension absorbs bumps well and is more sure-footed on rough pavement than the previous design. And strong stopping power with firm, progressive pedal action replaces mediocre brakes with a mushy pedal feel. Wind rush is noticeable though not intrusive. Tire noise is low for full-size SUVs, but still audible at highway speeds. Engines are throaty but refined-sounding under hard acceleration.

ACCOMMODATIONS The evolution-versus-revolution formula carries over into the interior of the 2000 Tahoe/Yukon and Suburban/Yukon XL. The slightly revised dashboard layout is logical and handy, with clear sightlines to gauges and easily accessed controls. The driver gets a commanding view of the road, while outward visibility and cargo room improve with the relocation of the spare tire from the wall of the cargo bay to beneath the rear undercarriage.

Seats are more comfortable and more substantial-feeling than before. Room in front is generous, even for the largest of occupants. Second-row seating is similarly spacious, with Tahoe/Yukon gaining 2.4 inches of rear leg room and Suburban/Yukon XL gaining 3. The difference between Tahoe/Yukon and the longer Suburban/Yukon XL is most obvious in the third-row seats, where Suburban and Yukon XL have ample head, shoulder, and leg room for two grownups. Leg and head clearance in the Tahoe/Yukon third-row seat is practical only for children or occasional adult use.

Modest door openings hamper rear ingress and egress somewhat. This is most evident on Tahoe/Yukon, where the openings are several inches smaller at the bottom than on Suburban/Yukon XL. Step-in is lower than on Expedition and Excursion, but higher than a typical minivan. Running boards are an option we recommend.

There's nearly 46 cubic feet of storage space behind the third-row seat in Suburban/Yukon XL; Tahoe/Yukon have only enough room for a single row of grocery bags, although their third-row seat is split 50/50, for slightly more versatility than the one-piece bench in Suburban/Yukon XL. The third-row seats on both models fold easily. They also remove, aided by roller wheels and safety belts mounted to the seat-frame rather than vehicle frame. Still, hoisting Suburban/Yukon XL's heavy bench in or out is a 2-person operation. Tahoe/Yukon's third-row seat removes in two 40-pound sections, making it more manageable. In either, cargo room is expansive with rear seats folded or removed.

VALUE FOR THE MONEY These impressive new full-size SUVs are capable, comfortable, and easy to live with. Their size fits nicely into gaps between Ford's Expedition and Excursion, and prices, which were unavailable in time for this issue, are not likely to increase much over the '99 models they replace.

ENGINES

	ohv V8	ohv V8	ohv V8
Size, liters/cu. in.	4.8/292	5.3/325	6.0/364
Horsepower @ rpm	275 @ 5200	285 @ 5200	300 @ 4800
Torque (lbs./ft.) @ rpm	290 @ 4000	325 @ 4000	355 @ 4000
Availability	S[1]	S[2]	S[3]

EPA city/highway mpg

4-speed OD automatic	NA

1. Base Tahoe. 2. Tahoe LS and LT, Suburban 1500. 3. Suburban 2500.

Prices, standard equipment, and options were unavailable at the time of publication.

CHEVROLET TRACKER

Chevrolet Tracker 4-door

Rear- or 4-wheel-drive compact sport-utility vehicle; similar to Suzuki Vitara

Base price range: $13,925-$16,250. Built in Canada. **Also consider:** Honda CR-V, Isuzu Amigo, Jeep Wrangler, Subaru Forester, Toyota RAV4

FOR • Maneuverability • Cargo room **AGAINST** • Rear-seat room • Rear visibility • Acceleration

A surf-motif appearance option for the convertible heads the short list of changes to the 2000 edition of Chevrolet's smallest sport-utility vehicle. Tracker was redesigned last year to be slightly longer and wider, with rounded styling. A 2-door convertible and 4-door wagon return, both built off a Suzuki-based design. This design is also used for Suzuki's Vitara models, which include the V6 Grand Vitara. Tracker offers only 4-cylinder engines: A 1.6 liter is standard in convertibles, a 2.0 liter is standard in wagons, optional in convertibles. Automatic transmission is available with the 2.0 liter only. Rear- or 4-wheel drive are available; the latter has separate 4-low gearing, but is for use on slippery surfaces only. The new convertible option package creates the Hang Ten Edition and includes special headrests, floormats, spare tire cover, and decals.

EVALUATION Both Tracker engines feel weak and gruff when worked hard, which is necessary most of the time. Real-world economy thus runs only about 18-20 mpg in our tests—nothing special for a small SUV. Neither are ride and handling; a Honda CR-V or Subaru Forester is far more composed and comfortable. Tracker is the better off-road choice, however, thanks to its low-range gearing and truck-style construction. Visibility isn't as commanding as in most SUVs, aft-cabin space is tight and rear entry/exit tricky, but there's good room and comfort up front. Stereo and climate controls sit too low for easy adjusting on the move, and the radio has tiny buttons. Neither body style has much cargo room, and tailgates swing right, hampering curbside loading. In all, Tracker is an also-ran among mini-SUVs. A CR-V, Forester, or Toyota RAV4 is more pleasant and enjoyable in the kind of driving most people do. They enjoy higher resale values, too.

ENGINES

	ohc I4	dohc I4
Size, liters/cu. in.	1.6/97	2.0/121
Horsepower @ rpm	97 @ 5200	127 @ 6000
Torque (lbs./ft.) @ rpm	103 @ 4000	134 @ 3000
Availability	S[1]	S[2]

EPA city/highway mpg

5-speed OD manual	25/28[3]	23/25[4]
4-speed OD automatic		24/26[5]

1. 2-door. 2. 4-door, optional 2-door. 3. 25/27 w/4WD. 4. 22/25 w/4WD. 5. 23/25 w/2-door or 4WD.

PRICES

Chevrolet Tracker	Retail Price	Dealer Invoice
2-door convertible, 2WD	$13925	$13117
2-door convertible, 4WD	15025	14154
4-door wagon, 2WD	15150	14271
4-door wagon, 4WD	16250	15308
Destination charge	400	400

Ratings begin on page 213. Specifications begin on page 220.
CONSUMER GUIDE™

STANDARD EQUIPMENT:

Convertible: 1.6-liter 4-cylinder engine, 5-speed manual transmission, driver- and passenger-side airbags, daytime running lights, power steering, cloth/vinyl front bucket seats, center console, cupholders, folding rear seat, AM/FM radio, digital clock, tachometer, variable intermittent wipers, passenger-side visor mirror, auxiliary power outlet, automatic headlights, floormats, dual outside mirrors, fuel-tank skid plate, front and rear tow hooks, rear-mounted full-size spare tire, 195/75R15 tires. **4WD** adds: part-time 4-wheel drive, 2-speed transfer case, 205/75R15 tires.

Wagon adds: 2.0-liter dohc 4-cylinder engine, split folding rear seat, rear defogger, cargo cover. **4WD** adds: part-time 4-wheel drive, 2-speed transfer case, 205/75R15 tires.

OPTIONAL EQUIPMENT:

	Retail Price	Dealer Invoice
Major Packages		
Preferred Equipment Group 2	$1545	$1375
Air conditioning, AM/FM/cassette, cruise control, tilt steering wheel, cargo storage compartment (convertible), rear washer/wiper (wagon).		
Convenience Pkg., wagon	730	650
Power mirrors, power windows and door locks, remote keyless entry. Requires Preferred Equipment Group 2.		
Hang Ten Edition, convertible	—	—
Hang Ten headrests, floormats, spare tire cover, and decals. Requires automatic transmission when ordered with 2.0-liter engine.		
Powertrains		
2.0-liter dohc 4-cylinder engine, convertible	400	356
4-speed automatic transmission	1000	890
Convertible requires 2.0-liter engine.		
Safety Features		
Antilock brakes	595	530
AM/FM/CD player	265	236
w/Preferred Equipment Group	100	89
Appearance and Miscellaneous		
Roof rack, wagon	126	112
Special Purpose, Wheels and Tires		
Alloy wheels	365	325

CHEVROLET VENTURE

RECOMMENDED

Chevrolet Venture LS

Front-wheel-drive minivan; similar to Oldsmobile Silhouette and Pontiac Montana

Base price range: $20,650-$28,995. Built in USA. **Also consider:** Dodge Caravan, Ford Windstar, Honda Odyssey, Toyota Sienna

FOR • Ride • Passenger and cargo room **AGAINST** • Fuel economy • Rear-seat comfort

Chevrolet's front-wheel-drive minivan loses its 3-door body for 2000, but adds a video-equipped model. Venture starts with the regular-length Value model and ascends through Plus and LS versions of both the regular and extended-length bodies. Topping the roster are extended-length LT and new video-system Warner Bros. models.

All Ventures have dual sliding side doors. A power right-side door is standard for LT and is optional on other models except the Value.

Seating for seven is standard. LT and LS are eligible for an 8-passenger setup. Front side airbags are standard.

A child safety seat built into the second-row bench is standard on the Warner Bros. and optional on other Ventures except the Value. A pair of integrated second-row child seats is optional on all but the Value.

The sole powerteam is an automatic transmission and a 3.4-liter V6 with 5 more horsepower this year. Traction control is newly standard on the LT model and remains optional on other Ventures except the Value. GM's OnStar assistance system has been temporarily dropped from the options list.

The Warner Bros. model has unique cloth/leather upholstery and a rear-seat entertainment package comprised of a video player, TV monitor, and an audio system with separate second- and third-row headphone jacks. The Value model offers few options, but includes air conditioning. Venture shares its design with the Oldsmobile Silhouette and Pontiac Montana, though only Chevy offers a cargo model.

PERFORMANCE Venture, Silhouette, and Montana have adequate acceleration, helped by a smooth, responsive transmission. Fuel economy is good for a minivan; most of our test models average around 18 mpg, though lots of city driving dropped a Montana to 15.7.

Chevy, Olds, or Pontiac, the basic suspension is the same. It allows these minivans to ride and handle much like cars. Most rivals do, too, but the GM models feel somewhat sportier than the minivan norm. Steering is accurate and communicative, cornering grippy and predictable, with only modest body lean. Most bumps are easily absorbed, and the highway ride is comfortable and stable. The load-leveling suspension available on all three brands has merit. Montana's sport suspension, part of the optional Sport Performance and Handling Package, slightly improves agility but makes the ride jittery on urban streets.

Stopping is controlled and progressive in any model, though a test Silhouette had slightly mushy brake feel. Wind noise is prominent around the mirrors at highway speed, but road and engine sounds are well-muffled.

ACCOMMODATIONS These minivans make efficient use of interior space, providing good head and leg room at all positions. Each second-row bucket seat weighs just 39 pounds and is easy to remove or relocate. Even the 45-pound rear bench isn't overly cumbersome. To get seats this light, however, GM uses less-substantial cushions than most rivals, and the seats are low enough that lanky adults sit with knees upright. Entry/exit is step-in easy, though it's still a squeeze to get to the rearmost seat.

The power passenger-side door is a convenience, though the Ford Windstar and Honda Odyssey offer power sliders on both sides. Storage bins and cup/juice-box holders abound, and there's a handy storage net between the front seats. With all seats in place, cargo room is tight on regular-length models, good on extended versions. The tailgate is easier to manage than most. Visibility is excellent, helped by large outside mirrors. Drivers also enjoy clear, handy gauges and controls.

All three GM minivans offer essentially the same video package. It has a screen that's easy to see in all light conditions, but the VCR is at the base of the dashboard at floor level and is difficult to operate while driving.

VALUE FOR THE MONEY Despite less-than-optimal rear-seat comfort, these minivans merit strong consideration. Venture is the best value of the three, but base prices on all are similar to direct Dodge, Plymouth, and Ford rivals—and GM's offerings come with more standard features.

ENGINES

	ohv V6
Size, liters/cu. in.	3.4/207
Horsepower @ rpm	185 @ 5200
Torque (lbs./ft.) @ rpm	210 @ 4000
Availability	S
EPA city/highway mpg	
4-speed OD automatic	18/25

PRICES

Chevrolet Venture	Retail Price	Dealer Invoice
Cargo extended 4-door van	$21950	$19865
Value regular length 4-door van	20650	19101
Plus regular length 4-door van	23350	21132
Plus extended 4-door van	24550	22218
LS regular length 4-door van	24550	22218
LS extended 4-door van	25550	23123
LT extended 4-door van	27950	25295

Prices are accurate at time of publication; subject to manufacturer's changes.

	Retail Price	Dealer Invoice
Warner Bros. Edition 4-door van	$28995	$26240
Destination charge	605	605

STANDARD EQUIPMENT:

Cargo: 3.4-liter V6 engine, 4-speed automatic transmission, driver- and passenger-side airbags, front side impact airbags, antilock brakes, daytime running lamps, front air conditioning, interior air filter, variable-assist power steering, tilt steering wheel, dual sliding rear doors, 2-passenger seating (vinyl front bucket seats), rubber floor covering, center storage console, overhead consolette, cupholders, automatic headlights, intermittent wipers, AM/FM radio, digital clock, heated power mirrors, power door locks, visor mirrors, auxiliary power outlet, rear defogger, intermittent rear wiper/washer, theft-deterrent system, 215/70R15 tires, wheel covers.

Value adds: power steering, cloth upholstery, 7-passenger seating (front bucket seats, center 2-passenger and rear 3-passenger bench seats), carpeting, deletes variable-assist power steering, heated power mirrors, rear defogger, rear wiper/washer, overhead consolette, interior air filter.

Plus adds: cruise control, heated power mirrors, power front windows, power door locks, remote keyless entry, center and third row split folding bench seats, overhead consolette, rear defogger, rear wiper/washer, floormats, deep-tinted rear glass.

LS adds: power rear quarter windows, AM/FM/cassette, interior air filter, driver information center, alloy wheels.

LT adds: traction control, front and rear air conditioning, 6-way power driver seat, two center row captain chairs, power passenger-side sliding rear door, AM/FM/cassette/CD player, rear radio controls, theft-deterrent system w/alarm, roof rack, air inflation kit, touring suspension.

Warner Bros. Edition adds: cloth/leather upholstery, three center-row bucket seats, two third-row bucket seats, integrated child seat, LCD screen, VCR player, remote control, deletes traction control, power passenger-side sliding rear door, air inflation kit, touring suspension.

OPTIONAL EQUIPMENT:

	Retail Price	Dealer Invoice
Major Packages		
Preferred Equipment Group 1, Cargo	$675	$581
Power windows, cruise control, remote keyless entry, deep-tinted glass (Passenger).		
Trailering Pkg., Cargo	465	399
LS, Warner	525	452
LS/Warner w/self-sealing tires	375	323
LT	165	142
Includes heavy-duty engine and transmission oil cooling, touring suspension.		
Powertrains		
Traction control, Cargo, LS, Warner	195	168
Safety Features		
Integrated child seat, Plus	125	108
LS, LT	NC	NC
NA with two center row captain chairs.		
Dual integrated child seats, Plus	225	194
LS, LT, Warner	100	86
NA with two center row captain chairs.		
Comfort and Convenience		
Front and rear air conditioning,		
Plus extended, LS extended	475	409
Power passenger-side sliding door, Plus	500	430
LS, Warner	450	387
Includes power rear quarter windows.		
6-way power driver seat, LS	270	232
8-passenger seating, LS	290	249
LT	NC	NC
Three center-row bucket seats, rear 3-passenger split folding bench seat. NA with leather upholstery.		
Seven bucket seats, LS	290	249
Two center-row captain chairs, LS	290	249
Includes front bucket seats and rear 3-passenger split folding bench seat.		
Leather upholstery, LT	895	770
AM/FM/cassette, Cargo, Plus	165	141
AM/FM/cassette w/automatic tone control,		
Cargo, Plus	270	232

	Retail Price	Dealer Invoice
AM/FM/CD player, Cargo, Plus	$370	$318
LS	100	86
AM/FM/cassette/CD player, Plus	470	404
LS	200	172
Rear-seat audio controls, LS	155	133
Includes headphone jacks. Requires optional radio.		
Rear defogger, Value	305	262
Roof rack, Cargo, Plus, LS	225	194
Touring Suspension, Cargo	300	258
LS, Warner	360	310
LS/Warner w/self-sealing tires	210	181
Load-leveling suspension, auxiliary air inflator (LS, Warner), 215/70R15 touring tires.		
Self-sealing 215/70R15 tires,		
LS, LT, Warner	300	258
Alloy wheels, Plus	295	254

CHRYSLER CIRRUS

Chrysler Cirrus LXi

Front-wheel-drive midsize car; similar to Chrysler Sebring, Dodge Stratus, and Plymouth Breeze
Base price: $19,935. Built in USA.   **Also consider:** Honda Accord, Saturn L-Series, Toyota Camry

FOR • Ride • Steering/handling • Passenger and cargo room
AGAINST • Noise • Rear visibility • Automatic transmission performance

This upscale version of the Dodge Stratus and Plymouth Breeze is once again available with a 4-cylinder engine. Chrysler dropped the 4-cylinder for 1998, leaving a V6 as the standard engine. For 2000, a 4-cylinder LX model joins the V6 LXi Cirrus. Both use automatic transmission. Antilock brakes are standard on LXi, optional on LX. Aluminum wheels and 8-speaker AM/FM cassette stereo are standard instead of optional for 2000 on the LXi. Rear child seat anchorages also are added to both models at no charge.

EVALUATION Cirrus corners with good grip and minimal body lean while providing a mostly comfortable ride. A 1999 Cirrus averaged a likable 21 mpg in our tests. While it doesn't have the low-speed muscle of larger-displacement V6s, the 2.5 provides good acceleration from a stop and in around-town driving, and adequate passing response on the highway. Suspension changes made during the '99 model year softened bigger bumps a bit while quieting the highway ride somewhat, but engine and exhaust noise remain intrusive. Passenger and cargo room are outstanding for the exterior size. Wide doors facilitate entry/exit, but the trunk opening is rather small. High-tail styling impedes visibility directly aft. In all, Cirrus is a capable family 4-door offering a touch of luxury at a reasonable price.

ENGINES

	dohc I4	ohc V6
Size, liters/cu. in.	2.4/148	2.5/152
Horsepower @ rpm	150 @ 5200	168 @ 5800
Torque (lbs./ft.) @ rpm	167 @ 4000	170 @ 4350
Availability	S[1]	S[2]
EPA city/highway mpg		
4-speed OD automatic	21/30	19/27

1. LX. 2. LXi.

PRICES

Chrysler Cirrus

	Retail Price	Dealer Invoice
LXi 4-door sedan	$19935	$18222
Destination charge	545	545

LX prices and equipment not available at time of publication.

STANDARD EQUIPMENT:

LXi: 2.5-liter V6 engine, 4-speed automatic transmission, driver- and passenger-side airbags, antilock 4-wheel disc brakes, emergency inside trunk release, variable-assist power steering, tilt steering column, leather-wrapped steering wheel, cruise control, air conditioning, cloth upholstery, front bucket seats w/lumbar adjusters, center console, cupholders, folding rear seat, AM/FM/cassette with six speakers, digital clock, tachometer, rear defogger, power mirrors, power windows, power door locks, remote keyless entry, speed-sensitive intermittent wipers, remote decklid release, universal garage-door opener, reading lights, auxiliary power outlet, illuminated visor mirrors, cargo net, floormats, fog lights, 195/65R15 tires, wheel covers.

OPTIONAL EQUIPMENT:

	Retail Price	Dealer Invoice
Major Packages		
Quick Order Pkg. 26K	$1635	$1455
Manufacturer's discount price	NC	NC
Leather upholstery, 8-way power driver seat, AM/FM/cassette w/CD changer controls and eight speakers, alloy wheels.		
Gold Pkg.	500	315
Gold trim and badging, chrome alloy wheels with gold accents.		
Comfort and Convenience		
Premium AM/FM/cassette w/6-disc CD changer	210	187
Power sunroof	580	516
Smoker's Pkg.	20	18
Sentry Key theft-deterrent system w/alarm	175	156

CHRYSLER CONCORDE

✓ **BEST BUY**

Chrysler Concorde LX

Front-wheel-drive full-size car; similar to Chrysler LHS and 300M and Dodge Intrepid

Base price range: $21,990-$26,235. Built in Canada. **Also consider:** Buick LeSabre, Pontiac Bonneville, Toyota Avalon

FOR • Passenger and cargo room • Ride • Steering/handling
AGAINST • Rear visibility • Trunk liftover

A sunroof is newly optional on the base model for 2000, and Concorde gets suspension changes designed to provide a quieter, smoother ride.

Concorde is similar to the Dodge Intrepid and is the foundation for Chrysler's luxury LHS and sporty 300M. It has standard seating for five and optional seating for six. The base LX model comes with a 200-horsepower 2.7 liter V6. The LXi gets a 225-hp 3.2-liter V6. Both use automatic transmission. Antilock brakes and traction control are optional on the LX, standard on LXi.

The sunroof was previously optional only with LXi trim. Also for 2000, the LX exchanges standard 15-inch wheels for the same 16-inchers used by the LXi. Among other changes are two exclusive LXi additions: standard vehicle-speed-sensitive variable-assist steering and an optional 4-disc in-dash CD changer.

PERFORMANCE Neither Concorde engine is as strong as General Motors' 3.8-liter V6, but the LXi's 3.2 liter has good power at low speeds and in passing situations. The LX's 2.7 provides adequate acceleration, but feels overworked in highway passing or merging. The 2.7 gives this large car impressive fuel economy: 26.2 mpg in our test of a '99 model that included lots of highway driving. The LXi averages about 21 mpg. Either Concorde steers responsively and changes direction with reasonable confidence. The suspension soaks up rough roads and provides a stable highway ride. Our test models did not display top-notch braking performance or feel, however. On the upside, Chrysler's efforts to reduce road noise have made Concorde as quiet as most similarly priced competitors.

ACCOMMODATIONS The spacious Concorde is among the few sedans wide enough to carry three adults in the back seat without uncomfortable squeezing. Still, the front passenger seat lacks enough leg room for 6-footers to stretch. Only children are comfortable in the front bench seat's middle position, and they should sit in back, anyway. There's slightly more rear head room than in the Intrepid, thanks to a different roofline. Doorways are big, but the rear door shape hampers entry.

Large, clear gauges and controls highlight the dashboard. The narrow rear window restricts the driver's view aft. Most interior materials are of good quality, though door panels are spartan and roof pillars are trimmed in hard plastic. The ample trunk has an opening wider than Intrepid's, but liftover is high. The rear seatback has a pass-through opening.

VALUE FOR THE MONEY Acceleration is ordinary, and its reputation for reliability lags behind that of such rivals as the Toyota Avalon and Buick LeSabre. But overall, Concorde is an impressive value with distinctive styling, loads of room, and fine handling.

ENGINES

	dohc V6	ohc V6
Size, liters/cu. in.	2.7/167	3.2/197
Horsepower @ rpm	200 @ 5800	225 @ 6300
Torque (lbs./ft.) @ rpm	190 @ 4850	225 @ 3800
Availability	S[1]	S[2]
EPA city/highway mpg		
4-speed OD automatic	21/30	19/29

1. LX. 2. LXi.

PRICES

Chrysler Concorde	Retail Price	Dealer Invoice
LX 4-door sedan	$21990	$20146
LXi 4-door sedan	26235	23924
Destination charge	560	560

STANDARD EQUIPMENT:

LX: 2.7-liter dohc V6 engine, 4-speed automatic transmission, driver- and passenger-side airbags, 4-wheel disc brakes, air conditioning, power steering, tilt steering wheel, cruise control, cloth upholstery, front bucket seats, 8-way power driver seat, driver seat manual lumbar adjustment, center console, cupholders, trunk pass-through, power mirrors, power windows, power door locks, remote keyless entry, tachometer, AM/FM/cassette with four speakers, illuminated visor mirrors, rear defogger, variable intermittent wipers, power decklid release, map lights, floormats, 225/60R16 tires, wheel covers.

LXi adds: 3.2-liter V6 engine, traction control, antilock brakes, variable-assist power steering, leather-wrapped steering wheel, leather upholstery, 8-way power passenger seat, automatic climate control, trip computer, universal garage door opener, theft-deterrent system, full-size spare tire, alloy wheels.

OPTIONAL EQUIPMENT:

	Retail	Dealer
Major Packages		
LX Pkg. 22D, LX	1125	1001
Eight-speaker sound system, automatic day/night mirror, universal garage door opener, trip computer, 8-way power passenger seat.		
Leather and Wheel Group, LX	1060	943
Manufacturer's discount price	760	676
Leather upholstery, leather-wrapped steering wheel, alloy wheels. Requires LX Pkg.22D.		
Powertrains		
Traction control, LX	175	156
Requires LX Pkg. 22D.		
Safety Features		
Antilock brakes, LX	600	534
Comfort and Convenience		
Power sunroof	895	797
Front split bench seat	100	89
AM/FM/cassette/CD player, LX	225	200
Includes eight speakers.		
AM/FM/cassette w/4-disc CD changer, LXi	500	445
Includes nine Infinity speakers.		
Smoker's group	20	18
Includes ashtrays and lighter.		
Chrome alloy wheels, LXi	600	534

Prices are accurate at time of publication; subject to manufacturer's changes.

CHRYSLER LHS AND 300M

Chrysler 300M

Front-wheel-drive near-luxury car; similar to Chrysler Concorde and Dodge Intrepid

Base price range: $28,090-$29,085. Built in Canada. **Also consider:** Acura TL, Audi A6, Lexus GS 300/400

FOR • Acceleration • Passenger and cargo room • Ride/handling
AGAINST • Rear visibility • Trunk liftover

The LHS and 300M are, respectively, luxury and sports versions of Chrysler's Concorde. For 2000, they get minor trim and option changes, including an available 4-disc in-dash CD changer and revised instrument lighting designed to improve readability. The LHS and 300M use the same front-wheel-drive chassis as the Concorde and similar Dodge Intrepid, but have distinct styling and shorter bodies. LHS and 300M share a 253-horsepower V6 and automatic transmission; the 300M uses Chrysler's AutoStick automatic, which has a separate gate for manual-shift capability. Antilock 4-wheel disc brakes and traction control are standard. Side airbags are unavailable.

Both have Chrysler's Sentry Key theft-deterrent system, which disables the ignition unless the proper key is used. The 300M has sportier suspension and steering settings, but the same tires and 17-inch wheels as the LHS; the Performance Handling option gives the 300M more-aggressive tires on 16-inch wheels, and is now available with chrome wheels.

PERFORMANCE Acceleration is a match for any direct rival—and a clear step ahead of Concorde and Intrepid. LHS and 300M fall short of such competitors as the Lexus GS 300 and Acura TL in overall refinement, however. Their engine isn't quite as smooth, and road and wind noise, while not objectionable, aren't as well-isolated. Over 11,698 miles, our extended-use-test 1999 LHS has averaged 20.5 mpg. A '99 300M we tested got just 14.4 in mostly city driving. The LHS has competent handling and a well-controlled ride. The 300M steers and turns with assertiveness and still absorbs bumps well. Both have strong brakes with fine pedal feel.

As for our extended-test LHS, at 40 mph, its transmission shifts in and out of overdrive with a modest jolt; a dealer service department said it could find no evidence of a transmission malfunction. There is also an intermittent thump from the center console when going through turns.

ACCOMMODATIONS Concorde and Intrepid offer a front bench seat for 6-passenger capacity, but LHS and 300M are 5-passenger cars. Leather upholstery and heated front seats are standard, and the 300M adds a 60/40 split folding rear seatback. No near-luxury rival equals their generous interior volume, though the 300M's slight rear leg-room deficiency compared to the LHS is apparent.

Instruments are tastefully designed, but we've previously criticized their nighttime readability; a full test will determine whether this year's changes in illumination solve the problem. Controls are well-placed and have good tactile feel. Interior materials and assembly are commendable, though not in a league with import rivals. Models with light-colored dashboard tops suffer annoying reflections in the windshield, and narrow rear windows make for poor aft visibility. The LHS's trunk is large and has a wide opening; the 300M's has less volume and a smaller opening.

VALUE FOR THE MONEY They give up a measure of refinement to the top competition, but LHS and 300M deliver more interior space and comparable performance at prices few rivals match. They have not, however, established the track record of reliability and customer service that are so important in this class.

ENGINES

	ohc V6
Size, liters/cu. in.	3.5/215
Horsepower @ rpm	253 @ 6400
Torque (lbs./ft.) @ rpm	255 @ 3950
Availability	S

EPA city/highway mpg

4-speed OD automatic	18/27

PRICES

Chrysler LHS and 300M	Retail Price	Dealer Invoice
LHS 4-door sedan	$28090	$25775
300M 4-door sedan	29085	26661
Destination charge	605	605

STANDARD EQUIPMENT:

LHS: 3.5-liter V6 engine, 4-speed automatic transmission, traction control, driver- and passenger-side airbags, antilock 4-wheel disc brakes, variable-assist power steering, leather-wrapped tilt steering wheel, cruise control, air conditioning w/automatic climate control, leather upholstery, heated 8-way power front bucket seats w/driver-side memory and manual lumbar adjustment, center console, cupholders, rear seat trunk pass-through, heated power mirrors w/memory, power windows, power door locks, remote keyless entry, AM/FM/cassette/CD player w/9-Infinity speakers and memory, analog clock, tachometer, trip computer, universal garage door opener, automatic day/night rearview mirror, rear defogger, power decklid release, variable intermittent wipers, illuminated visor mirrors, automatic headlights, front and rear reading lights, floormats, theft-deterrent system, fog lights, 225/55R17 tires, alloy wheels.

300M adds: 4-speed automatic transmission w/manual-shift capability, firm-feel power steering, split folding rear seat, deletes variable-assist power steering, and rear seat trunk pass-through.

OPTIONAL EQUIPMENT:
Major Packages

Performance Handling Group, 300M	500	445

Includes unlimited top speed engine controller, performance antilock 4-wheel disc brakes, performance power steering and suspension, 225/60VR16 tires.

Comfort and Convenience

Power sunroof	895	797
AM/FM/cassette w/4-disc CD changer	515	458
Includes 11-speaker Infinity sound system.		
Smoker's Group	20	18
Ashtrays, lighter.		
17-inch chrome alloy wheels	750	668
16-inch chrome alloy wheels, 300M	750	668
Requires Performance Handling Group.		

CHRYSLER SEBRING

RECOMMENDED

Chrysler Sebring JX

Front-wheel-drive sports coupe; similar to Chrysler Cirrus, Dodge Avenger and Stratus, and Plymouth Breeze

Base price range: $19,765-$26,560. Built in USA and Mexico.
Also consider: Chevrolet Monte Carlo, Honda Prelude, Volkswagen New Beetle

FOR • Passenger and cargo room • Steering/handling
AGAINST • Road noise • Rear visibility

Two significantly different cars share the Sebring badge. The Sebring convertible is based on the Chrysler Cirrus sedan and outsells the Sebring coupe 2-1. The coupe shares its Mitsubishi-based components with the Dodge Avenger. More standard equipment for the base-level coupe heads 2000's short list of changes.

The convertible comes in base JX and mid-level JXi models, and luxury JXi Limited trim; all have a power top with defrosted glass rear window. Coupes offer LX and LXi models. Convertibles use a Chrysler-made V6; coupes a Mitsubishi V6. All Sebrings have automatic transmission; JXi Limited equipment includes Chrysler's Autostick, an automatic that can be shifted manually. Antilock brakes are standard on Sebring convertibles, optional on coupes.

For 2000, convertibles offer an optional emergency escape release inside the trunk and gain additional body insulation designed to reduce noise and vibration. The LX coupe gets several features that previously were optional, including cruise control, power windows, 4-wheel disc brakes, and 16-inch wheels. The LXi and JXi Limited also have 4-wheel discs.

PERFORMANCE While they don't have the low-speed muscle of larger-displacement V6s, both 2.5-liter engines provide good acceleration from a stop and in around-town driving, and adequate passing response on the highway. Our test '99 JXi convertible averaged 21 mpg.

Handling, steering, and braking are satisfying, and blend with adequately damped suspensions to produce good all-around road manners. Too much road noise makes a long trip in either body style tiring, however. This year's added insulation makes convertibles significantly quieter with the top raised.

ACCOMMODATIONS Both coupe and convertible stand out among their respective competitors by offering relatively spacious interiors with rear seats that accommodate adults in reasonable comfort. Their dashboard designs differ, and the convertible's gets our nod for its more-accessible audio controls. The ragtop also integrates its front safety belts into the front seatbacks, so they move with the seats and always fit comfortably.

Both cars have visibility woes. The convertible's raised top blocks the driver's over-the-shoulder view, while the coupe has a high rear parcel shelf and bathtub-like seating. Long doors on both are a hindrance in parking lots. Rear entry and exit are better than on smaller 2-door cars, but still require stooping.

VALUE FOR THE MONEY Pleasant road manners and competitive pricing keep these cars interesting, but what sells them is their attractive styling: Both look richer and racier than their sticker prices would suggest.

ENGINES

	ohc V6	ohc V6
Size, liters/cu. in.	2.5/152	2.5/152
Horsepower @ rpm	163 @ 5500	168 @ 5800
Torque (lbs./ft.) @ rpm	170 @ 4350	170 @ 4350
Availability	S[1]	S[2]
EPA city/highway mpg		
4-speed OD automatic	19/27	19/27

1. LX, LXi. 2. JX, JXi, JXi Limited

PRICES

Chrysler Sebring	Retail Price	Dealer Invoice
LX 2-door coupe	$19765	$18121
LXi 2-door coupe	22100	20199
JX 2-door convertible	24245	22198
JXi 2-door convertible	26560	24258
Destination charge	545	545

STANDARD EQUIPMENT:

LX 2.5-liter V6 engine, 4-speed automatic transmission, driver- and passenger-side airbags, 4-wheel disc brakes, variable-assist power steering, tilt steering wheel, cruise control, air conditioning, cloth upholstery, front bucket seats, height-adjustable driver seat, center console, cupholders, split folding rear seat, power mirrors, power windows, power door locks, AM/FM/cassette, digital clock, tachometer, rear defogger, variable intermittent wipers, remote fuel-door and decklid releases, illuminated visor mirrors, map lights, floormats, fog lights, 205/55HR16 tires, wheel covers.

LXi adds: leather upholstery, leather-wrapped steering wheel, remote keyless entry, AM/FM/cassette/CD player, automatic day/night rearview mirror, compass, universal garage-door opener, theft-deterrent system, rear spoiler, 215/50HR17 tires, alloy wheels.

JX: 2.5-liter V6 engine, 4-speed automatic transmission, driver- and passenger-side airbags, antilock brakes, variable-assist power steering, tilt steering wheel, cruise control, air conditioning, front bucket seats w/6-way power driver seat, vinyl upholstery, console with storage armrest, cuphold-

ers, heated power mirrors, power windows, power door locks, remote keyless entry, AM/FM/cassette with CD changer controls and six speakers, digital clock, tachometer, variable intermittent wipers, auxiliary power outlet, automatic-off headlights, illuminated visor mirrors, map lights, power remote decklid release, power vinyl convertible top with glass rear window, rear defogger, floormats, 205/65R15 tires, wheel covers.

JXi adds: Firm Feel power steering, leather-wrapped steering wheel and shifter, leather upholstery, trip computer, 6-speaker Infinity sound system, touring suspension, cloth convertible top, theft-deterrent system, fog lights, 215/55R16 tires, alloy wheels.

OPTIONAL EQUIPMENT:

	Retail Price	Dealer Invoice
Major Packages		
Pkg. 24K, LXi	NC	NC
Manufacturer's discount price, (credit)	($630)	($531)
Standard equipment.		
Security Group, JX	175	156
Theft-deterrent system w/alarm system, programmable power door locks.		
16-inch Alloy Wheel Touring Group, JX	495	441
Firm Feel power steering, touring suspension, 215/55R16 tires, alloy wheels.		
Pkg. 26G Limited, JXi	1890	1682
Includes traction control, antilock 4-wheel disc brakes, 4-speed automatic transmission w/manual-shift capability, Limited Decor Group (luxury floormats, color-keyed grille, chrome alloy wheels), Luxury Convenience Group (universal garage door opener, automatic day/night inside mirror, map light).		
All Season Group, JXi	740	659
Manufacturer's discount price	490	436
Traction control, antilock 4-wheel disc brakes, AM/FM/cassette/CD player w/eight Infinity speakers and equalizer, universal garage door opener, automatic day/night rearview mirror, map light.		
Luxury Convenience Group, JXi	175	156
Universal garage-door opener, automatic day/night rearview mirror, map light.		
Powertrains		
2.5-liter V6 engine, LX	NC	NC
Manufacturer's discount price, (credit)	(675)	(601)
Safety Features		
Anti-lock brakes, LX, LXi	600	534
Comfort and Convenience		
Power sunroof, LX, LXi	685	610
AM/FM/cassette/CD player, LX	435	387
Includes graphic equalizer.		
Premium AM/FM/cassette/CD player, LX	760	676
Includes Infinity speakers and equalizer.		
Premium AM/FM/cassette/CD player, LXi	325	289
JX	340	303
Includes Infinity speakers and equalizer.		
6-disc CD changer, JXi	500	445
NA with All Season Group.		
Premium AM/FM/cassette w/6-disc CD changer, JXi	160	142
Requires Pkg. 26G Limited.		
Power driver seat, LX, LXi	205	182
Premium cloth upholstery, JX	95	85
Remote keyless entry, LX	305	271
Includes theft-deterrent system w/alarm.		

CHRYSLER TOWN & COUNTRY

Front- or all-wheel-drive minivan; similar to Dodge Caravan and Plymouth Voyager

Base price range: $26,360-$36,640. Built in USA. **Also consider:** Ford Windstar, Honda Odyssey, Oldsmobile Silhouette, Toyota Sienna

FOR • Acceleration (3.8 liter) • Ride • Passenger and cargo room
AGAINST • Fuel economy • Wind noise

Chrysler eliminates the regular-length version of its minivan for 2000. Town & Country is the luxury edition of the Dodge Caravan and Plymouth Voyager.

Extended-length LX, LXi, and Limited Town & Country models

Prices are accurate at time of publication; subject to manufacturer's changes.

Chrysler Town & Country LX

continue with new interior and exterior colors as their only changes. All seat seven and have sliding doors on both sides. Unique to the Limited are leather seats with simulated suede trim, a third-row bench with center armrest, chrome wheels, and body-color roof rack.

All Town & Countrys are available with an all-wheel-drive (AWD) system that automatically directs power to the rear wheels as needed. A 3.3-liter V6 is standard on LX and LXi models. A 3.8-liter V6 is standard on Limiteds and AWD models and is optional on the front-drive LXi. Automatic transmission, air conditioning, and antilock brakes are standard; AWD models get 4-wheel disc brakes. A load-leveling rear suspension is standard on Limited models, optional on LX and LXi, and included with AWD. Finally, newly available on Chrysler, Dodge, and Plymouth minivans is a dealer-installed video entertainment system. Called Rear Seat Video, it mounts above the front- or second-row seats and includes a VCR, 6.4-inch liquid crystal display screen, headphones, and remote control. Price, including installation, is $1500.

PERFORMANCE As do its less-costly siblings, Town & Country drives like a large car, with precise steering and reasonably balanced handling. Ride is firm yet supple, though the AWD and towing options have firmer damping that's mediocre at absorbing bumps. The 3.3-liter V6 has adequate power, but the 3.8's extra muscle makes expressway merging and uphill climbs noticeably easier, especially with a load. Our test '99 AWD model averaged 14.3 mpg; 3.3-liter models manage about 16 mpg overall. Tire noise is low, but wind rush is prominent at highway speeds. AWD works as advertised, but 3.8-liter front-drive models come with low-speed traction control that copes well with winter weather.

ACCOMMODATIONS Seating is comfortable, supportive, and roomy at all positions. Cargo space is ample with all seats in use. All seats are heavy and cumbersome to remove, though that's true of nearly all competitors, too. Step-in height is among the lowest in the class, so entry/exit is easy even with AWD. Double sliding doors are a standard convenience, but General Motors and Toyota rivals have a power right-side sliding door, and Ford and Honda offer two power sliders. Recent test T&Cs have been mechanically trouble-free, but some molded plastic looks low-budget, and the side door windows on our last test model rattled over bumps.

VALUE FOR THE MONEY Chrysler plans to offer the LX for under $27,000—less than last year's base regular-length model. That still doesn't make Town & Country the Best Buy value a Caravan/Voyager is, but as a minivan for the status-conscious, this Chrysler offers lots of posh for the price.

ENGINES

	ohv V6	ohv V6
Size, liters/cu. in.	3.3/202	3.8/231
Horsepower @ rpm	158 @ 4850	180 @ 4400
Torque (lbs./ft.) @ rpm	203 @ 3250	240 @ 3200
Availability	S[1]	S[2]

EPA city/highway mpg

4-speed OD automatic	18/24	17/24[3]

1. LX, LXi. 2. Standard, Limited and w/AWD; optional LXi. 3. 16/23 w/AWD.

PRICES

Chrysler Town & Country	Retail Price	Dealer Invoice
LX 4-door van, FWD	$26360	$23952
LX 4-door van, AWD	29525	26737
LXi 4-door van, FWD	28415	25760
LXi 4-door van, AWD	31590	28554
Limited 4-door van, FWD	34265	30908
Limited 4-door van, AWD	36640	32998
Destination charge	590	590

AWD denotes all-wheel drive. FWD denotes front-wheel drive.

STANDARD EQUIPMENT:

LX: 3.3-liter V6 engine, 4-speed automatic transmission, driver- and passenger-side airbags, antilock brakes, air conditioning w/manual dual-zone controls, power steering, tilt steering wheel, cruise control, dual sliding rear doors, cloth upholstery, seven passenger seating (reclining front bucket seats, reclining and folding middle bucket seats, 3-passenger rear seat w/recliner), 8-way power driver seat w/lumbar adjustment, center console, passenger-side underseat storage drawer, overhead console, compass, trip computer, AM/FM/cassette, digital clock, tachometer, heated power mirrors, power windows, power door locks, variable intermittent wipers, windshield wiper de-icer, rear defogger, variable intermittent rear wiper/washer, map lights, auxiliary power outlets, illuminated visor mirrors, floormats, deep-tinted rear glass, fog lights, 215/65R15 tires, wheel covers. **AWD** adds: permanent all-wheel drive, 3.8-liter engine, 4-wheel disc brakes, load-leveling suspension, 215/70R15 tires.

LXi adds: leather-wrapped steering wheel, remote keyless entry, AM/FM/cassette w/CD changer controls and 10-speaker Infinity sound system, automatic-off headlights, 215/65R16 tires. **AWD** adds: permanent all-wheel drive, 3.8-liter engine, 4-wheel disc brakes, load-leveling suspension.

Limited adds: 3.8-liter V6 engine (FWD and AWD), traction control, rear air conditioning and heater, leather/simulated suede upholstery, heated 8-way power front seats with driver-side memory, AM/FM/cassette/CD player with 10-speaker Infinity sound system, steering wheel radio controls, automatic day/night rearview and driver-side outside mirror, heated power mirrors w/memory, universal garage door opener, side seat storage bin, rear reading lights, automatic headlights, roof rack, theft-deterrent system w/alarm, load-leveling suspension (FWD and AWD), full-size spare tire, chrome alloy wheels, deletes passenger-side underseat storage drawer. **AWD** adds: permanent all-wheel drive, 4-wheel disc brakes, deletes traction control.

OPTIONAL EQUIPMENT:

Major Packages

	Retail Price	Dealer Invoice
Quick Order Pkg. 29Y, LXi FWD	$3525	$2996
Manufacturer's discount price	2525	2146
Quick Order Pkg. 29Y, LXi AWD	3350	2848
Manufacturer's discount price	2350	1998

Traction control (FWD), rear air conditioning and heater, AM/FM/cassette/CD player, steering wheel radio controls, universal garage door opener, heated power mirrors w/memory, leather upholstery, 8-way power front seats w/driver-side memory, seat side storage bin, theft-deterrent system w/alarm, roof rack, lower bodyside cladding, full-size spare tire, alloy wheels.

Value Plus Popular Equipment Group, LXi	1200	1020
Manufacturer's discount price	200	170

Rear air conditioning and heater, AM/FM/cassette/CD player, alloy wheels.

Wheel/Handling Group, LX FWD	360	306
LXi FWD	510	434

Front and rear stabilizer bars, heavy-duty suspension, 215/65R16 tires, alloy wheels.

Loading Group, LX, LXi	195	166

Includes heavy-duty suspension and full-size spare. NA with AWD.

Trailer Tow Group, LX FWD	370	315
LX AWD	300	255
LXi FWD, Limited FWD	245	208
LXi AWD, Limited AWD	175	149

Heavy-duty alternator, battery, radiator, brakes, and suspension; transmission oil cooler, trailer wiring harness, full-size spare tire.

Powertrains

3.8-liter V6 engine, LXi FWD	335	285
Manufacturer's discount price	285	242
Includes traction control.		
Traction Control, LXi FWD	175	149

Safety Features

Integrated child seat	125	106

Comfort and Convenience

Convenience Group IV, LX	240	204

Remote keyless entry, automatic-off headlights.

Convenience Group V, LX	390	332

Remote keyless entry, automatic-off headlights, theft-deterrent system w/alarm.

Ratings begin on page 213. Specifications begin on page 220. CONSUMER GUIDE™

	Retail Price	Dealer Invoice
Convenience Group VI, LXi	$240	$204
Universal garage door opener, theft-deterrent system w/alarm.		
Heated front seats, LXi	250	213
Requires Quick Order Pkg. 29Y.		
Value Plus Audio Group, LX	720	612
Manufacturer's discount price	270	229
AM/FM/cassette/CD player w/10-speaker Infinity sound system.		
Climate Group III, LX	475	404
Rear air conditioning and heater.		
Smoker's Group	20	17
Cigarette lighter, ashtrays.		

Appearance and Miscellaneous

	Retail Price	Dealer Invoice
Load-leveling suspension, LX/LXi FWD	290	247
Roof rack, LX, LXi	215	183
Alloy wheels, LX	265	225
Includes 215/65R16 tires.		

DAEWOO LANOS

Daewoo Lanos hatchback

Front-wheel-drive subcompact car

Base price range: $8,669-$12,519. Built in South Korea.
Also consider: Dodge/Plymouth Neon, Ford Escort/ZX2, Honda Civic

FOR • Fuel economy • Price **AGAINST** • Acceleration
• Automatic transmission performance • Rear-seat room

Lanos is the smallest of three cars from Daewoo, a South Korean automaker that entered the U.S. market in 1998. For 2000, all Lanos models get additional standard equipment but have base prices no higher than their 1999 counterparts. This front-wheel-drive subcompact comes as a 2-door hatchback in base S and SE trim, or a 4-door sedan in S and top-line SX trim. An SX hatchback and SE sedan are dropped for 2000. The only engine is a twincam 4-cylinder with manual or optional 4-speed automatic transmission. Traction control is not offered, but antilock brakes are optional on SE and SX models. For 2000, S models gain a standard height-adjustable driver's seat, center console, and remote fuel door/decklid release. SEs gain a rear spoiler, but no longer share with the SX a standard remote keyless entry theft-deterrent system. Daewoo's warranty includes roadside assistance and scheduled maintenance for 3 years/36,000 miles.

EVALUATION Though quite affordable, Lanos isn't inexpensive for a car that's only average in most respects and disappointing in several—namely acceleration, quietness, and rear-seat room. Perhaps its biggest disadvantage, is that Daewoo is a still a newcomer with a very uncertain future in the competitive U.S. market. But the company says it has more than 200 dealers, which makes this car a slightly less risky purchase than it was in '98, when Daewoo had just 16 sales and service outlets.

ENGINES

	dohc I4
Size, liters/cu. in.	1.6/98
Horsepower @ rpm	105 @ 5800
Torque (lbs./ft.) @ rpm	106 @ 3400
Availability	S

EPA city/highway mpg
5-speed OD manual	26/36
4-speed OD automatic	23/34

PRICES

Daewoo Lanos	Retail Price	Dealer Invoice
S 2-door hatchback, 5-speed	$8669	$7421
S 2-door hatchback, automatic	$9469	$8049
S 4-door sedan, 5-speed	9449	8032
S 4-door sedan, automatic	10249	8712
SE 2-door hatchback, 5-speed	10200	8670
SE 2-door hatchback, automatic	11000	9350
SX 4-door sedan, 5-speed	11719	9961
SX 4-door sedan, automatic	12519	10641
Destination charge	330	330

STANDARD EQUIPMENT:

S: 1.6-liter dohc 4-cylinder engine, 5-speed manual or 4-speed automatic transmission, driver- and passenger-side airbags, power steering, cloth upholstery, front bucket seats w/height-adjustable driver seat, center console, cupholders, split folding rear seat, AM/FM/cassette, digital clock, rear defogger, rear wiper/washer (hatchback), visor mirrors, remote fuel door/decklid release, dual outside mirrors, 185/60R14 tires.

SE adds: power passenger-side mirror, power windows, power door locks, rear spoiler.

SX adds: air conditioning, tilt steering wheel, AM/FM/cassette/CD player, remote keyless entry, theft-deterrent system, fog lights, alloy wheels, deletes rear spoiler.

OPTIONAL EQUIPMENT:
Safety Features
Antilock brakes, SE, SX	500	425

Comfort and Convenience
Air conditioning, S, SE	700	595
Power sunroof, SX	500	425

DAEWOO LEGANZA

Daewoo Leganza

Front-wheel-drive compact car

Base price range: $13,660-$18,660. Built in South Korea.
Also consider: Mazda 626, Mitsubishi Galant, Nissan Altima

FOR • Ride **AGAINST** • Acceleration (w/automatic transmission) • Automatic transmission performance

The base Leganza loses some standard equipment in exchange for an $880 price reduction, while other trim levels retain their '99 pricing for 2000. Leganza is a front-wheel-drive 4-door sedan that's priced and sized as a compact car, though Daewoo pitches it as an upscale sedan. Base SE, SX, and top-line CDX models are offered, all with a 2.2-liter 4-cylinder engine. Manual transmission is standard on the SE. A 4-speed automatic is optional on the SE and standard on SX and CDX. Antilock 4-wheel-disc brakes are unavailable on SEs for 2000, but remain standard on SXs and CDXs. The CDX also has traction control, alloy wheels, and a power sunroof. All models have standard air conditioning, and power windows and locks. Leganza's grille and alloy wheels are revised for 2000. Fog lamps and remote keyless entry are no longer available on SE models but remain standard on other Leganzas. SEs gain a height-adjustable driver's seat and variable intermittent wipers. SXs gain a leather-wrapped steering wheel and power antenna, but lose a standard 6-way power driver seat. Daewoo's warranty includes roadside assistance and scheduled maintenance for 3 years/36,000 miles.

EVALUATION Leganza is Daewoo's largest car, and like other Daewoos, is competitive in its class but no standout. It's a competent family 4-door with a smooth if pillowy ride, good room for four adults, decent braking, and soggy but safe handling. Less likable are its tepid acceleration, unexceptional 22.4-mpg average in our tests, and some odd interior design details. All models deliver lots of safety and convenience features for the money, but Daewoo is still an

---

Prices are accurate at time of publication; subject to manufacturer's changes.

unproven newcomer to the tough U.S. market, making Leganza a chancy proposition, particularly in resale value.

ENGINES

	dohc I4
Size, liters/cu. in.	2.2/134
Horsepower @ rpm	131 @ 5200
Torque (lbs./ft.) @ rpm	148 @ 2800
Availability	S

EPA city/highway mpg
5-speed OD manual	20/29
4-speed OD automatic	20/28

PRICES

Daewoo Leganza	Retail Price	Dealer Invoice
SE 4-door sedan, 5-speed	$13660	$11630
SE 4-door sedan, automatic	14460	12291
SX 4-door sedan, automatic	16660	14161
CDX 4-door sedan, automatic	18660	15861
Destination charge	330	330

STANDARD EQUIPMENT:

SE: 2.2-liter dohc 4-cylinder engine, 5-speed manual or 4-speed automatic transmission, driver- and passenger-side airbags, air conditioning, power steering, tilt steering wheel, cloth upholstery, front bucket seats w/height-adjustable driver seat, center console, cupholders, split folding rear seat, heated power mirrors, power windows, power door locks, AM/FM/cassette, digital clock, tachometer, rear defogger, illuminated visor mirrors, variable intermittent wipers, remote fuel door/decklid release, full-size spare tire, 205/60R15 tires.

SX adds: 4-speed automatic transmission, antilock 4-wheel disc brakes, variable-assist power steering, cruise control, leather upholstery, leather-wrapped steering wheel, AM/FM/cassette/CD player, power antenna, remote keyless entry, fog lights.

CDX adds: traction control, automatic climate control, power sunroof, 6-way power driver seat, theft-deterrent system, alloy wheels.

OPTIONAL EQUIPMENT:
Comfort and Convenience
Power sunroof, SX	500	425
6-disc CD changer, CDX	450	382
Includes graphic equalizer.		

Appearance and Miscellaneous
Alloy wheels, SX	400	340

DAEWOO NUBIRA

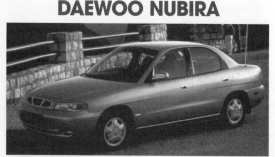
Daewoo Nubira 4-door sedan

Front-wheel-drive subcompact car
Base price range: $10,990-$14,960. Built in South Korea.
Also consider: Chevrolet Prizm, Honda Civic, Mazda Protege

Daewoo's senior subcompact is redesigned for 2000, adding a lower-priced base model but dropping the hatchback version. Wheelbase is the same, but the Nubira is now about an inch longer overall and several hundred pounds heavier. Trunk space is unchanged, but front-seat interior dimensions are slightly larger than last year. A 2.0-liter 4-cylinder continues as the only engine, with standard manual transmission or optional 4-speed automatic.

Nubira again comes in uplevel CDX sedan and wagon, but for 2000, the base SX version has been replaced by a new SE sedan. This model sells for $1260 less than the SX did, but doesn't include

air conditioning, heated power mirrors, power windows, power locks, and tilt steering wheel, which were standard on the SX. All are optionally available on the SE, though the price of these items negates the savings over the previous base model. This equipment is now standard on CDXs, which also have alloy wheels, fog lights, a CD player, and available leather seating. Antilock brakes are standard on CDXs, but unavailable on SEs. Daewoo's warranty includes roadside assistance and scheduled maintenance for 3 years/36,000 miles.

We have not yet tested the 2000 Nubira, and thus cannot provide an evaluation or ratings.

ENGINES
	dohc I4
Size, liters/cu. in.	2.0/122
Horsepower @ rpm	129 @ 5400
Torque (lbs./ft.) @ rpm	136 @ 4400
Availability	S

EPA city/highway mpg
5-speed OD manual	22/31
4-speed OD automatic	22/30

PRICES
Daewoo Nubira	Retail Price	Dealer Invoice
SE 4-door sedan, 5-speed	$10990	$9342
SE 4-door sedan, automatic	11790	10022
CDX 4-door sedan, 5-speed	13560	11526
CDX 4-door sedan, automatic	14360	12206
CDX 4-door wagon, 5-speed	14160	12036
CDX 4-door wagon, automatic	14960	12716
Destination charge	330	330

STANDARD EQUIPMENT:

SE: 2.0-liter dohc 4-cylinder, 5-speed manual or 4-speed automatic transmission, driver- and passenger-side airbags, 4-wheel disc brakes, power steering, cloth upholstery, front bucket seats w/height-adjustable driver seat, center console, cupholders, split folding rear seat, AM/FM/cassette, digital clock, tachometer, rear defogger, variable intermittent wipers, remote fuel door/decklid or hatch release, visor mirrors, 185/60R14 tires.

CDX adds: antilock brakes, air conditioning, tilt steering wheel, cruise control, AM/FM/cassette/CD player, heated power mirrors, power windows, power door locks, remote keyless entry, rear wiper/washer (wagon), theft-deterrent system, fog lights, roof rack (wagon), alloy wheels.

OPTIONAL EQUIPMENT:
Major Packages
Convenience Pkg., SE	560	476
Tilt steering wheel, heated power mirrors, power windows and door locks, remote keyless entry, theft-deterrent system, fog lights.		

Comfort and Convenience
Air conditioning, SE	700	595
Power sunroof, CDX	500	—
Leather upholstery, CDX	400	340

DODGE AVENGER

Dodge Avenger

Front-wheel-drive sports coupe; similar to Chrysler Sebring
Base price range: $18,970-$21,215. Built in USA. **Also consider:** Chevrolet Monte Carlo, Honda Prelude, Mitsubishi Eclipse

FOR • Steering/handling **AGAINST** • Noise • Rear visibility • Interior materials

Avenger for 2000 gets a host of standard features that previously were optional. Dodge's sports coupe comes with a V6 engine and automatic transmission. It shares its underskin design and powertrain with the Chrysler Sebring coupe, but differs in exterior styling. Both are built in Illinois by Mitsubishi. Both the Avenger base and ES models get standard power windows and locks for 2000. The base model also gains cruise control, 4-wheel disc brakes, and 16-inch wheels in place of 14s. The ES retains 17-inch wheels and now comes with the previously optional leather upholstery and keyless remote entry. It also adds a power driver's seat.

EVALUATION Rear-seat room and cargo space are good for a high-style 2-door, and the V6 delivers good acceleration. Base models have predictable front-drive handling, plus good ride comfort for the class. Firm suspension and performance tires make the ES more athletic, but also quite harsh on rough pavement. Debits include a low "bathtub" driving position, restricted rear visibility, and tricky backseat entry/exit. Workmanship is good but not great, prices are reasonable, and equipment fairly generous.

ENGINES

	ohc V6
Size, liters/cu. in.	2.5/152
Horsepower @ rpm	163 @ 5500
Torque (lbs./ft.) @ rpm	170 @ 4350
Availability	S

EPA city/highway mpg

4-speed OD automatic	19/27

PRICES

Dodge Avenger	Retail Price	Dealer Invoice
Base 2-door coupe	$18970	$17338
ES 2-door coupe	21215	19336
Destination charge	545	545

STANDARD EQUIPMENT:

Base: 2.5-liter V6 engine, 4-speed automatic transmission, driver- and passenger-side airbags, 4-wheel disc brakes, air conditioning, variable-assist power steering, tilt steering wheel, cruise control, cloth upholstery, front bucket seats, height-adjustable driver seat, center console, cupholders, split folding rear seat, power mirrors, power windows, power door locks, rear defogger, AM/FM/cassette w/six speakers, digital clock, tachometer, variable intermittent wipers, map lights, visor mirrors, remote fuel door/decklid release, floormats, rear spoiler, 205/55HR16 tires, wheel covers.

ES adds: leather upholstery, 6-way power driver seat, leather-wrapped steering wheel, remote keyless entry, AM/FM/cassette/CD player, universal garage door opener, theft-deterrent system, handling suspension, fog lights, 215/50HR17 tires, alloy wheels.

OPTIONAL EQUIPMENT:

Major Packages

Quick Order Pkg. 24F, ES	NC	NC
Manufacturer's discount price, (credit)	($630)	($531)
Standard equipment.		

Powertrains

2.5-liter V6 engine, Base	NC	NC
Manufacturer's discount price,		
Base (credit)	(675)	(601)

Safety Features

Antilock brakes, ES	600	534

Comfort and Convenience

AM/FM/cassette/CD player, Base	435	387
Infinity sound system, ES	325	289
Remote keyless entry, Base	305	271
Includes theft-deterrent system.		
Power sunroof	685	610

DODGE CARAVAN ✓ BEST BUY

Front- or all-wheel-drive minivan; similar to Chrysler Town & Country and Plymouth Voyager

Base price range: $18,685-$32,010. Built in USA and Canada. **Also consider:** Chevrolet Venture, Ford Windstar,

Dodge Grand Caravan ES

Honda Odyssey, Pontiac Montana, Toyota Sienna

FOR • Acceleration (3.8 liter) • Ride • Passenger and cargo room
AGAINST • Fuel economy • Wind noise

Dodge's popular minivan adds a Sport-badged version for 2000 and makes available a dealer-installed video system. Caravan shares its design with the Plymouth Voyager and Chrysler Town & Country. All come in extended-length models, but Dodge and Plymouth also sell regular-length versions.

Base and SE Caravans come in both body lengths. LE, ES, and the new Sport models are extended-length Grands. All models seat seven and include two front bucket seats, second-row bench or buckets, and a third-row bench. Up to two integrated second-row child safety seats are available. Two sliding side doors are standard except on the base regular-length model, where the left door is optional.

Regular-length models use a 4-cylinder engine or V6s of 3.0 and 3.3 liters. Grands get V6s of 3.0, 3.3 and 3.8 liters. The 4-cylinder comes with a 3-speed automatic transmission, the V6s with a 4-speed automatic. ES models get the 3.8 and Chrysler's Autostick automatic transmission, which can be shifted manually via a switch on the column shift lever. Front-wheel drive is standard. Traction control is standard on 3.8-liter ESs and optional on 3.8-liter LEs.

All-wheel drive (AWD) is optional on LE and ES Grand Caravans and is standard on the new Sport model. The Sport essentially replaces an SE AWD model and includes the 3.8 V6, load-levelling suspension, fog lights, and a rear spoiler. Antilock brakes are optional on base models, standard on the others. AWD models have 4-wheel discs.

For 2000, a cassette player and air conditioning are now standard instead of optional on base models. Newly available on Chrysler, Dodge, and Plymouth minivans is a dealer-installed video entertainment system. Called Rear Seat Video, it mounts above the front- or second-row seats and includes a VCR, 6.4-inch liquid crystal display screen, headphones, and remote control. Price, including installation, is $1500.

PERFORMANCE Caravan and Voyager are fine performers, but choose the right engine. Consider the weak 4-cylinder or the over-burdened 3.0-liter V6 only if you absolutely can't afford more power. The 3.3 provides adequate acceleration in regular-length models and is acceptable in the Grands. The 3.8 is the best overall choice, with enough power to pass and merge easily. Our test '99 3.8-liter Grand Caravan averaged 17.7 mpg. The 3.3 liter, which has to work that much harder, averaged 15.8 mpg in our test of a '99 Grand Voyager.

These minivans are maneuverable in the city, responsive on curves, and stable on the highway. Sudden stops dip the nose, but there's no loss of control, and braking power corresponds nicely to pedal pressure. Caravan and Voyager are quiet for minivans, but wind and road noise can be intrusive at highway speeds.

ACCOMMODATIONS Several fine rivals have come on the scene since the Caravan and Voyager were last redesigned for 1996, but these are still among the most comfortable, practical, and versatile minivans. Entry/exit is easy, the dashboard is user-friendly, and cupholders (some adjustable for size) abound, as do assorted bins and nooks.

The second- and third-row seats recline and their backrests tip forward to form a flat deck that can carry a 4x8-foot plywood sheet with the tailgate closed. There's also space beneath the seats for skis or 2x4s. Second- and third-row bench seats roll on built-in wheels, but weigh about 90 pounds each, so it takes two people to heft one in or out. Seats on Chevrolet, Oldsmobile, and Pontiac minivans weigh less, but don't offer the chair-like comfort of the Caravan/Voyager. Head and leg room are good at every position, and although the

---

Prices are accurate at time of publication; subject to manufacturer's changes.

third-row bench is somewhat cramped, it's not uncomfortable.

The twin sliding doors are very useful, although competitors from General Motors and Toyota offer one power-sliding door while mini-vans from Ford and Honda offer two. A low cowl and large windows contribute to outstanding visibility, and uplevel Caravans and Voyagers have electric windshield-wiper de-icers. The rear window's deep tint is difficult to see through in dim light, however.

VALUE FOR THE MONEY Caravan and Voyager are Best Buys, but rivals are getting closer, especially the Honda Odyssey and Toyota Sienna. Dodge and Plymouth dealers have taken notice. Use the competitive market to negotiate a good deal.

ENGINES

	dohc I4	ohc V6	ohv V6	ohv V6
Size, liters/cu. in.	2.4/148	3.0/181	3.3/202	3.8/231
Horsepower @ rpm	150 @ 5200	150 @ 5200	158 @ 4850	180 @ 4400
Torque (lbs./ft.) @ rpm	167 @ 4000	176 @ 4000	203 @ 3250	240 @ 3200
Availability	S[1]	S[2]	S[3]	S[4]
EPA city/highway mpg				
3-speed automatic	20/26			
4-speed OD automatic		19/26	18/24	17/24[5]

1. Base regular length. 2. Base Grand; optional on Base regular length. 3. SE and LE; optional on Base models. 4. Sport, ES; optional LE. 5. 16/23 w/AWD.

PRICES

Dodge Caravan	Retail Price	Dealer Invoice
Regular length Base 3-door van, FWD	$18685	$16978
Grand Base 4-door van, FWD	21790	19765
Regular length SE 4-door van, FWD	23085	20850
Grand SE 4-door van, FWD	24080	21780
Grand Sport 4-door van, AWD	28080	25300
Grand LE 4-door van, FWD	27195	24522
Grand LE 4-door van, AWD	30370	27316
Grand ES 4-door van, FWD	29405	26466
Grand ES 4-door van, AWD	32010	28759
Destination charge	590	590

AWD denotes all-wheel drive. FWD denotes front-wheel drive.

STANDARD EQUIPMENT:

Regular length Base: 2.4-liter dohc 4-cylinder engine, 3-speed automatic transmission, driver- and passenger-side airbags, power steering, 5-passenger seating, cloth reclining front bucket seats, 3-passenger second row bench seat, cupholders, variable intermittent wipers, variable intermittent rear wiper/washer, AM/FM/cassette, digital clock, front map lights, visor mirrors, auxiliary power outlets, dual outside mirrors, 205/75R14 tires, wheel covers.

Grand Base adds: 3.0-liter V6 engine, 4-speed automatic transmission, front air conditioning, sliding driver-side door, 7-passenger seating, front bucket seats, passenger-side underseat storage, 2-passenger second row bench seat, folding 3-passenger rear bench seat, rear floor silencer.

SE adds: 3.3-liter V6 engine, antilock brakes, tilt steering column, cruise control, 7-passenger seating w/third row bench seat, front seat cargo net, heated power mirrors, power windows, power door locks, tachometer, illuminated visor mirrors, rear defogger, windshield wiper de-icer, deluxe sound insulation, floormats, 215/65R15 tires, 4-wheel disc brakes, load-leveling suspension.

Sport adds: 3.8-liter V6 engine, permanent all-wheel drive, 4-wheel disc brakes, leather-wrapped steering wheel w/radio controls, deep-tinted glass, fog lights, rear spoiler, load-leveling suspension.

LE adds to SE: dual-zone manual climate control, 8-way power driver seat w/manual lumbar adjustment, overhead console (sunglass storage, trip computer, compass, outside temperature indicator), AM/FM/cassette w/CD changer controls and Infinity sound system, remote keyless entry, automatic headlights, deep-tinted glass. **AWD** models add: permanent all-wheel drive, 3.8-liter V6 engine, 4-wheel disc brakes, load-leveling suspension.

ES adds: 3.8-liter V6 engine, Autostick 4-speed automatic transmission, traction control, leather-wrapped steering wheel w/radio controls, AM/FM/cassette/CD player, automatic day/night rearview mirror and driver-side mirror, universal garage door opener, fog lights, rear spoiler, sport suspension, full-size spare tire, 215/60R17 tires, alloy wheels. **AWD** models add: permanent all-wheel drive, 4-wheel disc brakes, load-leveling suspension, 215/65R16 tires.

OPTIONAL EQUIPMENT:

Major Packages	Retail Price	Dealer Invoice
Pkg. 25T/26T/28T, reg. length Base	$1275	$1084
Manufacturer's discount price,		
w/2.4-liter engine	NC	NC
w/3.0- or 3.3-liter engine	515	438
Air conditioning, 7-passenger seating, underseat storage drawer, rear floor silencer.		
Value Plus V6 Group, Base	1170	995
Manufacturer's discount price	670	570
Tilt steering wheel, cruise control, power mirrors and windows, power door locks, deluxe interior door trim. Regular length Base requires Pkg. 25T/26T/28T.		
Sport Pkg. 25E/28E, SE	1205	1024
Manufacturer's discount price	930	790
Leather-wrapped steering wheel, fog lights, bodyside moldings, rear spoiler, deep-tinted glass, heavy-duty suspension, stabilizer bars, 215/65R16 tires.		
Sport Pkg. 25N/28N/29N, SE	2650	2253
Manufacturer's discount price	2275	1934
Pkg. 25E/28E plus quad bucket seats, 8-way power driver seat w/manual lumbar support, upgraded upholstery, overhead console w/trip computer, second row reading lights.		
Pkg. 25N/28N/29N, Sport	1445	1228
Manufacturer's discount price	1345	1143
Quad bucket seats, 8-way power driver seat w/manual lumbar support, upgraded upholstery, overhead console w/trip computer, second row reading lights.		
Value Plus Group, LE	1235	1050
Manufacturer's discount price	235	200
Rear air conditioning, rear heater, 7-passenger seating w/quad bucket seats.		
Value Plus Group, ES	1320	1122
Manufacturer's discount price	320	272
Rear air conditioning, rear heater, 7-passenger seating w/quad bucket seats, theft-deterrent system w/alarm.		
Climate Group II, Base	450	383
Deep-tinted glass. Requires option pkg.		
Value Plus Climate Group, SE	450	383
Manufacturer's discount price	NC	NC
Deep-tinted glass, wiper de-icer.		
Climate Group III, Grand SE	1230	1046
Sport	715	608
Rear air conditioning and heater with dual zone controls, deep-tinted glass (SE), overhead console w/trip computer.		
Loading Group, SE, LE FWD	195	166
Full-size spare tire, heavy load/firm ride suspension. SE requires option pkg.		
Trailer Tow Prep Group, Grand SE FWD, LE FWD	435	370
LE AWD	365	310
Sport	300	255
ES	175	149
Loading Group plus trailer wiring harness, heavy-duty alternator, battery, radiator, brakes, and transmission oil cooler. Grand SE FWD requires option pkg.		
Wheel/Handling Group, LE FWD	510	434
Front and rear stabilizer bars, heavy-duty suspension, 215/65R16 tires, alloy wheels.		

Powertrains		
3.0-liter V6 engine, reg. length Base	800	680
Requires 4-speed automatic transmission, option pkg. Not available in California, New York, or Massachusetts.		
3.3-liter V6 engine, reg. length Base	970	825
Grand Base	170	145
Regular length Base requires option pkg., 4-speed automatic transmission.		
3.8-liter engine w/traction control, LE	510	434
Manufacturer's discount price	460	391
4-speed automatic transmission, reg. length Base	200	170
Requires V6 engine.		
Traction control, FWD LE	175	149

Safety Features		
Anti-lock brakes, Base	565	480
Two integrated child seats, SE, Sport, LE, ES	225	191

	Retail Price	Dealer Invoice
Base	$235	$200

Includes reclining middle bench seat and integrated child seats. Base SWB and SE require option pkg.

Comfort and Convenience

Convenience Group I, Base	435	370

Cruise control, tilt steering column, power mirrors. Requires option pkg.

Convenience Group II, Base	750	638

Convenience Group I plus power door locks. Requires option pkg.

Convenience Group III, Base	1120	952

Convenience Group II, plus power door locks, power windows and rear quarter vent windows. Requires option pkg. NA AWD.

Convenience Group IV, SE, Sport	240	204

Remote keyless entry, illuminated entry, delay-off headlights. SE requires option pkg.

Convenience Group V, SE, Sport	390	332
LE, ES	150	128

Convenience Group IV (SE) plus theft-deterrent system w/alarm. Requires option pkg.

Sliding driver-side rear door, reg. length Base	595	506

Requires option pkg.

Rear defogger, Base	195	166

Includes heated outside mirrors, windshield wiper de-icer.

AM/FM/cassette/CD, LE	310	264
Value Plus Audio Group, SE, Sport	720	612
Manufacturer's discount price	270	229

AM/FM/cassette/CD player w/10-speaker Infinity sound system.

7-passenger seating w/quad bucket seats, SE, Sport	695	591

Front and middle reclining bucket seats, 3-passenger reclining rear bench seat with headrests.

7-passenger seating w/quad buckets and integrated child seat, SE, Sport, LE, ES	820	697
Leather upholstery, LE	890	757
ES	1245	1058

ES includes power passenger seat. Requires Climate Control Group III and 7-passenger seating w/quad bucket seats.

Heated front seats, ES	250	213

Requires leather upholstery.

Appearance and Miscellaneous

Load-leveling suspension, LE FWD, ES FWD	290	247
Roof rack, Base, SE, Sport, LE, ES	215	183
Body-colored roof rack, ES	260	221
15-inch alloy wheels, SE w/option pkg.	415	353
16-inch alloy wheels, LE	415	353
SE w/option pkg., Sport	265	225

DODGE DAKOTA

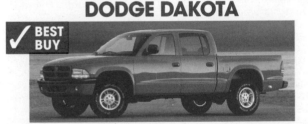

✓ BEST BUY

Dodge Dakota 4WD crew cab

Rear- or 4-wheel-drive compact pickup truck

Base price range: $13,555-$21,615. Built in USA. **Also consider:** Chevrolet S-10, Ford Ranger, Toyota Tacoma

FOR • Acceleration (V8) • Quietness • Ride **AGAINST** • Rear-seat comfort • Fuel economy (V8) • Acceleration (4-cylinder)

A V8 borrowed from the Jeep Grand Cherokee and the midyear introduction of a "crew cab" model with four front-hinged side doors highlight Dakota's 2000 season. Dakota is sized between compact pickups and full-size pickups and offers three cab styles.

Regular-cabs come with a 3-passenger bench seat. Extended-cab Club Cabs add a rear bench for 6-passenger capacity, but have only two doors. The new Quad Cab rides the same wheelbase as the Club Cab and also seats six, but its cab is longer and has two front-hinged rear doors. Along with the new Nissan Frontier Crew

Cab, it's the only compact pickup with front-hinged rear doors. For 2000, regular-cab Dakotas relinquish last year's available 8-foot cargo bed for the 6.5-foot bed used by the Club Cab. The Quad Cab has a 5.25-foot bed.

Dakota's base engine is a 4-cylinder. A V6 is standard on 4-wheel drive models and on Quad Cabs. Optional on all is a 235-horsepower overhead-cam 4.7-liter V8 similar to that used in the Grand Cherokee. It replaces a 230-hp 5.2-liter V8. A 250-hp 5.9-liter is optional on Quad Cabs and is required with the R/T package. Available on 2WD regular-cabs and Club Cabs, the R/T package includes a sport suspension, 17-inch alloy wheels, bucket seats, and distinct trim.

Dakota's 5.9 V8 comes only with automatic transmission; its other engines are available with manual or automatic. The base 4WD system is not for use on dry pavement. Available with the V8 engines is full-time 4WD, making Dakota the only compact pickup with 4WD that can be left engaged on all surfaces. Rear antilock brakes are standard; 4-wheel ABS is optional.

PERFORMANCE Dakota is a comfortable, refined, and highly capable truck. It's the only non-full-size pickup to offer a V8, and the new 4.7 smoothly furnishes strong acceleration. We've had no opportunity to calculate fuel economy, but the same V8 averaged 16.1 mpg in our test '99 Grand Cherokee in mostly highway driving. The 4-cylinder is too weak for a vehicle of this size, but the V6 provides adequate acceleration and is a sensible compromise in price and performance. The R/T has strong acceleration, but is hampered by a rough ride and lack of 4WD. Dakota feels impressively solid on rough roads. The 2WD models have a comfortable, stable ride that resists bounding on wavy surfaces. The 4x4s jiggle more over bumps. Our most-recent test Club Cab was quieter overall than some Dodge passenger cars.

ACCOMMODATIONS Dakota is slightly roomier than compact pickups, but the Club Cab's rear bench still doesn't have enough leg room for adults. Worse, lack of a third door means getting to that back seat is a squeeze, the tip/slide front passenger seat notwithstanding . The new Quad Cab's rear doors aren't technically full-size, but they open independently of the front doors and make entry and exit much more convenient. The Quad Cab also has more rear leg room than any rival's extended cab, although long-legged adults still will find their knees pressed into the front seatback.

Dakota's dashboard holds no surprises, and outward visibility is good. The quality of interior materials is equal to that of most rivals. The demise of the slow-selling 8-foot cargo bed demonstrates that Dakota's principle appeal is as a personal-use pickup rather than as a work-oriented hauler.

VALUE FOR THE MONEY Dakota is a good solution for those who don't need a full-size pickup but want more power, space, and towing capacity than a compact. With the advantages of optional V8 power, full-time 4WD, and the Quad Cab, it's a Best Buy.

ENGINES	ohv I4	ohv V6	ohc V8	ohv V8
Size, liters/cu. in.	2.5/150	3.9/239	4.7/287	5.9/360
Horsepower @ rpm	120 @ 5200	175 @ 4800	235 @ 4800	250 @ 4400
Torque (lbs./ft.) @ rpm	145 @ 3250	225 @ 3200	295 @ 3200	345 @ 3200
Availability	S	O[1]	O	O[2]
EPA city/highway mpg				
5-speed OD manual	20/25	16/22[3]	14/18	
4-speed OD automatic		16/21[4]	14/17	12/17

1. Standard in Quad Cab and 4WD models. 2. Quad Cab; required w/R/T package. 3. 15/19 w/4WD. 4. 14/18 w/4WD. 5. 13/16 w/4WD.

PRICES

Dodge Dakota	Retail Price	Dealer Invoice
2WD regular cab	$13555	$12348
4WD regular cab	17030	15436
2WD Club Cab	16750	15190
4WD Club Cab	19955	18040
2WD Quad Cab	18790	17174
4WD Quad Cab	21615	19521
Destination charge	520	520

STANDARD EQUIPMENT:

Regular cab: 2.5-liter 4-cylinder engine, 5-speed manual transmission,

Prices are accurate at time of publication; subject to manufacturer's changes.

driver- and passenger-side airbags, rear antilock brakes, power steering, vinyl bench seat, tachometer, AM/FM/cassette, digital clock, variable intermittent wipers, passenger-side visor mirror, black vinyl floor covering, manual outside mirrors, painted front and argent rear step bumper, 215/75R15 tires, full-size spare tire. **4WD** models add: part-time 4-wheel drive, two-speed transfer case, 3.9-liter V6 engine.

Club Cab adds: cloth upholstery, 40/20/40 split front bench seat, rear split folding bench seat, carpeting, behind-seat storage compartments, deep-tinted rear glass. **4WD** models add: part-time 4-wheel drive, two-speed transfer case, 3.9-liter V6 engine.

Quad Cab adds: 3.9-liter V6 engine, two rear doors, 215/75R15 white-letter tires, alloy wheels. **4WD** models add: part-time 4-wheel drive, 2-speed transfer case, 235/75R15 white letter tires.

OPTIONAL EQUIPMENT:
Major Packages

	Retail Price	Dealer Invoice
Bonus Discount,		
2WD Club Cab w/2.5-liter engine (credit)	($200)	($170)
2WD Club Cab w/3.9-liter or 4.7-liter engine (credit)	(560)	(476)
Quick Order Sport Pkg., 2WD regular cab	1635	1390
Manufacturer's discount price	985	837
Quick Order Sport Pkg., 4WD regular cab	1815	1543
Manufacturer's discount price	1165	990

Cloth 40/20/40 split bench seat (regular cab), upgraded door trim, carpeting (regular cab), Sport Group (color-keyed grille, front and rear color-keyed fascia, Sport badging, alloy wheels), 215/75R15 white-letter tires (2WD), 235/75R15 white-letter tires (4WD).

Quick Order Sport Pkg., 2WD Club Cab	980	833
Manufacturer's discount price	NC	NC
Quick Order Sport Pkg., 4WD Club Cab	1145	973
Manufacturer's discount price	NC	NC

Cloth 40/20/40 split bench seat (regular cab), upgraded door trim, carpeting (regular cab), Sport Group (color-keyed grille, front and rear color-keyed fascia, Sport badging, alloy wheels), 215/75R15 white-letter tires (2WD), 235/75R15 white-letter tires (4WD).

Quick Order Sport Plus Pkg.,		
2WD regular cab	1430	1216
Manufacturer's discount price	1145	973
Quick Order Sport Plus Pkg.,		
4WD regular cab	1465	1245
Manufacturer's discount price	1180	1003

Air conditioning, Light Group (regular cab, Club Cab), fog lights, rear stabilizer bar, 255/65R15 tires (2WD), 31x10.5R15 white-letter tires (4WD). Regular cab and Club Cab require Sport Pkg., 3.9-liter or 5.2-liter engine. NA with R/T Pkg.

Quick Order Sport Plus Pkg., 2WD Club Cab	1465	1245
Manufacturer's discount price	1115	947
Quick Order Sport Plus Pkg., 4WD Club Cab	1475	1254
Manufacturer's discount price	1125	956

Air conditioning, Light Group (regular cab, Club Cab), fog lights, rear stabilizer bar, 255/65R15 tires (2WD), 31x10.5R15 white-letter tires (4WD). Regular cab and Club Cab require Sport Pkg., 3.9-liter or 5.2-liter engine. NA with R/T Pkg.

Quick Order Sport Plus Pkg., 2WD Quad Cab	1310	1114
Manufacturer's discount price	960	816
Quick Order Sport Plus Pkg., 4WD Quad Cab	1320	1122
Manufacturer's discount price	970	824

Air conditioning, Light Group (regular cab, Club Cab), fog lights, rear stabilizer bar, 255/65R15 tires (2WD), 31x10.5R15 white-letter tires (4WD). Regular cab and Club Cab require Sport Pkg., 3.9-liter or 5.2-liter engine. NA with R/T Pkg.

Quick Order SLT Pkg., 2WD regular cab	3010	2559
Manufacturer's discount price	2340	1989
Quick Order SLT Pkg., 4WD regular cab	3190	2712
Manufacturer's discount price	2520	2142

Air conditioning, tilt steering wheel, cruise control, cloth 40/20/40 split bench seat (regular cab), upgraded door trim, up-shift light, carpeting (regular cab), front floormats, SLT Decor Group (heavy-duty sound insulation, chrome bumpers, bright grille, alloy wheels), Light Group (mini overhead console, glovebox and courtesy lights, cargo box and underhood lights, auxiliary power outlet), 215/75R15 white-letter tires (2WD), 235/75R15 white-letter tires (4WD). Requires optional engine.

Quick Order SLT Pkg., 2WD Club Cab	2325	1976
Manufacturer's discount price	1095	930
Quick Order SLT Pkg., 4WD Club Cab	2505	2129

	Retail Price	Dealer Invoice
Manufacturer's discount price	$1275	$1083

Air conditioning, tilt steering wheel, cruise control, cloth 40/20/40 split bench seat (regular cab), upgraded door trim, up-shift light, carpeting (regular cab), front floormats, SLT Decor Group (heavy-duty sound insulation, chrome bumpers, bright grille, alloy wheels), Light Group (mini overhead console, glovebox and courtesy lights, cargo box and underhood lights, auxiliary power outlet), 215/75R15 white-letter tires (2WD), 235/75R15 white-letter tires (4WD). Requires optional engine.

Quick Order SLT Pkg., Quad Cab	1220	1037
Manufacturer's discount price,		
2WD Quad Cab	955	812
4WD Quad Cab	1120	952

Air conditioning, tilt steering wheel, cruise control, floormats, hood insulation, chrome bumpers and grille.

Quick Order SLT Plus Pkg., 2WD regular cab	1075	914
Manufacturer's discount price	625	531
Quick Order SLT Plus Pkg., 2WD Club Cab	1100	935
Manufacturer's discount price	650	552
Quick Order SLT Plus Pkg., 4WD regular cab/Club Cab	1110	944
Manufacturer's discount price	860	731
Quick Order SLT Plus Pkg., 2WD Quad Cab	1275	1084
Manufacturer's discount price	825	701
Quick Order SLT Plus Pkg., 4WD Quad Cab	1285	1092
Manufacturer's discount price	1035	879

Power mirrors, power windows, power door locks, remote keyless entry, rear stabilizer bar, 255/65R15 tires (2WD), 31x10.5R15 white-letter tires (4WD). Requires SLT Pkg.

R/T Pkg., 2WD regular cab	2370	2015
2WD Club Cab	2410	2049

Includes limited-slip differential, lowered sport suspension, cloth high back bucket seats, upgraded door panels, leather-wrapped tilt steering wheel, cruise control, Light Group, heavy-duty sound insulation, fog lights, color-keyed bumpers, wheel flares, 255/55R17 tires. Requires Quick Order Sport Pkg., 5.9-liter V8 engine, 4-speed automatic transmission.

Deluxe Convenience Group	390	332

Cruise control, tilt steering column. NA 2.5-liter engine.

Power Convenience Group,		
regular cab, Club Cab	570	485
Quad Cab	745	633

Power windows and door locks, remote keyless entry. Requires Quick Order Pkg.

Power Overhead Convenience Group,		
regular cab/Club Cab w/SLT Pkg.	755	642
regular cab/Club Cab w/Sport Pkg.	785	667
Quad Cab	930	791

Power Convenience Group plus overhead console w/storage, trip computer, compass, outside temperature indicator, automatic day/night rearview mirror.

Light Group, regular cab	145	123
Club Cab	155	132

Mini overhead console, glovebox and courtesy lights, cargo box and underhood lights, auxiliary power outlet.

2WD Club Cab w/Quick Order Pkg.	185	157
Trailer Tow Group,		
4WD regular cab, Club Cab, Quad Cab	275	234

Class IV trailer-hitch receiver, 4-wire adapter. Requires Heavy Duty Service Group.

Powertrains

3.9-liter V6 engine, 2WD regular cab/Club Cab	560	476
4.7-liter V8 engine,		
2WD regular cab/Club Cab	1090	927
4WD regular cab/Club Cab, Quad Cab	590	502
Regular cab and Club Cab require Quick Order Pkg.		
5.9-liter V8 engine,		
2WD regular cab/Club Cab	1685	1432
2WD Quad Cab	1190	1012
4WD Quad Cab	1125	956

Requires 4-speed automatic transmission. Regular cab and Club Cab require Quick Order Sport Pkg., R/T Pkg.

Manual transmission, 2WD	NC	NC
Manufacturer's discount price,		
regular cab, Club Cab (credit)	(200)	(170)

Requires 2.5-liter engine.

	Retail Price	Dealer Invoice
4-speed automatic transmission	$975	$829

2WD regular cab requires 3.9- or 5.2-liter engine.

Optional axle ratio	40	34
Limited-slip differential	285	242

2WD requires optional axle ratio when ordered with V8 engine. 4WD requires optional axle ratio ordered with standard V6 engine.

Full-time 4WD, 4WD	395	336

Requires 4.7-liter engine, automatic transmission. Regular cab, Club Cab require Sport Pkg. or SLT Pkg.

Safety Features

Front and rear anti-lock brakes	495	421

Comfort and Convenience

Air conditioning	800	680
6-way power driver seat, Club Cab, Quad Cab	320	272

Club Cab requires Sport Pkg. or SLT Pkg.

Cloth/vinyl bucket seats	200	170

Includes center console. Requires Quick Order Pkg.

5x7 power mirrors	140	119

Regular cab and Club Cab require Quick Order Pkg.

AM/FM/cassette w/equalizer	300	255

Includes Infinity sound system. Regular cab and Club Cab require Quick Order Pkg.

AM/FM/CD player w/equalizer	480	408

Includes Infinity sound system. Regular cab and Club Cab require Quick Order Pkg.

AM/FM/cassette/CD player w/equalizer	660	561

Includes Infinity sound system. Regular cab and Club Cab require Quick Order Pkg.

Steering wheel radio controls	75	64

Requires leather-wrapped steering wheel and AM/FM/cassette/CD player.

Tilt steering wheel	140	119
Leather-wrapped steering wheel	50	43

Requires Deluxe Convenience Group.

Fog lights	120	102

Regular cab and Club Cab require Quick Order Pkg.

Sliding rear window	115	98

Special Purpose, Wheels and Tires

Heavy-duty engine cooling,		
ordered w/manual transmission	60	51
ordered w/automatic transmission	120	102
Heavy-Duty Service Group,		
ordered w/manual transmission	120	102
ordered w/automatic transmission	180	153

Includes heavy-duty engine cooling, transmission oil cooling, power steering fluid cooling, heavy-duty battery and alternator.

Tire and Handling Pkg., 2WD regular cab	365	310
2WD Club Cab/Quad Cab	390	332
4WD	400	340

Rear stabilizer bar (4WD regular cab, Club Cab), 255/65R15 tires (2WD), 31x10.5R15 white-letter tires, alloy wheels. Requires Quick Order Pkg. NA with 2.5-liter engine.

235/75R15 tires, regular cab, Club Cab	190	162
regular cab/Club Cab w/Quick Order Pkg., Quad Cab	65	55

DODGE DURANGO

RECOMMENDED

Dodge Durango 4WD Sport

Rear- or 4-wheel-drive midsize sport-utility vehicle
Base price range: $25,975-$27,975. Built in USA. **Also consider:** Chevrolet Blazer, Ford Explorer, Jeep Grand Cherokee

FOR • Passenger and cargo room • Acceleration (5.9-liter V8)
AGAINST • Rear-seat comfort • Fuel economy

Durango for 2000 shares a 4.7-liter V8 with the Jeep Grand Cherokee, and at midyear, introduces a sporty R/T version. In size and powertrains, Durango slots between the midsize and full-size SUV classes.

Durango comes with rear- or 4-wheel drive. The base 4WD system is for slippery surfaces only. Standard on R/T Durangos and optional on other 4X4s is a full-time system that allows 4WD to remain engaged on all surfaces. A 230-horsepower overhead valve 5.2-liter V8 is standard on 2WD Durangos. Newly standard on 4x4s, the 4.7-liter V8 has an overhead-cam design and 235 hp. Standard on the new R/T and available on Durangos equipped with the SLT option package is a 245-hp 5.9-liter V8. All engines use automatic transmission. Rear antilock brakes are standard, 4-wheel ABS is optional.

Front bucket seats and a 3-place rear bench are standard. A front bench is available, as is a 2-place third-row seat. Newly standard for 2000 is Chrysler's Enhanced Accident Response system, which lights the interior and unlocks power door locks when air bags deploy. A revised front suspension with rack and pinion steering also is new for 4x4s. The SLT package includes body-color exterior trim and fog lamps; the SLT Plus package for 4WD models adds leather upholstery and 31-inch tires with wheel-arch flares. The new R/T builds on the SLT Plus package, adding special 17-inch alloy wheels, R/T emblems, unique shock absorber tuning, and leather and suede interior trim, among other features.

PERFORMANCE The 4.7 V8 is smoother than the old 5.2, and just as strong—both have a towing capacity of around 6000 pounds. Stronger yet is the 5.9, which has a 7400-pound towing rating, similar to that of some full-size SUVs. The transmission used with the 4.7 is newer than the one used with the other V8s. Both automatics provide smooth, prompt upshifts, though 5.2- and 5.9-liter Durangos we tested suffered some sloppy, harsh downshifts. The 4.7 should do slightly better than the 12.4 mpg we averaged in a test of a 5.2-liter 4x4 Durango; a test 5.9-liter Durango averaged just 11.2 mpg.

Durango doesn't feel ponderous despite the usual SUV body lean and nose plowing in fast turns. Its ride is absorbent and composed even on bumpy roads, and directional stability is good. Durango has front-disc/rear-drum brakes and they don't stop this large vehicle with confidence. Braking is little improved with the 4-wheel ABS, which is standard on most rivals, but an option on Durango.

ACCOMMODATIONS Durango uses its size well, providing generous shoulder width and head room. Unfortunately, the available third-row seat is just as tight and hard to access as those in full-size SUVs. And seat padding is uncomfortably thin in both the second and third row. Demerits, too, for thick side pillars and rear headrests that impede driver vision, a climate system that won't feed air to floor and face vents simultaneously, and for an overly long stretch to the floor-mounted 4WD transfer-case lever.

On the plus side, large doors and modest step-in height make for easy entry/exit, there's enough space behind the third seat for a week's groceries, and the middle and rear benches fold flat in seconds to open up ample cargo room. Workmanship is solid, but the cabin is less dressy than most rivals, with an abundance of hard plastic surfaces and some exposed screw heads.

VALUE FOR THE MONEY Durango approaches full-size SUVs for roominess and power but sells at midsize-SUV prices. That merits our Recommended rating.

ENGINES	ohc V8	ohv V8	ohv V8
Size, liters/cu. in.	4.7/287	5.2/318	5.9/360
Horsepower @ rpm	235 @ 4800	230 @ 4400	245 @ 4000
Torque (lbs./ft.) @ rpm	295 @ 3200	300 @ 3200	335 @ 3200
Availability	S[1]	S[2]	O[3]
EPA city/highway mpg			
4-speed OD automatic	14/17	14/19	12/17[4]

1. 4WD. 2. 2WD. 3. requires SLT package; standard w/R/T 4. 12/16 w/4WD.

PRICES

Dodge Durango	Retail Price	Dealer Invoice
Base 4-door wagon 2WD	$25975	$23473

Prices are accurate at time of publication; subject to manufacturer's changes.

	Retail Price	Dealer Invoice
Base 4-door wagon 4WD	$27975	$25258
Destination charge	535	535

R/T equipment and prices not available at time of publication.

STANDARD EQUIPMENT:

Base: 5.2-liter V8 engine, 4-speed automatic transmission, driver- and passenger-side airbags, rear antilock brakes, front air conditioning, variable-assist power steering, tilt steering wheel, cruise control, cloth/vinyl upholstery, front split bench seat, split folding second row seat, cupholders, power 5x7-inch mirrors, power windows, power door locks, remote keyless entry, AM/FM/cassette w/four speakers, digital clock, visor mirrors, map lights, variable intermittent wipers, tachometer, auxiliary power outlets, rear defogger, intermittent rear wiper/washer, deep-tinted rear glass, full-size spare, 235/75R15 tires, 15x7 alloy wheels. **4WD** model adds: part-time 4-wheel drive, 4.7-liter V8 engine, front suspension skid plate.

OPTIONAL EQUIPMENT:
Major Packages

SLT Quick Order Pkg.	1230	1046
Manufacturer's discount price	915	778

Front bucket seats, 6-way power driver seat, center console, upgrade interior door panels, floormats, hood insulation, roof rack, fog lights, body-colored bumpers and bodyside moldings, 235/75R15 white-letter tires.

SLT Plus Quick Order Pkg., 2WD	2360	2006
Manufacturer's discount price, 2WD	2060	1751
SLT Plus Pkg., 4WD	2615	2223
Manufacturer's discount price, 4WD	2315	1968

Leather upholstery, AM/FM/cassette/CD player, Infinity sound system, steering wheel radio controls, woodgrain instrument panel, overhead console, trip computer, compass, outside temperature indicator, automatic day/night rearview mirror, illuminated visor mirrors, theft-deterrent system w/alarm, fender flares, 31x10.5R15 white-letter tires (4WD), 15x8 alloy wheels (2WD). Requires SLT Quick Order Pkg. 2WD deletes white letter tires.

Overhead Convenience Group	410	349

Includes illuminated visor mirrors, automatic day/night rearview mirror, overhead console, compass, trip computer, outside-temperature indicator, reading lights. Requires SLT Pkg.

Trailer Tow Prep Group	275	234

Includes 7-wire harness, platform hitch. Requires Heavy-Duty Service Group.

Powertrains

5.9-liter V8 engine	595	506
Requires SLT Pkg.		
Full-time 4WD, 4WD	395	336
Limited-slip differential	285	242

Safety Features

Front and rear anti-lock brakes	495	421

Comfort and Convenience

Rear air conditioning	430	366
Heated power 6x9-inch mirrors	75	64
Requires SLT Pkg.		
Third row seat	550	468
AM/FM/cassette/CD player	300	255
Infinity 8-speaker sound system	330	281

Appearance and Miscellaneous

Theft-deterrent system	150	128
Running boards	395	336
Requires SLT Pkg.		
Fog lights	120	102

Special Purpose, Wheels and Tires

Heavy-Duty Service Group	240	204
Heavy-duty alternator and battery, maximum engine cooling.		
Skid Plate Group, 4WD	130	111
Fuel tank and transfer case skid plates.		
Tire, Wheel and Flare Pkg., 2WD	250	213
Wheel flares, 235/75R15 tires, 15x8 alloy wheels.		
31x10.5R15 white-letter tires, 4WD	465	395
Includes fender flares.		

DODGE INTREPID

✓ **BEST BUY**

Dodge Intrepid ES

Front-wheel-drive full-size car; similar to Chrysler Concorde, LHS and 300M

Base price range: $20,390-$22,085. Built in Canada. **Also consider:** Buick LeSabre, Pontiac Bonneville, Toyota Avalon

FOR • Passenger and cargo room • Ride • Steering/handling
AGAINST • Trunk liftover • Rear visibility

A performance-oriented R/T model due in early calendar 2000 headlines changes to Dodge's full-size sedan. Intrepid shares its basic design with the Chrysler Concorde, but has different styling.

Base and ES versions return this fall. The base model gets standard 16 inch wheels in place of 15s and adds a power sunroof to its options list. On the ES, antilock brakes are no longer standard but are optional, as on the base model.

The standard 2.7-liter V6 makes 200 horsepower in the base model and 202 in the ES. Optional on the ES is a 225-hp 3.2-liter V6. The R/T will use a 242-hp 3.5-liter V6. The only transmission is a 4-speed automatic, but the ES and R/T get Chrysler's Autostick, an automatic that can be shifted manually.

Front bucket seats and a floor shift lever are standard on Intrepid, but the base model offers an optional front bench seat and column shift for 6-passenger seating. The R/T gets unique trim, standard antilock brakes, and 17-inch wheels.

PERFORMANCE Poised and controlled, Intrepid is among the best-handling full-size sedans, with a ride that is firm and stable without being harsh over rough pavement. Stops are short and straight, with fine pedal modulation.

The 2.7-liter engine in the '99 Intrepids we tested felt a bit sluggish. The 3.2 is no powerhouse, but Autostick helps it scoot through traffic, and passing and merging are surer. Our test '99 3.2-liter ES averaged 20.7 mpg; fuel economy with the 2.7 shouldn't be much different. Both engines are smooth and quiet. Road noise is par for the class, and wind noise is noticeable but not excessive. We have not yet tested an R/T.

ACCOMMODATIONS A spacious interior is an Intrepid high point, though the sloping roofline has tall rear-seaters brushing the headliner. Six-footers get enough leg room to be comfortable in all outboard positions, and the rear seat is wide enough for three adults. Rear entry is hurt by the back door's shape, but ingress and egress is otherwise great.

The radio is a stretch to reach and it takes some study to sort out, but other controls and gauges are close by and intelligently designed. Interior assembly is sound, though an abundance of hard plastic surfaces is at odds with the cabin's pleasing design. The ES's split folding rear seatback is a smart touch and the huge trunk has a flat floor that extends so far forward, a sliding cargo bin would be a great idea. Liftover is high, and the trunk opening is narrower than on the Concorde. Intrepid has a larger rear window than Concorde, but the high rear parcel shelf hurts visibility nonetheless.

VALUE FOR THE MONEY It doesn't have as strong a reputation for reliability as some competitors, but Intrepid is roomy, athletic, eye-catching, and competitively priced.

ENGINES

	dohc V6	ohc V6	ohc V6
Size, liters/cu. in.	2.7/167	3.2/197	3.5/215
Horsepower @ rpm	200 @ 5800	225 @ 6300	242 @ 6400
Torque (lbs./ft.) @ rpm	190 @ 4850	225 @ 3800	248 @ 3950
Availability	S[1]	O[2]	S[3]

EPA city/highway mpg			
4-speed OD automatic	21/30	18/28	NA

1. Base, ES. 2. ES. 3. R/T

PRICES

Dodge Intrepid	Retail Price	Dealer Invoice
Base 4-door sedan	$20390	$18677
ES 4-door sedan	22085	20186
Destination charge	560	560

R/T equipment and prices not available at time of publication.

STANDARD EQUIPMENT:

Base: 2.7-liter dohc V6 engine, 4-speed automatic transmission, driver- and passenger-side airbags, 4-wheel disc brakes, air conditioning, power steering, tilt steering wheel, cruise control, cloth upholstery, front bucket seats, center console, power mirrors, power windows, power door locks, rear defogger, variable intermittent wipers, AM/FM/cassette with four speakers, digital clock, tachometer, visor mirrors, map lights, power remote decklid release, automatic-off headlights, floormats, 225/60R16 tires, wheel covers.

ES adds: 4-speed automatic transmission w/manual-shift capability, 8-way power driver seat w/lumbar adjustment, split folding rear seat w/trunk pass-through, leather-wrapped steering wheel, remote keyless entry, fog lights, alloy wheels.

OPTIONAL EQUIPMENT:
Major Packages

	Retail	Dealer
Quick Order Pkg. 23/24L, ES	NC	NC
Manufacturer's discount price, (credit)	(115)	(102)
Standard Equipment.		
Quick Order Pkg. 24M, ES	3045	2710
Manufacturer's discount price	2560	2279

Leather upholstery, 8-way power front seats, automatic climate control, AM/FM/cassette w/4-disc CD changer and 9-speaker sound system, automatic day/night rearview mirror, trip computer, illuminated visor mirrors, universal garage door opener, theft-deterrent system w/alarm, full-size spare tire.

Powertrains

3.2-liter V6 engine, ES	500	445

Safety Features

Antilock brakes	600	534

ES with Quick Order Pkg. 24M includes traction control.

Comfort and Convenience

Power sunroof	895	797
Remote keyless entry, Base	225	200
AM/FM/cassette/CD player	575	512
Includes 8-speaker sound system.		
Front split bench seat, Base	100	89
8-way power driver seat, Base	380	338
Smoker's Group	20	18
Includes ashtrays and lighter.		

DODGE/PLYMOUTH NEON

RECOMMENDED

Dodge Neon 4-door

Front-wheel-drive subcompact car

Base price: $12,460. Built in USA . **Also consider:** Chevrolet Cavalier, Ford Focus, Honda Civic, Saturn S-Series, Toyota Corolla

FOR • Fuel economy • Steering/handling **AGAINST** • Noise • Automatic transmission performance

An in-dash 4-disc CD changer is a new option this fall on the little-changed Neon. This subcompact was redesigned for an early-1999

debut as a 2000 model and is sold in nearly identical form by Dodge and Plymouth dealers.

A 4-door sedan is the only body style and comes in base trim, called Highline, and as a better-equipped version called ES by Dodge and LX by Plymouth. The only engine is a 132-horsepower overhead-cam 4-cylinder. Manual transmission is standard, a 3-speed automatic is optional. The manual transmission gets revised gear ratios intended to improve performance and fuel economy. Antilock 4-wheel disc brakes are optional and are packaged with traction control. Unlike some competitors, Neon doesn't offer side airbags. Among new standard features this fall is a cassette player and a leather shift boot for the manual transmission.

PERFORMANCE Compared to the 1995-1999 generation, Neon's roughest edges have been smoothed out, but this version's modest acceleration remains a negative point. These subcompacts are lively enough with manual transmission, but highway passing demands a downshift from fifth gear to third. The optional 3-speed automatic drastically dulls off-the-line punch; most other cars in this class offer a 4-speed automatic for better acceleration from a stop. Our test Neons averaged a pleasant 24 mpg with automatic transmission and mostly highway driving, and 25.3 with manual transmission in a more-even mix of city and freeway work.

Neon absorbs most bumps well and its sporty steering and handling are true to the original's fun-to-drive character. Wind and road noise are noticeable but are not as intrusive as the engine, which groans loudly under hard throttle.

ACCOMMODATIONS Neon is roomy and comfortable for a subcompact, but it makes some concessions to its small size and low price. The driver sits in an alert, upright position. Both front buckets are comfortable and offer plenty of head room. In back, leg room is sufficient and seat comfort adequate, but head clearance is tight for those over 5-foot-8 or so.

Gauges are generously sized and look dressy, but lose contrast in dim light with the headlamps on. Available heated power mirrors are a nice feature in this price range, but the power-window option is for front windows only. A high parcel shelf restricts the driver's view directly aft.

Seat fabrics feel rich, and while there's a surplus of hard plastic on dashboard and doors, it doesn't look or feel cheap. Three cupholders are molded into the front console, with a fourth serving rear passengers when the console lid is open. Doorways are fairly large, but the rear-door shape hinders entry and exit. Trunk volume is good for this class, but liftover is high and the lid hinges dip into the load area.

VALUE FOR THE MONEY Tepid acceleration notwithstanding, Neon is a fairly refined and well-equipped subcompact that's priced attractively enough to earn our recommendation. Better yet for small-car shoppers, Neon sales are slower than expected, so great deals should be available on this Dodge/Plymouth sedan.

ENGINES

	ohc I4
Size, liters/cu. in.	2.0/122
Horsepower @ rpm	132 @ 5600
Torque (lbs./ft.) @ rpm	130 @ 4600
Availability	S

EPA city/highway mpg	
5-speed OD manual	29/39
3-speed automatic	23/32

PRICES

Dodge/Plymouth Neon	Retail Price	Dealer Invoice
Highline 4-door sedan	$12460	$11499
Destination charge	510	510

STANDARD EQUIPMENT:

Highline: 2.0-liter 4-cylinder engine, 5-speed manual transmission, driver- and passenger-side airbags, power steering, tilt steering wheel, cloth bucket seats, storage armrest, cupholders, split folding rear seat, AM/FM/cassette w/CD changer controls, variable intermittent wipers, rear defogger, passenger-side visor mirror, auxiliary power outlet, remote decklid release, floormats, dual outside mirrors, 185/65R14 tires, wheel covers.

OPTIONAL EQUIPMENT:
Major Packages

ES/LX Pkg.	2540	2261

Prices are accurate at time of publication; subject to manufacturer's changes.

	Retail Price	Dealer Invoice
Manufacturer's discount price	$1790	$1593

Air conditioning, leather-wrapped steering wheel and shift knob, upgraded upholstery, heated power mirrors, power front windows, Sentry Group (power door locks, remote keyless entry, power trunk release, tachometer, theft-deterrent system), fog lights, ES badging (Dodge), LX badging (Plymouth), 185/60R15 tires.

Value/Fun Group	1865	1660
Manufacturer's discount price	995	886

Power sunroof, heated power mirrors, power front windows and door locks, remote keyless entry, power decklid release, theft-deterrent system. Requires air conditioning.

Sentry Key Security Group	730	650
Manufacturer's discount price	315	281

Power door locks, remote keyless entry, power decklid release, tachometer, theft-deterrent system. Requires air conditioning.

Power Convenience Group	380	338

Power front windows, heated power mirrors. Requires Security Group, air conditioning.

Light Group	130	116

Illuminated visor mirrors, courtesy/reading lights, engine compartment light. Requires air conditioning.

Powertrains

3-speed automatic transmission	600	534

Safety Features

Anti-Lock Brake Group	840	748
ordered w/ES/LX Pkg.	740	659
Manufacturer's discount price	595	530

Antilock 4-wheel disc brakes, traction control, tachometer.

Comfort and Convenience

Air conditioning	1000	890
Cruise control	225	200
Requires ES/LX Pkg.		
4-disc CD changer	375	334
Smoker's Pkg.	20	18
Alloy wheels	410	365
ordered w/ES/LX Pkg.	355	316

Includes 185/60R15 tires. Requires air conditioning.

DODGE RAM 1500

RECOMMENDED

Dodge Ram 1500 4WD w/Off Road Group

Rear- or 4-wheel-drive full-size pickup truck; similar to Dodge Ram 2500/3500

Base price range: $14,895-$23,850. Built in USA and Mexico.
Also consider: Chevrolet Silverado 1500, Ford F-150, GMC Sierra 1500, Toyota Tundra

FOR • Interior room • Acceleration (V8s) **AGAINST** • Fuel economy • Acceleration (V6) • Rear-seat comfort

Introduction of an off-road option targets the tough side of Dodge's full-size pickup for 2000, while a new luxury package accentuates its softer side. All Rams get revised front suspension and steering systems aimed at improving ride and directional stability. This report covers the half-ton Ram 1500. Dodge also sells three-quarter ton 2500s and one-ton 3500 models.

Ram offers regular cabs and extended Club Cabs with two front doors. Quad Cabs are extended-cab models with two rear-hinged back doors. Regular cabs and Quad Cabs have a 6.5- or 8-foot cargo bed. Club Cabs get only the 6.5-foot bed for 2000; they had been available with both bed lengths. WS (Work Special) models come with a bench seat; all other Rams get a 40/20/40 split bench. Club and Quad Cabs have a 3-place rear bench seat for 6-passen-

ger capacity.

A 3.9-liter V6 is standard on the 2-wheel-drive regular cab. A 5.2-liter V8 is optional on that model and standard on all other Ram 1500s. A 5.9-liter V8 is optional on all. Manual transmission is standard with the V6 and 5.2 V8. Automatic is standard with the 5.9, optional with the other engines. Ram's 4-wheel drive is a part-time system not for use on dry pavement. Rear antilock brakes are standard, 4-wheel ABS is optional.

The new Off Road Group is for short-bed, regular-cab and Quad Cab 4WD Rams. It brings increased ground clearance and wheel travel, 17-inch alloy wheels, a limited-slip differential, tow hooks, skid plates, and other heavy-duty equipment. The new SLT Plus luxury package is optional on Quad Cabs. It includes power heated leather seats, a CD player with steering-wheel audio controls, and keyless entry with security alarm. A tachometer and underhood light are now standard on all models.

PERFORMANCE The V6 doesn't cut it in this full-size rig. Either V8 provides more-than-adequate acceleration, but the 5.9 is the better choice for hauling heavy loads or towing more than 4000 pounds. Our test 5.9-liter Rams averaged 12.4 mpg to 14.4 mpg—not great, but not much worse than the 5.2 averages. Ford and GM offer the convenience of shifting in and out of 4WD via a dashboard button; Ram has only a hard-to-reach floor lever. And the Chevy Silverado and GMC Sierra are alone among big pickups with 4WD that can be used on dry pavement. Spending $350 on Ram's 4-wheel ABS option is well worth the money. Rams don't take corners or absorb bumps quite as well as the new GM rigs, and their steering isn't as precise as the F-150's. But they perform most tasks with little drama.

ACCOMMODATIONS Ram has a roomy regular cab, with ample head space and leg room, plus adequate behind-the-seat storage via plastic bins, shelves, and a cargo net. With their rear doors, Quad Cabs afford much better access to the extended-cabin's rear compartment than do Club Cabs. But their rear-door handles are inside and are blocked by the front seatbacks. And there are no assist handles to help aft passengers climb in or out. As in the Ford F-Series and Toyota Tundra extended-cabs, the Ram's rear seat is hard, upright, and cramped; Silverado and Sierra are most comfortable in this regard. Ram's painted-on instrument markings and its interior materials shout low-budget, but workmanship is truck-tough.

VALUE FOR THE MONEY Popular because of its big-rig styling, Ram earns our recommendation for its functional design and competitive prices.

ENGINES

	ohv V6	ohv V8	ohv V8
Size, liters/cu. in.	3.9/239	5.2/318	5.9/360
Horsepower @ rpm	175 @ 4800	230 @ 4400	245 @ 4000
Torque (lbs./ft.) @ rpm	230 @ 3200	300 @ 3200	335 @ 3200
Availability	S[1]	S[2]	O[3]
EPA city/highway mpg			
5-speed OD manual...........................	15/21	13/18[4]	
4-speed OD automatic........................	15/20	13/19[5]	13/17[6]

1. 2WD exc. Lariat. 2. Lariat, 4WD SuperCab and SuperCrew; optional 2WD. 3. Lightning. 4. 15/18 w/4WD. 5. 14/17 w/4WD. 6. 13/16 w/4WD.

PRICES

Dodge Ram 1500	Retail Price	Dealer Invoice
WS 2WD regular cab short bed	$14895	$13613
WS 2WD regular cab long bed	15165	13850
ST 2WD regular cab short bed	16675	14679
ST 2WD regular cab long bed	16960	14921
ST 4WD regular cab short bed	20435	17925
ST 4WD regular cab long bed	20775	18214
ST 2WD Club Cab short bed	19460	17076
ST 4WD Club Cab short bed	22720	19982
ST 2WD Quad Cab short bed	20320	17827
ST 2WD Quad Cab long bed	20600	18065
ST 4WD Quad Cab short bed	23520	20572
ST 4WD Quad Cab long bed	23850	20853
Destination charge	650	650

STANDARD EQUIPMENT:

WS: 3.9-liter V6 engine, 5-speed manual transmission, antilock rear

Ratings begin on page 213. Specifications begin on page 220. CONSUMER GUIDE™

brakes, driver- and passenger-side airbags, variable-assist power steering, vinyl bench seat, cupholders, tachometer, variable intermittent wipers, auxiliary power outlet, black-rubber floor covering, manual 6x9-inch outside mirrors, removable tailgate, full-size spare tire, 225/75R16 tires.

ST regular cab adds: vinyl 40/20/40 split bench seat, AM/FM/cassette, digital clock, behind-seat modular storage system, cargo box light, chrome front and rear bumpers, bright wheel trim rings and chrome hub caps. **4WD** models add: part-time 4-wheel drive, 2-speed transfer case, 5.2-liter V8 engine.

ST Club Cab/ST Quad Cab adds: 5.2-liter V8 engine, rear folding bench seat, right- and left-side rear cab doors (Quad Cab). **4WD** models add: part-time 4-wheel drive, 2-speed transfer case, 245/75R16 tires.

OPTIONAL EQUIPMENT:

	Retail Price	Dealer Invoice
Major Packages		
SLT Pkg.,		
ST regular cab, 2WD Club/Quad Cab	$3000	$2550
Manufacturer's discount price	2300	1955

Laramie SLT Decor Group (leather-wrapped steering wheel, heated power mirrors, passenger-side visor mirror, premium cloth upholstery, carpeting, bodyside moldings, front-bumper sight shields, floormats), air conditioning, cruise control, tilt steering wheel, power windows and door locks, Light Group, 245/75R16 tires (2WD,4WD regular cab), alloy wheels. 2WD regular cab requires 5.2- or 5.9-liter engine.

SLT Pkg., 4WD Club Cab/Quad Cab	2870	2440
Manufacturer's discount price	2170	1845

Laramie SLT Decor Group (leather-wrapped steering wheel, heated power mirrors, passenger-side visor mirror, premium cloth upholstery, carpeting, bodyside moldings, front-bumper sight shields, floormats), air conditioning, cruise control, tilt steering wheel, power windows and door locks, Light Group, 245/75R16 tires (2WD,4WD regular cab), alloy wheels. 2WD regular cab requires 5.2- or 5.9-liter engine.

SLT Plus Pkg., 2WD Quad Cab	4855	4127
Manufacturer's discount price	4155	3532
SLT Plus Pkg., 4WD Quad Cab	4725	4016
Manufacturer's discount price	4025	3421

SLT Pkg. plus leather upholstery, woodgrain instrument panel, heated seats, heated power mirrors. Requires SLT Plus Decor Group, 5.9-liter V8 engine.

SLT Plus Decor Group, Quad Cab	2090	1777

Front and rear antilock brakes, AM/FM/cassette/CD player, Infinity sound system, steering wheel radio controls, remote keyless entry, overhead console, trip computer, automatic day/night rearview mirror, illuminated visor mirrors, rear underseat storage, theft-deterrent system w/alarm, fog lights. Requires SLT Plus Pkg.

Deluxe Convenience Group	390	332
Tilt steering wheel, cruise control.		
Sport Appearance Group, 2WD w/SLT Pkg.	505	429
4WD w/SLT Pkg.	790	672

Quad headlights, color-keyed front bumper and grille, color-keyed rear bumper, Sport decal, fog lights, 245/75R16 white-letter tires (2WD), 265/75R16 on/off-road white-letter tires (4WD), alloy wheels.

Off-Road Group,		
4WD short bed w/manual trans.	1615	1373

Limited-slip differential, performance axle ratio, Heavy Duty Service Group, skid plates, fog lights, tow hooks, LT275/70R17 on/off road tires. Requires SLT Pkg. NA with front and rear antilock brakes.

Off Road Group,		
4WD short bed w/automatic trans.	1745	1483

Limited-slip differential, performance axle ratio, Heavy Duty Service Group, skid plates, fog lights, tow hooks, LT275/70R17 on/off road tires. Requires SLT Pkg. NA with front and rear antilock brakes.

Travel Convenience Group, ST	345	293

Overhead console (includes trip computer, compass, outside-temperature indicator, reading lights), automatic day/night rearview mirror, illuminated visor mirrors. Requires SLT Pkg.

Leather Interior Group,		
regular cab w/SLT Pkg.	1450	1233
Club Cab/Quad Cab w/SLT Pkg.	1590	1352

Leather upholstery, 6-way power driver seat (regular cab) or 8-way power driver seat (Club Cab/Quad Cab), Travel Convenience Group.

Light Group, ST	90	77

Mini overhead console, deluxe headliner, glove box and map lights, underhood light.

	Retail Price	Dealer Invoice
Wheels Plus Group, 2WD ST	$745	$633
Manufacturer's discount price	345	293

Sliding rear window, chrome styled wheels, 245/75R16 white-letter tires.

Wheels Plus Group, 4WD Club/Quad Cab	760	646
4WD regular cab	890	672
Manufacturer's discount price	490	417

Sliding rear window, chrome styled wheels, 245/75R16 white-letter tires.

Snow Plow Prep Pkg.,		
4WD regular cab short bed	85	72
Manufacturer's discount price	NC	NC

Includes heavy-duty front suspension. Requires 5.2-liter engine, Heavy Duty Service Group, Trailer Tow Group.

Trailer Tow Group	275	234

Includes class IV trailer-hitch receiver, adapter plug, heavy-duty flasher. Requires Heavy Duty Service Group. NA with 3.9-liter engine.

Powertrains

5.2-liter V8 engine,		
2WD ST regular cab	590	502
5.9-liter V8 engine,		
2WD ST regular cab	1185	1007
4WD regular cab, Club Cab/Quad Cab	595	506
Requires 4-speed automatic transmission.		
4-speed automatic transmission	975	829
Limited-slip differential, 2WD	285	242

Safety Features

Front and rear antilock brakes	425	361

Comfort and Convenience

Air conditioning	805	684
Heated power 6x9-inch mirrors, ST	145	123
Requires air conditioning.		
Cloth 40/20/40 bench seat, ST	110	94
Cloth/vinyl bench seat, WS	110	94
6-way power driver seat,		
regular cab w/SLT Pkg.	320	272
8-way power driver seat,		
Club Cab/Quad Cab w/SLT Pkg.	360	306
AM/FM/cassette, WS	400	340
AM/FM/cassette w/equalizer,		
ordered w/SLT Pkg.	335	285
AM/FM/CD player w/equalizer,		
ordered w/SLT Pkg.	510	434
AM/FM/cassette/CD w/equalizer,		
ordered w/SLT Pkg.	690	587
Steering wheel radio controls, ST	75	64
Requires SLT Pkg., AM/FM/cassette/CD player, remote keyless entry.		
Remote keyless entry,		
ordered w/SLT Pkg.	190	162

Appearance and Miscellaneous

Fog lights, ordered w/SLT Pkg.	140	119
Sliding rear window	140	119
Theft-deterrent system w/alarm,		
ordered w/SLT Pkg.	150	128
Requires remote keyless entry and Travel Convenience Group.		
Argent rear bumper, WS	135	115

Special Purpose, Wheels and Tires

Heavy Duty Service Group, 2WD w/3.9-liter engine		
or 5.2-liter engine and manual transmission.	215	183
2WD w/5.2- or 5.9-liter engine and		
automatic transmission.	345	293
4WD	260	221

Heavy-duty alternator and battery, heavy-duty engine cooling (requires V8 and auto. trans.), heavy-duty transmission-oil cooler (requires auto. trans.), skid plates (4WD).

Chrome wheels, ST	345	293
245/75R16 tires,		
ST regular cab	130	111
245/75R16 on/off-road tires, 4WD	280	238
265/75R16 on/off-road white-letter tires,		
4WD w/SLT Pkg.	415	353

Prices are accurate at time of publication; subject to manufacturer's changes.

DODGE STRATUS

Dodge Stratus

Front-wheel-drive midsize car; similar to Chrysler Cirrus and Sebring, and Plymouth Breeze
Base price range: $15,930-$19,830. Built in USA. **Also consider:** Chevrolet Malibu, Ford Taurus, Honda Accord, Toyota Camry/Solara

FOR • Steering/handling • Passenger and cargo room
AGAINST • Noise • Rear visibility • Interior materials

Stratus for 2000 gets a new base model that includes the previously optional 150-horsepower 4-cylinder engine and automatic transmission. This is Dodge's version of the sedan also sold as the lower-priced Plymouth Breeze and as the costlier Chrysler Cirrus.

Called simply the base model last year, the new entry-level Stratus SE gets a 135-hp 2.0 liter 4-cylinder engine when ordered with manual transmission. Automatic-transmission SEs get the 150-hp 2.4 at no extra cost. The uplevel Stratus is again called the ES and it comes with a 168-hp Mitsubishi-built 2.5-liter V6 and Chrysler's Autostick automatic transmission, which has a separate gate for manual gear changes.

Antilock brakes are standard on the ES and include 4-wheel discs. ABS with rear drum brakes is optional on the SE. A new option is an emergency escape release inside the trunk.

PERFORMANCE Differing mainly in styling details and equipment availability, Stratus and Breeze have a similar driving feel. Both are agile-handling family sedans, though the compromise is a suspension that does a poor job of absorbing larger bumps and filtering out road noise. The ES's optional 4-wheel disc brakes improve pedal feel and modulation, but stopping power is no more than adequate.

Manual-transmission 2.0-liter 4-cylinders feel as lively as automatic-transmission 2.4s. Both furnish adequate acceleration and passing power, though neither runs quietly. The V6 is the best performer overall, but it's far from quiet and there's a frustrating pause before the automatic transmission downshifts for passing. We like Autostick's added degree of engine control. Fuel economy is good for this class. Our Autostick test '99 Stratus averaged 21 mpg. A 2.0-liter 5-speed test '99 Breeze returned 21.2 mpg.

ACCOMMODATIONS Stratus and Breeze are uncommonly roomy midsize sedans, and there's even enough rear-seat width for three medium-size adults to travel comfortably. Instruments and controls are well-placed, but the grade of materials used in the cabins is below average for this class, and loose rubber trim around a rear door window was a problem on more than one test car. The high parcel shelf hampers the view aft, but visibility is otherwise excellent. A large trunk with a flat floor and low liftover, plus the standard folding rear seatback, provides good cargo-carrying ability.

VALUE FOR THE MONEY They're not long on refinement, but Stratus and Breeze are roomy, competent sedans for the money. A loaded Stratus costs about as much as mid-level models in some rival lineups, while the Breeze is a downright bargain and qualifies for our Budget Buy label.

ENGINES

	ohc I4	dohc I4	ohc V6
Size, liters/cu. in.	2.0/122	2.4/148	2.5/152
Horsepower @ rpm	132 @	150 @	168 @
	6000	5200	5800
Torque (lbs./ft.) @ rpm	129 @	167 @	170 @
	4950	4000	4350
Availability	S[1]	O[1]	S[2]
EPA city/highway mpg			
5-speed OD manual	26/37		
4-speed OD automatic		21/30	19/27

1. SE. 2. ES.

PRICES

Dodge Stratus	Retail Price	Dealer Invoice
SE 4-door sedan	$15930	$14628
ES 4-door sedan	19830	18099
Destination charge	545	545

STANDARD EQUIPMENT:

SE: 2.0-liter 4-cylinder engine, 5-speed manual transmission, driver- and passenger-side airbags, air conditioning, power steering, tilt steering wheel, cloth upholstery, front bucket seats, height-adjustable driver seat, console, cupholders, folding rear bench seat, AM/FM/cassette w/six speakers, digital clock, tachometer, rear defogger, variable intermittent wipers, remote decklid release, auxiliary power outlet, visor mirrors, front floormats, dual remote mirrors, 195/70R14 tires, wheel covers.

ES adds: 2.5-liter V6 engine, 4-speed automatic transmission w/manual-shift capability, antilock 4-wheel disc brakes, cruise control, variable-assist power steering, leather-wrapped steering wheel and shift knob, cruise control, power mirrors, power windows, power door locks, map lights, illuminated visor mirrors, rear floormats, fog lights, 195/65R15 tires, alloy wheels.

OPTIONAL EQUIPMENT:
Major Packages

Quick Order Pkg. 24B, SE	1055	939
Manufacturer's discount price	NC	NC

Power windows and door locks, power mirrors, 8-way power driver seat, rear floormats. Requires 2.4-liter engine, 4-speed automatic transmission.

Quick Order Pkg. 26S, ES	1795	1598
Manufacturer's discount price	280	250

Leather upholstery, 8-way power driver seat, remote keyless entry, illuminated entry, premium AM/FM/cassette w/CD changer controls, cargo net, theft-deterrent system w/alarm.

Powertrains

2.4-liter dohc 4-cylinder engine, SE	450	401
Manufacturer's discount price	NC	NC

Requires 4-speed automatic transmission.

4-speed automatic transmission, SE	1050	935

Includes manual-shift capability, cruise control. Requires 2.4-liter engine.

Safety Features

Antilock brakes, SE	565	503

Comfort and Convenience

Power sunroof, SE	695	619
ES	580	516

Includes assist handles, map lights, illuminated visor mirrors (SE). SE requires Quick Order Pkg.

Remote/Illuminated Entry Group	170	151

Remote keyless entry, illuminated entry. SE requires Quick Order Pkg.

Premium AM/FM/cassette	340	303

Includes eight speakers, power amplifier, CD controls.

AM/FM/CD player, SE	200	178
Premium AM/FM/cassette and 6-disc CD changer	550	490
Smoker's Group	20	18

Ashtray, lighter.

Appearance and Miscellaneous

Theft-deterrent system w/alarm, ES	175	156

Requires Remote/Illuminated Entry Group.

DODGE VIPER

Rear-wheel-drive sports and GT car

Base price range: $65,725-$68,225. Built in USA. **Also consider:** Acura NSX, Chevrolet Corvette, Porsche 911

FOR • Acceleration • Steering/handling **AGAINST** • Noise • Fuel economy

Silver is a new exterior color for 2000 on Dodge's high-performance rear-drive 2-seat sports car. Viper comes as the GTS coupe and RT/10 convertible, the latter available with a removable solid roof panel. They share a 450-horsepower 8.0-liter V10, America's largest

Dodge Viper GTS

and most-powerful production automobile engine. A 6-speed manual is the sole transmission. Antilock brakes and traction control are unavailable. The American Club Racer package is available on the coupe and is intended for the race track.

EVALUATION Viper defines brutal performance, and ranks among the fastest and best-handling cars available. It's tiring to drive, however, has minimal luggage space, and poor fuel economy—just 14 mpg in our last GTS test. Still, don't expect much of a price discount: Dodge builds just enough to keep demand ahead of supply.

ENGINES

	ohv V10
Size, liters/cu. in.	8.0/488
Horsepower @ rpm	450 @ 5200
Torque (lbs./ft.) @ rpm	490 @ 3700
Availability	S

EPA city/highway mpg

6-speed OD manual	12/21

PRICES

1999 Dodge Viper	Retail Price	Dealer Invoice
RT/10 2-door convertible	$65725	$59038
GTS 2-door hatchback	68225	61238
Destination charge	700	700

Add Gas Guzzler Tax $3000.

STANDARD EQUIPMENT:

RT/10: 8.0-liter V10 engine, 6-speed manual transmission, limited-slip differential, driver- and passenger-side airbags, 4-wheel disc brakes, air conditioning, power steering, tilt steering wheel, leather-wrapped steering wheel and shifter knob, adjustable pedals, leather reclining front bucket seats with lumbar support adjuster, center console, power mirrors, power windows, power door locks, remote keyless entry, tachometer, AM/FM/CD player w/five speakers, map lights, fog lights, theft-deterrent system, removable folding soft top, 275/35ZR18 front tires, 335/30ZR18 rear tires, alloy wheels.

GTS adds: rear defogger, six speakers, overhead mesh storage pouches, trunk light, deletes removable folding soft top and map lights.

OPTIONAL EQUIPMENT:
Major Packages

Competition Pkg., GTS	10,000	8500

Includes five-point seat belts, low restriction air cleaner, special graphics, unique suspension, one-piece wheels. Deletes air conditioning, AM/FM/CD player, fog lights.

Comfort Group, GTS w/Competition Pkg.	910	774

Air conditioning, AM/FM/CD player.

Comfort and Convenience

Leather Pkg.	500	425

Cognac-colored leather seats and leather-wrapped steering wheel.

Appearance and Miscellaneous

Removable hardtop, RT/10	2500	2125
Tonneau cover, RT/10	250	213
Metallic stripe paint, GTS	2000	1700

FORD CONTOUR

Front-wheel-drive compact car; similar to Mercury Cougar

Base price range: $16,845-$22,715. Built in USA and Mexico.
Also consider: Mazda 626, Nissan Altima, Oldsmobile Alero

FOR • Acceleration (SVT) • Steering/handling **AGAINST**

Ford Contour

• Road noise • Rear-seat room

Contour scales back for 2000, slicing its roster to a single Sport model, with the high-performance SVT again available through selected Ford dealers. The Sport includes features that had been optional on last year's SE, including a 170-horsepower V6. A 5-speed manual transmission is standard. Automatic transmission, antilock brakes and traction control are optional. The SVT has a 200-hp V6, mandatory manual transmission, standard antilock 4-wheel disc brakes, sport suspension, and high-speed 16-inch tires. The Mercury Mystique, which shared Contour's basic design, has been discontinued.

EVALUATION Contour is based on the Ford Mondeo and reflects that European heritage with sporty road manners, but also a suspension that provides a tauter ride than most American compacts. The base V6 doesn't provide top-flank acceleration. We clocked a test '99 automatic V6 SE at a middling 9.3 seconds 0-60 mph, though its transmission downshifted promptly for good highway passing punch. That test car averaged 21.7 mpg. Manual V6 models feel stronger at all speeds—especially the SVT, which has genuine sport-sedan moves without riding significantly harder than an ordinary Contour. Road noise can be intrusive regardless of model. Stopping power is good with the optional antilock brakes and great with the SVT's 4-wheel discs. Front-seat room is competitive with other compacts, but Contour has only adequate rear leg room for medium-size adults, and rear head clearance is slim for those over 5-foot-8. Busy audio systems and power mirror controls semi-hidden to the left of the steering wheel detract from the otherwise well-designed dashboard. Though smaller inside than some rivals, Contour has polished road manners and reasonable prices—and discounts should be readily available.

ENGINES

	dohc V6	dohc V6
Size, liters/cu. in.	2.5/155	2.5/155
Horsepower @ rpm	170 @ 6250	200 @ 6700
Torque (lbs./ft.) @ rpm	165 @ 4250	165 @ 5625
Availability	S	S[1]

EPA city/highway mpg

5-speed OD manual	20/28	20/29
4-speed OD automatic	20/29	

1. SVT.

PRICES

Ford Contour	Retail Price	Dealer Invoice
Sport 4-door sedan	$16845	$15332
SVT 4-door sedan	22715	20556
Destination charge	560	560

Pricing and contents may vary in some regions.

STANDARD EQUIPMENT:

Sport: 2.5-liter dohc V6 170-horsepower engine, 5-speed manual transmission, driver- and passenger-side airbags, emergency inside trunk release, air conditioning, interior air filter, power steering, tilt steering wheel, leather-wrapped steering wheel, cruise control, cloth upholstery, front bucket seats, center console, cupholders, split folding rear seat, power mirrors, power windows, power door locks, remote keyless entry, AM/FM/cassette, digital clock, tachometer, illuminated visor mirrors, variable intermittent wipers, rear defogger, remote decklid release, auxiliary power outlet, floormats, theft-deterrent system, fog lights, rear spoiler, 205/60TR15 tires, alloy wheels.

SVT adds: 2.5-liter dohc V6 200-horsepower engine, antilock 4-wheel disc brakes, leather upholstery, 10-way power driver seat w/power lumbar adjustment, Premium Sound System, sport suspension, 215/50ZR16 tires.

Prices are accurate at time of publication; subject to manufacturer's changes.

OPTIONAL EQUIPMENT:

Powertrains

	Retail Price	Dealer Invoice
4-speed automatic transmission, Sport	$815	$725
Traction control, Sport	175	156

Safety Features

Antilock brakes, Sport	500	445

Comfort and Convenience

6-way power driver seat, Sport	350	312
Premium AM/FM/cassette, Sport	135	120
Premium AM/FM/CD player, Sport	275	245
SVT	NC	NC
Power sunroof, Sport	595	530
SVT	NC	NC
Smoker's Pkg.	15	13

Ashtray, cigarette lighter.

FORD CROWN VICTORIA

BUDGET BUY

Ford Crown Victoria

Rear-wheel-drive full-size car; similar to Mercury Grand Marquis

Base price range: $22,005-$24,120. Built in Canada. **Also consider:** Buick LeSabre, Dodge Intrepid, Toyota Avalon

FOR • Passenger and cargo room **AGAINST** • Fuel economy

If you want a big rear-drive American sedan, it has to be from Ford Motor Co., because the Crown Victoria, Mercury's similar Grand Marquis, and the related Lincoln Town Car are the only ones left. Changes for 2000 involve the addition of several safety features: an emergency trunk lid release inside the trunk, three child seat upper anchorages for the rear seat, and a chime that sounds to indicate an unbuckled seatbelt.

Crown Victoria comes in base and LX models with standard automatic transmission and a 200-horsepower 4.6-liter V8. Horsepower climbs to 215 with optional dual exhausts, which are part of a Handling and Performance Package that also includes firmer suspension, low-profile tires, and a higher numerical rear-axle ratio. Torque on both engines increases this year by 10 pound-feet. Antilock brakes are standard, traction control is optional.

PERFORMANCE Ford's overhead-cam V8 runs quietly and provides Crown Vic and Grand Marquis with smooth, strong acceleration and good passing power. The transmission is unobtrusive except for pronounced downshifts in passing situations. We averaged 14.7 mpg in a test of a 215-horsepower model; expect the base engine, with its more fuel-efficient axle ratio, to average 16-17 mpg.

Though not sloppy handlers, these big sedans don't change direction with as much poise as trimmer front-drive rivals from Dodge, Chrysler, or General Motors. The base suspension keeps float and wallow over pavement undulations to reasonable levels. While the Handling Package brings no improvement in road manners, neither does it hurt ride quality. Steering effort is too light for our tastes. The optional traction control system doesn't match the grip of front-wheel drive, but without it, these rear-drive sedans can become immobilized on slick roads.

ACCOMMODATIONS Crown Vic and Grand Marquis have that good-old big-car feel, with easy access to all seats and adult-size room front and rear. The center driveshaft tunnel intrudes on foot space, however, and the bench seats do a poor job holding occupants in place during fast turns.

We prefer the standard analog gauges, but the optional digital instruments are easy to read day or night. Controls are generously sized, though the driver must stretch to reach those for the climate system. A mix of plastic and vinyl panels and seats of cloth or leather create a con-

servative, serviceable interior decor. The trunk holds plenty of luggage, but the space is concentrated in a deep center well, so some bulky items are a tough fit.

VALUE FOR THE MONEY We favor the more-modern approach of front-wheel-drive rivals such as the Buick LeSabre and Dodge Intrepid, but rear-drive, V8 traditionalists won't be disappointed with the reasonably priced Crown Victoria and Grand Marquis.

ENGINES

	ohc V8	ohc V8
Size, liters/cu. in.	4.6/281	4.6/281
Horsepower @ rpm	200 @ 4250	215 @ 4500
Torque (lbs./ft.) @ rpm	275 @ 3000	285 @ 3000
Availability	S	O
EPA city/highway mpg		
4-speed OD automatic	17/24	17/24

PRICES

Ford Crown Victoria	Retail Price	Dealer Invoice
Base 4-door sedan	$22005	$20499
LX 4-door sedan	24120	22425
Destination charge	630	630

STANDARD EQUIPMENT:

Base: 4.6-liter V8 200-horsepower engine, 4-speed automatic transmission, driver- and passenger-side airbags, antilock 4-wheel disc brakes, emergency inside trunk release, air conditioning, variable-assist power steering, tilt steering wheel, cruise control, cloth reclining split bench seat, cupholders, AM/FM/cassette with four speakers, digital clock, power mirrors, power windows, power door locks, power decklid release, rear defogger, intermittent wipers, automatic headlights, rear heat ducts, theft-deterrent system, 225/60SR16 tires, wheel covers.

LX adds: upgraded interior trim, 6-way power driver seat with power recliner and power lumbar support, Light/Decor Group (illuminated visor mirrors, map lights, body striping), remote keyless entry.

OPTIONAL EQUIPMENT:

Major Packages

Comfort Group, LX	900	801

Automatic climate control, power passenger seat with power lumbar support, leather-wrapped steering wheel, automatic day/night mirror with compass, alloy wheels.

Comfort Plus Group, LX	2150	1914

Comfort Group plus leather upholstery, trip computer, digital instrumentation, Premium Audio System.

Handling and Performance Pkg., Base	935	832
LX	740	658
LX w/Comfort Group or Comfort Plus Group	615	547

Includes 215-horsepower engine, dual exhaust, performance springs, shocks and stabilizer bars, rear air suspension, 3.27 axle ratio, 225/60TR16 touring tires, alloy wheels.

Powertrains

Traction control	175	156

Comfort and Convenience

Remote keyless entry, Base	240	213
Leather upholstery, LX	735	654
Requires Comfort Group.		
6-way power driver seat, Base	360	321
AM/FM/CD player	140	124
6-disc CD changer, LX	350	312
Premium Audio System, LX	360	321

Upgraded amplifier and six speakers. Requires Comfort Group.

Universal garage door opener, LX	115	102
225/60SR16 whitewall tires	80	71

NA with Handling and Performance Pkg.

FORD ESCORT/ZX2

BUDGET BUY

Front-wheel-drive subcompact car

Base price range: $11,505-$11,760. Built in Mexico. **Also consider:** Chevrolet Cavalier, Honda Civic, Mazda Protege,

Ford Escort sedan

Saturn S-Series, Toyota Corolla

FOR • Fuel economy **AGAINST** • Rear-seat room • Noise

Ford launches its new subcompact Focus for 2000, and cuts back on its old subcompact Escort. Gone is the Escort wagon, leaving a 4-door sedan. Escort's 2-door coupe derivative, the ZX2, survives, and gains a performance S/R option later in the model year.

The sedan has a 114-horsepower 4-cylinder engine and standard manual or optional automatic transmission. ZX2 consolidates last year's "Cool" and "Hot" trim levels into a single model with a firmer suspension and a 130-hp twin-cam version of Escort's engine. Antilock brakes are optional on Escort and ZX2, and both have an emergency escape trunklid release. Newly standard on ZX2 are 185/60HR15 tires, a cassette player, power mirrors, and rear defroster. The S/R option includes a power increase (tentatively to 143 hp), 205/55ZR15 tires on specific alloy wheels, 4-wheel disc brakes, and upgraded exhaust and suspension parts. The current-generation Escort bowed for 1997 and will eventually be replaced by the slightly larger Focus.

PERFORMANCE Escorts get around nicely even with automatic transmission, though several test cars with the automatic suffered an annoying engine vibration at idle. A test 1999 automatic sedan averaged 23.9 mpg. Manual-shift models use less fuel and have much livelier acceleration. Escort's ride is firm but not jarring. Handing is competent, helped by power steering with good road feel. Noise levels can be intrusive, with high-rpm engine ruckus the worst offender.

ZX2s drive like slightly sportier Escorts, with added punch from the stronger engine and good grip and stability in turns. Again, manual versions are quicker than automatics, but the engine is busy and buzzy even at a moderate pace, and there's more road noise than in Escort sedans. Our test automatic ZX2 averaged a laudable 29.0 mpg, a 5-speed got 24.5 in harder driving.

ACCOMMODATIONS The sedan has adequate front-seat space, but in back, knee room is tight, and people over 5-foot-8 brush the headliner. The trunk is roomy for the car's exterior size. Escort and ZX2 have handy, logical controls, but the standard fixed steering wheel doesn't suit all drivers (a tilt wheel is an option). Both body styles suffer restricted over-the-shoulder visibility. The ZX2 has more rear-seat space than most sports coupes, but larger adults won't be happy there for long, and rear entry/exit is a real squeeze. Cargo room is good for a subcompact coupe, but the trunk opening narrows at bumper level and the lid hinges cut into load space.

VALUE FOR THE MONEY Escort lacks Focus's style, refinement, or roominess, but still qualifies as a sensible entry-level buy. The ZX2 looks sportier than it performs.

ENGINES

	ohc I4	dohc I4
Size, liters/cu. in.	2.0/121	2.0/121
Horsepower @ rpm	114 @ 5000	130 @ 5750
Torque (lbs./ft.) @ rpm	126 @ 3750	127 @ 4250
Availability	S[1]	S[2]
EPA city/highway mpg		
5-speed OD manual	28/37	25/33
4-speed OD automatic	25/34	25/33

1. Escort sedan. 2. ZX2.

PRICES

Ford Escort/ZX2	Retail Price	Dealer Invoice
SE 4-door sedan	$11505	$10769
ZX2 2-door coupe	11760	10967
Destination charge	440	440

STANDARD EQUIPMENT:

LX: 2.0-liter 4-cylinder engine, 5-speed manual transmission, driver- and passenger-side airbags, power steering, cloth upholstery, bucket seats, center console, cupholders, split folding rear seat, visor mirrors, AM/FM/cassette, digital clock, rear defogger, variable intermittent wipers, auxiliary power outlet, remote decklid release, dual outside mirrors, 185/65R14 tires, wheel covers.

ZX2 adds: power mirrors, tachometer, rear spoiler, 185/60R15 tires, alloy wheels.

OPTIONAL EQUIPMENT:

	Retail Price	Dealer Invoice
Major Packages		
Sport Group, ZX2	$1495	$1331

Performance exhaust and clutch, sport suspension, 4-wheel disc brakes, upgraded seats, 205/55ZR15 tires, special alloy wheels. Requires air conditioning. NA with Comfort Group, antilock brakes.

Power Group, ZX2	395	352

Power windows and door locks, remote keyless entry.

Comfort Group, ZX2	395	352

Cruise control, tilt leather-wrapped steering wheel, map lights.

Powertrains		
4-speed automatic transmission	815	725
Safety Features		
Antilock brakes	400	356
Comfort and Convenience		
Air conditioning	795	708
Power mirrors, SE	—	—
Leather upholstery, ZX2	395	352
Premium AM/FM/cassette w/6-disc CD changer, ZX2	295	263
Power sunroof, ZX2	595	530
Chrome alloy wheels, ZX2	595	530

FORD EXCURSION

Ford Excursion Limited

Rear- or 4-wheel-drive full-size sport-utility vehicle
Base price range: $33,460-$40,205. Built in USA. **Also consider:** Chevrolet Tahoe and Suburban, GMC Yukon and Yukon XL

FOR • Passenger and cargo room • Trailer towing capability • Seat comfort **AGAINST** • Fuel economy • Maneuverability • Rear visibility

Excursion debuts for 2000 as the world's biggest, heaviest sport-utility vehicle. It's 7.4 inches longer than a Chevrolet Suburban, 6 inches taller, some 1900 pounds heavier, and rides a 7-inch-longer wheelbase. Excursion is based on Ford's three-quarter-ton F-Series pickup truck. It seats up to nine and has four side doors. Its rear doors are center-opening half panels beneath a full-width top-hinged window. It comes in XLT and Limited trim levels and with 2- or 4-wheel drive. Automatic transmission and 4-wheel antilock disc brakes are standard.

A V8 is the base engine. A V10 is standard with 4WD and optional with 2WD. Available with either drivetrain is a turbocharged diesel V8. The 4WD system shifts between 2WD and 4WD via a dashboard switch and includes low-range gearing, but must be disengaged on dry pavement. General Motors rivals and Ford's Expedition offer full-time 4WD that can remain engaged on dry pavement.

Excursion has dashboard airbags, but no side airbags. Front bucket seats are standard on Limited and available in XLTs in lieu of

Prices are accurate at time of publication; subject to manufacturer's changes.

a 3-place bench. All models have a fold-down second-row bench and a removable third-row bench. Leather upholstery is standard on Limited, optional on XLT. An optional sensing system sounds an alert of objects in Excursion's path when backing up.

Responding to safety and environmental critics, Ford says Excursion engines meet low-emissions standards and that the SUV makes extensive use of recycled materials. Excursion also introduces Ford's BlockerBeam, a steel cross member below the front bumper designed to prevent cars from sliding under in a crash. In back is a standard trailer hitch intended for the same purpose.

PERFORMANCE Sixty percent of Excursions are ordered with 4WD, with the V10 XLT the top-selling version. Our initial test drives came with just a driver and up to four passengers. Under these conditions, either the V10 or the diesel engine gets this 7000-pound SUV to cruising speed fairly quickly. Highway passing response is adequate, too, aided by the transmission's smooth, prompt downshifts. A 2WD V10 Limited averaged 10.8 mpg in our tests, one of the lowest figures we've recorded. We have not tested a V8 model.

Excursion is a stable straight-line cruiser and isn't disturbed by most broken pavement, though bigger bumps and ridges register fairly sharply. On twisting roads or in traffic, this 19-foot-long, 6.6-foot-wide truck feels ponderous, responding lazily to steering inputs. The steering itself is as light as that of most cars, but curb-to-curb turning diameter is almost 50 feet, so it can be a chore to maneuver on side streets and in parking lots. The brakes are easily modulated and feel strong, but drivers need to reacclimate to longer stopping distances. Suppression of wind rush and road roar is quite good. The diesel idles noisily, but cruises without fuss, and the gas engines intrude only under full throttle.

ACCOMMODATIONS Excursion carries eight adults without painful squeezing. Second-row passengers get the roomiest accommodations, highlighted by exceptional leg space. The third-row seat is more confining, but not inhospitable to grownups. The driver's seat is comfortable, but the wide transmission tunnel intrudes somewhat into the front passenger's footwell.

Maximum cargo volume is an unmatched 146.4 cubic feet. Even with all seats in place, Excursion has a class-leading 48 cubic feet of luggage space. The one-piece third-row bench folds nearly flat, or it can be removed, though it's heavy and cumbersome despite small roller wheels. The second-row bench splits 70/30 and also folds. There are plenty of bins and cubbies, and up to 10 cupholders and 5 power outlets. The rear "Dutch" doors are a clever solution to cargo-bay access, though neither works with the liftglass closed.

Gauges are easy to see. Some of our testers had to stretch to reach the audio and climate controls, and the steering wheel partially hides the 4WD switch. The driver gets a big-rig perspective of the road, and notches cut into the forward portion of the front-door sills enhance the view out the side mirrors. But extra care is still need to be certain nothing's hiding along Excursion's long, tall flanks and tail. The reverse sensing system is a smart option, especially since the deep-tinted windows reduce rear visibility at night. Four-wheel-drive Excursions ride three inches higher than 2WD models, but ingress and egress are no harder than for other big SUVs, and easier than some. Standard running boards provide useful footholds, the rear doors are exceptionally long, and there's adequate clearance to the third-row seat.

VALUE FOR THE MONEY Excursion's size and weight are serious drawbacks if you're going to use it as a "suburban utility vehicle." But if you tow up to 10,000 pounds, need 4WD, and can abide abysmal fuel economy, base prices in $33,400-$41,000 range actually make it a good SUV value.

ENGINES

	ohc V8	ohc V10	Turbodiesel ohc V8
Size, liters/cu. in.	5.4/330	6.8/415	7.3/444
Horsepower @ rpm	255 @ 4500	310 @ 4250	235 @ 2700
Torque (lbs./ft.) @ rpm	350 @ 2500	425 @ 3250	500 @ 1600
Availability	S[1]	S[2]	O
EPA city/highway mpg			
4-speed OD automatic	NA	NA	15/18

1. 2WD. 2. 4WD; optional 2WD.

PRICES

Ford Excursion

	Retail Price	Dealer Invoice
XLT 4-door wagon, 2WD	$33460	$29201
XLT 4-door wagon, 4WD	$36775	$32018
Limited 4-door wagon, 2WD	37110	32303
Limited 4-door wagon, 4WD	40205	34934
Destination charge	700	700

STANDARD EQUIPMENT:

XLT: 5.4-liter V8 engine, 4-speed automatic transmission, driver- and passenger-side airbags, antilock 4-wheel disc brakes, front and rear air conditioning, power steering, tilt leather-wrapped steering wheel, cruise control, cloth upholstery, front split bench seat, second-row reclining split-folding bench seat, third row bench seat, cupholders, overhead console, heated power mirrors, power front windows, power door locks, remote keyless entry, AM/FM/cassette/CD player, digital clock, tachometer, automatic day/night rearview mirror, map lights, illuminated visor mirrors, intermittent wipers, rear defogger, auxiliary power outlets, intermittent rear wiper/washer, floormats, theft-deterrent system, rear liftgate w/lower Dutch doors, roof rack, privacy glass, running boards, front tow hooks, 4-lead trailer harness, Class IV trailer hitch, full-size spare tire, LT265/75R16D tires, wheel covers. **4WD** adds: part-time 4-wheel drive, 2-speed transfer case w/electronic control, 6.8-liter V10 engine.

Limited adds: leather upholstery, front captain chairs, 6-way power driver seat, center console, trip computer, rear audio controls, power rear quarter windows, illuminated running boards, LT265/75R16D white-letter tires, alloy wheels. **4WD** adds: part-time 4-wheel drive, 2-speed transfer case w/electronic control, 6.8-liter V10 engine.

OPTIONAL EQUIPMENT:
Major Packages

	Retail Price	Dealer Invoice
Comfort and Convenience Group, XLT	1160	986

Captain's chairs, 6-way power driver seat, trip computer, power rear quarter windows, illuminated running boards, bodyside stripes. NA with Special Services Group.

Special Services Group, XLT (credit)	(1995)	(1696)

Front bench seat, vinyl floor covering, manual outside mirrors, argent steel wheels. Deletes rear air conditioning, overhead console, automatic day/night rearview mirror, third row seat, cargo net, carpeting, floor mats, bodyside moldings, roof rack cross members, wheel covers.

Powertrains

6.8-liter V10 engine, 2WD	595	506
7.3-liter turbodiesel V8 engine, 2WD	4600	3901
4WD	4005	3404
5.4-liter V8 engine, 4WD	NC	NC
Limited-slip differential	250	213

Requires 6.8- or 7.3-liter engine.

Safety Features

Reverse Sensing System	245	208

Comfort and Convenience

Heated power trailer tow mirrors	60	51
Leather upholstery, XLT	1300	1105

Requires Comfort and Convenience Group.

Heated front seats, Limited	290	247
6-disc CD changer	495	421

XLT requires Comfort and Convenience Group.

Special Purpose, Wheels and Tires

Skid plates, 4WD	75	64
Alloy wheels, XLT	310	263

Requires optional tires. NA with Special Services Group.

LT265/75R16D all-terrain white-letter tires, XLT	255	217
Limited	130	111

XLT requires alloy wheels.

FORD EXPEDITION ✓ BEST BUY

Rear- or 4-wheel-drive full-size sport-utility vehicle; similar to Lincoln Navigator

Base price range: $29,655-$39,695. Built in USA. **Also consider:** Chevrolet Tahoe and Suburban, GMC Yukon and Yukon XL

FOR • Acceleration (5.4-liter) • Passenger and cargo room • Visibility • Towing ability • Build quality **AGAINST** • Fuel economy • Entry/exit (4WD models)

Ford Expedition

Second-row bucket seats, front side airbags, and a Reverse Sensing System are among new options for America's best-selling full-size sport-utility vehicle. Expedition is the basis for the luxury Lincoln Navigator and is slightly smaller than the Chevrolet Suburban/GMC Yukon XL.

Expedition offers XLT and Eddie Bauer models, both with a one-piece rear liftgate. Front bucket seats are standard on Eddie Bauer and optional on XLT in place of a front bench. A 3-passenger second-row bench seat is standard on both. Newly optional is a pair of second-row buckets (without a center console). Eddie Bauers add a 3-passenger third-row bench.

XLTs and 2-wheel-drive Eddie Bauers come with a 4.6-liter V8. Optional on those models and standard on 4WD Eddie Bauers is a 5.4-liter V8. Both are overhead-cam designs and team with automatic transmission. Expedition's 4WD system can be left engaged on dry pavement and has low-range gearing. Antilock 4-wheel disc brakes are standard. Maximum towing capacity is 8000 pounds.

Among other 2000 changes: power adjustable gas and brake pedals are standard instead of optional, the front center console is wider, and the radio antenna moves from the front fender to within the right rear glass. A power sunroof is now optional on XLT as well as Eddie Bauer, and the available outside mirrors with integrated turn-signal indicators are modified to include heated glass.

PERFORMANCE Expedition and Navigator aren't agile, but they're easy enough to drive for their size. Body lean is modest as long as cornering speeds are. Rear-drive models and XLT Expeditions with the 16-inch wheels have a stable, relatively soft ride. The 4x4s and versions with 17-inch wheels—Eddie Bauer Expeditions and all Navigators—ride stiffly and are not impressively composed over bumps.

The 5.4 V8 provides robust acceleration and is our recommendation if you order 4WD or tow trailers weighing more than 3000 pounds or so. Note that Navigator gets a twincam 5.4 with 300 horsepower, 40 more than Expedition's version. Expedition's 4.6 is adequate for most tasks, but doesn't have enough low-speed muscle for swift passing in this 2.5-ton wagon. In our most recent test, we averaged 12.6 mpg with a 5.4-liter Expedition and 12.5 in a Navigator. Wind and road noise are well-muffled, as is engine thrash except in hard acceleration.

ACCOMMODATIONS Front-seat space is bountiful, and Expedition and Navigator are wide enough for comfortable 3-across adult seating in the second row—and the nearly flat floor means no one straddles a hump. Navigator already offered the second-row buckets new to Expedition this year, though Lincoln fits a useful center console while Ford opts for a narrow channel to the third-row seat. That third-row seat is Crampsville for adults, and there's only a foot-wide trench of luggage space behind. However, cargo room gets ever-more cavernous as you fold or take out the second- and third-row benches. They're heavy, so removing either is a 2-person task. The tailgate glass opens separately, but the heavy liftgate is a chore to use, and side-opening cargo rear doors—as on General Motors rivals—aren't offered. Interior step-in is higher than on the big GM SUVs.

Navigator has fancier standard trim but the same user-friendly dashboard design as Expedition. A button adjacent to the steering column quickly powers the pedal cluster forward as much as three inches, enough travel to fine-tune the driving position: It's a welcome feature for shorter drivers. We also recommend the new reverse sensing system, which sounds a warning of unseen objects behind when backing up. Storage bins abound and include an enormous center-console box. Most of our test examples have had impressively solid build quality, but our last test Navigator suffered ill-fitting interior trim.

VALUE FOR THE MONEY Expedition and Navigator have strong new rivals in the redesigned 2000 Suburban and Yukon XL, while Ford's own Excursion may also draw away some sales. Expedition is our Best Buy value of the bunch, and all that competition should be to your benefit when negotiating a deal.

ENGINES

	ohc V8	ohc V8
Size, liters/cu. in.	4.6/281	5.4/330
Horsepower @ rpm	240 @ 4750	260 @ 4500
Torque (lbs./ft.) @ rpm	293 @ 3500	345 @ 2300
Availability	S[1]	S[2]
EPA city/highway mpg		
4-speed OD automatic	13/18[3]	13/18[3]

1. XLT and Eddie Bauer 2WD. 2. Eddie Bauer 4WD, optional others. 3. 12/16 w/4WD.

PRICES

Ford Expedition	Retail Price	Dealer Invoice
XLT 4-door wagon, 2WD	$29655	$25917
XLT 4-door wagon, 4WD	32525	28357
Eddie Bauer 4-door wagon, 2WD	35945	31263
Eddie Bauer 4-door wagon, 4WD	39695	34451
Destination charge	665	665

STANDARD EQUIPMENT:

XLT: 4.6-liter V8 engine, 4-speed automatic transmission, driver- and passenger-side airbags, antilock 4-wheel disc brakes, front air conditioning, rear heat ducts, variable-assist power steering, tilt steering wheel, cruise control, front cloth 40/60 split bench seat, 6-way power driver seat w/manual lumbar support, second-row split-folding-reclining bench seat, third row bench seat, cupholders, power adjustable pedals w/memory, power mirrors, power front windows, power door locks, remote keyless entry, key pad entry, AM/FM/cassette, digital clock, tachometer, map lights, passenger-side visor mirror, speed-sensitive intermittent wipers, rear defogger, rear wiper/washer, auxiliary power outlet, floormats, theft-deterrent system, rear liftgate with flip-up glass, roof rack, 4-lead trailer harness, full-size spare tire, 255/70R16 tires, styled steel wheels. **4WD adds:** Control Trac full-time 4-wheel drive, 2-speed transfer case, front tow hooks, 30-gallon fuel tank.

Eddie Bauer adds: automatic climate control, rear air conditioning and heater, leather upholstery, front captain chairs with manual lumbar support, driver seat memory, leather-wrapped steering wheel, front storage console (rear radio controls and headphone jacks, air conditioning/heater vent), overhead storage console (trip computer, compass, sunglass/garage door opener holder), heated power mirrors w/memory, automatic day/night rearview mirror, Mach audio system, illuminated visor mirrors, rear reading lights, power rear-quarter windows, automatic headlights, rear privacy glass, illuminated running boards, outside-mirror mounted turn signal lights, fog lights, 275/60R17 white-letter tires, chrome alloy wheels. **4WD adds:** Control Trac full-time 4-wheel drive, 2-speed transfer case, 5.4-liter V8 engine, front tow hooks, 30-gallon fuel tank, 265/70R17 all-terrain white-letter tires.

OPTIONAL EQUIPMENT:
Major Packages

Comfort/Convenience Pkg., XLT	2200	1870
Manufacturer's discount price	1495	1271

Captain's chairs, floor console, rear air conditioning and heater, automatic day/night rearview mirror, illuminated visor mirrors, rear privacy glass, illuminated running boards.

Premium Sport Appearance Group, XLT 2WD............	1295	1101
XLT 4WD	1395	1186

Captain's chairs, color-keyed bumpers and grille, side step bars, wheel lip moldings, fog lights, skid plates (4WD), 275/60R17 white-letter tires (2WD), 265/70R17 all-terrain white-letter tires, chrome steel wheels. Requires Comfort/Convenience Group.

Class III Trailer Tow Group, 2WD	880	748
4WD..	390	332

7-pin trailer wiring harness, frame-mounted hitch, auxiliary transmission-oil cooler, super engine cooling, heavy-duty battery, rear load-leveling suspension (2WD).

Powertrains

5.4-liter V8 engine, XLT, Eddie Bauer 2WD..................	695	591
Limited-slip differential	255	217

NA XLT 4WD with 4.6-liter engine.

Prices are accurate at time of publication; subject to manufacturer's changes.

Safety Features

	Retail Price	Dealer Invoice
Front side-impact airbags	$395	$335
XLT requires Comfort/Convenience Pkg.		
Reverse Sensing System	245	206
Requires front side-impact airbags.		

Comfort and Convenience

Heated mirrors, XLT	50	43
Eddie Bauer (credit)	(45)	(38)
Deletes outside-mirror mounted turn signal lights on Eddie Bauer.		
Power sunroof	800	680
XLT requires Premium Sport Appearance Group.		
Heated front seats, Eddie Bauer	295	251
Leather captain's chairs, XLT	1300	1105
Second row captain's chairs, Eddie Bauer	795	676
AM/FM/CD player, XLT	100	85
6-disc CD changer	495	421
Manufacturer's discount price, Eddie Bauer	NC	NC

Special Purpose, Wheels and Tires

Load-leveling suspension, 4WD	815	692
Skid plates, 4WD	105	89
255/70R16 all-terrain white-letter tires, XLT	230	196
Alloy wheels, XLT	250	213
Requires 265/70R17 all-terrain white-letter tires.		

FORD EXPLORER

✔ BEST BUY

Ford Explorer 4-door

Rear- or 4-wheel-drive midsize sport-utility vehicle; similar to Mercury Mountaineer

Base price range: $19,970-$34,375. Built in USA. **Also consider:** Chevrolet Blazer, Jeep Grand Cherokee, Mercedes-Benz M-Class, Toyota 4Runner

FOR • Acceleration (ohc V6, V8) • Cargo room • Visibility • Build quality **AGAINST** • Ride • Fuel economy • Engine noise (ohv V6)

America's best-selling sport-utility vehicle gets a new base trim level for 2000. Explorer shares its design with the Mercury Mountaineer, although only the Ford offers a 2-door body style. It's sold in Sport trim. Four-door Explorers come in XLS, XLT, Eddie Bauer, and Limited versions. XLS replaces last year's base XL model and includes as standard power mirrors, windows, and locks, which had been optional. All Explorers have standard antilock brakes and 2- or 4-wheel drive.

Available engines are a 160-horsepower overhead-valve V6, a 210-hp overhead-cam V6, and, for XLT, Eddie Bauer, and Limited, a 215-hp V8. Manual transmission is standard with the base V6. A 5-speed automatic is optional on the base V6 and required with the overhead-cam V6. The V8 gets only a 4-speed automatic. V6 4x4s use Ford's Control Trac system with 4WD that need not be disengaged on dry pavement. V8 4x4s have permanently engaged all-wheel-drive. Front side airbags are optional on all models.

Among other options is a Reverse Sensing System that audibly warns of obstacles when backing up. Rear load-leveling is an option for 4WD XLT, Eddie Bauer, and Limited models.

PERFORMANCE The overhead-cam V6 is the best overall Explorer/Mountaineer engine. It's smoother than Explorer's gruff base V6 and more powerful, too. It doesn't match the V8's muscle, but the 5-speed automatic does an admirable job of keeping the ohc six in its power band. Expect mileage to average around 15-16 mpg with either V6, versus the abysmal 12.4 mpg we got in a test of an AWD V8 model.

Like rival systems from General Motors, Jeep, and Dodge, Control Trac automatically sends power to the wheels with the best traction so the driver doesn't need to constantly evaluate road conditions and decide whether the vehicle should be in 2WD or 4WD. The AWD system on V8s affords similar freedom.

Explorer and Mountaineer corner confidently, with moderate body lean, but the ride is less-forgiving and more trucklike than that of its main competition.

ACCOMMODATIONS Explorer and Mountaineer have ample space for four adults, and three can fit in back with some squeezing. Unfortunately, the rear bench has a split seatback that, as in most of these wagons, is hard and lacks shoulder support. Step-in height is taller than in GM rivals, so it's a little more work to get in or out. Power window and headlight switches are illuminated for easy nighttime use, but it's a slight stretch to the climate controls. Available side airbags and the new reverse-warning system are laudable features and rare in this class. Deep side and rear windows and well-placed outside mirrors provide a clear view of surrounding traffic. The liftgate's rear glass opens separately. Cargo room is good, thanks to undercarriage spare-tire storage. And the split rear seatback folds in a single motion without removing the headrests.

VALUE FOR THE MONEY An array of engine and 4WD choices, sound ergonomics, and competitive pricing keep Explorer and Mountaineer among our Best Buys. But competition is tougher than ever, so angle for a good deal.

ENGINES

	ohv V6	ohc V6	ohv V8
Size, liters/cu. in.	4.0/245	4.0/245	5.0/302
Horsepower @ rpm	160 @ 4200	210 @ 5250	215 @ 4200
Torque (lbs./ft.) @ rpm	225 @ 2750	240 @ 3250	288 @ 3300
Availability	S[1]	S[2]	O[3]
EPA city/highway mpg			
5-speed OD manual	18/23[4]		
4-speed OD automatic			14/19
5-speed OD automatic	16/20[5]	16/21[5]	

1. Sport and XLT. 2. Eddie Bauer and Limited; optional Sport and XLT. 3. XLT, Eddie Bauer, and Limited. 4. 16/20 w/4WD. 5. 15/19 w/4WD.

PRICES

Ford Explorer	Retail Price	Dealer Invoice
Sport 2-door wagon, 2WD	$19970	$18153
Sport 2-door wagon, 4WD	23070	20881
XLS 4-door wagon, 2WD	23290	21075
XLS 4-door wagon, 4WD	25170	22729
XLT 4-door wagon, 2WD	27185	24503
XLT 4-door wagon, 4WD	29150	26233
XLT 4-door wagon, AWD	29900	26892
Eddie Bauer 4-door wagon, 2WD	31740	28511
Eddie Bauer 4-door wagon, 4WD	33705	30240
Eddie Bauer 4-door wagon, AWD	34120	30606
Limited 4-door wagon, 2WD	31995	28736
Limited 4-door wagon, 4WD	33960	30465
Limited 4-door wagon, AWD	34375	30830
Destination charge	550	550

XLT, Eddie Bauer, and Limited require a Series Code Pkg.

STANDARD EQUIPMENT:

Sport/XLS: 4.0-liter V6 engine, 5-speed manual transmission, antilock 4-wheel disc brakes, driver- and passenger-side airbags, air conditioning, power steering, cloth front captain's chairs, center console, split folding rear seat, power mirrors, power windows, power door locks, power liftgate release, intermittent wipers, auxiliary power outlet, tachometer, AM/FM/cassette, digital clock, map light, rear defogger, intermittent rear wiper/washer, passenger-side visor mirror, theft-deterrent system, roof rack, rear privacy glass (Sport), full-size spare tire, 235/75R15 all-terrain white-letter tires, alloy wheels. **4WD** adds: Control Trac full-time 4-wheel drive, transfer-case skid plate.

XLT adds: leather-wrapped tilt steering wheel, cruise control, cloth sport front bucket seats w/manual lumbar support, 6-way power driver seat, high series floor console (armrest, cupholders, rear radio/air conditioning controls), overhead console (compass, outside temperature display, front and rear reading lights), remote keyless entry, AM/FM/CD player, illuminated visor mirrors, cargo cover, floormats, fog lights, roof rack. **4WD**

models add: Control Trac full-time 4-wheel drive, transfer-case skid plate.
AWD adds: permanent 4-wheel drive, 5.0-liter V8 engine, 4-speed automatic transmission.

Eddie Bauer adds: 4.0-liter ohc V6 engine, 5-speed automatic transmission, automatic climate control, steering wheel radio/climate controls, automatic day/night rearview mirror, universal garage door opener, Travelnote digital memo recorder, automatic headlights, illuminated running boards, 255/70R16 all-terrain white-letter tires. **4WD** adds: Control Trac full-time 4-wheel drive, transfer-case skid plate. **AWD** adds: permanent 4-wheel drive, 5.0-liter V8 engine, 4-speed automatic transmission.

Limited adds: heated power mirrors w/puddle lights, wood interior trim.
4WD adds: Control Trac full-time 4-wheel drive, transfer-case skid plate.
AWD adds: permanent 4-wheel drive, 5.0-liter V8 engine, 4-speed automatic transmission.

OPTIONAL EQUIPMENT:

	Retail Price	Dealer Invoice
Major Packages		
Comfort Group, Sport	$2945	$2503
Manufacturer's discount price	1850	1572

Cloth sport bucket front seats, 6-way power driver seat, AM/FM/CD player, high series floor console (cupholders, armrest, rear radio and air conditioning controls) overhead console (compass, outside temperature display, front and rear reading lights), illuminated visor mirrors, automatic day/night rearview mirror, key pad entry, puddle lights. Requires automatic transmission and Convenience Group.

Premium Sport Group, Sport	1600	1360
Manufacturer's discount price	1100	935

Fog lights, platinum-painted bumpers, side bars, wheel lip moldings, front tow hooks, special axle ratio, chrome steel wheels (2WD), machined alloy wheels (4WD), 255/70R16 all-terrain white-letter tires (4WD).

Convenience Group, Sport, XLS	750	638
Manufacturer's discount price, Sport	395	336

Tilt steering wheel, cruise control, cargo cover, floormats (Sport), rear privacy glass (XLS).

Sport Group, XLS	1500	1275
Manufacturer's discount price	1000	850

Special cloth captain's chairs, AM/FM/CD player, storage bag, side step bars, fog lights, wheel lip moldings, chrome steel wheels.

Series Code Pkg., XLT	1095	931
Manufacturer's discount price	NC	NC

5-speed automatic transmission. NA AWD.

Sport Group, XLT	1095	931
Manufacturer's discount price	795	676

Color-keyed grille, platinum-colored bumpers and wheel lip moldings, side step bars, limited slip differential (w/5.0-liter engine), special axle ratio, Eddie Bauer-style wheels, 255/70R16 tires.

Series Code Pkg., Eddie Bauer	1615	1373
Manufacturer's discount price	NC	NC

AM/FM/cassette/CD player w/Mach Audio System, leather upholstery, 6-way power passenger seat.

Series Code Pkg., Limited	1870	1590
Manufacturer's discount price	NC	NC

AM/FM/cassette/CD player, Mach Audio System, leather upholstery, heated front seats, power passenger seat, driver seat memory.

Trailer Towing Prep Group	355	302

Wiring harness, heavy-duty flasher, limited-slip differential, special axle ratio.

Powertrains

4.0-liter ohc V6 engine,		
Sport, 2WD/4WD XLT	540	459

Requires 5-speed automatic transmission.

5.0-liter V8 engine, XLT 2WD	775	659
Eddie Bauer 2WD, Limited 2WD	421	358

Requires 4-speed automatic transmission, Trailer Towing Pkg., AM/FM/cassette/CD player.

4-speed automatic transmission,		
XLT, Eddie Bauer, Limited	NC	NC

NA 4WD. Requires 5.0-liter V8 engine.

5-speed automatic transmission, Sport, XLS	1095	931

NA with 5.0-liter engine. Sport requires Comfort Group.

Safety Features

Front side-impact air bags	395	336

Sport requires leather sport bucket seats.

	Retail Price	Dealer Invoice
Reverse Sensing System,		
XLT, Eddie Bauer, Limited	$255	$217
Comfort and Convenience		
Cloth sport bucket seats, XLS	280	238
Leather sport bucket seats, Sport	655	557
XLT	950	808

Includes power front seats. Sport requires Comfort Group.

Heated seats, Eddie Bauer	255	217
Automatic day/night mirror, XLT	185	158

Includes automatic headlights.

Power sunroof,		
Sport, XLT, Eddie Bauer, Limited	800	680

Includes front overhead console with rear reading lamps. Sport requires Comfort Group and Premium Sport Group.

AM/FM/CD player, Sport, XLS	100	85
AM/FM/cassette/CD player, Sport	230	196
Sport w/Comfort Group, XLS, XLT	130	111
AM/FM/cassette/CD player, Sport, XLT	665	565

Includes Mach Audio System. Sport requires automatic transmission and Comfort Group.

6-disc CD changer,		
Sport, XLT, Eddie Bauer, Limited	395	336

Sport requires automatic transmission and Comfort Group.

Universal garage door opener, XLT	215	185

Includes Travelnote digital memo recorder.

Appearance and Miscellaneous

Side-step bar, Sport, XLS	295	251
Running boards, XLT	395	336
Rear privacy glass,		
XLS, XLT, Eddie Bauer, Limited	295	251

Special Purpose, Wheels and Tires

Rear load leveling suspension,		
XLT, Eddie Bauer, Limited	350	298

NA 2WD, AWD. XLT requires leather sport bucket seats.

FORD FOCUS

Ford Focus 4-door sedan

Front-wheel-drive subcompact car

Base price range: $11,865-$15,380. Built in USA. **Also consider:** Dodge/Plymouth Neon, Honda Civic, Mazda Protege, Toyota Corolla

FOR • Control layout • Handling/roadholding • Fuel economy • Cargo room (wagon) **AGAINST** • Acceleration • Engine noise

Ford's new subcompact is slightly larger than its aging Escort and offers three body styles, all with the company's "new-edge" styling. Focus comes as a 2-door hatchback in sporty ZX3 trim, a 4-door sedan in LX, SE, and top ZTS form, and as a 4-door SE wagon.

A 110-horsepower version of Escort's single-cam 4-cylinder engine is standard in LX and SE models. Standard in ZTS and ZX3 and optional for SE is a 130-hp twincam four, as in the Escort-based ZX2 coupe. Both engines team with manual transmission or 4-speed automatic. Antilock brakes are standard on ZTS, optional on other models. Head/chest front side airbags are optional, and all models come with rear child-seat anchors.

Focus will eventually replace the Escort line. Comparing sedans, Focus is 3 inches taller than the Escort and some 4.5 inches longer in wheelbase and overall length.

PERFORMANCE Focus has terrific road manners tempered by ordinary engine performance. It tackles twisty roads with linear, com-

Prices are accurate at time of publication; subject to manufacturer's changes.

municative steering, well-controlled body lean, and outstanding grip from the 15-inch tires standard on most models. All versions have a firm suspension and a flat highway ride. Bumps register with a thump, as in many European cars, but their impact seldom disturbs the cabin. The brakes feel strong, but nosedive is pronounced in "panic" stops, and some early test models concentrated too much assist in the first few inches of pedal travel.

Ford expects the SE sedan to be the most-popular Focus, accounting for nearly 50 percent of sales. The SE wagon will snare another 17 percent. SE buyers should spring for the $200 twincam option. It provides slightly better acceleration than the tepid base 2.0, but both are merely adequate at merging with fast-moving freeway traffic or pulling steadily up long grades, even with manual transmission. Automatic transmission dulls off-the-line snap, but provides fuss-free gear changes and is not a big detriment to everyday performance. We have not yet measured fuel economy.

Ford used the Honda Civic as a performance benchmark, and while Civic has less lateral tire grip, it rides softer and is quieter than Focus. Our pre-production test Focuses suffered noticeable wind rush around the front side windows and a ragged engine note at high rpm, but noise levels were otherwise unobjectionable.

ACCOMMODATIONS No subcompact is roomier overall. Occupants sit comfortably upright on chairlike cushions, get outstanding head room, and more rear leg clearance than in any other car in the class. Ford says most Focus buyers will be women and it pitches the standard height-adjustable driver's seat as a selling point. That feature enhances already-confident outward visibility, but the height-adjusting crank is inconveniently positioned on the front of the lower cushion, so getting situated requires trial and error. An available tilt/telescope steering wheel further tunes the driving position.

The dashboard echoes Focus's new-edge styling, and works well. Controls are conspicuous and smooth-working, air ducts prominent, and the air conditioner operates in all vent modes. The removable radio-station-button panel is a clever theft deterrent. No gauge is obstructed, though we'd have included a redline on the tachometer in the sporty ZX3 and ZTS, and would have avoided the oddly redundant power door lock switches and buttons.

Stirrup-type door handles and large front-door frames help entry/exit, though rear doors should open wider. All body types, the wagon in particular, have generous cargo holds and rear seats that flip/fold flat. Liftovers are low, and the sedan's trunklid uses strut-type hinges that don't intrude into the luggage area—a feature many costlier cars lack.

VALUE FOR THE MONEY Focus is not as refined as a Civic or quite as polished as the more-conservative Toyota Corolla. But no rival has more room, style, or body types. Ford's newest is fun to drive, too, despite the timid engines, and prices are competitive. Don't buy a small car without checking out Focus.

ENGINES

	ohc I4	dohc I4
Size, liters/cu. in.	2.0/121	2.0/121
Horsepower @ rpm	110 @ 5000	130 @ 5300
Torque (lbs./ft.) @ rpm	125 @ 3750	135 @ 4500
Availability	S	O[1]
EPA city/highway mpg		
5-speed OD manual	28/38	25/34
4-speed OD automatic	27/35	24/32

1. SE; standard ZX3 and ZTS.

PRICES

Ford Focus	Retail Price	Dealer Invoice
LX 4-door sedan	$12125	$11319
SE 4-door sedan	13565	12629
SE 4-door wagon	15380	14280
ZTS 4-door sedan	15165	14085
ZX3 2-door hatchback	11865	11082
Destination charge	415	415

STANDARD EQUIPMENT:

LX: 2.0-liter 4-cylinder engine, 5-speed manual transmission, driver- and passenger-side airbags, emergency inside trunk release, power steering, cloth upholstery, front bucket seats, height-adjustable driver seat, center console, cupholders, split folding rear seat, AM/FM/cassette, digital clock, auxiliary power outlet, visor mirrors, rear defogger, intermittent wipers,

remote decklid release, dual outside mirrors, 185/65R14 tires, wheel covers.

ZX3 adds: 2.0-liter dohc 4-cylinder engine, AM/FM/CD player, leather-wrapped steering wheel, tachometer, rear wiper/washer, fog lights, 195/60R15 tires, alloy wheels.

SE sedan adds to LX: air conditioning, power mirrors, power door locks, remote keyless entry, variable intermittent wipers, 195/60R15 tires, alloy wheels.

SE wagon adds: 4-speed automatic transmission, cargo cover, rear wiper/washer, roof rack.

ZTS adds to SE sedan: 2.0-liter dohc 4-cylinder engine, antilock brakes, tilt/telescoping leather-wrapped steering wheel, cruise control, power windows, AM/FM/CD player, tachometer, front armrest, map lights.

OPTIONAL EQUIPMENT:

	Retail Price	Dealer Invoice
Major Packages		
Comfort Group, SE	$395	$352
Cruise control, tilt/telescoping steering wheel, center armrest, map lights.		
Sport Group, SE sedan	425	379
2.0-liter dohc 4-cylinder engine, tachometer, rear spoiler, fog lights.		
Powertrains		
2.0-liter dohc 4-cylinder engine, SE	200	178
4-speed automatic transmission	815	725
Std. SE wagon.		
Safety Features		
Antilock brakes, LX, SE, ZX3	400	356
Front side-impact airbags	350	312
Comfort and Convenience		
Air conditioning, LX, ZX3	795	708
Leather upholstery, ZTS	695	619
Power windows, SE	295	263
Remote keyless entry, LX, ZX3	395	352
Includes power door locks.		
AM/FM/CD player, LX, SE	140	124
AM/FM/cassette, ZX3	—	—
Smoker's Pkg.	15	13
Includes ashtray, lighter.		
Alloy wheels, LX	360	321
Includes 195/60R15 tires.		

FORD F-150

Ford F-150 crew cab

Rear- or 4-wheel-drive full-size pickup truck; similar to Ford F-250

Base price range: $15,285-$30,255. Built in USA and Canada. **Also consider:** Chevrolet Silverado 1500, Dodge Ram 1500, GMC Sierra 1500, Toyota Tundra

FOR • Acceleration (V8s) • Build quality **AGAINST** • Acceleration (V6) • Fuel economy • Noise (V6) • Rear-seat comfort • Ride

Midyear additions of power-adjustable pedals and a class-exclusive cab style make news for America's perennial top-selling vehicle. The new cab style is called the SuperCrew and it has four regular-size front-opening doors. This "crew cab" configuration is traditionally reserved for three-quarter-ton and one-ton pickups, but Ford is the first to offer it in the more-popular half-ton format. The SuperCrew is to debut in early calendar 2000 as a 2001 model.

As for 2000-model F-150s, gas and brake pedals that power fore and aft several inches to accommodate drivers of different heights will be available in trucks built after November. And Ford drops the related light-duty F-250 in favor of a new heavy-duty F-150 with similar payload ratings. The separate Super Duty F-Series line has unique styling and is aimed at commercial and serious recreational users. This report focuses on the F-150.

F-150 regular cab and extended SuperCabs come with flush-fender Styleside cargo boxes in 6.5- and 8-foot lengths or a Flareside bulge-fender 6-foot box. SuperCrews will use a 5.5-foot Styleside box with an available tube-frame partition that effectively extends the bed with the tailgate lowered.

SuperCabs have back-hinged rear half-doors that open and close in conjunction with the front doors. They come with a 3-place split rear bench seat, which this year is reclined a few additional degrees in an effort to improve room and comfort. The SuperCrew's overall length is similar to that of a short-bed SuperCab, but its cab is 12 inches longer and includes a full-size 3-passenger split-folding rear seat.

All models are offered with rear- or 4-wheel drive. The 4x4s come with a floor-mounted transfer case lever; electronic control via a dashboard switch is optional. Unlike the system in the Chevrolet Silverado and GMC Sierra, the F-150's 4WD can't be used on dry pavement. Available engines are a base 4.2-liter V6, and V8s of 4.6 and 5.4 liters. The first two come with manual or automatic transmission, the 5.4 with automatic only.

All F-150s have a passenger-side air bag with a key-operated disable switch. Rear-wheel antilock brakes are standard; antilock 4-wheel disc brakes are optional on Work and XL models and included at no extra cost on XLT and top-line Lariat. Maximum payload is 2435 pounds, towing capacity 8200 pounds.

The SuperCrew will come in XLT or Lariat trim with V8 power only and will offer a power glass moonroof.

The new adjustable pedals are offered only with automatic transmission and are controlled by a dashboard switch. They're standard on the new SuperCrew and on Lariats, and optional on XLT models.

Among other 2000 changes, an overhead console with compass and outside temperature gauge is standard on all but XL and Work models, while the Lariat gets standard 17-inch wheels in place of 16s, plus turn-signal lights mounted in the outside mirrors. Ford also offers the limited-edition, high-performance Lightning. This 2WD regular-cab Flareside has a special supercharged 5.4 V8, a sport suspension, unique 18-inch alloy wheels, and the turn-signal mirrors.

PERFORMANCE The noisy base V6 provides only adequate acceleration. The smoother 4.6 V8 is sufficient for light-duty work, and the 5.4 is satisfyingly strong. No big pickup delivers good fuel economy. Our test 4.6-liter SuperCab 4x4 averaged just 12.5 mpg; expect about the same from the 5.4. The exciting Lightning is a fast, maneuverable, stiff-riding muscle truck that averaged 14.1 mpg in our test.

Most F-150s have a stable, relatively comfortable ride. The rear axle resists juddering even when the cargo bed is empty. Off-road and heavy-duty-payload suspensions give a less-forgiving ride. In any version, wind and road noise are moderate by pickup standards. Stopping power and pedal feel are good—and improve with the rear disc brakes, though Silverado and Sierra have standard antilock 4-wheel discs.

ACCOMMODATIONS Interiors range from Work-version stark to Lariat luxurious, but all have handy driving controls, plenty of small-items stowage, and ample front passenger room. As usual, entry/exit is higher in 4x4s versus 2WD models.

The SuperCab is the most-popular body style and while its back doors ease rear access, its rear seat isn't nearly as comfortable as that in Silverado and Sierra. Adults get loads of head room, but just-adequate leg room, and the seatback is still too upright for best comfort. It does fold flat to provide good in-cab cargo space. And the front-seat shoulder belt hangs in the rear doorway to act as a kind of grab handle. We have not yet tested a SuperCrew.

Build quality and workmanship has been solid on the F-150s we've tested.

VALUE FOR THE MONEY F-150 earns its Best Buy status with a keen blend of carlike manners and true-truck muscle. The new SuperCrew gets the drop on GM, but Silverado and Sierra match up well otherwise and offer a more accommodating extended cab. Shop Ford and the GM models for the best deal on the combination of virtues that suits you.

ENGINES

	ohv V6	ohc V8	ohc V8	Supercharged ohc V8
Size, liters/cu. in.	4.2/256	4.6/281	5.4/330	5.4/330
Horsepower @ rpm	205 @ 4750	220 @ 4500	260 @ 4500	360 @ 4750
Torque (lbs./ft.) @ rpm	250 @ 3000	290 @ 3250	345 @ 2300	440 @ 3000

	ohv V6	ohc V8	ohc V8	Supercharged ohc V8
Availability	S[1]	S[2]	O	S[3]
EPA city/highway mpg				
5-speed OD manual	15/21[4]	14/19[5]		
4-speed OD automatic	16/20[4]	15/19[5]	13/17[6]	14/21

1. 2WD exc. Lariat. 2. Lariat, 4WD SuperCab and SuperCrew; optional 2WD. 3. Lightning. 4. 15/18 w/4WD. 5. 14/17 w/4WD. 6. 13/16 w/4WD.

PRICES

Ford F-150

	Retail Price	Dealer Invoice
Work Styleside 2WD regular cab, short bed	$15285	$13916
Work Styleside 2WD regular cab, long bed	15575	14171
XL Styleside 2WD regular cab, short bed	16220	14252
XL Styleside 2WD regular cab, long bed	16520	14507
XL Flareside 2WD regular cab, short bed	17230	15111
XLT Styleside 2WD regular cab, short bed	19175	16763
XLT Styleside 2WD regular cab, long bed	19470	17014
XLT Flareside 2WD regular cab, short bed	20185	17623
SVT Lightning Flareside		
2WD regular cab, short bed	30710	26568
Work Styleside 4WD regular cab, short bed	18505	16749
Work Styleside 4WD regular cab, long bed	18795	17005
XL Styleside 4WD regular cab, short bed	19560	17091
XL Styleside 4WD regular cab, long bed	19860	17346
XL Flareside 4WD regular cab, short bed	20570	17949
XLT Styleside 4WD regular cab, short bed	22590	19667
XLT Styleside 4WD regular cab, long bed	22900	19930
XLT Flareside 4WD regular cab, short bed	23600	20525
Work Styleside 2WD SuperCab, short bed	17875	16195
Work Styleside 2WD SuperCab, long bed	18165	16450
XL Styleside 2WD SuperCab, short bed	18905	16534
XL Styleside 2WD SuperCab, long bed	19205	16789
XL Flareside 2WD SuperCab, short bed	19915	17392
XLT Styleside 2WD SuperCab, short bed	21905	19084
XLT Styleside 2WD SuperCab, long bed	22205	19339
XLT Flareside 2WD SuperCab, short bed	22915	19942
Lariat Styleside 2WD SuperCab, short bed	25690	22302
Lariat Styleside 2WD SuperCab, long bed	25990	22557
Lariat Flareside 2WD SuperCab, short bed	26700	23160
Work Styleside 4WD SuperCab, short bed	21605	19477
Work Styleside 4WD SuperCab, long bed	21895	19733
XL Styleside 4WD SuperCab, short bed	22770	19819
XL Styleside 4WD SuperCab, long bed	23070	20074
XL Flareside 4WD SuperCab, short bed	23780	20678
XLT Styleside 4WD SuperCab, short bed	25715	22322
XLT Styleside 4WD SuperCab, long bed	26015	22577
XLT Flareside 4WD SuperCab, short bed	26730	23186
Lariat Styleside 4WD SuperCab, short bed	28985	25103
Lariat Styleside 4WD SuperCab, long bed	29285	25358
Lariat Flareside 4WD SuperCab, short bed	29995	25961
Destination charge	665	665

XLT and Lariat require a Series Code Pkg.

STANDARD EQUIPMENT:

Work: 4.2-liter V6 engine, 5-speed manual transmission, driver- and passenger-side airbags, rear antilock brakes, power steering, AM/FM radio, digital clock, rear doors (SuperCab), vinyl bench seat, rear split folding seat (SuperCab), cupholders, cargo box light, black vinyl floor covering, intermittent wipers, auxiliary power outlet, theft-deterrent system, argent front bumper and rear step bumper, dual outside mirrors, 4-lead trailering harness, full-size spare, 235/70R16 tires, argent steel wheels. **4WD** models add: part-time 4-wheel drive, 2-speed transfer case, 4.6-liter V8 engine (SuperCab).

XL adds: cloth bench seat, passenger-side visor mirror, map lights, underhood light, chrome bumpers, styled steel wheels. **4WD** models add: part-time 4-wheel drive, 2-speed transfer case, 4.6-liter V8 engine (SuperCab).

XLT adds: tilt steering wheel, cruise control, split bench seat w/driver-side manual lumbar support, center storage console, power mirrors, power windows, power door locks, AM/FM/cassette, tachometer, speed-sensitive intermittent wipers, overhead console, compass, outside temperature indicator, visor mirrors, carpeting, floormats, rear privacy glass (SuperCab), swing-out rear quarter windows (SuperCab), tailgate locks, alloy wheels. **4WD** models add:

Prices are accurate at time of publication; subject to manufacturer's changes.

part-time 4-wheel drive, 2-speed transfer case, 4.6-liter V8 engine (SuperCab), fog lights, front tow hooks.

Lariat adds: air conditioning, leather upholstery, 6-way power driver seat, leather-wrapped steering wheel, automatic headlights, remote keyless entry, AM/FM/CD player, outside-mirror mounted turn signal lights, 275/60R17 white-letter tires, chrome steel wheels. **4WD** models add: part-time 4-wheel drive, 2-speed transfer case, tow hooks, fog lights, 265/70R17 all-terrain white-letter tires.

SVT Lightning adds: supercharged 5.4-liter V8 engine, 4-speed automatic transmission, limited-slip differential, antilock 4-wheel disc brakes, cloth and leather upholstery, sliding rear window w/deep-tinted glass, Heavy-Duty Electrical/Cooling Pkg., sport suspension, 295/45ZR18 tires, alloy wheels, deletes outside-mirror mounted turn signal lights, rear privacy glass.

OPTIONAL EQUIPMENT:
Major Packages

	Retail Price	Dealer Invoice
Special discount, SuperCab (credit)	($500)	($425)

Requires manual transmission and air conditioning. NA Lariat.

Convenience Group, XL	420	357

Tilt steering wheel, cruise control, overhead console, tailgate locks.

Sport Group, 2WD XL short bed	495	421
4WD XL short bed, XLT short bed	595	506

Color-keyed bumpers and grille, color-keyed mirrors, power mirrors (XLT), tachometer (4WD XL), fog lights (4WD XL), 3.55 axle ratio, polished alloy wheels, 255/70R16 white-letter tires (XL), 275/60R17 white-letter tires (XLT regular cab), 265/70R17 all-terrain white-letter tires (4WD XLT SuperCab), 275/60R17 white-letter tires (2WD XLT SuperCab).

Series Code 507A, XLT	1180	1003
Manufacturer's discount price	NC	NC

Air conditioning, front and rear antilock 4-wheel disc brakes.

Series Code 508A, Lariat	1470	1250
Manufacturer's discount price	NC	NC

4.6-liter V8 engine, 4-speed automatic transmission, front and rear antilock 4-wheel disc brakes.

Diamondplate Accessories Pkg.	995	846

Diamondplate running boards, front mud flaps, toolbox, bedrail caps, and tailgate protector. Black hard plastic bedliner. NA Flareside, SVT Lightning.

Top Three Accessories Pkg.	750	638

Color-keyed running boards, wraparound hood deflector. NA long bed, SVT Lightning.

Off-Road Equipment, 4WD XLT	995	846
4WD Lariat	450	383

Skid plates, heavy-duty shock absorbers, fog lights, 3.55 axle ratio, 265/70R17 all-terrain white-letter tires, alloy wheels (Lariat). NA with 4.2-liter V6 engine.

Class III Trailer Towing Group, Work, XL, XLT, Lariat	400	340

Heavy-Duty Electrical/Cooling Pkg., 7-wire trailer harness, trailer hitch, heavy-duty shock absorbers.

Class III Trailer Towing Group, Lightning	245	208

Seven-wire trailer harness, trailer hitch, heavy-duty shock absorbers.

Powertrains

4.2-liter V6 engine, Work (credit)	(500)	(425)

NA w/Off-Road Equipment, 4WD SuperCab.

4.6-liter V8 engine, Work, XL, XLT	750	638

Std. 4WD SuperCab.

5.4-liter V8 engine, Work, XL, XLT	1550	1318
Lariat, 4WD SuperCab	800	680

Requires automatic transmission. Includes front and rear antilock brakes.

4-speed automatic transmission, Work, XL, XLT	1095	931
Electronic transfer case, 4WD XLT/Lariat	160	136

Requires 4.6-liter or 5.4-liter engine and 4-speed automatic transmission.

3.55 rear axle ratio	50	43

Std. Lightning.

Limited-slip differential	285	243

Std. Lightning.

Safety Features

	Retail Price	Dealer Invoice
Front and rear anti-lock brakes, Work, XL	$375	$319

Includes 4-wheel disc brakes.

Comfort and Convenience

Air conditioning, Work, XL	805	684
Remote keyless entry, XLT	150	128
Cruise control and tilt steering wheel, Work	385	328
Cloth bench seat, Work	250	213
Cloth split bench seat, XL	260	221
Cloth captain's chairs, XLT	490	417

Includes floor console.

Leather captain's chairs, Lariat	490	417

Includes floor console.

Power driver seat, XLT	360	306

Includes automatic headlights. Requires automatic transmission when ordered with captain chairs.

AM/FM/cassette, XL	130	111
AM/FM/CD player, XL	320	273
XLT	190	162
AM/FM/cassette w/6-disc CD changer, XLT	400	340
Lariat, Lightning	210	178

Appearance and Miscellaneous

Sliding rear window	125	107

Std. Lightning

Cab steps, XL regular cab Flareside, XL 4WD regular cab Styleside, XLT/Lariat Flareside, 4WD XLT/Lariat	350	298
XL 2WD regular cab Styleside, XLT/Lariat 2WD Styleside	250	215
Fog lights, XL 4WD	140	119
Tonneau cover	150	128

Special Purpose, Wheels and Tires

Skid plates, 4WD SuperCab, 4WD regular cab long bed	160	136
4WD regular cab short bed	80	68
Heavy-Duty Electrical/Cooling Pkg.	210	178

Heavy-duty battery, heavy-duty alternator (w/4.2-liter V6 engine), super engine cooling, auxiliary transmission-oil cooler (w/automatic transmission), engine oil cooler (w/5.4-liter V8 engine). Std. Lightning.

Alloy wheels, XL	200	170
LT245/75R16 all-terrain white-letter tires, 4WD Work/XL/XLT	695	591

FORD MUSTANG

BUDGET BUY

Ford Mustang coupe

Rear-wheel-drive sports and GT car

Base price range: $16,520-$31,605. Built in USA. **Also consider:** Chevrolet Camaro, Pontiac Firebird

FOR • Acceleration (GT, Cobra) • Steering/handling • Fuel economy (GT, Cobra) • Rear-seat room • Wet weather traction (without traction control) **AGAINST**

A Sport appearance option for the V6 version tops the short list of additions to the 2000 Mustang. Base, GT, and Cobra models return as coupes or as convertibles with a power top and defrosted glass rear window. Base Mustangs have a 190-hp 3.8-liter V6. GTs use a 260-hp 4.6-liter single-overhead-cam V8. The Cobra gets a 320-hp twin-cam 4.6 V8. A 5-speed manual transmission is standard, automatic is optional on base and GT. The Cobra has an independent rear suspension, the other models use a less-sophisticated solid rear-axle design. Traction control is standard on Cobra and optional on base and GT models. All models have standard 4-wheel disc brakes; antilock

Ratings begin on page 213. Specifications begin on page 220.

control is standard on the GT and Cobra, optional on the base.

For 2000, all models get two rear child safety-seat anchors and, on the front fenders, a tri-color-bar emblem. Base versions are available with new 6-spoke 15-inch alloy wheels and, for the first time, with the same 16-inch alloy wheel and tire size used on the GT. The new Sport appearance group includes a rear spoiler, bright alloys, and body stripes.

PERFORMANCE Mustang proves there's still some life in one of Detroit's oldest designs. V6 versions account for 60 percent of sales, and even they accelerate strongly. The GT's V8 has tire-smoking muscle and effortless passing power, but you'll need the Cobra to keep up with a Chevrolet Camaro or Pontiac Firebird equipped with GM's larger, overhead-valve V8. Our test 5-speed GT coupe averaged 15.6 mpg.

Mustang has a ride-comfort edge over those GM rivals, though bad pavement comes through distinctly in the stiff-riding GT. And all these cars tend to get skittish in bumpy corners. There's plenty of lateral grip, and steering feel is good. Traction control enhances wet-weather safety; we recommend it. Stopping power is strong, pedal modulation good with the standard 4-wheel discs—although ABS is optional here and standard on Camaro and Firebird. Wind noise is low, but hard acceleration brings out lots of engine noise and, with the V-8, substantial exhaust roar. The convertible has enough top insulation to keep it from being uncomfortably noisy with its roof raised.

ACCOMMODATIONS With its relatively upright design, Mustang is easier to get into and out of than most competitors, although its long doors and tight rear-seat entry/exit are common coupe drawbacks. Mustang has a relatively airy cabin, and a higher seating position than its GM rivals. The front seats offer good room for two and are reasonably supportive. The rear bench best suits children. Unfortunately, hard plastic is the dominant theme inside. The convertible top's thick rear "pillars" restrict over-the-shoulder vision. Trunk space is meager, and convertibles lack the coupe's handy split folding rear seatback.

VALUE FOR THE MONEY Mustang handily outsells its GM competition because its appeal is broader-based. It's still an impractical car, but Mustang's never been better at its core mission: accelerate, handle, and look sporty for a reasonable price.

ENGINES

	ohv V6	ohc V8	dohc V8
Size, liters/cu. in.	3.8/232	4.6/281	4.6/281
Horsepower @ rpm	190 @ 5250	260 @ 5250	320 @ 6000
Torque (lbs./ft.) @ rpm	220 @ 2750	300 @ 4000	315 @ 4750
Availability	S[1]	S[2]	S[3]
EPA city/highway mpg			
5-speed OD manual	20/29	17/24	NA
4-speed OD automatic	20/27	17/23	

1. Base. 2. GT. 3. Cobra.

PRICES

Ford Mustang	Retail Price	Dealer Invoice
Base 2-door coupe	$16520	$15123
Base 2-door convertible	21370	19439
GT 2-door coupe	21015	19123
GT 2-door convertible	25270	22910
Cobra 2-door coupe	27605	24988
Cobra 2-door convertible	31605	28548
Destination charge	550	550

STANDARD EQUIPMENT:

Base coupe: 3.8-liter V6 engine, 5-speed manual transmission, driver- and passenger-side airbags, 4-wheel disc brakes, emergency inside trunk release, power steering, tilt steering wheel, air conditioning, cloth upholstery, bucket seats, split folding rear seat, center console, cupholders, power mirrors, power windows, power door locks, remote keyless entry, AM/FM/cassette/CD player, digital clock, tachometer, visor mirrors, intermittent wipers, auxiliary power outlet, power remote decklid release, theft-deterrent system, 205/65R15 tires, alloy wheels.

Base convertible adds: power convertible top, illuminated visor mirrors, deletes split folding rear seat.

GT coupe adds to base coupe: 4.6-liter V8 engine, limited-slip differen-

tial, antilock 4-wheel disc brakes, leather-wrapped steering wheel, fog lights, rear spoiler, GT Suspension Pkg., 225/55HR16 tires.

GT convertible adds to GT coupe: power convertible top, illuminated visor mirrors, deletes split folding rear seat.

Cobra adds to GT coupe: 4.6-liter dohc V8 engine, traction control, cruise control, leather upholstery, 6-way power driver seat, Mach audio system, illuminated visor mirrors, rear defogger, front floormats, folding convertible top (convertible), Cobra Suspension Pkg. w/independent rear suspension, 245/45ZR17 tires, deletes rear spoiler, convertible deletes split folding rear seat.

OPTIONAL EQUIPMENT:

	Retail Price	Dealer Invoice
Major Packages		
Convenience Group, Base, GT	$550	$490
Cruise control, 6-way power driver seat, rear defogger, front floormats. GT includes front power lumbar support when ordered with leather upholstery.		
V6 Sport Appearance Group, Base	550	490
Leather-wrapped steering wheel, rear spoiler, body stripes, bright alloy wheels.		
Powertrains		
4-speed automatic transmission, Base, GT	815	725
Traction control, Base, GT	230	205
Base requires antilock brakes.		
Safety Features		
Antilock brakes, Base	500	445
Comfort and Convenience		
Leather upholstery, Base, GT	500	445
Mach 460 sound system, Base, GT	395	352
Includes equalized amplifier, premium speakers.		
Illuminated visor mirrors, Base/GT coupe	95	85
Smoker's Pkg.	15	13
Cigarette lighter, ash tray.		
Rear spoiler, Base, Cobra	195	174
17-inch alloy wheels, GT	500	445
Includes 245/45ZR17 tires.		
225/55R16 tires, Base	190	169
Requires V6 Sport Appearance Group.		

FORD RANGER

Ford Ranger XLT ext. cab

Rear- or 4-wheel-drive compact pickup truck; similar to Mazda B-Series
Base price range: $11,485-$19,690. Built in USA. **Also consider:** Chevrolet S-10, Dodge Dakota, GMC Sonoma

FOR • Acceleration (4.0-liter V6) • Build quality • 4-door extended-cab **AGAINST** • Rear-seat comfort • Acceleration (4-cylinder) • Interior room (regular cab) • Ride

America's best-selling compact pickup adds a 4x4-look 2WD model for 2000 and also extends the 4-door cab style to the base trim level.

Ranger returns with regular-cab or extended SuperCab bodies, both in XL and uplevel XLT trim. SuperCabs are available with two rear doors; they're hinged at the back and open in conjunction with the front doors. The rear doors are now offered on both trim levels after being exclusive to the XLT. XLT 4-door SuperCabs, however, continue with a pair of fold-down rear jump seats; XL versions delete the jump seats. Regular-cabs get a 6- or 7-foot cargo bed, SuperCabs the 6-foot box. A flare-fender Flareside short-bed is optional.

Prices are accurate at time of publication; subject to manufacturer's changes.

Two-wheel-drive Rangers come with a 4-cylinder engine. A 3.0-liter V6 is optional on 2WD models, standard on 4x4s. A 4.0-liter V6 is optional across the board. Manual transmission is standard. The 4-cylinder and 3.0 V6 offer a 4-speed automatic option, the 4.0 a 5-speed automatic.

The new XL Trailhead option gives the 2WD regular cab XL short-bed the raised suspension, 16-inch wheels, and exterior trim used by 4WD Rangers. Also for 2000, front bucket seats are available on 2WD XLT models; they had been an option exclusive to 4WD XLTs. Mazda's B-Series pickups are built by Ford to the basic Ranger design but have slightly different styling.

PERFORMANCE Loaded with cargo or aimed uphill, 4-cylinder Rangers and B-Series Mazdas labor to gain speed, especially with automatic transmission. Even with manual, our test 2WD Mazda took nearly 13 seconds 0-60 mph, though it did average a friendly 20.1 mpg. We recommend the 4.0-liter V6, which is only a bit thirstier than the 3.0 and doesn't cost much more. It performs well and meshes nicely with the 5-speed automatic. Over its first 3200 miles, our extended-use-test 4.0/automatic SuperCab 4x4 is averaging 15.6 mpg. It has required no unscheduled service, though it does have an intrusive amount of drivetrain whine. None of these engines is quiet, though the sixes are slightly smoother than the four.

Regardless of engine or brand name, these little haulers have decent ride and handling for trucks. They jiggle some on rough roads, but absorb big bumps well and display stable cornering. Only Dodge's compact pickup offers 4WD that can be used on dry pavement, so this Ford system isn't as convenient as Dakota's.

ACCOMMODATIONS The 4-door option is a nice Ford/Mazda plus. Dakota and Nissan's Frontier offer two forward-opening rear doors and GM offers 3-door extended-cab compacts, but other competitors still have only two doors. Even so, all these rear-hinged doors are narrow and can't be opened unless a front door is first. And in any of these compact pickups, the rear-seat area is best used for toddlers or cargo. The regular-cab Ranger/B-Series does provide slightly more storage space, seat travel, and seatback recline than its competitors.

In any model, three adults are a squeeze in front, and entry/exit can be awkward in the higher-riding 4x4s. On the plus side, Ranger and B-Series have a convenient dashboard, solid overall assembly, and good-quality interior materials.

VALUE FOR THE MONEY Dodge's larger Dakota offers brawny V8s and full-time 4WD, but these Ford-built trucks have plenty of assets of their own and are without glaring faults. Ranger is justifiably a best-seller, but note that the functionally interchangeable but less-popular B-Series is likely to carry deeper discounts.

ENGINES

	ohc I4	ohv V6	ohv V6
Size, liters/cu. in.	2.5/153	3.0/182	4.0/245
Horsepower @ rpm	119 @ 5000	150 @ 4750	160 @ 4200
Torque (lbs./ft.) @ rpm	146 @ 3000	190 @ 3650	225 @ 2750
Availability	S[1]	S[2]	O
EPA city/highway mpg			
5-speed OD manual	22/27	18/23[3]	16/21[5]
4-speed OD automatic	20/25	17/22[4]	
5-speed OD automatic			17/22[6]

1. 2WD. 2. 4WD, optional 2WD. 3. 18/21 w/4WD. 4. 15/19 w/4WD. 5. 16/20 w/4WD. 6. 17/20 w/4WD.

PRICES

Ford Ranger

	Retail Price	Dealer Invoice
XL 2WD regular cab, short bed	$11485	$10912
XL 2WD regular cab, long bed	11955	11344
XLT 2WD regular cab, short bed	13560	12278
XLT 2WD regular cab, long bed	14110	12761
XL 4WD regular cab, short bed	15825	14904
XL 4WD regular cab, long bed	16295	15337
XLT 4WD regular cab, short bed	17975	16163
XLT 4WD regular cab, long bed	18545	16664
XL 2WD SuperCab	15145	13672
XLT 2WD SuperCab	15795	14244
XL 4WD SuperCab	17435	15688
XLT 4WD SuperCab	19690	17672
Destination charge	535	535

STANDARD EQUIPMENT:

XL: 2.5-liter 4-cylinder engine, 5-speed manual transmission, antilock rear brakes, driver- and passenger-side airbags, power steering, vinyl split bench seat, cloth split bench seat and rear jump seats (SuperCab), floor console, cupholders, AM/FM radio, digital clock, black vinyl floor covering, intermittent wipers, auxiliary power outlet, Styleside bed, painted bumpers, dual outside mirrors, trailer tow wire harness, full-size spare tire, 225/70R15SL tires, styled steel wheels. **4WD** models add: part-time 4-wheel drive, 3.0-liter V6 engine, tachometer, wheel flares, heavy-duty gas shock absorbers, front tow hooks, 215/75R15SL all-terrain white-letter tires.

XLT adds: cloth split bench seat, carpeting, AM/FM/CD player, cargo box and map lights, passenger-side visor mirror, behind-seat storage tray, chrome bumpers. **4WD** models add: part-time 4-wheel drive, 3.0-liter V6 engine, front and rear antilock brakes, tachometer, theft-deterrent system, fog lights, wheel flares, heavy-duty gas shock absorbers, front tow hooks, 235/75R15SL white-letter all-terrain tires, alloy wheels.

OPTIONAL EQUIPMENT:

Major Packages

	Retail Price	Dealer Invoice
XL Sport Appearance Pkg., XL 2WD	$395	$336
Color-keyed grille and bumpers, 225/70R15SL white-letter tires, sliver styled steel wheels.		
Trailhead Group, XL 2WD regular cab shortbed	1595	1356
Argent grille and bumpers, tachometer, fog lights, special axle ratio, front tow hooks, Payload Pkg. 2, heavy-duty front springs, 245/75R16SL all-terrain white-letter tires, alloy wheels.		
XLT Series Code 846A, XLT	805	695
Manufacturer's discount price, XLT	NC	NC
Air conditioning.		
XLT Sport Appearance Pkg.,		
XLT 2WD w/4-cylinder engine	435	370
XLT 2WD w/V6 engine	495	421
XLT 4WD	395	336
Color-keyed grille and bumpers, tachometer (2WD), fog lights (V6), 225/70R15SL white-letter tires (2WD), 245/75R16SL all-terrain white-letter tires (4WD), chrome styled steel wheels (2WD).		
Power Equipment Group, XLT	535	455
Power mirrors, power windows and door locks, remote keyless entry.		
4x4 Off-Road Pkg., XLT 4WD	395	336
4.10 axle ratio, off-road shock absorbers, skid plates, "4x4 Off-road" decal, 245/75R16SL all-terrain white-letter tires, 5-spoke alloy wheels.		
Wheel and Tire Group, XLT 2WD SuperCab	325	277
Manufacturer's discount price, ordered without flareside bed	NC	NC
Chrome styled steel wheels, 225/70R15SL white-letter tires.		

Powertrains

3.0-liter V6, 2WD	395	336
4.0-liter V6, 2WD XLT	1295	1101
4WD XLT	695	592
4-speed automatic transmission	1095	931
NA with 4.0-liter engine.		
5-speed automatic transmission, XLT	1145	973
Requires 4.0-liter engine.		
Limited-slip rear axle	295	251
Requires V6 engine. Includes auxiliary transmission-oil cooler.		

Safety Features

4-wheel antilock brakes, XL, XLT 2WD	300	255

Comfort and Convenience

Two rear doors, XLT SuperCab	695	591
XL SuperCab	575	488
Requires V6 engine. XL deletes jumps seat.		
Air conditioning, XL	805	684
Cruise control and tilt leather-wrapped steering wheel	395	336
Cloth split bench seat, XL regular cab	295	251
Cloth sport bucket seats, XLT	360	306
AM/FM/cassette, XL	140	119
AM/FM/CD player, XL	240	204
AM/FM/cassette/CD player, XLT	130	111

Appearance and Miscellaneous

Flareside bed	495	421
Manufacturer's discount price,		
XL 2WD SuperCab, XLT SuperCab	NC	NC
NA regular cab long bed. NA with Trailhead Group.		

	Retail Price	Dealer Invoice
Sliding rear window........................	$125	$107

Includes rear privacy glass.

Side step bars, XL/XLT 2WD regular cab short bed,
XLT 4WD, XLT SuperCab .... | 295 | 250 |

XL requires Trailhead Group. XLT 2WD regular cab short bed require XLT Sport Appearance Pkg.

Special Purpose, Wheels and Tires

Class III trailer hitch, ordered w/V6 engine .... | 215 | 182 |

FORD TAURUS

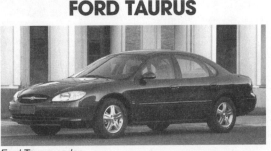

Ford Taurus sedan

Front-wheel-drive midsize car; similar to Mercury Sable
Base price range: $17,695-$20,895. Built in USA. **Also consider:** Chevrolet Impala, Honda Accord, Pontiac Grand Prix, Toyota Camry/Solara

FOR • Handling/roadholding • Rear-seat comfort • Cargo room
AGAINST • Low-speed acceleration

Ford's best-selling car sheds some controversial styling in a major 2000-model revamp. Taurus's exterior dimensions change little, but oval styling themes give way to conventional shapes that bring added head room and trunk space. Inside is a more-traditional dashboard and available adjustable foot pedals.

The V8 Taurus SHO disappears, leaving an LX sedan and uplevel SE sedan and wagon, all with V6 engines. Taurus continues to seat six with the available front bench, or five with optional front console. The wagon again offers a 2-place third-row seat. The new adjustable gas and brake pedals power fore and aft about three inches; they're a $120 option for SE models equipped with the power driver's seat.

Ford uses safety as a 2000 Taurus selling point. Head/chest front side airbags are a first-time option, and Ford's new Advanced Restraints System is standard. This is designed to minimize airbag injuries to front-seat occupants by gauging the severity of a crash, recognizing variables such as seat position, then deciding whether to deploy the front airbags and at what power. Initially, the system works only for the driver's side, but will later become operative for the passenger side. The system does not control the side airbags, but does modulate the new seatbelt pretensioners for both front seats. Sedans get a release inside the trunk designed to free trapped occupants. And both body styles have rear child-seat anchors. Antilock brakes are standard for SE Value and Comfort models, optional on other Tauruses.

The base overhead-valve V6 has 155 horsepower. Standard on the SE Comfort and optional on other SEs is a 200-hp twincam V6. A 4-speed automatic remains the only transmission, but traction control is a new option. Standard 16-inch wheels replace 15s. Taurus again shares its underskin design and mechanical components with the similarly renovated Mercury Sable.

PERFORMANCE Taurus delivers all the performance one could ask of a mainstream midsize car, as long as that doesn't include class-leading acceleration. Both engines are smooth runners, but neither furnishes top-notch midrange pulling power: press the accelerator at 25-50 mph, and Taurus takes precious moments to gather speed while the 4-speed automatic downshifts a gear or two and the engines spool up. Neither V6 matches the throttle response of Chevrolet Impala's 3.4-liter V6. Floor the gas from a standing start, however, and Taurus reaches highway speeds with little fuss. We've had no opportunity to measure fuel economy, but expect it to be similar to our '99 tests, where we averaged 18.9 mpg with the base engine and 17.1 with the twincam. Ford V6s use regular-grade gas.

No apologies about Taurus's road manners. LX and SE share tires and suspension settings and feel balanced, secure, and predictable even in rapid changes of direction. The steering—no longer variable assist—has fine on-center sense, but its turning effort is not as linear as some drivers may like. And two pre-production models we tested seemed acutely sensitive to road-surface texture, frequently transmitting vibrations through the steering-wheel rim in 65-mph cruising.

Resistance to wallow and float is impressive, but preview drives were mostly on smooth pavement, so a final verdict on ride comfort awaits a full road test. Although we'd like to see 4-wheel disc brakes available on Taurus sedans (only the wagon has them), stopping power feels strong and easily modulated. Increased insulation deadens engine and road noise to levels that make wind rush the most prominent sound at highway speeds, but it doesn't require a raised voice to overcome.

ACCOMMODATIONS Taurus is synonymous with "family car," and the 2000 shines in this roll. Particularly notable is back-seat comfort, where head clearance is generous, increasing almost 2 inches thanks to the new roof shape, and leg and foot space also is plentiful. The rear seat itself is substantial and comfortably contoured, though only leather-trimmed models get a center armrest. The wagon's rear-facing fold-away third seat is designed for children under 80 pounds.

Front outboard seating positions are uncrowded and adequately bolstered. The bench's center position suits only toddlers—who shouldn't ride in front anyway—but it flip-folds into a handy console/armrest that doesn't block the lower instrument panel, as did the previous Taurus's. The movable pedals adjust easily via a control on the outboard seat bottom. They team with the standard tilt steering wheel to provide an easily tailored driving position, and they permit shorter drivers to sit further from the steering-wheel airbag. The SE's driver-seat lumbar adjustment also helps comfort, but its control knob is awkwardly located on the seat front.

Gauges include a tachometer and are unobstructed, but their analog markings may be too small for all drivers to easily read at a glance. And on bucket-seat models, the transmission-position readout isn't repeated within the instrument pod. Audio and climate controls are easy to see and use, though there are no selectable air conditioning or recirculation modes.

Luggage room in both body styles is generous. The sedan's trunk is among the largest in class, and includes useful grocery-bag hooks, though the trunklid's hinges and adjustment brackets intrude into the cargo area. Available split folding rear seatbacks increase sedan cargo versatility, but don't lock to isolate cabin from trunk.

VALUE FOR THE MONEY Taurus returns to its roots as family transportation that doesn't compromise function for styling. Yet, it's fully contemporary, with fine road manners, an array of safety features, and competitive prices. Acceleration isn't always impressive, but the 2000 Taurus merits a place on any midsize-car shopping list.

ENGINES	ohv V6	dohc V6
Size, liters/cu. in.	3.0/182	3.0/181
Horsepower @ rpm	155 @ 4900	200 @ 5650
Torque (lbs./ft.) @ rpm	185 @ 3950	200 @ 4400
Availability	S	O
EPA city/highway mpg		
4-speed OD automatic	19/28	20/28

PRICES Ford Taurus	Retail Price	Dealer Invoice
LX 4-door sedan	$17695	$16306
SE 4-door sedan	18745	17063
SE 4-door wagon	19900	18091
SE Special Value Group 4-door sedan	19620	17842
SE Comfort 4-door sedan	20895	18977
Destination charge	550	550

STANDARD EQUIPMENT:

LX: 3.0-liter V6 engine, 4-speed automatic transmission, driver- and passenger-side airbags, emergency inside trunk release, air conditioning, variable-assist power steering, tilt steering wheel, cloth upholstery, 5-passenger seating, front bucket seats, column shift, center console, cupholders, power mirrors, power windows, AM/FM radio, digital clock, tachome-

Prices are accurate at time of publication; subject to manufacturer's changes.

ter, variable intermittent wipers, auxiliary power outlets, visor mirrors, rear defogger, remote decklid release, theft-deterrent system, 215/60R16 tires, wheel covers.

SE adds: 4-wheel disc brakes (wagon), power door locks, remote keyless entry, cruise control, 6-passenger seating (wagon), split folding rear seat (wagon), AM/FM/cassette, power antenna (wagon), rear/wiper washer (wagon), roof rack (wagon), alloy wheels.

SE Special Value Group adds: antilock brakes, 6-passenger seating, 6-way power driver seat w/lumbar adjustment, split folding rear seat, illuminated visor mirrors.

SE Comfort adds: 3.0-liter dohc V6 engine, leather-wrapped steering wheel, automatic climate control, remote keyless entry w/keypad, heated power mirrors, automatic headlights.

OPTIONAL EQUIPMENT:

	Retail Price	Dealer Invoice

Major Packages
LX Plus Pkg., LX $750 $668
Cruise control, power door locks, remote keyless entry, AM/FM/cassette, alloy wheels. Available only in California, Hawaii, and Orlando region.
Special Value Group, SE wagon 900 801
Antilock brakes, 6-way power driver seat, illuminated visor mirrors. Requires Wagon Group.
Wagon Group, SE wagon 300 267
Rear facing third seat, cargo cover.
SVG Comfort Plus Group, SE Wagon 325 290
3.0-liter dohc V6 engine, power-adjustable pedals. Available only in California, Hawaii, and Orlando region.
SVG Plus Group, SE Special Value Group 325 290
3.0-liter V6 engine, power-adjustable pedals, 5-passenger seating, console, floor shift. Available only in California, Hawaii, and Orlando region.
Comfort Plus Group, SE Comfort 150 134
Power-adjustable pedals, 5-passenger seating, console, floor shift, Mach Audio system, 6-disc CD changer. Available only in California, Hawaii, and Orlando region.

Powertrains
3.0-liter dohc V6 engine,
SE wagon, SE Special Value Group 695 619
Traction control,
SE, SE Special Value Group, SE Comfort...... 175 156
Requires antilock brakes. SE wagon requires SE Special Value Group.

Safety Features
Front side-impact airbags 390 347
LX requires power door locks.
Antilock brakes, LX, SE sedan 600 534

Comfort and Convenience
6-passenger seating, LX, SE sedan .... NC NC
5-passenger seating,
SE Special Value Group, SE Comfort 105 93
Includes floor shift.
Leather upholstery,
SE wagon, SE Special Value Group,
SE Comfort 895 797
Includes 5-passenger seating. Wagon requires Special Value Group.
6-way power driver seat, SE 395 352
Includes lumbar adjustment.
6-way power passenger seat, SE Comfort Group 350 312
Requires leather upholstery and front side-impact airbags.
Split folding rear seat, SE sedan 140 124
Power door locks, LX 275 245
Requires side-impact air bags.
Power-adjustable pedals 120 107
NA LX. SE requires power driver seat.
Audio Group, SE wagon, SE Special Value Group,
SE Comfort....................................... 670 596
6-disc CD changer, Mach Audio system. Wagon requires Special Value Group and Wagon Group.
Power sunroof,
SE Special Value Group, SE Comfort 840 747
Heated power mirrors,
SE wagon, SE Special Value Group 35 31

FORD WINDSTAR

RECOMMENDED

Ford Windstar

Front-wheel-drive minivan
Base price range: $19,815-$30,515. Built in Canada. **Also consider:** Chevrolet Venture, Dodge Caravan, Honda Odyssey, Toyota Sienna

FOR • Passenger and cargo room **AGAINST** • Fuel economy

Adjustable gas and brake pedals and a rear-seat video system are new options for the 2000 Windstar. Ford's minivan was revamped for '99, gaining new styling and sliding doors on both sides.

All Windstars have automatic transmission and a V6 engine. A 3.8-liter is standard on the SE and luxury SEL models and optional on the base and LX models. Base and LX come with a 3.0. Dual sliding doors are standard on SE and SEL, optional elsewhere. Power operation for both doors is standard on SEL and optional on SE; power operation for just the right-side door is optional on all but the base model. Head/chest front side airbags are optional on all Windstars. Antilock brakes are standard, traction control optional.

Windstar seats up to seven. The second-row bench on 3.0L and LX models can be positioned on the left or right side of the vehicle. SE and SEL come with second-row buckets. Windstar's 3-passenger third-row bench can be used as the second-row seat. Among options on 4-door models is a Reverse Sensing System that sounds a warning of obstacles while backing up.

Adjustable pedals that power fore and aft over a 4-inch span are a new option for XL, SE, and SEL. Optional on models with second-row bucket seats is an entertainment system that includes a VCR and flip-down 6.4-inch LCD TV screen; it's for use by rear passengers. Seatback grocery hooks are added to the rear bench for 2000. Windstar also comes as a 3-door cargo version.

PERFORMANCE This is a pretty good performer with the strong 3.8-liter engine, which furnishes sufficient power even with a full load of passengers. The 3.0 struggles to provide adequate acceleration, and both engines are gruff under hard throttle In mostly city driving. Our 3.8-liter tester averaged 14.8 mpg—below average for a minivan, but we doubt the overworked 3.0 would do better.

Windstar's wheelbase is among the longest of any minivan and helps provide a stable, carlike ride. Still, this Ford doesn't absorb bumps quite as well as the Toyota Sienna. Handling is confident and better than Sienna's, though Windstar's steering feels artificial and doesn't respond as quickly as that of the Honda Odyssey or General Motors minivans. And our 3.8-liter test model exhibited annoying torque steer—a tug on the steering wheel in fast take-offs. Brake-pedal feel is good, but overall stopping power is mid-pack.

ACCOMMODATIONS Windstar has a generally friendly dashboard design and roomy seating. The power side doors are a convenience, and even the manual sliders are unusually easy to open and close thanks to easy-grip interior handles. Likewise, the rear hatch raises and lowers with a light touch, although separate-opening rear glass isn't available.

The power adjustable pedals are a minivan first and should help a range of drivers position themselves a safe distance from the steering wheel airbag. Some of our testers find the driver's seat itself uncomfortable. The second- and third-row seats are substantial and supportive, but they're heavy—the benches weigh more than 100 pounds apiece, the second-row buckets 65 pounds each—so removal and installation demand muscle and technique. Second- and third-row seatbacks fold forward and even recline for great cargo and passenger versatility. The second-row outboard shoulder belts are height-adjustable. No integrated child seat is offered.

Audio controls are too busy, but we like the climate system's ability to run air conditioning in all vent modes. Switches for the available power-operated rear quarter windows are on the driver's door panel and are inaccessible to the front passenger. The Reverse Sensing System is worth considering because the base of Windstar's rear window is not visible to the driver, complicating backing up. We haven't tried Windstar's new video system, but similar setups in test GM minivans pleased passengers and didn't distract drivers.

VALUE FOR THE MONEY Minivans from Dodge, Plymouth, and Honda are our Best Buys, but the roomy Windstar boasts some noteworthy safety and convenience features.

ENGINES

	ohv V6	ohv V6
Size, liters/cu. in.	3.0/182	3.8/232
Horsepower @ rpm	150 @ 5000	200 @ 4900
Torque (lbs./ft.) @ rpm	186 @ 3750	240 @ 3600
Availability	S[1]	S[2]
EPA city/highway mpg		
4-speed OD automatic	17/23	17/23

1. 3.0L. 2. LX, SE, SEL, Cargo.

PRICES

Ford Windstar	Retail Price	Dealer Invoice
Cargo 3-door van	$19815	$17962
Base 3-door van	21315	19708
LX 3-door van	23965	21615
SE 4-door van	27615	24826
SEL 4-door van	30515	27378
Destination charge	605	605

LX requires 3.8-liter V6 engine.

STANDARD EQUIPMENT:

Cargo: 3.8-liter V6 engine, 4-speed automatic transmission, driver- and passenger-side airbags, antilock brakes, air conditioning, power steering, 2-passenger seating (cloth front buckets), front passenger area carpeting and cloth headliner, cupholders, power mirrors, power windows, power door locks, AM/FM radio, digital clock, intermittent wipers, rear defogger, rear wiper/washer, tachometer, auxiliary power outlets, visor mirrors, full-size spare tire, 215/70R15 tires, wheel covers.

Base adds: 3.0-liter V6 engine, 7-passenger seating (front bucket seats, 2-place middle seat and 3-place bench seats), rear passenger area carpeting and cloth headliner, interior air filter, theft-deterrent system, 205/70R15 tires, deletes full-size spare.

LX adds: tilt steering wheel, cruise control, remote keyless entry, second and third row adjustable seat-tracks and rollers, AM/FM/cassette, Light Group (front map/dome lights, glovebox light, second row reading and B-pillar lights, Sleeping Baby Mode lights).

SE adds: 3.8-liter V6 engine, driver-side sliding rear door, automatic climate control, rear air conditioning w/rear climate controls, leather-wrapped steering wheel, quad bucket seats, 6-way power driver seat w/power lumbar adjustment, heated power mirrors, overhead console (conversation mirror, coin holder, garage door opener/sunglasses holders, dome/reading lights), illuminated visor mirrors, floormats, roof rack, rear privacy glass, cornering lights, 215/70R15 tires, alloy wheels.

SEL adds: power sliding rear doors, leather upholstery, 6-way power passenger seat w/power lumbar adjustment, premium AM/FM/cassette/CD player w/rear audio controls, automatic day/night rearview mirror, universal garage door opener, compass, third row reading lights, automatic headlights, 225/60R16 tires.

OPTIONAL EQUIPMENT:

Major Packages

	Retail Price	Dealer Invoice
Comfort Group, LX	965	820
Rear air conditioning, automatic climate control, rear climate controls, roof rack, privacy glass.		
Family Security Pkg., LX	480	408
SE	435	370
SEL	275	234
Traction control, heated power mirrors (LX), theft-deterrent system w/perimeter alarm, self-sealing tires (LX, SE).		
Enhanced Seating Group, Base	410	348
Reclining second and third row seats, additional cupholders, second and third row adjustable tracks and rollers, map pockets on front seatbacks.		
Electronics Group, SE	535	455
Automatic day/night rearview mirror, universal garage door opener, compass, additional warning messages, automatic headlights.		

	Retail Price	Dealer Invoice
Class I Trailer Tow Electrical Pkg.	$35	$30
Module, trailer tow wiring harness.		
Class II Trailer Towing Pkg., LX, SE, SEL	470	400
Class I Trailer Towing Electrical Pkg. plus heavy-duty cooling and battery, transmission oil cooler, heavy-duty halfshafts, full-size spare tire, 215/70R15 tires.		

Powertrains

	Retail Price	Dealer Invoice
3.8-liter V6 engine, Base, LX	685	583
Manufacturer's discount price, LX	NC	NC

Safety Features

	Retail Price	Dealer Invoice
Front side-impact air bags	390	332
NA Cargo. Base requires Enhanced Seating Group.		
Reverse Sensing System, LX, SE, SEL	245	208
LX requires driver-side rear door.		

Comfort and Convenience

	Retail Price	Dealer Invoice
Rear Seat Entertainment System	1295	1101
Videocassette player, LCD screen, two headphones. NA Cargo. NA w/floor console.		
Driver-side sliding rear door, Base, LX	500	425
LX requires alloy wheels.		
Power passenger-side and manual driver-side sliding rear doors,		
LX	1000	850
SE	500	425
LX requires Comfort Group, full overhead console.		
Power driver- and passenger-side sliding rear doors,		
SE	900	765
Cruise control/tilt steering wheel, Cargo, Base	375	319
Floor console, LX, SE, SEL	155	132
Includes cupholders and covered storage bin.		
Full overhead console, LX	100	85
Storage, conversation mirror, map light, dome light. Requires driver-side sliding rear door.		
Remote keyless entry, Base	250	213
Includes Light Group.		
AM/FM/cassette, Cargo, Base	170	144
Premium AM/FM/cassette/CD player, LX, SE	300	255
Power adjustable pedals, LX, SE, SEL	120	102
LX requires power driver seat.		
Power driver seat, LX	325	277
Requires Comfort Group, driver-side rear door.		
Quad bucket seats, LX	745	633
SE, SEL	NC	NC
LX requires Comfort Group, alloy wheels.		
Quad bucket seats w/power driver seat, LX	1070	910
Requires Comfort Group, driver-side rear door.		
Leather upholstery, SE	865	735
Includes power passenger seat.		
Alloy wheels, LX	415	352
Includes 215/70R15 tires.		
Bright alloy wheels, SE	225	192
Includes 225/60R16 tires.		

GMC JIMMY/ENVOY

GMC Jimmy 4-door

Rear- or 4-wheel-drive midsize sport-utility vehicle; similar to Chevrolet Blazer and Oldsmobile Bravada
Base price range: $19,070-$34,270. Built in USA. **Also consider:** Ford Explorer, Jeep Grand Cherokee, Toyota 4Runner

FOR • Acceleration • Cargo room   **AGAINST** • Rear-seat comfort • Fuel economy

Prices are accurate at time of publication; subject to manufacturer's changes.

GMC's slightly upscale versions of the Chevrolet Blazer lose their base models for 2000 but gain an upgraded base suspension. Two- and 4-door Jimmys return, both with a drop-down tailgate with top-hinged rear window; 4-doors offer an alternative one-piece liftgate with opening window.

Gone are the SL trim levels, leaving better-equipped SLS 2-doors and SLE 4-doors. A special Diamond Edition 4-door bowed as an early 2000 model and returns to mark Jimmy's 30th birthday with brushed-aluminum exterior accents and specific interior trim. Again topping the line is Envoy, a luxury 4-door with monochrome exterior cladding, 2-tone leather-and-wood interior, load-leveling suspension, high-intensity headlamps, and other standard amenities. All models come with antilock 4-wheel disc brakes. The previously optional "Luxury Ride Suspension" package with its gas-charged shock absorbers and front and rear stabilizer bars is now standard on all 4-door models.

The only engine is a 4.3-liter V6. Manual transmission is standard on 2-doors; 4-doors come with an automatic that has a "Tow/Haul" mode designed to optimize shift points for heavy loads and towing; Blazer does not offer the Tow/Haul feature. Maximum towing capacity increases 400 pounds, to 5900 pounds, for 2000.

Jimmy's basic InstaTrac 4WD is for use only on slippery surfaces. Optional on Jimmy and standard on Envoy and the Diamond Edition is GM's Autotrac. It can be used on all surfaces and normally runs in 2WD but automatically engages the front axle when rear-wheel slip is detected; it also has 4-high and 4-low modes. GM's OnStar communication system is optional. The performance and accommodations of Jimmy and Envoy models mirror those of similarly equipped Blazers.

The Chevrolet Blazer report includes an evaluation of the Jimmy/Envoy.

ENGINES

	ohv V6
Size, liters/cu. in.	4.3/262
Horsepower @ rpm	190 @ 4400
Torque (lbs./ft.) @ rpm	250 @ 2800
Availability	S
EPA city/highway mpg	
5-speed OD manual	17/23[1]
4-speed OD automatic	16/21[2]

1. 15/18 w4WD. 2. 16/20 w/4WD.

PRICES

GMC Jimmy/Envoy	Retail Price	Dealer Invoice
Jimmy SLS 2-door wagon, 2WD	$19070	$17258
Jimmy SLS 2-door wagon, 4WD	22070	19973
Jimmy SLS Convenience 2-door wagon, 2WD	21970	19883
Jimmy SLS Convenience 2-door wagon, 4WD	24970	22598
Jimmy SLE 4-door wagon, 2WD	26570	24046
Jimmy SLE 4-door wagon, 4WD	28570	25856
Jimmy SLT 4-door wagon, 2WD	27870	25222
Jimmy SLT 4-door wagon, 4WD	29870	27032
Jimmy Diamond Edition 4-door wagon, 2WD	29570	26761
Jimmy Diamond Edition w/1SH 4-door wagon, 4WD	31570	28571
Jimmy Diamond Edition w/1SK 4-door wagon, 4WD	33370	30200
Envoy 4-door wagon, 4WD	34270	31014
Destination charge	550	550

Diamond Edition w/1SK requires Marketing Pkg.

STANDARD EQUIPMENT:

Jimmy SLS: 4.3-liter V6 engine, 5-speed manual transmission, limited-slip differential, driver- and passenger-side airbags, antilock 4-wheel disc brakes, daytime running lights, air conditioning, variable-assist power steering, reclining cloth front bucket seats with lumbar adjusters, center storage console, cupholders, split folding rear seat, tachometer, AM/FM/cassette, digital clock, automatic headlights, intermittent wipers, passenger-side visor mirror, floormats, theft-deterrent system, dual outside manual mirrors, black roof rack, deep-tinted rear side glass, tailgate, Euro-Ride Suspension, full-size spare tire, 235/70R15 tires, alloy wheels. **4WD** adds: part-time 4-wheel drive with electronic transfer case, front tow hooks.

Jimmy SLS Convenience/SLE add: 4-speed automatic transmission, tilt leather-wrapped steering wheel, cruise control, 8-way power driver seat (SLE), AM/FM/CD player, heated power mirrors, driver-side auto-matic day/night mirror (SLS Convenience), power windows, power door locks, remote keyless entry, illuminated visor mirrors, auxiliary power outlets, overhead console w/storage, compass, outside temperature indicator, map lights, cargo cover (SLE), rear defogger, rear intermittent wiper/washer, power remote liftgate release, deep-tinted tailgate glass, liftgate/liftglass (SLE), Luxury Ride Suspension (SLE), deletes limited-slip differential. **4WD** adds: part-time 4-wheel drive with electronic transfer case, front tow hooks.

Jimmy SLT adds: leather upholstery, 8-way power driver seat, cargo cover, fog lights, liftgate/liftglass, Luxury Ride Suspension, deletes automatic day/night driver-side and rearview mirrors. **4WD** adds: Autotrac full-time 4-wheel drive with electronic transfer case, front tow hooks.

Jimmy Diamond Edition adds: leather upholstery w/special diamond pattern stitching, special trim and badging, brushed aluminum roof rack, 7-wire trailering harness, heavy-duty hitch platform and flasher. **4WD** models adds: Autotrac full-time 4-wheel drive w/electronic transfer case, front tow hooks, 235/75R15 on/off-road tires.

Envoy adds to Jimmy SLT: Autotrac full-time 4-wheel drive, electronic transfer case, automatic climate control, heated front seats w/power lumbar adjustment, driver seat memory, 8-way power passenger seat, wood interior trim, heated power mirrors w/driver-side automatic day/night, Bose AM/FM/cassette w/6-disc CD changer, steering wheel radio controls, trip computer, universal garage door opener, automatic day/night rearview mirror, intermittent rear wiper/washer, rear liftgate/liftglass, high-intensity headlights, load-leveling suspension, front tow hooks, 7-wire trailering harness, heavy-duty hitch platform and flasher.

OPTIONAL EQUIPMENT:

Major Packages	Retail Price	Dealer Invoice
1SD SLE Luxury Marketing Pkg., SLE	—	—
Manufacturer's discount price	$1250	$1075

Automatic day/night rearview and driver-side mirrors, 8-way power passenger seat, Bose sound system, steering wheel radio controls, trip computer, universal garage door opener.

	Retail Price	Dealer Invoice
1SF SLT Luxury Marketing Pkg., SLT	—	—
Manufacturer's discount price	1800	1548

Automatic climate control, heated front seats, driver seat memory, 8-way power passenger seat, Bose sound system, steering wheel radio controls, automatic day/night rearview and driver-side mirrors.

	Retail Price	Dealer Invoice
1SJ Diamond Edition Special Marketing Pkg., 2WD Diamond Edition, 4WD Diamond Edition w/1SH	1800	1548

Automatic climate control, heated front seats, driver seat memory, 8-way power passenger seat, Bose sound system, steering wheel radio controls, automatic day/night rearview and driver-side mirrors.

	Retail Price	Dealer Invoice
1SK Diamond Edition Special Marketing Pkg., 4WD Diamond Edition w/1SK	1250	1075

1SJ Diamond Edition Special Marketing Pkg. plus AM/FM/cassette w/automatic tone control, 6-disc CD changer, rear seat radio controls, high-intensity headlights, load-leveling suspension.

	Retail Price	Dealer Invoice
ZQ3 Convenience Pkg., SLS	395	340

Cruise control, tilt steering wheel.

	Retail Price	Dealer Invoice
ZQ6 Convenience Pkg., SLS	535	460

Heated power mirrors, power windows and door locks.

	Retail Price	Dealer Invoice
Rear Window Convenience Pkg., SLS	322	277

Power remote tailgate/liftgate release, rear defogger, rear intermittent wiper/washer.

	Retail Price	Dealer Invoice
Heavy-duty trailering equipment, SLS, SLS Convenience, SLE, SLT	210	181

Weight distributing hitch platform, 7-lead wiring harness, heavy-duty flasher.

Powertrains

	Retail Price	Dealer Invoice
5-speed manual transmission, SLS Convenience (credit)	(1000)	(860)
4-speed automatic transmission, SLS	1000	860

Deletes limited-slip differential.

	Retail Price	Dealer Invoice
Autotrac full-time 4WD, 4WD SLS Convenience, 4WD SLE	225	194
Optional axle ratio, Jimmy	NC	NC
Limited-slip differential	270	232

Comfort and Convenience

	Retail Price	Dealer Invoice
OnStar System	695	—

Includes Global Positioning System, roadside assistance, emergency services. Requires annual service charge. Price may vary.

	Retail Price	Dealer Invoice
Power sunroof	$750	$645
NA SLS.		
6-way power driver seat, SLS Convenience	240	206
Overhead console, SLS	147	126
Includes storage, outside temperature indicator, compass.		
Deluxe overhead console, SLS Convenience	130	112
Includes storage, trip computer, universal garage door opener, outside temperature indicator, compass.		
AM/FM/cassette, 2-door	80	69
Includes automatic tone control.		
AM/FM/CD player, SLS	180	155
AM/FM/cassette/CD player, 2-door	100	86
6-disc CD changer	395	340
Std. Diamond Edition w/1SK, Envoy. NA with 5-speed manual transmission.		
Bose sound system, 2-door	495	426
NA w/5-speed manual transmission, AM/FM/cassette/CD player.		
Steering wheel radio controls, SLS Convenience	125	108
NA with 5-speed manual transmission.		

Appearance and Miscellaneous

Tailgate, SLE, SLT, Diamond Edition	NC	NC
Fog lights, 2WD SLS Convenience	115	99

Special Purpose, Wheels and Tires

Shield Pkg., Jimmy 4WD	126	108
Front differential skid plates, transfer-case, steering-linkage and fuel-tank shields.		
Euro-Ride Suspension Pkg., SLE, SLT, 2WD Diamond Edition	NC	NC
Bilstein gas shock absorbers (2WD), DeCarbon shock absorbers (4WD), larger stabilizer bars, heavy-duty springs.		
Off-Road Suspension Pkg., 4WD SLS Convenience	245	211
Bilstein gas shock absorbers, heavy-duty springs and body mounts, larger stabilizer bars. Requires 235/75R15 on/off-road white-letter tires.		
235/70R15 white-letter tires, 2-door, 2WD SLE, 2WD SLT	133	114
235/75R15 on/off-road white-letter tires, 4WD 2-door	168	144
Exterior spare-tire carrier, 4WD 2-door	159	137

GMC SAFARI

GMC Safari

Rear- or all-wheel-drive minivan; similar to Chevrolet Astro

Base price range: $20,104-$23,751. Built in USA. **Also consider:** Chevrolet Venture, Ford Windstar, Plymouth Voyager

FOR • Passenger and cargo room • Trailer towing capability
AGAINST • Fuel economy • Entry/exit • Ride

Safari and its Chevrolet Astro twin are America's only rear-wheel-drive truck-based minivans. Both come as passenger and cargo versions in a single body length with passenger-side sliding door and are available with rear-wheel drive or all-surface all-wheel drive (AWD). Passenger models offer the choice of two side-hinged panel doors at the back or swing-out half-height "Dutch" doors below a glass hatch. Antilock brakes and daytime running lights are standard.

This year, Safari gains rear child-seat anchors, a standard third-row bench seat allowing 7- or 8-passenger capacity, and a 2-gallon-larger fuel tank made of plastic instead of metal. Other new standards include headlamps that switch on automatically in low-light conditions, "flash-to-pass" headlights, battery-rundown protection, and retained accessory power that permits operating electrical accessories after the ignition is turned off or until a door is opened. Also new is a Tow/Haul mode that optimizes shift points on the mandatory automatic transmission for heavy hauling and towing. The only engine remains a 4.3-liter V6 that's mildly updated for quieter operation and lower emissions. Safari's optional AWD drives the rear wheels until they start to slip, when it automatically engages the front axle to restore traction. Finally, maximum trailering capacities are increased this year—by 500 pounds to 6000 for 2WD models and by 800 pounds to 5800 with AWD. Safari's performance and accommodations mirror those of similarly equipped Astros.

The Chevrolet Astro report includes an evaluation of the Safari.

ENGINES

	ohv V6
Size, liters/cu. in.	4.3/262
Horsepower @ rpm	190 @ 4400
Torque (lbs./ft.) @ rpm	250 @ 2800
Availability	S

EPA city/highway mpg

4-speed OD automatic	16/20[1]

1. 15/19 with AWD

PRICES

GMC Safari	Retail Price	Dealer Invoice
Cargo 3-door van	$20104	$18194
Cargo AWD 3-door van	22504	20360
Passenger 3-door van	21451	19413
Passenger AWD 3-door van	23751	21495
Destination charge	595	595

AWD denotes all-wheel drive.

STANDARD EQUIPMENT:

Cargo: 4.3-liter V6 engine, 4-speed automatic transmission, antilock brakes, driver- and passenger-side airbags, daytime running lights, variable-assist power steering, front air conditioning, 2-passenger seating (front reclining vinyl bucket seats), cupholders, AM/FM radio, digital clock, rubber floor covering, front cloth headliner, intermittent wipers, remote fuel-door release, auxiliary power outlets, theft-deterrent system, rear panel doors, dual outside mirrors, 215/75R15 tires. **AWD** adds: Autotrac permanent 4-wheel drive.

Passenger adds: 8-passenger seating (cloth front bucket seats, two folding bench seats), carpeting, full cloth headliner, visor mirrors, storage bin, 6-wire trailering harness. **AWD** adds: Autotrac permanent 4-wheel drive.

OPTIONAL EQUIPMENT:

Major Packages

SLE Option Pkg. 2, Passenger	3356	2886
Manufacturer's Discount Price,		
2WD Passenger	1179	1014
AWD Passenger	679	584

Power mirrors, power windows and door locks, remote keyless entry, tilt steering wheel, cruise control, overhead console/electronics (storage, reading lights, compass, outside temperature indicator, trip computer, illuminated visor mirrors), AM/FM/cassette, Seat Pkg. (front inboard/outboard armrests, map pockets, manual lumbar support), under passenger-seat storage, cargo net, floormats, roof rack, chrome accent grille, composite headlights, swing-out rear door glass, deep-tinted glass, lower bodyside cladding, chrome-appearance styled wheels.

SLT Option Pkg. 3, Passenger	6683	5747
Manufacturer's discount price	5883	5059

SLE Option Pkg. 2 plus front and rear air conditioning, rear heater, 6-way power driver seat, fold-down center console, leather-wrapped steering wheel, upgraded upholstery, AM/FM/cassette/CD player, additional cupholders, Dutch doors, alloy wheels.

ZQ2 Convenience Pkg.	474	408
Power door locks, power windows.		
ZQ3 Convenience Pkg.	383	329
Tilt steering wheel, cruise control.		

Prices are accurate at time of publication; subject to manufacturer's changes.

	Retail Price	Dealer Invoice
Trailer towing equipment	$309	$266

Platform hitch, 8-lead wiring harness.

Powertrains
Locking differential	252	217

Comfort and Convenience
Rear air conditioning, Passenger	523	450
Rear heater	205	176
Rear defogger	154	132

Requires rear Dutch doors.

Rear Dutch doors	518	445
w/SLE Pkg.	459	395

Includes rear wiper/washer. Passenger requires power door locks.

7-passenger seating, w/SLE Pkg.	318	273
w/SLT Pkg.	NC	NC

Front reclining bucket seats w/lumbar support and armrests, middle bucket seats, 3-passenger rear seat (split folding with SLT Pkg.).

6-way front power seat, each, Passenger	240	206

Requires SLE or SLT Pkg. Power passenger seat deletes under passenger-seat storage.

Seat Pkg.	168	144

Front armrests, front lumbar support, map pocket. Requires Option Pkg. 2. NA with vinyl upholstery.

Leather upholstery, w/SLT Pkg.	950	817
Overhead console, Passenger	223	192

Includes storage, compass, trip computer, outside temperature indicator, reading lights, illuminated visor mirrors.

Overhead console w/electronics, Passenger	223	192

Includes storage, map lights, compass, outside temperature display, trip computer, illuminated visor mirrors.

Power door locks, Cargo	223	192
Remote keyless entry	170	146

Requires power door locks.

AM/FM/cassette	147	126
Upgraded AM/FM/cassette	160	138

Includes automatic tone control. Cargo requires Convenience Pkg. ZQ2. Passenger requires SLE Pkg.

AM/FM/CD player	407	350

Includes automatic tone control. Cargo requires Convenience Pkg. ZQ2. Passenger requires SLE or SLT Pkg.

AM/FM/cassette/CD player	507	436

Includes automatic tone control. Cargo requires Convenience Pkg. ZQ2. Passenger requires SLE or SLT Pkg.

Rear headphone jacks/radio controls, Passenger	125	108

Requires SLE or SLT Pkg.

Universal garage-door opener, Passenger	115	99

Requires overhead console or option pkg.

Appearance and Miscellaneous
Chrome accent grille	220	189

Includes composite headlights.

Running boards, Passenger	400	344

Requires alloy wheels.

Deep-tinted glass, Passenger	290	249
Cargo w/ZW6 Glass Pkg.	262	225
ZW6 Glass Pkg., Cargo	368	316

Complete body glass.

Alloy wheels, Passenger	365	314
w/SLE Pkg.	25	21
Chrome-appearance styled wheels	340	292

GMC SIERRA 1500 ✓ BEST BUY

Rear- or 4-wheel-drive full-size pickup truck; similar to Chevrolet Silverado 1500

Base price range: $16,000-$27,861. Built in USA and Canada. **Also consider:** Dodge Ram 1500, Ford F-150, Toyota Tundra

FOR • Acceleration (V8s) • Instruments/controls **AGAINST** • Fuel economy • Ride

Sierra's big news for 2000 is the arrival of an optional fourth side door for extended-cab models. GMC's full-size pickup returns from its

GMC Sierra 1500 regular cab

1999 redesign in half-ton 1500-series models and light-duty three-quarter-ton 2500s. This report covers the 1500s, which offer SL, SLE, and top-line SLT trim levels. Heavy-duty 2500s and one-ton 3500s continue with GM's previous big-truck design as Sierra Classics, which are cousins to Chevy C/K models.

Like Chevy's near-identical Silverado, Sierra offers regular and extended cabs with 6.5- or 8.1-foot Wideside cargo beds. A factory-installed tonneau cover is a new Wideside-bed option. A flare-fender Sportside short-bed is also available. As on the 3-door extended-cab, the new fourth door is hinged at the rear and does not open or close independently of the front door. The extra door will initially be a "mandatory option" before becoming standard at midyear. That's about the time Ford will introduce its new SuperCrew, the first half-ton pickup with four conventional front-hinged rear doors.

A 4.3-liter V6 is the base engine, with available V8s of 4.8 and 5.3 liters. Both V8s gain 15 horsepower for 2000. Manual and automatic transmissions continue, the latter with a "Tow/Haul" mode that reduces shifting under heavy loads. Maximum towing capacity increases for 2000 by 700 pounds, to 11,200 pounds. Sierra's optional Autotrac 4-wheel drive can be used on dry pavement, automatically engaging the front axle when rear-wheel slip is detected. It also has locked-in 4WD high and low ranges. Antilock 4-wheel disc brakes are standard. Sierra's performance and accommodations mirror those of comparably equipped Silverados.

The Chevrolet Silverado report includes an evaluation of the Sierra 1500.

ENGINES
	ohv V6	ohv V8	ohv V8
Size, liters/cu. in.	4.3/262	4.8/294	5.3/325
Horsepower @ rpm	200 @ 4600	270 @ 5200	285 @ 5200
Torque (lbs./ft.) @ rpm	260 @ 2800	285 @ 4000	325 @ 4000
Availability	S	O	O
EPA city/highway mpg			
5-speed OD manual	17/23	16/20[1]	
4-speed OD automatic	16/20[2]	16/21[2]	16/20[2]

1. 15/19 w/4WD. 2. 15/18 w/4wd.

PRICES
GMC Sierra 1500
	Retail Price	Dealer Invoice
2WD SL Wideside regular cab, short bed	$16000	$14480
2WD SL Wideside regular cab, long bed	16300	14752
2WD SLE Wideside regular cab, short bed	19864	17381
2WD SLE Wideside regular cab, long bed	20164	17644
4WD SL Wideside regular cab, short bed	19077	17265
4WD SL Wideside regular cab, long bed	19377	17536
4WD SLE Wideside regular cab, short bed	22926	20060
4WD SLE Wideside regular cab, long bed	23226	20323
2WD SL Wideside extended cab, short bed	22259	19477
2WD SL Wideside extended cab, long bed	22559	19739
2WD SLE Wideside extended cab, short bed	24499	21437
2WD SLE Wideside extended cab, long bed	24799	21699
2WD SLT Wideside extended cab, short bed	24499	21437
2WD SLT Wideside extended cab, long bed	24799	21699
4WD SL Wideside extended cab, short bed	25321	22156
4WD SL Wideside extended cab, long bed	25621	22418
4WD SLE Wideside extended cab, short bed	27561	24116
4WD SLE Wideside extended cab, long bed	27861	24378
4WD SLT Wideside extended cab, short bed	27561	24116
4WD SLT Wideside extended cab, long bed	27861	24378
Destination charge	665	665

SLT models require a Marketing Option Pkg.

STANDARD EQUIPMENT:

SL regular cab: 4.3-liter V6 engine, 5-speed manual transmission, driver- and passenger-side airbags, antilock 4-wheel disc brakes, daytime running lights, power steering, tilt steering wheel, cloth split bench seat, AM/FM radio, digital clock, cupholders, auxiliary power outlets, tachometer, engine hour meter, passenger-side visor mirror, cargo box light, intermittent wipers, automatic headlights, carpeting, floormats, theft-deterrent system, dual outside mirrors, chrome front bumper, painted rear step bumper, 7-lead trailering harness, front tow hooks, full-size spare tire, 235/75R16 tires. **4WD** models add: part-time 4-wheel drive, 2-speed transfer case, 245/75R16 tires.

SL extended cab adds: 4.8-liter V8 engine, 4-speed automatic transmission, third door, reclining front seat, folding rear bench seat, swing-out rear quarter windows. **4WD** models add: part-time 4-wheel drive, 2-speed transfer case, 245/75R16 tires.

SLE regular cab adds to SL regular cab: air conditioning, interior air filter, cruise control, leather-wrapped steering wheel, AM/FM/CD player, power mirrors, power windows, power door locks, remote keyless entry, chrome rear bumper, chrome steel wheels. **4WD** models add: part-time 4-wheel drive, 2-speed transfer case, 245/75R16 tires.

SLE extended cab/SLT adds: 4.8-liter V8 engine, 4-speed automatic transmission, third door, reclining front seat, folding rear bench seat, swing out rear quarter windows. **4WD** models add: part-time 4-wheel drive (SLE), Autotrac full-time 4-wheel drive (SLT), 2-speed transfer case, 245/75R16 tires.

OPTIONAL EQUIPMENT:
Major Packages

	Retail Price	Dealer Invoice
Marketing Option Pkg., SL	$625	$538
Chrome grill surround, chrome rear step bumper, bodyside moldings, painted alloy wheels.		
Commercial Group,		
SL regular cab w/cloth seat	995	856
SL extended cab w/cloth seat (credit)	(100)	(86)
SL regular cab w/vinyl seat	713	613
SL extended cab w/vinyl seat (credit)	(382)	(329)
4-speed automatic transmission (regular cab), cloth or vinyl split bench seat. Deletes carpeting, seat recliners (extended cab), armrests, map pockets.		
Convenience Group, SL regular cab	1397	1201
SL extended cab	1377	1184
Air conditioning, cruise control, power door locks, AM/FM/cassette.		
Convenience Plus Group, 2WD SLE	655	563
4WD SLE	1030	886
Dual power front seats, automatic day/night rearview mirror, compass, outside temperature indicator, active transfer case (4WD).		
Marketing Option Pkg. 1SD, 2WD SLT	1750	1505
4WD SLT	2125	1828
Leather upholstery, 6-way power front seats, AM/FM/CD player, automatic day/night rearview mirror, compass, outside temperature indicator, active transfer case (4WD), 255/70R16 tires (2WD), alloy wheels.		
Comfort Group, SLT	775	667
Heated bucket seats, AM/FM/cassette/CD player.		
Snow Plow Prep Pkg.,		
4WD regular cab short bed w/automatic transmission	285	245
4WD regular cab short bed w/manual transmission or Trailering Equipment	190	163
Larger front springs, heavy-duty automatic transmission cooler, heavy-duty alternator, electrical supply/connections and mounting equipment, emergency lights.		
Off-Road Chassis Pkg., 4WD SLE	395	340
Includes larger springs and shock absorbers, jounce bumpers, stabilizer bars, high capacity air cleaner. Requires 265/R16 all-terrain tires or LT245/75R16C on/off-road tires.		
Firm Ride/Heavy Duty Suspension Pkg.	95	82
SLT	NC	NC
Includes heavy-duty shock absorbers, heavy-duty engine oil cooler, transmission oil cooler (automatic transmission). Requires 255/70R16 tires.		
Special Heavy-Duty Trailering Equipment	285	245
Trailer hitch platform, 7-wire trailering harness, heavy-duty auxiliary transmission oil cooler. Requires 4.8-liter or 5.3-liter engines and automatic transmission, Firm Ride/Heavy Duty Suspension.		

Powertrains	Retail Price	Dealer Invoice
4.8-liter V8 engine, regular cab	$695	$598
5.3-liter V8 engine, regular cab	1495	1286
extended cab	800	688
4-speed automatic transmission, regular cab	1095	942
Locking differential	285	245
Autotrac full-time 4WD, 4WD SLE	375	323

Comfort and Convenience		
Fourth door, extended cab	330	289
Air conditioning, SL	825	710
AM/FM/cassette, SL regular cab	170	146
SL extended cab	150	129
AM/FM/cassette/CD player, SLE/SLT extended cab	100	86
Requires bucket seats. 4WD SLE requires active transfer case.		
Bucket seats, SLE, SLT	375	323
Includes floor and overhead consoles.		
Rear defogger	175	151
NA w/sliding rear window. SL requires air conditioning.		
Automatic day/night rearview mirror, SLE	175	151
Includes compass and outside temperature indicator.		
Heated power mirrors, SLE, SLT	42	36
Requires rear defogger.		
Cruise control, SL	240	206
Power door locks, SL	162	139

Appearance and Miscellaneous		
Sportside body, SL short bed	895	770
SLE/SLT short bed	795	684
SL includes chrome rear step bumper.		
Tonneau cover, Wideside	240	206
Fog lights, SLE, SLT	140	120
Fender flares, 4WD	180	155
Deep-tinted glass, regular cab	50	43
extended cab	107	92
Requires sliding rear window or rear defogger.		
Sliding rear window	125	108

Special Purpose, Wheels and Tires		
Skid plates, 4WD	95	82
Ride Control Suspension Pkg., 2WD SLE	420	361
2WD SLT	325	280
Alloy wheels, SLE	110	95
235/75R16 white-letter tires, 2WD SL, 2WD SLE	125	108
245/75R16 white-letter tires, 4WD	125	108
245/75R16 all-terrain white-letter tires, 4WD	230	198
LT245/75R16 on/off-road white-letter tires, 4WD	286	246
255/75R16 white-letter tires, 2WD SL, 2WD SLE	295	254
265/75R16 all-terrain white-letter tires, SLE/SLT 4WD	365	314

GMC SONOMA

RECOMMENDED

GMC Sonoma extended cab

Rear- or 4-wheel-drive compact pickup truck; similar to Chevrolet S-10 and Isuzu Hombre

Base price range: $12,619-$20,231. Built in USA. **Also consider:** Dodge Dakota, Ford Ranger, Toyota Tacoma

FOR • Acceleration (V6) • Instruments/controls **AGAINST** • Ride • Rear-seat comfort

Extra V6 horsepower and a standard handling/trailering suspension for 4-wheel-drive models top the year-2000 news for Sonoma, a mechanical twin of the Chevrolet S-10 and Isuzu Hombre.

Prices are accurate at time of publication; subject to manufacturer's changes.

Regular- and extended-cab Sonomas return in SL and upscale SLS trim, while last year's SLE option package is now considered the new top-line model. A driver-side rear door is optional for extended cabs. Cargo beds of 6 and 7.3 feet are offered. Both come in flush-fender Wideside form, with the 6-foot bed available as a flare-fender Sportside. Front seating is a 3-place bench seat or extra-cost buckets. For 2000, the buckets are standard on 4WD SLS and SLE regular cabs and on 4WD extended-cabs. Extended cabs add two rear jump seats, with the left one eliminated on 3-door models. Antilock brakes are standard; 4x4s have 4-wheel discs.

Base power is a 2.2-liter 4-cylinder. Optional on 2WD Sonomas and standard on 4x4s is a 4.3-liter V6 with 180 or 190 horsepower, respectively. The base V6 previously had 175 hp. Both engines team with manual or optional automatic transmission. Maximum towing capacity is 6400 pounds. Sonoma 4x4s use GM's InstaTrac system, which is not for use on dry pavement but offers on-the-fly shifting at any speed via a dashboard switch. Like this year's S-10s, Sonomas get alterations to the V6 and manual transmission aimed at smoother, quieter operation. Sonoma's performance and accommodations mirror those of equivalent S-10s.

The Chevrolet S-10 report includes an evaluation of the Sonoma.

ENGINES

	ohv I4	ohv V6	ohv V6
Size, liters/cu. in.	2.2/134	4.3/262	4.3/262
Horsepower @ rpm	120 @	180 @	190 @
	5000	4400	4400
Torque (lbs./ft.) @ rpm	140 @	245 @	250 @
	3600	2800	2800
Availability	S[1]	O[1]	S[2]
EPA city/highway mpg			
5-speed OD manual	23/29	17/21	17/23
4-speed OD automatic	19/26	16/21	17/23

1. 2WD. 2. 4WD.

PRICES

GMC Sonoma	Retail Price	Dealer Invoice
22WD SL Wideside regular cab, short bed	$12619	$11925
2WD SL Wideside regular cab, long bed	12970	12257
2WD SLS Wideside regular cab, short bed	13777	12468
2WD SLS Wideside regular cab, long bed	14128	12786
2WD SLE Wideside regular cab, short bed	13777	12468
4WD SL Wideside regular cab, short bed	16853	15926
4WD SLS Wideside regular cab, short bed	18181	16454
4WD SLE Wideside regular cab, short bed	18181	16454
2WD SL Wideside extended cab, short bed	15508	14035
2WD SLS Wideside extended cab, short bed	16078	14551
2WD SLE Wideside extended cab, short bed	16078	14551
4WD SL Wideside extended cab, short bed	18777	17744
4WD SLS Wideside extended cab, short bed	20231	18309
4WD SLE Wideside extended cab, short bed	20231	18309
Destination charge	535	535

STANDARD EQUIPMENT:

SL: 2.2-liter 4-cylinder engine (2WD), 5-speed manual transmission, driver- and passenger-side airbags, antilock brakes, daytime running lights, air conditioning (extended cab), variable-assist power steering, vinyl or cloth bench seat (regular cab), split folding bench seat w/storage armrest (extended cab), rear jump seats (extended cab), cupholders, AM/FM radio, digital clock, passenger-side visor mirror, intermittent wipers, automatic headlights, black vinyl floor covering, theft-deterrent system, dual outside mirrors, painted front bumper and rear step bumper, Smooth Ride Suspension Pkg. (regular cab short bed), Z85 Heavy Duty Suspension Pkg. (regular cab long bed, extended cab), 205/75R15 tires. **4WD** models add: 4.3-liter V6 190-horsepower engine, part-time 4-wheel drive, electric 2-speed transfer case, 4-wheel disc brakes, front bucket seats (extended cab), center console (extended cab), tachometer, front tow hooks, Z85 Heavy Duty Suspension Pkg., 235/70R15 tires.
SLS adds: cloth split bench seat w/storage armrest, upgraded door trim, carpeting, auxiliary power outlets, floormats. **4WD** models add: 4.3-liter V6 190-horsepower engine, part-time 4-wheel drive, electric 2-speed transfer case, 4-wheel disc brakes, front bucket seats, center console, tachometer, front tow hooks, Z85 Heavy Duty Suspension Pkg., 235/70R15 tires.
SLE adds: illuminated visor mirrors, map lights, alloy wheels. **4WD** mod-

els add: 4.3-liter V6 190-horsepower engine, part-time 4-wheel drive, electric 2-speed transfer case, 4-wheel disc brakes, front bucket seats, center console, tachometer, front tow hooks, Z85 Heavy Duty Suspension Pkg., 235/70R15 tires.

OPTIONAL EQUIPMENT:

	Retail Price	Dealer Invoice
Major Packages		
Marketing Option Pkg. 1SA, SL	$450	$387
Manufacturer's discount price	NC	NC
Standard equipment.		
Marketing Option Pkg. 1SC, SLS	450	387
Manufacturer's discount price	NC	NC
Standard equipment.		
Marketing Option Pkg. 1SE,		
2WD SLS regular cab short bed	1841	1583
Manufacturer's discount price,		
w/manual transmission	841	723
w/automatic transmission	516	444

Air conditioning, cruise control, tilt steering wheel, AM/FM/CD player, tachometer, alloy wheels. NA with 4.3-liter engine, ZQ6 Convenience Pkg., bucket seats, leather-wrapped steering wheel, fog lights, Z85 Heavy Duty Suspension.

Marketing Option Pkg. 1SF,		
2WD SLS extended cab	2156	1854
Manufacturer's discount price,		
w/manual transmission	1156	994
w/automatic transmission	831	715

Third door, cruise control, tilt steering wheel, AM/FM/CD player, tachometer, deep-tinted glass, alloy wheels. NA with 4.3-liter engine, bucket seats, leather-wrapped steering wheel, fog lights.

Marketing Option Pkg. 1SG,		
2WD SLS extended cab	4602	3958
Manufacturer's discount price	3277	2818

4.3-liter V6 180-horsepower engine, 4-speed automatic transmission, 3.42 axle ratio, third door, cruise control, tilt steering wheel, AM/FM/CD player, tachometer, deep-tinted glass, alloy wheels. NA with leather-wrapped steering wheel.

Marketing Option 1SH, 4WD SLS extended cab	3057	2630
Manufacturer's discount price	1732	1490

4-speed automatic transmission, 3.42 axle ratio, third door, cruise control, tilt steering wheel, AM/FM/CD player, tachometer, deep-tinted glass, alloy wheels. NA with Sportside bed, Highrider Suspension, Underbody Shield Pkg.

Marketing Option Pkg. 1SJ, 4WD SLS extended cab	6421	5522
Manufacturer's discount price	5096	4382

Marketing Option Pkg. 1SH plus limited-slip differential, 3.73 axle ratio, heated power mirrors, power windows and door locks, remote keyless entry, leather-wrapped steering wheel, ZR2 Highrider Suspension Pkg. NA with Sportside bed, fog lights.

ZQ6 Convenience Pkg., SLS, SLE	795	684

Heated power mirrors, power windows and door locks, remote keyless entry. Regular cab requires air conditioning.

ZQ3 Convenience Pkg.	395	340

Tilt steering wheel, cruise control.

ZQ8 Sport Suspension Pkg.,		
2WD SLS short bed	735	632

DeCarbon shock absorbers, special coil springs, heavy-duty front and rear stabilizer bars, urethane jounce bumpers, 235/55R16 tires, unique alloy wheels. Requires tachometer.

ZR2 Highrider Suspension Pkg.,		
4WD SLS extended cab	1895	1630

Includes Shield Pkg., Bilstein shock absorbers, heavy-duty springs, wheel flares, 31x10.5R15 on/off-road tires, chassis enhancements for increased height and width. Requires locking differential, bucket seats. NA with Sportside bed, fog lights.

Powertrains

4.3-liter V6 180-horsepower engine, 2WD	1295	1114

Includes engine oil cooler, tachometer. Transmission oil cooler when ordered w/automatic transmission.

4-speed automatic transmission	1095	942
Locking differential	270	232

Comfort and Convenience

Third door, extended cab	315	271
Deletes driver-side jump seat.		
Air conditioning, regular cab	805	692

	Retail Price	Dealer Invoice
Bucket seats, 2WD SLS, 2WD SLE..........	$341	$293
Includes center console.		
Leather-wrapped steering wheel, SLS, SLE..........	54	46
Tachometer, 2WD..........	59	51
AM/FM/cassette..........	122	105
AM/FM/CD player, SLS, SLE..........	302	260
Includes automatic tone control.		
AM/FM/cassette/CD player, SLS, SLE..........	402	346
SLS w/Option Pkg. 1SG/1SH/1SJ..........	100	86
Includes automatic tone control.		

Appearance and Miscellaneous

Sportside bed, SLS short bed..........	475	409
Sliding rear window..........	120	103
Deep-tinted rear glass, regular cab..........	75	65
extended cab..........	115	99
Fog lights, SLS, SLE..........	115	99

Special Purpose, Wheels and Tires

Underbody Shield Pkg., 4WD..........	126	108
Transfer case, front differential, fuel tank, and steering linkage skid plates.		
Heavy Duty Suspension Pkg., 2WD regular cab short bed..........	256	220
Heavy-duty shock absorbers and rear springs.		
Alloy wheels, SL 2WD..........	372	320
Cast alloy wheels, 4WD SL..........	372	320
4WD SLS..........	280	241
235/75R15 on/off-road white-letter tires, 4WD..........	218	187

GMC YUKON AND YUKON XL

GMC Yukon XL

Rear- or 4-wheel-drive full-size sport-utility vehicle; similar to Chevrolet Tahoe and Suburban

Base price range: NA. Built in USA and Mexico. **Also consider:** Ford Expedition, Lincoln Navigator, Toyota Land Cruiser

FOR • Passenger and cargo room • Trailer towing capability
AGAINST • Fuel economy

General Motors redesigns its full-size SUVs for 2000, and GMC's offerings are again basically retrimmed versions of the Chevrolet Tahoe and Suburban. Yukon mirrors the Tahoe, while Yukon XL is the new name for GMC's take on the Suburban.

All are 4-door wagons that are about an inch shorter in wheelbase and overall length than their predecessors, but are two inches wider, two inches taller, and some 300 pounds lighter. Yukon gains third-row seating, for 9-passenger capacity, same as the XL. Both come with side-opening rear cargo doors or a new aluminum liftgate with independent-opening glass hatch. Front side airbags are new standard features. Yukon XL again comes in half-ton 1500 and three-quarter-ton 2500 versions.

As in the latest full-size GM pickups that parent all these SUVs, a 5.7-liter V8 gives way to 4.8-, 5.3-, and 6.0-liter V8s. Yukon comes with the 4.8 and offers the 5.3 as an option. Yukon XL 1500s come wit the 5.3 and offer the 6.0 as an option. Yukon XL 2500s come only with the 6.0. The only transmission is a 4-speed automatic with GM's "Tow/Haul" mode that adjusts shift points to accommodate heavy loads or trailers.

All models offer rear-wheel drive or GM's Autotrac 4WD with an "Auto 4WD" mode that can be used on dry pavement. Autotrac is controlled by a dashboard switch and includes locked-in 4WD high and low ranges. Traction control is a new option for 2WD models. All models have standard 4-wheel antilock brakes.

Newly available features include automatic climate control, power sunroof, rear audio controls, self-leveling rear suspension and, for XL, second-row reclining bucket seats. GM's OnStar communications system is to become an XL option during the model year. Yukons and Yukon XLs have performance and accommodations similar to those of like-equipped 2000 Tahoes and Suburbans.

The Chevrolet Tahoe and Suburban report includes an evaluation of the Yukon and Yukon XL.

ENGINES	ohv V8	ohv V8	ohv V8
Size, liters/cu. in.	4.8/294	5.3/325	6.0/364
Horsepower @ rpm	275 @ 5200	285 @ 5200	300 @ 4800
Torque (lbs./ft.) @ rpm	290 @ 4000	325 @ 4000	355 @ 4000
Availability	S	S[1]	S[2]

EPA city/highway mpg

1. Yukon XL 1500; optional Yukon. 2. Yukon XL 2500.

Prices, standard equipment, and options were unavailable at the time of publication.

GMC YUKON DENALI

GMC Yukon Denali

4-wheel-drive full-size sport-utility vehicle; similar to Cadillac Escalade and Chevrolet Tahoe Limited and Z71

Base price: $43,535. Built in USA. **Also consider:** Lexus LX 470, Lincoln Navigator

FOR • Passenger and cargo room • Trailer towing capability
AGAINST • Fuel economy • Entry/exit

While its Yukon stablemate is redesigned for 2000, the luxury Yukon Denali continues to use General Motors' previous-generation full-size SUV platform and powertrain. Denali shares this holdover status with the similar 2000 Cadillac Escalade and the Chevrolet Tahoe Z71 and Limited.

GM's OnStar communications system is standard for 2000, so the sole Denali option is a no-cost choice between a rear liftgate/tailgate or twin side-opening rear doors.

Unlike its redesigned GM cousins, which can seat up to nine passengers, Denali offers only a 5-place seating arrangement: power front bucket seats and a split/folding rear seat. Standard equipment dictated by Denali's luxury mission includes heated front and outboard rear leather seats, wood interior trim, a CD audio system with 6-disc CD changer and rear-seat audio controls, and power heated outside mirrors.

Its redesigned cousins get new engines, but Denali continues with a 5.7-liter V8, plus automatic transmission and Autotrac full-time 4-wheel drive that can be left engaged on dry pavement. Denali's standard towing rating is 6600 pounds. Performance and accommodations mirror those of the Cadillac Escalade.

The Cadillac Escalade report includes an evaluation of the Yukon Denali.

ENGINES	ohv V8
Size, liters/cu. in.	5.7/350
Horsepower @ rpm	255 @ 4600
Torque (lbs./ft.) @ rpm	330 @ 2800
Availability	S

EPA city/highway mpg
4-speed OD automatic 13/16

Prices are accurate at time of publication; subject to manufacturer's changes.

PRICES

GMC Yukon Denali	Retail Price	Dealer Invoice
Base 4-door wagon	$43535	$38093
Destination charge	675	675

STANDARD EQUIPMENT:

Base: 5.7-liter V8 engine, 4-speed automatic transmission, Autotrac full-time 4-wheel drive, locking rear differential, driver- and passenger-side airbags, antilock brakes, daytime running lights, OnStar System (Global Positioning System, roadside assistance, emergency services), front and rear air conditioning w/manual dual-zone controls, variable-assist power steering, tilt leather-wrapped steering wheel, cruise control, leather upholstery, 6-way power front bucket seats, center console, cupholders, split folding rear seat, heated front and rear seats, wood interior trim, heated power mirrors w/automatic day/night, power windows, power door locks, remote keyless entry, overhead console (universal garage door opener, rear audio controls, storage), automatic day/night rearview mirror, compass, outside temperature indicator, Bose AM/FM/cassette/CD player, 6-disc CD changer, tachometer, intermittent wipres, illuminated visor mirrors, map lights, auxiliary power outlets, rear defogger, rear wiper/washer (ordered with rear tailgate), automatic headlights, cargo cover, floormats, theft-deterrent system, fog lights, running boards, rear privacy glass, transmission oil cooler, trailer hitch, 8-lead trailer wiring harness, heavy-duty flasher, 265/70R16 tires, chrome alloy wheels.

OPTIONAL EQUIPMENT:
Appearance and Miscellaneous

Rear panel doors	NC	NC
Deletes rear wiper/washer.		

HONDA ACCORD

✓ BEST BUY

Honda Accord LX 4-door

Front-wheel-drive midsize car; similar to Acura TL
Base price range: $15,350-$24,550. Built in USA. **Also consider:** Dodge Stratus, Ford Taurus, Oldsmobile Intrigue, Toyota Camry/Solara

FOR • Acceleration (V6 models) • Quietness • Instruments/controls • Steering/handling • Build quality • Exterior finish • Interior materials **AGAINST** • Automatic transmission performance

The addition of front side airbags to some versions of the 2000 Accord is the big news for Honda's top-selling car line. Accord returns with coupe and sedan body styles in LX and upscale EX trim with 4-cylinder or V6 power, along with a price-leader 4-cylinder DX sedan. The 2.3-liter 4-cylinder makes 135 horsepower in the DX and 150 in LX and EX models. Accord's 3.0-liter V6 develops 200 hp.

Four-cylinder models come with manual or extra-cost automatic transmission, the V6 comes only with automatic. Antilock brakes remain standard on V6s and 4-cylinder EXs, optional for the automatic 4-cylinder LX sedan. Leather upholstery is included on EX V6s and available for 4-cylinder EXs.

The new front side air bags are standard on V6 models and on leather-equipped 4-cylinder EXs. All Accords gain a dual-stage passenger-side dashboard airbag for 2000. This airbag deploys with normal or reduced force depending on input from seat-mounted sensors that monitor the size and position of the passenger. The system can also deactivate the airbag if the sensors determine the passenger is too small or out of position.

PERFORMANCE Both Accord engines are silky, revvy, quiet, and punchy. We timed an 5-speed 4-cylinder EX at 8.5 seconds to 60 mph, a V6 EX sedan at 7.6. However, Accord's automatic transmis-

sion sometimes shifts with a jolt and can be painfully slow to downshift for passing. Typical of Hondas, economy is good. Our extended-use 4-cylinder manual coupe returned 23.8 mpg over more than 8100 city/highway miles. We've also averaged 24.7 mpg with an automatic I4 sedan and between 20.7-24 mpg with V6 sedans.

Ride is firm but comfortable and controlled. Accords are capable handlers, too, with precise steering and fine balance, though ultimate cornering grip is modest on 4-cylinder models because of relatively narrow tires. Braking is short, quick, and stable, though one V6 test sedan suffered unusually heavy nosedive in simulated panic stops. Wind rush is modest, but tire hum intrudes on coarse pavement and overall noise suppression is only average. Accords impress as solid and carefully constructed. Our extended-use car was trouble-free, though a recent test sedan's power front-passenger window worked only intermittently.

ACCOMMODATIONS Accord sedans are about as spacious as 4-door Toyota Camrys, but neither Honda body style seats five large adults without squeezing. Seat comfort itself is first-rate, especially up front. Several rival midsize cars offer front side airbags, but Accord joins the 2000 Ford Taurus as one of the few mid-priced models to offer the "smart" airbag system designed to reduce airbag-induced injuries.

Accord's dashboard design is very user-friendly, although the power window and lock switches aren't illuminated, and the ill-defined detent between the automatic transmission's top two gears may have many drivers cruising in third instead of fourth. Outward vision is good except over-the-shoulder, where a high parcel shelf inhibits sightlines. Entry/exit is easy on sedans, crouch-and-crawl to the rear in coupes. Interior storage space is decent, and both body styles have wide, flat-floor trunks. Liftover is a bit high in coupes, which also have slightly less cargo volume.

VALUE FOR THE MONEY Accord is a must-see midsize: roomy, very well built from top-grade materials, and with road manners a cut above the family-car norm. Demand is strong, so don't expect much discounting, but reliability and resale value are terrific.

ENGINES

	ohc I4	ohc I4	ohc V6
Size, liters/cu. in.	2.3/137	2.3/137	3.0/183
Horsepower @ rpm	135 @ 5400	150 @ 5700	200 @ 5500
Torque (lbs./ft.) @ rpm	145 @ 4700	152 @ 4900	195 @ 4700
Availability	S[1]	S[2]	S[3]
EPA city/highway mpg			
5-speed OD manual.............................	23/30	25/31	
4-speed OD automatic..........................	22/29	23/30	20/28

1. DX models. 2. LX, EX models. 3. V-6 models.

PRICES

Honda Accord	Retail Price	Dealer Invoice
DX 4-door sedan, 5-speed	$15350	$13661
DX 4-door sedan, automatic	16150	14371
LX 2-door coupe, 5-speed	18540	16495
LX 2-door coupe, automatic	19340	17206
LX 4-door sedan, 5-speed	18540	16495
LX 4-door sedan, automatic	19340	17206
LX 4-door sedan w/ABS, automatic	19940	17739
SE 4-door sedan w/ABS, automatic	20490	18228
LX V6 2-door coupe, automatic	21950	19526
LX V6 4-door sedan, automatic	21950	19526
EX 2-door coupe, 5-speed	21050	18726
EX 2-door coupe, automatic	21850	19437
EX 2-door coupe w/leather, 5-speed	22300	19837
EX 2-door coupe w/leather, automatic	23100	20547
EX 4-door sedan, 5-speed	21050	18726
EX 4-door sedan, automatic	21850	19437
EX 4-door sedan w/leather, 5-speed	22300	19837
EX 4-door sedan w/leather, automatic	23100	20547
EX V6 2-door coupe, automatic	24550	21836
EX V6 4-door sedan, automatic	24550	21836
Destination charge	415	415

ABS denotes antilock 4-wheel disc brakes.

STANDARD EQUIPMENT:

DX: 2.3-liter 4-cylinder 135-horsepower engine, 5-speed manual or

Ratings begin on page 213. Specifications begin on page 220.

CONSUMER GUIDE™

4-speed automatic transmission, driver- and passenger-side airbags, variable-assist power steering, tilt steering wheel, cloth reclining front bucket seats, folding rear seat, storage console with armrest, tachometer, maintenance interval indicator, AM/FM/cassette w/two speakers, integrated antenna, digital clock, cupholder, intermittent wipers, rear defogger, remote fuel-door and decklid releases, visor mirrors, dual outside mirrors, theft-deterrent system, 195/70R14 tires, wheel covers.

LX/SE add: 2.3-liter 4-cylinder VTEC 150-horsepower engine, cruise control, air conditioning, interior air filter, power mirrors, power windows, power door locks, illuminated visor mirrors, driver seat manual height adjustment, map lights, rear armrest w/trunk pass-through (4-door), split folding rear seat (2-door), variable intermittent wipers, 4-speaker sound system, floormats (SE), 195/65HR15 tires, alloy wheels (SE).

LX V6 adds: 3.0-liter V6 engine, 4-speed automatic transmission, front side-impact airbags, antilock 4-wheel disc brakes, 8-way power driver seat, 205/65R15 tires, deletes floormats, alloy wheels.

EX adds to LX/SE: antilock 4-wheel disc brakes, power sunroof, remote keyless entry, driver seat power height adjustment, driver seat adjustable lumbar support, AM/FM/CD player with six speakers, automatic-off headlights, power decklid release, alloy wheels, deletes floormats.

EX w/leather adds: front side-impact airbags, leather upholstery, leather-wrapped steering wheel, 8-way power driver seat.

EX V6 adds: 3.0-liter V6-cylinder engine, 4-speed automatic transmission, automatic climate control, steering wheel radio controls, universal garage door opener, 205/65R15 tires (4-door), 205/60R16 tires (2-door).

Options are available as dealer-installed accessories.

HONDA CIVIC

Honda Civic EX 4-door

Front-wheel-drive subcompact car
Base price range: $10,750-$17,630. Built in USA, Canada, and Japan. **Also consider:** Ford Focus, Mazda Protege, Toyota Corolla, Volkswagen Jetta/Golf

FOR • Fuel economy • Visibility • Build quality • Exterior finish • Ride **AGAINST** • Rear-seat entry/exit • Road noise

Redesigned Civics are due for 2001, so the addition of a standard tilt steering wheel to the base CX model and a few paint-color changes are the only changes for 2000. Civic offers 2-door coupes and hatchbacks and 4-door sedans, all with 1.6-liter 4-cylinder engines. CX, DX, and LX models have 106 horsepower, EX models 127, and the mileage-minded HX coupe 115. The sporty Si coupe has 160 hp, standard 4-wheel disc brakes, and low-profile tires on 15-inch alloy wheels (versus 14s elsewhere). Antilock brakes are standard on the EX sedan and optional on EX coupes equipped with automatic transmission. All models come with manual transmission, and all but the Si offer optional automatic. On the HX, the automatic option is Honda's CVT continuously variable transmission, which uses a belt-and-pulley system to provide infinite gear ratios.

Likely on sale in fall 2000, the 2001 Civics are slightly wider and longer than the current models and will have more-powerful 4-cylinder engines. Coupes and sedans are definite. It's uncertain whether hatchbacks will return, although there may be a Civic wagon positioned as a sort of bantam sport-utility vehicle below the CR-V.

PERFORMANCE All Civics have at least adequate acceleration, and the Si is quick. We timed a DX hatchback at 10.2 seconds 0-60 mph—brisk for an automatic-transmission subcompact. That test car averaged 29.1 mpg, despite gas-eating performance tests. EX models border on lively with their extra power yet are hardly less frugal; a test automatic sedan averaged 25.8 mpg. Our test Si did 0-60 in 7.8 seconds and averaged 26 mpg on the required premium fuel; other models use regular. Alas, the Si's high-strung engine demands lots of shifting for best performance and is geared for overly busy revving even at modest cruising pace. At least the manual gearbox in any Civic is a pleasure to use, while the conventional automatic is

generally smooth and responds quickly to large throttle inputs. The CVT works well, too, though its behavior takes getting used to. On all models, engine noise is intrusive at high rpm, and road noise is prominent on coarse pavement.

Civic's smooth, absorbent ride sets the small-car standard. About the only flaw is some short-wheelbase chop on freeways, especially in the tautly damped Si. All models are nimble and fun to drive, with terrific steering and a tight turning circle. However, the skinny tires on lesser models tend to roll too easily onto their sidewalls in high-speed cornering, thus compromising control. A more serious criticism is limiting ABS to the highest-priced models. Other Civics deserve it too, at least as an option.

ACCOMMODATIONS Civic sedans qualify as compact-class cars based on interior volume, while hatchbacks and coupes fall into the subcompact category. All have enough aft cabin space for up to 6-footers, although leg room is limited without the front seats moved way up, and rear entry/exit is nothing special even on sedans. Thin roof pillars and large windows make for fine all-round visibility. The driving position is low but comfortable, the dash a model of simple, intuitive design. A split-fold rear seatback expands cargo capacity in all models. No Civic is really luxurious, but workmanship is thorough, materials solid.

VALUE FOR THE MONEY These Hondas are far from the cheapest subcompacts, but they're very practical, they top the charts for refinement, and they offer plenty of driving fun. Add a proven record of reliability, durability, and high resale value, and any Civic rates as a Best Buy.

ENGINES

	ohc I4	ohc I4	ohc I4	dohc I4
Size, liters/cu. in.	1.6/97	1.6/97	1.6/97	1.6/97
Horsepower @ rpm	106 @ 6200	115 @ 6300	127 @ 6600	160 @ 7600
Torque (lbs./ft.) @ rpm	103 @ 4600	104 @ 5400	107 @ 5500	111 @ 7000
Availability	S[1]	S[2]	S[3]	S[4]
EPA city/highway mpg				
5-speed OD manual	32/37	35/43	30/35	26/31
4-speed OD automatic	28/35		28/35	

1. CX, DX, VP, LX. 2. HX. 3. EX. 4. Si.

PRICES

Honda Civic	Retail Price	Dealer Invoice
CX 2-door hatchback, 5-speed	$10750	$10157
CX 2-door hatchback, automatic	11750	11100
DX 2-door hatchback, 5-speed	12200	11027
DX 2-door hatchback, automatic	13000	11749
DX 2-door coupe, 5-speed	12680	11460
DX 2-door coupe, automatic	13480	12182
DX 4-door sedan, 5-speed	12885	11645
DX 4-door sedan, automatic	13685	12367
VP 4-door sedan, automatic	14730	13309
HX 2-door coupe, 5-speed	13500	12200
HX 2-door coupe, CVT	14500	13102
LX 4-door sedan, 5-speed	14930	13223
LX 4-door sedan, automatic	15730	13945
EX 2-door coupe, 5-speed	15550	14049
EX 2-door coupe, automatic	16350	14771
EX 2-door coupe w/ABS, automatic	16950	15312
EX 4-door sedan, 5-speed	16830	15204
EX 4-door sedan, automatic	17630	15926
Si 2-door coupe, 5-speed	17545	15849
Destination charge	415	415

ABS denotes antilock brakes.

STANDARD EQUIPMENT:
CX: 1.6-liter 4-cylinder 106-horsepower engine, 5-speed manual or 4-speed automatic transmission, driver- and passenger-side airbags, power steering (requires automatic transmission), tilt steering wheel, cloth upholstery front bucket seats, split folding rear seat, cupholders, remote fuel-door and hatch releases, rear defogger, intermittent wipers, visor mirrors, rear spoiler, dual remote outside mirrors, 185/65R14 tires.

DX hatchback adds: power steering, rear wiper/washer, AM/FM radio, digital clock, cargo cover, wheel covers.

Prices are accurate at time of publication; subject to manufacturer's changes.

DX sedan/coupe adds to CX: power steering, AM/FM radio, digital clock, rear heat ducts, remote trunk release, rear map pocket, wheel covers, deletes cargo cover, rear spoiler.

VP adds: 4-speed automatic transmission, air conditioning, power door locks, remote keyless entry, front storage console with armrest, AM/FM/CD player.

HX adds to DX sedan/coupe: 1.6-liter 4-cylinder VTEC 115-horsepower engine, 5-speed manual or Continuously Variable Transmission (CVT), power mirrors, power windows, power door locks, front storage console with armrest, tachometer, alloy wheels.

LX adds to DX sedan/coupe: air conditioning, cruise control, power mirrors, power windows, power door locks, height-adjustable driver seat, tachometer, front storage console with armrest.

EX adds to LX: 1.6-liter 4-cylinder VTEC 127-horsepower engine, antilock brakes (sedan), power sunroof, AM/FM/CD player, remote keyless entry.

Si adds: 1.6-liter 4-cylinder VTEC 160 horsepower engine, 4-wheel disc brakes, leather-wrapped steering wheel, sport suspension, 195/55VR15 tires, alloy wheels, deletes antilock brakes.

Options are available as dealer-installed accessories.

HONDA CR-V

✓ BEST BUY

Honda CR-V EX 4WD

Front- or 4-wheel-drive compact sport-utility vehicle
1999 base price range: $18,550-$21,250. Built in Japan.
Also consider: Kia Sportage, Subaru Forester, Toyota RAV4

FOR • Steering/handling • Cargo room • Build quality • Exterior finish **AGAINST** • Rear-seat entry/exit • Acceleration

Except for one new paint color, Honda's compact sport-utility vehicle is a rerun for 2000. CR-V continues as a 4-door wagon in three versions. The base LX comes with front-wheel drive and column-shift automatic transmission. There's also an LX and top-line EX with 4-wheel drive and manual or extra-cost automatic. Honda's Real-Time 4WD normally drives the front wheels, but will direct power to the rear if the front tires lose traction. No CR-V is intended for hard off-road use, and 4x4s lack separate low-range gearing. The only engine remains a 2.0-liter 4-cylinder, which gained 20 horsepower last year and is unchanged this year.

PERFORMANCE CR-V's smallish engine is still no powerhouse despite last year's upgrading, but it's adequate for the vehicle's weight, capable of 9.3 seconds to 60 mph with manual shift and 4WD—and only the driver aboard. Interestingly, that's a few ticks better than our clocking of a new 2WD Nissan Xterra V6 with automatic. We'd avoid the automatic Honda, as that transmission saps low-rpm torque and thus lengthens both standing-start acceleration and mid-range passing, especially in the heavier 4x4s. Despite a so-so power-to-weight ratio, our '99 manual-shift EX averaged 22.5 mpg—respectable, all things considered.

Being based on Honda's Civic instead of a truck, the CR-V is more carlike to drive than most low-priced SUVs. Steering is a bit inert on-center, but precise enough. Body lean is modest in tight turns, so the CR-V can be tossed around much like any small wagon. Ride comfort is good except for annoying hop over undulations and freeway expansion joints. Wind noise and tire thrum are low, but engine boom around 4000 rpm—which equals about 70 mph—is wearing on long trips.

ACCOMMODATIONS The CR-V is roomy for its exterior size, with ample head and leg room, but not enough interior width for three adults in back. Step-in height is reasonable given the 8-inch ground clearance, but rear doorways are narrow for larger folk. A standard tilt steering wheel and manual seat-height adjuster help tailor a basi-

cally good driving position, but the wiper stalk gets in the way of the automatic's column shifter.

All models have a 50/50 split rear seat that double-folds to form a flat load floor; put the seat up, however, and there's space behind for only about 10 grocery bags. A nice touch is the plastic cargo-floor panel that transforms into a picnic table with fold-down legs. Just as nice, workmanship is solid and rattle-free, with fine detail finish and sturdy—though not fancy—interior decor.

VALUE FOR THE MONEY The handy, well built CR-V is still very easy to like, but we'd like it even better with a bigger, stronger, and quieter engine. It remains a Best Buy among baby SUVs, but can't match the space, brawn, or off-road prowess of larger 4x4s. That includes Nissan's new midsize Xterra, which is more trucklike but usefully roomier—and sells for similar money.

ENGINES

	dohc I4
Size, liters/cu. in.	2.0/122
Horsepower @ rpm	146 @ 6200
Torque (lbs./ft.) @ rpm	133 @ 4500
Availability	S

EPA city/highway mpg
5-speed manual	NA
4-speed OD automatic	NA

PRICES

1999 Honda CR-V	Retail Price	Dealer Invoice
LX 2WD 4-door wagon, automatic	$18550	$16945
LX 4WD 4-door wagon, 5-speed	18950	17310
LX 4WD 4-door wagon, automatic	19750	18040
EX 4WD 4-door wagon, 5-speed	20450	18679
EX 4WD 4-door wagon, automatic	21250	19409
Destination charge	415	415

STANDARD EQUIPMENT:

LX: 2.0-liter dohc 4-cylinder engine, 5-speed manual or 4-speed automatic transmission, driver- and passenger-side airbags, air conditioning, interior air filter, rear heat ducts, variable-assist power steering, tilt steering column, cruise control, reclining front bucket seats w/driver-seat height adjustment, split folding rear bench seat, cupholders, power mirrors, power windows, power door locks, tachometer, AM/FM/cassette, digital clock, rear defogger, intermittent rear wiper/washer, visor mirrors, map lights, remote fuel filler/hatch release, lift-out folding picnic table, auxiliary power outlets, intermittent wipers, outside-mounted full-size spare tire, 205/70R15 tires. **4WD** models add: permanent all-wheel drive.

EX adds: permanent all-wheel drive, antilock brakes, AM/FM/CD player, remote keyless entry, alloy wheels.

Options are available as dealer-installed accessories.

HONDA INSIGHT

Honda Insight

Front-wheel-drive subcompact car
Base price range: NA. Built in Japan. **Also consider:** Ford Focus, Honda Civic, Mitsubishi Eclipse, Volkswagen New Beetle

FOR • Fuel economy • Passenger room **AGAINST** • Acceleration • Rear visibility • Road noise

Thanks to its lightweight aluminum construction and gas/electric hybrid powerplant, the new Honda Insight is the King of Economy, with EPA mileage estimates of 61 mpg city/70 mpg highway. A small electric motor kicks in during hard acceleration to supplement a 1.0-liter 3-cylinder gasoline engine, producing a combined total of 73 horsepower and 91 pound-feet of torque. Upon deceleration, the electric motor becomes a generator that recharges its nickel-metal-hydride battery pack. There is no need to plug into an electric outlet to recharge the batteries. A 5-speed manual is the only transmission. At 1856 pounds, the 2-seat Insight is the lightest car sold in America. Only 4000 are expected to be exported to the U.S. annually. Insight beats Toyota's Prius gas/electric hybrid to the U.S. market. Due in July 2000 as a 2001 model, Prius is a 4-door subcompact that can run on its electric motor, its 4-cylinder gas engine, or a combination of both.

EVALUATION There is a price to be paid for the Insight's lofty fuel economy. While around-town acceleration is adequate, any kind of hill—encountered at virtually any speed—radically slows progress and usually requires a downshift of at least two gears. Ditto for highway passing. Aiding around-town fuel economy is an "idle-stop" feature that shuts the engine off under certain conditions while sitting still in traffic. Despite the light weight and short wheelbase, Insight rides quite smoothly, becoming harsh only over larger bumps. There's little body lean in turns, and the skinny tires cling well even in the wet. The aerodynamic body produces little wind noise on the highway, but a shortage of soundproofing allows copious road noise. Insight's interior offers plenty of head and leg room for tall adults. The seats are fairly comfortable, but they're mounted lower than in other Hondas. Radio and climate controls are clear and easy to reach. The instrument panel includes a battery-level indicator along with digital and bar-graph gauges for fuel-economy and a readout showing whether the electric motor is in power or regenerative mode. Cargo space beneath the hatch lid is meager. A high tail and slanted roof pillars block the view aft, though a narrow glass panel at the base of the hatch lid aids in parking maneuvers. Insight's appeal is as much high-tech conversation piece as high-mileage commuter, but it seems far more practical at this point than any purely electric vehicle.

ENGINES

	ohc I3/Electric
Size, liters/cu. in.	1.0/61
Horsepower @ rpm	73 @ 5700
Torque (lbs./ft.) @ rpm	91 @ 2000
Availability	S

EPA city/highway mpg

5-speed OD manual	61/70

Prices, standard equipment, and options were unavailable at the time of publication.

HONDA ODYSSEY

✓ BEST BUY

Honda Odyssey EX

Front-wheel-drive minivan

Base price range: $23,400-$28,000. Built in Canada. **Also consider:** Chevrolet Venture, Dodge Caravan, Ford Windstar, Toyota Sienna

FOR • Entry/exit • Passenger and cargo room **AGAINST** • Rear visibility

A strong seller in its first year as a traditional minivan, Odyssey returns for its second season with a class exclusive: an optional navigation system.

Odyssey is among the biggest minivans and its 210-horsepower V6 is one of the most powerful minivan engines. LX and uplevel EX models are offered, both with standard automatic transmission, antilock brakes, and dual sliding rear side doors; the EX adds traction control and dual power sliding doors. Both models seat seven with front buckets, a pair of removable second-row buckets that can slide together to make a bench seat, and a third-row bench that folds away into the floor.

Odyssey's navigator is available only on the EX and uses a six-inch-wide in-dash color touch screen to display a map or driving directions; the latter can also be provided as audio prompts. The

$2000 system employs satellite positioning and DVD mapping, and is similar to that available in the RL and TL sedans from Honda's upscale Acura division.

PERFORMANCE Odyssey's performance is top of the class. It's alert and confident in changes of direction, with good steering feel. Ride is taut, so some big bumps jolt, and there's marked wheel patter on expansion joints and pavement breaks—but that's with just a driver aboard. Add some weight and Odyssey absorbs most rough stuff with fine comfort and control.

Acceleration is spirited for a minivan. Our test EX did 0-60 mph in just over 9 seconds, though throttle response at low and midrange speeds is hampered by a transmission that's a bit slow to downshift. Fuel economy is about par for the field. We averaged 18.6 mpg with lots of highway miles, 16.8 mpg in hard city/freeway driving. Honda recommends premium fuel, but says the V6 will tolerate regular with a slight loss of power

This engine is always smooth and quiet, and only the Toyota Sienna exceeds Odyssey for overall minivan powertrain refinement. Wind noise is low, but there's tire rumble and even body drumming on coarse or broken pavement. Stopping ability is strong and stable, although one test model's rear brakes squealed in low-speed stops.

ACCOMMODATIONS Odyssey's spacious cabin is easy to get into and out of thanks to a low step-in and large doorways. The EX's power-sliding side doors are convenient, if slower-acting than those in Ford and General Motors rivals.

Drivers have a commanding view ahead, but a headrest at every seating position leaves few clear rear sightlines. The driver's seat has too much backrest bolstering for some of our testers, too little for others, and it seems too firm or too soft to suit all body types. Control placement is generally good, but the column-mount shifter tends to slide past Drive into third gear when moving from Park; it also blocks the driver's reach to some audio controls. And the power outlet is mounted at nearly floor level. We have not tested an EX with the new navigation system, but it's a worthwhile feature in a family vehicle.

Second-row passengers get plenty of room, and we like the bench/bucket format. The third-row bench is a squeeze for three unless they're children, and leg room is tight unless the second-row seats are moved well forward. The hideaway third-row seat is a smart idea, but stowing it exposes two metal sidewall anchors that could damage cargo. The design also mandates a "space-saver" spare tire stored in a covered well behind the front seats, which means a flat full-size tire must be carried in the passenger or cargo area.

All passengers get a reading light and an air vent, and power rear vent windows are standard. Less likable were the interior rattles that afflicted one test Odyssey, including a persistent clicking from that versatile second-row seat.

VALUE FOR THE MONEY It's not perfect, but Honda's minivan is a solid Best Buy: roomy, refined, reasonably priced, and a fine performer. No wonder it's been a virtual sell-out.

ENGINES

	ohc V6
Size, liters/cu. in.	3.5/212
Horsepower @ rpm	210 @ 5200
Torque (lbs./ft.) @ rpm	229 @ 4300
Availability	S

EPA city/highway mpg

4-speed OD automatic	18/25

PRICES

Honda Odyssey	Retail Price	Dealer Invoice
LX 4-door van	$23400	$20814
EX 4-door van	26000	23124
EX 4-door van w/navigation system	28000	24902
Destination charge	415	415

STANDARD EQUIPMENT:

LX: 3.5-liter V6 engine, 4-speed automatic transmission, driver- and passenger-side airbags, antilock brakes, front and rear air conditioning, interior air filter, power steering, tilt steering wheel, cruise control, cloth upholstery, 7-passenger seating, front bucket seats, two second-row bucket seats, third row 3-passenger folding bench seat, center storage console, cupholders, AM/FM/cassette, digital clock, power mirrors, power windows, power door locks, remote fuel door release, tachometer, variable

Prices are accurate at time of publication; subject to manufacturer's changes.

intermittent wipers, rear defogger, rear wiper/washer, illuminated visor mirrors, reading lights, auxiliary power outlet, theft-deterrent system, rear privacy glass, 215/65R16 tires, wheel covers.

EX adds: traction control, 8-way power driver seat w/lumbar adjustment, dual power-sliding rear doors, remote keyless entry, automatic climate control, AM/FM/CD player, steering wheel radio controls, universal garage door opener, automatic-off headlights, roof rails, alloy wheels.

Options are available as dealer-installed accessories.

HONDA PASSPORT

Honda Passport EXL 4WD

Rear- or 4-wheel-drive midsize sport-utility vehicle; similar to Isuzu Rodeo

1999 base price range: $22,700-$29,950. Built in USA.
Also consider: Chevrolet Blazer, Ford Explorer, Toyota 4Runner

FOR • Cargo room • Acceleration **AGAINST** • Road and wind noise • Fuel economy • Ride

A new top-trim model and minor front and rear appearance alterations make news for the 2000 Passport. This is Honda's version of the Isuzu Rodeo and it returns LX and ritzier EX models with rear- or 4-wheel drive, and adds the new luxury EX-L. The EX-L comes with leather upholstery, two-tone paint, color-matched fender flares and bodyside moldings, and in-dash 6-disc CD changer. Also for 2000, 2WD LXs join other models with standard 16-inch wheels (versus 15s).

The only engine is an Isuzu-designed V6. LXs come with manual transmission and offer an optional automatic that's standard on other models. Towing capacity is 4500 pounds. Passport's 4WD system isn't for dry pavement but shifts between 2WD and 4-high via a dashboard button; it also has separate low-range gearing. All Passports have standard antilock brakes and a left-hinged tailgate below a glass liftgate. LXs stow their spare tire under the rear cargo floor; other models have a swing-away external carrier.

Passport is built alongside Rodeo at the Subaru-Isuzu plant in Indiana, though the Isuzu version outsells it almost 3 to 1. Rodeo for 2000 offers an electronically controlled shock absorber system, but Passport's performance and accommodations otherwise mirror those of comparably equipped Rodeos.

The Isuzu Rodeo report includes an evaluation of the Passport.

ENGINES

	dohc V6
Size, liters/cu. in.	3.2/193
Horsepower @ rpm	205 @ 5400
Torque (lbs./ft.) @ rpm	214 @ 3000
Availability	S

EPA city/highway mpg

5-speed OD manual	16/20
4-speed OD automatic	16/21[1]

1. 16/20 w4WD.

PRICES

1999 Honda Passport	Retail Price	Dealer Invoice
LX 2WD 4-door wagon, 5-speed	$22700	$20268
LX 2WD 4-door wagon, automatic	23850	21294
LX 4WD 4-door wagon, 5-speed	25450	22721
LX 4WD 4-door wagon with 16-inch Wheel Pkg., 5-speed	25850	23078
LX 4WD 4-door wagon, automatic	26600	23747
LX 4WD 4-door wagon with 16-inch Wheel Pkg., automatic	27000	24104

	Retail Price	Dealer Invoice
EX 2WD 4-door wagon, automatic	$26500	$23658
EX 2WD 4-door wagon w/leather, automatic	27500	24550
EX 4WD 4-door wagon, automatic	28950	25843
EX 4WD 4-door wagon w/leather, automatic	29950	26735
Destination charge	415	415

STANDARD EQUIPMENT:

LX 2WD: 3.2-liter V6 engine, 5-speed manual or 4-speed automatic transmission, driver- and passenger-side airbags, antilock brakes, air conditioning, variable-assist power steering, tilt steering wheel, cruise control, reclining front bucket seats, center storage console, cupholders, split folding rear bench seat, heated power mirrors, power windows, power door locks, tachometer, AM/FM/cassette, digital clock, visor mirrors, variable intermittent wipers, power tailgate release, cargo cover, rear defogger, rear wiper/washer, roof rack, skid plate, full-size spare tire, 235/75R15 tires.

LX 4WD adds: part-time 4-wheel drive, automatic locking front hubs, 2-speed transfer case, 4-wheel disc brakes, transfer case skid plate, alloy wheels.

LX 4WD w/16-inch Wheel Pkg. adds: limited-slip differential, flared wheel openings, splash guards, outside-mounted spare tire, 245/70R16 tires.

EX 2WD adds to LX 2WD: power sunroof, leather upholstery (w/leather models), leather-wrapped steering wheel, illuminated visor mirrors, map lights, theft-deterrent system, fog lights, rear privacy glass, 16-inch Wheel Pkg. (245/70R16 tires, alloy wheels, flared wheel openings, splash guards, outside-mounted spare tire).

EX 4WD adds: part-time 4-wheel drive, limited-slip differential, automatic locking front hubs, 2-speed transfer case, 4-wheel disc brakes, transfer-case skid plate.

Options are available as dealer-installed accessories.

HONDA PRELUDE

✓ BEST BUY

Honda Prelude SH

Front-wheel-drive sports coupe

Base price range: $23,500-$26,000. Built in Japan. **Also consider:** Mitsubishi Eclipse, Toyota Celica, Volkswagen New Beetle

FOR • Acceleration • Steering/handling • Build quality • Exterior finish **AGAINST** • Road noise • Rear-seat room

Unchanged for 2000, Honda's sporty Prelude coupe returns in base and SH models with twincam 4-cylinder power and standard manual transmission. Only the base model offers optional automatic, Honda's Sequential SportShift with manual shift capability. Exclusive to the SH is the Active Torque Transfer System that counters the tendency of front-drive cars to plow, or understeer, in hard cornering.

EVALUATION Prelude's 2.2 liter makes more low-end torque than most like-size twincam fours, but it still needs to rev for best performance. We timed 0-60 in about 8 seconds with automatic, just over 7 with manual. We averaged around 23 mpg, but premium fuel is mandatory. We prefer the slick-shifting 5-speed, but SportShift works well enough, though high-rpm down shifts can induce a jerky lunge. Handling is go-kart sharp. The torque-transfer system keeps the SH from running wide in hard turns, but it's no substitute for proper traction control, which isn't available. Ride is reasonably supple for a sports coupe; still, every bump comes through. Drivers sit low in a well-bolstered seat and enjoy good visibility and a convenient dashboard spoiled only by cheap-feeling slider-type climate controls. Rear-seat space is limited, as is trunk room. The pricey Prelude is in a sales free-fall, but we're impressed by its polished road manners and sophisticated engineering.

 Ratings begin on page 213. Specifications begin on page 220. CONSUMER GUIDE™

ENGINES

	dohc I4
Size, liters/cu. in.	2.2/132
Horsepower @ rpm	200 @ 7000
Torque (lbs./ft.) @ rpm	156 @ 5250
Availability	S[1]

EPA city/highway mpg

5-speed OD manual	22/27
4-speed OD automatic	21/26

1. 195 hp @ 6600 rpm with automatic transmission.

PRICES

Honda Prelude	Retail Price	Dealer Invoice
Base 2-door coupe, 5-speed	$23500	$20982
Base 2-door coupe, automatic	24500	21874
SH 2-door coupe, 5-speed	26000	23212
Destination charge	415	415

STANDARD EQUIPMENT:

Base: 2.2-liter 4-cylinder dohc engine, 5-speed manual or 4-speed automatic transmission w/manual-shift capability, driver- and passenger-side airbags, antilock 4-wheel disc brakes, air conditioning, interior air filter, variable-assist power steering, leather-wrapped tilt steering wheel, cruise control, cloth upholstery, front bucket seats w/driver-seat height adjustment, folding rear seat, center console, cupholders, power mirrors, power windows, power door locks, remote keyless entry, power sunroof, AM/FM/CD player, digital clock, tachometer, visor mirrors, map lights, rear defogger, remote fuel-door and decklid release, variable intermittent wipers, auxiliary power outlet, theft-deterrent system, 205/50VR16 tires, alloy wheels.

SH adds: 5-speed manual transmission, Active Torque Transfer System, leather-wrapped shifter, rear spoiler.

Options are available as dealer-installed accessories.

HONDA S2000

Honda S2000 Roadster

Rear-wheel-drive sports and GT car

Base price: $32,000. Built in Japan. **Also consider:** BMW Z3 Series, Chevrolet Corvette, Mazda Miata

FOR • Acceleration • Steering/handling • Brake performance • Seat comfort **AGAINST** • Engine noise • Ride • Passenger and cargo room

Honda breaks into the traditional sports car ranks with the S2000, a high-performance rear-wheel-drive 2-seater. It uses a new 240-horsepower 2.0-liter 4-cylinder engine and a 6-speed manual transmission. Also included are antilock 4-wheel disc brakes, air conditioning, and a power folding soft top with a plastic rear window.

EVALUATION Acceleration is breathtaking, brakes extraordinarily powerful, and handling razor-sharp. But the engine has a dizzying 9000-rpm redline and makes little usable power below 5000 rpm, so this new Honda must be driven aggressively to extract real performance. Gear changes are wrist-flick quick, and the steering follows every command. Traction control is unavailable, limiting the S2000's appeal in snowy climates. The ride is stiff but not harsh and while wind buffeting is modest, engine and exhaust combine for high noise levels in all but gentle cruising. There's adequate room for two, but trunk and cabin storage space is minimal. Most controls are close by, and the unique digital dashboard readouts are readable even in direct sunlight. The audio system has poor sound reproduction, however, and the air conditioning struggles to keep the interior cool. Packed with performance and Honda quality, the exciting S2000 is a

bargain at $32,000. But with Honda limiting supply to 5000 annually, the story here is likely to be high demand and inflated selling prices.

ENGINES

	dohc I4
Size, liters/cu. in.	2.0/122
Horsepower @ rpm	240 @ 8300
Torque (lbs./ft.) @ rpm	153 @ 7500
Availability	S

EPA city/highway mpg

6-speed OD manual	20/26

PRICES

Honda S2000	Retail Price	Dealer Invoice
Base 2-door convertible	$32000	$28456
Destination charge	415	415

STANDARD EQUIPMENT:

Base: 2.0-liter dohc 4-cylinder engine, 6-speed manual transmission, limited slip differential, driver- and passenger-side air bags, antilock 4-wheel disc brakes, air conditioning, interior air filter, variable-assist power steering, cruise control, leather upholstery, bucket seats, center console, cupholders, power mirrors, power windows, power door locks, remote keyless entry, AM/FM/CD player, digital clock, tachometer, intermittent wipers, auxiliary power outlet, power convertible top, remote fuel filler release, theft-deterrent system, 205/55VR16 front tires, 225/50VR16 rear tires, alloy wheels.

Options are available as dealer installed accessories.

HYUNDAI ACCENT

Hyundai Accent 4-door

Front-wheel-drive subcompact car

Base price range: $8,999-$10,299. Built in South Korea.
Also consider: Ford Escort/ZX2, Mitsubishi Mirage, Nissan Sentra

FOR • Fuel economy • Visibility **AGAINST** • Noise • Acceleration • Ride

Hyundai redesigns its lowest-priced car for 2000, enlarging Accent slightly and giving it new styling. Two-door hatchback and 4-door sedan body styles return on a wheelbase longer by 1.6 inches. The cars are longer by about 5 inches, wider by almost 2, and up to 192 pounds heavier, depending on model. Interior and cargo volume are little changed. Hatchbacks come in base L or GS trim, the sedan in top-level GL form. A 1.5-liter 4-cylinder returns as the sole engine. Manual transmission is standard. Optional on GS and GL is a 4-speed automatic models with Hyundai's Adaptive Logic, which is designed to limit unnecessary gear changes on grades or in deceleration. Accent remains among the few mainstream passenger cars that does not offer antilock brakes. For 2000, power steering is standard on all models; it had been unavailable on the L version. The L also gains the GS and GL's slightly wider tires, and the GS loses its standard remote trunk release. Hyundai's basic warranty is among the industry's longest: 5-years/60,000-miles bumper-to-bumper, 10-years/100,000-miles powertrain.

EVALUATION Engine and road noise still intrude on Accent's interior, but the 2000 is noticeably quieter than previous models. Acceleration is adequate above 3500-4000 rpm, where this 4-cylinder gets buzzy. The automatic transmission performs well, and Hyundai's Adaptive Logic does reduce erratic shifting on hills. Expect little change from our test 5-speed '99, which did 0-60 mph in just under 11 seconds and averaged 28.6 mpg; an automatic '99 got 23.7 mpg. Cornering grip is limited by the conservative tires, but Accent changes direction without drama.

Prices are accurate at time of publication; subject to manufacturer's changes.

Except for some jitter on bumpy pavement, the ride is as comfortable as that of most subcompacts. The slightly larger interior dimensions aren't noticeable, but there's ample room for two adults in back, and the redesigned front seats are comfortable. Dashboard layout and outward vision are good, though the view through back window is a bit pinched. Preview models we tested were solid and carefully assembled, with good paint finishes. Accent is a low-priced car that doesn't feel excessively cheap, although resale values of cars from this South Korean automaker are weak.

ENGINES

	ohc I4
Size, liters/cu. in.	1.5/91
Horsepower @ rpm	92 @ 5500
Torque (lbs./ft.) @ rpm	97 @ 4000
Availability	S

EPA city/highway mpg

5-speed OD manual	28/36
4-speed OD automatic	26/34

PRICES

Hyundai Accent	Retail Price	Dealer Invoice
L 2-door hatchback, 5-speed	$8999	$8610
GS 2-door hatchback, 5-speed	9599	8985
GS 2-door hatchback, automatic	10199	9547
GL 4-door sedan, 5-speed	9699	9078
GL 4-door sedan, automatic	10299	9640
Destination charge	435	435

STANDARD EQUIPMENT:

L: 1.5-liter 4-cylinder engine, 5-speed manual transmission, driver- and passenger-side airbags, power steering, cloth upholstery, front bucket seats, center console, cupholders, folding rear seat, AM/FM/cassette, rear defogger, remote fuel-door release, passenger-side visor mirror, variable intermittent wipers, auxiliary power outlet, remote outside mirrors, 175/70R13 tires, wheel covers.

GS and GL add: 5-speed manual or 4-speed automatic transmission, height-adjustable driver seat w/lumbar support, split folding rear seat, tachometer, digital clock, remote decklid release (GL), rear wiper/washer (GS).

OPTIONAL EQUIPMENT:
Major Packages

Option Pkg. 2, GS, GL	750	686
Air conditioning		
Option Pkg. 3, GS, GL	1250	1141
Air conditioning, power mirrors, power windows and door locks, AM/FM/CD player.		

Appearance and Miscellaneous

Rear spoiler	405	273

Post production options also available.

HYUNDAI ELANTRA

Hyundai Elantra sedan

Front-wheel-drive subcompact car
Base price range: $11,799-$13,249. Built in South Korea.
Also consider: Chevrolet Cavalier, Dodge/Plymouth Neon, Ford Escort/ZX2, Mitsubishi Mirage

FOR • Cargo room (wagon) • Fuel economy   **AGAINST**

• Engine noise • Automatic transmission performance

Elantra restores its uplevel GLS model for 2000 and shelves the entry-level GL trim. Hyundai's "senior" subcompact sedans and wagons are somewhat larger and costlier than its entry-level Accent subcompact. Elantra also uses a larger 4-cylinder engine linked to manual or optional automatic transmission.

Elantra comes only in GLS trim, which had been dropped during the 1999 model year. A split-folding rear seatback and power windows, mirrors, and locks are standard, as is a rear window wiper on the wagon. Four-wheel disc brakes are standard; antilock brakes are optional. Hyundai's basic warranty is among the industry's longest: 5-years/60,000-miles bumper-to-bumper, 10-years/100,000-miles powertrain.

PERFORMANCE Elantra rides and handles more competently than many small cars. The suspension is taut enough to deliver almost sporty cornering, yet ride is firm without being harsh, though marked thumping occurs on freeway expansion joints, and body lean is noticeable in quick direction changes. Braking is stable, but 60-mph panic stops were a tad long with our wagon, which lacked the optional ABS and was prone to sudden rear-wheel locking.

Few subcompacts match Elantra's horsepower, and a test wagon with automatic transmission ran 0-60 mph in a respectable 9.6 seconds. It averaged 22.4 mpg in hard city/freeway driving. Hyundai's 2.0 feels sleepy at low engine speeds, however, and hard acceleration can cause the automatic to "hang" in second gear, a nuisance in some situations. And the engine is boomy and gruff-sounding—enough to drown out most wind and road noise.

ACCOMMODATIONS Even 6-footers get decent front head room, plus firm, well-shaped bucket seats with enough fore-aft travel. The rear seat has surprisingly good head and leg room, but isn't wide enough to take three grownups without squeezing. Rear entry/exit is fairly easy despite rather narrow doors. Drivers enjoy good all-around visibility and mostly simple controls. Audio switches are small, poorly marked, and hard to reach while driving. The sedan's low-liftover trunk is roomy for the subcompact class, and both body styles have a useful split-fold rear seat. Workmanship is neat and solid, but not top-of-the-class.

VALUE FOR THE MONEY Elantra is nowhere near as refined as the Honda Civic or Toyota Corolla, but it's roomier and offers more features for the money. This South Korean automaker is still establishing itself in the U.S., but value-conscious shoppers should at least consider Hyundai's Elantra.

ENGINES

	dohc I4
Size, liters/cu. in.	2.0/122
Horsepower @ rpm	140 @ 6000
Torque (lbs./ft.) @ rpm	133 @ 4800
Availability	S

EPA city/highway mpg

5-speed OD manual	24/33
4-speed OD automatic	22/31

PRICES

Hyundai Elantra	Retail Price	Dealer Invoice
GLS 4-door sedan, 5-speed	$11799	$10860
GLS 4-door sedan, automatic	12549	11546
GLS 4-door wagon, 5-speed	12499	11504
GLS 4-door wagon, automatic	13249	12190
Destination charge	435	435

STANDARD EQUIPMENT:

GLS: 2.0-liter dohc 4-cylinder engine, 5-speed manual or 4-speed automatic transmission, driver- and passenger-side airbags, 4-wheel disc brakes, air conditioning, variable-assist power steering, tilt steering column, cloth reclining front bucket seats, manual 6-way adjustable driver seat, front storage console, split folding rear seat, AM/FM/cassette, digital clock, tachometer, power mirrors, power windows, power door locks, passenger-side visor mirror, variable intermittent wipers, rear defogger, remote fuel-door and decklid release, map lights, cargo cover (wagon), rear wiper/washer (wagon), 195/60HR14 tires, wheel covers.

Ratings begin on page 213. Specifications begin on page 220. CONSUMER GUIDE™

OPTIONAL EQUIPMENT:
Major Packages

	Retail Price	Dealer Invoice
Option Pkg. 2	$200	$166
Cruise control.		
Option Pkg. 3, sedan	850	707
Cruise control, power sunroof.		
Option Pkg. 4	925	767
Cruise control, AM/FM/CD player, alloy wheels.		
Option Pkg. 5	1400	1251
Antilock brakes, cruise control, AM/FM/CD player.		
Option Pkg. 6, sedan	1775	1475
Cruise control, AM/FM/CD player, power sunroof, rear spoiler, alloy wheels.		

Comfort and Convenience
Driver door remote keyless entry	365	232
Includes theft-deterrent system.		

Appearance and Miscellaneous
Theft-deterrent system	260	162
Roof rack cross rails, wagon	140	85
Rear spoiler, sedan	395	264

Other options are available as port installed items.

HYUNDAI SONATA

BUDGET BUY

Hyundai Sonata GLS

Front-wheel-drive compact car
Base price range: $14,999-$17,499. Built in South Korea.
Also consider: Chevrolet Malibu, Dodge Stratus, Honda Accord, Mazda 626, Toyota Camry/Solara

FOR • Ride **AGAINST** • Automatic transmission performance • Wind noise • Rear-seat comfort

Cruise control, a folding rear seatback, and 15-inch wheels are newly standard on the base version of Hyundai's largest sedan for 2000. The base Sonata continues with a 4-cylinder engine, the uplevel GLS model with a V6. Both get manual or automatic transmission. Both models have standard front side airbags, but only the GLS includes 4-wheel disc brakes and offers optional antilock brakes and traction control. Cruise control, the folding seatback, and 15-inch wheels were previously GLS exclusives. Hyundai's basic warranty is among the industry's longest: 5-years/60,000-miles bumper-to-bumper, 10-years/100,000-miles powertrain.

EVALUATION Sonata's suspension easily irons out most bumps, and rivals larger, costlier cars for overall comfort. The downside is poor control of body motions: Dips and crests send the Sonata bounding, and lane changes at highway speeds are sloppy. The V6 automatic has decent acceleration—0-60 mph in 9 seconds in our tests. But lack of midrange power makes it feel lazy around town. Our test GLS averaged 22.4 mpg. The GLS's 4-wheel disc brakes provide stable, reasonably short stops even without ABS. There's tire thrum on coarse pavement and some wind noise from the door mirrors, but this is otherwise a fairly quiet car. Front seating is roomy and supportive, but rear head room is tight for 6-footers, and the cushion is short and low. Pluses include trunk room, good visibility, and a convenient dashboard layout. Mediocre resale value and Hyundai's uncertain long-term viability in the U.S. market are drawbacks. But Sonata is a well-equipped compact for the price of a premium subcompact, and its warranty is solid. It qualifies as a compact-class Budget Buy.

ENGINES
	dohc I4	dohc V6
Size, liters/cu. in.	2.4/146	2.5/152
Horsepower @ rpm	149 @ 5500	170 @ 6000
Torque (lbs./ft.) @ rpm	156 @ 3000	166 @ 4000
Availability	S[1]	S[2]
EPA city/highway mpg		
5-speed OD manual	21/29	20/28
4-speed OD automatic	21/28	20/27

1. Base. 2. GLS.

PRICES
Hyundai Sonata
	Retail Price	Dealer Invoice
Base 4-door sedan, 5-speed	$14999	$13805
Base 4-door sedan, automatic	15499	14304
GLS 4-door sedan, 5-speed	16999	15116
GLS 4-door sedan, automatic	17499	15615
Destination charge	435	435

STANDARD EQUIPMENT:
Base: 2.4-liter dohc 4-cylinder engine, 5-speed manual or 4-speed automatic transmission, driver- and passenger-side airbags, front side-impact airbags, air conditioning, rear heat ducts, power steering, tilt steering wheel, cruise control, cloth upholstery, front bucket seats w/manual 4-way adjustable driver seat, front storage console, cupholders, split folding rear seat, power mirrors, power windows, power door locks, tachometer, AM/FM/cassette, digital clock, illuminated passenger-side visor mirror, remote fuel-door and decklid releases, rear defogger, variable intermittent wipers, 205/60R15 tires, alloy wheels.

GLS adds: 2.5-liter dohc V6 engine, 4-wheel disc brakes, heated power mirrors, manual 6-way adjustable driver seat, console armrest, interior air filter, AM/FM/CD player, power antenna, map lights.

OPTIONAL EQUIPMENT:
Major Packages
Option Pkg. 2, Base	800	679
Power sunroof, AM/FM/CD player.		
Option Pkg. 10, GLS	975	834
Power sunroof, AM/FM/cassette/CD player.		
Option Pkg. 11, GLS	1325	1171
Leather upholstery, power driver seat, AM/FM/cassette/CD player.		
Option Pkg. 12, GLS	1875	1629
Power sunroof, AM/FM/cassette/CD player, leather upholstery, power driver seat.		
Option Pkg. 13, GLS	2575	2284
Option Pkg. 12 plus antilock brakes, traction control.		

Comfort and Convenience
Remote keyless entry	180	107

Appearance and Miscellaneous
Rear spoiler	440	295

Other options are available as port installed items.

HYUNDAI TIBURON

Hyundai Tiburon

Front-wheel-drive sports coupe
Base price range: $13,999-$14,749. Built in South Korea.
Also consider: Ford Escort/ZX2, Honda Civic, Saturn S-Series

FOR • Steering/handling • Ride **AGAINST** • Passing power (automatic transmission) • Rear-seat room • Entry/exit

Hyundai gives its sporty coupe a facelift and a simplified lineup for 2000. Gone is the uplevel FX model, leaving a base version with a revamped nose, including standard fog lamps, and a new-look tail.

Prices are accurate at time of publication; subject to manufacturer's changes.

Tiburon has a 4-cylinder engine and manual or automatic transmission. Previously exclusive to the FX model, 4-wheel disc brakes and 15-inch alloy wheels in place of 14-inch steel wheels are standard. Antilock brakes are optional. Power windows are a new feature and are standard. Hyundai's basic warranty is among the industry's longest: 5-years/60,000-miles bumper-to-bumper, 10-years/ 100,000-miles powertrain.

EVALUATION Handling is Tiburon's strong point, and its ride is taut without being harsh. But acceleration is weak with automatic transmission, which also reduces this car's sportiness. Typical of small coupes, Tiburon has a low, snug driving position and a rear seat better suited to small parcels than people. Along with the exterior facelift comes a redesigned dashboard; it works well and is interesting to look at, though there are some oddly shaped controls whose workings are not intuitive. Distinctive styling and good road manners aside, there are better sports coupes than this, but few match Tiburon's low price.

ENGINES

	dohc I4
Size, liters/cu. in.	2.0/122
Horsepower @ rpm	140 @ 6000
Torque (lbs./ft.) @ rpm	133 @ 4800
Availability	S

EPA city/highway mpg

5-speed OD manual	23/32
4-speed OD automatic	22/30

PRICES

Hyundai Tiburon	Retail Price	Dealer Invoice
Base 2-door hatchback, 5-speed	$13999	$12739
Base 2-door hatchback, automatic	14749	13425
Destination charge	435	435

STANDARD EQUIPMENT:

Base: 2.0-liter dohc 4-cylinder engine, 5-speed manual or 4-speed automatic transmission, driver- and passenger-side airbags, 4-wheel disc brakes, air conditioning, power steering, tilt steering wheel, cloth upholstery, front bucket seats, front storage console, split folding rear seat, cupholders, power mirrors, power windows, power door locks, tachometer, AM/FM/cassette, digital clock, rear defogger, remote hatch and fuel-door releases, variable intermittent wipers, map lights, cargo cover, 195/55HR15 tires, alloy wheels.

OPTIONAL EQUIPMENT:
Major Packages

Option Pkg. 2	1300	1082
Power sunroof, AM/FM/cassette/CD player.		
Option Pkg. 3	2475	2143
Power sunroof, AM/FM/cassette/CD player, leather upholstery, rear spoiler.		
Option Pkg. 4	3250	2868
Option Pkg. 3 plus antilock brakes.		

Comfort and Convenience

Driver door remote keyless entry	385	242
Includes theft-deterrent system.		
Rear spoiler	450	293

Other options are available as port installed items.

INFINITI G20

Infiniti G20

Front-wheel-drive near-luxury car
Base price range: $21,395-$23,695. Built in Japan. **Also**

consider: Acura TL, Audi A4, Volvo 40 series

FOR • Steering/handling • Instruments/controls • Visibility • Exterior finish **AGAINST** • Automatic transmission performance • Engine noise

The entry-level sedan from Nissan's upscale division gets minor revisions for 2000. Luxury and sportier Touring (G20t) models return, both with a 2.0-liter 4-cylinder engine with 145 horsepower, a gain of 5 hp from 1999. Infiniti also says revised ratios on both the manual and optional automatic transmissions help performance. Both G20s have front side airbags and antilock 4-wheel disc brakes. New features for both models include a remote power trunk release operable from the dash or key fob, one-touch up/down driver's window (versus down only), and retained accessory power. Newly optional for the Touring model only is Infiniti's cell phone/satellite assistance and communications system.

EVALUATION Don't count on significantly better acceleration from this year's powertrain changes. The G20 is peppy enough once up to speed, but a relative lack of torque means lackluster acceleration—an unimpressive 10-plus seconds 0-60 mph in our tests of '99 models. At least fuel economy is better than the near-luxury norm, averaging between 22.8 and 26.9 mpg in our tests. Mountain road or Interstate, the G20 feels stable and maneuverable. It also absorbs large bumps and tar strips pretty well. Panic stops are swift and sure. The engine is vocal when worked hard and never sounds that pleasant, while tire roar is noticed on coarse pavement. G20's seats are comfortable, but rear leg room is only adequate for larger adults, and head room is tight anywhere with the optional moonroof. Most near-luxury cars have more interior space. Gauges and controls are where you'd expect, and the G20t's standard automatic climate system is a nice feature at this price. Standard split folding rear seatbacks augment a roomy trunk. Exterior fit and finish are excellent, but interiors have a faint economy-car look and feel even with the available leather upholstery. Infiniti gives great customer service, but, overall, this well-equipped 4-cylinder compact is not a better value than a similarly equipped and priced midsize Honda Accord or Toyota Camry.

ENGINES

	dohc I4
Size, liters/cu. in.	2.0/122
Horsepower @ rpm	145 @ 6000
Torque (lbs./ft.) @ rpm	136 @ 4800
Availability	S

EPA city/highway mpg

4-speed OD automatic	23/30
5-speed OD automatic	24/31

PRICES

Infiniti G20	Retail Price	Dealer Invoice
Luxury 4-door sedan, 5-speed	$21395	$19422
Luxury 4-door sedan, automatic	22195	20152
Touring 4-door sedan, 5-speed	22895	20560
Touring 4-door sedan, automatic	23695	21282
Destination charge	525	525

STANDARD EQUIPMENT:

Luxury: 2.0-liter dohc 4-cylinder engine, 5-speed manual or 4-speed automatic transmission, driver- and passenger-side airbags, front side-impact airbags, antilock 4-wheel disc brakes, air conditioning, variable-assist power steering, tilt steering wheel, cruise control, cloth upholstery, front bucket seats, center console, split folding rear seat, cupholders, Bose AM/FM/cassette/CD player, power antenna, steering wheel radio controls, digital clock, power mirrors, power windows, power door locks, remote keyless entry, rear defogger, remote fuel door release, power decklid release, illuminated-visor mirrors, variable intermittent wipers, cargo net, automatic-off headlights, floormats, theft-deterrent system, 195/65R15 tires, alloy wheels.

Touring adds: limited-slip differential, automatic climate control, leather-wrapped steering wheel, fog lights, rear spoiler, 195/60R15 tires.

OPTIONAL EQUIPMENT:
Major Packages

Leather and Convenience Pkg.,		
Luxury automatic	1500	1132

	Retail Price	Dealer Invoice
Touring	$1200	$904

Leather upholstery, power driver seat, leather-wrapped steering wheel (Luxury), automatic climate control (Luxury), power sunroof, universal garage door opener.

Seat Pkg., Luxury automatic, Touring	420	362

Heated front seats, heated mirrors. Requires Leather and Convenience Pkg.

Comfort and Convenience

Infiniti Communicator, Luxury automatic, Touring	1599	1378

Includes Global Positioning System, cellular telephone, roadside assistance, emergency services, four years service fees. Requires Leather and Convenience Pkg.

Power sunroof, Touring	950	819
6-disc CD changer	718	340

Requires Leather and Convenience Pkg.

INFINITI I30

RECOMMENDED

Infiniti I30

Front-wheel-drive near-luxury car; similar to Nissan Maxima

Base price range: $29,465-$31,540. Built in Japan. **Also consider:** Acura TL, BMW 3-Series, Lexus ES 300

FOR • Acceleration • Build quality • Instruments/controls • Quietness • Seat comfort • Handling/roadholding **AGAINST** • Rear visibility

Nissan's Maxima is redesigned for 2000, so the upscale Infiniti model that shares its platform and engine is, too. The new I30 offers some features Maxima doesn't, plus its own more conservative styling. Like the revamped Maxima, I30 is larger, gaining 2 inches in wheelbase and 4.1 inches overall (it's also 3.2 inches longer than the Nissan). Rear leg room increases nearly 2 inches.

Revisions to the carried-over V6 engine increase horsepower by 37, to 227 (that's 5 more than in the Maxima). Manual transmission is no longer offered, leaving a 4-speed automatic.

Base and sportier I30t Touring models return. Standard front head/chest side airbags are joined by active front head restraints designed to minimize whiplash injury. Antilock 4-wheel disc brakes are standard. Traction control is optional and teams with heated front seats.

The I30t is expected to account for about 25 percent of sales. It gets 17-inch wheels in place of the base 16s, and a firmer suspension. Standard on all I30s are a power sunroof, power rear-window sunshade (unavailable on Maxima), leather upholstery, automatic climate control, and remote keyless entry. A cell phone/satellite navigation and assistance system is optional.

PERFORMANCE While Maxima attempts a return to its "4-door sports car" heyday, I30 takes a softer, gentler approach befitting its near-luxury mission. More sound insulation makes it quieter than Maxima, and isolation from road, wind, and engine noise is better than in an Acura TL, but not as complete as in the class-leading Lexus ES 300. Ride is firm but absorbent and again falls between the taut TL and the softer ES. Handling does, as well, with the I30 exhibiting fine grip and balance in turns, despite noticeable body lean. The I30t's tighter suspension settings and larger tires provide crisper steering and sharper cornering than the base model, with little penalty in ride.

Acceleration and throttle response are rewarding around town and on the freeway, and are an easy match for either of the above-mentioned rivals. Without the optional traction control, though, the

I30 suffers bothersome torque steer—pulling to one side—in brisk getaways. We averaged 20.9 mpg on the recommended premium fuel. Braking power and feel is very good, and the I30s we tested felt solid and rattle-free over the largest bumps.

ACCOMMODATIONS Outside, the styled-in-Japan I30 shares only its window glass and roof panel with the styled-in-America Maxima. Inside, differences are more subtle. The Infiniti gets modestly different seat padding, and it's comfortable and supportive. The dashboard is the same efficient design, but climate and audio controls are slightly rearranged; their size and markings are excellent. Also, the I30 gets a foot-pedal parking brake, Maxima a sportier floor lever.

This is a roomy cabin, with plenty of adult-size leg space front and rear. In back, head clearance is tight for those over 5-foot-10 but the seat cushion is nicely contoured. Conveniences include a height-adjustable center front armrest and a right-front cupholder positioned so a dashboard vent can cool (or heat) its beverage. The rear sunshade is another thoughtful touch. Still, the interior lacks any particularly imaginative design element, and the plastic wood trim looks low-budget. Standard split folding rear seatbacks augment the large trunk, though trunk-lid hinges dip deeply into the luggage area. The test cars were not equipped with the cell-phone/satellite communications system.

VALUE FOR THE MONEY We're disappointed that heated seats and traction control aren't standard, but the I30 counts among its many assets fine performance, comfort, solidity, and reasonable prices. Add in Infiniti's sterling reputation for customer satisfaction and this new sedan is a sound near-luxury buy.

ENGINES

	dohc V6
Size, liters/cu. in.	3.0/181
Horsepower @ rpm	227 @ 6400
Torque (lbs./ft.) @ rpm	217 @ 4000
Availability	S
EPA city/highway mpg	
4-speed OD automatic	20/28

PRICES

Infiniti I30	Retail Price	Dealer Invoice
I30 4-door sedan	$29465	$26835
I30t 4-door sedan	31540	27979
Destination charge	525	525

STANDARD EQUIPMENT:

I30: 3.0-liter dohc V6 engine, 4-speed automatic transmission, driver- and passenger-side airbags, front side-impact airbags, front seat active head restraints, antilock 4-wheel disc brakes, air conditioning w/automatic climate control, variable-assist power steering, leather-wrapped tilt steering wheel, cruise control, leather upholstery, front bucket seats, 8-way power driver seat w/manual lumbar adjustment and memory, 4-way power passenger seat, center console, cupholders, split folding rear seat, power mirrors, power windows, power door locks, remote keyless entry, power sunroof, Bose AM/FM/cassette/CD player, analog clock, rear defogger, automatic day/night rearview mirror, outside temperature indicator, tachometer, variable intermittent wipers, illuminated visor mirrors, universal garage door opener, auxiliary power outlet, power rear sunshade, automatic headlights, remote fuel door and decklid release, theft-deterrent system, fog lights, cornering lights, 215/55R16 tires, alloy wheels.

I30t adds: limited-slip differential, Xenon headlights, sport suspension, 225/50R17 tires.

OPTIONAL EQUIPMENT:
Major Packages

Heated Seats Pkg.	420	374

Heated front seats, heated mirrors.

Touring Sport Pkg., I30t	1000	887

Rear spoiler, side sill spoilers.

Sunroof and Sunshade Pkg. delete, (credit)	(1000)	(868)

Deletes power sunroof, power rear sunshade.

Powertrains

Traction control	300	268

Requires Heated Seats Pkg.

Prices are accurate at time of publication; subject to manufacturer's changes.

Comfort and Convenience

	Retail Price	Dealer Invoice
In Vehicle Communications System	$1599	$1378

Includes Global Positioning System, cellular telephone, roadside assistance, emergency services.

6-disc CD changer	718	340

INFINITI QX4

Infiniti QX4

4-wheel-drive midsize sport-utility vehicle; similar to Nissan Pathfinder

Base price: $35,550. Built in Japan. **Also consider:** Lexus RX 300, Mercedes-Benz M-Class

FOR • Cargo room • Steering/handling • Build quality • Exterior finish • Interior materials **AGAINST** • Rear-seat entry/exit • Rear leg room • Engine noise • Fuel economy

QX4 follows its "1999½" makeover with a revamped "2000½" model due in Spring 2000. It will have altered styling and a new 3.5-liter version of the familiar Nissan/Infiniti 3.0-liter passenger-car V6. Until then, this sport-utility vehicle continues with a truck-based 3.3-liter V6, automatic transmission, and Nissan's All-Mode full-time 4WD that allows using 4-wheel drive on dry pavement and also has separate 4WD-low gearing for off-road use. QX4 is the luxury version of the Nissan Pathfinder. It gained standard front side airbags among several updates for "1999½," when Pathfinder got a more visible makeover and optional side airbags.

EVALUATION QX4 drives more like a car than many sport-utility vehicles, but its luxury billing is undercut by a mediocre ride over sharp bumps and ridges, plus a marginally overworked V6 that's relatively loud and sounds a bit crude. Front-seat room is good, but rear-seat space is limited and step-in is high. Overall, the QX4 just doesn't impress like the roomier, smoother-riding Mercedes M-Class and Lexus's carlike RX 300. A carefully optioned Pathfinder offers the same basic package for less money, though you'll pay extra for side airbags and miss out on full-time 4WD and Infiniti's red-carpet service.

ENGINES

	ohc V6
Size, liters/cu. in.	3.3/200
Horsepower @ rpm	170 @ 4800
Torque (lbs./ft.) @ rpm	200 @ 2800
Availability	S

EPA city/highway mpg

4-speed OD automatic	15/18

PRICES

Infiniti QX4	Retail Price	Dealer Invoice
Base 4-door wagon	$35550	$32153
Destination charge	525	525

STANDARD EQUIPMENT:

Base: 3.3-liter V6 engine, 4-speed automatic transmission, full-time 4-wheel drive, driver- and passenger-side airbags, front side-impact airbags, antilock brakes, air conditioning w/automatic climate control, interior air filter, variable-assist power steering, tilt steering wheel, leather-wrapped steering wheel w/radio controls, cruise control, leather upholstery, power front bucket seats, reclining split-folding rear seat, center storage console w/armrest, overhead storage console (includes outside-temperature indicator, compass, map lights), wood interior trim, cupholders, heated power mirrors, power windows, power door locks, remote keyless entry, tachometer, Bose AM/FM/cassette/CD player, digital clock, power antenna, variable intermittent wipers, intermittent rear wiper/washer, rear defogger, remote fuel-door and hatch releases, auxiliary power

outlets, universal garage door opener, illuminated visor mirrors, automatic-off headlights, cargo cover, floormats, fog lights, theft-deterrent system, rear privacy glass, step rails, roof rack, fuel-tank skid plates, full-size spare tire, 255/65R16 tires, alloy wheels.

OPTIONAL EQUIPMENT:
Major Packages

	Retail Price	Dealer Invoice
Premium Sport Pkg.	$700	$632

Limited-slip rear differential, heavy-duty battery, heated front seats. Requires Sunroof Preferred Pkg.

Sunroof Preferred Pkg.	1250	1129

Power sunroof, 6-disc CD changer, rear window wind deflector.

Comfort and Convenience

Infiniti Communicator	1599	1378

Includes Global Positioning System, cellular telephone, roadside assistance, emergency services. Includes four years of service fees.

Heated front seats	400	361
Power sunroof	950	858

Special Purpose, Wheels and Tires

Tow hitch	390	294

INFINITI Q45

Infiniti Q45t

Rear-wheel-drive luxury car

Base price range: $48,895-$50,595. Built in Japan. **Also consider:** Cadillac Seville, Lexus LS 400, Mercedes-Benz E-Class

FOR • Acceleration • Quietness • Build quality • Exterior finish • Interior materials

AGAINST • Fuel economy • Cargo room

Though due to be redesigned for 2001, Nissan's luxury-division flagship sedan gets some equipment alterations and a "birthday special" for 2000. Q45 offers regular and sportier Touring (Q45t) models whose 4.1-liter V8 gets platinum-tip spark plugs good for 100,000-miles between tuneups. Also new are active front head restraints designed to minimize whiplash injury in rear-end collisions. Rear child-seat anchors are new, as is one-touch open/close for the standard moonroof and all power windows. A newly optional in-car navigation system with dashboard touch-screen and a satellite/cell-phone link replaces a simpler, non-video system. Available on a limited basis is a 10th Anniversary Touring edition with machine-finish road wheels, special badges and upholstery, wood/leather steering wheel, and bird's-eye maple interior accents.

EVALUATION The Q45 offers lush accommodations for front-seat passengers, but isn't as roomy in back as some competitors. It also comes up short in trunk space. Pluses include strong acceleration (0-60 mph in 7.2 seconds in our tests), a refined automatic transmission, a soft ride (with better body control but worse bump absorption in the Touring), and competent if not sporty road manners. Economy is so-so; we've averaged 15.4-17.6 mpg depending on driver and conditions. Overall, the Q45 is an impressive car, but not as compelling as some comparably priced alternatives, one reason it's been a sales disappointment—and why it's being replaced after a fairly short 4-year lifespan.

ENGINES

	dohc V8
Size, liters/cu. in.	4.1/252
Horsepower @ rpm	266 @ 5600
Torque (lbs./ft.) @ rpm	278 @ 4000
Availability	S

EPA city/highway mpg

4-speed OD automatic	18/23

Ratings begin on page 213. Specifications begin on page 220.
CONSUMER GUIDE™

PRICES

Infiniti Q45

	Retail Price	Dealer Invoice
Q45 4-door sedan	$48895	$43914
Q45t 4-door sedan	50595	44939
Destination charge	525	525

10th Anniversary Edition price and equipment not available at time of publication.

STANDARD EQUIPMENT:

Q45: 4.1-liter dohc V8 engine, 4-speed automatic transmission, traction control system, limited-slip differential, driver- and passenger-side airbags, front side-impact airbags, front seat active head restraints, antilock 4-wheel disc brakes, air conditioning w/automatic climate control, interior air filter, variable-assist power steering, power tilt/telescopic steering wheel w/memory, leather-wrapped steering wheel and shifter, cruise control, leather upholstery, 8-way power front bucket seats w/power lumbar adjustment, memory driver seat, folding rear seat, center console, auxiliary power outlet, cupholders, Bose AM/FM/cassette/CD player, power antenna, steering wheel radio controls, analog clock, power sunroof, heated power mirrors w/memory, power windows, power door locks, remote keyless entry, tachometer, outside temperature indicator, automatic day/night rearview mirror, rear defogger, remote power fuel-door and decklid releases w/decklid pull-down, illuminated visor mirrors, map lights, variable intermittent wipers, automatic headlights, universal garage-door opener, power rear window sunshade, floormats, theft-deterrent system, Xenon headlights, fog lights, 215/60VR16 tires, alloy wheels.

Q45t adds: leather-wrapped sport steering wheel, electronically-controlled suspension w/driver adjustment, 225/50VR17 tires.

OPTIONAL EQUIPMENT:
Comfort and Convenience

Infiniti Communicator	1599	1378

Includes Global Positioning System, cellular telephone, roadside assistance, emergency services. Includes four years of Infiniti Response Center Service.

Heated front seats	420	378
6-disc CD changer	718	340

Appearance and Miscellaneous

Rear spoiler	529	395
Two-tone paint	500	431

Other options are available as port installed items.

ISUZU AMIGO

Isuzu Amigo

Rear- or 4-wheel-drive compact sport-utility vehicle
1999 base price range: $15,810-$20,250. Built in USA. **Also consider:** Chevrolet Tracker, Jeep Wrangler, Toyota RAV4

FOR • Cargo room • Acceleration (V6) **AGAINST** • Acceleration (4-cyl) • Ride • Noise • Entry/exit

Optional adjustable shock absorbers and a restyled nose and tail top changes to the 2000 Amigo. This is essentially a 2-door version of Isuzu's Rodeo and comes two ways: as a semi-convertible model with a folding soft top over the back seat and a pop-up sunroof, and as a hardtop with a pop-up sunroof over the rear seat. Both offer rear- and 4-wheel-drive and a 4-cylinder engine or a V6. Manual transmission is standard, automatic is optional on V6 models, which gain standard cruise control for 2000. Amigo's 4WD isn't for use on dry pavement but has pushbutton shift-on-the-fly between 2WD and 4WD, plus separate low-range gearing. Four-wheel antilock brakes are standard. New for V6 Amigos equipped with the Preferred Equipment package is an Ironman appearance package named for Isuzu's sponsorship of the Ironman triathlon competition. Isuzu's Intelligent Suspension Control is optional on V6 models with the Ironman package and uses a dashboard switch to choose sport or normal shock damping. In other changes, the previously optional 16-inch wheels replace 15s as standard, a plastic/vinyl spare tire cover is newly standard, and fender flares are new options. Also, Isuzu has doubled its powertrain warranty to 10 years/120,000 miles on Amigo, Trooper, and VehiCross.

EVALUATION Our test V6 5-speed 4x4 Amigo convertible ran 0-60 mph in 8.5 seconds—impressive for a compact SUV. It averaged 17.3 mpg. An automatic V6 averaged 16.9. We haven't tested an Amigo with the new Intelligent Suspension Control. With the standard suspension, small bumps are easily absorbed, but Amigo bounces and bounds over wavy pavement, potholes, and frost heaves. Room in front is adequate, but there's a high step-up into the interior and the rear seat is tough to get to and not very spacious for adults. Working the vinyl soft-top is a chore. Amigo is far from perfect, though it is more substantial than some other small SUVs, and more refined than a Jeep Wrangler.

ENGINES

	dohc I4	dohc V6
Size, liters/cu. in.	2.2/134	3.2/193
Horsepower @ rpm	130 @ 5200	205 @ 5400
Torque (lbs./ft.) @ rpm	144 @ 4000	214 @ 3000
Availability	S	O
EPA city/highway mpg		
5-speed OD manual	21/24[1]	18/21
4-speed OD automatic		17/21

1. 20/23 w/4WD.

PRICES

1999 Isuzu Amigo	Retail Price	Dealer Invoice
2WD S 4-cylinder 2-door convertible, 5-speed	$15810	$14861
2WD S 4-cylinder 2-door wagon, 5-speed	15810	14861
4WD S 4-cylinder 2-door convertible, 5-speed	18330	17230
2WD S V6 2-door convertible, automatic	17950	16514
2WD S V6 2-door wagon, automatic	17950	16514
4WD S V6 2-door convertible, 5-speed	19470	17913
4WD S V6 2-door convertible, automatic	20250	18630
4WD S V6 2-door wagon, automatic	20250	18630
Destination charge	495	495

STANDARD EQUIPMENT:

2WD S 4-cylinder: 2.2-liter dohc 4-cylinder engine, 5-speed manual transmission, driver- and passenger-side airbags, antilock brakes, variable-assist power steering, cloth upholstery, front reclining bucket seats, folding rear seat, center console, tachometer, AM/FM/cassette w/four speakers, manual front sunroof, auxiliary power outlets, driver-side visor mirror, intermittent wipers, map lights, rear folding top, skid plates, outside-mounted full-size spare tire, 235/75R15 tires. **4WD** models add: part-time 4-wheel drive, 2-speed transfer case, limited-slip differential, 4-wheel disc brakes.

S 4-cylinder wagon adds: manual rear sunroof, rear defogger, rear intermittent wiper, deletes rear folding top.

S V6 adds to S 4-cylinder convertible and S 4-cylinder wagon: 3.2-liter dohc V6 engine, tilt steering wheel. **4WD** models add: part-time 4-wheel drive, 2-speed transfer case, limited-slip differential, 4-wheel disc brakes.

OPTIONAL EQUIPMENT:
Major Packages

Preferred Equipment Pkg. 2, V6	2110	1842

Air conditioning, power mirrors, power windows and door locks, remote keyless entry, variable intermittent wipers, 6-speaker sound system, center armrest pad, courtesy lights, cargo net, floormats, theft-deterrent system.

Comfort and Convenience

Air conditioning	950	845
Deluxe CD player	500	395
Premium CD player, V6 w/Preferred Pkg.	550	434

Includes 6-speakers.

Prices are accurate at time of publication; subject to manufacturer's changes.

	Retail Price	Dealer Invoice
6-disc CD player, V6 w/Preferred Pkg.	$650	$513
Cargo cover	180	142

Appearance and Miscellaneous
Fog lights, 4WD V6	70	56
Requires Preferred Pkg. and alloy wheels.		
Sport side steps	355	281
Brush guard	298	236

Special Purpose, Wheels and Tires
Trailer hitch	253	200
Alloy wheels	600	534
Includes 245/R16 tires.		

Other options are available as port installed items.

ISUZU HOMBRE

Isuzu Hombre ext. cab

Rear- or 4-wheel-drive compact pickup truck; similar to Chevrolet S-10 and GMC Sonoma

1999 base price range: $11,545-$21,145. Built in USA.
Also consider: Dodge Dakota, Ford Ranger, Toyota Tacoma

FOR • Acceleration (V6) **AGAINST** • Rear-seat comfort • Ride

Stronger V6 engines and a greater number of Spacecab variations highlight changes to Isuzu's version of the Chevrolet S-10/GMC Sonoma compact pickup truck. Hombre wears distinct front-end sheetmetal, but is otherwise virtually identical to its General Motors' cousins. Model choices are expanded for 2000 to include V6 Spacecabs (extended-cabs) in base S trim. Spacecabs were previously offered only in pricier XS guise. However, Hombre still lacks some combinations available in the GM models, such as V6 regular cabs and 2WD V6 extended-cabs with manual transmission. It also has fewer options.

Hombre comes in regular-cab and Spacecab models, the latter offering an optional driver-side third door. Both have a 6-foot long cargo bed; the 7.3-foot bed available on the GM versions is not offered. Engines are GM's 2.2-liter 4-cylinder or 4.3-liter V6 with manual or automatic transmission. For 2000, the V6 gains 5 horsepower in 2WD applications, 10 in 4WD models.

Four-wheel-drive versions have GM's shift-on-the-fly, slippery surfaces-only 4WD system. Antilock brakes are standard, and 4WD models add rear discs. In other model-year 2000 changes, the Performance Package heavy-duty suspension previously optional on 2WD regular-cab S models is now standard across the line, and 4X4s get taller 235/75R15 tires in place of 235/70R15s. Hombre's performance and accommodations mirror those of similarly equipped S-10s and Sonomas.

The Chevrolet S-10 report includes an evaluation of the Hombre.

ENGINES
	dohc I4	ohv V6
Size, liters/cu. in.	2.2/134	4.3/262
Horsepower @ rpm	120 @ 5000	180 @ 4400
Torque (lbs./ft.) @ rpm	140 @ 3600	245 @ 2800
Availability	S[1]	O[2]
EPA city/highway mpg		
5-speed OD manual	23/29	17/23[3]
4-speed OD automatic	19/26	16/21

1. 2WD. 2. SpaceCab. 190 hp and 250 lb-ft with 4WD. 3. 17/21 w/4WD.

PRICES
1999 Isuzu Hombre
	Retail Price	Dealer Invoice
2WD S regular cab, 5-speed	$11545	$11083

	Retail Price	Dealer Invoice
2WD S regular cab, automatic	$12615	$12111
4WD S regular cab, 5-speed	17200	16168
2WD XS regular cab, 5-speed	11955	11238
2WD XS regular cab, automatic	13025	12244
2WD XS Spacecab 4-cylinder, 5-speed	15200	13680
2WD XS Spacecab 4-cylinder, automatic	16270	14643
2WD XS Spacecab V6, automatic	17420	15678
4WD XS Spacecab V6, 5-speed	20075	18068
4WD XS Spacecab V6, automatic	21145	19031
Destination charge	495	495

STANDARD EQUIPMENT:

S: 2.2-liter 4-cylinder engine, 5-speed manual or 4-speed automatic transmission, driver- and passenger-side airbags, antilock brakes, daytime running lights, variable-assist power steering, 3-passenger cloth bench seat, front storage console, cupholder, variable-intermittent wipers, theft-deterrent system, dual outside mirrors, 205/75R15 tires. **4WD** adds: part-time 4-wheel drive, 4.3-liter V6 engine, 4-wheel disc brakes, AM/FM radio, tachometer, heavy-duty suspension, full-size spare tire, 235/70R15 tires, alloy wheels.

XS regular cab adds: split bench seat, carpeting, illuminated visor mirrors, map lights, rear bumper, heavy-duty suspension. **4WD** adds: part-time 4-wheel drive, 4.3-liter V6 engine, 4-wheel disc brakes, AM/FM radio, tachometer, full-size spare tire, 235/70R15 tires, alloy wheels.

XS Spacecab 4-cylinder adds: AM/FM radio, digital clock, center armrest w/storage, dual vinyl rear jump seats, swing-out rear quarter windows. **4WD** models add: part-time 4WD, 4.3-liter V6 engine, tachometer, full-size spare tire, 235/70R15 tires, alloy wheels.

XS Spacecab V6 adds: 4.3-liter V6 engine, 4-speed automatic transmission. **4WD** models add: part-time 4WD, 5-speed manual or 4-speed automatic transmission, tachometer, full-size spare tire, 235/70R15 tires, alloy wheels.

OPTIONAL EQUIPMENT:
Major Packages
	Retail	Dealer
Preferred Equipment Pkg., 2WD XS regular cab	1429	1271
Manufacturer's discount price	1143	1086
Air conditioning, AM/FM/cassette, sliding rear window, tachometer (2WD), floormats.		
Preferred Equipment Pkg., 2WD XS Spacecab	1194	1062
Manufacturer's discount price	955	907
Preferred Equipment Pkg., 4WD XS Spacecab	1135	1017
Manufacturer's discount price	908	862
Air conditioning, AM/FM/cassette, sliding rear window, tachometer (2WD), floormats.		
Convenience Pkg., XS Spacecab V6	525	468
Manufacturer's discount price	425	404
Tilt steering wheel, cruise control.		
Power Pkg., XS Spacecab V6	750	666
Manufacturer's discount price	650	618
Heated power mirrors, power windows and door locks.		

Comfort and Convenience
Third door, Spacecab	375	333
Air conditioning	835	743
AM/FM radio, 2WD S regular cab	235	209
AM/FM/cassette, 4WD S	145	129

Appearance and Miscellaneous
Rear bumper, S	60	53

Special Purpose, Wheels and Tires
Performance Pkg., 4-cylinder	65	58
Alloy wheels, 2WD XS Spacecab	280	249

ISUZU RODEO

Rear- or 4-wheel-drive midsize sport-utility vehicle; similar to Honda Passport

1999 base price range: $18,180-$30,650. Built in USA.
Also consider: Chevrolet Blazer, Ford Explorer, Jeep Grand Cherokee, Toyota 4Runner

FOR • Cargo room • Acceleration (V6) **AGAINST** • Road and

Isuzu Rodeo

wind noise • Fuel economy • Ride

Adjustable shock absorbers and a minor front and rear restyle are among additions to Rodeo for 2000. This 4-door wagon offers rear- or 4-wheel drive in S, LS, and LSE trim levels. A new Ironman package for the LS marks Isuzu's sponsorship of the Ironman triathlon competition and includes white or black paint over grey lower body panels and special graphics.

All Rodeos have a side-hinged tailgate with separate flip-up rear window. An outside-mount spare tire is standard on 4WD LSEs and a no-charge option on other models in place of the regular position beneath the cargo area. A 4-cylinder engine is standard on the S model. A V6 is optional on the S and standard on other Rodeos and now includes cruise control. Manual transmission is available with both engines. Automatic is available only with the V6, and is now standard on the LSE. The 4WD system shifts on the fly via a dashboard button but is not for use on dry pavement. Maximum towing capacity is 4500 pounds. Antilock brakes are standard.

For 2000, all models have standard 16-inch wheels; 16s had been standard on the LSE, optional on LS, and unavailable on the S. Isuzu's new Intelligent Suspension Control system is standard on the LSE and optional on the LS. A dashboard button switches between Sport and Normal settings. Finally, Isuzu has doubled its powertrain warranty to 10 years/120,000 miles on Amigo, Trooper, and VehiCross. Honda sells a retrimmed Rodeo as the Passport. Both are built from an Isuzu design at a factory in Indiana, but Passport does not offer the adjustable shock absorbers.

PERFORMANCE We haven't tested the new Intelligent Suspension Control, but Rodeo and its Passport companion could use an improvement in ride quality. They're choppy over small road imperfections and harsh over big bumps and potholes. They are, however, among the more agile midsize SUVs, despite suffering plenty of body lean and tire squeal in tight turns. V6 models deliver brisk acceleration and good passing power, and the automatic transmission shifts smoothly and quickly. Our test 1999 4WD LS Rodeo averaged 15.8 mpg. The Isuzu-engineered part-time push-button 4WD is convenient to engage, but most rivals offer 4WD systems that don't need to be disengaged on dry pavement.

ACCOMMODATIONS There's a shortage of rear toe space, but otherwise, Rodeo and Passport have good passenger room. The driver's seat isn't height-adjustable and its positioning doesn't suit all our testers, although the firmly padded seat itself gets high marks. Undersized audio controls mar the simple dashboard layout. Durable-feeling but unadorned trim gives the interior a spartan feel, although the available leather upholstery dresses things up.

Step-in height is a little lower than the midsize-SUV norm, but narrow rear-door openings hinder back-seat exits. Forward visibility is excellent thanks to a low cowl, but the outside spare tire interferes with the rear view. The side-opening tailgate demands cumbersome two-handed operation: To open it you must first raise the window; to close it, you must reach into the hinge area and release a lever to free the door.

VALUE FOR THE MONEY The spry V6 Rodeos and Passports emphasize the sport in sport-utility. But prices are no bargain and overall, there's no outstanding feature that sets either above the competition.

ENGINES

	dohc I4	dohc V6
Size, liters/cu. in.	2.2/134	3.2/193
Horsepower @ rpm	129 @ 5200	205 @ 5400
Torque (lbs./ft.) @ rpm	144 @ 4000	214 @ 3000
Availability	S[1]	S[2]

EPA city/highway mpg		
5-speed OD manual	21/24	16/20
4-speed OD automatic		18/21[3]

1. 2WD S. 2. S V-6, LS, LSE. 3. 18/20 w/4WD.

PRICES

1999 Isuzu Rodeo	Retail Price	Dealer Invoice
S 4-cylinder 2WD 4-door wagon, 5-speed	$18180	$17089
S V6 2WD 4-door wagon, 5-speed	21140	19026
S V6 2WD 4-door wagon, automatic	22140	19925
S V6 4WD 4-door wagon, 5-speed	23690	21321
S V6 4WD 4-door wagon, automatic	24690	22220
LS 2WD 4-door wagon, 5-speed	23540	21196
LS 2WD 4-door wagon, automatic	24540	22086
LS 4WD 4-door wagon, 5-speed	26490	23841
LS 4WD 4-door wagon, automatic	27490	24741
LSE 2WD 4-door wagon, 5-speed	28150	25194
LSE 4WD 4-door wagon, automatic	30650	27432
Destination charge	495	495

STANDARD EQUIPMENT:

S: 2.2-liter 4-cylinder engine, 5-speed manual transmission, driver- and passenger-side airbags, antilock brakes, variable-assist power steering, cloth and vinyl reclining front bucket seats, center storage console, split folding rear seat, 4-speaker AM/FM/cassette, tachometer, intermittent wipers, driver-side visor mirror, cupholders, rear defogger, rear wiper/washer, auxiliary power outlet, dual outside mirrors, skid plates, full-size spare tire, 235/75R15 tires.

S V6 adds: 3.2-liter V6 engine, 5-speed manual or 4-speed automatic transmission, tilt steering wheel. **4WD** adds: part-time 4-wheel drive, automatic locking hubs, limited-slip differential, 4-wheel disc brakes, transfer-case skid plate.

LS adds: air conditioning, cloth upholstery, cruise control, heated power mirrors, power windows, power door locks, remote keyless entry, AM/FM/cassette w/CD changer controls, variable intermittent wipers, power hatchgate release, map and courtesy lights, cargo net and cover, floormats, theft-deterrent system, roof rack. **4WD** adds: part-time 4-wheel drive, automatic locking hubs, limited-slip differential, 4-wheel disc brakes, transfer-case skid plate, alloy wheels.

LSE adds: leather upholstery, leather-wrapped steering wheel, center console armrest, power sunroof, illuminated visor mirrors, fog lights, rear privacy glass, alloy wheels. **4WD** adds: part-time 4-wheel drive, automatic locking hubs, limited-slip differential, 4-wheel disc brakes, transfer-case skid plate, outside spare tire carrier, 245/70R16 tires.

OPTIONAL EQUIPMENT:
Major Packages

Preferred Equipment Pkg. 1, S, S V6	1010	899
Air conditioning, roof rack.		
Gold Pkg., LSE	400	316
Gold badging, 245/70R16 tires, special alloy wheels. Requires outside spare tire carrier.		
Power sunroof, LS 2WD automatic, LS 4WD	700	623
CD player, LS, LSE	550	434
6-disc CD changer, LS, LSE	650	513

Appearance and Miscellaneous

Brush guard	298	236
Running boards	360	283
Side steps	355	281

Special Purpose, Wheels and Tires

Trailer hitch	253	200
15-inch alloy wheels, LS 2WD automatic	400	356
16-inch alloy wheels, LS 2WD	600	534
LS 4WD, LSE 2WD	200	178
Includes 245/70R16 tires.		

Other options are available as port installed items.

ISUZU TROOPER
Rear- or 4-wheel-drive full-size sport-utility vehicle
1999 base price range: $27,100-$28,650. Built in Japan.
Also consider: Chevrolet Tahoe and Suburban, Ford Expedition, Toyota Land Cruiser

Prices are accurate at time of publication; subject to manufacturer's changes.

Isuzu Trooper

FOR • Passenger and cargo room **AGAINST** • Fuel economy • Ride • Entry/exit

Isuzu's SUV flagship adds rear-wheel-drive, a new grille and taillights, and an expanded lineup for 2000. This 4-door wagon has swing-out rear doors split 70/30. S, LS, and Limited models replace last year's lone S model. A 3.5-liter V6 linked to manual or automatic transmission repeats, but all models now offer rear- or 4-wheel drive; 4WD had been standard. Manual-transmission 4WD Troopers get a part-time system not for use on dry pavement; those with automatic use Isuzu's Torque On Demand 4WD, which does not require that 4WD be disengaged on dry pavement. Antilock 4-wheel disc brakes are standard. Maximum towing capacity is 5000 pounds. Among other 2000 changes, automatic climate control is standard, and automatic transmissions are revised in an effort to minimize gear changes on grades. Finally, Isuzu has doubled its powertrain warranty to 10 years/120,000 miles on Amigo, Trooper, and VehiCross. Isuzu had provided Honda's upscale Acura division with a Trooper clone for sale as the SLX, but Acura has dropped that model for 2000.

EVALUATION Trooper displays fine throttle response throughout the speed range and Torque On Demand allows 2WD cruising or set-and-forget 4WD convenience. But our automatic-transmission test model averaged a poor 13.5 mpg. Handling is competent, although Trooper's tall build makes it feel more top-heavy than most SUVs in tight turns and it hurts directional stability in crosswinds. It also contributes to considerable wind noise at highway speeds. Ride is stable, but big bumps can register with a jolt. There's loads of passenger space and back-seat width for three adults. Step-in height is not unreasonable, and the tall build combines with large windows for fine outward visibility. Some testers object to the steering wheel's bus-like angle, and others complain of insufficient fore-aft driver-seat travel. Some minor controls are haphazardly placed, and the audio system is too recessed and has undersized buttons. Overall, this is a roomy SUV with a smooth powertrain, but its priced against even larger V8 rivals that seat more than five.

ENGINES

	dohc V6
Size, liters/cu. in.	3.5/213
Horsepower @ rpm	215 @ 5400
Torque (lbs./ft.) @ rpm	230 @ 3000
Availability	S
EPA city/highway mpg	
5-speed OD manual	16/19
4-speed OD automatic	15/19

PRICES

1999 Isuzu Trooper	Retail Price	Dealer Invoice
S 4-door 4WD wagon, 5-speed	$27100	$24255
S 4-door 4WD wagon, automatic	28650	25642
Destination charge	495	495

STANDARD EQUIPMENT:

S: 3.5-liter dohc V6 engine, 5-speed manual or 4-speed automatic transmission, limited-slip differential, part-time 4-wheel drive with automatic locking front hubs (manual transmission), full-time 4-wheel drive (automatic transmission), 2-speed transfer case, driver- and passenger-side airbags, antilock 4-wheel disc brakes, air conditioning, variable-assist power steering, tilt steering wheel, cruise control, cloth reclining front bucket seats, storage console, split folding and reclining rear seat, cupholders, AM/FM/cassette w/six speakers, digital clock, heated power mirrors, power windows, power door locks, remote keyless entry, rear defogger, rear wiper/washer, remote fuel door release, intermittent wipers, tachometer, illuminated visor mirrors, cargo cover, cornering lights, theft-deterrent system, first aid kit, skid plates, outside-mounted

full-size spare tire, 245/70R16 tires, alloy wheels.

OPTIONAL EQUIPMENT:	Retail Price	Dealer Invoice
Major Packages		
Performance Pkg., w/automatic transmission	$1400	$1176

Leather-wrapped steering wheel, height/angle adjustable front seats, variable intermittent wipers, map lights, rear-passenger foot rests, cargo floor rails, diversity antenna, rear privacy glass, fog lights, color-keyed bumpers and overfenders, color-keyed mirrors, bodyside moldings, alloy spare wheel.

Luxury Pkg., w/automatic transmission	4300	3612

Leather upholstery, heated front bucket seats, 8-way power driver seat, 4-way power passenger seat, leather-wrapped shifter and handbrake, woodgrain interior trim, 6-disc CD player, multi-meter, power sunroof, two-tone paint, chrome mirrors. Requires Performance Pkg.

Gold Pkg., w/automatic transmission	400	316

Includes gold badging, gold alloy wheels. Requires Performance Pkg.

Comfort and Convenience

Power sunroof, w/automatic transmission	1100	979
Requires Performance Pkg.		
Leather power/heated front seats, w/automatic transmission	2250	2002
Requires Performance Pkg.		
AM/FM/CD player	550	434
6-disc CD changer	650	513
Multi-meter gauge, w/automatic transmission	200	178
Requires Performance Pkg.		

Appearance and Miscellaneous

Running boards	340	269
Ski rack	293	231

Special Purpose, Wheels and Tires

Trailer hitch	253	200

Other options are available as port installed items.

ISUZU VEHICROSS

Isuzu VehiCross

4-wheel-drive compact sport-utility vehicle

1999 base price: $28,900. Built in Japan. **Also consider:** Isuzu Amigo, Jeep Wrangler, Subaru Forester

FOR • Cargo room • Acceleration • Maneuverability **AGAINST** • Entry/exit • Visibility • Noise

This limited-edition, 4-seat, 2-door sport-utility vehicle starts the 2000 model year with some new colors as its only change, but midyear, Isuzu plans to replace VehiCross's 16-inch wheels with 18s. At the same time, the standard air conditioning will be upgraded to automatic climate control. About five inches shorter in wheelbase and overall length than its Amigo stablemate, VehiCross's body is metal with unpainted plastic lower cladding. The tailgate encloses the spare tire and swings open to the left beneath a top-hinged rear window. VehiCross shares Trooper's V6, automatic transmission, and Torque On Demand full-time 4WD system. Antilock 4-wheel disc brakes are standard. For 2000, Isuzu has doubled its powertrain warranty to 10 years/120,000 miles on Amigo, Trooper, and VehiCross.

EVALUATION Its looks may be unorthodox, but VehiCross is among the better-performing SUVs, with good acceleration, accurate steering, and good grip and balance in turns, without excessive body lean. Our test model averaged 14.7 mpg. The V6 sounds coarse under even moderate throttle, however, and our test example suffered lots of intrusive gear whine and a wind leak from the driver's window. Ride is choppy over uneven pavement, but most bumps are easily absorbed. Braking performance and pedal feel are nothing special. A high step-in and low roofline make for difficult entry and exit, though the seats are comfortable (especially the Recaro-brand front buckets) and the cabin is roomy enough. The dashboard is shared with Amigo and has hard-to-reach audio and climate controls. The rear bench splits 50/50 and folds down, but cargo room is tight. Outward visibility is dangerously obstructed over the shoulder and the slit-like rear window and intrusive spare-tire shell conspire to hide virtually all objects behind. VehiCross is an answer to a question no one has asked. Priced against roomier, more traditional 4-door SUVs, any value it has is emotional, not rational.

ENGINES

	dohc V6
Size, liters/cu. in.	3.5/213
Horsepower @ rpm	215 @ 5400
Torque (lbs./ft.) @ rpm	230 @ 3000
Availability	S
EPA city/highway mpg	
4-speed OD automatic	15/19

PRICES

1999 Isuzu VehiCross	Retail Price	Dealer Invoice
Base 2-door wagon	$28900	$25866
Destination charge	695	695

STANDARD EQUIPMENT:

Base: 3.5-liter dohc V6 engine, 4-speed automatic transmission, permanent 4-wheel drive, limited-slip differential, driver- and passenger-side airbags, antilock 4-wheel disc brakes, air conditioning, variable-assist power steering, leather-wrapped tilt steering wheel, cruise control, leather upholstery, front bucket seats, split folding rear seat, cupholders, heated power mirrors, power windows, power door locks, remote keyless entry, intermittent wipers, AM/FM/cassette w/6-disc CD changer, tachometer, rear defogger, rear wiper/washer, floormats, roof rails, rear spoiler, 245/70R16 tires, alloy wheels.

OPTIONAL EQUIPMENT:
Major Packages

Ironman Pkg.	995	886

Includes cargo mat, roof rack, badging and graphics.

Appearance and Miscellaneous

Roof rack	293	232

JAGUAR S-TYPE

RECOMMENDED

Jaguar S-Type

Rear-wheel-drive luxury car; similar to Lincoln LS
Base price range: $42,500-$48,000. Built in England. **Also consider:** BMW 5-Series, Lexus GS 300/400, Mercedes-Benz E-Class

FOR • Acceleration (V8) • Handling/roadholding • Quietness • Ride **AGAINST** • Automatic transmission performance (V6) • Cargo room

Jaguar's smaller sedan gets minor trim changes following its introduction as a 2000 model in spring '99. Jaguar is part of Ford, and the rear-wheel drive S-Type shares its platform with the Lincoln LS, though the S-Type is built in Britain with mostly Jaguar-specific components.

The 3.0 model has a 3.0-liter V6 derived from a Ford design. The S-Type 4.0 uses a 4.0-liter Jaguar V8. The Lincoln LS shares versions of these engines. The only transmission is a Ford/Jaguar 5-speed automatic. Standard are traction control, antilock 4-wheel disc brakes, and front head/chest side airbags. Options include a Weather Package with Jaguar's antiskid Dynamic Stability Control, and a Sport Package that features computer-controlled shock absorbers and 17-inch wheels with high-speed tires. A Deluxe Communications Package adds an in-dash navigation display, satellite/cell-phone assistance system, and voice-activated control for telephone, audio, and climate functions. Also optional is Reverse Park Control, which sounds an alert as the car backs toward an obstacle.

Running additions include a trunk pull-down strap, redesigned alloy wheels, and redundant radio controls on the steering wheel. Also, the front door armrests and center console lid are raised slightly and their height equalized.

PERFORMANCE Jaguar says the V6 S-Type does 0-60 mph in 8 seconds, the V8 in 6.6. Those are good numbers, and they ring true after our initial testing. Our V6 test car averaged 19.5 mpg. We haven't measured fuel economy with a V8 version, but both engines require premium fuel. As expected of Jaguars, the base suspension delivers a plush, supple ride with excellent bump absorption and little tire rumble even on rough pavement. Large humps induce a trace of float, yet body lean is modest in fast corners, where the car grips well and inspires confidence. Steering is quick and informative, but we'd prefer a tad more effort for best high-speed control. The Sport Package doesn't increase steering effort, but sharpens most other reflexes and provides wider tires with still more grip at only a slight penalty in ride quality and road noise. Both engines are smooth and hushed, rising to a muted, expensive-sounding growl when worked hard.

The main dynamic fault is the automatic transmission's tendency to change gears willy-nilly in hard driving. And it sometimes takes a second or three to do so, even when using the manual mode of the slightly awkward "J-gate" shifter. The problem is more pronounced with the V6. When it's cooperating, the automatic shifts promptly and smoothly enough.

ACCOMMODATIONS Passenger and cargo space isn't a Jaguar priority, but at least 6-footers have decent head clearance all-around, unlike in the older and larger XJ sedans. Tall occupants sit knees-up in back, though foot room is adequate and the seat is properly firm and contoured. Three adults can squeeze in the rear seat, but they best be very chummy. Up-front ambience is cozy, too, but front-seat comfort is excellent. Rear visibility isn't the best, though large door mirrors partly compensate.

Numerous adjustments help tailor a good driving position. The all-button audio and climate controls are handy but busy; add the optional navigator and the center dash gets complex. The voice-activation system may simplify your life, but it's part of a pricey $4300 option package. Other lapses include a glovebox that's tough to access, and an optional cell phone that effectively eliminates one front cupholder. Interior storage is so-so. The trunk is small by class standards, but usefully shaped and easy to load. Test S-Types felt substantial, but one suffered a minor front-window air leak, another a rattle from the dashboard. Despite leather and wood appointments, the interior's plastic trim imparts a generic feel absent in other Jaguars—and in such rivals as Audi and Lexus.

VALUE FOR THE MONEY A good value in an upper-crust sedan, the S-Type blends traditional Jaguar charm with modern engineering and—we hope—Ford reliability. It's not as sporty as a BMW 5-Series, but should easily achieve its expected 18,000 annual U.S. sales.

ENGINES

	dohc V6	dohc V8
Size, liters/cu. in.	3.0/181	4.0/244
Horsepower @ rpm	240 @ 6800	281 @ 6100
Torque (lbs./ft.) @ rpm	221 @ 4500	287 @ 4300
Availability	S	O
EPA city/highway mpg		
5-speed OD automatic	18/26	17/23

PRICES

Jaguar S-Type	Retail Price	Dealer Invoice
3.0 4-door sedan	$42500	$37128
4.0 4-door sedan	48000	41932
Destination charge	595	595

Prices are accurate at time of publication; subject to manufacturer's changes.

STANDARD EQUIPMENT:

3.0: 3.0-liter dohc V6 engine, 5-speed automatic transmission, traction control, driver- and passenger-side airbags, front side-impact airbags, antilock 4-wheel disc brakes, air conditioning w/dual-zone automatic climate control, interior air filter, variable-assist power steering, tilt/telescoping steering wheel, wood/leather-wrapped steering wheel, cruise control, leather upholstery, 8-way power front bucket seats, split folding rear seat, wood interior trim, power mirrors, power windows, power door locks, remote keyless entry, AM/FM/cassette w/CD changer controls, steering wheel radio controls, digital clock, tachometer, trip computer, rear defogger, heated wiper park, automatic headlights, floormats, theft-deterrent system, front and rear fog lights, full-sized spare tire, 225/55HR16 tires, alloy wheels.

4.0 adds: 4.0-liter dohc V8 engine, power sunroof, memory driver seat and mirrors, front seat power lumbar supports, power tilt/telescoping steering w/memory, automatic day/night rearview mirror, compass, universal garage door opener.

OPTIONAL EQUIPMENT:
Major Packages

	Retail Price	Dealer Invoice
Power/Memory Pkg., 3.0	$1900	$1596

Power sunroof, memory driver seat and mirrors, front seat lumbar supports, power tilt/telescoping steering wheel w/memory, automatic day/night rearview mirror, compass, universal garage door opener.

Deluxe Communications Pkg.	4300	3644

Integrated navigation system, emergency services, voice activated controls (telephone, climate control, audio), portable cellular telephone.

Sport Pkg.	1100	924

Computer-controlled shock absorbers, 235/50ZR17 tires, special alloy wheels.

Weather Pkg.	1200	1008

Anti-skid system, heated front seats, rain-sensing wipers, heated windshield, headlight washers, engine block heater.

Safety Features

Reverse park control	400	336

Comfort and Convenience

Integrated navigation system	2000	1680
6-disc CD changer w/premium sound system	1500	1260

JAGUAR XJ SEDAN

Jaguar XJ8

Rear-wheel-drive luxury car

Base price range: $55,650-$80,650. Built in England. **Also consider:** Cadillac Seville, Infiniti Q45, Lexus LS 400

FOR • Ride • Acceleration • Quietness • Build quality • Exterior finish • Interior materials **AGAINST** • Fuel economy • Cargo space

Jaguar's flagship sedan gains a supercharged ultra-luxury model and an optional satellite navigation system for 2000. Joining the XJ8, XJ8L, luxury-oriented Vanden Plas, and high-performance XJR, is the Vanden Plas Supercharged model. All are 4-door sedans that seat five, but the XJ8L and Vanden Plas models have a 4.9-inch longer wheelbase than the XJ8 and XJR. The XJ8, XJ8L, and Vanden Plas have a 290-horsepower 4.0-liter V8. XJR and the Vanden Plas Supercharged add a supercharger for 370 hp. A 5-speed automatic is the only transmission. Antilock 4-wheel disc brakes and front side airbags are standard. The standard traction control system now modulates throttle and brakes, instead of just varying throttle to maintain grip. The new satellite navigation system is operated from a touch-screen display mounted in the dashboard and is optional on all models. Also new for 2000 are rain-sensing windshield wipers. Newly standard on the XJR and optional on the other models is a 320 watt Alpine stereo, and the XJR gets redesigned alloy wheels.

EVALUATION Jaguar's silky V8 moves these 2-ton cars with authority. Ride is as comfortable and compliant as any rival's, and noise levels are very low. There's less body lean in corners with the XJR, but all these Jags grip well. Straight-line stability in crosswinds could be better, though. Most dashboard controls are haphazardly arranged, and the sleek styling dictates some compromises. Head room is cozy for 6-footers and rear leg space is tight in the XJ8 and XJR, almost generous in the L and Vanden Plas versions. However, rear-seat cushions on all are too low to be comfortable. The low roof hinders entry and exit, visibility is hampered by the back-seat headrests, and cargo space is subpar for the class. All things considered, however, these are attractive alternatives to more staid luxury sedans, such as the Lexus LS 400 and Mercedes-Benz E-Class—especially with Jaguar's rising customer-satisfaction ratings since the British automaker became part of Ford in 1989.

ENGINES

	dohc V8	Supercharged dohc V8
Size, liters/cu. in.	4.0/244	4.0/244
Horsepower @ rpm	290 @ 6100	370 @ 6150
Torque (lbs./ft.) @ rpm	290 @ 4250	387 @ 3600
Availability	S[1]	S[2]

EPA city/highway mpg

5-speed OD automatic	17/24	16/22

1. XJ8, XJ8L, Vanden Plas. 2. XJR, Vanden Plas Supercharged.

PRICES

Jaguar XJ Sedan

	Retail Price	Dealer Invoice
XJ8 4-door sedan	$55650	$48616
XJ8L 4-door sedan	60700	53028
Vanden Plas 4-door sedan	64750	56566
XJR 4-door sedan	68550	59886
Vanden Plas Supercharged 4-door sedan	80650	70456
Destination charge	595	595

XJR and Vanden Plas Supercharged retail price includes $1300 Gas Guzzler tax.

STANDARD EQUIPMENT:

XJ8: 4.0-liter dohc V8 engine, 5-speed automatic transmission, traction control, driver- and passenger-side side airbags, front side-impact airbags, antilock 4-wheel disc brakes, variable-assist power steering, power tilt/telescopic steering wheel, cruise control, air conditioning w/automatic climate control, leather upholstery, wood interior trim, 12-way power front bucket seats with power lumbar adjusters, front storage console, overhead console, cupholders, driver memory system (driver seat, steering wheel, outside mirrors), automatic headlights, power sunroof, heated power mirrors, power windows, power door locks, remote keyless entry, trip computer, outside-temperature indicator, automatic day/night rearview mirror, AM/FM/cassette, steering wheel radio controls, analog clock, rear defogger, remote fuel-door and decklid releases, illuminated visor mirrors, universal garage-door opener, map lights, rain-sensing variable intermittent wipers, floormats, theft-deterrent system, chrome hood ornament, front and rear fog lights, full-size spare tire, 225/60ZR16 tires, alloy wheels.

XJ8L adds: 4.9-inch longer wheelbase.

Vanden Plas adds: wood and leather-wrapped steering wheel, wood shift knob, wood picnic trays on front seatbacks, upgraded leather upholstery and wood interior trim, lambswool floormats.

XJR adds to XJ8: supercharged 4.0-liter dohc V8 engine, Alpine sound system w/6-disc CD changer, heated front seats, wood and leather-wrapped steering wheel, sport suspension, 255/40ZR18 tires.

Vanden Plas Supercharged adds to Vanden Plas: supercharged 4.0-liter dohc V8 engine, heated front and rear seats, Alpine sound system w/6-disc CD changer, Computer Active Technology Suspension, 235/50ZR17 tires.

OPTIONAL EQUIPMENT:
Comfort and Convenience

Navigation system	1500	1260

XJ8, XJ8L requires Alpine sound system or CD changer.

Heated front and rear seats,		
XJ8, XJ8L, Vanden Plas	500	420
6-disc CD changer, XK8, XL8L, Vanden Plas	800	672
Alpine sound system w/CD changer,		
XJ8, XJ8L, Vanden Plas	1800	1512

JAGUAR XK8

Jaguar XK8 coupe

Rear-wheel-drive luxury car
Base price range: $66,200-$81,800. Built in England. **Also consider:** Cadillac Eldorado, Lexus SC 300/400, Mercedes-Benz SL-Class

FOR • Acceleration • Ride • Quietness • Build quality • Exterior finish • Interior materials **AGAINST** • Passenger and cargo room • Entry/exit • Rear visibility

Jaguar adds a supercharged high-performance model and an optional satellite navigation system to its XK line for 2000. These 4-passenger luxury sports cars offer a coupe body style or a convertible with a power soft top and glass rear window with defroster. All use a 4.0-liter V8 that makes 290 horsepower in XK8s. The supercharged XKR has 370 hp, plus functional hood louvers and a rear spoiler. A 5-speed automatic is the only transmission. Antilock 4-wheel disc brakes are standard, and 18-inch wheels are newly optional in place of the XK8's standard 17s. Traction control is standard, but this year uses the previously optional design that modulates throttle and brakes. This replaces a throttle-only system. The satellite navigation system operates from a dashboard touch-screen.

EVALUATION Any XK8 is too heavy to be a real sports car, but every one is entertaining on twisty roads. XKRs don't match the XK8's impressively absorbent ride, but aren't harsh. Jaguar's V8 is a gem: nearly silent at idle and never louder than a muted, expensive-sounding snarl. Our test XK8 coupe vaulted from 0-60 mph in under 7 seconds and averaged 15 mpg. The XKR convertible we tested felt true to Jaguar's claim of 0-60 in under 6 seconds; it averaged 16.2 mpg. Beware the XK8 if you're tall or claustrophobic; room is tight even in front. The back seat is toddler size. Entry/exit is difficult, thanks to a low body, wide door sills, and an outboard handbrake lever on the driver's side. But the seats are comfortable, and the attractive dash has logical switches and large, legible gauges. Ford owns Jaguar, and it shows in the XK8's solid, all-of-a-piece feel, convertible included. And it's competitively priced, all things considered.

ENGINES

	dohc V8	Supercharged dohc V8
Size, liters/cu. in.	4.0/244	4.0/244
Horsepower @ rpm	290 @ 6100	370 @ 6150
Torque (lbs./ft.) @ rpm	290 @ 4250	387 @ 3600
Availability	S[1]	S[2]
EPA city/highway mpg		
5-speed OD automatic	17/25[3]	16/23

1. XK8. 2. XKR. 3. 17/24 w/convertible.

PRICES

Jaguar XK8	Retail Price	Dealer Invoice
XK8 2-door coupe	$66200	$57832
XK8 2-door convertible	71200	62200
XKR 2-door coupe	76800	67092
XKR 2-door convertible	81800	71460
Destination charge	595	595

STANDARD EQUIPMENT:

XK8: 4.0-liter dohc V8 engine, 5-speed automatic transmission, traction control, driver- and passenger-side airbags, antilock 4-wheel disc brakes, air conditioning w/automatic climate control, variable-assist power steering, power tilt/telescopic steering wheel, wood/leather-wrapped steering wheel, cruise control, power top (convertible), leather upholstery, 12-way power front bucket seats w/power lumbar support, memory system (driver seat, steering wheel, outside mirrors), cupholders, wood interior trim and shifter, tachometer, trip computer, outside-temperature indicator, automatic headlights, AM/FM/cassette, steering wheel radio controls,

analog clock, heated power mirrors, power windows, power door locks, remote keyless entry, universal garage-door opener, illuminated visor mirrors, automatic day/night rearview mirror, rear defogger, remote fuel-door and decklid release, rain-sensing variable intermittent windshield wipers, map lights, floormats, theft-deterrent system, front and rear fog lights, full-size spare tire, 245/50ZR17 tires, alloy wheels.

XKR adds: supercharged 4.0-liter dohc V8 engine, heated front seats, Alpine sound system, 6-disc CD changer, headlight washers, Computer Active Technology Suspension, 245/45ZR18 front tires, 255/45ZR18 rear tires, deletes full-size spare tire.

OPTIONAL EQUIPMENT:

	Retail Price	Dealer Invoice
Major Packages		
All-Weather Pkg., XK8	$500	$420
Heated front seats, headlight washers.		
Comfort and Convenience		
Navigation system	2400	2016
XK8 requires Alpine sound system or CD changer.		
6-disc CD changer, XK8	800	672
Alpine sound system w/CD changer, XK8	1800	1512
Appearance and Miscellaneous		
18-inch alloy wheels, XK8	500	420
Includes 245/45ZR18 front tires, 255/45ZR18 rear tires, space-saver spare tire.		

JEEP CHEROKEE

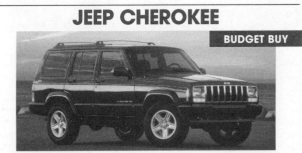

BUDGET BUY

Jeep Cherokee Limited 4-door

Rear- or 4-wheel-drive midsize sport-utility vehicle
Base price range: $16,445-$25,210. Built in USA. **Also consider:** Chevrolet Blazer, Nissan Xterra

FOR • Acceleration (6-cylinder) • Cargo room **AGAINST** • Fuel economy • Acceleration (4-cylinder) • Ride

Cherokee's big change for 2000 is fancier duds for its top-line Limited model. SE and Sport models come as 2- and 4-door wagons. Classic and Limited are 4-door only. Limited is promoted to a separate model from an option package.

SEs have a standard 4-cylinder engine with manual transmission or optional 3-speed automatic. Optional for SEs and standard on other Cherokees is an inline 6-cylinder engine with revisions designed to make it quieter and reduce exhaust emissions. Its standard manual transmission gets modifications aimed at smoother shifts. A 4-speed automatic is optional with the six. Cherokee offers rear-wheel drive and two 4WD systems: part-time Command-Trac and full-time Selec-Trac. Selec-Trac does not require that 4WD be disengaged on dry pavement and is available only on 6-cylinder models, as are antilock brakes.

Limited's new look includes a chrome grille and headlight surrounds, bright silver alloy wheels, and a chrome rear license-plate brow. New standard features on all models include headlights Jeep says are brighter and longer-lasting, a cassette player, and rear child-seat anchors. Classic and Limited also get a new 16-inch cast wheel design.

PERFORMANCE Cherokee's 4-cylinder provides adequate acceleration with manual transmission, but feels underpowered with automatic in anything but gentle cruising. Most buyers order the six. It's strong throughout the speed range with fuel economy typical for a midsize SUV: about 15 mpg with automatic, 17 with manual in our tests.

Good balance and tidy dimensions make Cherokee quite maneuverable in most situations. The base suspension absorbs most bumps without jarring. The Up Country option makes for a rough ride; spend instead for optional antilock brakes. Cherokee suffers powertrain and road resonances absent in most rivals. Wind noise at speed also is high.

ACCOMMODATIONS Cherokee shows its age in a low-roof passenger compartment with no surplus of front shoulder room, a shortage of rear knee clearance, and fairly lofty step-in. Another sign: Rear entry/exit is tight, thanks to narrow lower doorways. The dashboard is convenient, and outward vision is good, though larger door mirrors would help lane-changing. Mounting the spare tire inside eats up cargo room, but there's still decent space with the rear seat in use, and a long load floor with it folded. An outside spare is available through Jeep dealers. Recent test Cherokees had occasional interior rattles and wide panel gaps around the hood and tailgate.

VALUE FOR THE MONEY Cherokee is capable on-road and off, and not too expensive, provided you go easy on options. Still, being way behind the times in room, ride, and refinement, this is the "blue light special" of midsize SUVs.

ENGINES

	ohv I4	ohv I6
Size, liters/cu. in.	2.5/150	4.0/242
Horsepower @ rpm	125 @ 5400	190 @ 4600
Torque (lbs./ft.) @ rpm	150 @ 3250	225 @ 3000
Availability	S[1]	S[2]
EPA city/highway mpg		
5-speed OD manual	21/25[3]	18/24[4]
3-speed automatic	18/22	
4-speed OD automatic		16/22[5]

1. SE. 2. Sport, Limited; optional SE. 3. 18/20 w/4WD. 4. 17/22 w/4WD. 5. 16/21 w/4WD.

PRICES

Jeep Cherokee	Retail Price	Dealer Invoice
SE 2-door wagon 2WD	$16445	$15455
SE 2-door wagon 4WD	17960	16854
SE 4-door wagon 2WD	17485	16421
SE 4-door wagon 4WD	18995	17815
Sport 2-door wagon 2WD	18870	17096
Sport 2-door wagon 4WD	20380	18444
Sport 4-door wagon 2WD	19905	18026
Sport 4-door wagon 4WD	21415	19375
Classic 4-door wagon 2WD	21370	19316
Classic 4-door wagon 4WD	22885	20669
Limited 4-door wagon 2WD	23090	20829
Limited 4-door wagon 4WD	25210	23250
Destination charge	535	535

Sport, Classic, Limited require a quick order pkg.

STANDARD EQUIPMENT:

SE: 2.5-liter 4-cylinder engine, 5-speed manual transmission, driver- and passenger-side airbags, power steering, vinyl upholstery, front bucket seats, folding rear seat, floor console, cupholders, AM/FM/cassette, digital clock, intermittent wipers, auxiliary power outlets, rear defogger, remote outside mirrors, 215/75R15 tires. **4WD** models add: Command-Trac part-time 4-wheel drive.

Sport adds: 4.0-liter 6-cylinder engine, cloth/vinyl upholstery, tachometer, cargo-area light, spare-tire cover, 225/75R15 white-letter all-terrain tires. **4WD** models add: Command-Trac part-time 4-wheel drive.

Classic adds: 4-speed automatic transmission, cloth upholstery, leather-wrapped steering wheel, power mirrors, intermittent rear wiper/washer, floormats, roof rack, 225/70R16 tires, alloy wheels. **4WD** adds: Command-Trac part-time 4-wheel drive.

Limited adds: air conditioning, overhead console, compass, trip computer, cargo cover, deep-tinted glass. **4WD** adds: Selec-Trac full-time 4-wheel drive, full-size spare tire.

OPTIONAL EQUIPMENT:

Major Packages

	Retail Price	Dealer Invoice
Trailer Tow Group	365	310
4WD w/Up Country Suspension Group	245	208

Equalizer hitch, 7-wire receptacle, 4-wire trailer adapter, maximum engine cooling. SE and Sport require automatic transmission and full-size spare tire. Classic requires full-size spare tire.

Up Country Suspension Group, Classic, Limited	725	616
Sport 4WD w/alloy wheels, automatic	845	718
Sport 4WD w/alloy wheels, manual	$805	$684
Sport 4WD w/automatic	780	663
Sport 4WD w/manual	740	629

Limited-slip rear differential, maximum engine cooling, off-road suspension, tow hooks, Skid Plate Group, rear stabilizer bar delete, full-size spare tire.

Quick Order Pkg. 23B/25B/26B, SE	1275	1084
Manufacturer's discount price	NC	NC

Air conditioning, cloth and vinyl high-back bucket seats, power mirrors, intermittent rear wiper/washer.

Quick Order Pkg. 25J/26J, Sport 2-door	2170	1845
Sport 4-door	2345	1993
Manufacturer's discount price	NC	NC

Air conditioning, Light Group (automatic-off headlights, illuminated visor mirrors, map lights, underhood light), power mirrors, power windows and door locks, remote keyless entry, intermittent rear wiper/washer, leather-wrapped tilt steering wheel, floormats, roof rack.

Quick Order Pkg. 26S, Classic	1825	1551
Manufacturer's discount price	NC	NC

Air conditioning, Light Group (On Time Delay headlights, illuminated visor mirrors, map lights, underhood light), power windows and door locks, remote keyless entry, tilt steering wheel.

Quick Order Pkg. 26H, Limited	2060	1751
Manufacturer's discount price	NC	NC

Leather upholstery, 6-way power driver seat, power windows and door locks, remote keyless entry, tilt steering wheel, cruise control, Light Group (automatic-off headlights, illuminated visor mirrors, map lights, underhood light).

Convenience Group, SE	440	374

Tilt leather-wrapped steering wheel, cruise control. Requires quick order pkg.

Powertrains

4.0-liter 6-cylinder engine, SE	995	846
3-speed automatic transmission, SE 2WD	625	531

Requires 2.5-liter engine.

4-speed automatic transmission, SE, Sport	945	803

SE requires 4.0-liter 6-cylinder engine.

Selec-Trac full-time 4WD, Sport 4WD w/automatic, Classic	540	459
Limited-slip rear differential	285	242

Requires full-size spare tire.

Safety Features

Antilock brakes	600	510

SE requires 4.0-liter 6-cylinder engine.

6-way power driver seat, Classic	300	255
Heated front seats, Limited	550	468
Overhead console, Classic	235	200

Outside temperature indicator, trip computer, sunglasses/garage door opener holder.

Cruise control, Sport, Classic	250	213
Heated power mirrors, Sport, Classic, Limited	45	38
AM/FM/cassette/CD player, Sport, Classic, Limited	410	349
Infinity sound system, Classic, Limited	350	298

Requires AM/FM/cassette/CD player.

Cargo cover, Sport, Classic	75	64
Smokers Group	20	17

Ash tray, lighter.

Appearance and Miscellaneous

Theft-deterrent system	75	64

SE requires quick order pkg.

Deep-tinted glass, Sport 2-door	375	319
Sport 4-door, Classic	270	230
Fog lights, Sport, Classic, Limited	110	94
Roof rack, SE, Sport	140	119

SE requires quick order pkg.

Special Purpose, Wheels and Tires

Wheel Plus Group, SE	875	744

Full-size spare, 225/75R15 all-terrain white-letter tires, alloy wheels. Requires quick order pkg.

Alloy wheels, Sport	245	208

JEEP GRAND CHEROKEE

Jeep Grand Cherokee Laredo

Rear- or 4-wheel-drive midsize sport-utility vehicle
Base price range: $26,570-$34,345. Built in USA. **Also consider:** Lexus RX 300, Mercedes-Benz M-Class, Mercury Mountaineer

FOR • Acceleration • Cargo room **AGAINST** • Fuel economy

Two-wheel-drive Grand Cherokees are available with a V8 engine for 2000, keynoting the changes to Jeep's flagship SUV. Laredo and Limited models return, both with a standard inline 6-cylinder engine or an optional 4.7-liter V8. Both use a 4-speed automatic transmission, though the V8's has an extra gear ratio between second and third gears designed to improve passing response and provide smoother downshifts.

Rear-wheel drive had been exclusive to 6-cylinder models, but now both engines come with rear-drive or one of three 4WD systems, all of which are usable on dry pavement. Selec-Trac provides 2WD or full-time 4WD and for 2000, is available with the V8 after being limited to the six. Permanently engaged Quadra-Trac II apportions power between front and rear axles. Quadra-Drive is also permanently engaged, but can send 100 percent of the engine's power to any one wheel to maintain traction.

Among other additions for 2000 are standard front seat-belt pretensioners, sun-visor extensions, and a "Headlights On" indicator.

PERFORMANCE Ride, handling, and off-road ability are Grand Cherokee strong points, rating at or near the top of the class. The suspension easily absorbs most large bumps and potholes, though smaller, sharp road imperfections register through the seats. There's fine balance and control in quick directional changes despite a fair amount of body lean and some lingering side-to-side pitching motions over bumps. Steering feel is natural, though frequent corrections are needed at highway speeds

Acceleration is adequate with the 6-cylinder, robust with the V8. Our test 6-cylinder model averaged 15.9 mpg, about par for a midsize SUV. Our test V8 averaged 16.1 mpg in mostly highway driving. Transmissions shift with prompt smoothness, especially the V8's. No SUV offers this range of 4WD systems, and all provide Grand Cherokee with excellent traction on-road and off. Our Quadra-Drive V8 test models, however, suffered lots of gear whine at highway speeds and drivetrain binding in tight turns at low speeds. And there was a pronounced shudder through one test model's Quadra-Drive powertrain when coming to a stop.

Braking is strong and smooth, pedal modulation good. Engines are well-muffled, but wind rush and tire roar can intrude at highway speeds.

ACCOMMODATIONS Four adults fit easily, but Grand Cherokee isn't wide enough to seat three grownups comfortably in the rear. Moreover, the rear seatback is too upright for best comfort and there's little toe space under the front seats. The dashboard has simple radio and climate controls mounted fairly close to the driver, and Limited adds handy steering-wheel audio controls. Roof pillars are too thick for best outward vision, though large outside mirrors help. Bins and pockets provide plenty of small-items storage. Cargo room, though adequate, is at the low end for this class, and most SUVs have easier-to-fold rear seatbacks. The overall structure feels solid, and interior materials are appropriate for these prices.

VALUE FOR THE MONEY Grand Cherokee's performance and solidity are top-notch, and prices are competitive. But questions about this otherwise-impressive Jeep's long-term mechanical reliability keep it from our Best Buy category.

ENGINES

	ohv I6	ohc V8
Size, liters/cu. in.	4.0/242	4.7/284
Horsepower @ rpm	195 @ 4600	235 @ 4600
Torque (lbs./ft.) @ rpm	230 @ 2400	295 @ 3200
Availability	S	O
EPA city/highway mpg		
4-speed OD automatic	16/21	15/20[1]

1. 15/19 w/4WD

PRICES

Jeep Grand Cherokee	Retail Price	Dealer Invoice
Laredo 4-door wagon 2WD	$26570	$24087
Laredo 4-door wagon 4WD	28540	25855
Limited 4-door wagon 2WD	31915	28790
Limited 4-door wagon 4WD	34345	30964
Destination charge	535	535

STANDARD EQUIPMENT:

Laredo: 4.0-liter 6-cylinder engine, 4-speed automatic transmission, driver- and passenger-side airbags, antilock 4-wheel disc brakes, air conditioning, power steering, tilt steering wheel, cruise control, cloth front bucket seats, split folding rear seat, storage console w/armrest, cupholders, overhead console (compass, trip computer, outside temperature indicator, map lights), power mirrors, power windows, power door locks, tachometer, AM/FM/cassette, variable intermittent wipers, auxiliary power outlet, visor mirrors, rear defogger, rear wiper/washer, theft-deterrent system, deep-tinted rear glass, roof rack, 225/75R16 tires, alloy wheels. **4WD** adds: Selec-Trac full-time 4-wheel drive.

Limited adds: dual-zone automatic climate control, leather upholstery, leather-wrapped steering wheel w/radio controls, 10-way power front seats w/driver-side memory, heated power mirrors w/driver-side memory and automatic day/night, remote keyless entry, AM/FM/cassette/CD player w/Infinity sound system, automatic day/night rearview mirror, universal garage door opener, illuminated visor mirrors, automatic headlights, cargo cover, floormats, fog lights, 245/70R16 tires. **4WD** adds: Quadra-Trac II permanent 4-wheel drive.

OPTIONAL EQUIPMENT:
Major Packages

Pkg. 26F/28F, Laredo	2910	2474
Manufacturer's discount price	2110	1794
Remote keyless entry, 6-way power front seats, automatic day/night rearview mirror, automatic headlights, leather-wrapped steering wheel, heated power mirrors, AM/FM/cassette CD player w/Infinity sound system, universal garage door opener, illuminated visor mirrors, cargo cover and net, floormats, fog lights, theft-deterrent system w/alarm, 225/75R16 white-letter tires.		
Pkg. 26K/28K, Limited	1050	893
Heated front seats, power sunroof.		
Luxury Group, Laredo	750	638
6-way power front seats, automatic day/night rearview mirror, automatic headlights. Requires Infinity sound system.		
Cold Weather Group, Laredo	300	255
Limited	250	213
Heated power mirrors, heated 10-way power front seats. Laredo requires leather upholstery.		
Convenience Group, Laredo	640	544
Manufacturer's discount price	140	119
Remote keyless entry, cargo cover and net, floormats, 225/75R16 white-letter tires.		
Up-Country Suspension Group, Laredo 4WD	575	489
Limited 4WD	390	332
Heavy-duty shock absorbers, Skid Plate Group, full-size spare tire, 245/70R16 all-terrain white-letter tires.		
Class III Trailer Tow Prep Group	105	89
Trailer wiring harness, mechanical cooling fan. Requires 4.0-liter engine.		
Trailer Tow Group	360	306
Frame mounted receiver hitch, 7-wire connector, 7-way round to 4-way flat plug adapter, power steering cooler. Requires 4.0-liter engine.		
Trailer Tow Group IV, 4WD	255	217
Trailer Tow Group ordered with 4.7-liter engine. Laredo requires option pkg.		

Powertrains

4.7-liter V8 engine, Laredo 4WD	1165	990

Prices are accurate at time of publication; subject to manufacturer's changes.

	Retail Price	Dealer Invoice
Laredo 2WD, Limited......................................	$1070	$910
Includes multi-speed automatic transmission.		
Quadra-Trac II permanent 4WD, Laredo 4WD............	445	378
Quadra-Drive permanent 4WD,		
Laredo w/4.0 liter engine	995	846
Laredo w/4.7-liter engine, Limited.............................	550	468
Quadra-Trac II plus Vari-Lok progressive axles.		
Trak-Lok differential, Laredo	285	242
NA with 4.7-liter engine or Quadra-Trak II permanent 4WD.		

Comfort and Convenience

Power sunroof	800	680
Leather upholstery, Laredo	580	493
Requires option pkg. or Luxury Group.		
AM/FM/cassette/CD player, Laredo	335	285
10-disc CD changer, Laredo	1045	888
Laredo w/Pkg. 26F/28F, Limited	300	255
Laredo includes Infinity sounds system.		
Infinity sound system, Laredo	410	349
Requires AM/FM/cassette/CD player.		

Appearance and Miscellaneous

Theft-deterrent system, Laredo...........................	150	128
Fog lights, Laredo	120	102

Special Purpose, Wheels and Tires

Skid Plate/Tow Hook Group, 4WD	200	170
245/75R16 all-terrain white-letter tires,		
Laredo...	435	370
Laredo w/option pkg.	185	157

JEEP WRANGLER

BUDGET BUY

Jeep Wrangler Sahara

4-wheel-drive compact sport-utility vehicle

Base price range: $14,430-$20,345. Built in USA. **Also consider:** Chevrolet Tracker, Honda CR-V, Isuzu Amigo, Toyota RAV4

FOR • Cargo room • Maneuverability **AGAINST** • Fuel economy • Acceleration (4-cylinder w/automatic) • Noise • Ride

The 6-cylinder engine in Jeep's tradition-bound SUV gets modifications aimed at smoother operation, standard radios are upgraded, and child-seat tethers are added to the rear seat for 2000.

Wranglers come with a soft top and plastic side windows; a hardtop with glass windows is optional. The base SE model has a 4-cylinder engine. Uplevel Sports and Saharas use Jeep's inline 6-cylinder. Manual transmission is standard; a 3-speed automatic is optional. All Wranglers have 4-wheel drive for use only on slippery surfaces. Antilock brakes are optional on 6-cylinder models.

For 2000, the Sport's standard AM/FM radio adds a cassette player and a pair of speakers mounted in the roll bar, and the Sahara exchanges a cassette player for a CD player. Also, the optional tilt steering wheel on SE and Sport is now the same leather-covered unit that's standard on Sahara.

PERFORMANCE Wrangler is fun to drive, but not if you like comfort or quiet. A short wheelbase and off-road-ready suspension trigger abrupt vertical ride motions even on apparently smooth roads. Likewise, cornering is skittish on bumpy surfaces and the steering isn't very precise. Wrangler is quite maneuverable, however, and the optional antilock brakes stop it with fine control. Sound insulation is sparse, so wind noise can be deafening in the convertible, even with the top up. It's less brutal in the hardtop, but that only allows copious tire noise to drum through.

The 4-cylinder feels underpowered with automatic transmission. It accelerates well enough in town with manual shift, but must be worked to its limits on short freeway on-ramps and in two-lane passing. The 6-cylinder delivers fine power with either transmission but doesn't make the 3000-pound Wranglera hot rod. The six isn't particularly gruff, but we haven't tested a 2000 and can't say how this year's changes effect smoothness. Our test 5-speed Sahara averaged 15.2 mpg —slightly better than we average with the 4-cylinder.

ACCOMMODATIONS Head room is terrific with either top, and front seats are chair-height comfortable. Two adults fit in back without touching shoulders, but knee room is tight and the seat isn't much more comfortable than a park bench. Gauges and controls are logically grouped, and outward vision suffers no serious impediments. A few grocery bags fit behind the back seat, which folds or removes for steamer-trunk-sized load space. Raising or lowering the soft top requires a time-consuming struggle with zippers, fasteners, and struts. Workmanship and materials are on the paramilitary side.

VALUE FOR THE MONEY Wrangler isn't comfortable, but few vehicles have more personality or better off-road ability. Six-cylinder models can quickly top $20,000, but all versions have strong resale value.

ENGINES

	ohv I4	ohv I6
Size, liters/cu. in.	2.5/150	4.0/242
Horsepower @ rpm	120 @ 5400	181 @ 4600
Torque (lbs./ft.) @ rpm	140 @ 3500	222 @ 2800
Availability	S[1]	S[2]
EPA city/highway mpg		
5-speed OD manual	18/20	16/19
3-speed automatic	16/18	15/18

1. SE. 2. Sport, Sahara.

PRICES

Jeep Wrangler	Retail Price	Dealer Invoice
SE 2-door convertible	$14430	$13840
Sport 2-door convertible	18415	16625
Sahara 2-door convertible	20345	18324
Destination charge	535	535

STANDARD EQUIPMENT:

SE: 2.5-liter 4-cylinder engine, 5-speed manual transmission, Command-Trac part-time 4-wheel drive, driver- and passenger-side airbags, power steering, reclining front vinyl bucket seats, tachometer, front carpeting, mini floor console, cupholder, auxiliary power outlet, dual outside mirrors, fender flares, skid plates, 205/75R15 all-terrain tires, styled steel wheels.

Sport adds: 4.0-liter 6-cylinder engine, folding rear bench seat, AM/FM/cassette with rear sound bar and speakers, digital clock, rear carpeting, 215/75R15 all-terrain tires.

Sahara adds: tilt leather-wrapped steering wheel, cloth upholstery, full storage console, courtesy and underhood lights, variable intermittent wipers, AM/FM/CD player, front floormats, fog lights, bodyside steps, spare-tire cover, heavy-duty suspension, front and rear tow hooks, 225/75R15 all-terrain tires, alloy wheels.

OPTIONAL EQUIPMENT:
Major Packages

Pkg. 22N/23N, SE..	1310	1114
AM/FM/cassette, rear sound bar w/speakers, high back bucket seats, folding rear seat, rear carpeting.		
Pkg. 24D/25D, Sport......................................	525	446
Tilt leather-wrapped steering wheel, intermittent wipers, Convenience Group, full-size spare tire.		
Convenience Group, SE, Sport	165	140
Full storage console w/cupholders, courtesy and underhood lights.		

Powertrains

3-speed automatic transmission	625	531
Trac-Loc rear differential...	285	242
Requires full-size spare tire, 5-speed transmission.		
Dana 44 rear axle, Sport, Sahara.................................	595	506
Requires full-size spare. NA with antilock brakes. Includes Trac-Loc rear differential.		

Safety Features	Retail Price	Dealer Invoice
Antilock brakes, Sport, Sahara	$600	$510

Comfort and Convenience

Hard top, SE, Sport..	755	642
Sahara	1160	986

Includes full metal doors with roll-up windows, rear wiper/washer, deep-tinted glass (Sahara), rear defogger (Sahara), cargo light.

Soft and hard tops, SE, Sport	1395	1186
Sahara	1800	1560

Includes hard doors.

Full metal doors w/roll-up windows...............................	125	106
Air conditioning...	895	761
Cloth/vinyl reclining front bucket seats with rear seat,		
SE	745	633
SE w/22N/23N, Sport	150	128

SE includes rear carpeting.

Convenience Group 1, SE, Sport	245	208

Includes tilt leather-wrapped steering wheel, intermittent wipers.

Cruise control, SE, Sport	300	255
Sahara	250	213

Includes leather-wrapped steering wheel.

Rear defogger for hardtop, SE, Sport...........................	165	140

Requires Heavy Duty Electrical Group.

AM/FM/cassette, SE	715	608

Includes rear sound bar with speakers.

AM/FM/CD player, SE	840	714
SE w/22N/23N, Sport	125	106

Includes rear sound bar with speakers.

Appearance and Miscellaneous

Theft-deterrent system...	75	64
Add-A-Trunk lockable storage.......................................	125	106

SE requires rear seat.

Deep-tinted rear-quarter and liftgate glass,		
SE, Sport	405	344

Includes rear defogger. Requires hardtop.

Bodyside steps, SE, Sport	75	64
Fog lights, Sport	120	102

Requires Heavy Duty Electrical Group or air conditioning.

Spare-tire cover, SE, Sport..	50	43

NA with full-size spare tire. NA with SE when ordered with optional tires.

Special Purpose, Wheels and Tires

Heavy-duty shock absorbers, SE, Sport	90	77

SE requires optional tires.

Heavy-Duty Electrical Group, SE, Sport	135	115

Heavy-duty battery and alternator. Std. Sahara.

Front and rear tow hooks, SE, Sport............................	60	51
225/75R15 white-letter all-terrain tires,		
SE	470	400
Sport	425	361
Sport w/Pkg. 25D/24D...	310	264

SE requires full-face steel or alloy wheels.

Tire and Wheel Pkg., Sport	785	667
Sport w/Pkg. 25D/24D...	670	570
Sahara	360	306

Five alloy wheels, full-size spare, 30x9.5R15 white-letter tires. Sport includes heavy-duty shock absorbers. Deletes spare-tire cover on Sahara.

Full-face steel wheels, SE...	230	196

Requires optional tires.

Alloy wheels, SE...	495	421
Sport	265	225

Requires optional tires.

KIA SEPHIA

Front-wheel-drive subcompact car

Base price range: $9,995-$12,750. Built in South Korea. **Also consider:** Chevrolet Prizm, Honda Civic, Saturn S-Series

FOR • Fuel economy **AGAINST** • Noise • Rear seat room • Cargo room • Build quality • Interior materials

The base Sephia keeps its '99 pricing for 2000, but comes with pre-

Kia Sephia

viously optional equipment that cost $855 last year. The LS gets a $600 price increase, but now includes options totalling $1600. Kia, the South Korean automaker recently purchased by former rival Hyundai, is known here mostly for its Sportage compact SUV. The only car it sells in the U.S. is the Sephia, a front-wheel-drive subcompact sedan available in base, LS, and LS with Power Package models. All offer manual or optional automatic transmission and a Kia-designed 4-cylinder engine. Antilock brakes are optional except on the base model. For 2000, power steering, AM/FM cassette, and a split fold-down rear seat are standard instead of optional on the base Sephia. Power windows and locks, air conditioning, AM/FM cassette, and tachometer are now standard instead of optional on LS models.

EVALUATION Overall, Sephia is a mediocre performer compared to most budget-range rivals. Acceleration is so-so, as are ride and handling. Fuel economy is also unremarkable, our test 5-speed LS averaging 22.7 mpg. Noise is a problem, too, and refinement lags way behind that of the class-leading Hondas and Toyotas. Starting prices are attractive, but workmanship and resale values aren't.

ENGINES

	dohc I4
Size, liters/cu. in.	1.8/109
Horsepower @ rpm	125 @ 6000
Torque (lbs./ft.) @ rpm	108 @ 4500
Availability	S

EPA city/highway mpg

5-speed OD manual	24/31
4-speed OD automatic	23/31

PRICES

Kia Sephia	Retail Price	Dealer Invoice
Base 4-door sedan, 5-speed	$9995	$8996
Base 4-door sedan, automatic	10970	9856
LS 4-door sedan, 5-speed	11595	10359
LS 4-door sedan, automatic	12750	11219
Destination charge	450	450

STANDARD EQUIPMENT:

Base: 1.8-liter dohc 4-cylinder engine, 5-speed manual or 4-speed automatic transmission, driver- and passenger-side airbags, variable-assist power steering, cloth upholstery, front bucket seats, center console, cupholders, split folding rear seat, AM/FM/cassette, rear defogger, remote fuel-door/decklid release, intermittent wipers, dual remote outside mirrors, 185/65R14 tires, wheel covers.

LS adds: air conditioning, tilt steering wheel, cruise control, driver seat front cushion tilt, power mirrors, power windows, power door locks, tachometer, variable intermittent wipers, passenger-side visor mirror.

OPTIONAL EQUIPMENT:

Safety Features

Antilock brakes, LS	800	745

Includes 4-wheel disc brakes.

Comfort and Convenience

Air conditioning, Base	900	745
AM/FM/CD player, LS	295	248

Prices are accurate at time of publication; subject to manufacturer's changes.

Appearance and Miscellaneous

	Retail Price	Dealer Invoice
Rear spoiler	$175	$132
Alloy wheels, LS	340	274

KIA SPORTAGE

Kia Sportage 2-door

Rear- or 4-wheel-drive compact sport-utility vehicle

Base price range: $13,995-$19,595. Built in South Korea.
Also consider: Chevrolet Tracker, Honda CR-V, Subaru Forester, Suzuki Vitara, Toyota RAV4

FOR • Cargo room • Maneuverability • Visibility **AGAINST** • Acceleration (4-door) • Ride • Noise • Interior materials

A bolder-sounding horn, driver's left footrest, and newly optional remote keyless entry are among the few changes to Sportage for 2000. Base prices are unchanged from 1999. This compact sport-utility vehicle comes as a 4-door wagon and as a shorter 2-door semi-convertible. The wagon seats five, the convertible seats four and has a manual-folding soft top over the rear seat. All Sportages have a 2.0-liter 4-cylinder engine and offer rear-wheel drive or on-demand 4-wheel drive. The 4WD isn't for use on dry pavement, but has separate low-range gearing. Wagons come with manual or optional automatic transmission; 2WD convertibles use automatic, 4x4s manual.

EVALUATION Wagons have adequate room for four adults, but the convertible's back seat is best left to kids. Getting decent cargo space in either requires folding the back seat. Both versions handle well for small SUVs, but the body-on-frame Sportage has a more "trucky" ride than the rival car-based unibody Honda CR-V and Toyota RAV4. Acceleration is sluggish even for this class, particularly with automatic, and the engine is loud and gruff when worked even moderately hard. We averaged 19 mpg with a 4WD 5-speed wagon, which is just slightly less than we've logged with CR-Vs and RAV4s. The Honda and Toyota also score over this Kia with their all-surface 4WD. And most automakers rate far better than Kia in consumer surveys of reliability and satisfaction. Still, materials and workmanship have improved lately, so you may find the Sportage appealing as a lower-cost alternative to a CR-V or RAV4—though we don't.

ENGINES

	dohc I4
Size, liters/cu. in.	2.0/122
Horsepower @ rpm	130 @ 5500
Torque (lbs./ft.) @ rpm	127 @ 4000
Availability	S

EPA city/highway mpg	
5-speed OD manual	19/23
4-speed OD automatic	19/23

PRICES

Kia Sportage	Retail Price	Dealer Invoice
2WD Base 2-door convertible, automatic	$13995	$12724
2WD Base 4-door wagon, 5-speed	14795	13441
2WD Base 4-door wagon, automatic	15795	14351
4WD Base 2-door convertible, 5-speed	14495	13058
4WD Base 4-door wagon, 5-speed	16295	14670
4WD Base 4-door wagon, automatic	17295	15580
2WD EX 4-door wagon, 5-speed	17395	15680

	Retail Price	Dealer Invoice
2WD EX 4-door wagon, automatic	$18395	$16590
4WD EX 4-door wagon, 5-speed	18595	16600
4WD EX 4-door wagon, automatic	19595	17510
Destination charge	450	450

STANDARD EQUIPMENT:

Base: 2.0-liter dohc 4-cylinder engine, 5-speed manual or 4-speed automatic transmission, driver- and passenger-side airbags, driver-side knee airbag, variable-assist power steering, tilt steering wheel, cloth upholstery, front bucket seats w/driver-side lumbar adjuster, console w/armrest, cupholders, folding rear seat (convertible), split folding rear seat (wagon), power mirrors, power windows, power door locks, tachometer, digital clock, rear defogger (wagon), remote fuel-door release, intermittent wipers, rear folding soft top (convertible), theft-deterrent system, full-size spare with cover, rear spare-tire carrier, 205/75R15 tires. **4WD** models add: part-time 4-wheel drive, 2-speed transfer case, alloy wheels.

EX adds: air conditioning, cruise control, AM/FM/CD player, passenger-side visor mirror, variable intermittent wipers, rear wiper/washer, rear privacy glass, roof rack, alloy wheels. **4WD** models add: part-time 4-wheel drive, 2-speed transfer case.

OPTIONAL EQUIPMENT:

Safety Features

Antilock brakes	490	410

Comfort and Convenience

Air conditioning, Base	900	745
Cruise control, convertible	260	200
AM/FM/cassette, Base	320	250
AM/FM/CD player, Base	475	375
Remote keyless entry	225	140
Leather upholstery, EX	900	760
Includes leather door-panel inserts, leather-wrapped steering wheel.		
Rear wiper/washer, Base 4-door	125	100

Appearance and Miscellaneous

Sport appearance graphics, Base	95	60
Rear spoiler	189	143
Roof rack, Base wagon	195	150

Special Purpose, Wheels and Tires

Alloy wheels, 2WD Base	340	274

LAND ROVER DISCOVERY

Land Rover Discovery Series II

4-wheel-drive midsize sport-utility vehicle

1999 base price: $34,150. Built in England. **Also consider:** Ford Explorer, Lexus RX 300, Mercedes-Benz M-Class

FOR • Ride • Exterior finish • Cargo room **AGAINST** • Fuel economy • Noise • Entry/exit

Addition of an integrated compass to the rear-view mirror is the only change of note to Land Rover's lower-priced sport-utility vehicle for 2000. Discovery comes as a 4-door wagon with permanently engaged 4-wheel drive and standard seating for five. An optional third-row seat expands capacity to seven. A 4.0-liter V8, 4-speed automatic transmission, and antilock 4-wheel disc brakes are standard. The 4WD system is designed to apply each brake individually to limit wheel spin in severe conditions. It also employs Land Rover's Hill Descent Control, which applies the brakes to slow the vehicle when descending steep grades in 4-wheel low range. Land Rover's optional Active Cornering Enhancement (ACE) system replaces the usual anti-roll bars with hydraulic rams to reduce body lean in hard turns. Self-Leveling Suspension is also available. In addition to the compass, Discovery gets a fuel filler door indicator on the instrument panel and new shades of red and green paint for 2000. Britain's Land Rover is owned by BMW, and the German automaker is introducing its own SUV, the X5.

EVALUATION Without ACE, this tall, relatively narrow SUV suffers copious body lean in tight turns. With ACE, it corners with fine control and balance; too bad the effective new technology is available only in a pricey option package. Ride is choppy on closely spaced bumps, but most imperfections are soaked up without jarring. Braking is sure, and acceleration okay for the class; our '99 Discovery did 0-60 mph in 10.2 seconds, but wind, engine, and axle noise can intrude, and we averaged just 12.5 mpg on required premium fuel. The optional third-row seat feels cramped, but overall, people and package space are good. A tall step-in and narrow doorways make entry/exit tough even for an SUV, especially to the rear. One of our test examples suffered numerous squeaks and rattles. Discovery's optional 7-seat capacity is a plus, but the Mercedes M-Class offers the same, and is a better performer. The polished Lexus RX 300 is the top alternative in a less-trucky 5-passenger SUV.

ENGINES

	ohv V8
Size, liters/cu. in.	4.0/241
Horsepower @ rpm	188 @ 4750
Torque (lbs./ft.) @ rpm	250 @ 2600
Availability	S
EPA city/highway mpg	
4-speed OD automatic	13/17

PRICES

1999 Land Rover Discovery	Retail Price	Dealer Invoice
Base 4-door wagon	$34150	$30394
Destination charge	625	625

STANDARD EQUIPMENT:

Base: 4.0-liter V8 engine, 4-speed automatic transmission, permanent 4-wheel drive, 2-speed transfer case, traction control, Hill Descent Control, driver- and passenger-side airbags, antilock 4-wheel disc brakes, air conditioning w/dual-zone control, outside temperature indicator, power steering, leather-wrapped tilt steering wheel, cruise control, wood interior trim, cloth front bucket seats w/adjustable lumbar support, split folding rear seat, front storage console, cupholders, heated power mirrors, power windows, power door locks, remote keyless entry, tachometer, Harman/Kardon AM/FM/cassette with CD changer controls, diversity antenna, steering wheel radio controls, rear defogger, rear wiper/washer, illuminated visor mirrors, automatic day/night rearview mirror, map lights, variable intermittent wipers, cargo cover, remote fuel-door release, front and rear fog lights, headlight washers, theft-deterrent system, Class III towing hitch receiver, rear-mounted full-size spare tire, 255/65HR16 tires, alloy wheels.

OPTIONAL EQUIPMENT:

Major Packages

Leather Pkg.	1950	1735

Leather upholstery, 8-way power front seats, additional wood interior trim, upgraded Harman/Kardon sound system w/rear audio controls.

Rear Seat Pkg.	1750	1588

Forward-facing third-row seats, rear step, self-leveling rear suspension.

Performance Pkg.	2900	2581

Active Cornering Enhancement, 255/55HR18 tires, special alloy wheels.

Cold Climate Pkg.	500	445

Heated windshield, heated front seats.

Comfort and Convenience

Dual sunroofs	1500	1335

Requires Leather Pkg.

Rear air conditioning	750	668

Requires Leather Pkg. and Rear Seat Pkg.

6-disc CD changer	625	525

Special Purpose, Wheels and Tires

Self-leveling rear suspension	750	668

LAND ROVER RANGE ROVER

Land Rover Range Rover 4.0 SE

4-wheel-drive full-size sport-utility vehicle
1999 base price range: $58,000-$66,000. Built in England.
Also consider: Lexus LX 470, Lincoln Navigator

FOR • Ride • Passenger and cargo room • Interior materials • Build quality • Exterior finish **AGAINST** • Fuel economy • Entry/exit

Body-colored bumpers and new-look alloy wheels for the base model keynote appearance changes to Range Rover for 2000. This is the ultra-luxury companion to the smaller, less-expensive Discovery. Both these British-built SUVs are products of England's Land Rover, which is owned by BMW of Germany. Range Rover is a 5-passenger, 4-door wagon that comes in two models, the 4.0 SE and 4.6 HSE. Both have permanent 4-wheel drive, automatic transmission, and a V8 engine. The 4.0 SE uses a 4.0 liter, the 4.6 HSE a 4.6. Antilock 4-wheel disc brakes, traction control, front side airbags, and a driver-adjustable self-leveling suspension are standard. For 2000, Range Rover gets standard auto-dimming outside mirrors, tinted turn signal lenses, and revised instrument graphics. The 4.0 SE's alloy wheels are redesigned, and both models get body-colored bumpers and mirrors, and more interior brightwork, including a chrome gearshift surround. Land Rover offered a small run of high-performance Callaway versions during 1999 and plans to offer a series of limited-production appearance packages beginning in Spring 2000.

EVALUATION Range Rovers are marvelous off-road, comfortable on-road, and well-suited to their role as transport for the foxes-and-hounds set. But they're quite thirsty, and acceleration in the SE borders on sluggish. In short, there's nothing of tangible value that you can't get in rival SUVs for thousands less.

ENGINES

	ohv V8	ohv V8
Size, liters/cu. in.	4.0/241	4.6/278
Horsepower @ rpm	188 @ 4750	222 @ 4750
Torque (lbs./ft.) @ rpm	250 @ 2600	300 @ 2600
Availability	S[1]	S[2]
EPA city/highway mpg		
4-speed OD automatic	13/17	13/15

1. 4.0 SE. 2. 4.6 HSE.

PRICES

1999 Land Rover Range Rover	Retail Price	Dealer Invoice
4.0 SE 4-door wagon	$58000	$51330
4.6 HSE 4-door wagon	66000	58410
Destination charge	625	625

STANDARD EQUIPMENT:

4.0 SE: 4.0-liter V8 engine, 4-speed automatic transmission, permanent 4-wheel drive, electronic 2-speed transfer case, locking center differential, front and rear traction control, driver- and passenger-side airbags, front side-impact airbags, antilock 4-wheel disc brakes, variable-assist power steering, leather-wrapped tilt/telescopic steering wheel, leather-wrapped shifter, cruise control, air conditioning w/dual-zone automatic climate control, interior air filter, leather upholstery, wood interior trim, heated 10-way power front bucket seats w/memory feature, split folding rear seat, front storage console, cupholders, heated power mirrors w/memory and automatic day/night, outside mirror tilt-down back-up aid, power windows, power door locks, remote keyless entry, power sunroof, trip computer, computer message center, Alpine AM/FM/weatherband/cassette w/6-disc CD changer, steering-wheel radio controls, integrated

Prices are accurate at time of publication; subject to manufacturer's changes.

diversity antenna, automatic day/night rearview mirror, universal garage-door opener, remote fuel-door release, heated windshield and rear window, variable intermittent wipers w/heated washer nozzles, rear wiper/washer, illuminated visor mirrors, map lights, cargo cover, theft-deterrent system, heated headlight wiper/washers, front and rear fog lights, automatic load-leveling suspension, trailer hitch and wiring harness, 265/65HR16 tires, full-size spare tire, alloy wheels.

4.6 HSE adds: 4.6-liter V8 engine, overhead storage console, 255/55HR18 tires.

OPTIONAL EQUIPMENT:
Comfort and Convenience

	Retail Price	Dealer Invoice
Navigation System	$2995	$2650

LEXUS ES 300

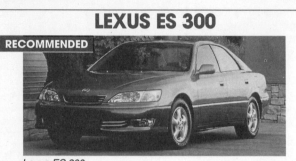

RECOMMENDED

Lexus ES 300

Front-wheel-drive near-luxury car; similar to Toyota Camry/Solara

Base price: $31,405. Built in Japan.   **Also consider:** Acura TL, Audi A6, BMW 3-Series, Infiniti I30

FOR • Acceleration • Ride • Quietness • Build quality • Exterior finish • Interior materials   **AGAINST** • Rear visibility • Steering feel

Traditionally the entry-level sedan from Toyota's luxury brand, the ES 300 gets a mild revamp—including altered front and rear styling—in advance of the spring 2000 debut of a smaller, less expensive rear-wheel-drive stablemate, the IS 300.

The front-drive ES remains a visually distinct underskin cousin to the V6 Toyota Camry 4-door, but has slightly more power and torque, plus more standard features including front side airbags and traction control. Lengthening the list for 2000 are rear child-seat anchors, electrochromic inside and driver's mirrors, a trunk pass-through lock, and automatic volume control for the sound system. In addition, the available driver's-seat memory now incorporates mirror settings, the optional heated seats go from one to two warmth levels, and the extra-cost Vehicle Skid Control system is bolstered by a new Lexus Brake Assist feature that automatically provides full hydraulic power in response to strong, quick brake-pedal movements. New options include 16-inch wheels, high-intensity discharge headlamps, and ventilation microfilter. The 2000 ES also sports minor front and rear styling changes, plus more wood dashboard trim.

PERFORMANCE Quietness and comfort remain the ES 300's signature assets. Wind and road noise are muted, and the V6 is silent at idle, silken under power. Acceleration is equally impressive at under 7.5 seconds 0-60 mph. Less likeable is a standard automatic transmission that's reluctant to kickdown from overdrive fourth at midrange speeds, which frustrates passing maneuvers. Economy is acceptable but not outstanding; we averaged 20.5 mpg overall on the required premium fuel. Braking is swift and vice-free save marked nosedive in "panic" stops, something the new Brake Assist feature will do nothing to cure.

In ride and handling, the ES 300 is more "little limo" than sports sedan. Steering is quick but short on road feel, and though the car corners capably, there's marked body lean and relatively modest grip. Ride is soft and isolating, but some sharp bumps do register. The optional Adaptive Variable Suspension—basically computer-controlled shock absorbers—has little functional advantage over the normal chassis, but experience in senior Lexus models shows the VSC antiskid system to be worth its extra cost.

ACCOMMODATIONS As always, the ES interior is an inviting place for four adults. Six-footers can sit comfortably in tandem, although those in back must ride knees-up and have little toe room

beneath the front seats. The modestly sized trunk is usefully shaped and benefits from a low liftover. Thoughtful features include a convenient glovebox mounting for the available CD changer. Drivers get ample seat and steering-wheel adjustments, clear gauges, and handy switchgear. Outward visibility is fine except for hard-to-see rear corners, a penalty of the high-tail styling. Workmanship and materials are generally first-rate, although the last ES 300 we sampled suffered some misaligned dashboard panels—very un-Lexus.

VALUE FOR THE MONEY The ES is beginning to feel dated against newer-design rivals like the Acura TL and BMW 3-Series, and it's pricey against Infiniti's I30. But if you value comfort and elegance over sporty road manners in your near-luxury car, this Lexus is still hard to beat, and its resale values are golden.

ENGINES

	dohc V6
Size, liters/cu. in.	3.0/181
Horsepower @ rpm	210 @ 5800
Torque (lbs./ft.) @ rpm	220 @ 4400
Availability	S
EPA city/highway mpg	
4-speed OD automatic	19/26

PRICES

Lexus ES 300	Retail Price	Dealer Invoice
Base 4-door sedan	$31405	$27278
Destination charge	495	495

STANDARD EQUIPMENT:

Base: 3.0-liter dohc V6 engine, 4-speed automatic transmission, traction control, driver- and passenger-side airbags, front side-impact airbags, antilock 4-wheel disc brakes, daytime running lights, air conditioning w/automatic climate control, variable-assist power steering, tilt steering wheel, cruise control, cloth upholstery, power front bucket seats, driver-side power lumbar support, rear seat trunk pass-through, wood interior trim, front console, auxiliary power outlet, overhead console, cupholders, heated power mirrors w/driver-side automatic day/night, power windows, power door locks, remote keyless entry, AM/FM cassette, digital clock, tachometer, automatic day/night rearview mirror, outside-temperature indicator, rear defogger, variable intermittent wipers, illuminated visor mirrors, remote fuel-door and decklid releases, first-aid kit, automatic headlights, floormats, theft-deterrent system, fog lights, full-size spare tire, 205/65VR15 tires, alloy wheels.

OPTIONAL EQUIPMENT:
Major Packages

Leather Trim Pkg.	1885	1508
Leather upholstery, leather-wrapped steering wheel, memory driver seat and outside mirrors, interior air filter, universal garage door opener.		
Value Pkg.	2465	2215
Leather Trim Pkg. plus power sunroof, 6-disc CD changer.		
Value Pkg. w/Nakamichi Audio	3015	2711
Value Pkg. plus Nakamichi premium audio system.		

Safety Features

Antiskid system	550	440

Comfort and Convenience

Power sunroof	1000	800
Heated front seats	440	352
Requires Leather Trim Pkg.		
Nakamichi premium audio system	1630	1277
Includes 6-disc CD changer.		
6-disc CD changer	1080	864

Appearance and Miscellaneous

High intensity headlights	515	412
Adaptive Variable Suspension	620	496
Requires Leather Trim Pkg.		
Chrome alloy wheels	1740	870
Includes 205/60VR16 tires.		
205/60VR16 tires	40	32

Other options are available as port installed items.

LEXUS GS 300/400

RECOMMENDED

Lexus GS 300

Rear-wheel-drive luxury car

Base price range: $37,605-$46,005. Built in Japan. **Also consider:** Acura RL, BMW 5-Series, Jaguar S-Type, Mercedes-Benz E-Class

FOR • Acceleration • Steering/handling • Quietness • Build quality • Exterior finish • Interior materials **AGAINST** • Fuel economy • Navigation system controls

A standard **Brake** Assist feature is the main 2000-model news for Lexus's midrange sedans. The GS 300 retains an inline 3.0-liter six, the GS 400 a 4.0-liter V8 shared with the larger flagship LS 400 sedan. Both come with 5-speed automatic transmission; the 400 adds Lexus's E-shift, a quartet of steering-wheel buttons allowing sequential manual gear selection. Front side airbags are standard, as is a Vehicle Stability Control (VSC) anti-skid system integrated with standard antilock brakes and traction control.

For 2000, the VSC incorporates a Mercedeslike Brake Assist that automatically provides full hydraulic power in response to quick, strong brake-pedal movement. The only other notable change is the addition of child-seat anchors to the rear parcel shelf.

PERFORMANCE V8 or six, the GS delivers swift, silky acceleration and powerful braking. Our test 400 ran 0-60 mph in only 6 seconds; the 300 takes around 7.6. GS 400s averaged 17.9-19.0 mpg in our tests; a 300 returned 17.2 with lots of city driving. Both require premium fuel. The GS automatic transmission is smooth and responsive. Some of our testers laud the 400's E-shift system, but others feel it offers no advantages.

Wind and mechanical noise are low enough to make tire roar noticeable, especially with the optional low-profile 17-inch rubber. Unlike other Lexus sedans, the GS corners with grippy precision and noticeably less body lean, aided by firm, responsive steering. Even so, overall ride, handling, and brake-pedal feel don't quite match those of the best European sports sedans. The suspension is comfortably supple on most surfaces, though the 400 turns fidgety and thumpy over tar strips and expansion joints. The last 400 we tested suffered a vibration at highway speeds, but a dealer service department claimed there was nothing wrong with the steering or suspension.

ACCOMMODATIONS The GS design affords terrific space for four adults, though three in back is a cozy fit and 6-footers have no surplus rear head room. Doors open exceptionally wide and all seats are supportive and just soft enough. One 6-foot-plus tester had trouble finding a satisfactory relationship between steering wheel, pedals, and instruments, but other drivers fit perfectly, aided by the standard power tilt/telescopic steering wheel. The tall rear deck interferes with vision astern for everyone.

Per Lexus custom, gauges and most minor controls are large and handy, but trunk and fuel-door releases are semi-hidden at the base of the dashboard. The optional in-dash navigator complicates driving because some audio and climate functions are controlled from its touch-screen display. The trunk isn't exceptionally roomy, but it's sufficient for long weekends. Cabins are trimmed in supple leather and gorgeous wood, and overall workmanship is top-notch, though recent test cars have suffered some minor rattles inside and one had ripply-looking paint beneath its glossy clearcoat.

VALUE FOR THE MONEY Either GS makes a satisfying alternative to taut-handling German sports sedans, yet they're every inch the posh, feature-laden Lexus. In the rarefied arena of import V8 sedans, we prefer the BMW 540i and Mercedes-Benz E430 over the GS 400, making the GS 300 our pick as the better value of the Lexus pair.

ENGINES

	dohc I6	dohc V8
Size, liters/cu. in.	3.0/183	4.0/242
Horsepower @ rpm	220 @ 5800	300 @ 6000
Torque (lbs./ft.) @ rpm	220 @ 3800	310 @ 4000
Availability	S[1]	S[2]
EPA city/highway mpg		
5-speed OD automatic	20/25	17/24

1. GS 300. 2. GS 400.

PRICES

Lexus GS 300/400	Retail Price	Dealer Invoice
GS 300 4-door sedan	$37605	$32663
GS 400 4-door sedan	46005	39495
Destination charge	495	495

STANDARD EQUIPMENT:

GS 300: 3.0-liter dohc 6-cylinder engine, 5-speed automatic transmission, traction control, driver- and passenger-side airbags, front side-impact airbags, antilock 4-wheel disc brakes, daytime running lights, anti-skid system, air conditioning w/automatic dual-zone climate control, variable-assist power steering, power tilt/telescopic leather-wrapped steering wheel, cruise control, cloth upholstery, 10-way power front bucket seats with power lumbar support, front storage console, wood interior trim, cupholder, heated power mirrors, power windows, power door locks, remote keyless entry, automatic day/night rearview mirror, AM/FM/cassette, digital clock, variable intermittent wipers, rear defogger, outside-temperature indicator, illuminated visor mirrors, universal garage door opener, remote fuel-door and trunk releases, front and rear reading lights, automatic headlights, floormats, theft-deterrent system, fog lights, tool kit, first-aid kit, 215/60VR16 tires, alloy wheels.

GS 400 adds: 4.0-liter dohc V8 engine, 5-speed automatic transmission w/manual shift-capability, leather upholstery, memory system (driver seat, steering wheel, outside mirrors), automatic day/night outside mirrors, 225/55VR16 tires.

OPTIONAL EQUIPMENT:
Major Packages

Leather Trim Pkg., GS 300	1760	1408

Leather upholstery, memory system (driver seat, steering wheel, outside mirrors).

Premium Pkg., GS 300	3860	3088

Leather Trim Pkg., power sunroof, 6-disc CD changer, automatic day/night outside mirrors.

Premium Pkg., GS 400	3055	2444

Heated front seats, power sunroof, 6-disc CD changer, high intensity headlights.

Navigation Pkg., GS 300	7065	5765
GS 400	5305	4357

Navigation system, Premium Pkg., heated front seats, high intensity headlights.

Nakamichi Audio System Pkg., GS 300	6015	4752
GS 400	4255	3344

Nakamichi premium radio system, Premium Pkg., heated front seats, automatic day/night outside mirrors (GS 300), high intensity headlights.

Comfort and Convenience

Heated front seats, GS 300	440	352

Requires Premium Pkg.

6-disc CD changer	1080	864
Power sunroof	1020	816

Appearance and Miscellaneous

Rear spoiler, GS 400	440	352

Requires Premium Pkg.

Chrome alloy wheels	1700	850
GS 400	1915	958

Other options are available as port installed items.

LEXUS LS 400

✓ BEST BUY

Rear-wheel-drive luxury car

1999 base price: $53,805. Built in Japan. **Also consider:** Audi A8, BMW 7-Series, Mercedes-Benz S-Class

FOR • Acceleration • Ride • Quietness • Build quality • Exterior

Prices are accurate at time of publication; subject to manufacturer's changes.

Lexus LS 400

finish • Interior materials **AGAINST** • Steering feel • Navigation system controls

Toyota's luxury-division flagship sedan makes do with a new Brake Assist feature and rear child-seat anchors in its last season before being redesigned for 2001. The LS 400 continues with a V8, 5-speed automatic transmission, front side airbags, antilock 4-wheel disc brakes, traction control, and Lexus's Vehicle Stability Control antiskid system. Brake Assist automatically applies full braking power when sensors detect rapid brake-pedal movement consistent with a panic stop. Options again include power moonroof, heated front seats, premium Nakamichi audio, high-intensity headlamps, electronic air suspension with rear self-leveling, and a satellite navigation system with in-dash screen.

EVALUATION The LS 400 defines smooth, quick, and quiet. Acceleration is strong at 6.1 seconds 0-60 mph in our tests, highway passing ability impressive. We averaged a surprising 19.0 mpg. Ride comfort is outstanding overall, yet certain peaked bumps register sharply, and high speeds induce some float over big humps. Too large and softly damped to be nimble, the LS 400 nonetheless has good grip and balance, plus only modest cornering lean. Vehicle Stability Control keeps you safely on track when the going gets slippery, and the antilock brakes are reassuringly strong. One of the world's quietest cars, the LS coddles with comfortable seats and only a slight tightness in rear head room and an intrusive transmission hump to detract. Electroluminescent gauges are easy to read even in direct sunlight, and most controls are convenient. The helpful navigation system's touch-screen display incorporates some radio and climate functions, making adjustments complicated and distracting. Thick rear pillars can impede lane changes. Trunk space is inadequate only for cross-country hauls. Handsome materials and solid assembly support this car's lofty reputation. It's easily $60,000 with options, but few cars match the LS's formidable blend of luxury and performance, reliability and blue-chip resale value.

ENGINES

	dohc V8
Size, liters/cu. in.	4.0/242
Horsepower @ rpm	290 @ 6000
Torque (lbs./ft.) @ rpm	300 @ 4000
Availability	S

EPA city/highway mpg	
5-speed OD automatic	18/25

PRICES

1999 Lexus LS 400	Retail Price	Dealer Invoice
Base 4-door sedan	$53805	$45648
Destination charge	495	495

STANDARD EQUIPMENT:

Base: 4.0-liter dohc V8 engine, 5-speed automatic transmission, traction control, driver- and passenger-side airbags, front side-impact airbags, antilock 4-wheel disc brakes, daytime running lights, variable-assist power steering, power tilt/telescopic steering wheel, leather-wrapped/wood steering wheel and shifter, cruise control, air conditioning w/dual-zone automatic climate control, interior air filter, leather upholstery, power front bucket seats with power lumbar support, memory system (driver seat, steering wheel, outside mirrors), front storage console with auxiliary power outlet, cupholders, wood interior trim, heated power mirrors w/passenger-side back-up aid, automatic day/night inside and outside mirrors, power windows, power door locks, remote keyless entry, Lexus/Pioneer AM/FM/cassette with seven speakers, diversity antenna, digital clock, tachometer, outside-temperature indicator, trip computer, rear defogger, remote fuel-door and decklid releases, illuminated visor mirrors, universal garage door opener, speed-sensitive variable intermittent wipers, automatic headlights, first-aid kit, floormats, theft-deterrent system, fog lights, tool kit, skid control, full-size spare tire, 225/60VR16 tires, alloy wheels.

OPTIONAL EQUIPMENT:

	Retail Price	Dealer Invoice
Major Packages		
Premium Pkg.	$2715	$2172
Power sunroof, 6-disc CD changer, high intensity headlights.		
Navigation System Pkg.	5405	4437
Navigation system, Premium Pkg., heated front seats.		
Radio System Pkg.	4355	3424
Nakamichi Premium Radio System, Premium Pkg., heated front seats.		
Comfort and Convenience		
Power sunroof	1120	896
Heated front seats	440	352
6-disc CD changer	1080	864
Appearance and Miscellaneous		
High intensity headlights	500	400
Electronic air suspension	1905	1524
Includes ride control and automatic load leveling. Requires Radio System Pkg. or Navigation System Pkg.		
Chrome alloy wheels	1700	850

Other options are available as port installed items.

LEXUS LX 470

Lexus LX 470

4-wheel-drive full-size sport-utility vehicle; similar to Toyota Land Cruiser

Base price: $59,005. Built in Japan. **Also consider:** Land Rover Range Rover, Lincoln Navigator

FOR • Acceleration • Passenger and cargo room • Ride • Build quality • Exterior finish • Interior materials **AGAINST** • Fuel economy • Rear entry/exit

A standard antiskid system heads a short list of year-2000 changes to this upscale version of the Toyota Land Cruiser. The LX 470 stands apart with Lexus styling cues, a higher price, and more standard equipment, but both of these big sport-utility vehicles come with V8 power, traction control, antilock brakes, and permanent 4-wheel drive with low-range gearing and locking center differential.

Among LX features not shared with the Land Cruiser are a standard Adaptive Variable Suspension—computer-controlled shock absorbers that automatically vary among 16 damping levels to match surface conditions within driver-selected firm, normal, and soft modes. Another exclusive is Automatic Height Control with three driver-selectable elevations. Other LX standards include exterior running boards that are newly illuminated for 2000, plus leather-and-wood interior trim, rear air conditioning, and in-dash CD changer. A power sunroof joins the standard-equipment list (it cost extra before), as does a version of Lexus's Vehicle Stability Control (VSC) antiskid system incorporating Lexus's new Brake Assist feature, which automatically supplies full hydraulic power in response to quick, strong brake-pedal movement. A leather-and-wood steering wheel is also a new option. Performance and accommodations are similar to those of the Land Cruiser.

The Toyota Land Cruiser report includes an evaluation of the LX 470.

ENGINES

	dohc V8
Size, liters/cu. in.	4.7/285
Horsepower @ rpm	230 @ 4800
Torque (lbs./ft.) @ rpm	320 @ 3400
Availability	S

EPA city/highway mpg	
4-speed OD automatic	13/16

PRICES
Lexus LX 470

	Retail Price	Dealer Invoice
Base 4-door wagon	$59005	$50656
Destination charge	500	500

STANDARD EQUIPMENT:

Base: 4.7-liter dohc V8 engine, 4-speed automatic transmission, permanent 4-wheel drive, locking center differential and limited-slip rear differential, traction control, driver- and passenger-side airbags, antilock 4-wheel disc brakes, antiskid system, daytime running lights, front and rear air conditioning w/front and rear automatic climate controls, interior air filter, variable-assist power steering, power tilt and telescoping steering wheel w/memory, leather-wrapped steering wheel and shifter, cruise control, leather upholstery, heated power front bucket seats with driver-side lumbar support and memory, reclining and split folding middle seat, split folding rear seat, universal garage door opener, front storage console, cupholders, overhead console, wood interior trim, AM/FM/cassette with 6-disc CD changer and seven speakers, power antenna, digital clock, heated power mirrors w/driver-side automatic day/night and memory, passenger-side mirror w/tilt-down back-up aid, power windows, power door locks, remote keyless entry, power sunroof, rear defogger, intermittent rear wiper/washer, tachometer, outside temperature display, auxiliary power outlets, automatic day/night rearview mirror, illuminated visor mirrors, map lights, variable intermittent wipers, automatic headlights, remote fuel-door release, floormats, running boards, rear privacy glass, fog lights, theft-deterrent system, first-aid and tool kits, adaptive-variable and height-adjustable suspension, full-size spare tire, 275/70HR16 tires, alloy wheels.

OPTIONAL EQUIPMENT:
Comfort and Convenience

Nakamichi premium sound system	1200	900
Leather-wrapped and wood steering wheel	330	264
Includes wood shift knob.		

Other options are available as port installed items.

LEXUS RX 300

✓ BEST BUY

Lexus RX 300

Front- or 4-wheel-drive midsize sport-utility vehicle

Base price range: $32,505-$33,905. Built in Japan. **Also consider:** Ford Explorer, Jeep Grand Cherokee, Mercedes-Benz M-Class

FOR • Ride • Passenger and cargo room • Build quality • Exterior finish • Interior materials **AGAINST** • Wind noise

This **midsize sport-utility** vehicle debuted as an early '99 model and quickly became the new top-seller for Toyota's luxury brand. No surprise, then, that the RX 300 stands pat for 2000 except for the addition of a standard trailer hitch.

A pioneer of the so-called hybrid SUVs based partly on passenger-car platforms, it continues as a 5-passenger, 4-door wagon available with front-wheel drive or permanent all-wheel drive. There's no separate 4-low-range gearing because the RX isn't designed for severe off-road duty. The sole powertrain comprises a 4-speed automatic transmission linked to a 3.0-liter V6 with variable valve timing. Towing capacity is 3500 pounds. Front side airbags and antilock 4-wheel disc brakes are standard.

PERFORMANCE The front-drive RX is snappy off the line—we clocked one at 8.2 seconds to 60 mph—and has good power throughout the speed range. The slightly heavier AWD version does almost as well. The V6 is a model of refinement, but the transmissions in two AWD test units exhibited some uneven shifting until warmed up, after which they were flawless. Between those two vehicles we averaged 16.3 mpg, just slightly better than the midsize SUV norm, but a front-drive model returned 19.2 despite hard running.

The RX behaves like no other SUV—more like a luxury car or minivan. Though too big and heavy to have sporty handling, it corners with fine stability and little body lean for an SUV, helped by responsive steering. Ride is even more impressive, the RX smothering bumps large and small with ease—better than many cars, in fact. Routine braking is good, though some of our testers find pedal action a trifle spongy. Tire noise is noticed on coarse pavement, but the RX is pleasingly quiet overall—except with the sunroof open at highway speeds, when the pop-up air deflector creates mighty wind roar.

ACCOMMODATIONS Entry/exit is a simple matter, and there's ample room and comfort for five adults, even at the middle-rear position. Drivers sit commandingly high, but some may find the roof pillars too thick for best outward vision, even in front, and the tilt steering wheel doesn't go up high enough to suit our 6-foot testers. The unusual video-type display for climate and audio settings is slightly gimmicky, though it works well enough. Other instruments and controls are large, clear and close by.

Handy touches include full auto-up/down power windows, a pair of useful drawers in the center console, and large map pockets in each door—but there are no rear cupholders. Out back, two small underfloor bins flank a covered spare-tire well. Rear-seat conversion is convenient, but the load deck isn't that long with the seat up, and liftover is relatively high even on the 2WD version.

VALUE FOR THE MONEY More "suburban utility vehicle" than traditional SUV, the RX 300 is posh, refined, roomy, and pleasant to drive. The main drawback to this Best Buy is that discounts are nearly non-existent in the face of justifiably strong demand.

ENGINES

	dohc V6
Size, liters/cu. in.	3.0/183
Horsepower @ rpm	220 @ 5800
Torque (lbs./ft.) @ rpm	222 @ 4400
Availability	S
EPA city/highway mpg	
4-speed OD automatic	19/24[1]

1. 19/22 w/4WD.

PRICES
Lexus RX 300

	Retail Price	Dealer Invoice
Base 2WD 4-door wagon	$32505	$28234
Base 4WD 4-door wagon	33905	29450
Destination charge	500	500

STANDARD EQUIPMENT:

Base: 3.0-liter dohc V6 engine, 4-speed automatic transmission, driver- and passenger-side airbags, front side-impact airbags, antilock 4-wheel disc brakes, daytime running lights, air conditioning w/automatic climate control, variable-assist power steering, leather-wrapped steering wheel and shifter, tilt steering wheel, cruise control, cloth upholstery, power front bucket seats w/driver-side power lumbar support, front center console, split folding rear seat, wood interior trim, AM/FM/cassette w/seven speakers, power antenna, digital clock, heated power mirrors, power windows, power door locks, remote keyless entry, variable intermittent wipers, trip computer, outside temperature display, illuminated visor mirrors, rear defogger, intermittent rear wiper/washer, remote fuel door release, automatic headlights, map lights, cupholders, auxiliary power outlets, overhead console with sunglass holder, cargo cover, theft-deterrent system, rear privacy glass, trailer hitch, trailer wiring harness, 225/70SR16 tires, alloy wheels. **4WD** model adds: permanent 4-wheel drive.

OPTIONAL EQUIPMENT:
Major Packages

Limited Pkg.	1820	1456
Includes Leather Trim Pkg., driver seat memory, universal garage door opener, interior air filter.		
Premium Pkg.	1920	1536
Limited Pkg. plus automatic day/night rear view and outside mirrors.		
Convenience Pkg.	516	323
Roof rack, rear wind deflector.		

Prices are accurate at time of publication; subject to manufacturer's changes.

Powertrains

	Retail Price	Dealer Invoice
Traction control, 2WD	$300	$240
Locking rear differential, 4WD	390	312

Comfort and Convenience

Power moonroof	1000	800
Leather Trim Pkg.	1280	1024
Heated front seats	440	352
Requires Limited or Premium Pkg.		
6-disc CD changer	1080	864
Premium audio system	1630	1277
Includes 6-disc CD changer, upgraded speakers, and amplifiers.		

Other options are available as port installed items.

LEXUS SC 300/400

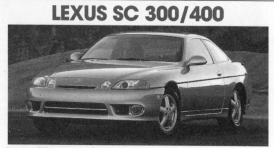

Lexus SC 400

Rear-wheel-drive luxury car

Base price range: $43,405-$55,905. Built in Japan. **Also consider:** Cadillac Eldorado, Jaguar XK8, Mercedes-Benz SL-Class

FOR • Quietness • Acceleration • Steering/handling • Build quality • Exterior finish • Interior materials **AGAINST** • Fuel economy • Rear-seat room • Cargo room

Though sales continue to decline, Toyota's luxury-division coupes carry into the new century with only a new paint shade and new perforated leather upholstery. As before, the SC 300 uses an inline 6-cylinder engine and 4-speed automatic transmission, while the V8 SC 400 comes with 5-speed automatic. Both models include dual front airbags and antilock brakes, but traction control remains an option and side airbags still aren't available.

EVALUATION The SCs offer luxurious accommodations for two adults; rear seats are big enough only for tots. Long, heavy doors hurt entry/exit in tight spaces, and taller drivers might lack headroom with the optional moonroof. Despite their size and weight, the SCs corner with precision and stability. They don't ride as smoothly as Lexus sedans and aren't as quiet, but are far above average in both respects. Acceleration is brisk with either engine, mechanical refinement high, fuel economy so-so. Luxury cars don't have to be practical and the Lexus coupes aren't, but they make few compromises in comfort, convenience, or performance while ranking at the top in quality and customer satisfaction.

ENGINES

	dohc I6	dohc V8
Size, liters/cu. in.	3.0/183	4.0/242
Horsepower @ rpm	225 @ 6000	290 @ 6000
Torque (lbs./ft.) @ rpm	220 @ 4000	300 @ 4000
Availability	S[1]	S[2]

EPA city/highway mpg

4-speed OD automatic	19/24	
5-speed OD automatic		18/25

1. SC 300. 2. SC 400.

PRICES

Lexus SC 300/400	Retail Price	Dealer Invoice
SC 300 2-door coupe	$43405	$37701
SC 400 2-door coupe	55905	47994
Destination charge	495	495

STANDARD EQUIPMENT:

SC 300: 3.0-liter dohc 6-cylinder engine, 4-speed automatic transmission, driver- and passenger-side airbags, antilock 4-wheel disc brakes, daytime running lights, air conditioning w/automatic climate control, variable-assist power steering, tilt/telescoping leather-wrapped steering wheel, cruise control, cloth upholstery, 10-way power front bucket seats, center console, cupholders, wood interior trim, heated power mirrors, power windows, power door locks, remote keyless entry, AM/FM/cassette w/6-disc CD changer, power antenna, digital clock, tachometer, trip computer, outside-temperature indicator, rear defogger, illuminated visor mirrors, remote fuel-door and decklid releases, variable intermittent wipers, automatic day/night rearview mirror, automatic headlights, floormats, theft-deterrent system, fog lights, tool kit, first aid kit, full-size spare tire, 225/55VR16 tires, alloy wheels.

SC 400 adds: 4.0-liter dohc V8 engine, 5-speed automatic transmission, leather upholstery, memory driver seat, power tilt/telescoping steering column w/memory, automatic day/night outside mirrors w/memory.

OPTIONAL EQUIPMENT:

	Retail Price	Dealer Invoice
Major Packages		
Leather Trim Pkg., SC 300	$2110	$1688
Leather upholstery, automatic day/night outside mirrors, memory system (driver seat, steering column, outside mirrors), color-keyed bumpers and mirrors.		
Powertrains		
Traction control system w/heated front seats	1240	992
SC 300 requires Leather Trim Pkg.		
Comfort and Convenience		
Power sunroof	1130	904
Nakamichi Sound System	1200	900
Appearance and Miscellaneous		
Rear spoiler	440	352
Chrome alloy wheels	1700	850

Other options are available as port installed items.

LINCOLN CONTINENTAL

Lincoln Continental

Front-wheel-drive luxury car

Base price: $38,880. Built in USA. **Also consider:** Acura RL, Buick Park Avenue, Cadillac Seville

FOR • Acceleration • Passenger and cargo room **AGAINST** • Rear-seat comfort

The only front-wheel-drive Lincoln has three new safety features for 2000: rear child-seat anchors; a manual emergency release inside the trunk; and BeltMinder, a chime and warning light to encourage buckling up. Continental again comes with V8 power, automatic transmission, traction control, antilock 4-wheel disc brakes, and front side airbags. Normal shock absorbers with automatic rear leveling are standard, as are three levels of power-steering assist. An optional Driver Select System includes an electronic suspension and memory for steering/suspension settings. Options include tire-pressure alert, run-flat tires, and Lincoln's RESCU emergency assistance and concierge service.

EVALUATION Though not as brawny or smooth as Cadillac's Northstar V8, Continental's engine provides fine acceleration, effortless cruising, and acceptable thrift: 18.5 mpg in our extended-use test. We prefer the base suspension. The Driver Select setup doesn't work as well on most settings. Stopping power is strong, but tire and wind noise are a bit high for a luxury car. The interior has ample room for four adults, but the soft seat cushions don't give anyone good long-distance support. Headrests and hefty roof pillars impede vision to the rear corners. Our extended-use test car developed a dashboard rattle, but was otherwise trouble-free. Continental is

Ratings begin on page 213. Specifications begin on page 220.

CONSUMER GUIDE™

worth considering, but only if you can get a hefty discount on this slow seller.

ENGINES

	dohc V8
Size, liters/cu. in.	4.6/281
Horsepower @ rpm	275 @ 5750
Torque (lbs./ft.) @ rpm	275 @ 4750
Availability	S

EPA city/highway mpg

4-speed OD automatic	17/25

PRICES

Lincoln Continental	Retail Price	Dealer Invoice
Base 4-door sedan	$38880	$35408
Destination charge	695	695

STANDARD EQUIPMENT:

Base: 4.6-liter dohc V8 engine, 4-speed automatic transmission, traction control, driver- and passenger-side airbags, front side-impact airbags, antilock 4-wheel disc brakes, emergency inside trunk release, programmable variable-assist power steering, leather-wrapped tilt steering wheel, cruise control, air conditioning w/automatic climate control, interior air-filter, leather upholstery, reclining front bucket seats with power lumbar adjusters, 6-way power front seats, memory system for driver seat and outside mirrors, center console, overhead console, wood interior trim, heated power mirrors w/tilt-down back-up aid, power windows, power door locks, remote keyless entry, key pad entry, rear defogger, automatic day/night rearview mirror w/compass, variable intermittent wipers, tachometer, AM/FM/cassette, analog clock, remote fuel-door and decklid releases, reading lights, auxiliary power outlet, illuminated visor mirrors, automatic headlights, floormats, automatic load leveling, theft-deterrent system, cornering lights, 225/60R16 tires, alloy wheels.

OPTIONAL EQUIPMENT:
Major Packages

Personal Security Pkg.	750	646

Run-flat tires with low-pressure alert, universal garage-door opener. Requires polished alloy wheels.

Driver Select System	595	512

Semi-active suspension, selectable ride control, Memory Profile System (includes power steering assist and ride control), steering wheel with radio and climate controls, automatic day/night outside mirrors. Requires Alpine sound system.

Luxury Appearance Pkg.	1095	942

Wood steering wheel, unique seat trim and floormats, special grille, chrome alloy wheels. Requires Driver Select System.

RESCU Pkg.	2345	2016
ordered w/Personal Security Pkg.	2225	1914

Global-positioning system, Alpine Audio System, universal garage-door opener, and voice-activated cellular telephone.

Comfort and Convenience

Power sunroof	1515	1302

Requires universal garage-door opener.

Front split bench seat	NC	NC
Heated front seats	290	250
Voice-activated cellular telephone	790	680

Requires Alpine Audio System.

Alpine Audio System	565	486

Digital signal processing, subwoofer amplifier, additional speakers.

6-disc CD changer	595	512

Requires Alpine Audio System.

Universal garage-door opener	120	104
Chrome alloy wheels	845	726
Polished alloy wheels	350	302

LINCOLN LS

Rear-wheel-drive near-luxury car; similar to Jaguar S-Type

Base price range: $30,915-$34,690. Built in USA. **Also consider:** Acura TL, Lexus ES 300, Lexus GS 300/400

FOR • Acceleration (V8) • Ride/handling • Seat comfort **AGAINST** • Automatic transmission performance • Climate controls

Lincoln LS

Lincoln's latest luxury/sport sedan shares a platform with Jaguar's new S-Type, but the LS is built in Michigan and differs from the British car in many ways. The LS's 3.0-liter V6 is based on that in Ford's Taurus, its 3.9-liter V8 on Jaguar's 4.0-liter V8. Both team with a new 5-speed automatic transmission (also used by the S-Type), and the V6 can be ordered with a 5-speed manual. Front side airbags, antilock 4-wheel disc brakes, wood and leather interior trim, and power tilt/telescopic steering wheel are standard. Automatic-transmission models include traction control and can be optionally equipped with Lincoln's new AdvanceTrac antiskid system. A firmer-suspension Sport Package replaces 16-inch wheels with 17s and high-performance tires. All manual transmission LSs have the Sport Package; automatic models with the option get a separate shift gate that facilitates manual gear changes. Options include power moon-roof and Lincoln's RESCU cell phone/satellite assistance system.

PERFORMANCE The LS is the dynamic equal of some costlier import sedans. Low-speed steering feel could be firmer, but the LS turns in crisply and corners with grippy precision and modest lean. The optional Sport Package enhances body control without harming the impressively supple ride. Engines are muted too, but tire noise intrudes on some coarse surfaces. Braking is swift and sure.

Acceleration with the V8 feels strong in all situations; Lincoln claims 0-60 mph in 7.7 seconds, good for this class. It says an automatic V6 needs 9.3 seconds. That's not outstanding, but the V6 feels adequate except on steep inclines or when real passing punch is required. Alas, the automatic transmission is slow to downshift to provide more passing power, though it's more responsive than in S-Type Jaguars we've tested. And neither the manual nor automatic changes gears with a smoothness befitting a near-luxury car. We averaged 16.3 mpg in a test of a V8 LS and 19.6 with a manual V6; Lincoln recommends premium fuel for both.

ACCOMMODATIONS Though the LS feels less cramped than the S-Type, four adults is the practical limit. Head clearance is so-so, but there's good rear leg space even behind tall front occupants. Some test drivers couldn't dial in a comfortable seat/pedal/steering wheel relationship in the manual-transmission test car, and nobody found the all-button climate system easy to use. Large door mirrors offset visibility lost to thickish rear roof pillars. Interior storage is confined to small door map pockets and a puny center-console bin. The optional CD changer mounts conveniently in the glovebox but fills most of it. And manual-transmission and SelectShift models have but a single front cupholder. Cargo space looks good on paper, but only small suitcases can stand upright, and there's not much fore/aft depth.

Our test cars felt solid and had fine detail finish, but coarse pavement brought out some minor body drumming. Compared to other near-luxury cars, the LS's interior is unimaginative in design and disappointing in decor, with lightweight plastic switchgear and many unpadded panels.

VALUE FOR THE MONEY The LS has lots of features for the money, and is among the few near-luxury cars available with a V8 engine. Capable road manners help offset ordinary interior furnishings, and on balance, Lincoln's newest begs comparison with sedans costing thousands more.

ENGINES

	dohc V6	dohc V8
Size, liters/cu. in.	3.0/181	3.9/235
Horsepower @ rpm	210 @ 6500	252 @ 6100
Torque (lbs./ft.) @ rpm	205 @ 4750	267 @ 4300
Availability	S[1]	S[2]

EPA city/highway mpg

5-speed manual	18/25	
5-speed OD automatic	18/25	17/23

1. LS V6. 2. LS V8.

Prices are accurate at time of publication; subject to manufacturer's changes.

PRICES

Lincoln LS

	Retail Price	Dealer Invoice
LS V6 4-door sedan, automatic	$30915	$28264
LS V6 4-door sedan, manual	31715	28976
LS V8 4-door sedan, automatic	34690	31624
Destination charge	560	560

STANDARD EQUIPMENT:

LS V6 automatic: 3.0-liter dohc V6 engine, 5-speed automatic transmission, traction control, driver- and passenger-side airbags, front side-impact airbags, antilock 4-wheel disc brakes, emergency inside trunk release, air conditioning w/dual-zone automatic climate control, variable-assist power steering, power tilt/telescoping wood/leather-wrapped steering wheel, cruise control, leather upholstery, 8-way power driver seat, 6-way power passenger seat, center console, split folding rear seat, cupholders, heated power mirrors, power windows, power door locks, remote keyless entry, AM/FM/cassette, steering wheel radio controls, tachometer, map lights, illuminated visor mirrors, rear defogger, variable intermittent wipers, automatic headlights, remote fuel door/decklid release, floormats, theft-deterrent system, fog lights, 215/60HR16 tires, brushed alloy wheels.

LS manual adds: 5-speed manual transmission, Sport Pkg. (leather-wrapped steering wheel, color-keyed bumpers, engine oil cooler, sport suspension, full-size spare tire, 235/50VR17 Super Silver Alloy Wheels), deletes traction control, wood/leather-wrapped steering wheel.

LS V8 adds to LS V6 automatic: 3.9-liter dohc V8 engine, memory driver seat, memory steering wheel and mirrors, front power lumbar supports, automatic day/night rearview mirror, universal garage door opener, moisture-sensing wipers, trip computer, compass, 215/60VR16 tires.

OPTIONAL EQUIPMENT:
Major Packages

Sport Pkg., automatics	1000	860

Leather-wrapped steering wheel, automatic transmission w/manual-shift capability, color-keyed bumpers, engine oil cooler, sport suspension, 235/50VR17 Super Silver Alloy Wheels.

Convenience Pkg., LS V6	850	732

Memory driver seat, memory steering wheel and mirrors, front power lumbar supports, automatic day/night rearview mirror, universal garage door opener, moisture-sensing wipers.

Safety Features

Antiskid system, automatics	725	624

Comfort and Convenience

Messaging System, LS V8	960	826

RESCU global positioning system, roadside emergency assistance, portable cellular telephone.

Power sunroof	995	856
Heated front seats	290	250
Portable cellular telephone	695	598
Alpine Audiophile Radio System	565	486
6-disc CD changer	595	512
Polished alloy wheels, automatics	395	340

LINCOLN NAVIGATOR

Lincoln Navigator

Rear- or 4-wheel-drive full-size sport-utility vehicle; similar to Ford Expedition

Base price range: $42,110-$45,860. Built in USA. **Also consider:** GMC Yukon and Yukon XL, Land Rover Range Rover, Toyota Land Cruiser

FOR • Passenger and cargo room • Instruments/controls • Build quality • Interior materials **AGAINST** • Fuel economy

• Entry/exit • Maneuverability

Front side airbags keynote standard-equipment additions, while "climate-controlled" front seats and a navigation system are among new options for Lincoln's luxury version of the Ford Expedition.

Navigator comes with a 300-horsepower edition of the 260-hp 5.4-liter V8 available in Expedition. Automatic transmission, self-leveling shock absorbers, and antilock 4-wheel disc brakes are standard. Rear-wheel drive or Ford's all-surface Control Trac 4-wheel drive are available. Standard seating consists of front- and second-row buckets, each with a center console, and a 3-passenger third-row bench. A 3-passenger second-row bench is available at no charge. The standard power-adjustable pedal cluster is linked to the driver-seat memory system.

For 2000, Navigator gets revised door mirrors with built-in turn indicators and an available power-fold mechanism. The previously optional 17-inch wheels replace 16s as standard. New inside is more wood trim, softer leather upholstery, a redesigned center console with more and larger cupholders, and second- and third-row child-seat anchors. An automatic parking brake release and front-seat power-lumbar adjustment are newly standard, too.

New options include a satellite navigation system with an in-dash CD-ROM-based map display screen. New at $495 are "climate-controlled" front seats that include a small internal fan and heat pump. Another new option is a reverse sensing system that provides an audible warning as the vehicle approaches an obstacle while reversing.

Expedition doesn't offer the navigation system or 300-hp engine, but Navigator's performance and accommodations are otherwise comparable to those of the Ford version.

The Ford Expedition report includes an evaluation of the Navigator.

ENGINES

	dohc V8
Size, liters/cu. in.	5.4/330
Horsepower @ rpm	300 @ 5000
Torque (lbs./ft.) @ rpm	355 @ 2750
Availability	S

EPA city/highway mpg

4-speed OD automatic	13/18

PRICES

Lincoln Navigator

	Retail Price	Dealer Invoice
4-door wagon, 2WD	$42110	$36728
4-door wagon, 4WD	45860	39916
Destination charge	665	665

STANDARD EQUIPMENT:

2WD: 5.4-liter dohc V8 engine, 4-speed automatic transmission, limited-slip differential, antilock 4-wheel disc brakes, driver- and passenger-side airbags, front side-impact airbags, air conditioning w/automatic climate control, variable-assist power steering, wood/leather-wrapped steering wheel w/radio and climate controls, tilt steering column, cruise control, power adjustable pedals w/memory, leather upholstery, 7-passenger seating w/quad bucket seats, 6-way power front seats w/power lumbar adjustment, driver seat memory, third row folding bench seat, wood interior trim, front floor console (rear audio controls and headphone jack, rear air conditioning/heater outlet), second row floor console, overhead console (sunglass/garage-door opener holder, trip computer, compass), cupholders, heated power mirrors w/memory and turn signal lights, power windows, power door locks, remote keyless entry, key pad entry, tachometer, automatic day/night rearview mirror, AM/FM/cassette, digital clock, illuminated visor mirrors, auxiliary power outlets, universal garage door opener, automatic headlights, variable intermittent wipers, rear defogger, intermittent rear wiper/washer, floormats, theft-deterrent system, rear privacy glass, fog lights, roof rack, running boards, rear self-leveling suspension, Trailer Towing Group (7-wire harness, hitch, heavy-duty flasher, engine-oil cooler, auxiliary transmission-oil cooler), full-size spare tire, 275/60R17 white-letter tires, alloy wheels.

4WD adds: Control Trac full-time 4-wheel drive, front and rear self-leveling suspension, front tow hooks, 255/75R17 all-terrain white-letter tires.

OPTIONAL EQUIPMENT:
Safety Features

Reverse Sensing System	245	208

Requires rear air conditioning.

Comfort and Convenience

	Retail Price	Dealer Invoice
Navigation system	$1995	$1696
Rear air conditioning	705	599
Power sunroof	1495	1271
Replaces overhead console with mini overhead console. Requires rear air conditioning. NA with navigation system.		
Climate control front seats	495	421
Heated front seats	290	247
8-passenger seating	NC	NC
Second row 3-passenger split bench seat.		
Alpine AM/FM/cassette	570	484
6-disc CD changer	595	506
Voice activated cellular telephone	650	553
Requires CD changer.		
Power folding mirrors	145	123
Chrome alloy wheels	595	506

LINCOLN TOWN CAR

Lincoln Town Car

Rear-wheel-drive luxury car

Base price range: $38,630-$43,130. Built in USA. **Also consider:** Cadillac DeVille, Jaguar XJ Sedan, Lexus LS 400

FOR • Passenger and cargo room • Quietness **AGAINST** • Fuel economy • Rear visibility

A trio of safety enhancements marks the 2000 edition of the last American-brand, rear-drive full-size luxury sedan. Redesigned two years ago, Town Car continues with a 4.6-liter V8 that makes 200 horsepower in the base Executive and mid-level Signature models, 20 more with standard dual exhausts in the line-topping Cartier. A Signature Touring Sedan package includes the 220-hp engine, plus firmer suspension. All models again have standard four-speed automatic transmission, all-disc antilock brakes, traction control, leather upholstery, and 40/20/40 front bench seat.

Like other Ford Motor Company cars for 2000, Lincoln's biggest sedan gains an emergency escape release inside the trunk, rear child-seat anchors, and BeltMinder, a chime and warning light to encourage seat-belt usage.

PERFORMANCE This big 4-door suffers more cornering lean and less grip than imported luxury sedans allow—enough that you'll want to slow down for tight turns. But the steering is reasonably accurate, if too light for our tastes. Ride is absorbent and hushed, spoiled by mild float over humps and minor tire pattering on some freeway surfaces. Refinement is a plus, with little road noise and just a muted engine note. Wind rush rises above 60 mph, but doesn't intrude.

Town Car can't match Cadillac DeVille for acceleration, but it's sufficiently quick: 9.5 seconds 0-60 mph for our test Cartier. The transmission provides seamless upshifts and prompt downshifts, though the latter sometimes require a deep helping of throttle. Fuel economy is about par for the class at 17.3 mpg in our tests.

Standard traction control enhances grip, but Town Car isn't as mobile in deep snow as front-drive rivals, and the system can sometimes interrupt engine power enough to cause anxious moments when accelerating across a slippery intersection. "Panic" braking is surprisingly short and stable for such a softly sprung heavyweight, but pedal action isn't progressive and nosedive is more than moderate.

ACCOMMODATIONS A 1998 redesign cut nearly 200 pounds, but also cost Town Car some roominess. Head clearance is generous all-around, but leg space is good rather than great and the interior isn't wide enough for six adults without squeezing. Entry/exit is still easy, though. Trunk volume looks fine on paper, but is concentrated in a deep center well that

makes loading and unloading heavy objects a strain. Gauges are analog and legible, climate and audio controls handy and user-friendly. Visibility is compromised by thick side and rear pillars and a high rear deck. Workmanship on our test Cartier was flawless, though interior materials are less substantial than those in Cadillacs and imported luxury cars.

VALUE FOR THE MONEY The new DeVille is a better car, but Town Car delivers traditional American luxury-car values of spaciousness and isolation and its base prices are the lowest in this class.

ENGINES

	ohc V8	ohc V8
Size, liters/cu. in.	4.6/281	4.6/281
Horsepower @ rpm	200 @ 4500	220 @ 4500
Torque (lbs./ft.) @ rpm	265 @ 3500	275 @ 3500
Availability	S[1]	S[2]
EPA city/highway mpg		
4-speed OD automatic	17/24	17/24

1. Executive, Signature. 2. Cartier; optional Signature.

PRICES

Lincoln Town Car	Retail Price	Dealer Invoice
Executive 4-door sedan	$38630	$35186
Signature 4-door sedan	40630	36966
Cartier 4-door sedan	43130	39191
Destination charge	695	695

STANDARD EQUIPMENT:

Executive: 4.6-liter V8, 4-speed automatic transmission, traction assist, driver- and passenger-side airbags, front side-impact airbags, antilock 4-wheel disc brakes, emergency inside trunk release, variable-assist power steering, leather-wrapped tilt steering wheel, cruise control, air conditioning w/automatic climate control, leather upholstery, 8-way power 40/20/40 split front seat with dual power recliners, heated power mirrors, power windows, power door locks, remote keyless entry, auxiliary power outlet, rear defogger, AM/FM/cassette, diversity antenna, digital clock, remote fuel-door release, power decklid pulldown, intermittent wipers, illuminated visor mirrors, automatic headlights, floormats, theft-deterrent system, cornering lights, 225/60SR16 tires, alloy wheels.

Signature adds: memory driver-seat, power lumbar support, memory mirrors, automatic day/night rearview and driver-side mirrors, compass, universal garage-door opener, Alpine audio system, steering-wheel radio and climate controls.

Cartier adds: upgraded leather upholstery, heated front seats, upgraded door trim panels, analog clock, gold pkg., dual exhaust, chrome alloy wheels.

OPTIONAL EQUIPMENT:
Major Packages

	Retail	Dealer
Mirrors and Compass Group, Executive	245	210
Automatic day/night driver-side and rearview mirrors, compass.		
Touring Pkg., Signature	700	602
Upgraded suspension, dual exhaust, performance axle ratio and torque converter, perforated leather upholstery, 235/60TR16 tires, chrome alloy wheels.		
Premium Pkg., Signature, Cartier	2110	1814
Manufacturer's discount price	1595	1372
CD changer, power sunroof.		

Comfort and Convenience

Power sunroof, Signature, Cartier	1515	1302
Heated front seats, Signature	290	250
CD changer, Signature, Cartier	595	512
Voice-activated cellular telephone, Signature, Cartier	790	680

MAZDA B-SERIES ✓ BEST BUY

Rear- or 4-wheel-drive compact pickup truck; similar to Ford Ranger

Base price range: $11,495-$23,640. Built in USA. **Also consider:** Chevrolet S-10, Dodge Dakota, GMC Sonoma

FOR • Acceleration (B4000) • Build quality **AGAINST** • Engine noise • Acceleration (B2500) • Rear-seat comfort • Ride

Prices are accurate at time of publication; subject to manufacturer's changes.

Mazda B-Series Cab Plus 4

Trim and equipment revisions account for the changes to Mazda's compact pickup for 2000. The B-Series borrows its mechanical design from the Ford Ranger but has its own front-end styling.

B2500 models have a 2.5-liter 4-cylinder engine, B3000s a 3.0-liter V6, and B4000s a 4.0-liter V6. Manual transmission is standard on all models. For 2000, automatic transmission is standard on B4000 2-wheel-drive models and continues as optional on the other B-Series trucks. B2500s and B3000s get a 4-speed automatic, while the B4000s use a 5-speed automatic. B3000s and B4000s are available with 4-wheel drive that's not for use on dry pavement. All B-Series models have rear antilock brakes; and 4-wheel ABS is optional only on 4WD B4000s.

B2500 and B3000 versions come as regular cabs and as Cab Plus extended-cab models, both with two side doors. Available in B3000 trim and mandatory with B4000s is the Cab Plus 4, an extended-cab with two rear-hinged rear doors that work in conjunction with the front doors. Cab Plus and Cab Plus 4 models have two folding rear jump seats.

SX, SE, and TL trim levels are offered. The last is named for Troy Lee, a designer of extreme-sports equipment. It includes bodyside graphics, fender flares, fog lights, unique alloy wheels, and other items. TLs come only as Cab Plus 4 models in B3000 2WD or B4000 4WD form. Among other changes for 2000, a trailer hitch is standard instead of optional on 4WD B4000s, and a leather-wrapped steering wheel and fog lamps are standard on all 4x4s.

B-Series pickups are built by Ford, and their performance and accommodations mirror those of similarly equipped Rangers.

The Ford Ranger report includes an evaluation of the B-Series.

ENGINES

	ohc I4	ohv V6	ohv V6
Size, liters/cu. in.	2.5/152	3.0/182	4.0/245
Horsepower @ rpm	119 @ 5000	150 @ 4750	160 @ 4200
Torque (lbs./ft.) @ rpm	146 @ 3000	190 @ 3650	225 @ 2750
Availability	S[1]	S[2]	S[3]
EPA city/highway mpg			
5-speed OD manual	22/27	18/23[4]	17/22[6]
4-speed OD automatic	20/25	17/22[5]	
5-speed OD automatic			16/22[7]

1. B2500. 2. B3000. 3. B4000. 4. 18/21 w/4WD. 5. 15/19 w/4WD. 6. 17/20 w/4WD. 7. 16/20 w/4WD.

PRICES

Mazda B-Series

	Retail Price	Dealer Invoice
B2500 SX 2WD regular cab	$11495	$10764
B3000 SX 2WD regular cab	11890	11132
B2500 SE 2WD regular cab	13805	12849
B3000 SE 2WD regular cab	14200	12846
B3000 SE 4WD regular cab	17725	16025
B2500 SE 2WD Cab Plus	15995	14469
B3000 SE 2WD Cab Plus	16465	14892
B3000 SE 2WD Cab Plus 4	17205	15559
B3000 TL 2WD Cab Plus 4	18610	16827
B4000 SE 2WD Cab Plus 4	20630	18649
B3000 SE 4WD Cab Plus 4	20210	18270
B4000 SE 4WD Cab Plus 4	22540	20370
B4000 TL 4WD Cab Plus 4	23640	21362
Destination charge	510	510

Prices are for vehicles distributed by Mazda Motor of America, Inc. Prices may be higher in areas served by independent distributors.

STANDARD EQUIPMENT:

B2500 SX/ B3000 SX: 2.5-liter 4-cylinder engine (B2500), 3.0-liter V6 engine (B3000), 5-speed manual transmission, rear antilock brakes, driver- and passenger-side airbags, power steering, floor consolette, cupholders, vinyl split bench seat, AM/FM radio, digital clock, variable intermittent wipers, auxiliary power outlet, black vinyl floor covering, theft-deterrent system (B3000), dual outside mirrors, argent front bumper and rear step bumper, 4-wire trailer harness, 225/70R15 tires.

B2500 SE/B3000 SE adds: air conditioning, rear doors (Cab Plus 4), cloth upholstery, rear jump seat (Cab Plus/Cab Plus 4), AM/FM/CD player, tachometer, map light, carpeting, cargo box light, passenger-side visor mirror, floormats, rear privacy glass (Cab Plus 4), chrome bumpers, alloy wheels. **4WD** models add: part-time 4-wheel drive, 2-speed transfer case, leather-wrapped steering wheel, fog lights, fender flares, skid plates, tow hooks, 235/75R15 tires.

B3000 TL 2WD Cab Plus 4 adds: leather-wrapped steering wheel, rear privacy glass, Troy Lee bodyside graphics, fender flares, fog lights, raised suspension, 245/75R16 white letter tires, special alloy wheels.

B4000 SE adds to B2500 SE/B3000 SE: 4.0-liter V6 engine, 5-speed automatic transmission, tilt steering wheel, cruise control, power mirrors, power windows, power door locks, remote keyless entry, sliding rear window, bedliner. **4WD** models add: part-time 4-wheel drive, 2-speed transfer case, 5-speed manual transmission, leather-wrapped steering wheel, fog lights, fender flares, skid plates, front tow hooks, trailer hitch, 265/75R15 all-terrain white-letter tires.

B4000 4WD TL Cab Plus 4 adds to B4000 SE 4WD: leather upholstery, Troy Lee bodyside graphics, 245/75R16 all-terrain white-letter tires, special alloy wheels.

OPTIONAL EQUIPMENT:

Major Packages

	Retail Price	Dealer Invoice
Convenience Pkg., B2500 SE, B3000 SE/TL	$700	$574

Tilt steering wheel, cruise control, swing out rear quarter windows (Cab Plus), sliding rear window, bedliner.

	Retail Price	Dealer Invoice
Power Pkg., B2500 SE, B3000 SE/TL	535	439

Power mirrors, power windows and door locks, remote keyless entry. Requires Convenience Pkg.

	Retail Price	Dealer Invoice
Traction Pkg., B4000 4WD	600	492

Front and rear antilock brakes, limited-slip differential.

Powertrains

4-speed automatic transmission, B2500, B3000	1095	898

SX requires air conditioning.

5-speed automatic transmission, B4000 4WD	1145	939

Comfort and Convenience

Air conditioning, B2500 SX	805	660
Sport bucket seats, B4000 SE	360	115

Special Purpose, Wheels and Tires

Trailer hitch, B4000 2WD	140	115

MAZDA MIATA

Mazda Miata

Rear-wheel-drive sports and GT car

Base price range: $21,245-$23,995. Built in Japan. **Also consider:** BMW Z3 Series, Chevrolet Camaro, Ford Mustang, Honda S2000

FOR • Acceleration • Steering/handling • Fuel economy
AGAINST • Cargo room • Noise

Miata gains a new uplevel model for 2000, while some previously optional equipment becomes standard. Mazda's 2-seat sports car uses a 1.8-liter 4-cylinder engine with 5-speed manual transmission or optional automatic. The 6-speed manual on last year's 10th Anniversary model is unavailable for 2000, but the anniversary car's lower-body aero styling survives as a new option for other Miatas. Taking the anniversary model's place as the top-line Miata is the new LS, which comes with leather upholstery, power door locks, cruise control, 15-inch wheels (instead of 14s) and a limited-slip differential. All but the leather are available as options on the base Miata. Previously optional features now standard on both include alloy wheels, power steering, power windows, and a leather-wrapped Nardi steering wheel. Four-wheel disc brakes are standard. Antilock brakes are optional only on the LS for 2000; they had been optional on the base model. A manual-folding soft top with defrosted glass rear window is standard and a removable hardtop is optional. Orange joins available colors for 2000.

EVALUATION Acceleration is brisk; Mazda says 0-60 mph takes 8.0 seconds with manual transmission, and that feels about right based on our tests. Automatic-transmission versions aren't as responsive. Our extended-use-test '99 5-speed averaged 25.8 mpg over 10,000 miles. Road, wind, and engine noise are all prominent in this soft-top sports car. The brakes are strong and easily modulated, handling a delight, steering a model of accuracy. The factory tires furnish poor traction in snow, so we installed four Goodyear Ultra Grip Ice winter tires on our Chicago-based extended-use test car. They provided unerring bite in snow and adequate cornering grip on dry surfaces. Miata has decent room for two adults, though it's tight for 6-footers. Entry/exit requires bending and twisting. Short side windows and a small back window hamper visibility. The cargo limit is a couple of soft overnight bags. Rippled pavement and railroad crossings trigger some body flex, but workmanship is good, with quality materials and tight assembly. You can spend more and get a higher level of performance, but Miata is unmatched among sports cars on the fun-per-dollar scale.

ENGINES

	dohc I4
Size, liters/cu. in.	1.8/112
Horsepower @ rpm	140 @ 6500
Torque (lbs./ft.) @ rpm	119 @ 5500
Availability	S

EPA city/highway mpg	
5-speed OD manual	25/29
4-speed OD automatic	23/28

PRICES

Mazda Miata	Retail Price	Dealer Invoice
Base 2-door convertible	$21245	$19499
LS 2-door convertible	23995	22018
Destination charge	450	450

STANDARD EQUIPMENT:

Base: 1.8-liter dohc 4-cylinder engine, 5-speed manual transmission, driver- and passenger-side airbags, 4-wheel disc brakes, variable-assist power steering, leather-wrapped steering wheel, cloth upholstery, bucket seats, center console, cupholders, power mirrors, power windows, AM/FM/CD player, power antenna, digital clock, tachometer, intermittent wipers, rear defogger, remote fuel-door and decklid releases, passenger-side visor mirror, 185/60R14 tires, alloy wheels.

LS adds: limited-slip differential, cruise control, leather upholstery, power door locks, Bose AM/FM/cassette/CD player, floormats, windblock panel, 195/50VR15 tires.

OPTIONAL EQUIPMENT:

Major Packages

Convenience Pkg., Base	795	668

Cruise control, power door locks, upgraded sound system, windblock panel.

Suspension Pkg., Base	995	836
LS	495	416

Sport suspension w/Bilstein shock absorbers, limited slip differential (Base), 195/50VR15 tires (Base).

Appearance Pkg.	595	476

Side sills, front air dam, rear mud guards.

Powertrains

4-speed automatic transmission, Base	900	872

	Retail Price	Dealer Invoice
Limited-slip differential, Base	$395	$332

Safety Features

Antilock brakes, LS	550	468

Comfort and Convenience

Air conditioning	900	720
AM/FM/cassette/CD player, Base	250	213

Appearance and Miscellaneous

Detachable hardtop	1500	1215

Requires option pkg. NA w/Sport Pkg.

Fog lights	250	200
Wind block panel, Base	150	120
Rear spoiler	295	236

MAZDA MILLENIA

Mazda Millenia S

Front-wheel-drive near-luxury car

Base price range: $24,995-$29,995. Built in Japan. **Also consider:** Infiniti I30, Lexus ES 300, Mitsubishi Diamante

FOR • Acceleration (S model) • Steering/handling • Build quality • Exterior finish • Interior materials **AGAINST** • Transmission performance • Rear visibility

Remote keyless entry is standard instead of optional for 2000, a model year that sees few changes to Mazda's top-line car. Millenia comes in base and uplevel S models. Both have a V6 engine, the base version a 2.5-liter with 170 horsepower, the S a supercharged 2.3 with 210. The only transmission is a 4-speed automatic. Traction control is standard on the S, optional on the base model. Antilock brakes are standard on both, but neither offers side airbags. For 2000, the Millenia also gets a lighted ignition switch, along with steering gear revisions intended to improve handling stability.

EVALUATION Acceleration is adequate in the base Millenia, which did 0-60 mph in a respectable 9.4 seconds in our tests. Our test S model did 0-60 mph in just 7.8 seconds, despite some throttle lag. The S averaged 18.9 mpg in mostly highway driving; we didn't have an opportunity to measure fuel economy with the base model. Millenia exhibits fine road manners with stable cornering, an absorbent ride, and relatively little wind or road noise. The tastefully designed cabin has good room in front, but space is tight in back for larger adults, and three across is a squeeze. Millenia debuted for 1995 and is among the oldest near-luxury cars. It's eclipsed overall by the Lexus ES 300, Infiniti I30, and Acura TL, but is still a good entry-luxury choice for those who don't follow the crowd.

ENGINES

	dohc V6	Supercharged dohc V6
Size, liters/cu. in.	2.5/152	2.3/138
Horsepower @ rpm	170 @ 5800	210 @ 5300
Torque (lbs./ft.) @ rpm	160 @ 4800	210 @ 3500
Availability	S[1]	S[2]
EPA city/highway mpg		
4-speed OD automatic	20/27	20/28

1. Base. 2. S model.

PRICES

Mazda Millenia	Retail Price	Dealer Invoice
Base 4-door sedan	$24995	$22840
S 4-door sedan	29995	27400
Destination charge	450	450

Prices are accurate at time of publication; subject to manufacturer's changes.

Prices are for vehicles distributed by Mazda Motor America, Inc. Prices may be higher in areas served by independent distributors.

STANDARD EQUIPMENT:

Base: 2.5-liter dohc V6 engine, 4-speed automatic transmission, driver- and passenger-side airbags, antilock 4-wheel disc brakes, air conditioning w/automatic climate control, variable-assist power steering, leather-wrapped power tilt steering wheel w/memory, cruise control, cloth upholstery, front bucket seats, 8-way power driver seat, front storage console, cupholders, tachometer, outside-temperature indicator, power mirrors, power windows, power door locks, remote keyless entry, variable intermittent wipers, AM/FM/cassette/CD player, steering wheel radio controls, digital clock, illuminated visor mirrors, rear defogger, auxiliary power outlet, automatic-off headlights, remote fuel-door and decklid releases, floormats, theft-deterrent system, fog lights, 215/55VR16 tires, alloy wheels.

S adds: 2.3-liter dohc supercharged V6 engine, traction control, leather upholstery, 8-way power front passenger seat, power sunroof, Bose sound system, 215/50VR17 tires.

OPTIONAL EQUIPMENT:
Major Packages

	Retail Price	Dealer Invoice
Premium Pkg., Base	$2000	$1720

Leather upholstery, power passenger seat, power sunroof.

4-Seasons Pkg., Base	600	504
S	300	252

Traction control (Base), heated front seats, heavy-duty wipers, heavy-duty battery, extra-capacity windshield-washer tank. Base requires Premium Pkg.

Comfort and Convenience

Bose audio system, Base	700	588
Chrome alloy wheels, S	500	420

MAZDA MPV

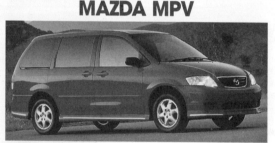

2000 Mazda MPV ES

Front-wheel-drive minivan

Base price range: $19,995-$25,550. Built in Japan. **Also consider:** Dodge Caravan, Honda Odyssey, Toyota Sienna

FOR • Handling/roadholding • Passenger and cargo room • Instruments/controls **AGAINST** • Acceleration • Automatic transmission performance

Mazda's minivan is redesigned for the first time since its 1989 premiere and now has front-wheel drive and sliding rear side doors instead of rear-wheel drive and swing-out side doors.

The 2000 MPV comes in DX, mid-level LX, and luxury-oriented ES versions. All use a 2.5-liter dual-overhead cam V6 based on a design from Ford, Mazda's parent company. A 4-speed automatic is the only transmission. Antilock brakes are standard on the LX and ES, unavailable on DX. Front side airbags are standard on the ES and optional on LX.

MPV's dual sliding side doors have roll-down windows, a minivan first. Power operation for the doors is not offered. All models seat seven and have second-row bucket seats that slide together to create a 2-passenger bench seat. The 3-place third-row bench folds flat into the floor. Optional on LX and ES is a sporty appearance package with fog lights and aero body addenda. Leather upholstery is an ES exclusive.

PERFORMANCE This Japanese-built minivan serves Mazda worldwide, and although 40 percent come to the U.S., MPV's exterior dimensions are sized for Europe and Asia. That means MPV is smaller than most American minivans, but this has performance advantages—good handling foremost among them. In particular, MPVs with the 16-inch wheels carve corners with outstanding balance and grip. Close-quarters maneuverability is great, too. Steering is faithful and communicative, the antilock brakes linear and strong. Ride is flat at speed and absorbent over bumps.

MPV's engine is among the smallest in any minivan, however, and acceleration suffers. Progress is good from a standing start and in most flatland cruising. But MPV feels underpowered in hilly terrain and in passing maneuvers, especially when asked to accelerate briskly with several passengers aboard and the air conditioning on. Moreover, the transmission tends to settle in the least-optimal gear, then downshifts too late to be of much use. We haven't yet measured fuel economy, but EPA estimates are no better than those of rivals with larger, stronger engines. And this Ford V6 emits a coarse growl under even moderate throttle, disturbing what are otherwise pleasantly low noise levels.

ACCOMMODATIONS Despite its relative compactness, the MPV doesn't feel cramped. Front seating is spacious, and front- and second-row cushions are comfortably thick and supportive, though the third-row bench is flat and hard. The sliding second-row arrangement is useful, but exposed floor tracks will likely collect debris, interfering with seat movement. Second- and third-row knee clearance is adequate for 6-footers. The second-row seats slide forward a few inches, but their base remains stationary, so there's no gain in third-row foot space. The clever "tumble under" rear bench (as in Honda's Odyssey) flips to create rear-facing tailgate-party seating.

In its standard position, the rear bench frees up a floor well that creates 17.2 cubic feet of carrying room, so cargo space is better than in most minivans of this length. That bench folds with little effort, and the easily removable second-row seats weigh just 37 pounds apiece.

The dashboard attractively arranges readable gauges and simple controls, though the transmission lever blocks the driver's view of some radio buttons. Entry and exit are less convenient than in longer-wheelbase rivals because MPV's side doors don't open as far. Plus, step-in height is taller than today's minivan norm.

VALUE FOR THE MONEY Its small engine is easily overtaxed, but sporty-handling MPV does an admirable job of people and parcel packaging. The well-equipped ES lists for less than competitors' topline models, but 70 percent of MPV sales will be the LX. It starts at a reasonable $22,050, but similar money buys a Dodge Grand Caravan or base Honda Odyssey, both of which are roomier and more powerful.

ENGINES

	dohc V6
Size, liters/cu. in.	2.5/152
Horsepower @ rpm	170 @ 6250
Torque (lbs./ft.) @ rpm	165 @ 4250
Availability	S

EPA city/highway mpg

4-speed OD automatic	18/23

PRICES

Mazda MPV	Retail Price	Dealer Invoice
DX 4-door van	$19995	$18379
LX 4-door van	22050	20151
ES 4-door van	25550	23343
Destination charge	480	480

STANDARD EQUIPMENT:

DX: 2.5-liter dohc V6 engine, 4-speed automatic transmission, driver- and passenger-side airbags, front air conditioning, variable-assist power steering, tilt steering wheel, cloth upholstery, front bucket seats, center console, cupholders, two center row bucket seats, third row 3-passenger bench seat, overhead console, visor mirrors, variable intermittent wipers, AM/FM/CD player, digital clock, tachometer, rear intermittent wiper, auxiliary power outlet, 205/65R15 tires, wheel covers.

LX adds: antilock brakes, heated power mirrors, power windows, power door locks, cruise control, height-adjustable driver seat, illuminated visor mirrors, rear privacy glass.

ES adds: front side-impact airbags, front and rear air conditioning, leather upholstery, leather-wrapped steering wheel, remote keyless entry, AM/FM/cassette/CD player w/premium sound system, floormats, theft-deterrent system, 215/60R16 tires, alloy wheels.

OPTIONAL EQUIPMENT:
Major Packages

	Retail Price	Dealer Invoice
DX Power Pkg., DX	$1325	$1140
Cruise control, heated power mirrors, power windows, power door locks, floormats, bodyside moldings, alloy wheels.		
LX Security Pkg., LX	1100	946
Front side-impact airbags, remote keyless entry system, floormats, theft-deterrent system, alloy wheels.		
LX Touring Pkg., LX	1975	1699
Premium sound system with 9 speakers, wood-tone interior trim, 215/60R16 tires, alloy wheels.		
1GT GFX Pkg., LX, ES	900	774
Front spoiler, fog lights, side sill extensions, rear underspoiler.		
2GT GFX Pkg., LX	1200	1032
1GT GFX Pkg. plus 215/60HR16 tires, alloy wheels.		
4-Seasons Pkg., LX, ES	400	344
Rear heater, heavy-duty rear defogger, larger washer tank, transmission oil cooler, heavy-duty battery and radiator, additional cooling fan. LX requires Security Pkg. or Touring Pkg.		

Comfort and Convenience

Rear air conditioning, DX, LX	595	512
DX requires Power Pkg.		
Power sunroof, LX, ES	702	602
LX requires Touring Pkg.		
6-disc CD changer, LX, ES	600	516
LX requires Touring Pkg.		

Appearance and Miscellaneous

Roof Rack	200	172
Fog lights	250	215

MAZDA PROTEGE

RECOMMENDED

Mazda Protege ES

Front-wheel-drive subcompact car

Base price range: $11,970-$15,040. Built in Japan. **Also consider:** Chevrolet Prizm, Ford Focus, Honda Civic

FOR • Fuel economy • Ride • Quietness **AGAINST** • Noise • Acceleration (with automatic transmission)

Optional front side airbags are the big change to Mazda's smallest sedan for 2000. Protege comes in base DX, uplevel LX, and top-line ES models. All have a 4-cylinder engine. The DX and LX have a 105-horsepower 1.6 liter, the ES a 122-hp 1.8. Manual transmission is standard, automatic is optional. Antilock brakes are optional on the LS and ES and are unavailable on the DX.

The front side airbags are part of the Premium option package available on LX and ES models. Mazda also adds some chrome trim to the interior.

PERFORMANCE Protege has sportier road manners than many subcompacts, including the class-leading Honda Civic and Toyota Corolla/Chevrolet Prizm. But the tradeoff is a slightly stiffer ride and a markedly higher level of engine, road, and wind noise than most rivals, especially compared to those class leaders. DX and LX Proteges take most bumps with firm control and provide accurate steering and agile handling. The ES shares the same suspension and adds lower-profile tires that sharpen handling, but allow road imperfections to be felt more.

Acceleration is adequate with the manual transmission, but disappointing with the automatic; the 5-speed ES can scoot through traffic well enough, but neither engine has good highway passing power. Our test '99 5-speed ES averaged 26.6 mpg with lots of high-

way driving. The 2000s should yield similar results. Visibility is good to all corners. Assembly and paintwork on the cars we tested were nearly the equal of Honda and Toyota.

ACCOMMODATIONS Protege remains one of the most spacious subcompact sedans, with relatively abundant front head room and rear leg room. The dashboard is well laid out, though the climate system's rotary knobs are just out of the driver's easy reach and a bit too small to easily use. Interior storage space is good, with open and covered bins, two cupholders, front-door map pockets, and a large glovebox. Trunk space is about average for the class, though all models come with a 60/40 split folding rear seatback for carrying longer items. The Protege is attractively finished, and even the base DX is fitted with a nice blend of fabrics and textured plastic surfaces.

VALUE FOR THE MONEY Protege tends to be overlooked by subcompact buyers. That's a shame, because in terms of room and driving pleasure it equals—even exceeds—such standouts and the Honda Civic and Toyota Corolla. It's easy to recommend, with the DX in particular a cut above most base-model subcompacts.

ENGINES

	dohc I4	dohc I4
Size, liters/cu. in.	1.6/97	1.8/110
Horsepower @ rpm	105 @ 5500	122 @ 6000
Torque (lbs./ft.) @ rpm	107 @ 4000	120 @ 4000
Availability	S[1]	S[2]
EPA city/highway mpg		
5-speed OD manual	29/34	26/30
4-speed OD automatic	26/33	24/29

1. DX, LX. 2. ES.

PRICES

Mazda Protege	Retail Price	Dealer Invoice
DX 4-door sedan	$11970	$11445
LX 4-door sedan	13245	12389
ES 4-door sedan	15040	13909
Destination charge	450	450

Prices are for vehicles distributed by Mazda Motor of America, Inc. Prices may be higher in areas served by independent distributors.

STANDARD EQUIPMENT:

DX: 1.6-liter dohc 4-cylinder engine, 5-speed manual transmission, driver- and passenger-side airbags, variable-assist power steering, tilt steering wheel, cloth reclining front bucket seats, center console, split folding rear seat, cupholders, rear defogger, remote fuel-door release, intermittent wipers, visor mirrors, auxiliary power outlet, remote outside mirrors, 185/65R14 tires, wheel covers.

LX adds: cruise control, AM/FM/CD, digital clock, sport front bucket seats w/height adjustment, remote decklid release, tachometer, power mirrors, power windows, power door locks, map lights.

ES adds: 1.8-liter dohc 4-cylinder engine, air conditioning, remote keyless entry, theft-deterrent system, 195/55R15 tires, alloy wheels.

OPTIONAL EQUIPMENT:
Major Packages

Convenience Pkg., DX	1575	1292
Air conditioning, AM/FM/CD player, digital clock, floormats.		
Comfort Pkg., LX	1145	939
Air conditioning, floormats.		
Premium Pkg., LX	1600	1312
Front side-impact airbags, power sunroof, remote keyless entry, antilock brakes. Requires Comfort Pkg.		
Premium Pkg., ES	1580	1296
Front side-impact airbags, power sunroof, floormats, antilock brakes.		

Powertrains

4-speed automatic transmission	800	720

Comfort and Convenience

Power sunroof, LX, ES	700	560
LX requires remote keyless entry.		
AM/FM/cassette/CD player	250	213
DX requires Convenience Pkg.		
Remote keyless entry, LX	100	80
Includes theft-deterrent system.		

Prices are accurate at time of publication; subject to manufacturer's changes.

Appearance and Miscellaneous

	Retail Price	Dealer Invoice
Rear spoiler	$330	$246

MAZDA 626

✓ BEST BUY

Mazda 626

Front-wheel-drive compact car
Base price range: $18,245-$22,445. Built in USA.
Also consider: Mitsubishi Galant, Nissan Altima, Oldsmobile Alero, Volkswagen Passat

FOR • Acceleration (V6) • Steering/handling • Build quality

AGAINST • Automatic transmission performance • Road noise

Optional front side airbags top the model-2000 changes to Mazda's best-selling car. The 626 is a 4-door sedan that comes in LX and uplevel ES trim. Both models are available with a 4-cylinder engine or a V6. The 4-cylinder gains 5 horsepower this year, for a total of 130. The V6 continues with 170. The 4-cylinder ES model comes standard with automatic transmission, but all other models offer manual or optional automatic.

All 626s except the 4-cylinder LX model have standard 4-wheel disc brakes. Antilock brakes are optional on all models and include traction control for V6 versions. The new front side airbags are included in the ABS option package. Among other 2000 alterations, LX 4-cylinders get 15-inch wheels, replacing 14s, and 16-inch alloy wheels replace 15s as standard on the ES V6 and optional on the LX V6. All models gain rear-seat heater ducts. Heated outside mirrors also are new and are standard on the ES V6, optional on the others.

PERFORMANCE Four-cylinder 626s have adequate acceleration with manual transmission, but feel sluggish with automatic. V6s are lively with either transmission, but most enjoyable with manual. Regardless of engine, Mazda's automatic sometimes downshifts with a jolt. We got a pleasing 22.5 mpg in a test of a manual-transmission V6 model. Expect slightly less with automatic. We did not have an opportunity to measure fuel economy with a 4-cylinder 626.

Wind noise is well-muffled, though tire roar is intrusive over coarse pavement. Ride is absorbent, but high-speed dips induce some floating. Directional changes aren't sport-sedan crisp, though body lean in turns is mild. Braking performance is good, with little nosedive and steady tracking in hard stops.

ACCOMMODATIONS Technically, the 626 is a compact-sized car, but it rivals some midsize sedans in allowing 6-footers to sit one behind the other without the rear passenger's knees digging into the front seats. There's also good underseat foot room and adequate rear head clearance even for 6-footers. Still, tall drivers might want a little more rearward seat travel to get further from the steering wheel. And the cabin is a bit narrow for uncrowded 3-abreast travel in back, but larger doorways make for easy entry/exit all around.

Outward visibility, driver seating, and dash layout? The 626 is competitive but no more. Interior materials are better than the compact-class norm and this Mazda feels solid on the road and exhibits fine detail finish.

VALUE FOR THE MONEY The 626 isn't the sportiest compact sedan, but it's a highly competent family 4-door and our Best Buy in its class. LX models are the top 626 values, but plenty of competition means you shouldn't have to pay full retail for any of these Mazdas.

ENGINES

	dohc I4	dohc V6
Size, liters/cu. in.	2.0/122	2.5/152
Horsepower @ rpm	130 @ 5500	170 @ 6000
Torque (lbs./ft.) @ rpm	127 @ 3000	163 @ 5000
Availability	S[1]	S[2]

EPA city/highway mpg

5-speed OD manual	26/33	21/27
4-speed OD automatic	22/29	20/26

1. LX 4-cylinder, ES 4-cylinder. 2. LX V6, ES V6.

PRICES

Mazda 626

	Retail Price	Dealer Invoice
LX 4-cylinder 4-door sedan	$18245	$16642
LX V6 4-door sedan	19445	17735
ES 4-cylinder 4-door sedan	20445	18645
ES V6 4-door sedan	22445	20465
Destination charge	450	450

Prices are for vehicles distributed by Mazda Motor of America, Inc. Prices may be higher in areas served by independent distributors.

STANDARD EQUIPMENT:

LX: 2.0-liter dohc 4-cylinder engine, 5-speed manual transmission, driver- and passenger-side airbags, air conditioning, variable-assist power steering, tilt steering wheel, cruise control, cloth upholstery, front bucket seats w/driver seat height adjustment, storage console with armrest, cupholders, split folding rear seat, power mirrors, power windows, power door locks, remote keyless entry, AM/FM/CD player, digital clock, tachometer, variable intermittent wipers, rear defogger, auxiliary power outlets, map lights, illuminated visor mirrors, automatic headlights, remote fuel-door and decklid releases, 205/60R15 tires, wheel covers.

LX V6 adds: 2.5-liter dohc V6 engine, 4-wheel disc brakes.

ES adds to LX: 4-speed automatic transmission, leather upholstery, leather-wrapped steering wheel and shifter, floormats, alloy wheels.

ES V6 adds: 2.5-liter dohc V6 engine, 5-speed manual transmission, 4-wheel disc brakes, 6-way power driver seat, Bose AM/FM/cassette/CD player, heated mirrors, power sunroof, theft-deterrent system, 205/55R16 tires.

OPTIONAL EQUIPMENT:
Major Packages

	Retail	Dealer
Luxury Pkg., LX 4-cylinder	1800	1440
ES 4-cylinder	1300	1040

Power sunroof, 6-way power driver seat, heated mirrors, theft-deterrent system w/alarm, floormats (LX), alloy wheels (LX).

Premium Pkg., LX V6	1850	1480

Power sunroof, 6-way power driver seat, heated mirrors, floormats, theft-deterrent system w/alarm, 205/55R16 tires, alloy wheels.

Powertrains

4-speed automatic transmission, LX, ES V6	800	696

Safety Features

Antilock brakes, LX V6, ES V6	950	760
LX 4-cylinder, ES 4-cylinder	800	640

Includes front side-impact airbags. V6 models include traction control.

Comfort and Convenience

AM/FM/cassette/CD player, LX, ES 4-cylinder	200	170
Audio Pkg., LX V6	600	480

AM/FM/cassette/CD player, w/Bose sound system.

6-disc CD changer, ES V6	225	180

Appearance and Miscellaneous

Rear spoiler	395	295
Fog lights, LX, ES 4-cylinder	—	—
Alloy wheels, LX 4-cylinder	450	383
16-inch alloy wheels, LX V6	595	505

Includes 205/55R16 tires.

MERCEDES-BENZ C-CLASS

Rear-wheel-drive near-luxury car; similar to Mercedes-Benz CLK

Base price range: $31,750-$53,000. Built in Germany. **Also consider:** Acura TL, Audi A6, Infiniti I30, Lexus ES 300

FOR • Steering/handling • Acceleration (C280, C43) • Build quality **AGAINST** • Road noise • Rear-seat and cargo room

Mercedes' smallest sedan gets manual shift capability for its automatic transmission, and a telescoping steering column and antiskid

Mercedes-Benz C230 w/Sport Package

control are standard instead of optional for 2000.

The C-Class line consists of the C230 Kompressor with a supercharged 2.3 liter 4-cylinder, the mid-level C280 with a 2.8-liter V6, and the limited-production C43 with a high-performance 4.3-liter V8. All use a 5-speed automatic transmission, which this year gains Mercedes' Touch Shift with a separate gate for manual shifting.

Traction control is standard, as is Mercedes' Electronic Stability Program antiskid control. Also standard are front side airbags, antilock 4-wheel disc brakes, and Mercedes' TeleAid emergency assistance system. All Mercedes vehicles now include free scheduled maintenance with the 4-year/50,000-mile basic warranty.

PERFORMANCE Solid and well-balanced, C-Class models behave much like bigger Mercedes sedans, with two exceptions: a choppier ride over rough pavement and more road noise than is warranted at these prices.

Our Kompressor test car ran 0-60 mph in 7.5 seconds, slightly faster than the V6 C280. But the V6 is more refined than the 4-cylinder and doesn't suffer the supercharged engine's momentary delay in acceleration. The C43 is just plain fast; Mercedes lists a 0-60-mph time of 5.9 seconds. Our test C280 averaged 21.9 mpg in hard driving, a C230 22.8 in mostly highway work. We haven't measured a C43's fuel economy.

Regardless of model, Mercedes' 5-speed automatic transmission has a gear for every need and shifts with smooth authority. Kudos for the standard antiskid system, but the C-Class's traction control works partly by reducing engine power, which can cause anxious moments crossing a slippery intersection. Braking power and feel is excellent. Handling is responsive and stable, though just short of BMW's 3-Series rivals. The ride isn't harsh, but is decidedly firm and occasionally abrupt on bumpy pavement.

ACCOMMODATIONS The C-Class suffers skimpy back-seat leg room and tight rear entry/exit for larger adults. All-around head room for 6-footers is just adequate. Cargo space isn't great either, but what's there is usable. Drivers should find the accommodations comfortable, but despite being within easy reach, the audio controls are difficult to decipher and some switches are inconveniently located. Visibility is generally good all-round. Workmanship and materials are in line with sticker prices and Mercedes' reputation, though charging $1000 just to order Xenon headlights or a ski sack seems greedy.

VALUE FOR THE MONEY Performance and engineering earn the C-Class sedans our respect, but a bit too much noise and small interiors for the price keep them from earning our recommendation. Still, these are Mercedes-Benzes, with all that implies for prestige and resale value.

ENGINES

	Supercharged dohc I4	ohc V6	ohc V8
Size, liters/cu. in.	2.3/140	2.8/171	4.3/260
Horsepower @ rpm	185 @ 5300	194 @ 5800	302 @ 5850
Torque (lbs./ft.) @ rpm	200 @ 2500	195 @ 3000	302 @ 3250
Availability	S[1]	S[2]	S[3]
EPA city/highway mpg 5-speed OD automatic	21/29	21/27	18/23

1. C230. 2. C280. 3. C43.

PRICES

Mercedes-Benz C-Class

	Retail Price	Dealer Invoice
C230 Kompressor 4-door sedan	$31750	$29528
C280 4-door sedan	35950	33434
C43 4-door sedan	53000	46290
Destination charge	595	595

STANDARD EQUIPMENT:

C230: 2.3-liter dohc supercharged 4-cylinder engine, 5-speed automatic transmission w/manual-shift capability, traction control, driver- and passenger-side airbags w/automatic child seat recognition system, front side-impact airbags, antilock 4-wheel disc brakes, antiskid system, TeleAid emergency assistance system, power steering, telescoping leather-wrapped steering wheel, cruise control, air conditioning w/manual dual-zone control, interior air filter, leather and vinyl upholstery, front bucket seats, 10-way power driver seat, 10-way manual adjustable passenger seat, center storage console, cupholders, wood interior trim, heated power mirrors w/driver-side automatic day/night, power windows, power door locks, remote keyless entry, AM/FM/cassette w/CD changer controls, digital clock, tachometer, outside-temperature indicator, automatic day/night rearview mirror, remote fuel door/decklid release, illuminated visor mirrors, rear defogger, universal garage-door opener, first-aid kit, floormats, theft-deterrent system, front and rear fog lights, full-size spare, 205/60HR15 tires, alloy wheels.

C280 adds: 2.8-liter V6 engine, dual-zone automatic climate control, 10-way power passenger seat, Bose sound system.

C43 adds: 4.3-liter V8 engine, full leather upholstery, multi-contour/heated front seats, split folding rear seat, memory system for driver seat and outside mirrors, power sunroof, sport suspension, 225/45R17 front tires, 245/40R17 rear tires.

OPTIONAL EQUIPMENT:
Major Packages

	Retail Price	Dealer Invoice
Option Pkg. C1	$450	$419
Headlight washer/wiper, rain-sensing automatic wipers.		
Option Pkg. C2, C230	1700	1581
C280	1270	1181
Power sunroof, 10-way power passenger seat (C230), split-folding rear seat.		
Sport Option Pkg. C6, C230, C280	900	837
Full leather upholstery, front sport bucket seats, sport interior trim, bodyside moldings, sport suspension, 205/55HR16 tires.		
Option Pkg. K2	1795	1454
Integrated portable cellular telephone, 6-disc CD changer.		

Comfort and Convenience

	Retail Price	Dealer Invoice
Power sunroof, C230, C280	1130	1051
Full leather upholstery, C230, C280	1345	1251
Multi-contour front seats, C230, C280	710	—
Requires special order charge. NA with Option Pkg. C6.		
Heated front seats, C230, C280	605	563
Bose sound system, C230	580	539
Ski sack	200	
Requires special order charge.		

Appearance and Miscellaneous

	Retail Price	Dealer Invoice
Xenon headlights	950	
Requires special order charge.		
Special order charge	1000	1000
Fee for one or more options requiring special order charge.		

MERCEDES-BENZ CLK

RECOMMENDED

Mercedes-Benz CLK430 coupe

Rear-wheel-drive luxury car; similar to Mercedes-Benz C-Class

1999 base price range: $40,600-$47,900. Built in Germany.
Also consider: BMW 3-Series, Saab 9-3, Volvo 70 series

FOR • Steering/handling • Acceleration **AGAINST** • Rear-seat and cargo room • Rear-seat entry/exit

Prices are accurate at time of publication; subject to manufacturer's changes.

These sporty 2-door coupes and convertibles are offshoots of Mercedes' compact C-Class sedan. For 2000, both body styles are available with a V8 engine; the convertible had been available only with a V6. And an antiskid system is now standard on all models. Convertibles have a power top and defrosted-glass rear window. Both come as the CLK320, with a 3.2-liter V6 engine, and as the CLK430, with a 4.3-liter V8. A 5-speed automatic is the only transmission and this year gains Mercedes' Touch Shift with a separate gate for manual shifting. Also standard are antilock brakes, traction control, front side airbags, and Mercedes' TeleAid emergency assistance system. Mercedes' antiskid Electronic Stability Program had been standard on the CLK430, optional the CLK320, but this year is standard on all CLKs. Also for 2000, CLK320s gain new front and rear body-color aprons and new-look alloy wheels. CLK430s have larger brakes than CLK320s, firmer suspension, 17-inch wheels and performance tires (versus 16s), and different lower-body cladding. All Mercedes vehicles now include free scheduled maintenance along with the 4-year/50,000-mile basic warranty.

EVALUATION These are polished performers, with V8 models being a sort of German pony-car hot rod. Our test CLK320 coupe ran 0-60 mph in just under 7 seconds and averaged 21.6 mpg. Structural stiffening that makes the convertible unusually solid over bumps also adds enough weight to make it feel noticeably slower than the CLK320 coupe. CLK430s feel sleepy off the line, then rocket away; Mercedes says 0-60 in 6.1 seconds. Our test 430 coupe averaged 20.2 mpg. All CLKs enjoy a weighty Mercedes driving feel, handle well, and have a firm yet absorbent ride. The CLK430's performance tire tread furnishes virtually no grip in snow, however, despite the standard traction control. Noise levels are low, but tires thump over expansion joints and rumble on rough pavement. Front-seat room is snug for larger occupants, and rear room is tight. Interior decor is tasteful. However, the steering wheel telescopes but doesn't tilt, and some controls are poorly marked and placed. The convertible's trunk shrinks to just 5.8 cubic feet with the top lowered. Solid and comfortable, CLKs are highly capable tourers, with typical Mercedes virtues—and prices.

ENGINES

	ohc V6	ohc V8
Size, liters/cu. in.	3.2/195	4.3/260
Horsepower @ rpm	215 @ 5700	275 @ 5750
Torque (lbs./ft.) @ rpm	229 @ 3000	295 @ 3000
Availability	S[1]	S[2]
EPA city/highway mpg		
5-speed OD automatic	21/29[3]	18/25[4]

1. CLK 320. 2. CLK 430. 3. 19/28 w/convertible. 4. 17/25 w/convertible.

PRICES

1999 Mercedes-Benz CLK

	Retail Price	Dealer Invoice
CLK320 2-door coupe	$40600	$35320
CLK320 2-door convertible	47200	41060
CLK430 2-door coupe	47900	41670
Destination charge	595	595

STANDARD EQUIPMENT:

CLK320: 3.2-liter V6 engine, 5-speed automatic transmission, traction control, driver- and passenger-side airbags w/automatic child seat recognition system, front side-impact airbags, antilock 4-wheel disc brakes, automatic roll bar (convertible), air conditioning w/dual-zone automatic climate control, interior air filter, power steering, tilt and telescoping leather-wrapped steering wheel, cruise control, leather upholstery, 10-way power front seats w/driver seat memory, split folding rear seat, wood interior trim, cupholders, heated power mirrors w/passenger-side tilt-down back-up aid, power windows, power door locks, remote keyless entry, power convertible top (convertible), AM/FM/cassette w/Bose sound system, digital clock, tachometer, intermittent wipers, illuminated visor mirrors, universal garage door opener, floormats, theft-deterrent system, front and rear fog lights, 205/55R16 tires, alloy wheels.

CLK430 adds: 4.3-liter V8 engine, anti-skid system, lower-body cladding, 225/45ZR17 front tires, 245/40ZR17 rear tires.

OPTIONAL EQUIPMENT:
Major Packages

	Retail	Dealer
Option Pkg. K2	1595	1293

Integrated portable cellular telephone, 6-disc CD changer.

	Retail Price	Dealer Invoice
Option Pkg. K3, coupes	$1290	$1122

Sunroof, automatic day/night driver-side and rearview mirrors, power rear window sunshade.

Option Pkg. K4	1495	1301

Heated front seats, Xenon headlights w/washers.

Safety Features

Electronic Stability Program anti-skid system, CLK320	1000	870

Comfort and Convenience

Multi-contour front seats	700	609

MERCEDES-BENZ E-CLASS

✓ BEST BUY

Mercedes-Benz E320 sedan

Rear- or all-wheel-drive luxury car

Base price range: $47,100-$69,800. Built in Germany. **Also consider:** Audi A6, BMW 5-Series, Lexus GS 300/400

FOR • Cargo room (wagon) • Acceleration • Steering/handling • Ride • Available all-wheel drive • Build quality • Exterior finish
AGAINST • Fuel economy (E430, E55) • Instruments/controls

Mercedes drops the diesel E-Class model for 2000, but adds an all-wheel-drive V8 sedan and standard rear side airbags. All E-Class models also get minor styling revisions and new communications options.

Discontinued is the E300 and its 174-horsepower turbocharged 6-cylinder diesel engine; this was the lowest-priced E-Class. The E320 sedan and wagon continue with a 221-hp 3.2-liter V6. The E430 is a sedan with a 275-hp 4.3-liter V8. The limited-production E55 sedan uses a 349-hp 5.4-liter V8. A 5-speed automatic is the sole transmission and this year gains Mercedes' Touch Shift with a separate gate for manual shifting. Wagons have a rear-facing third-row seat for 7-passenger capacity.

E320 sedans and wagons, and now the E430 sedan, are available with Mercedes' 4Matic all-wheel drive. Mercedes' anti-skid Electronic Stability Program is standard on all models for 2000; it was optional on E320s. Also standard is Mercedes' TeleAid emergency assistance system. All models have "curtain" side airbags that drop from above the side windows to limit head injuries in side collisions. Joining front lower-body side airbags as standard for 2000 are lower-body rear side airbags. New options include a voice-activated cellular phone, in-dash navigation system and screen, and an audible parking-warning system. Appearance changes include new wheels and lower-body styling. And all Mercedes vehicles now include free scheduled maintenance along with the 4-year/50,000-mile basic warranty.

PERFORMANCE Any E-Class is more athletic than the typical 4-door luxury car, if not so nimble as a 5-Series BMW. Steering is firm and precise and body lean modest in hard cornering. A model blend of ride comfort and control, the suspension is stable at high speeds and easily smothers most bumps. Quietness is another asset. 4Matic furnishes superb traction but adds about 200 pounds for a slight sacrifice in acceleration and fuel economy.

Acceleration is satisfying in any version. Fine performance during our test drives lends credence to Mercedes' claims of 7.1 seconds 0-60 mph for the E320 and 7.8 for the E320 wagon. AWD adds about a half-second. Mercedes says the E430 does 0-60 in 6.4 seconds. It does feel usefully faster around town than the E320 and delivers outstanding highway passing power. The E55 has stirring acceleration—5.4 seconds 0-60, says Mercedes—and handles better than some sports cars.

ACCOMMODATIONS There's ample room for four adults; the transmission tunnel precludes long-distance comfort for a rear center-seater. All models have good cargo capacity, flat load floors, and low liftovers. The wagon's third seat folds easily for cargo, and is sized for kids. Gauges and controls are generally well laid out, though too many buttons are poorly marked, and console-mounted power window controls may not be to everyone's liking. All models offer good visibility from a comfortable, easily tailored driver's post, plus craftsmanship that's solid on the road and nearly impeccable to the eye.

VALUE FOR THE MONEY Quality, resale value, performance, and safety features make E-Class models unqualified luxury car Best Buys. The wagon and available AWD are added attractions for superior traction and/or increased cargo capacity. E320s are the best values, with the E430 a stellar rival for the Lexus LS 400 and BMW 540i.

ENGINES

	ohc V6	ohc V8	ohc V8
Size, liters/cu. in.	3.2/195	4.3/260	5.4/322
Horsepower @ rpm	221 @ 5500	275 @ 5750	349 @ 5500
Torque (lbs./ft.) @ rpm	232 @ 3000	295 @ 3000	391 @ 3000
Availability	S[1]	S[2]	S[3]
EPA city/highway mpg			
5-speed OD automatic	21/30[4]	18/24[5]	16/23

1. E320. 2. E430. 3. E55 AMG. 4. 20/27 w/wagon, 20/26 w/4matic wagon, 20/28 w/4Matic sedan. 5. 17/23 w/4matic.

PRICES

Mercedes-Benz E-Class	Retail Price	Dealer Invoice
E320 4-door sedan	$47100	$43803
E320 4-door wagon	47950	44594
E320 AWD 4-door sedan	49900	46407
E320 AWD 4-door wagon	50750	47198
E430 4-door sedan	52450	48779
E430 AWD 4-door sedan	55250	51383
E55 4-door sedan	69800	64914
Destination charge	595	595

AWD denotes all-wheel drive. E55 add gas guzzler tax $1000.

STANDARD EQUIPMENT:

E320 sedan: 3.2-liter V6 engine, 5-speed automatic transmission w/manual-shift capability, traction control, driver- and passenger-side airbags w/automatic child seat recognition system, front and rear side-impact airbags, front and rear side head-protection, antilock 4-wheel disc brakes, anti-skid system, TeleAid emergency assistance system, air conditioning w/dual-zone automatic climate control, interior air filter, variable-assist power steering, power tilt/telescopic steering wheel with memory feature, leather-wrapped steering wheel, cruise control, leather upholstery, 10-way power front bucket seats with memory feature, center console, cupholders, wood interior trim, heated power mirrors with memory feature and driver-side automatic day/night, passenger-side mirror tilt-down parking aid, power windows, power door locks, remote keyless entry, automatic day/night rearview mirror, outside-temperature indicator, AM/FM/cassette w/CD changer controls, digital clock, tachometer, rear defogger, illuminated visor mirrors, auxiliary power outlet, remote fuel door and decklid releases, universal garage-door opener, variable intermittent wipers, reading lights, floormats, front and rear fog lights, theft-deterrent system, first-aid kit, full-size spare tire, 215/55HR16 tires, alloy wheels. **AWD** adds: permanent all-wheel drive.

E320 wagon adds: cloth and leather upholstery, folding third seat, cargo cover, intermittent rear wiper and heated washer, automatic rear load leveling suspension, roof rails. **AWD** adds: permanent all-wheel drive.

E430 adds to E320 sedan: 4.3-liter V8 engine, Bose sound system, 235/45WR17 tires. **AWD** adds: permanent all-wheel drive.

E55 adds: 5.4-liter V8 engine, power sunroof, heated multi-contour front seats, rain-sensing automatic wipers, power rear window sunshade, aerodynamics package, Xenon headlights w/washers, projector beam fog lights, sport suspension, 245/40ZR18 front tires, 275/35ZR18 rear tires.

OPTIONAL EQUIPMENT:
Major Packages

	Retail Price	Dealer Invoice
E1 Option Pkg., E320, E430	1575	1465

Heated front seats, Xenon headlamps, heated headlight washers.

	Retail Price	Dealer Invoice
E2 Option Pkg., E320	$1575	$1465

Bose sound system, power sunroof, rain-sensing wipers.

E3 Option Pkg., E430	4010	3729

Front air dam, side sill skirts, rear apron, projector beam fog lights, special alloy wheels. NA 430 AWD.

K2 Option Pkg.	1795	1454

Integrated portable cellular telephone, 6-disc CD changer.

K2A Option Pkg.	2190	1774

Voice-activated integrated portable cellular telephone, 6-disc CD changer.

Designo Expresso Edition, E320 sedan, E430	5900	5487
E320 wagon	6500	6045
E55	5200	4836

Elm wood console trim, elm wood/charcoal leather steering wheel, Nappa leather upholstery (E320, E430), charcoal/light brown floormats. Requires heated front seats. Not available AWD.

Designo Silver Edition, E320 sedan, E430	5900	5487
E320 wagon	6500	6045
E55	5200	4836

Maple wood console trim, maple wood/charcoal leather steering wheel, Nappa leather upholstery (E320, E430), charcoal/dark green floormats. Requires heated front seats. Not available AWD.

Command System	1995	1855

Navigation system, AM/FM/CD player, steering wheel radio controls.

Comfort and Convenience

Power sunroof, E320, E430	1130	1051
Full leather upholstery, E320 wagon	1345	1251
Nappa leather upholstery, E320 sedan, E430	700	651
E320 wagon	2045	1902

Requires special order charge.

Multi-contour power front seats, E320, E430	710	660
Heated front seats, E320, E430	605	563
Power rear window sunshade, E320 sedan, E430	410	381
Parktronic System, E320, E430	975	907

Requires special order charge. Not available AWD.

Appearance and Miscellaneous

Roof rack, E320 wagon	450	419
Special order charge	1000	1000

Fee for one or more options requiring special order charge.

MERCEDES-BENZ M-CLASS

Mercedes-Benz ML55 AMG

4-wheel-drive midsize sport-utility vehicle

Base price range: $35,300-$64,900. Built in USA. **Also consider:** Ford Explorer, Jeep Grand Cherokee, Lexus RX 300, Toyota 4Runner

FOR • Steering/handling • Build quality • Exterior finish • Cargo room **AGAINST** • Fuel economy • Ride (ML430, ML55 AMG)

Mercedes' sport-utility vehicle gets rear side airbags, optional third-row seating, an available navigation system, and a new high-performance model for 2000.

The ML320 has a 215-horsepower 3.2-liter V6, the ML430 a 268-hp 4.3-liter V8, and the new limited-edition ML55 a 342-hp 5.4-liter V8. A 5-speed automatic is the only transmission and this year gains Mercedes' Touch Shift with a separate gate for manual shifting. The standard permanent 4-wheel drive has separate low-range gearing controlled by a dashboard button. Antilock 4-wheel disc brakes also are standard.

Prices are accurate at time of publication; subject to manufacturer's changes.

Rear side airbags are new for 2000 and are standard along with front side airbags. Newly optional is a 2-passenger third-row seat; it's available on the ML320 and ML430 and increases seating capacity to seven. Interior revisions include new door panels, footwell lights, and lower-dashboard padding, and ML320s now come with the same wood trim and leather-covered steering wheel used by V8 models. ML320s also gain the V8's body-colored bumpers and trim, but retain a separate wheel design. Also new is a 5-inch-diameter dashboard video display that controls the audio system and a new satellite navigation system. It's standard on V8 models, with the navigation component a dealer-installed ML320 option.

ML55s include more-powerful brakes, exclusive 18-inch wheels with low profile tires, and sport front bucket seats. Just 1500 are planned for model-year 2000. All Mercedes vehicles now include free scheduled maintenance along with the 4-year/50,000-mile basic warranty.

PERFORMANCE Although the Lexus RX 300 is more carlike, few true SUVs are more pleasant to drive than the M-Class. The smooth automatic transmission helps the ML320 do 0-60 mph in a decent 9.1 seconds in our tests, though acceleration slows discernably with heavier loads aboard. Our test ML320s averaged 13.9-15 mpg, typical of 6-cylinder SUVs.

V8 models are noticeably faster; Mercedes pegs the ML430 at 8 seconds 0-60. Acceleration off the line isn't head-snapping, but the 430 gathers speed quickly and has fine highway passing power. The ML55 mirrors those characteristics, and delivers even more thrust once underway; 0-60 in a class-leading 6.4 seconds, says Mercedes. The V6 sounds coarse when pushed. Both V8s emit a throaty roar. Over its first 8800 miles, our extended-use 1999 ML430 is averaging 16.2 mpg, which is better than we get with most V8 SUVs. It requires premium fuel.

MLs are poised and stable for SUVs, with less body lean in corners than most. Steering is precise and linear, though it must be guided back to center after tight turns. The ML320 has an absorbent ride, but the ML430 and ML55 have low-profile tires that generate impact harshness over bumps and sharply broken pavement.

Employing the antilock brakes to check slipping wheels, the 4WD system works well, though it isn't as effective as some more-traditional 4x4 systems in the most-severe back-trail conditions. Wind and road noise are higher than in a family sedan—or in the RX 300—but low for an SUV. Braking is strong and stable, especially the ML55's. Our extended-use ML430 has been mechanically trouble-free, but suffers poor AM radio reception in urban areas.

ACCOMMODATIONS The M-Class has a manageably low step-up for an SUV, exceptionally wide doors, and room enough for five adults—though rear leg space gets tight with the front seats fully aft. The M-Class is now among the few midsize SUVs with third-row seating; as in the others, it's intended for children or occasional adult use. Markings on some controls are not obvious, but ergonomics are otherwise good. So is visibility, except directly aft due to the rear headrests. Load volume is ample, but it takes some practice to master the complex mechanism that folds the second-row seat. The interior is now more in line with Mercedes-level expectations, looking and feeling more upscale, with softer available leather and revised trim. A sturdy driving feel and careful detail finish are evident, despite the rare minor body shuddering on rough pavement.

VALUE FOR THE MONEY Among true SUVs, the M-Class is at the forefront in refinement, handling, and overall competence. Prices are steep, but high resale values boost this Best Buy's overall value.

ENGINES

	ohc V6	ohc V8	ohc V8
Size, liters/cu. in.	3.2/195	4.3/260	5.4/332
Horsepower @ rpm	215 @ 5500	268 @ 5500	342 @ 5500
Torque (lbs./ft.) @ rpm	233 @ 3000	288 @ 3000	376 @ 3000
Availability	S[1]	S[2]	S[3]
EPA city/highway mpg			
5-speed OD automatic	16/20	15/19	14/18

1. ML320. 2. ML430. 3. ML55 AMG.

PRICES

Mercedes-Benz M-Class	Retail Price	Dealer Invoice
ML320 4-door wagon	$35300	$32829
ML430 4-door wagon	43750	40688
ML55 4-door wagon	$64900	$60357
Destination charge	595	595

STANDARD EQUIPMENT:

ML320: 3.2-liter V6 engine, 5-speed automatic transmission w/manual-shift capability, permanent 4-wheel drive, traction control, driver- and passenger-side airbags w/automatic child seat recognition system, front and rear side-impact airbags, anti-skid system, antilock 4-wheel disc brakes, air conditioning w/interior air filter, power steering, tilt leather-wrapped steering wheel, cruise control, cloth upholstery, manual 6-way front bucket seats, center console, split folding rear seat, cupholders, wood interior trim, heated power mirrors, power windows, power door locks, intermittent wipers, remote keyless entry, rear window defogger, rear wiper/washer, AM/FM/cassette w/CD changer controls, digital clock, tachometer, universal garage door opener, auxiliary power outlets, illuminated visor mirrors, cargo cover, floormats, theft-deterrent system, roof rack, rear fog lights, front and rear tow hooks, 255/65R16 tires, alloy wheels.

ML430 adds: 4.3-liter V8 engine, navigation system, leather upholstery, heated 8-way power front seats, passenger-side under-seat storage drawer, automatic day/night outside and rearview mirrors, trip computer, rear privacy glass, 275/55R17 tires.

ML55 adds: 5.5-liter V8 engine, power sunroof, dual front seat memory, 6-disc CD changer w/Bose sound system, power rear quarter windows, Xenon headlights, front fog lights, 285/50WR18 tires.

OPTIONAL EQUIPMENT:
Major Packages

	Retail	Dealer
M1 Luxury Pkg., ML320	1500	1395

Leather upholstery, heated 8-way power front seats, rear privacy glass. Requires sunroof or Skyview roof.

M2 Convenience Pkg., ML320	995	925

Trip computer, automatic day/night outside and rearview mirrors, dual front seat memory, locking under-passenger-seat compartment. Requires M1 Luxury Pkg.

M3 Convenience Pkg., ML430	495	460

Dual front seat memory. Requires sunroof or Skyview roof.

M4 Off-Road Pkg.	1595	1483

Brush guard, side bars, polished stainless steel exterior trim, mud guards, front skid plate. Requires sunroof or Skyview roof.

M7 Seat Pkg., ML320	1150	1350
ML320 w/M1 Pkg., ML430	1350	1256

Two third row seats, power rear quarter windows.

Comfort and Convenience

Power sunroof, ML320, ML430	1095	1018
Skyview roof, ML320, ML430	2395	2227

8-square foot power sunroof.

Bose sound system, ML320, ML430	1050	977

Includes 6-disc CD changer. ML320 requires M1 Luxury Pkg.

Heated front seats, ML320	605	563

MERCEDES-BENZ S-CLASS/CL500

Mercedes-Benz S-Class

Rear-wheel-drive luxury car

Base price range: $69,700-$77,850. Built in Germany. **Also consider:** Audi A8, BMW 7-Series, Lexus LS 400

FOR • Acceleration • Build quality • Exterior finish • Entry/exit • Interior materials • Passenger room • Refinement • Ride
AGAINST • Fuel economy • Navigation system controls

The **redesigned 2000** version of Mercedes-Benz's flagship was introduced in spring '99, with trimmer dimensions and even more leading-edge technology. In January, Mercedes added a coupe companion, the CL500.

The S-Class sedan is 1-2 inches smaller in nearly all dimensions than its predecessor, and some 500 pounds lighter. There's marginally less front head room but slightly more rear leg room. Two V8 sedans are offered, the 4.3-liter S430 and the 5.0-liter S500.

The CL500 coupe also follows a downsized formula compared to its predecessor and uses the same V8 as the S500. All models have a 5-speed automatic transmission with a separate gate for manual shifting. Antilock 4-wheel disc brakes with Mercedes' Brake Assist are standard, as is traction control and an antiskid system. The sedans' suspension uses air bladders that adjust damping to suit the road surface, and features driver-adjusted sport and normal settings, plus automatic level control. The CL500 retains coil springs, but adds Mercedes' Active Body Control, which uses hydraulic rams to automatically reduce body roll in turns.

Rear side airbags are standard on sedans, and both body styles come with curtain airbags that deploy along all side windows to protect head and shoulders in a side impact. A satellite-based navigation system with an in-dash video display and voice-command response also is standard. The cruise control system uses radar to automatically maintain a preset distance behind other cars. Also standard is TeleAid, Mercedes' emergency assistance system. All Mercedes vehicles now include free scheduled maintenance along with the 4-year/50,000-mile basic warranty.

PERFORMANCE We haven't yet tested a CL500, but Mercedes has met its goal of a leaner, sportier-feeling flagship sedan. The S-Class is still too large and heavy to qualify as nimble, but it is responsive, and its formidable technology breeds confidence under virtually all conditions. The only flaws of note in our testing were a trace of wobble on the freeway in the wake of large trucks and some side-to-side pitching on uneven pavement. Mild float over big pavement dips at speed is cured with a dashboard button that switches the suspension to its firmer damping schedule. In any mode, the S-Class confronts rough pavement with granite solidity and a firm ride that doesn't ignore bumps and ruts, but filters out unpleasant harshness.

Acceleration with either V8 is swift, smooth, nearly seamless. Mercedes says the S430 does 0-60 mph in 6.9 seconds, the S500 in just 6.1. Our S500 test car averaged 16.6 mpg, impressive for the high-luxury class. We haven't measured an S430's fuel economy. Braking is strong and easily modulated, and to driver and passengers the sounds of engine, road, and wind are mostly rumors. The new radar cruise control was unavailable for testing.

ACCOMMODATIONS You don't so much occupy the S-Class's interior as interact with it. The daunting array of seat, climate, audio, and communications features is useful, but takes time to learn. The navigation system provides instructions graphically and audibly, and it conveniently projects route guidance within the main instrument cluster. But its operation is complex and far from intuitive, and its main screen in the center of the dashboard washes out in certain light conditions.

Seating is supportive and long-distance comfortable, though the optional "pulsating" front seatbacks are dubious. Head room is generous, and leg room limolike front and rear, but the new, narrower cabin isn't as inviting for 3-across rear seating. Outward visibility is outstanding. Main gauges are unobstructed, but their electronic presentation is one-dimensional and doesn't dim enough at night. Both the plastic storage housings below the front seats and the front-seat cupholders intrude into passenger space. The trunk is efficiently sized, though not expansive. Most materials are of very high quality; the plastic glovebox door and plastic front-seat valances are exceptions.

VALUE FOR THE MONEY The new S-Class is hard to fault dynamically, but it does trade its predecessors' unapologetic size and uncompromised materials for technological sophistication. Prices drop in the bargain. The S430 lists for $4200 less than the S420 it replaces, and the S500 starts at $9650 below last year's S500.

ENGINES

	ohc V8	ohc V8
Size, liters/cu. in.	4.3/260	5.0/303
Horsepower @ rpm	275 @ 5750	302 @ 5600
Torque (lbs./ft.) @ rpm	295 @ 3000	339 @ 2700
Availability	S[1]	S[2]
EPA city/highway mpg		
5-speed OD automatic	17/24	16/23

1. S430. 2. S500, CL500.

PRICES

Mercedes-Benz S-Class/CL500	Retail Price	Dealer Invoice
S430 4-door sedan	$69700	$64821
S500 4-door sedan	77850	72400
Destination charge	595	595

CL500 prices, standard equipment, and options not available at time of publication. S500 add Gas Guzzler Tax $1000.

STANDARD EQUIPMENT:

S430: 4.3-liter V8 engine, 5-speed automatic transmission w/manual-shift capability, ASR traction control, driver- and passenger-side airbags w/automatic child recognition system, front and rear side-impact airbags, front and rear side head protection system, anti-skid system, antilock 4-wheel disc brakes, TeleAid emergency assistance system, air conditioning w/dual-zone automatic climate control, variable-assist power steering, power tilt and telescoping leather-wrapped steering wheel w/memory, cruise control, leather upholstery, heated 14-way power front bucket seats w/adjustable lumbar support and memory, wood interior trim, heated power mirrors w/memory and driver-side automatic day/night, power windows, power door locks, remote keyless entry, power sunroof, automatic day/night rearview mirror, voice-activated cellular telephone, AM/FM/cassette/CD player w/Bose sound system, steering wheel radio controls, automatic headlights, outside-mirror mounted turn signal lights, self-leveling air suspension, 225/60R16 tires, alloy wheels.

S500 adds: 5.0-liter V8 engine, upgraded leather upholstery, Xenon headlights, headlight washers.

OPTIONAL EQUIPMENT:
Major Packages

S4 Convenience Pkg.	3775	3511

Distronic cruise control with distance control, Parktronic system, rear window sunshade.

Designo Expresso Edition, S430	9300	8649
S500	8500	7905

Special light brown leather seat trim w/two-tone door panels, elm wood interior trim, unique floormats, Designo Expresso paint. Requires climate comfort rear seats or heated rear seats.

Designo Silver Edition, S430	10250	9533
S500	9550	8882

Shell-colored leather interior trim, maple wood interior trim, unique floormats, Designo Silver paint. Requires climate comfort rear seats or heated rear seats, power reclining rear seatback, power rear sunshade.

Comfort and Convenience

S3 Comfort Pkg.	1940	1804

Multi-contour front seats with internal ventilation, pulsating air chambers, and active lumbar support.

Rear compartment climate control	1800	1674
Power reclining rear seatback	1750	1627
Four Place Seating Pkg., S500	5540	5152

Includes rear bucket seats, power reclining seatbacks.

Rear Climate Comfort Seats	1500	1395

Heated rear seats with internal ventilation and pulsating air chambers. Requires power reclining rear seatback or Four Place Seating Pkg.

Heated rear seats	595	553
Parktronic	975	907
Power rear window sunshade	495	460

Appearance and Miscellaneous

Xenon headlights w/washers, S430	1105	1028
Special order charge	1000	1000

Fee for car ordered with one or more options requiring special order charge.

MERCEDES-BENZ SL-CLASS
Rear-wheel-drive luxury car

Base price range: $82,600-$128,950. Built in Germany. **Also consider:** Jaguar XK8, Lexus SC 300/400

FOR • Acceleration • Steering/handling • Braking • Build quality • Exterior finish • Interior materials **AGAINST** • Fuel economy • Cargo space

Heated seats and an adaptive suspension are new options for the V8 version of Mercedes' top-line convertible. Both the V8 SL500 and

Prices are accurate at time of publication; subject to manufacturer's changes.

Mercedes-Benz SL500

the V12 SL600 have a power soft top and a removable aluminum hard-top. Antilock brakes, front side airbags, and Mercedes' ESP antiskid system are included, and newly standard is Mercedes' TeleAid emergency assistance system. A glass-roof Panorama hardtop is available, as is a Sport Package with new-design 18-inch wheels, high-performance tires, and different lower-body styling. Both SLs again include Mercedes' Brake Assist and BabySmart child-seat recognition system. Also standard is a roll bar that automatically pops up when sensors detect an impending rollover. Again standard on the SL600 and newly optional for the SL500 are heated seats and Mercedes' Adaptive Damping System, which automatically adjusts shock-absorber firmness to suit driving conditions. All Mercedes vehicles now include 4-year/50,000-mile free scheduled maintenance.

EVALUATION SLs are beautifully finished, refined road cars with strong performance, solid engineering, and luxurious trappings. They're too heavy to be sports cars (the lighter of the pair weighs over two tons), but precious few cars provide open-air motoring with this much comfort, safety, style, and speed.

ENGINES

	ohc V8	dohc V12
Size, liters/cu. in.	5.0/303	6.0/365
Horsepower @ rpm	302 @ 5600	389 @ 5200
Torque (lbs./ft.) @ rpm	339 @ 2700	420 @ 3800
Availability	S[1]	S[2]
EPA city/highway mpg		
5-speed OD automatic	16/23	13/19

1. SL500. 2. SL600.

PRICES

Mercedes-Benz SL-Class	Retail Price	Dealer Invoice
SL500 2-door convertible	$82600	$76818
SL600 2-door convertible	128950	119924
Destination charge	595	595

SL500 add Gas Guzzler Tax $1000. SL600 add Gas Guzzler Tax $2600.

STANDARD EQUIPMENT:

SL500: 5.0-liter V8 engine, 5-speed automatic transmission, traction control, driver- and passenger-side airbags w/automatic child recognition system, side-impact airbags, anti-skid system, pop-up roll bar, antilock 4-wheel disc brakes, TeleAid emergency assistance system, air conditioning w/automatic climate control, interior air filter, power steering, power tilt/telescopic steering wheel w/memory, leather-wrapped steering wheel and shifter, cruise control, leather upholstery, 10-way power front seats w/memory, center console, cupholders, wood interior trim, Bose AM/FM/cassette w/CD changer controls, power antenna, analog clock, heated power mirrors w/memory, driver-side mirror w/automatic day/night, power windows, power door locks, remote keyless entry, tachometer, illuminated visor mirrors, remote decklid and fuel-door release, rear defogger, universal garage-door opener, rain-sensing variable intermittent wipers, automatic day/night rearview mirror, map lights, floormats, power convertible top, removable hardtop, theft-deterrent system, heated headlight wipers/washers, front and rear fog lights, 245/45ZR17 tires, alloy wheels.

SL600 adds: 6.0-liter dohc V12 engine, upgraded leather upholstery, heated front seats, leather-wrapped/wood steering wheel, leather and wood shift knob, 6-disc CD changer, portable cellular telephone, Adaptive Damping System, Xenon headlights w/automatic levelling.

OPTIONAL EQUIPMENT:
Major Packages

	Retail Price	Dealer Invoice
Sport Option Pkg. SL1	4995	5301

Ground effects, badging, mesh air dam, projector beam fog lights, 245/40ZR18 front tires, 275/35ZR18 rear tires, monoblock alloy wheels.

	Retail Price	Dealer Invoice
Sport Option Pkg. SL2, SL500	$1820	$1693

Heated front seats, 6-disc CD changer, Xenon headlights w/automatic levelling.

Designo Black Diamond Edition	4900	4557

Red/black leather-wrapped steering wheel and floormats, black carbon fiber center console trim. SL500 requires heated seats.

Designo Slate Blue Edition	5700	5301

Charcoal leather-wrapped/wood steering wheel, maple charcoal wood center console trim, black/blue floormats. SL500 requires heated seat.

Comfort and Convenience

Multi-contour power front seats	710	660
Heated front seats, SL500	605	563
Leather-wrapped/wood steering wheel, SL500	590	—
Requires special order charge.		
Special wood and interior color combination	NC	NC
Requires special order charge.		

Appearance and Miscellaneous

Removable panorama roof	3850	3581
Includes power sunshade. Replaces removable hardtop.		
Adaptive Damping System, SL500	4000	—
Requires special order charge.		
Special order charge	1000	1000
Fee for car ordered with one or more options requiring special order charge.		

MERCEDES-BENZ SLK230

RECOMMENDED

Mercedes-Benz SLK230 w/Sport Package

Rear-wheel-drive sports and GT car

Base price: $41,000. Built in Germany. **Also consider:** BMW Z3 Series, Chevrolet Corvette, Porsche Boxster

FOR • Acceleration • Steering/handling • Build quality • Exterior finish • Interior materials **AGAINST** • Cargo room

An optional voice-activated cellular phone and new "designer" packages are main additions to the smaller of Mercedes' two convertibles for 2000. The SLK230 uses a supercharged 2.3-liter 4-cylinder engine with manual or optional 5-speed automatic transmission. It's metal roof powers down into the trunk. Standard on this 2-seater are side airbags, antilock brakes, traction control, and Mercedes' BabySmart feature that deactivates the right-side airbags when a special Mercedes child seat is installed. An available Sport package includes performance tires on 17-inch wheels in place of the standard 16-inchers, and different lower-body cladding. The voice-actived cell phone is part of a new option package that also includes a 6-disc CD changer. "Designo" appearance packages include special paint and interior trim, plus sports seats; similar packages are offered on other Mercedes cars this year. Like all Mercedes vehicles, the SLK now comes with free scheduled maintenance along with the 4-year/50,000 mile basic warranty.

EVALUATION The SLK230 entertains with fine handling and adroit overall balance, though the ride is stiff over sharp bumps. Standing starts are a bit leisurely, there's occasional, irritating throttle lag, and the engine growls coarsely when worked hard. But speed gathers quickly once the supercharger delivers full boost. The manual transmission doesn't shift as crisply as some, but makes the car feel sportier. Our test automatic averaged 24.2 mpg. Wind noise is modest with the top and windows raised. Road rumble is prominent except on glassy asphalt. A low, compact body means tricky entry/exit and a snug cockpit, but 6-footers won't complain about the firm, comfortable seats. Door windows stick up an annoying half-inch when fully lowered. The hardtop drops quickly, but cuts trunk space from passable to little more than three cubic feet. Workmanship is exemplary except for a rickety pop-out cupholder and minor body tremors on very rough roads. The SLK is a coupe, a convertible, a Mercedes, and fun, which is why demand is strong and discounts rare.

ENGINES

	Supercharged dohc I4
Size, liters/cu. in.	2.3/140
Horsepower @ rpm	185 @ 5300
Torque (lbs./ft.) @ rpm	200 @ 2500
Availability	S
EPA city/highway mpg	
5-speed OD manual	21/31
5-speed OD automatic	22/30

PRICES

Mercedes-Benz SLK230	Retail Price	Dealer Invoice
SLK 2-door convertible	$41000	$38130
Destination charge	595	595

STANDARD EQUIPMENT:

SLK: 2.3-liter supercharged dohc 4-cylinder engine, 5-speed manual transmission, traction control, driver- and passenger-side airbags with automatic child recognition system, front side-impact airbags, antilock 4-wheel disc brakes, air conditioning w/dual-zone automatic climate control, interior air filter, power steering, telescoping leather-wrapped steering wheel, cruise control, leather upholstery, bucket seats, center console, cupholders, rear defogger, universal garage door opener, heated power mirrors w/driver-side automatic day/night, power windows, power locks, remote keyless entry, automatic day/night rearview mirror, outside temperature indicator, Bose AM/FM/cassette w/CD changer controls, remote decklid release, tachometer, visor mirrors, floormats, power retractable steel hardtop, theft-deterrent system, heated headlight washers, front and rear fog lights, 205/55VR16 front tires, 225/50VR16 rear tires, alloy wheels.

OPTIONAL EQUIPMENT:
Major Packages

Sport Pkg. SP1	4050	3767

Sculpted front and rear fascias, bodyside skirts, projector beam fog lights, 225/45ZR17 front tires, 245/40ZR17 rear tires, monoblock alloy wheels.

K2 Pkg.	1795	1454

Includes integrated portable cellular telephone and 6-disc CD changer.

K2A Pkg.	2190	—

Includes integrated portable voice-activated cellular telephone and 6-disc CD changer.

Designo Copper Edition	4700	4371

Copper-colored sport seats, center console, and roll bar trim, copper/charcoal steering wheel and floormats. Requires heated seats.

Designo Electric Green Edition	4250	3953

Sport seats, charcoal-colored steering wheel and center console, charcoal/light green floormats. Requires heated seats.

Powertrains

5-speed automatic transmission	900	837

Comfort and Convenience

Heated seats	605	563

MERCURY COUGAR

Front-wheel-drive sports coupe; similar to Ford Contour
Base price range: $16,445-$16,945. Built in USA. **Also consider:** Acura CL, Honda Prelude, Mitsubishi Eclipse, Volkswagen New Beetle

FOR • Exterior finish **AGAINST** • Rear visibility • Rear-seat room

This compact 4-seat hatchback based on the Ford Contour sedan debuted for '99 and is little changed for 2000. The base 4-cylinder Cougar comes only with manual transmission, the plusher V6 gets

Mercury Cougar

manual or automatic. Options include front side airbags, antilock brakes, and, with the V6, traction control. A V6 Sport Group includes rear disc brakes (versus drums) and 16-inch wheels in place of 15s. For 2000, the driver's door map pocket is deleted, the ashtray and cigarette lighter become optional, and, as on other 2000 Ford Motor Company cars, an emergency escape release with glow-in-the-dark handle is added to the cargo area.

EVALUATION Cougar's base powerteam is reasonably peppy. The V6 adds some low-end muscle, but its passing power is unimpressive, as is its 0-60-mph acceleration (9.9 seconds for our automatic test car). Neither engine matches comparable Japanese units for refinement or high-revving fun. A 5-speed V6 averaged 19.9 mph in our tests, an automatic V6 20.7. Cougar handles well, but lacks the twisty-road agility of most import-brand rivals. The V6 Sport Group improves roadability at the expense of a thumpy, nervous ride. Brake-pedal feel is inconsistent—mushy on one test car, touchy on another—though stopping power is adequate. Road rumble and exhaust noise are intrusive. Most sport-coupe interiors feel claustrophobic and Cougar's is no exception. Front head and leg room are adequate and the bucket seats afford good lateral support, though none of our drivers gives them high marks for comfort. The cramped rear seat is a preteen environment, and the cabin abounds with hard, cheap-looking plastic. The hatchback design and split-folding seatbacks provide generous cargo space, but liftover is high. Cougar costs substantially less than a Honda Prelude, but its biggest competitive threat is probably Mitsubishi's 2000 Eclipse.

ENGINES

	dohc I4	dohc V6
Size, liters/cu. in.	2.0/121	2.5/155
Horsepower @ rpm	125 @ 5500	170 @ 6250
Torque (lbs./ft.) @ rpm	130 @ 4000	165 @ 4250
Availability	S	O
EPA city/highway mpg		
5-speed OD manual	24/34	19/28
4-speed OD automatic		20/29

PRICES

Mercury Cougar	Retail Price	Dealer Invoice
4-cylinder 2-door hatchback	$16445	$15021
V6 2-door hatchback	16945	15466
Destination charge	425	425

STANDARD EQUIPMENT:

4-cylinder: 2.0-liter dohc 4-cylinder engine, 5-speed manual transmission, driver- and passenger-side airbags, emergency inside trunk release, air conditioning, interior air filter, variable-assist power steering, tilt steering wheel, cloth front bucket seats, power height-adjustable driver seat, split folding rear seat, heated power mirrors, power windows, power door locks, AM/FM/cassette, digital clock, tachometer, trip computer, auxiliary power outlet, driver-side illuminated visor mirror, passenger-side visor mirror, rear defogger, cupholder, variable intermittent wipers, power decklid release, front floormats, theft-deterrent system, 205/60R15 tires, alloy wheels.
V6 adds: 2.5-liter dohc V6 engine, upgraded suspension.

OPTIONAL EQUIPMENT:
Major Packages

Convenience Group, 4-cylinder	615	547

Cruise control, remote keyless entry, rear wiper/washer.

Convenience Group, V6	720	641

Cruise control, remote keyless entry, rear wiper/washer, AM/FM/CD player.

Prices are accurate at time of publication; subject to manufacturer's changes.

	Retail Price	Dealer Invoice
Sport Group, V6	$815	$725

Leather-wrapped steering wheel and shift knob, upgraded sport seats w/driver-side manual lumbar adjustment, center console w/storage, reading lights, glove box light, additional warning lights, illuminated visor mirrors, fog lights, rear spoiler, 4-wheel disc brakes, 215/60R16 tires.

Powertrains

4-speed automatic transmission, V6	815	725
Traction control, V6	235	209
Requires antilock brakes.		

Safety Features

Antilock brakes	500	445
Front side-impact airbags	390	347

Comfort and Convenience

Power sunroof	615	547
6-way power driver seat, V6	235	209
Requires Sport Group.		
Leather upholstery, V6	895	797
Requires Sport Group and power driver seat.		
AM/FM/CD player	140	124
AM/FM/cassette/CD player	220	196
V6 w/Convenience Group	80	71
CD changer	350	312
NA with AM/FM/cassette/CD player.		
Smoker's Pkg.	15	13
Includes ashtray, lighter.		

Appearance and Miscellaneous

Rear spoiler, 4-cylinder	235	209
Polished alloy wheels, V6	250	223
Requires Sport Group.		

MERCURY GRAND MARQUIS

Mercury Grand Marquis

Rear-wheel-drive full-size car; similar to Ford Crown Victoria

Base price range: $22,415-$24,315. Built in Canada. **Also consider:** Buick LeSabre, Chrysler Concorde, Toyota Avalon

FOR • Passenger and cargo room **AGAINST** • Fuel economy

Redesigned two years ago, Mercury's largest car remains closely related to the Ford Crown Victoria and Lincoln Town Car—the only traditional full-size rear-drive sedans available from a North American manufacturer. Grand Marquis comes in GS and uplevel LS versions with a 200-horsepower V8 and automatic transmission. An optional Handling Package includes dual exhausts that add 15 horsepower, a numerically higher rear-axle ratio for faster getaways, performance tires, firmer damping, and rear load-leveling air springs. Four-wheel disc brakes are standard. Antilock brakes and traction control are optional. Maximum trailer weight is 2000 pounds.

Like other Ford Motor Company cars for 2000, Grand Marquis adds rear child-seat anchors and an emergency manual release with glow-in-the-dark emergency release handle for persons trapped in the trunk. Also new is BeltMinder, a chime and warning light to encourage buckling up. Grand Marquis' performance and accommodations mirror those of the Crown Victoria.

The Ford Crown Victoria report includes an evaluation of the Grand Marquis.

ENGINES

	ohc V8	ohc V8
Size, liters/cu. in.	4.6/281	4.6/281
Horsepower @ rpm	200 @ 4250	215 @ 4500
Torque (lbs./ft.) @ rpm	265 @ 3000	275 @ 3000
Availability	S	O

EPA city/highway mpg

4-speed OD automatic	17/24	17/24

PRICES

Mercury Grand Marquis	Retail Price	Dealer Invoice
GS 4-door sedan	$22415	$20897
LS 4-door sedan	24315	22626
Destination charge	630	630

STANDARD EQUIPMENT:

GS: 4.6-liter V8 engine, 4-speed automatic transmission, driver- and passenger-side airbags, 4-wheel disc brakes, emergency inside trunk release, air conditioning, variable-assist power steering, tilt steering wheel, cruise control, cloth front split bench seat, 8-way power driver seat, dual power recliners, cupholders, power mirrors, power windows, power door locks, AM/FM/cassette, integrated rear-window antenna, digital clock, variable intermittent wipers, rear defogger, passenger-side visor mirror, automatic headlights, power remote decklid release, floormats, theft-deterrent system, cornering lights, 225/60R16 tires, wheel covers.

LS adds to GS: upgraded upholstery, power driver-seat lumbar adjuster, remote keyless entry, key pad entry, Luxury Light Group (front and rear reading lights, illuminated visor mirrors), bodyside stripes.

OPTIONAL EQUIPMENT:

Major Packages

Handling Pkg., GS, LS	855	761
LS w/Premium Pkg.	535	476
Upgraded suspension, load-leveling rear air-suspension, performance axle ratio, dual exhaust, 225/60R16 handling tires, alloy wheels.		
Premium Pkg., LS	1000	890
Automatic climate control, power passenger seat w/power lumbar, leather-wrapped steering wheel, automatic day/night rearview mirror, compass, alloy wheels.		
Ultimate Pkg., LS	2400	2136
Premium Pkg. plus antilock brakes, traction control, electronic instrumentation, premium AM/FM/cassette.		

Safety Features

Antilock brakes	600	534
Antilock brakes w/traction control	775	690

Comfort and Convenience

Automatic climate control, LS	175	156
Includes outside-temperature indicator.		
Electronic instrumentation, LS	425	379
Digital instrumentation, tripminder computer. Requires automatic climate control.		
Luxury Light Group, GS	190	169
Includes front and rear reading lights, visors, illuminated visor mirrors.		
Remote keyless entry, GS	240	213
Includes key pad entry.		
Universal garage door opener, LS	115	102
Leather upholstery, LS	735	654
Requires Premium Pkg. or Ultimate Pkg.		
Premium AM/FM/cassette, LS	360	321
Requires automatic climate control.		
AM/FM/CD player, GS	140	124
6-disc CD player, LS	350	312
Requires Ultimate Pkg.		
Rear air suspension, LS	270	240
Tuned for softer ride.		
Alloy wheels, LS	320	285

MERCURY MOUNTAINEER   `RECOMMENDED`

Rear- or 4-wheel-drive midsize sport-utility vehicle; similar to Ford Explorer

Base price range: $27,370-$29,835. Built in USA. **Also consider:** Jeep Grand Cherokee, Mercedes-Benz M-Class, Toyota 4Runner

Mercury Mountaineer

FOR • Acceleration • Cargo room • Visibility • Build quality
AGAINST • Fuel economy • Ride

Mercury's upscale version of the 4-door Ford Explorer adds a couple of luxury options groups for 2000. Mountaineer offers rear- and 4-wheel drive with a choice of an overhead-cam V6 with a 5-speed automatic transmission or a V8 with 4-speed automatic. V6 models with 4WD get Ford's Control Trac system, which need not be disengaged on dry pavement. V8 versions have permanently engaged 4WD. Options include front side airbags, rear load-leveling suspension, and Ford Motor Company's Reverse Sensing System, which signals an audible warning when the vehicle backs up close to an object.

The new luxury options groups are called Monterey and, for V8 models only, Premiere. Both include woodgrain interior trim and color-keyed bodyside moldings, running boards, and bumpers, among other amenities. The Premiere adds steering-wheel audio controls, a color-keyed grille, special spruce green paint, and exclusively, 16-inch tires on 5-spoke alloy wheels (compared to 15s on other models). Mountaineer's performance and accommodations mirror those of comparably equipped Explorers.

The Ford Explorer report includes an evaluation of the Mountaineer.

ENGINES

	ohc V6	ohv V8
Size, liters/cu. in.	4.0/245	5.0/302
Horsepower @ rpm	210 @ 5250	215 @ 4200
Torque (lbs./ft.) @ rpm	240 @ 3250	288 @ 3300
Availability	S	O
EPA city/highway mpg		
4-speed OD automatic		14/19
5-speed automatic	15/20[1]	

1. 15/19 w/4WD.

PRICES

Mercury Mountaineer	Retail Price	Dealer Invoice
4-door wagon, 2WD	$27370	$24706
4-door wagon, 4WD	29370	26466
4-door wagon, AWD	29835	26876
Destination charge	550	550

STANDARD EQUIPMENT:

2WD: 4.0-liter V6 engine, 5-speed automatic transmission, driver- and passenger-side airbags, antilock 4-wheel disc brakes, air conditioning, power steering, tilt leather-wrapped steering wheel, cruise control, cloth front captain chairs, split folding rear seat, floor console, cupholders, power mirrors, power windows, power door locks, intermittent rear wiper/washer, rear defogger, AM/FM/cassette, digital clock, tachometer, illuminated visor mirrors, variable intermittent wipers, auxiliary power outlets, cargo cover, map lights, floormats, theft-deterrent system, running boards, roof rack, two-tone paint, rear privacy glass, fog lights, full-size spare tire, 225/70R15 tires, alloy wheels.

4WD adds: Control Trac full-time 4-wheel drive, 2-speed transfer case.

AWD adds: 5.0-liter V8 engine, 4-speed automatic transmission, permanent 4-wheel drive, limited-slip differential, Trailer Tow Pkg. (heavy-duty flasher, trailering harness), 235/75R15 all-terrain white-letter tires.

OPTIONAL EQUIPMENT:
Major Packages

	Retail	Dealer
Luxury Group	1745	1483

Leather upholstery, 6-way power front sport bucket seats, automatic climate control, Mach AM/FM/cassette/CD player, unique two-tone paint. Requires Convenience Group.

	Retail Price	Dealer Invoice
Convenience Group	$1195	$1016

Cloth sport bucket seats, 6-way power driver seat, AM/FM/cassette/CD player, rear radio controls, remote keyless entry, key pad entry, autolock/relock system, overhead console w/compass and outside temperature indicator, automatic day/night rearview mirror, high series floor console, rear vent w/fan, automatic headlights, puddle lights.

Monterey Feature Group	495	421

Woodgrain interior trim, special carpeting, unique floormats, two-tone paint, color-keyed bodyside moldings, running boards and bumpers. Requires Convenience Group and Luxury Group.

Premiere Feature Group, 2WD, AWD	595	506

Universal garage door opener, Travelnote digital memo recorder, steering wheel radio controls, woodgrain interior trim, unique floormats, Spruce Green metallic paint, color-keyed grille, bodyside moldings, bumpers and running boards, 255/70R16 white letter tires. Requires Convenience Group, Luxury Group. 2WD requires 5.0-liter engine.

Powertrains

5.0-liter V8 engine, 2WD	465	395

Includes 4-speed automatic transmission, limited-slip differential, 3.73 axle ratio, 235/75R15 all-terrain tires. NA 4WD.

Limited-slip differential, 2WD, 4WD	355	302

Includes Trailer Tow Pkg. (heavy-duty flasher, trailering harness) and 3.73 axle ratio.

Safety Features

Front side-impact air bags	390	332

Requires Convenience Group.

Reverse Sensing System	245	208

Requires Convenience Group.

Comfort and Convenience

Automatic climate control	275	234

Includes steering wheel climate/radio controls. Requires Convenience Group and Mach AM/FM/cassette/CD player.

Leather sport bucket seats	950	808

Includes 6-way power front seats. Requires Convenience Group.

Universal garage door opener	215	182

Includes Travelnote digital memo recorder.

Power sunroof	800	680

Requires Convenience Group.

6-disc CD changer	370	314

Requires Convenience Group.

Mach AM/FM/cassette/CD player	440	374

Requires Convenience Group.

Special Purpose, Wheels and Tires

Skid plates, 4WD, AWD	105	89
Rear load-leveling suspension, 4WD, AWD	395	336

Requires Convenience Group, leather sport bucket seats.

Chrome alloy wheels	495	421
235/75R15 all-terrain white-letter tires, 2WD, 4WD	230	196

MERCURY SABLE

Mercury Sable sedan

Front-wheel-drive midsize car; similar to Ford Taurus
Base price range: $18,845-$22,345. Built in USA. **Also consider:** Chrysler Cirrus, Honda Accord, Oldsmobile Intrigue, Toyota Camry

Because Ford's Taurus gets a major update for year-2000, the

Prices are accurate at time of publication; subject to manufacturer's changes.

functionally identical Sable does too. Appearance changes include a new grille and hood, and new tail styling.

Sedans and wagons return and come in base GS and uplevel LS trim. Standard is a 153-horsepower overhead-valve 3.0-liter V6; a 200-hp twincam V6 is an LS option. A 4-speed automatic is the only transmission. Antilock brakes are optional, and traction control is newly available. Standard 16-inch wheels replace 15s and the chassis is revised in an effort to improve ride and handling.

Five-passenger seating with front buckets or 6-passenger seating with a front bench are available. Unlike its Taurus cousin, the Sable wagon does not offer a 2-place third-row seat. Like the Taurus, Sable gets a revised dashboard and extra in-cabin storage. Power-adjusting foot pedals are standard on LS and optional on GS.

Front head/chest side airbags are a first-time option, and all Sables get Ford's Advanced Restraints System. This is designed to minimize airbag injuries to front-seat occupants by gauging the severity of a crash, recognizing variables such as seat position, then deciding whether to deploy the front airbags and at what power. Initially, the system works only for the driver's side, but will later become operative for the passenger side. The system does not control the side airbags, but does modulate the new seatbelt pretensioners for both front seats. Sedans get an emergency trunklid release designed to free anyone trapped in the trunk. And all modes gain built-in rear child-seat anchors.

We have not yet tested the 2000 Sable, but its performance and accommodations are likely to mirror those of similarly equipped Tauruses. See the Taurus report for our evaluation of the Ford-badged version of these new cars.

ENGINES

	ohv V6	dohc V6
Size, liters/cu. in.	3.0/182	3.0/181
Horsepower @ rpm	153 @ 5000	200 @ 5750
Torque (lbs./ft.) @ rpm	182 @ 4000	200 @ 4500
Availability	S	O
EPA city/highway mpg		
4-speed OD automatic	NA	NA

PRICES

Mercury Sable	Retail Price	Dealer Invoice
GS 4-door sedan	$18845	$17177
GS 4-door wagon	20645	18779
LS 4-door sedan	19945	18156
LS Premium 4-door sedan	21245	19313
LS Premium 4-door wagon	22345	20292
Destination charge	550	550

STANDARD EQUIPMENT:

GS: 3.0-liter V6 engine, 4-speed automatic transmission, driver- and passenger-side air bags, 4-wheel disc brakes (wagon), emergency inside trunk release, air conditioning, variable-assist power steering, tilt steering wheel, cruise control, cloth upholstery, 6-passenger seating w/driver seat manual lumbar adjustment, column shift, split folding rear seat (wagon), third row seat (wagon), cupholders, power mirrors, power windows, power door locks, remote keyless entry, AM/FM/cassette, digital clock, power antenna (wagon), tachometer, variable intermittent wipers, rear defogger, visor mirrors, auxiliary power outlets, remote decklid release (sedan), cargo cover (wagon), rear wiper/washer (wagon), floormats, theft-deterrent system, roof rack (wagon), 215/60R16 tires, wheel covers (sedan), alloy wheels (wagon).

LS adds: 5-passenger seating w/front bucket seats, center console, floor shift, power driver seat w/power lumbar adjustment, split folding rear seat, power adjustable pedals, leather-wrapped steering wheel, alloy wheels.

LS Premium adds: 3.0-liter dohc V6 engine, automatic climate control, leather upholstery, remote keyless entry w/keypad, heated power mirrors, remote tailgate release, illuminated visor mirrors, automatic headlights, theft-deterrent system w/alarm, fog lights.

OPTIONAL EQUIPMENT:

Powertrains

3.0-liter dohc V6 engine, LS	695	619
Traction control, LS, LS Premium	175	156
Requires antilock brakes.		

Safety Features

Front side-impact airbags	390	347
Antilock brakes	600	534

Comfort and Convenience	Retail Price	Dealer Invoice
5-passenger seating, GS sedan	$105	$93
Includes center console, floor shift.		
6-passenger seating, LS Premium	NC	NC
Power driver seat, GS	395	352
Includes power lumbar support		
Power passenger seat, LS Premium	350	312
Requires front side-impact airbags.		
Power adjustable pedals, GS	120	107
Power sunroof, LS, LS Premium	840	747
Audio Group, LS, LS Premium	670	597
6-disc CD changer, Mach sound system.		

Appearance and Miscellaneous		
Alloy wheels, GS sedan	395	352
Chrome alloy wheels, LS, LS Premium	295	263

MERCURY VILLAGER

Mercury Villager

Front-wheel-drive minivan; similar to Nissan Quest

Base price range: $22,415-$27,115. Built in USA. **Also consider:** Chevrolet Venture, Dodge Caravan, Honda Odyssey, Toyota Sienna

FOR • Passenger and cargo room • Control layout **AGAINST** • Interior materials • Fuel economy

Villager offers an optional rear seat video entertainment system for 2000. Mercury's minivan was revamped for 1999, along with the Nissan Quest, with which it shares its design.

Villager returns in base, Sport, and luxury Estate models. All have dual sliding rear doors, a 3.3-liter V6 engine, automatic transmission, and front bucket seats. All models seat seven. Base versions get a second-row bench seat, Sport and Estate have a pair of standard second-row bucket seats. A 3-person second-row bench seat is a no-charge option on base and Sport models; this bench had been standard on the base model. Twin integrated second-row child seats are no longer available, however. All Villagers have a third-row bench seat that slides on built-in floor tracks. Available behind the third-row seat is a rear parcel shelf that adjusts to several heights. Side airbags and power sliding doors aren't available, but all models gain rear child-seat anchors for 2000.

The new optional $1295 entertainment system is for use by rear passengers and includes a VCR, 6.4-inch flip-down LCD screen, and multi-channel audio with three headphone jacks. Unlike similar setups in other minivans, this one includes remote VCR operation. Quest also offers this system, but at no extra charge. Also for 2000, remote keyless entry/alarm becomes standard on all Villagers, and leather upholstery is now standard on the Estate.

PERFORMANCE Villager and Quest are reasonably snappy away from a stop. But power in the 35-55-mph range is unimpressive, and highway passing response borders on inadequate with a full load and the air conditioning on. As in Nissan trucks that use this 3.3-liter V6, there's marked engine roar under heavy throttle. Wind and tire noise are par for the class, as is fuel economy. Our test Quest averaged 16.9 mpg.

On the upside, the relatively compact Villager and Quest have above-average minivan maneuverability, abetted by firm steering with ample feel. Base models have 15-inch tires, but the 16s on the Villager Estate and Sport and Quest SE provide notably crisper cornering response. All use the same suspension and it soaks up sharp bumps decently well, but overall ride quality doesn't match that of longer-wheelbase minivans like Dodge Grand Caravan and Toyota Sienna.

ACCOMMODATIONS These minivans are relatively cozy, with scant clearance between any of the seats. The front seatbacks are narrow, although supportive cushions make for good overall comfort. Step-in is low, but third-row entry/exit is tighter than in most minivans due to a lowish roof and narrow passageways.

Cargo room is slim with the third seat in its normal position, though the handy available adjustable-height rear parcel shelf greatly enhances versatility in stowing smaller items. The third-row bench doesn't remove, but can slide up to the front seats to free up a large cargo hold; too bad its release handle is so difficult to reach. The second-row seats are easy to take in and out, and maximum cargo space is good for the exterior size.

Interior storage includes a removable net between the front seats, double front-door pockets, and numerous bins and beverage holders, including a dual front cupholder that doesn't block any controls when in use.

Villager and Quest target an upscale audience but undercut that goal with an abundance of hard-surfaced interior plastic, industrial-looking switchgear, unfinished edges around door handles and map pockets, and some sharp-edge seat mounts. The Villager we tested also suffered a rattling rear seat.

VALUE FOR THE MONEY Like Mazda's MPV, Villager and Quest are smaller outside and inside than most rivals, but are more maneuverable. The absence of available side airbags and power sliding doors in the Mercury and Nissan are telling omissions for modern minivans, however. And acceleration and refinement need to be more competitive, too.

ENGINES
	ohc V6
Size, liters/cu. in.	3.3/200
Horsepower @ rpm	170 @ 4800
Torque (lbs./ft.) @ rpm	200 @ 2800
Availability	S

EPA city/highway mpg
4-speed OD automatic	17/24

PRICES
Mercury Villager	Retail Price	Dealer Invoice
Base 4-door van	$22415	$20230
Sport 4-door van	25415	22870
Estate 4-door van	27115	24366
Destination charge	605	605

STANDARD EQUIPMENT:
Base: 3.3-liter V6 engine, 4-speed automatic transmission, driver- and passenger-side airbags, interior air filter, front air conditioning, power steering, tilt steering wheel, cruise control, cloth upholstery, 7-passenger seating (front bucket seats, 2-passenger second row bench seat, 3-passenger third row folding bench seat), center console, cupholders, dual sliding rear doors, power mirrors, power front windows, power door locks, remote keyless entry, AM/FM/cassette, tachometer, variable intermittent wipers, illuminated visor mirrors, rear defogger, intermittent rear wiper/washer, auxiliary power outlets, floormats, theft-deterrent system, roof rack, cornering lights, 215/70R15 tires, wheel covers.

Sport adds: front and rear air conditioning, power driver seat, second row bucket seats, leather-wrapped steering wheel w/radio controls, rear radio controls, power rear quarter windows, overhead console w/conversation mirror, adjustable rear parcel shelf, map lights, rear reading lights, privacy glass, flip-open liftgate, two-tone paint, handling suspension, 225/60R16 tires, alloy wheels.

Estate adds: leather upholstery, memory driver seat and mirrors, power passenger seat, Premium sound system, heated power mirrors, universal garage door opener, Travelnote digital memo recorder, automatic headlights.

OPTIONAL EQUIPMENT:
Major Packages
Convenience Group, Base	995	846

Rear air conditioning w/rear controls, interior air filter, rear audio controls, overhead console, power rear windows, 6-way power driver seat, map lights, rear reading lights, additional courtesy lights, flip-open liftgate, privacy glass.

Rear Seat Entertainment System	1295	1101

Videocassette player, headphones, remote control, video game outlet, rear passenger controls, headphones.

	Retail Price	Dealer Invoice
Trailer Tow Prep Group	$250	$213

Trailer tow module and jumper harness, heavy-duty battery, full-size spare tire.

Safety Features
Antilock brakes	590	502

Comfort and Convenience
Rear air conditioning, Base	495	421
Automatic climate control, Sport, Estate	245	208
Power sunroof, Sport, Estate	775	659

NA w/7-passenger seating w/middle bench seat.

Electronic instrument cluster, Estate	295	251

Digital speedometer, digital odometer and dual trip odometers, outside temperature indicator, trip computer. Requires automatic air conditioning and Supersound AM/FM/cassette/CD player.

Premium AM/FM/cassette, Base	310	263
Supersound AM/FM/cassette/CD player, Sport, Estate	865	735

Includes 6-disc CD changer. Requires Electronic instrument cluster and automatic climate control.

6-disc CD changer	370	314
Leather upholstery, Sport	795	676
7-passenger seating w/second row bench seat, Sport	NC	NC
Alloy wheels, Base	395	336

MITSUBISHI DIAMANTE

Mitsubishi Diamante

Front-wheel-drive near-luxury car

Base price range: $24,997-$27,897. Built in Australia. **Also consider:** Acura TL, Infiniti I30, Lexus ES 300

FOR • Acceleration • Quietness • Ride **AGAINST** • Rear head room

Trimmed to a single offering last year, Mitsubishi's flagship sedan resurrects its former ES and LS model designations for 2000. The Diamante ES carries last year's base-level standard equipment but substitutes a CD player for a cassette player. The LS adds such features as leather upholstery, power sunroof, and 16-inch alloy wheels to ES's model's 15-inch steel wheels. Fog lamps, heated mirrors and front seats, and traction control are combined in an All-Weather option package for the LS. Antilock 4-wheel disc brakes are standard, but side airbags are unavailable. The sole powertrain is a 3.5-liter V6 engine and a 4-speed automatic transmission. A standard anti-theft engine immobilizer and an optional in-dash 6-disc CD changer are new for both models.

EVALUATION This torquey V6 provides satisfying go. We timed a Diamante at 8.1 seconds 0-60 mph and averaged 19.7 mpg with a healthy dose of highway driving. We recommend the optional traction control because the front tires can spin wildly on damp pavement; too bad this safety feature only comes grouped in an option package for the top model. Wind and road noise are low, but the engine isn't as smooth as the near-luxury norm. Most bumps are easily absorbed, but there's some float over fast humpbacks, and marked body lean in tight turns. Inside, four adults won't lack leg or foot space, but head clearance is marginal for 6-footers beneath the LS's standard power sunroof. Interior storage space is subpar, and the pop-out cupholders flimsy. The dashboard layout is rather busy and saddled with too-small radio buttons. Outward visibility is good. The trunk is usefully roomy and easy to load, though the lid hinges dip into the cargo area. Detail assembly is thorough and materials generally look good, but door closings are a bit tinny. In a very com-

Prices are accurate at time of publication; subject to manufacturer's changes.

petitive class, Diamante survives mostly on a feature-per-dollar basis.

ENGINES

	ohc V6
Size, liters/cu. in.	3.5/213
Horsepower @ rpm	210 @ 5000
Torque (lbs./ft.) @ rpm	231 @ 4000
Availability	S

EPA city/highway mpg

4-speed OD automatic	18/24

PRICES

Mitsubishi Diamante	Retail Price	Dealer Invoice
ES 4-door sedan	$24997	—
LS 4-door sedan	27897	—
Destination charge	470	470

Dealer invoice prices not available at time of publication.

STANDARD EQUIPMENT:

ES: 3.5-liter V6 engine, 4-speed automatic transmission, driver- and passenger-side airbags, antilock 4-wheel disc brakes, air conditioning w/automatic climate control, power steering, tilt steering wheel, cruise control, cloth upholstery, manual 10-way adjustable front bucket seats, center console, cupholders, power mirrors, power windows, power door locks, remote keyless entry, variable intermittent wipers, AM/FM/CD player, power antenna, digital clock, tachometer, illuminated visor mirrors, rear defogger, map lights, remote fuel-door and decklid releases, theft-deterrent system, full-size spare tire, 205/65HR15 tires, wheel covers.

LS adds: leather upholstery, 8-way power driver seat w/memory and power lumbar support, 4-way power passenger seat, leather-wrapped steering wheel w/radio controls, Infinity sound system, power sunroof, universal garage door opener, 215/60VR16 tires, alloy wheels.

OPTIONAL EQUIPMENT:
Major Packages

All Weather Pkg., LS	840	684

Traction control, heated front seats and mirrors, fog lights.

MITSUBISHI ECLIPSE

Mitsubishi Eclipse GS

Front-wheel-drive sports coupe

Base price range: $17,697-$21,187. Built in USA. **Also consider:** Acura Integra, Honda Prelude, Volkswagen New Beetle

FOR • Acceleration • Handling/roadholding • Instruments/controls • Front-seat comfort **AGAINST** • Road noise • Rear-seat room • Rear visibility

Mitsubishi redesigns its top U.S. seller for 2000, dropping turbocharging and all-wheel drive, but making a V6 available for the first time. The Japanese company's American-built Eclipse debuts as a front-wheel-drive hatchback coupe that's 2 inches longer in wheelbase, 3 inches longer overall, and some 2 inches taller than the car it replaces.

RS and GS models use a 4-cylinder engine, the top-line GT gets Eclipse's first V6. Both have power similar to the engines they replace and are related to the engines in Mitsubishi's Galant, which also lends the Eclipse its basic platform. Manual transmission is standard. Automatic is optional and, on the GS and GT, includes Mitsubishi's Sportronic manual-shift mode.

Front side air bags and antilock brakes are exclusive to the GT as part of a Premium Package option that also includes leather upholstery. Standard features include alloy wheels, air conditioning, CD

stereo, and power windows and locks. The RS has 15-inch wheels, the GS 16, and the GT 17. The GT adds aerodynamic body trim and has rear disc brakes instead of drums.

PERFORMANCE Proving that "bad boys" can grow up, the latest Eclipses are more refined than any of their predecessors. The old rough-and-tumble gives way to a pliant, comfortable sporty-coupe ride regardless of tire size. Handling remains alert and responsive, with little cornering lean and grippy front-drive predictability. There's still wheel patter on washboard roads, but it's not bothersome. Braking is good, too, but ABS should be available on all models, not just the GT with a pricey option package.

Eclipse's new engines are a big improvement. Where the old 2.0-liter fours were throbby and loud, the 2.4 is generally smooth and quiet. Even better, it packs respectable punch, at least with manual shift, which itself is now a pleasure to use. The automatic is responsive enough, and "Sportronic" helps get the most out of either engine. The V6 GT doesn't rocket away like the old turbocharged 4-cylinder models, but it's plenty quick—and suffers no irritating "turbo lag." An automatic GT averaged 23 mpg in our tests. Surprisingly, the V6 is hardly quieter than the 4-cylinder, while the hatchback build captures too much exhaust drone and admits noticeable tire noise except on glassy pavement. Wind rush, by contrast, is nicely tamed despite the retention of frameless door glass.

ACCOMMODATIONS Despite a more spacious cabin feel and a tad more actual head room and rear leg room, Eclipse remains a cozy 2+2 with a Yoda-size rear seat and limbo-dancer entry/exit. At least the front buckets hug the torso and are comfortable on long rides.

The driving position is low-slung, and visibility still difficult directly aft and over-the-shoulder. Taller drivers might wish the standard tilt steering wheel adjusted higher, but all models have a seat-height control. Gauges and most switchgear are clear and handy. Clock/audio readouts are eye-level in a remote central pod; the unorthodox location isn't as annoying as their too-dim daytime illumination. A similar lighting problem affects the air conditioner and recirculation buttons.

Cost-cutting is evident in the abundance of lightweight plastic interior panels. In-cabin storage is acceptable, and luggage space with the rear seat folded is generous, but the load lip is lofty and the hatch lid rather heavy. The doors are bulky, and closed with a tinny clang on models we tested.

VALUE FOR THE MONEY A maturing market dictated a more mature sporty coupe, and the new Eclipse is that. Not as inspiring as Honda's Prelude or as solid as Volkswagen's New Beetle, it still should easily find an audience. A GT would be our pick, but you won't feel penalized in one of the less expensive 4-cylinder models.

ENGINES

	ohc I4	ohc V6
Size, liters/cu. in.	2.4/143	3.0/181
Horsepower @ rpm	154 @ 5500	205 @ 5500
Torque (lbs./ft.) @ rpm	163 @ 4500	205 @ 4500
Availability	S[1]	S[2]

EPA city/highway mpg

5-speed OD manual	23/31	20/28
4-speed OD automatic	20/28	20/27

1. RS, GS; 145 horsepower and 155 lb-ft with automatic transmission. 2. GT; 200 horsepower with automatic transmission.

PRICES

Mitsubishi Eclipse	Retail Price	Dealer Invoice
RS 2-door hatchback, 5-speed	$17697	$16193
RS 2-door hatchback, automatic	18497	16295
GS 2-door hatchback, 5-speed	19047	17428
GS 2-door hatchback, automatic	20047	18343
GT 2-door hatchback, 5-speed	20187	18471
GT 2-door hatchback, automatic	21187	19385
Destination charge	435	435

STANDARD EQUIPMENT:

RS: 2.4-liter 4-cylinder engine, 5-speed manual or 4-speed automatic transmission, driver- and passenger-side airbags, variable-assist power steering, tilt steering wheel, air conditioning, interior air filter, cloth upholstery, front bucket seat w/driver height adjustment, front storage console, cupholders, folding rear seat, power windows, power door locks,

AM/FM/CD player, digital clock, tachometer, variable-intermittent wipers, auxiliary power outlets, rear defogger, automatic headlights, theft-deterrent system, dual outside mirrors, 195/65HR15 tires, alloy wheels.

GS adds: 5-speed manual or 4-speed automatic transmission w/manual-shift capability, cruise control, remote keyless entry, leather-wrapped steering wheel, power mirrors, power sunroof, split folding rear seat, front lumbar adjustments, fog lights, 205/55HR16 tires.

GT adds: 3.0-liter V6 engine, 4-wheel disc brakes, sport suspension, 215/50VR17 tires, deletes sunroof, fog lights.

OPTIONAL EQUIPMENT:
Major Packages

	Retail Price	Dealer Invoice
Sport and Sound Pkg., GS	$700	$609

AM/FM/cassette/CD player w/Infinity sound system, theft-deterrent system w/alarm, rear spoiler.

Premium Pkg., GT 5-speed	2600	2262
GT automatic	2890	2512

Antilock brakes, traction control (automatic), leather upholstery, front side-impact airbags, power driver seat, power sunroof, AM/FM/cassette/CD player w/Infinity sound system, 4-disc CD changer, rear wiper/washer, theft-deterrent system w/alarm.

Sun and Sound Pkg., GT	1350	1175

AM/FM/cassette/CD player w/Infinity sound system, power sunroof, theft-deterrent system w/alarm.

MITSUBISHI GALANT

RECOMMENDED

Mitsubishi Galant ES V6

Front-wheel-drive compact car

Base price range: $17,357-$23,757. Built in USA. **Also consider:** Mazda 626, Nissan Altima, Oldsmobile Alero

FOR • Ride • Quietness • Steering/handling **AGAINST** • Rear-seat entry/exit

Traction control is newly available on the 2000 version of Mitsubishi's compact sedan. Base DE and step-up ES Galants use a 2.4-liter 4-cylinder engine. The ES V6, LS, and sporty GTZ models get a 3.0-liter V6. All come only with a 4-speed automatic transmission. Front side airbags are standard for LS and GTZ, optional for ES. Antilock brakes are standard on V6 models and optional on the 4-cylinder ES. The GTZ stands apart with a body-color grille, rear-deck spoiler, and white-faced gauges.

Traction control is introduced to the line as a standard feature on LS and GTZ models; it is unavailable on other Galants. For 2000, all Galants gain a rear center 3-point safety belt, and all models save the DE get a standard anti-theft system and driver-seat lumbar adjustment. An in-dash 6-disc CD changer is a new option.

PERFORMANCE This is a surprisingly entertaining compact sedan, especially with the V6 engine. Both engines are smooth performers. The 4-cylinder is decently brisk and becomes vocal only at higher rpm. Our test example managed 0-60 mph in 10.3 seconds. The V6 is smoother and quieter and took our test GTZ to 60 mph in 8.3 seconds. It also works in harmony with the automatic transmission to provide throttle response as good as any in this class. The V6 is fairly thrifty too, averaging between 21 mpg and 22.2 in our tests, though it requires premium fuel. In slightly more highway driving, our 4-cylinder automatic ES averaged 24 mpg on regular gas.

There's some tail hop over sharp lateral ridges, but Galant's ride is comfortably compliant and controlled. Handling is predictable and balanced, and straight-line tracking is good. The GTZ telegraphs small bumps more clearly than other models, but has slightly less body lean in tight corners and more precise steering. "Panic" stops are short, true, and level, even without antilock control. Wind rush is muted, but tire roar intrudes on coarse pavement.

ACCOMMODATIONS Galant has only average compact-class room for four adults, five in a pinch. Rear entry/exit could be better, but front seats are long-haul supportive. As usual with compacts, adult rear seaters have just enough head room for comfort, but not enough leg space to avoid riding knees-up.

Gauges and controls are well placed and obvious, while visibility is hindered only to the rear by the high-tail styling. The flat-floor low-liftover trunk is spacious enough, and all models except the base DE come with a folding rear seatback—though only the right side folds. Galant's driving feel is satisfyingly solid, though the trunk lid feels flimsy, and minor dash rattles plagued two examples we tested. Exterior finish appears fine across the board. Interior materials are pedestrian but pleasant, falling just shy of "upscale" even on the toney LS and GTZ.

VALUE FOR THE MONEY An agreeable, competent family 4-door, Galant mimics much of the driving satisfaction—if not the top-notch engineering—of a Honda Accord or Toyota Camry at lower cost. Put it on your shopping list.

ENGINES

	ohc I4	ohc V6
Size, liters/cu. in.	2.4/143	3.0/181
Horsepower @ rpm	145 @ 5500	195 @ 5500
Torque (lbs./ft.) @ rpm	155 @ 3000	205 @ 4500
Availability	S[1]	S[2]
EPA city/highway mpg		
4-speed OD automatic	21/28	20/27

1. DE, ES. 2. ES V6, LS, GTZ.

PRICES

Mitsubishi Galant	Retail Price	Dealer Invoice
DE 4-door sedan, automatic	$17357	$15963
ES 4-door sedan, automatic	18257	16615
ES V6 4-door sedan, automatic	20157	18338
LS 4-door sedan, automatic	23657	21524
GTZ 4-door, automatic	23757	21617
Destination charge	435	435

STANDARD EQUIPMENT:

DE: 2.4-liter 4-cylinder engine, 4-speed automatic transmission, driver- and passenger-side airbags, air conditioning, interior air filter, power steering, tilt steering wheel, cloth upholstery, front bucket seats, manual 8-way adjustable driver seat, center console, cupholders, power windows, power door locks, AM/FM/CD player, digital clock, automatic-off headlights, auxiliary power outlet, tachometer, rear defogger, variable intermittent wipers, remote fuel door and decklid releases, floormats, remote outside mirrors, 195/60HR15 tires, wheel covers.

ES adds: cruise control, leather-wrapped steering wheel, remote keyless entry, driver seat lumbar adjustment, split folding rear seat, power mirrors, illuminated visor mirrors, theft-deterrent system w/alarm, fog lights.

ES V6 adds: 3.0-liter V6 engine, antilock 4-wheel disc brakes, 205/55HR16 tires.

LS adds: traction control, front side-impact airbags, leather upholstery, 8-way power driver seat, power sunroof, Infinity sound system w/seven speakers, universal garage door opener, alloy wheels.

GTZ adds: sport suspension, rear spoiler, deletes universal garage door opener.

OPTIONAL EQUIPMENT:
Major Packages

Premium Pkg., ES 4-cylinder	2600	2257
ES V6	2400	2087

Front side-impact airbags, antilock brakes (ES 4-cylinder), power sunroof, Infinity sound system, heated mirrors, alloy wheels.

Comfort and Convenience

Power sunroof, ES	850	697
6-disc CD changer	—	—

MITSUBISHI MIRAGE

Front-wheel-drive subcompact car

Base price range: $11,757-$16,947. Built in Japan. **Also consider:** Ford Escort/ZX2, Honda Civic, Toyota Corolla

FOR • Fuel economy • Steering/handling **AGAINST**

Prices are accurate at time of publication; subject to manufacturer's changes.

Mitsubishi Mirage LS 4-door

• Acceleration (DE coupe) • Rear-seat room (coupes)

Antilock brakes are no longer available, but the standard-features list grows on 2000 versions of this entry-level subcompact. Mirage offers coupes and sedans in DE and LS trim. DE coupes retain a 92-horsepower 4-cylinder engine, while the DE sedan now shares a 113-hp 4-cylinder with the LS models. A 5-speed manual transmission is standard. A 4-speed automatic is optional on all but the LS sedan, where it's standard. ABS had been an LS option. For 2000, DEs exchange standard 13-inch wheels for the 14s used by LEs, and also get the tilt steering column previously exclusive to LEs. Air conditioning and power windows and locks are now standard instead of optional on the DE sedan, and a CD player is newly standard. Likewise, the LS sedan comes with a power sunroof and alloy wheels, which had cost extra.

EVALUATION Mirage is competitive but unremarkable. There's little difference between its engines for performance or economy, but the underpowered DE coupe qualifies as no more than an urban runabout, especially with automatic transmission. Fuel economy is a plus: the manual-shift LS coupe we tested averaged 30.9 mpg in mostly highway driving. Moderate-speed cornering is agile and predictable, but the ride is choppy on broken surfaces. Engine noise is relatively high, as is tire thrum. Interiors offer a tidy dash and clear outward vision, but also tight rear leg room and, on coupes, poor rear-seat entry/exit. All models have decently roomy trunks, and a split-fold rear seatback is now standard on all but the DE coupe, where it's optional. Workmanship is good, though interior materials are low-buck. Mirage doesn't challenge Honda or Toyota for refinement or overall value, but prices are right if you scrimp on options—and slow sales should bring healthy discounts.

ENGINES

	ohc I4	ohc I4
Size, liters/cu. in.	1.5/90	1.8/112
Horsepower @ rpm	92 @ 5500	113 @ 5500
Torque (lbs./ft.) @ rpm	93 @ 3000	116 @ 4500
Availability	S[1]	S[2]
EPA city/highway mpg		
5-speed OD manual	33/40	28/36
4-speed OD automatic	28/36	26/33

1. DE coupe. 2. DE sedan and LS models.

PRICES

Mitsubishi Mirage	Retail Price	Dealer Invoice
DE 2-door coupe, 5-speed	$11757	$10815
DE 2-door coupe, automatic	12557	11550
DE 4-door sedan, 5-speed	13987	12870
DE 4-door sedan, automatic	14787	13599
LS 2-door coupe, 5-speed	14607	13433
LS 2-door coupe, automatic	15407	14172
LS 4-door sedan, automatic	16947	15587
Destination charge	425	425

STANDARD EQUIPMENT:

DE coupe: 1.5-liter 4-cylinder engine, 5-speed manual or 4-speed automatic transmission, driver- and passenger-side airbags, power steering, tilt steering wheel, cloth/vinyl upholstery, front bucket seats, height-adjustable driver seat, front storage console, cupholders, rear defogger, auxiliary power outlet, visor mirrors, digital clock, remote fuel-door and decklid release, dual outside mirrors, 175/65R14 tires, wheel covers. **DE sedan** adds: 1.8-liter 4-cylinder engine, air conditioning, power windows, power door locks, AM/FM/CD player, cloth upholstery, split folding rear seat, intermittent wipers. **LS** adds: cruise control, power mirrors, power sunroof (sedan), variable

intermittent wipers, tachometer, map lights, 185/65R14 tires, alloy wheels (sedan).

OPTIONAL EQUIPMENT:

Major Packages	Retail Price	Dealer Invoice
Convenience Pkg., DE coupe	$1820	$1491

Air conditioning, power windows and door locks, AM/FM/CD player, cloth upholstery, split folding rear seat.

Premium Pkg., DE sedan	410	336

Cruise control, power mirrors, variable intermittent wipers, tachometer, map lights.

Sport Pkg., LS coupe	1030	844

Fog lights, rear spoiler, alloy wheels.

Comfort and Convenience

Air conditioning, DE coupe	880	720
Power sunroof, LS coupe	793	650
AM/FM/cassette, DE	352	247
AM/FM/CD player, DE coupe	473	333
LS sedan	399	299

LS sedan requires Value Pkg.

Remote keyless entry, DE sedan, LS	248	161

DE requires Power and Convenience Pkg. LS coupe requires Convenience Pkg.

Other options are available as port installed items.

MITSUBISHI MONTERO

Mitsubishi Montero

4-wheel-drive full-size sport-utility vehicle
1999 base price: $31,370. Built in Japan. **Also consider:** Ford Expedition, Isuzu Trooper

FOR • Passenger/cargo room **AGAINST** • Fuel economy • Entry/exit • Ride

Mitsubishi's "senior" sport-utility vehicle gains an up-level Endeavor edition for 2000, and adds some previously optional equipment to the base model. Standard on both are antilock brakes, rear jump seats for 7-passenger capacity, and, new this year, a security system with keyless entry, a CD player, and a roof rack. The new Endeavor comes standard with many items previously offered in the optional Value, Luxury, and All Weather packages, including wood interior trim, heated leather seats, power driver's seat, heated mirrors, and power sunroof.

EVALUATION The sole powertrain, a 3.5-liter V6 with 4-speed automatic transmission, feels strong enough in everyday duty, but Montero's 0-60-mph acceleration is mid-pack at about 10 seconds. We like the convenience of the standard "Active Trac" on-demand 4-wheel drive, which is usable on dry pavement and allows on-the-fly shifts between 2WD and 4-high. Still, Montero feels ponderous and leans heavily in turns, bumps come through with authority, and the tall body falls victim to crosswinds. There's abundant passenger and cargo space along with commanding visibility. However, interior materials don't match the lofty price, step-in is high, and the rear doors are hard to climb through. Overall, Montero's dated design shows its age, and slow sales reflect it. Most all rivals offer better value.

ENGINES

	ohc V6
Size, liters/cu. in.	3.5/213
Horsepower @ rpm	200 @ 5000
Torque (lbs./ft.) @ rpm	228 @ 3500
Availability	S
EPA city/highway mpg	
4-speed OD automatic	16/19

Ratings begin on page 213. Specifications begin on page 220.

PRICES

1999 Mitsubishi Montero	Retail Price	Dealer Invoice
Base 4-door wagon	$31370	$27916
Destination charge	455	455

STANDARD EQUIPMENT:

Base: 3.5-liter V6 engine, 4-speed automatic transmission, Active-Trac permanent 4-wheel drive, driver- and passenger-side airbags, antilock 4-wheel disc brakes, air conditioning, power steering, leather-wrapped tilt steering wheel, cruise control, cloth reclining front bucket seats, split folding second-row seat, split folding third-row seat, front storage console, cupholders, power mirrors, power windows, power door locks, tachometer, multi-meter (oil-pressure gauge, compass, outside-temperature indicator, voltmeter), map lights, AM/FM/cassette, power antenna, digital clock, variable intermittent wipers, rear defogger, intermittent rear wiper/washer, remote fuel-door release, auxiliary power outlets, visor mirrors, fog lights, side steps, rear privacy glass, engine oil cooler, tool kit, front and rear tow hooks, skid plates, full-size spare tire, 265/70R15 tires, alloy wheels.

OPTIONAL EQUIPMENT:
Major Packages

Value Pkg.	2300	1467
Manufacturer's discount price	1120	967

Remote keyless entry, theft-deterrent system, 10-disc CD changer, wood interior trim kit, floormats, cargo mat, cargo cover, roof rack, spare tire cover, wheel locks.

Luxury Pkg.	2826	2285

Leather upholstery, power driver seat, Infinity sound system w/amplifier and CD changer control, power sunroof.

Premium Pkg.	1110	910

Adjustable shocks, sport suspension, chrome alloy wheels.

All Weather Pkg.	774	635

Heated front seats, heated mirrors, headlight washers, locking rear differential.

Comfort and Convenience

CD player..	399	299

Special Purpose, Wheels and Tires

Trailer hitch w/harness..............................	252	164

MITSUBISHI MONTERO SPORT

Mitsubishi Montero Sport XLS

Rear- or 4-wheel-drive midsize sport-utility vehicle

Base price range: $22,527-$31,357. Built in Japan. **Also consider:** Ford Explorer, Honda Passport, Nissan Pathfinder, Toyota 4Runner

FOR • Cargo room • Instruments/controls • Build quality **AGAINST** • Fuel economy • Rear-seat entry/exit • Engine noise • Ride/handling

Mitsubishi's junior sport-utility wagon began its 2000 model year in the summer with a mild facelift and several new features. Montero Sport continues in ES, LS, XLS, and top-line Limited trim. All get a new front-end look and black tailgate trim instead of reflectorized red. The Limited also gets a new monochrome exterior. Interiors are revised with two-tone color schemes and larger front cupholders in a modified center console. Mechanically, rear coil springs replace leaf springs. All but the price-leader ES get larger front brakes and standard 16-inch wheels. Antilock 4-wheel disc brakes are standard on

Limiteds and on 4-wheel-drive LS and XLS models.

For 2000, the ES drops its 4-cylinder engine in favor of the 3.0-liter V6 that powers LS and XLS. The Limited's 3.5-liter V6 is borrowed from the "senior" Montero. ES is rear-wheel drive only; the others offer 4WD that's not for use on dry pavement. The ES also loses its manual transmission, so all models have standard automatic, which gains electronic shift control that adapts to driving style. Other linewide additions include an anti-theft engine immobilizer integrated with the ignition key, and standard CD audio. A limited-slip differential is included on Limited and available for XLS, replacing the previous locking-rear-differential option.

PERFORMANCE On- and off-road test drives show the new rear suspension makes for much smoother going, reducing tail jiggle on washboard surfaces and improving body control over large humps and dips. Springs and shock absorbers remain truck-tight, however, so don't expect a carlike ride. Same goes for handling, which is okay for a high-built SUV but doesn't inspire confidence on fast twisty roads, thanks to fairly vague steering and a somewhat tippy feel on the tall tires. Crosswind-stability at highway speeds isn't great on most SUVs, and it isn't here. There's also marked wind rush above about 60 mph. Road noise, by contrast, is fairly low.

Acceleration is nothing special. The 3.0-liter models move rather lazily from a standstill but cruise comfortably and have decent passing punch. The Limited's 3.5 liter delivers fine acceleration at all speeds, though it's scarcely quieter than the smaller V6, suffering marked fan noise when worked hard. Fuel economy should match our previous test averages: 14-17 mpg with the 3.0 liter, 16.8 with a 2WD Limited.

ACCOMMODATIONS The high floor and low roof that give Montero Sport a somewhat distinctive look pay no dividends in room or comfort. Ingress and egress are a tad tough, thanks to a fairly lofty step-in and, in back, narrow lower door openings. Tubular side steps are standard on LS, XLS, and Limited, but are mostly decorative. Aft head clearance is only adequate for 6-footers, and the rear bench is short in the backrest and too narrow for uncrowded three-adult travel. However, rear legroom is generous even behind a tall front-seater. The cargo load floor is rather high, but the available space is useful and rear-seat folding straightforward.

Drivers enjoy a carlike dash, but the front seats are low to the floor, forcing a legs-out position. Visibility suffers some from thickish rear roof pillars. All models have a tilt steering wheel, but it doesn't raise high enough to give taller drivers an unobstructed view of the gauges. Montero Sport retains a reassuring trucklike solidity, backed up by fine detail finish and attractive interior materials.

VALUE FOR THE MONEY It's a bit noisy, stiff-riding, and, in 3.0-liter form, slightly underpowered. But Montero Sport is priced right and should carry deeper discounts than more-popular rivals like Ford Explorer or Toyota 4Runner.

ENGINES

	ohc V6	ohc V6
Size, liters/cu. in.	3.0/181	3.5/213
Horsepower @ rpm	173 @ 5250	200 @ 5000
Torque (lbs./ft.) @ rpm	188 @ 4000	228 @ 3500
Availability	S[1]	S[2]
EPA city/highway mpg		
4-speed OD automatic	19/22[3]	17/20[4]

1. ES, LS, XLS. 2. Limited. 3. 18/21 w/4WD. 4. 16/20 w/4WD.

PRICES

Mitsubishi Montero Sport	Retail Price	Dealer Invoice
ES 2WD 4-door wagon	$22527	$20493
LS 2WD 4-door wagon	24777	22534
LS 4WD 4-door wagon	26807	24384
XLS 2WD 4-door wagon	27417	24936
XLS 4WD 4-door wagon	29327	26678
Limited 2WD 4-door wagon	29907	27203
Limited 4WD 4-door wagon	31357	28524
Destination charge	455	455

STANDARD EQUIPMENT:

ES: 3.0-liter V6 engine, 4-speed automatic transmission, driver- and passenger-side airbags, air conditioning, power steering, tilt steering wheel, cloth upholstery, front bucket seats, center console, cupholders, folding

---

Prices are accurate at time of publication; subject to manufacturer's changes.

rear seat, overhead console, power mirrors, power windows, power door locks, AM/FM/CD player, digital clock, tachometer, auxiliary power outlets, intermittent wipers, rear defogger, map lights, visor mirrors, floormats, theft-deterrent system, front and rear tow hooks, skid plates, full-size spare, 235/75R15 tires.

LS adds: cruise control, split folding rear seat, variable-intermittent wipers, rear wiper/washer, rear privacy glass, 255/70R16 tires, alloy wheels. **4WD** adds: part-time 4-wheel drive, 2-speed transfer case, anti-lock 4-wheel disc brakes.

XLS adds: leather-wrapped steering wheel, remote keyless entry, automatic day/night rearview mirror, compass, outside temperature indicator, power antenna, cargo cover, fog lights, roof rack. **4WD** adds: part-time 4-wheel drive, 2-speed transfer case, anti-lock 4-wheel disc brakes.

Limited adds: 3.5-liter V6 engine, limited-slip differential, antilock 4-wheel disc brakes, heated mirrors, Infinity sound system, power sunroof, illuminated visor mirrors, rear heater, side steps. **4WD** adds: part-time 4-wheel drive, 2-speed transfer case.

OPTIONAL EQUIPMENT:

	Retail Price	Dealer Invoice
Major Packages		
Preferred Pkg., LS	$755	$505
Side steps, roof rack, rear deflector.		
Premium Pkg., XLS	2655	2171
Leather upholstery, power sunroof, Infinity sound system, limited-slip differential.		
Leather Seating Pkg., Limited	1235	1008
Leather upholstery, heated front seats.		
Comfort and Convenience		
Remote keyless entry, LS	305	250
Includes theft-deterrent system w/alarm.		

NISSAN ALTIMA

RECOMMENDED

Nissan Altima SE

Front-wheel-drive compact car

Base price range: $15,140-$20,390. Built in USA. **Also consider:** Mazda 626, Mitsubishi Galant, Oldsmobile Alero

FOR • Steering/handling • Instruments/controls **AGAINST** • Rear-seat comfort • Automatic transmission performance

Nissan's best-selling car line gets a makeover for 2000, including first-time availability of front side airbags. Altima continues in base XE, volume GXE, sporty SE, and luxury GLE sedans, all with a 2.4-liter 4-cylinder engine that gains 5 horsepower. All come with manual or automatic transmission, except the GLE, which comes only with automatic. Antilock brakes are optional except for the base Altima.

Front side airbags are standard on GLE and optional for GXE and SE. Among other changes, SE and GLE gain standard 16-inch wheels and tires instead of 15s, plus a cross-car brace in the engine bay. All Altimas get revisions to steering and suspension, as well as fresh front and rear fascias, a new center console with automatic transmission, and the addition of rear cupholders. A new Appearance and Convenience Package gives the GXE the GLE's suspension and 16-inch wheels, among other items. Leather upholstery is standard for GLE, optional for SE.

PERFORMANCE This year's engineering work pays dividends. Altima's engine is smoother and free of its previous high-rpm boom. Ride is more controlled, thanks to firmer mounts for steering and suspension and new shock absorbers that provide max-

imum damping only on sharp bumps. There's less body lean and better all-around poise, especially on the 16-inch tires. Steering remains a bit numb on-center and requires more correcting than we like in straightline highway cruising. Wind noise is greatly reduced, and although Altima isn't as quiet as a Honda Civic, even its sport-tuned SE chassis soaks up rough stuff without thumpiness or drumming while still providing a reasonably absorbent ride.

Acceleration feels much stronger. We had no opportunity to clock our 2000 test cars, but Nissan says revised gearing clips almost a second from 0-60 mph sprints. That would be welcome because the 1999 automatic GLE we tested took a sleepy 10 seconds. Alas, the automatic transmission remains hesitant to downshift at midrange speeds, and sometimes slurs upshifts. The 5-speed GXE we tested averaged 20.4 mpg, compared to 23.4 for that '99 GXE automatic. Brakes are unchanged, so panic stops are undramatic but not exceptionally short.

ACCOMMODATIONS The 2000 makeover doesn't change Altima's interior dimensions, so front-seat room is good, even for 6-footers. Rear knee clearance is compatible with 6-footers, too, though toe space beneath the front seats is tight, and the back seat itself is short and too soft and ill-shaped to offer much support. Narrow lower rear door openings make for tight entry/exit, but that's true of most like-sized rivals.

The dashboard has convenient, guess-free controls that complement a well-judged driving position, enhanced for 2000 by more supportive, better bolstered bucket seats. Drivers also enjoy a standard front/rear cushion tilt except on base models, though its dual handwheel adjusters aren't the most convenient. Visibility suffers some from high-tail styling and wide roof posts. Trunk space remains good, though a broad sill can make for back-straining reaches and the lid hinges intrude into the load area. The 2000 Altimas we sampled had a more solid on-road feel than our '99 test cars and showed the same good all-around fit-and-finish.

VALUE FOR THE MONEY This year's changes add welcome spice to what was a competent if bland family compact. It's part of Nissan's image-building campaign and makes Altima a stronger class contender, especially as the many improvements come with virtually no price increase. Unfortunately, the 2000s probably won't be discounted as much as the '99s, which is also part of Nissan's plan.

ENGINES

	dohc I4
Size, liters/cu. in.	2.4/146
Horsepower @ rpm	155 @ 5600
Torque (lbs./ft.) @ rpm	156 @ 4400
Availability	S
EPA city/highway mpg	
5-speed OD manual	23/30
4-speed OD automatic	21/28

PRICES

Nissan Altima	Retail Price	Dealer Invoice
XE 4-door sedan, 5-speed	$15140	$14547
XE 4-door sedan, automatic	15940	15315
GXE 4-door sedan, 5-speed	16340	15016
GXE 4-door sedan, automatic	17140	15751
SE 4-door sedan, 5-speed	18640	16935
SE 4-door sedan, automatic	19440	17662
GLE 4-door sedan, automatic	20390	18525
Destination charge	520	520

STANDARD EQUIPMENT:

XE: 2.4-liter 4-cylinder engine, 5-speed manual or 4-speed automatic transmission, driver- and passenger-side airbags, power steering, tilt steering wheel, cloth upholstery, front bucket seats, center console, cupholders, power mirrors, power windows, tachometer, intermittent wipers, rear defogger, passenger-side visor mirror, remote fuel door and decklid release, theft-deterrent system, 195/65R15 tires, wheel covers.

GXE adds: split folding rear seat, 205/60R15 tires.

SE adds: 4-wheel disc brakes, air conditioning, leather-wrapped steering wheel and manual shift knob, cruise control, power door locks, remote keyless entry, AM/FM/cassette/CD player, digital clock, variable intermittent wipers, illuminated visor mirrors, universal garage door opener, auxiliary power outlet, sport-tuned suspension, fog lights, rear spoiler, 205/55R16 tires, alloy wheels.

GLE adds to GXE: 4-speed automatic transmission, front side-impact airbags, leather upholstery, 8-way power driver seat, luxury suspension, 205/55TR16 tires, deletes 4-wheel disc brakes, rear spoiler.

OPTIONAL EQUIPMENT:

	Retail Price	Dealer Invoice

Major Packages

	Retail Price	Dealer Invoice
XE Option Pkg., XE	$1999	$1734

AM/FM/CD player with digital clock, air conditioning, cruise control.

Value Option Pkg., GXE	999	918

Air conditioning, AM/FM/CD player, power door locks, remote keyless entry, illuminated visor mirrors, rear cupholders (automatic), variable intermittent wipers, auxiliary power outlet (automatic), glove box and map lights.

Appearance and Convenience Pkg., GXE	599	519

AM/FM/cassette/CD player, cargo net, luxury suspension, 16-inch alloy wheels. Requires Value Option Pkg.

Safety Features

Antilock brakes, GXE, SE, GLE	499	454

GXE, SE require front side-impact airbags.

Front side-impact airbags, GXE, SE	249	227

Comfort and Convenience

Leather upholstery, SE	1299	1126

Includes 8-way power driver seat.

Power sunroof, GXE, SE, GLE	849	737

GXE requires Value Option Pkg., Appearance and Convenience Pkg.

Appearance and Miscellaneous

Rear spoiler, GXE, GLE	409	289
Fog lights, XE, GXE	299	234

NISSAN FRONTIER

RECOMMENDED

Nissan Frontier crew cab

Rear- or 4-wheel-drive compact pickup truck

Base price range: $11,590-$22,240. Built in USA. **Also consider:** Chevrolet S-10, Ford Ranger, Toyota Tacoma

FOR • 4-door extended cab • Handling **AGAINST** • Rear-seat comfort • Acceleration (4-cylinder)

Introduction of a Crew Cab with independent, front-opening rear doors highlights the 2000 model year for Nissan's compact pickup.

Frontier Crew Cabs have front bucket seats and a 3-person rear bench. The cargo bed is only 4.6-feet long, but an optional tube-frame enclosure extends the bed, allowing longer loads to be carried with the tailgate down. Regular-cab Frontiers have a 6.5-foot bed. King Cabs, which are extended-cab models with no rear doors, have a 6.2-foot bed and two rear jump seats.

Regular cabs come only in XE trim with a 4-cylinder engine and 2-wheel drive. A V6 is standard in Crew Cabs and optional in King Cabs; both offer XE and uplevel SE trim. Automatic transmission is optional. Also new is the Desert Runner, a 2WD V6 King Cab built on the higher-riding 4x4 chassis also used by Crew Cabs.

Frontier's 4WD allows on-the-fly shifts up to 50 mph, but is not for dry pavement. Four-wheel antilock brakes are standard on 4x4s, Desert Runner, and all Crew Cabs; other 2WD Frontiers have rear-only ABS. Among competitors, the Dodge Dakota offers a crew cab, while Ford Ranger/Mazda B-Series offer rear-hinged doors that don't open independently of the front doors.

PERFORMANCE Frontier ranks with the best small pickups for ride and handling. That applies to the new Crew Cabs, which are the same length as the 2-door Kings and just as easy to maneuver. All models take bumps in stride and show only moderate body lean in hard turns, but beware the optional Off-Road Package, which makes the going much bouncier. Stopping power is only adequate with the rear-only ABS, swift and stable with the all-wheel system.

The 4-cylinder provides only adequate pep in 2WD models and bogs down in the weightier 4x4s. The V6 is stronger, but still less robust than those of most rivals. We timed a 4x4 V6 King Cab at a leisurely 11.2 seconds to 60 mph, and that with manual shift. Both engines are on the noisy side—especially the four, which is none too smooth, either. Wind and tire ruckus are also higher than the compact-truck norm. We averaged 18.5 mpg with an automatic 2WD regular-cab but only 14 mpg with two manual 4x4s, though in admittedly hard driving.

ACCOMMODATIONS Front-opening doors give Crew Cabs more-convenient rear access than the rear-hinged doors on Ranger/B-Series. Still, Crew Cabs' aft entryways are quite narrow, and there's little leg room ahead of the hard back bench unless a front seat is shoved far forward. Front room in any model is generous, but the King Cab's rear jump seats are just as small and tough to reach as any rival's.

We like Frontier's convenient carlike dash, but not the pull-out umbrella-style hand brake. And the automatic transmission's column shifter on bench-seat models interferes with the nearby wiper stalk and the driver's view of the climate controls. Materials and workmanship stand comparison with any brand's.

VALUE FOR THE MONEY Always competent and comfortable, Frontier is coming abreast of competitors with the new Crew Cabs and wider V6 availability. It's still not the brawniest or most-refined small truck, however, and 4-wheel ABS should be offered on more models. But prices are attractive enough to warrant our Recommended stamp.

ENGINES

	dohc I4	ohc V6
Size, liters/cu. in.	2.4/146	3.3/201
Horsepower @ rpm	143 @ 5200	170 @ 4800
Torque (lbs./ft.) @ rpm	154 @ 4000	200 @ 2800
Availability	S	S[1]

EPA city/highway mpg

5-speed OD manual	22/26[2]	16/19
4-speed OD automatic	20/24	15/19

1. Desert Runner, Crew Cab; optional, King Cab. 2. 18/21 w/4WD.

PRICES

Nissan Frontier	Retail Price	Dealer Invoice
XE 2WD regular cab, 5-speed	$11590	$10900
XE 2WD regular cab, automatic	12640	11888
XE 2WD King Cab, 5-speed	13540	12594
XE 2WD King Cab, automatic	14590	13570
XE 4WD King Cab, 5-Speed	17340	15946
XE 4WD King Cab V6, 5-speed	18340	16865
XE 4WD King Cab V6, automatic	19390	17831
SE 4WD King Cab V6, 5-speed	20490	18628
SE 4WD King Cab V6, automatic	21540	19583
XE Desert Runner 2WD King Cab, 5-speed	15740	14639
XE Desert Runner 2WD King Cab, automatic	16790	15615
SE Desert Runner 2WD King Cab, 5-speed	17890	16451
XE Desert Runner 2WD King Cab, automatic	18940	17417
XE 2WD Crew Cab, 5-speed	17290	16081
XE 2WD Crew Cab, automatic	18340	17058
XE 4WD Crew Cab, 5-speed	19890	18291
XE 4WD Crew Cab, automatic	20940	19256
SE 2WD Crew Cab, 5-speed	18590	17095
SE 2WD Crew Cab, automatic	19640	18060
SE 4WD Crew Cab, 5-speed	21190	19265
SE 4WD Crew Cab, automatic	22240	20219
Destination charge	520	520

Prices are accurate at time of publication; subject to manufacturer's changes.

STANDARD EQUIPMENT:

XE: 2.4-liter dohc 4-cylinder engine, 5-speed manual or 4-speed automatic transmission, driver- and passenger-side airbags, rear antilock brakes, power steering, cloth bench seat (regular Cab), split bench seat (King Cab), rear jump seats (King Cab), cupholder, carpeting, AM/FM/cassette, digital clock, tachometer, intermittent wipers, auxiliary power outlet, black bumpers, dual outside mirrors, skid plates, 215/65R15 tires. **4WD** adds: part-time 4-wheel drive, manually locking front hubs, 2-speed transfer case, 5-speed manual transmission, front and rear antilock brakes, center console, fender flares, full-size spare tire, 235/70R15 tires.

XE 4WD King Cab V6 adds to XE 4WD: 3.3-liter V6 engine, 5-speed manual or 4-speed automatic transmission, automatic locking front hubs, front bucket seats, center console, fender flares.

SE 4WD King Cab adds: air conditioning, tilt leather-wrapped steering wheel, cruise control, deluxe AM/FM/CD player, map lights, variable intermittent wipers, passenger-side visor mirror, chrome bumpers, cargo box light, privacy glass, sliding rear window, fog lights, step rails, 265/70R15 tires, alloy wheels.

XE Desert Runner King Cab adds to XE: 3.3-liter V6 engine, front and rear antilock brakes, front bucket seats, center console, sliding rear window, fender flares, raised suspension, full-size spare tire, 235/70R15 tires.

SE Desert Runner King Cab adds: air conditioning, tilt leather-wrapped steering wheel, cruise control, deluxe AM/FM/CD player, map lights, variable intermittent wipers, passenger-side visor mirror, chrome bumpers, cargo box light, rear privacy glass, fog lights, step rails, 255/65R16 tires, alloy wheels.

XE Crew Cab adds to XE King Cab: 3.3-liter V6 engine, front and rear antilock brakes, air conditioning, front bucket seats, center console, cloth rear bench seat, rear privacy glass, sliding rear window, fender flares, chrome bumpers, full-size spare tire, 235/70R15 tires. **4WD** adds: part-time 4-wheel drive, automatic locking hubs, 2-speed transfer case.

SE Crew Cab adds: tilt leather-wrapped steering wheel, variable intermittent wipers, passenger-side visor mirror, AM/FM/CD player, fog lights, color-keyed bumpers, step rails, 255/65R16 tires, alloy wheels. **4WD** adds: part-time 4-wheel drive, automatic locking hubs, 2-speed transfer case.

OPTIONAL EQUIPMENT:
Major Packages

	Retail Price	Dealer Invoice
Value Truck Pkg., XE regular cab	$549	$516
XE King Cab, XE Desert Runner	949	893

Air conditioning, deluxe AM/FM/cassette, rear privacy glass and sliding rear window (King Cab), cargo box light (King Cab), chrome bumpers, chrome grille, alloy wheels (King Cab).

Power Pkg., King Cab	980	849
Crew Cab	1080	936

Power mirrors, power windows and door locks, remote keyless entry, cruise control, theft-deterrent system.

Popular Equipment Pkg., XE regular cab/King Cab, XE Desert Runner	1399	1213

Air conditioning, deluxe AM/FM/cassette, chrome bumpers and grille.

Value Plus Pkg., XE regular cab	649	563

Bucket seats, center console, sliding rear window, fender flares, alloy wheels. Requires Value Truck Pkg.

Value Plus Pkg., XE 2WD King Cab	349	303

Bucket seats, center console, tilt steering wheel, variable intermittent wipers, passenger side visor mirror, map lights, tailgate finisher, fender flares, alloy wheels. Requires Value Truck Pkg.

Value Plus Pkg., XE Desert Runner	699	606

Tilt steering wheel, variable intermittent wipers, passenger-side visor mirror, limited-slip differential, tailgate finisher, 265/70R15 tires. Requires Value Truck Pkg.

Value Plus Pkg., XE 2WD Crew Cab	599	519
XE 4WD Crew Cab	799	693

Tilt steering wheel, variable intermittent wipers, passenger-side visor mirror, limited-slip differential (4WD), Tailgate finisher, 265/70R15 tires, alloy wheels.

Sport Pkg., SE Crew Cab, SE King Cab, SE Desert Runner	749	650

Manual sunroof, AM/FM/cassette/CD player.

	Retail Price	Dealer Invoice
Appearance Pkg., XE King Cab, XE Desert Runner	$650	$564

Sliding rear window, cargo box light, privacy glass, alloy wheels.

Off-Road Pkg., 4WD King Cab V6	649	563

Limited-slip differential, tilt steering wheel, variable intermittent wipers, passenger-side visor mirror, 265/70R15 tires. Requires Value Truck Pkg.

Utility Pkg., 2WD SE Crew Cab	250	217
4WD Se Crew Cab	450	391

Roof rack, limited-slip differential (4WD).

Powertrains

Limited-slip differential, SE King Cab V6, Desert Runner	200	173
AM/FM/CD player, XE	469	310

Appearance and Miscellaneous

Bedliner	299	148
Bed extender	229	166

Post production options also available.

NISSAN MAXIMA

RECOMMENDED

Nissan Maxima SE

Front-wheel-drive midsize car; similar to Infiniti I30
Base price range: $21,049-$26,249. Built in Japan. **Also consider:** Honda Accord, Oldsmobile Intrigue, Toyota Camry/Solara

FOR • Acceleration • Steering/handling • Ride **AGAINST** • Manual shift action

A redesigned 2000 Maxima debuted last spring with revised styling, added power, and more features. Nissan's flagship sedan remains a front-drive midsize car, but adds 2 inches to its wheelbase for slightly more interior and trunk volume. A 3.0-liter V6 returns, but with 222 horsepower, an increase of 32, and with maintenance intervals extended to 100,000 miles.

Three models are offered. GXE and sporty SE come with a 5-speed manual transmission or extra-cost 4-speed automatic. The automatic is standard on the top-line GLE. Antilock brakes are now standard rather than optional on all, and front side airbags are a first-time option. Traction control is optional for SE and GLE.

The SE again comes with a rear spoiler and firmer suspension and offers a 17-inch wheel/tire option. Sixteen-inch alloy wheels are standard on SE and GLE and optional in place of 15s on the GXE. Leather upholstery is standard on GLE, optional on SE, and unavailable on GXE. An anti-theft engine immobilizer is now part of the standard remote keyless-entry system.

PERFORMANCE The 2000 redesign improves an already smooth, swift, and polished performer. Maxima corners with grippy assurance and only mild body lean. The SE is a tad crisper in turns thanks to its sport suspension, but all models are agile and have quick, informative steering. That SE suspension results in a somewhat choppy ride over bumps that other models comfortably absorb. Credit Nissan for standardizing antilock brakes and for adopting rear discs for all models, plus slightly larger brakes all-around. The 2000 scrubs off speed quickly and consistently with excellent control.

We timed a 2000 GXE at 7.9 seconds 0-60 mph, same as our 1999 test model. But while it's no quicker than earlier models, Maxima continues to shine for its responsive powertrain. This V6 feels downright muscular, with fine punch off the line and enticingly strong passing power. And fuel economy is improved: Our 2000 test models averaged 20-22.5 mpg, versus 18.2 for the previous model.

Most Maximas are sold with automatic transmission, and our 2000 test models were free of the annoying lurch in full-throttle downshifts we criticized before. However, the manual transmission still suffers imprecise clutch takeup and slightly stiff shift action. Another dynamic quibble is annoying steering-wheel tug in hard takeoffs unless the front wheels are perfectly straight. This torque-steer effect isn't entirely cancelled even with the available traction control—which should be at least offered on the base GXE.

ACCOMMODATIONS Maxima remains a practical 4-seater for grownups, but the 2000 gives everyone a bit more wiggle room. Taller adults get enough head clearance beneath the optional moonroof to avoid challenging their haircuts (a problem in the old Maxima), and a more upright rear seatback pays comfort dividends on long trips. There's also a little extra aft leg space, but 6-footers still need to ride knees-up behind a similarly tall front occupant.

Gauges and switchgear remain simple and generally inviting, though lookalike knobs for audio volume and temperature are potentially confusing, and some of our test drivers found it a stretch to the main radio and climate system controls. Useful improvements include more rearward seat travel than even the lankiest drivers should need, easier-to-reach power seat controls, and a lower windshield base for slightly better visibility. A 60/40 folding rear seatback improves on the previous narrow pass-through, and the slightly larger trunk has a wider opening. Our test models were generally solid and well-finished, but we noticed minor body shudder over rough disturbances, plus a couple of annoying rattles inside.

VALUE FOR THE MONEY Maxima's natural rivals tend to be top-line V6 Toyota Camrys and Honda Accords, and the quiet, athletic 2000 fares well against these tough adversaries. Better still, Maxima base prices are down as much as $650 from '99, making this an outstanding value.

ENGINES

	dohc V6
Size, liters/cu. in.	3.0/183
Horsepower @ rpm	222 @ 6400
Torque (lbs./ft.) @ rpm	217 @ 4000
Availability	S
EPA city/highway mpg	
5-speed OD manual	22/28
4-speed OD automatic	20/28

PRICES

Nissan Maxima	Retail Price	Dealer Invoice
GXE 4-door sedan, 5-speed	$21049	$19247
GXE 4-door sedan, automatic	22749	20563
SE 4-door sedan, 5-speed	23649	21253
SE 4-door sedan, automatic	24149	21703
GLE 4-door sedan, automatic	26249	23590
Destination charge	520	520

STANDARD EQUIPMENT:

GXE: 3.0-liter dohc V6 engine, 5-speed manual or 4-speed automatic transmission, driver- and passenger-side airbags, antilock 4-wheel disc brakes, air conditioning, variable-assist power steering, tilt steering wheel, cruise control, cloth upholstery, front bucket seats, front console, cupholders, split folding rear seat, power mirrors, power windows, power door locks, remote keyless entry, tachometer, 4-speaker AM/FM/cassette, power antenna, digital clock, auxiliary power outlets, illuminated visor mirrors, intermittent wipers, rear defogger, automatic headlights, remote decklid and fuel door releases, map lights, theft-deterrent system, 205/65R15 tires, wheel covers.
SE adds: AM/FM/cassette/CD player w/6-speaker sound system, leather-wrapped steering wheel, floormats, fog lights, rear spoiler, sport-tuned suspension, 215/55R16 tires, alloy wheels.
GLE adds to GXE: 4-speed automatic transmission, air conditioning w/automatic climate control, outside temperature display, leather upholstery, 8-way power driver seat, 4-way power passenger seat,

leather-wrapped steering wheel, variable intermittent wipers, AM/FM/cassette/CD player w/Bose 7-speaker sound system, universal garage door opener, power decklid release, fog lights, 215/55R16 tires, alloy wheels.

OPTIONAL EQUIPMENT:

Major Packages	Retail Price	Dealer Invoice
GXE Comfort and Convenience Pkg., GXE automatic	$1069	$950

AM/FM/cassette/CD player w/6-speaker sound system, 8-way power driver seat, variable intermittent wipers, universal garage door opener, cargo net, 215/55R16 tires, alloy wheels.

SE Comfort and Convenience Pkg., SE	1799	1598

Power sunroof, 8-way power driver seat, universal garage door opener, variable intermittent wipers, cargo net, 225/50VR17 tires (SE).

Deluxe Seating Pkg., GXE automatic, SE, GLE	539	467

Front side-impact airbags, heated front seats and mirrors, low washer fluid warning light, special trunk lid trim. GXE and SE require Comfort and Convenience Pkg.

SE Leather Trim Pkg., SE	1349	1171

Leather upholstery, 4-way power passenger seat, automatic climate control, outside temperature display.

Meridian Edition, GXE automatic, SE, GLE	539	467

Front side-impact airbags, heated front seats and mirrors, low windshield washer fluid warning light. GXE and SE requires Comfort and Convenience Pkg.

Powertrains

Traction control, SE automatic, GLE	299	259

Comfort and Convenience

Bose sound system, SE	899	798
Requires Comfort and Convenience Pkg.		
AM/FM/cassette/CD player, GXE	—	—
6-disc CD changer, GXE automatic, GLE	719	338
GXE requires Comfort and Convenience Pkg.		
Power sunroof, GXE automatic, GLE	899	779
GXE requires Comfort and Convenience Pkg.		

Appearance and Miscellaneous

Rear spoiler, GXE, GLE	479	361

Post production options also available.

NISSAN PATHFINDER

Nissan Pathfinder LE

Rear- or 4-wheel-drive midsize sport-utility vehicle; similar to Infiniti QX4
Base price range: $26,399-$31,299. Built in Japan. **Also consider:** Ford Explorer, Toyota 4Runner

FOR • Steering/handling • Cargo room • Build quality **AGAINST** • Rear-seat entry/exit • Rear-seat room • Engine noise

Pathfinder is in for a short 2000 model year after a "1999½" update featuring revised styling and first-time availability of side airbags. With arrival this fall of the lower-priced Xterra, Pathfinder becomes Nissan's "senior" SUV, aimed at older, more affluent buyers. The 2001 Pathfinders bow in Spring 2000 with changes expected to include a more powerful engine, likely a 3.5-liter V6.

Until then, XE, SE, and LE models carry over with a 3.3-liter V6 and 2- or 4-wheel drive. XE and LE models have automatic transmission, while SE offers automatic or manual, plus its own eggcrate grille. Maximum towing capacity is 5000 pounds.

Prices are accurate at time of publication; subject to manufacturer's changes.

Antilock brakes and 16-inch wheels are standard. Pathfinder's 4WD system has a floor-mounted transfer-case lever and on-the-fly shifting up to 50 mph, but must be disengaged on dry pavement. Front side airbags are included in a leather upholstery option package for SE and LE models; the package lists for almost $2000. Dropped for 2000 is an optional Off Road Package with outside spare tire. Pathfinder is the basis for the luxury QX4 from Nissan's Infiniti division.

PERFORMANCE Although the mid-'99 revisions included a little more power and torque, they also added more than 200 pounds, so Pathfinder's acceleration remains unimpressive. Low-speed throttle response is good, but 0-60 mph takes about 10.5 seconds for 2WD versions, 11.2 for 4x4s—both mediocre figures. In our tests, an early 1999 automatic 4x4 averaged 14.1 mpg, also on the low side for a 6-cylinder midsize SUV.

Pathfinder's tight suspension and linear steering aid driver control—a good thing, because there's marked body lean and tire squeal in fast turns. Ride is firm but not jarring over bumps. Wind and road noise are not intrusive, but Pathfinder's V6 is rather gruff and growly when worked hard. And unlike an increasing number of rivals, its 4WD still lacks electronic shifting and dry-pavement capability. Those conveniences are reserved for the pricier QX4.

ACCOMMODATIONS Head room is good all around, but rear leg space is barely adequate for those over 5-foot-10. Ride height is rather lofty, and narrow rear-door openings further complicate entry/exit. The dashboard is attractive and functional, but the driver's over-the-shoulder vision is impeded by thick roof pillars. Cargo volume is good, but rear-seat conversion is a bit tedious. Fit, finish, and materials are top-notch.

VALUE FOR THE MONEY It's solidly built, and the available front side airbags are a safety plus. But Pathfinder costs more than some domestic rivals, yet doesn't match their room, power, or the convenience of available full-time 4WD. The 2001 models will need to correct some of those competitive deficits.

ENGINES

	ohc V6
Size, liters/cu. in.	3.3/200
Horsepower @ rpm	170 @ 4800
Torque (lbs./ft.) @ rpm	200 @ 2800
Availability	S
EPA city/highway mpg	
5-speed OD manual	17/19[1]
4-speed OD automatic	16/19[2]

1. 16/18 w/4WD. 2. 15/19 w/4WD.

PRICES

Nissan Pathfinder	Retail Price	Dealer Invoice
XE 2WD 4-door wagon, automatic	$26399	$24001
XE 4WD 4-door wagon, automatic	28399	25819
SE 2WD 4-door wagon, 5-speed	27349	24865
SE 2WD 4-door wagon, automatic	28349	25774
SE 4WD 4-door wagon, 5-speed	29349	26683
SE 4WD 4-door wagon, automatic	30349	27592
LE 2WD 4-door wagon, automatic	29299	26637
LE 4WD 4-door wagon, automatic	31299	28455
Destination charge	520	520

STANDARD EQUIPMENT:

XE: 3.3-liter V6 engine, 4-speed automatic transmission, driver- and passenger-side airbags, antilock brakes, power steering, tilt steering wheel, air conditioning, cloth upholstery, height-adjustable front bucket seats w/adjustable lumbar support, center storage console with armrest, split folding and reclining rear seat, cupholders, AM/FM/CD player, digital clock, tachometer, passenger-side visor mirror, variable intermittent wipers, rear defogger, rear intermittent wiper/washer, remote fuel-door release, auxiliary power outlets, map lights, theft-deterrent system, dual outside mirrors, rear privacy glass, roof rails, full-size spare tire, 245/70R16 tires, alloy wheels. **4WD** models add: part-time 4-wheel drive, 2-speed transfer case.

SE adds: 5-speed manual or 4-speed automatic transmission, cruise control, leather-wrapped steering wheel, suede-look upholstery, 8-way manual driver seat w/height and lumbar adjustment, 4-way

manual passenger seat, heated power mirrors, power windows, power door locks, remote keyless entry, cargo cover, theft-deterrent system w/alarm, roof rack, fender flares, tubular step rails, tow hooks, 255/65R16 tires. **4WD** models add: part-time 4-wheel drive, 2-speed transfer case.

LE adds: 4-speed automatic transmission, automatic climate control, outside temperature display, compass, Bose AM/FM/cassette/CD player, power antenna, universal garage-door opener, illuminated visor mirrors, running boards, fog lights, deletes tubular step rails. **4WD** adds: part-time 4-wheel drive, 2-speed transfer case.

OPTIONAL EQUIPMENT:

Major Packages	Retail Price	Dealer Invoice
Popular Pkg., XE	$1250	$1085

Cruise control, leather-wrapped steering wheel, heated power mirrors, power windows and door locks, remote keyless entry, theft-deterrent system w/alarm, cargo net and cover.

Popular Pkg., SE	NC	NC

Bose AM/FM/cassette/CD player, power antenna, cargo net, fog lights, rear air deflector.

Sunroof Pkg., SE	1099	953

Power sunroof, illuminated visor mirrors, universal garage door opener, outside-temperature display, compass. Requires Popular Pkg.

Sunroof Pkg., LE	NC	NC

Power sunroof.

Leather Pkg., SE 2WD automatic, LE 2WD	1799	1560
SE 4WD automatic, LE 4WD	1999	1734

Leather upholstery, 8-way power driver seat, 4-way power passenger seat, heated front seats (4WD), side-impact airbags. SE requires Sunroof Pkg.

Powertrains

Limited-slip differential, SE 4WD, LE 4WD	249	216

Requires Sunroof Pkg.

Comfort and Convenience

6-disc CD changer	719	338

Special Purpose, Wheels and Tires

Tow hitch	389	294

Post production options also available.

NISSAN QUEST

Nissan Quest

Front-wheel-drive minivan; similar to Mercury Villager
Base price range: $22,259-$26,699. Built in USA. **Also consider:** Dodge Caravan, Ford Windstar, Honda Odyssey, Toyota Sienna

FOR • Passenger and cargo room • Control layout
AGAINST • Interior materials

A video entertainment system is available at no extra cost on the 2000 version of Nissan's minivan. Quest shares its design with the Mercury Villager and both got a heavy makeover for 1999. A single body size is offered in GXE, sporty SE, and luxury GLE models. All have a Nissan V6 engine, automatic transmission, and dual rear sliding side doors. Antilock brakes are standard, but side airbags and power sliding doors are unavailable.

All Quests have a 3-person third-row bench seat that slides fore and aft on built-in floor tracks. SE and GLE get two second-row bucket seats. The GXE has a removable 2-place second-row bench that can be optionally fitted with child safety seats.

The SE model has a firmer suspension with 16-inch wheels

Ratings begin on page 213. Specifications begin on page 220.
CONSUMER GUIDE™

and performance tires; other models have 15-inch wheels. GLEs have leather upholstery, power front seats and, new for 2000, a rear stabilizer bar and simulated woodgrain interior trim. Other changes include perforated upholstery for the SE's available Leather Package. The new entertainment system is for use by rear passengers and includes a VCR, 6.4-inch flip-down LCD screen, and multi-channel audio with three headphone jacks. Unlike similar setups in other minivans, this one includes remote VCR operation. Villager also offers this system, but as a $1295 option. Quest and Villager are assembled by Ford in Ohio using a high percentage of Nissan parts. Quest's performance and accommodations mirror those of similarly equipped Villagers.

The Mercury Villager report includes an evaluation of the Quest.

ENGINES

	ohc V6
Size, liters/cu. in.	3.3/201
Horsepower @ rpm	170 @ 4800
Torque (lbs./ft.) @ rpm	200 @ 2800
Availability	S

EPA city/highway mpg

4-speed OD automatic	17/24

PRICES

Nissan Quest	Retail Price	Dealer Invoice
GXE 4-door van	$22259	$20236
SE w/cloth 4-door van	24399	21927
SE w/leather 4-door van	26699	23994
GLE 4-door van	26399	23725
Destination charge	520	520

STANDARD EQUIPMENT:

GXE: 3.3-liter V6 engine, 4-speed automatic transmission, driver- and passenger-side airbags, antilock brakes, front air conditioning, variable-assist power steering, tilt steering wheel, cruise control, cloth upholstery, 7-passenger seating, front bucket seats, second-row 2-passenger bench seat, third-row sliding 3-passenger bench seat, front storage console, under passenger-seat storage, cupholders, two sliding rear doors, heated power mirrors, power front windows, power door locks, remote keyless entry, AM/FM/cassette, digital clock, tachometer, variable intermittent wipers, illuminated visor mirrors, rear defogger, intermittent rear wiper/washer, remote fuel door/hatch releases, floormats, theft-deterrent system, rear privacy glass, cornering lights, roof rack, 215/70R15 tires, wheel covers.

SE w/cloth adds: rear air conditioning, interior air filter, rear climate controls, AM/FM/cassette/CD player, leather-wrapped steering wheel w/radio controls, rear audio controls, conversation mirror, reading lights, second row captain chairs, auxiliary power outlet, automatic headlights, sport suspension, 225/60R16 tires, alloy wheels.

SE w/leather adds: leather upholstery, 6-way power driver seat w/manual lumbar support, 4-way power passenger seat, memory system for driver seat and mirrors, reclining second row captain chairs, power rear quarter windows, universal garage door opener, adjustable rear parcel shelf, flip-up rear hatch glass.

GLE adds: automatic climate control w/front and rear controls, 215/70R15 tires, deletes adjustable rear parcel shelf, flip-up rear glass hatch, sport suspension.

OPTIONAL EQUIPMENT:

Major Packages

	Retail Price	Dealer Invoice
Comfort Plus Pkg., GXE	899	779

Leather-wrapped steering wheel w/radio controls, rear air conditioning controls, reading lights, conversation mirror, auxiliary power outlet, adjustable rear parcel shelf, heavy-duty battery, alloy wheels.

Convenience Pkg., SE w/cloth	799	693

6-way power driver seat w/lumbar adjustment, power rear quarter windows, universal garage door opener, automatic headlights, adjustable rear parcel shelf, flip-up rear hatch glass.

Popular Pkg., GLE	500	433

Adjustable rear parcel shelf, 6-disc CD changer, flip-up rear hatch glass, full-size spare tire, trailer wiring harness.

Audio Upgrade Pkg., GXE	349	303

AM/FM/cassette/CD player. Requires Comfort Plus Pkg.

	Retail Price	Dealer Invoice
Audio Upgrade Pkg., SE	$359	$311

6-disc CD changer. Requires sunroof. SE w/cloth requires Convenience Pkg.

Towing Pkg., GXE, SE	169	—

Full-size spare tire, trailering harness.

Safety Features

Two integrated child seats, GXE	229	199

NA with Audio Upgrade Pkg.

Comfort and Convenience

Video Entertainment System	1099	—
Manufacturer's discount price	NC	NC

Videocassette player, LCD screen, jacks for headphones and games.

Power sunroof, SE, GLE	899	779

SE requires Convenience Pkg.

Appearance and Miscellaneous

Fog lights, GXE	379	283
SE, GLE	389	287
Running boards w/bumper step pad	529	373
Tow hitch	419	305

GXE and SE requires Towing Pkg. GLE requires Popular Pkg.

NISSAN XTERRA

Nissan Xterra SE

Rear- or 4-wheel-drive midsize sport-utility vehicle
Base price range: $17,349-$25,549. Built in USA. **Also consider:** Honda CR-V, Jeep Cherokee, Toyota RAV4

FOR • Cargo room **AGAINST** • Acceleration (4-cyl.) • Rear-seat entry/exit • Wind noise • Ride/handling

Priced against compacts such as the Honda CR-V, Nissan's new Xterra is a midsize SUV based on the Frontier pickup truck. It's designed to appeal to young buyers who favor function and a rugged appearance over comfort amenities.

The base Xterra XE has a 4-cylinder engine, manual transmission, and 2-wheel drive. XE V6 and top-line SE models get the 3.3-liter V6 used by Nissan's more upscale Pathfinder SUV. They come with manual or automatic transmission, 2WD or 4WD. Xterra's 4WD system is not for use on dry pavement. Standard features include antilock brakes, air conditioning, and engine/transmission skid plates. SEs add a manual sunroof.

PERFORMANCE Xterra aims to be back-pack functional and hip-hop cool, yet it's rather stodgy in some ways. Acceleration is plodding with the 4-cylinder, but adequate with the V6. Our test automatic 2WD SE did 0-60 mph in 9.6 seconds; still, the manual-transmission 4WD CR-V we tested clocked a 9.3. Xterra's automatic transmission works well, as do the brakes.

Even in 2WD form, Xterra's suspension is stiff enough to cause noticeable jiggle on bumpy pavement, though rough stuff won't pummel your kidneys. Cornering grip is decent for a high, narrowish SUV, but the steering is vague on-center, and Xterra is easily outmaneuvered by true compact SUVs. Fuel economy is assuredly midsize SUV: 14.6-17.2 mpg in the 2WD V6 models we tested. That test 5-speed CR-V averaged 22.5 mpg.

While it doesn't match CR-V or Toyota's RAV4 with the convenience of all-surface 4WD, Xterra is designed to better them in off-road capability and includes a 4WD-low range that the Honda and Toyota do not. Indeed, Xterra made short work of difficult mountain trails in our tests. Xterra is no quieter than a com-

Prices are accurate at time of publication; subject to manufacturer's changes.

pact SUV, though. Its V6 drones under hard throttle, and a nagging wind whistle from the prominent roof rack adds to intrusive highway noise levels.

ACCOMMODATIONS Xterra's nothing-you-don't-need approach is evident in utilitarian cabin furnishings. To keep prices down, for example, there's no folding mechanism for the rear seat cushions. They simply lift out to allow the rear seatbacks to flop forward. Likewise, most interior trim panels are noticeably thin, as is the door glass, though seat fabrics look durable.

The simple dashboard comes from the Frontier and generally works well. Lanky drivers might wish for more rearward seat travel, and the "umbrella handle" parking brake is an old-fashioned chore. Lowish front bucket seats mean good front head room for tall occupants, but also a slightly legs-out posture that's tough on long-distance comfort. Head room is terrific in back, where the kicked-up roofline allows the bench seat to stand higher than the front buckets, giving riders a better view ahead. Alas, three grownups won't fit in back without crowding, and rear leg room is minimal without the front seats pushed up some. The rear bench is both hard and short on leg support, too. Step-in is high, and narrow rear door bottoms hamper entry/exit. Cargo space is better than in a CR-V or RAV4 with the rear seat up, and ample with it fully stowed.

VALUE FOR THE MONEY It's less pleasant than the CR-V and RAV4 in everyday driving, but Xterra offers truck toughness and off-road ability, plus V6 power those car-based rivals lack. Better still, a V6 Xterra is priced lower than those less-roomy 4-cylinder competitors.

ENGINES

	ohc I4	ohc V6
Size, liters/cu. in.	2.4/146	3.3/200
Horsepower @ rpm	143 @ 5200	170 @ 4800
Torque (lbs./ft.) @ rpm	154 @ 4000	200 @ 2800
Availability	S[1]	S[2]
EPA city/highway mpg		
5-speed OD manual	19/24	16/18
4-speed OD automatic		15/19

1. XE. 2. XE V6, SE.

PRICES

Nissan Xterra

	Retail Price	Dealer Invoice
2WD XE 4-door wagon, 5-speed	$17349	$16136
2WD XE V6 4-door wagon, 5-speed	18499	17205
2WD XE V6 4-door wagon, automatic	19499	18135
4WD XE V6 4-door wagon, 5-speed	20499	19065
4WD XE V6 4-door wagon, automatic	21499	19995
2WD SE 4-door wagon, 5-speed	22549	20736
2WD SE 4-door wagon, automatic	23549	21656
4WD SE 4-wagon, 5-speed	24549	22575
4WD SE 4-wagon, automatic	25549	23494
Destination charge	520	520

STANDARD EQUIPMENT:

XE: 2.4-liter dohc 4-cylinder engine, 5-speed manual transmission, driver- and passenger-side airbags, antilock brakes, air conditioning, power steering, cloth upholstery, front bucket seats, center console w/armrest, split folding rear seat, AM/FM/cassette, digital clock, cupholders, tachometer, rear defogger, rear privacy glass, skid plates, full-size spare tire, 235/70R15 tires.

XE V6 adds: 3.3-liter V6 engine, 5-speed manual or 4-speed automatic transmission, AM/FM/CD player. **4WD** models add: part-time 4-wheel drive, 2-speed transfer case, upgraded antilock brakes.

SE adds: limited-slip differential, power mirrors, power windows, power door locks, remote keyless entry, manual sunroof, tilt leather-wrapped steering wheel, cruise control, AM/FM/cassette/CD player, auxiliary power outlets, passenger-side visor mirror, variable intermittent wipers, map lights, cargo cover, rear wiper, theft-deterrent system, roof rack, tubular step rails, first aid kit, fog lights, front tow hooks, 265/70R15 tires, alloy wheels. **4WD** models add: part-time 4-wheel drive, 2-speed transfer case, upgraded antilock brakes.

OPTIONAL EQUIPMENT:
Major Packages

	Retail	Dealer
Utility Pkg., XE	899	779
	Retail Price	Dealer Invoice
XE V6	$999	$866

Tilt steering wheel, variable intermittent wipers, cargo cover, rear wiper, ceiling tie clips, first aid kit, auxiliary power outlets, roof rack, tubular step rails, fender lip moldings (XE V6), 265/70R15 tires (XE V6).

Power Pkg., XE V6	1299	1126

Power mirrors, power windows, power door locks, remote keyless entry, cruise control, map lights, cloth door inserts, theft-deterrent system. Requires Utility Pkg.

Sport Pkg., XE V6	799	693

Fog lights, limited-slip differential, front tow hooks, alloy wheels. Requires Utility Pkg.

Comfort and Convenience

CD player, XE	469	370

Special Purpose, Wheels and Tires

Tow hitch, manual transmission	399	289
automatic transmission	349	238
Alloy wheels, XE, XE V6	599	434

Post production options also available.

OLDSMOBILE ALERO

Oldsmobile Alero 2-door

Front-wheel-drive compact car; similar to Pontiac Grand Am

Base price range: $16,005-$21,545. Built in USA. **Also consider:** Chrysler Sebring, Mazda 626, Nissan Altima, Subaru Legacy

FOR • Acceleration (V6) • Control layout • Passenger and cargo room • Quietness **AGAINST** • Engine noise (4-cylinder) • Rear visibility (coupe)

Oldsmobile's compact coupe and sedan is available with manual transmission for 2000, and mid-level models can now be equipped with the sport suspension. Alero shares its basic design with the Pontiac Grand Am.

Base GX Aleros and GL 1 and 2 models use a dual camshaft 4-cylinder engine. GL3 models and the top-line GLS get a 3.4-liter V6. The new manual transmission, a 5-speed supplied by the German manufacturer Getrag, is standard on GX and GL1 models. Automatic transmission is optional on those and standard on other Aleros. All come with antilock 4-wheel disc brakes and traction control, and all but GXs have a tire-pressure monitor.

Three child-seat anchors on the rear parcel shelf are new for 2000. And a new Sport option package for GLs includes the firmer performance suspension previously reserved for the GLS; it includes 16-inch alloy wheels (versus steel 15s) and wider performance tires. Finally, gold-color exterior badges are a new option.

PERFORMANCE Acceleration with the V6 engine is perhaps Alero's best feature. The 3.4 feels gutsy off the line and responds quickly in passing situations. At around 8 seconds 0-60 mph, a V6 Alero is among the faster compacts. The downside? Torque steer—sideways pulling under hard acceleration—and a lack of refinement compared to rival Japanese V6s. Alero's 4-cylinder isn't nearly as fast, but it's okay in most everyday tasks. Test V6 Aleros averaged 21.6-23.7 mpg; we have not measured the 4-cylinder's fuel economy. With either engine, the automatic transmission provides smooth, prompt downshifts. The manual transmission adds a dash of sportiness to 4-cylinder Aleros, but it doesn't shift as smoothly as that in such rivals as Honda and Toyota.

Ratings begin on page 213. Specifications begin on page 220.

Alero's ride and handling won't be confused with those of an import-brand sport sedan, either. There's good grip in steady-state cornering. But the steering feels artificially heavy and is somewhat nervous on center, and Alero can feel unsure in quick transitions. Neither suspension rides harshly over bumps, but neither impresses with its compliance or ability to enhance control. Some of our test drivers said moderate bumps upset cornering stability in the Sport package GL3 we tested. Others noticed no such flaw.

Braking is drama-free and pedal action reassuringly firm, but stopping power feels no more than adequate. Both engines sound and feel coarse under hard throttle, and the 4-cylinder we tested vibrated at idle. Wind noise is modest, though the tires drum and thrum on any but the smoothest of pavement.

ACCOMMODATIONS Gauges are clear and compact. Major controls are nicely grouped around the driver, and the easy-to-use climate system features independent air conditioning and recirculation modes. There's no indicator that the available fog lamps are on, however, and no control feels particularly rich or satisfying to use. Padded dashboard and door panels are a nice touch, but at odds with Alero's upscale aspirations are the dashboard vents, which suffer a crude, notchy movement and can't be aimed above the horizontal. Visibility is good in sedans but hampered in coupes by thick roof pillars.

Front head and leg room are good, and rear-seat space rivals that of a few midsize cars. However, seat comfort is compromised by insubstantial foam padding that offers little long-distance support. Rear-seat entry/exit is the usual squeeze in the coupes. Trunks are wide and deep but don't extend that far forward and have smallish openings. All models come with split-fold rear seatbacks to expand the cargo area. Aleros we tested felt solid and rattle-free.

VALUE FOR THE MONEY Strong V6 acceleration and overall solidity are Alero's principal virtues, and it feels more mature than cousin Grand Am. A long list of standard features at competitive prices help make this Olds a Recommended compact-class value.

ENGINES

	dohc I4	ohv V6
Size, liters/cu. in.	2.4/146	3.4/207
Horsepower @ rpm	150 @ 5600	170 @ 4800
Torque (lbs./ft.) @ rpm	155 @ 4400	200 @ 4000
Availability	S[1]	S[2]

EPA city/highway mpg

5-speed OD manual	22/31	
4-speed OD automatic	22/30	20/32

1. GX and GL. 2. GLS, optional GL.

PRICES

Oldsmobile Alero

	Retail Price	Dealer Invoice
GX 2-door coupe	$16005	$14965
GX 4-door sedan	16005	14965
GL1 2-door coupe	17820	16305
GL1 4-door sedan	17820	16305
GL2 2-door coupe	18270	16717
GL2 4-door sedan	18270	16717
GL3 2-door coupe	18875	17271
GL3 4-door sedan	18875	17271
GLS 2-door coupe	21545	19498
GLS 4-door sedan	21545	19498
Destination charge	550	550

STANDARD EQUIPMENT:

GX: 2.4-liter dohc 4-cylinder engine, 5-speed manual transmission, traction control, driver- and passenger-side airbags, antilock 4-wheel disc brakes, daytime running lights, air conditioning, power steering, tilt steering wheel, cloth front bucket seats, split folding rear seat, power door locks, AM/FM radio, tachometer, intermittent wipers, auxiliary power outlets, rear defogger, visor mirrors, power decklid release, automatic headlights, floormats, theft-deterrent system, dual outside mirrors, 215/60R15 tires, wheel covers.

GL1/GL2/GL3 add: 3.4-liter V-6 engine (GL3), 4-speed automatic transmission (GL2/GL3), low tire-inflation warning system, variable-assist power steering, cruise control, power mirrors, power windows,

AM/FM/cassette, driver seat w/power height adjustment and manual lumbar support, 215/60R15 tires (GL2/GL3).

GLS adds: 3.4-liter V6 engine, 4-speed automatic transmission, remote keyless entry, leather upholstery, 6-way power driver seat, leather-wrapped steering wheel, AM/FM/cassette/CD player, fog lights, 225/50R16 tires, polished alloy wheels.

OPTIONAL EQUIPMENT:

	Retail Price	Dealer Invoice
Major Packages		
Feature Pkg., GL	$925	$823
Manufacturer's discount price	625	556
Remote keyless entry, leather-wrapped steering wheel, fog lights, alloy wheels.		
Sport Pkg., GL	925	824
Manufacturer's discount price	450	401
Dynamic bass audio system, rear spoiler, performance sport suspension, 225/50VR16 tires. Requires Feature Pkg.		
Leather Pkg., GL1, GL2	1455	1295
Manufacturer's discount price	1025	912
Leather upholstery, 6-way power driver seat, AM/FM/cassette/CD player. Requires Feature Pkg.		
Performance Suspension Pkg., GLS	250	223
Performance sport suspension, 225/50VR16 tires.		
Gold Pkg., GL, GLS	150	134
Gold badging.		
Powertrains		
4-speed automatic transmission, GX	785	699
Comfort and Convenience		
Power sunroof, GL, GLS	650	579
6-way power driver seat, GL	305	271
Cruise control, GX	225	200
AM/FM/cassette, GX	220	196
AM/FM/cassette/CD player, GX	480	427
GL	200	178
Includes dynamic bass audio system.		
Dynamic bass audio system, GL, GLS	150	134
GL requires Feature Pkg.		
Appearance and Miscellaneous		
Rear spoiler, GL, GLS	225	200

OLDSMOBILE BRAVADA

Oldsmobile Bravada

4-wheel-drive midsize sport-utility vehicle; similar to Chevrolet Blazer and GMC Jimmy/Envoy

Base price: $31,498. Built in USA. **Also consider:** Ford Explorer, Jeep Grand Cherokee, Lexus RX 300, Mercedes-Benz M-Class

FOR • Acceleration • Cargo room • Ride **AGAINST** • Fuel economy • Rear-seat comfort

A "cargo management" system" with vertical dividers to keep small items in place is a new option for the 2000 Bravada. This is a luxury version of the 4-door Chevrolet Blazer/GMC Jimmy and uses the same V6 engine, automatic transmission, and standard antilock brakes. Bravada comes standard with their optional Autotrac 4-wheel drive system. Called SmartTrak by Olds, it drives the rear wheels until they slip, then automatically engages the front axle to maintain traction. SmartTrak does not have Autotrac's locked-in 2WD and 4-low settings. Optional for 2000 is GM's OnStar assistance system. Back from a mid-'99 introduction is a Platinum Edition option group with pewter-colored body cladding among its features.

Prices are accurate at time of publication; subject to manufacturer's changes.

EVALUATION Like its siblings, Bravada has good acceleration, adequate stopping power, and is reasonably quiet, though the V6 sounds gruff until it warms up. The suspension furnishes a more compliant on-road ride than the Chevy/GMC tuning, but also allows some wallow over big dips. Visibility is good, although the standard tinted rear glass makes things murky at night. There's sufficient room for four adults and step-in height is modest, but rear doorways are tight and the rear seat cushion too low for best comfort. Soft-feel interior surfaces and lots of standard equipment help justify Bravada's upscale pricing, but this is an aging SUV that offers nothing of substance over the more reasonably priced Chevy and GMC versions.

ENGINES

	ohv V6
Size, liters/cu. in.	4.3/262
Horsepower @ rpm	190 @ 4400
Torque (lbs./ft.) @ rpm	250 @ 2800
Availability	S

EPA city/highway mpg

4-speed OD automatic	16/20

PRICES

Oldsmobile Bravada	Retail Price	Dealer Invoice
Base 4-door wagon	$31498	$28506
Destination charge	550	550

STANDARD EQUIPMENT:

Base: 4.3-liter V6 engine, 4-speed automatic transmission, permanent 4-wheel drive with active electronic transfer case, limited-slip rear differential, driver- and passenger-side airbags, antilock 4-wheel disc brakes, daytime running lamps, air conditioning w/automatic climate control, variable-assist power steering, tilt steering wheel, cruise control, leather upholstery, front reclining bucket seats with power lumbar adjustment, 8-way power driver seat w/power recliner, split folding rear seat, center console with storage armrest, cupholders, overhead storage console (trip computer, compass, reading lights, outside temperature indicator, universal garage-door opener), AM/FM/cassette/CD player, digital clock, rear defogger, rear wiper/washer, automatic day/night rearview mirror, tachometer, heated power mirrors, power windows, power door locks, remote keyless entry, illuminated visor mirrors, intermittent wipers, automatic headlights, auxiliary power outlets, cargo net and cover, floormats, theft-deterrent system, rear liftgate, deep-tinted rear glass, fog lights, roof rack, front tow hooks, full-size spare tire, 235/70R15 tires, alloy wheels.

OPTIONAL EQUIPMENT:

Major Packages

Convenience Pkg.	757	651
Manufacturer's discount price	57	49

Driver seat memory, power passenger seat, heated and automatic day/night driver-side outside-mirror, Towing Pkg., white-letter tires.

Platinum Edition	939	808
Manufacturer's discount price	239	206

Convenience Pkg. plus pewter-colored lower bodyside cladding, badging.

Towing Pkg.	210	181

Heavy-duty suspension and hazard lights, 8-wire electrical harness, platform hitch, engine oil cooler.

Comfort and Convenience

OnStar System	695	—

Includes Global Positioning System, roadside assistance, emergency services. Requires annual service charge. Price may vary.

Heated front seats	250	215

Requires option pkg.

Power sunroof	750	645
Bose sound system	495	426
CD changer	395	340
Steering-wheel radio and climate controls	125	108
Cargo management system	125	108

OLDSMOBILE INTRIGUE

RECOMMENDED

Oldsmobile Intrigue

Front-wheel-drive midsize car; similar to Chevrolet Impala, Buick Regal and Century, and Pontiac Grand Prix

Base price range: $22,090-$25,720. Built in USA. **Also consider:** Honda Accord, Nissan Maxima, Toyota Camry/Solara

FOR • Acceleration • Passenger and cargo room • Ride • Steering/handling **AGAINST** • Climate controls

An optional anti-skid system tops the short list of additions to Oldsmobile's import-flavored midsize sedan. Intrigue returns in GX, GL, and top-line GLS models. All have a double overhead-cam 3.5-liter V6, automatic transmission, antilock 4-wheel disc brakes, and traction control.

The new anti-skid device is called the Precision Control System (PCS). It's designed to help keep the car on its intended path by selective braking of one or more individual wheels. PCS is optional on all 2000 Intrigues, but requires GX buyers to order the optional traction control that's already standard on the GL and GLS. Rounding out this year's changes are standard retained accessory power, an optional gold-trim package, and, for GLS, standard heated power front seats. Intrigue is built from the same design as the Buick Regal and Pontiac Grand Prix, although those cars use an overhead-valve 3.8 V6.

PERFORMANCE We haven't yet tested the new Precision Control System, but experience with similar traction aids in other cars suggests it's a worthwhile option that should enhance an already capable performer. Intrigue's twincam V6 doesn't deliver quite as much off-the-line snap as the older 3.8 in its corporate siblings, but it's a smoother, quieter engine that provides fine highway passing response and complements a well-behaved transmission. It's also pretty thrifty, returning between 17.7 and 19.5 mpg in our tests—and on regular gas; rivals like Honda Accord and Toyota Camry offer smaller twincam V6s that require premium fuel and make less horsepower.

A solid structure and taut suspension give Intrigue a stable ride and capable handling. Grip and balance in turns is good, and there's little float or wallow over uneven pavement. To some testers, the speed-sensitive steering feels artificially heavy off-center, however. Ride is firm but comfortable. Stopping power is strong, but some testers find brake-pedal feel is numb. Wind noise is generally well-muffled, but tires and suspension thump over sharp bumps and ridges.

ACCOMMODATIONS Intrigue's front bucket seats are firm and supportive, though some of our testers find the lumbar bolster to be too prominent. There's more-than-adequate adult-size head room front and rear, and good back-seat leg space with the front seats moved anywhere short of fully aft. Wide doors provide easy entry/exit. The dashboard has a modern, attractive design, but the automatic climate control standard on GL and GLS models suffers from poorly marked, low-mounted controls that aren't easy to use while driving. We've also found that this system has had trouble defogging the windows in some chilly, damp conditions. Thoughtful touches include dual cupholders front and rear, handy in-dash ignition switch, and non-protruding trunk hinges that don't rob space or scuff luggage. Exterior finish and interior materials are impressive for the price.

VALUE FOR THE MONEY Intrigue feels more grown up than Grand Prix, more sophisticated than Regal. It's a smart blend of features and performance at prices that generally undercut competing midsize import brands. For that, it earns our Recommended rating.

Ratings begin on page 213. Specifications begin on page 220.
CONSUMER GUIDE™

ENGINES

	dohc V6
Size, liters/cu. in.	3.5/211
Horsepower @ rpm	215 @ 5500
Torque (lbs./ft.) @ rpm	230 @ 4400
Availability	S

EPA city/highway mpg	
4-speed OD automatic	19/27

PRICES

Oldsmobile Intrigue	Retail Price	Dealer Invoice
GX 4-door sedan	$22090	$20212
GL 4-door sedan	23720	21704
GLS 4-door sedan	25720	23534
Destination charge	560	560

STANDARD EQUIPMENT:

GX: 3.5-liter dohc V6 engine, 4-speed automatic transmission, traction control, antilock 4-wheel disc brakes, driver- and passenger side airbags, daytime running lamps, variable-assist power steering, tilt steering wheel, cruise control, air conditioning, cloth reclining front bucket seats, center console, cupholders, AM/FM/cassette, digital clock, tachometer, power mirrors, power windows, power door locks, rear defogger, remote trunk and fuel door release, visor mirrors, map lights, floormats, theft-deterrent system, cornering lights, 225/60R16 tires, alloy wheels.

GL adds: full-function traction control, remote keyless entry, dual-zone automatic climate control, heated power mirrors, 6-way power driver seat, split-folding rear seat, leather-wrapped steering wheel/armrest/shifter, 6-speaker sound system, illuminated visor mirrors, fog lights.

GLS adds: leather upholstery, heated front seats, power passenger seat, AM/FM/cassette/CD player, steering-wheel radio controls, automatic day/night rearview mirror, compass.

OPTIONAL EQUIPMENT:
Major Packages

Precision Control System..	595	530

Anti-skid system, performance axle ratio, 225/60HR16 performance tires. GX requires full-function traction control.

Powertrains

Full-function traction control, GX.............................	145	129

Comfort and Convenience

Power Sunroof..	750	668
AM/FM/cassette/CD player, GX	270	240
GL	200	178

Includes six speakers.

Bose cassette/CD player,		
GL, GLS	500	445

Includes eight speakers, automatic tone control, amplifier.

12-disc CD changer, GL, GLS	460	409
Steering wheel radio controls, GL..........................	125	111
Remote keyless entry, GX.......................................	150	134
Leather-wrapped steering wheel, GX......................	120	107

Includes leather shifter and armrest.

6-way power driver seat, GX...................................	305	271
6-way power passenger seat, GL	305	271
Leather upholstery, GL	995	886
Split folding rear seat, GX	150	134
Heated front seats, GL..	295	263

Requires leather upholstery, power passenger seat.

Appearance and Miscellaneous

Rear spoiler..	225	200
Gold emblems	150	134
Chrome alloy wheels, GL, GLS...............................	695	619

OLDSMOBILE SILHOUETTE

Front-wheel-drive minivan; similar to Chevrolet Venture and Pontiac Montana

Base price range: $25,195-$31,595. Built in USA. **Also consider:** Chrysler Town & Country, Ford Windstar, Honda

Oldsmobile Silhouette Premier

Odyssey, Toyota Sienna

FOR • Ride • Passenger and cargo room **AGAINST** • Fuel economy

Silhouette loses the shorter of its two body lengths for 2000 and now carries a maximum of seven passengers, not eight.

This upscale version of the Chevrolet Venture and Pontiac Montana comes in GL, GLS, and top-line Premiere models. With loss of last year's short-body GS model, Silhouette uses the longer Venture/Montana body and features dual sliding side doors. Optional for GL and standard elsewhere are a power right-side sliding door, rear air conditioning, leather upholstery, and traction control. The 3-bucket middle-row setup is shelved, so all Silhouettes now carry seven in a 2-2-3 arrangement. Middle-row child safety seats also have been dropped.

The sole powertrain is a 3.4-liter V6 and automatic transmission. Antilock brakes and front side airbags are standard. Included on Premiere and optional on other models is a touring suspension with automatic load leveling. Exclusive to Premiere is a rear audio/video package with VCR, TV monitor, and 3-channel sound system.

Among other 2000 changes are a revised gauge cluster with a dot-matrix data display, new-design audio units with Radio Data System (RDS) capability, and standard second-row reading lamps. Heated front seats are newly optional for GLS and Premier. Silhouette's performance and accommodations are similar to those of like-equipped Ventures.

The Chevrolet Venture report includes an evaluation of the Silhouette.

ENGINES

	ohv V6
Size, liters/cu. in.	3.4/207
Horsepower @ rpm	185 @ 5200
Torque (lbs./ft.) @ rpm	210 @ 4000
Availability	S

EPA city/highway mpg	
4-speed OD automatic...	19/26

PRICES

Oldsmobile Silhouette	Retail Price	Dealer Invoice
GL 4-door van	$25195	$22801
GLS 4-door van	28895	26150
Premiere Edition 4-door van	31595	28593
Destination charge	605	605

STANDARD EQUIPMENT:

GL: 3.4-liter V6 engine, 4-speed automatic transmission, driver- and passenger-side airbags, front side-impact airbags, antilock brakes, daytime running lights, front air conditioning, interior air filter, power steering, tilt steering wheel, cruise control, reclining front bucket seats w/lumbar adjustment and folding armrests, 4-way manually-adjustable driver seat, second-row 2-passenger split-folding bench seat, third-row 3-passenger split-folding bench seat, front storage console, overhead console, map lights, cupholders, heated power mirrors, power windows, power door locks, tachometer, AM/FM/cassette, digital clock, intermittent wipers, rear wiper/washer, rear defogger, automatic headlights, visor mirrors, rear reading lights, auxiliary power outlets, floormats, sliding driver-side door, rear deep-tinted glass, theft-deterrent system, fog lights, roof rack, 215/70R15 tires, wheel covers.

GLS adds: traction control, remote keyless entry, leather upholstery, 6-way power front seats, second-row captain's chairs, power sliding

---

Prices are accurate at time of publication; subject to manufacturer's changes.

passenger-side door, overhead storage console (includes compass, outside temperature indicator, driver information center), rear air conditioning and heater, leather-wrapped steering wheel w/radio controls, rear-seat radio controls, headphones, illuminated visor mirrors, 215/70R15 touring tires, alloy wheels.

Premiere Edition adds: LCD color screen/videocassette player, input jacks for video games or video camera, AM/FM/cassette/CD player, touring suspension w/automatic load leveling, air inflation kit.

OPTIONAL EQUIPMENT:
Major Packages

	Retail Price	Dealer Invoice
Personal Convenience Pkg., GL	$1305	$1122

AM/FM/cassette/CD player, two center row captain's chairs, 6-way power front seats, remote keyless entry, theft-deterrent system w/alarm.

Towing Pkg., GL, GLS	370	318
Premiere	85	73

Includes touring suspension and automatic load leveling (GL, GLS), engine-oil cooler, heavy-duty alternator and radiator, heavy-duty flasher, 5-lead wiring harness.

Powertrains

Traction control, GL	195	168

Comfort and Convenience

Power sliding passenger-side door, GL	450	387

Requires remote keyless entry.

Rear air conditioning, GL	450	387

Includes rear heater. Requires rear radio controls.

6-way power front seats, GL	575	495
Heated front seats, GLS, Premiere Edition	195	168
AM/FM/CD player, GL, GLS	100	86

Includes automatic tone control.

Rear radio controls, GL	125	108
Remote keyless entry, GL	235	202

Includes theft-deterrent system w/alarm.

Touring suspension, GL, GLS	270	232

Includes automatic load leveling, air inflation kit.

Alloy wheels, GL	295	254

PLYMOUTH BREEZE

BUDGET BUY

Plymouth Breeze

Front-wheel-drive midsize car; similar to Chrysler Cirrus and Sebring and Dodge Stratus

Base price: $15,910. Built in USA. **Also consider:** Chevrolet Malibu, Honda Accord, Saturn L-Series

FOR • Steering/handling **AGAINST** • Noise • Rear visibility

Breeze includes several previously optional features at no extra cost for 2000, including an 8-way power-adjustable driver seat. This 4-door midsize sedan is the low-priced version of the Dodge Stratus and the luxury-oriented Chrysler Cirrus.

Breeze comes in a single trim level with a 132-horsepower 2.0 liter 4-cylinder engine and manual transmission. A 150-hp 2.4-liter four now comes at no charge with the optional automatic transmission, which isn't available with the 2.0. The 2.4 comes only with automatic. Stratus shares these 4-cylinder engines, but also offers a V6. Antilock brakes are available, but Breeze doesn't offer the 4-wheel disc brakes that are optional on Stratus and standard on Cirrus.

New safety features for 2000 include an optional emergency escape release inside the trunk and standard child seat rear anchorages. And a cassette player is now standard instead of optional. Breeze has performance and accommodations similar

to those of comparably equipped Stratuses.

The Dodge Stratus report includes an evaluation of the Breeze.

ENGINES

	ohc I4	dohc I4
Size, liters/cu. in.	2.0/122	2.4/148
Horsepower @ rpm	132 @ 6000	150 @ 5200
Torque (lbs./ft.) @ rpm	129 @ 4950	167 @ 4000
Availability	S	O
EPA city/highway mpg		
5-speed OD manual	26/36	
4-speed OD automatic		21/30

PRICES

Plymouth Breeze	Retail Price	Dealer Invoice
Base 4-door sedan	$15910	$14585
Destination charge	535	535

STANDARD EQUIPMENT:

Base: 2.0-liter 4-cylinder engine, 5-speed manual transmission, driver- and passenger-side airbags, air conditioning, power steering, tilt steering wheel, cloth upholstery, front bucket seats, folding rear seat, center storage console, cupholders, tachometer, 6-speaker AM/FM/cassette, digital clock, rear defogger, variable intermittent wipers, auxiliary power outlet, remote decklid release, visor mirrors, front floormats, dual remote mirrors, 195/70R14 tires, wheel covers.

OPTIONAL EQUIPMENT:
Major Packages

Quick Order Pkg. 24B	1055	939
Manufacturer's discount price	NC	NC

Power mirrors, power door locks and windows, 8-way power driver seat, rear floormats. Requires 2.4-liter engine, automatic transmission.

Powertrains

2.4-liter dohc 4-cylinder engine	450	401
Manufacturer's discount price	NC	NC

Requires Quick Order Pkg. 24B, automatic transmission.

4-speed automatic transmission	1050	935

Includes cruise control. Requires Pkg. 24B, 2.4-liter engine.

Safety Features

Antilock brakes	565	503

Comfort and Convenience

Power sunroof	695	619

Includes map lights, illuminated visor mirrors. Requires Quick Order Pkg. 24B.

Remote keyless entry	170	151

Requires Quick Order Pkg. 24B.

Premium AM/FM/CD player	200	178
Premium AM/FM/cassette and 6-disc CD changer	550	490
Smoker's Pkg.	20	18

Lighter, ashtray.

PLYMOUTH PROWLER

Plymouth Prowler

Rear-wheel-drive sports and GT car

Base price: $42,700. Built in USA. **Also consider:** BMW Z3 Series, Chevrolet Corvette, Mercedes-Benz SLK230

FOR • Acceleration • Steering/handling **AGAINST** • Cargo room • Visibility • Entry/exit • Ride

Plymouth's limited-production hot rod changes color and gets suspension revisions for 2000. This rear-wheel-drive 2-seat roadster uses the 253-horsepower 3.5-liter V6 from the Chrysler LHS and 300M. The only transmission is a rear-mounted automatic with Chrysler's Autostick, which allows limited manual shifting. Four-wheel disc brakes are standard, but antilock brakes and traction control are unavailable. New for 2000 are softer springs and recalibrated shock absorbers intended to improve ride and handling. Prowler is available in red, black, and now silver, which replaces yellow and purple. And the standard alloy wheels are chromed for 2000. Also new are a chrome bezel and leather boot for the shifter, a trip computer, and an automatic-dimming mirror with integral compass.

EVALUATION Prowler's light weight gives it impressive acceleration despite its somewhat mainstream passenger-car engine; Plymouth claims 0-60 mph times of around 6 seconds. Fuel economy is decent as well, with our '99 test car averaging 22.1 mpg. Handling is a strong point. Ride is not, nor is interior room or outward visibility with the top up. And there's only enough luggage space for one slim briefcase. Of course, those negatives are of little consequence to Prowler buyers. This is a sunny-day toy, a lifestyle statement, and buyers snap them up as fast as Plymouth builds them.

ENGINES

	ohc V6 3.5/215
Size, liters/cu. in.	3.5/215
Horsepower @ rpm	253 @ 6400
Torque (lbs./ft.) @ rpm	255 @ 3950
Availability	S

EPA city/highway mpg
4-speed OD automatic 17/23

PRICES

Plymouth Prowler	Retail Price	Dealer Invoice
Base 2-door convertible	$42700	$39882
Destination charge	700	700

STANDARD EQUIPMENT:

Base: 3.5-liter V6 engine, 4-speed automatic transmission w/manual-shift capability, driver- and passenger-side airbags, 4-wheel disc brakes, air conditioning, power steering, tilt leather-wrapped steering wheel, cruise control, leather upholstery, bucket seats, 6-way manual driver seat w/height adjuster, center console, cupholder, power mirrors, power windows, power door locks, remote keyless entry, tachometer, Infinity AM/FM cassette player, 6-disc CD changer, steering-wheel radio controls, auxiliary power outlet, automatic day/night rearview mirror, compass, trip computer, intermittent wipers, tire-pressure monitor, rear defogger, floormats, theft-deterrent system, manual cloth convertible top, extended mobility tires (225/45HR17 front, 295/40HR20 rear), chrome alloy wheels.

Options are available as dealer-installed accessories.

PLYMOUTH VOYAGER

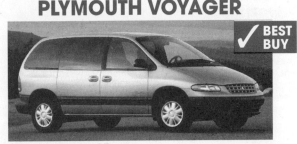

✓ BEST BUY

Plymouth Voyager SE

Front-wheel-drive minivan; similar to Chrysler Town & Country and Dodge Caravan
Base price range: $18,685-$24,080. Built in USA and Canada. **Also consider:** Chevrolet Venture, Ford Windstar, Honda Odyssey, Toyota Sienna

FOR • Ride • Passenger and cargo room **AGAINST** • Fuel economy • Wind noise

Air conditioning and 7-passenger seating are standard instead of optional on the lowest-priced Voyager for 2000, and a video system is newly available on all models. Voyager shares its design with the Dodge Caravan and Chrysler Town & Country, but offers fewer trim and option choices, in keeping with the Plymouth brand's no-frills approach.

Like Caravan, Voyager comes in regular-length and extended-length models, the latter called Grands. Both body lengths come in base and uplevel SE trim. All Voyagers now seat seven, with front buckets and second- and third-row benches standard. The third-row bench (along with air conditioning) is now a no-cost option on base models with the standard 4-cylinder engine. Two second-row bucket seats are optional on SE Voyagers. And up to two integrated middle-row child safety seats are available.

A 4-cylinder is standard on the base regular-length Voyager. A 3.0-liter V6 is standard on base Grands, optional on base regular-length models. A 3.3-liter V6 is standard on SEs, optional on base models. Plymouth briefly offered a 3.8 liter V6 in the 1999 Voyager, but discontinues it for 2000. All engines come with automatic transmission. Antilock brakes are standard on SEs, optional on base models. Traction control is unavailable.

Finally, new for Chrysler, Dodge, and Plymouth minivans is a dealer-installed video entertainment system. Called Rear Seat Video, it mounts between the front- or second-row seats and includes a VCR, 6.4-inch liquid crystal display screen, headphones, and remote control. Price, including installation, is $1500. Voyager's performance and accommodations mirror those of similarly equipped Caravans.

The Dodge Caravan report includes an evaluation of the Voyager.

ENGINES

	dohc I4	ohc V6	ohv V6
Size, liters/cu. in.	2.4/148	3.0/181	3.3/202
Horsepower @ rpm	150 @ 5200	150 @ 5200	158 @ 4850
Torque (lbs./ft.) @ rpm	167 @ 4000	176 @ 4000	203 @ 3250
Availability	S¹	S²	S³

EPA city/highway mpg
3-speed automatic 20/26
4-speed OD automatic 19/26 18/24

1. Base regular length. 2. Base Grand; optional Base regular length. 3. SE; optional Base regular length, Base Grand.

PRICES

Plymouth Voyager	Retail Price	Dealer Invoice
Base regular length 3-door van	$18685	$16978
Base Grand 4-door van	21790	19750
SE regular length 4-door van	23085	20850
Grand SE 4-door van	24080	21765
Destination charge	590	590

STANDARD EQUIPMENT:

Base regular length: 2.4-liter dohc 4-cylinder engine, 3-speed automatic transmission, driver- and passenger-side airbags, power steering, 5-passenger seating w/cloth reclining front bucket seats, 3-passenger rear bench seat, AM/FM/cassette, digital clock, variable intermittent wipers, intermittent rear wiper/washer, passenger-side visor mirror, auxiliary power outlet, dual outside mirrors, 205/75R14 tires, wheel covers.

Base Grand adds: 3.0-liter V6 engine, 4-speed automatic transmission, sliding driver side door, front air conditioning, 7-passenger seating w/folding 2-passenger middle bench seat, folding 3-passenger rear bench seat, passenger-side under-seat storage.

SE adds: 3.3-liter V6 engine, antilock brakes, tilt steering wheel, cruise control, power mirrors, power windows, power door locks, rear defogger, tachometer, illuminated visor mirrors, floormats, 215/65R15 tires.

OPTIONAL EQUIPMENT:
Major Packages
Pkg. 22T/25T/26T/28T,		
Base reg. length	1275	1084

Prices are accurate at time of publication; subject to manufacturer's changes.

	Retail Price	Dealer Invoice
Manufacturer's discount price, w/2.4-liter...............	NC	NC
Manufacturer's discount price, w/3.0-liter or 3.3-liter	$515	$438

Front air conditioning, CYE 7-passenger Seating Group (folding 2-passenger middle bench seat, folding 3-passenger rear bench seat), rear sound insulation, storage drawer below passenger seat, cargo net.

V6 Value Plus Group, Base.....................................	670	570

Cruise control, tilt steering wheel, power mirrors and windows, power door locks, upgraded door panel trim. Base regular length requires V6 engine, Pkg. 25T/26T/28T.

Pkg. 25L/28L/29L, SE	1445	1228
Manufacturer's discount price	1345	1143

Premium cloth upholstery, CYS Deluxe 7-passenger Seating Group (reclining/folding middle bucket seats, and rear 3-passenger bench seat with adjustable headrests), 8-way power driver seat, overhead console, trip computer.

Climate Group II, Base..	450	383

Sunscreen glass, windshield wiper de-icer.

Climate Group III, Grand SE	1230	1046
Manufacturer's discount price	780	663

Sunscreen glass, rear heater and air conditioning w/dual controls, overhead console, trip computer.

Climate Group III, Grand SE w/Trailer Tow Prep	1165	991
Manufacturer's discount price	715	608

Sunscreen glass, rear heater and air conditioning w/dual controls, overhead console, trip computer.

Loading Group, SE..	195	166

Heavy-duty suspension, full-size spare tire.

Trailer Tow Prep Group, Grand SE	435	370

Loading Group plus heavy-duty battery, alternator, brakes, radiator, and transmission-oil cooler, trailer wiring harness.

Powertrains

3.0-liter V6 engine, Base reg. length......................	800	680

Requires 4-speed automatic transmission and option pkg.

3.3-liter V6 engine, Base reg. length......................	970	825
Base Grand...	170	145

Base regular length requires 4-speed automatic transmission and option pkg.

4-speed automatic transmission, Base reg. length	200	170

Requires V6 engine.

Safety Features

Antilock brakes, Base	565	480
Dual integrated child seats, Base	235	209
Integrated child seat, SE.......................................	125	106

Comfort and Convenience

Convenience Group I, Base	435	370

Cruise control, tilt steering column, power mirrors. Requires option pkg.

Convenience Group II, Base	750	638

Group I plus power locks. Requires option pkg.

Convenience Group III, Base	1120	952

Cruise control, tilt steering wheel, power mirrors and windows, power door locks. Requires option pkg.

Convenience Group IV, SE	240	204

Remote keyless entry, illuminated entry, headlight-off delay. Requires option pkg.

Convenience Group V, SE	390	332

Group III plus theft-deterrent system.

CYR Deluxe 7-passenger Seating Group, SE	225	191

Deluxe 7-passenger Seating Group with two integrated child seats in middle bench. NA with Pkg. 25L/28L/29L.

CYS 7-passenger Quad Seating Group, SE..........	695	591

Reclining/folding middle bucket seats and rear 3-passenger bench seat with adjustable headrests.

CYT 7-passenger Quad Seating Group, SE	820	697

CYS Quad Seating Group with integrated child seat.

Rear defogger, Base	195	166
Base w/Convenience Group	230	196

Includes windshield wiper de-icer.

Sliding driver-side door, Base reg. length	595	506

Requires option pkg.

	Retail Price	Dealer Invoice
AM/FM/cassette/CD w/equalizer, SE	$720	$612

Includes 10-speaker Infinity sound system.

Smoker's Group	20	17

Cigarette lighter, ashtrays.

Appearance and Miscellaneous

Roof rack..	215	183

Base requires option pkg.

Value Plus Climate Group, SE	NC	NC

Sunscreen glass.

Load-leveling suspension, Grand SE......................	290	247
Alloy wheels, SE	415	353

PONTIAC BONNEVILLE

Pontiac Bonneville

Front-wheel-drive full-size car; similar to Buick LeSabre

Base price range: $23,680–$31,635. Built in USA. **Also consider:** Dodge Intrepid, Toyota Avalon

FOR • Acceleration • Passenger and cargo room • Ride/handling **AGAINST** • Fuel economy • Rear-seat comfort

Pontiac's full-size sedan is redesigned for 2000 with new styling but carried-over powertrains. Front side airbags are among new standard features, and General Motors' StabiliTrak antiskid system is included on the top-line model.

Wheelbase and overall length increase nearly two inches, but interior leg room is unchanged and head room shrinks slightly.

SE, SLE, and SSEi trim levels are offered. All come with front bucket seats, but the SE offers an optional bench for 6-passenger capacity. The only engine is a 3.8-liter V6. SE and SLE models have 205 horsepower, the supercharged SSEi 240. The only transmission is a 4-speed automatic. Traction control is standard on SSEi, optional elsewhere. Antilock 4-wheel disc brakes replace a disc/drum setup, and a tire-inflation monitor is a new standard feature. The SSEi's StabiliTrak system is designed to selectively brake the front wheels to counteract skids in turns. That model also comes with GM's EyeCue head-up display, which projects main instrument readings onto the windshield. A revised version of GM's OnStar assistance system is to become available on the SSEi later in the 2000 model year.

PERFORMANCE Unchanged powertrains pull slightly more weight this year, but acceleration remains strong in the SE and SLE, with good throttle response throughout the speed range. The SSEi's supercharged engine again has outstanding power, and we believe Pontiac's claim of 7.0 seconds 0-60 mph, a good figure and about the same as last year. As before, the supercharged version requires premium fuel. With either engine, the transmission changes gears smoothly and downshifts quickly for passing.

SEs ride a bit more softly than the sportier SLE and SSEi, but all are comfortable over bumps and nearly devoid of the front-end bobbing that sometimes plagued previous Bonnevilles. Also helping ride stability is the standard load-leveling rear suspension, which was previously unavailable on SEs.

Balanced and composed, handling is likewise impressive. SLE and SSEi feel sharpest, thanks in part to their lower-profile 17-inch tires; last year's versions wore 16 inchers. (The 16s are now standard on SE models in place of 15s.) Though the SSEi's StabiliTrak can get confused by rapid sawing of the steering wheel, it benefits Cadillacs we've tested, and should help this Bonneville stay on course in emergency maneuvers. Stopping power with the new 4-wheel disc brakes feels strong and sure, though pedal modulation is not uniform in hard stops.

ACCOMMODATIONS Bonneville's spacious interior, like the rest of the car, has a sportier flair than that of most full size sedans. There's plenty of room for four adults, though the lost inch of rear headroom will be missed by taller passengers. The rear seatback's protruding center section discourages 3-across seating, and the entire cusion is too soft and poorly shaped to provide comfortable support.

Gauges include a tachometer, and an inlaid effect gives them a richer look than last year's painted-on graphics. The instruments are grouped closer to the driver, too, though the steering wheel hides the odometer. Two-tone surfaces also improve the dashboard's appearance, but its plastic panels still feel low budget, and numerous curved cut lines and eight air vents clutter the overall look. Controls for audio and climate systems are easy to reach and decipher.

Front-seat comfort is generally good, helped by safety belts newly integrated into the seats. The SSEi's leather-covered buckets still have 12 separate position settings and still aren't as supportive as they should be, but at least they now include power memory. Entry/exit is easy through large doors, but the cloth upholstery in the SE and SLE is so grippy that it can hinder getting out of the seats. There are numerous interior storage cubbies, though the front cupholders won't hold large cups. The rear seat has a fold-down armrest and a trunk pass through. The trunk is large, but the lid's hinges dip into the load area.

VALUE FOR THE MONEY A $25,000 SE is a good big-car value, and is expected to account for 65 percent of Bonneville sales. We like its supercharged power, but a loaded SSEi can top $34,000—well into the near-luxury realm, where most cars have more panache and refinement.

ENGINES

	ohv V6	Supercharged ohv V6
Size, liters/cu. in.	3.8/231	3.8/231
Horsepower @ rpm	205 @ 5200	240 @ 5200
Torque (lbs./ft.) @ rpm	230 @ 4000	280 @ 3600
Availability	S[1]	S[2]
EPA city/highway mpg		
4-speed OD automatic	19/30	17/28

1. SE, SLE. 2. SSEi.

PRICES

Pontiac Bonneville

	Retail Price	Dealer Invoice
SE 4-door sedan	$23680	$21667
SLE 4-door sedan	27380	25053
SSEi 4-door sedan	31635	28946
Destination charge	630	630

STANDARD EQUIPMENT:

SE: 3.8-liter V6 engine, 4-speed automatic transmission, driver- and passenger-side airbags, front side-impact airbags, antilock 4-wheel disc brakes, daytime running lights, air conditioning, variable-assist power steering, tilt steering wheel, cruise control, cloth upholstery, front bucket seats, center console, rear seat trunk pass-through, power mirrors, power windows, power door locks, AM/FM/cassette, digital clock, tachometer, overhead console, map lights, intermittent wipers, visor mirrors, automatic headlights, floormats, theft-deterrent system, fog lights, 225/60R16 tires, wheel covers.

SLE adds: heated power mirrors, leather-wrapped steering wheel w/radio controls, dual-zone automatic climate control, interior air filter, 6-way power driver seat w/manual lumbar adjustment, remote keyless entry, upgraded sound system, illuminated visor mirrors, tire pressure monitor, compass, outside temperature indicator, remote decklid release, alloy wheels, rear spoiler, performance suspension, 235/55R17 tires.

SSEi adds: 3.8-liter V6 supercharged engine, traction control, anti-skid system, magnetic variable-assist power steering, leather upholstery, articulating 12-way power front seats, EyeCue Head-Up instrument display, AM/FM/cassette/CD player w/Bose sound system, automatic day/night rearview mirror, universal garage door opener, park-assist passenger-side mirror.

OPTIONAL EQUIPMENT:

	Retail Price	Dealer Invoice
Major Packages		
Option Group 2, SE	$835	$743
Remote keyless entry, 6-way power driver seat, illuminated visor mirrors, remote decklid release, cargo net, theft-deterrent system w/alarm.		
Option Group 3, SE	2655	2363
Option Group 2 plus leather upholstery, leather-wrapped steering wheel w/radio controls, dual-zone automatic climate control, upgraded sound system, performance axle ratio, painted alloy wheels.		
Powertrains		
Traction control, SE, SLE	175	156
SE requires option group.		
Comfort and Convenience		
Power sunroof	980	872
SE requires option group and universal garage door opener.		
6-way power passenger seat, SE, SLE	305	271
SE requires option group.		
Leather upholstery, SE, SLE	850	757
SE require Option Group 2.		
Front split bench seat, SE	150	134
NA with Option Group 3.		
Heated front seats, SSEi	195	174
AM/FM/CD player, SE, SLE	100	89
SE requires option group.		
AM/FM/cassette/CD player, SE, SLE	200	178
SE requires option group.		
12-disc CD changer	595	530
SE requires Option Group 3.		
Leather-wrapped steering wheel w/radio controls, SE	175	156
Requires Option Group 2.		
Universal garage door opener, SE, SLE	100	89
SE requires Option Group 3.		
Appearance and Miscellaneous		
Rear spoiler, SE	110	98
Painted alloy wheels, SE	285	254
Chrome alloy wheels, SLE, SSEi	595	530

PONTIAC FIREBIRD

Pontiac Firebird Tran Am coupe w/Ram Air

Rear-wheel-drive sports and GT car; similar to Chevrolet Camaro

Base price range: $18,590-$30,950. Built in Canada.
Also consider: Chevrolet Corvette, Ford Mustang, Mazda Miata

FOR • Acceleration • Handling **AGAINST** • Fuel economy (V8 models) • Ride (V8 models) • Rear-seat room • Rear visibility • Wet-weather traction (without traction control)

Pontiac's performance leader survives into 2000 despite rumors of its imminent demise due to declining sales. Changes are limited to colors, the addition of rear child-seat anchors, and new-design 17-inch aluminum wheels for the high-performance WS6 package. Firebird offers hatchback coupes in base, Formula, and Trans Am trim, plus base and Trans Am convertibles with standard power top and glass rear window. Firebirds ladle unique styling around the same platform and powertrains used by Chevrolet Camaros.

A 3.8-liter V6 powers base models. Formulas and Trans Ams

Prices are accurate at time of publication; subject to manufacturer's changes.

have a 5.7-liter V8 derived from the Chevrolet Corvette engine. The WS6 Ram Air option boosts V8 horsepower by 15 and includes a functional hood scoop. All engines meet low-emission vehicle standards for 2000. V6 models have a 5-speed manual transmission or optional automatic. V8s get the automatic or a 6-speed manual at no extra charge; a Hurst-brand shifter is a stand-alone option with the 6-speed. Antilock 4-wheel disc brakes are standard, traction control is optional. Firebird's performance and accommodations are similar to those of like-equipped Camaros.

The Chevrolet Camaro report includes an evaluation of the Firebird.

ENGINES

	ohv V6	ohv V8	ohv V8
Size, liters/cu. in.	3.8/231	5.7/346	5.7/346
Horsepower @ rpm	200 @	305 @	320 @
	5200	5200	5200
Torque (lbs./ft.) @ rpm	225 @	335 @	345 @
	4000	4000	4400
Availability	S[1]	S[2]	O[2]
EPA city/highway mpg			
5-speed OD manual	19/30		
6-speed OD manual		19/28	16/26
4-speed OD automatic	19/29	17/23	18/24

1. Base. 2. Formula, Trans Am.

PRICES

Pontiac Firebird	Retail Price	Dealer Invoice
Base 2-door hatchback	$18590	$17010
Base 2-door convertible	25210	23067
Formula 2-door hatchback	23770	21750
Trans Am 2-door hatchback	26880	24595
Trans Am 2-door convertible	30950	28319
Destination charge	550	550

STANDARD EQUIPMENT:

Base hatchback: 3.8-liter V6 engine, 5-speed manual transmission, driver- and passenger-side airbags, antilock 4-wheel disc brakes, daytime running lights, air conditioning, power steering, tilt steering wheel, cruise control, cloth reclining front bucket seats, folding rear seat, center console, auxiliary power outlet, cupholders, AM/FM/CD player, digital clock, tachometer, intermittent wipers, map lights, visor mirrors, remote hatch release, rear defogger, automatic headlights, floormats, left remote and right manual mirrors, theft-deterrent system, fog lights, rear spoiler, 215/60R16 tires, alloy wheels.

Base convertible adds: power mirrors, power windows, power door locks, remote keyless entry, leather-wrapped steering wheel w/radio controls, leather-wrapped shifter and handbrake, 6-way power driver seat, Monsoon sound system, power antenna, rear decklid release, power convertible top, theft-deterrent system w/alarm.

Formula adds to Base hatchback: 5.7-liter V8 305-horsepower engine, 4-speed automatic transmission, limited-slip differential, power mirrors, power windows, power door locks, leather-wrapped steering wheel w/radio controls, leather-wrapped shifter and parking brake, Monsoon sound system, power antenna, performance suspension, 245/50ZR16 tires.

Trans Am hatchback adds to Formula: 6-way power driver seat, leather upholstery, remote keyless entry, removable hatch roof, theft-deterrent system w/alarm.

Trans Am convertible adds: power convertible top, rear decklid release, deletes removable hatch roof.

OPTIONAL EQUIPMENT:
Major Packages

	Retail Price	Dealer Invoice
Option Group 1SB, Base hatchback	1510	1344

4-speed automatic transmission, power mirrors, power windows, power door locks, power antenna.

| Option Group 1SC, Base hatchback | 2450 | 2181 |

Group 1SB plus Monsoon sound system, leather-wrapped steering wheel w/radio controls, 6-way power driver seat, remote keyless entry, theft-deterrent system w/alarm.

| Option Group 1SB, Formula | 1505 | 1339 |

4-speed automatic transmission, removable hatch roof, 6-way power driver seat, remote keyless entry, power antenna, theft-deterrent system w/alarm.

	Retail Price	Dealer Invoice
3800 Performance Pkg., Base	$490	$436

Limited-slip differential, faster ratio steering gear, dual exhaust, 3.42 rear axle ratio (with automatic transmission), 235/55R16 tires.

| SLP Firehawk Pkg., Formula, Trans Am | 3999 | 3439 |

Forced-air induction system, hood-mounted heat extractors, special hood w/scoops, 327-horsepower engine, special key fobs and dash plaque, upgraded suspension, 275/40ZR17 tires, painted alloy wheels.

| WS6 Ram Air Performance and Handling Pkg., Formula, Trans Am | 3150 | 2804 |

Ram air induction system, functional hood scoops, 320-horsepower engine, upgraded suspension, power steering fluid cooler, bright exhaust outlets, 275/40ZR17 tires, high-polished alloy wheels.

| Sport Appearance Pkg., Base | 1040 | 926 |

Specific Aero Appearance Pkg., dual exhaust. Requires automatic transmission. Hatchback requires option group. Convertible requires 235/55R16 tires.

| Security Pkg., Base hatchback, Formula | 240 | 214 |

Remote keyless entry, theft-deterrent system w/alarm. Base requires Group 1SB.

Powertrains

	Retail Price	Dealer Invoice
5-speed manual transmission, Base hatchback, (credit)	(815)	(725)

Requires option group.

| 6-speed manual transmission, Formula, Trans Am | NC | NC |
| Hurst shifter, Formula, Trans Am | 325 | 289 |

Requires 6-speed manual transmission.

4-speed automatic transmission, Base	815	725
Traction control, Base	250	223
Formula, Trans Am	450	401
Rear performance axle, Formula, Trans Am	300	267

Includes 3.23 axle ratio, performance tires.

Comfort and Convenience

	Retail Price	Dealer Invoice
Monsoon AM/FM/cassette, Base hatchback w/Group 1SB	330	294
Base hatchback w/Group 1SC, Base convertible, Formula, Trans Am (credit)	(100)	(89)

Base hatchback includes leather-wrapped steering wheel with radio controls.

| Monsoon sound system, Base hatchback w/Group 1SB | 430 | 383 |

Includes leather-wrapped steering with radio controls.

| 12-disc CD changer | 595 | 530 |

Base requires Group 1SC.

| Leather upholstery, Base, Formula | 575 | 512 |

Base hatchback requires Group 1SC. Formula requires Group 1SB.

| Articulating bucket seats, Trans Am | 185 | 165 |
| 6-way power driver seat, Base hatchback, Formula | 270 | 240 |

Appearance and Miscellaneous

	Retail Price	Dealer Invoice
Removable locking hatch roof, Base hatchback, Formula	995	886

Includes sunshades, lock, and stowage.

| 235/55R16 tires, Base | 135 | 120 |
| Chromed alloy wheels | 595 | 530 |

Base hatchback and Formula require option group. NA with Ram Air Performance and Handling Pkg.

PONTIAC GRAND AM
Front-wheel-drive compact car; similar to Oldsmobile Alero

Base price range: $16,040-$21,470. Built in USA. Also consider: Mitsubishi Galant, Nissan Altima, Volkswagen Passat

FOR • Acceleration (V6) • Steering/handling **AGAINST** • Engine noise (4-cylinder) • Ride • Radio controls

Pontiac's sales champ and America's best-selling compact car

Ratings begin on page 213. Specifications begin on page 220.
CONSUMER GUIDE™

Pontiac Grand Am GT 2-door

sails into 2000 with new colors, standard rear child-seat anchors, and an available 5-speed manual transmission as its principal changes. Back from mid-1999 are Grand Am's "Solid" option packages that deliver popular extra-cost items at special reduced prices.

Coupes and sedans are offered in ascending levels of trim called SE, SE1, SE2, and sportier GT and GT1. A 4-cylinder engine remains standard for SE and SE1, with a 3.4-liter V6 optional for SE1 and standard elsewhere. The V6 makes 175 horsepower in GTs, 170 in SEs. Both engines now meet low-emission-vehicle (LEV) standards. The 4-cylinder now teams with a standard Getrag 5-speed manual transmission. A 4-speed automatic is now optional instead of standard. The V6 comes only with automatic. Antilock brakes and traction control remain standard for all models. Oldsmobile's Alero shares the Grand Am's chassis and powertrains, but targets a slightly more upscale, import-oriented clientele.

PERFORMANCE Grand Am isn't underpowered, but it looks faster than it is. The 4-cylinder has adequate spunk and should average at least 20 mpg, though it shakes at idle and groans under hard throttle. The V6 is quieter, smoother, quicker around town, and returned 19.4-21.5 mpg in our tests. The new manual transmission gives 4-cylinder models a sportier feel, despite its somewhat notchy shift action. The well-behaved automatic downshifts quickly and rarely hunts between gears. Both engines have a sporty exhaust note that quickly grows tiresome. Wind noise isn't objectionable, but tires thrum intrusively on rough surfaces and thump loudly over tar strips.

Grand Am's ride is firm without being harsh, though it gets a bit choppy over broken pavement. Handling isn't Eurosedan precise, but turn-in is reasonably quick, there's good grip and balance in corners, and the steering is pleasantly firm. Stopping power is adequate, pedal feel good.

ACCOMMODATIONS Unlike Alero, the Grand Am is as over-styled inside as it is outside. Gauges are deeply recessed and not that legible, the small audio switches are difficult to operate, and some of our drivers find the steering wheel protrudes too far. Front-seat room is sufficient, and two adults won't mind riding in the sedan's rear seat, but coupes are much tighter in back and more difficult to enter or exit. Rear visibility isn't the best, especially with the available rear spoiler, but aft "cornering" lamps help with backing up at night. Trunks are spacious, but suffer from small openings and unusually high sills. Most interior surfaces are covered by padded vinyl and sturdy feeling plastics, but an SE sedan we tested suffered creaks in body and cabin trim.

VALUE FOR THE MONEY Grand Am has "expressive" styling, but we wish similar resources had been spent on its engineering and construction. Unless sporty looks are your top priority in a family compact, you'd be well advised to scout the competition.

ENGINES

	dohc I4	ohv V6	ohv V6
Size, liters/cu. in.	2.4/146	3.4/207	3.4/207
Horsepower @ rpm	150 @ 5600	170 @ 5200	175 @ 5200
Torque (lbs./ft.) @ rpm	155 @ 4400	195 @ 4000	205 @ 4000
Availability	S[1]	S[2]	S[3]
EPA city/highway mpg			
5-speed OD manual	22/31		
4-speed OD automatic	22/30	20/32	20/32

1. SE, SE1. 2. SE2; optional SE1. 3. GT, GT1.

PRICES

Pontiac Grand Am	Retail Price	Dealer Invoice
SE 2-door coupe	$16040	$14677
SE1 2-door coupe	17250	15784
SE2 2-door coupe	19580	17916
SE 4-door sedan	16340	14951
SE1 4-door sedan	17550	16058
SE2 4-door sedan	19880	18190
GT 2-door coupe	19670	17998
GT1 2-door coupe	21170	19371
GT 4-door sedan	19970	18273
GT1 4-door sedan	21470	19645
Destination charge	550	550

STANDARD EQUIPMENT:

SE: 2.4-liter dohc 4-cylinder engine, 5-speed manual transmission, traction control, driver- and passenger-side airbags, antilock brakes, daytime running lights, air conditioning, power steering, tilt steering wheel, cloth reclining front bucket seats, center console, cupholders, AM/FM/cassette, power door locks, remote fuel door and decklid release, variable intermittent wipers, rear defogger, tachometer, illuminated entry, automatic headlights, visor mirrors, floormats, dual outside mirrors, theft-deterrent system, fog lights, tinted glass, 215/60R15 tires, wheel covers.

SE1 adds: power mirrors, power windows, cruise control, 4-way manual driver seat w/power height adjustment, split folding rear seat, alloy wheels.

SE2 adds: 3.4-liter V6 engine, 4-speed automatic transmission, variable-assist power steering, remote keyless entry, Sport Interior Group (upgraded upholstery, leather-wrapped steering wheel and shift knob, driver seat manual lumbar adjustment, seatback pockets, map lights, cargo net), AM/FM/CD player, High Performance sound system w/six speakers, steering-wheel radio controls, 225/50R16 tires.

GT adds: 4-wheel disc brakes, AM/FM/cassette, tire inflation monitor, rear spoiler, upgraded suspension, deletes remote keyless entry, AM/FM/CD player, High Performance sound system w/six speakers, steering-wheel radio controls.

GT1 adds: 6-way power driver seat, remote keyless entry, power sunroof, AM/FM/CD player, High Performance sound system w/six speakers, steering wheel radio controls.

OPTIONAL EQUIPMENT:
Major Packages

Solid Style Appearance Pkg., SE1	1695	1508
Manufacturer's discount price	1070	952

Remote keyless entry, power sunroof, AM/FM/CD player, rear spoiler. NA with 3.4-liter V6 engine.

Solid Sun Appearance Pkg., GT	1915	1704
Manufacturer's discount price	1290	1148

Remote keyless entry, power sunroof, chrome alloy wheels.

Solid Sound Appearance Pkg., GT1	1315	1171
Manufacturer's discount price	995	886

Leather upholstery, AM/FM/cassette/CD player, chrome alloy wheels.

Powertrains

3.4-liter V6 engine, SE1	655	583

Includes variable-assist power steering. Requires 4-speed automatic transmission.

4-speed automatic transmission, SE, SE1	785	699

Comfort and Convenience

Power sunroof, SE2, GT	650	579
Power driver seat, SE2, GT	265	236
Leather upholstery, SE2, GT, GT1	475	423
AM/FM/CD player w/six speakers, SE, SE1, GT	210	187
AM/FM/CD player w/High Performance sound system, SE, SE1, GT	275	245

Includes six speakers.

AM/FM/cassette/CD player, SE, SE1, GT	470	418
SE2, GT1	195	174

Includes High Performance six-speaker sound system.

Prices are accurate at time of publication; subject to manufacturer's changes.

	Retail Price	Dealer Invoice
Remote keyless entry, SE1, GT	$150	$134
Cruise control, SE	235	209

Appearance and Miscellaneous

Rear spoiler, SE, SE1, SE2	195	174
Alloy wheels, SE1	490	436
Chrome alloy wheels, GT, GT1	645	574

PONTIAC GRAND PRIX

RECOMMENDED

Pontiac Grand Prix SE 4-door

Front-wheel-drive midsize car; similar to Buick Century and Regal, Chevrolet Impala, and Oldsmobile Intrigue

Base price range: $19,935-$24,430. Built in USA. **Also consider:** Ford Taurus, Honda Accord, Nissan Maxima, Toyota Camry/Solara

FOR • Acceleration • Steering/handling **AGAINST** • Fuel economy (supercharged engine)

A more powerful base engine, revised wheels and nose styling, and a limited-edition Daytona 500 pace car replica head the changes for Pontiac's 2000 midsize line.

Grand Prix again offers a base SE sedan, sportier GT coupe and sedan, and high-performance GTP coupe and sedan. All have V6 engines. For 2000, the SE's standard 3.1 liter gains 15 horsepower, to 175. A 200-hp 3.8 is optional on the SE and standard on GTs. GTPs continue with a 240-hp supercharged 3.8. Automatic transmission, antilock 4-wheel disc brakes, and traction control are standard. Rear child-seat anchors and an anti-theft system that disables the starter unless the proper ignition key is used are newly standard for 2000. A simplified version of GM's OnStar assistance system is to be phased in during the year.

Only 2000 pace car replicas are planned, all silver coupes with unique 16-inch aluminum wheels, functional hood vents, decklid spoiler, bright exhaust tips, and Daytona decals. Inside are distinctive trim plates, contrasting-color upholstery, and embroidered Daytona emblems. Grand Prix shares its platform and some running gear with the Buick Century and Regal, Oldsmobile Intrigue, and Chevrolet Impala, but only Pontiac offers a coupe body style in addition to a sedan.

PERFORMANCE Grand Prix plays its sporty role well. Acceleration is adequate with the 3.1 V6, strong with the 3.8, and muscular with the supercharged 3.8. Transmissions are admirably smooth and downshift quickly for passing. Fuel economy is so-so. A test 3.8-liter SE averaged 22.7 mpg in mostly highway driving but only 15 in urban commuting. A test GTP managed 18 mpg overall on the required premium gas.

The firm SE and GT suspensions deliver a stable, comfortable ride with little bounce over undulations. Their handling is capable, their steering firm and direct. The GTP's tauter chassis provides still sharper, flatter cornering, but also more tire thump and small-bump harshness. Braking is strong in any model, though modulation is mediocre. Wind and engine noise are low, but tire thrum frequently intrudes.

ACCOMMODATIONS Like its siblings, Grand Prix has good room for four adults, five in a pinch. Front-seat comfort is adequate, but the rear bench is low to the floor and provides little support. Doors open wide, but foot clearance through the rear doors is tight. Gauges and controls are easy to see and reach, but the overall look of the dashboard is busy and cluttered. Pontiac's EyeCue head-up display projects key instrument read-

ings onto the windshield. Some testers find the option useful, others consider it gimmicky and take advantage of its off-switch.

A high parcel shelf limits vision astern for parking. The trunk is wide and has a long, flat floor, but the opening is narrow and liftover high. Grand Prixs we've tested have been impressively solid over rough roads, a feeling of substance at odds with the overuse of glossy, budget-grade plastic trim inside.

VALUE FOR THE MONEY Grand Prix is a capable, sporty midsize that challenges the class leaders in overall value. Like the related Intrigue, it earns our Recommended nod, with the Pontiac feeling more the brash American to the Oldsmobile's import-flavored approach.

ENGINES

	ohv V6	ohv V6	Supercharged ohv V6
Size, liters/cu. in.	3.1/191	3.8/231	3.8/231
Horsepower @ rpm	175 @ 5200	200 @ 5200	240 @ 5200
Torque (lbs./ft.) @ rpm	195 @ 4000	225 @ 4000	280 @ 3200
Availability	S[1]	S[2]	S[3]
EPA city/highway mpg			
4-speed OD automatic	20/29	19/30	18/28

1. SE. 2. GT; optional, SE. 3. GTP.

PRICES

Pontiac Grand Prix	Retail Price	Dealer Invoice
SE 4-door sedan	$19935	$18240
GT 2-door coupe	21515	19686
GT 4-door sedan	21665	19823
GTP 2-door coupe	24280	22216
GTP 4-door sedan	24430	22353
Destination charge	560	560

STANDARD EQUIPMENT:

SE: 3.1-liter V6 engine, 4-speed automatic transmission, enhanced traction control, antilock 4-wheel disc brakes, driver- and passenger-side airbags, daytime running lights, air conditioning, power steering, tilt steering wheel, cloth front bucket seats, front console, cupholders, auxiliary power outlet, AM/FM/cassette, power mirrors, power windows, power door locks, tachometer, visor mirrors, intermittent wipers, rear defogger, automatic headlights, floormats, fog lights, 205/70R15 tires, wheel covers.

GT adds to SE: 3.8-liter V6 engine, variable-assist power steering, cruise control, remote decklid release, rear spoiler, 225/60R16 tires, alloy wheels.

GTP adds: 3.8-liter supercharged V6 engine, full-function traction control, dual-zone automatic climate control, 6-way power driver seat, remote keyless entry, AM/FM/CD player w/equalizer, leather-wrapped steering wheel w/radio controls, rear seat trunk pass-through, overhead console, trip computer, sport suspension.

OPTIONAL EQUIPMENT:
Major Packages

Option Group 1SB, SE	345	307

Cruise control, rear seat trunk pass-through, remote decklid release.

Option Group 1SC, SE	1285	1144

Group 1SB plus overhead console, leather-wrapped steering wheel w/radio controls, 6-way power driver's seat, cargo net, remote keyless entry, rear spoiler, theft-deterrent system w/alarm. Requires 3.8-liter engine, 225/60R16 tires.

Option Group 1SB, GT	815	725

Rear seat trunk pass-through, leather-wrapped steering wheel w/radio controls, 6-way power driver's seat, cargo net, remote keyless entry, overhead console, theft-deterrent system w/alarm.

Option Group 1SC, GT sedan...............................	1390	1237
GT coupe	1360	1210

Group 1SB plus trip computer, dual-zone automatic climate control, automatic day/night rearview mirror, illuminated visor mirrors, rear reading lights (sedan).

Option Group 1SD, GT sedan...............................	2860	2545
GT coupe	2830	2519

Group 1SC plus leather upholstery, heated driver seat, 4-way power lumbar support, Head-up instrument display, power sunroof.

Ratings begin on page 213. Specifications begin on page 220.

CONSUMER GUIDE™

	Retail Price	Dealer Invoice
Option Group 1SB, GTP sedan	$555	$494
GTP coupe	525	467

Head-up instrument display, 4-power driver seat lumbar support, illuminated visor mirrors, front-door courtesy lamps, rear reading lights (sedan), assist grip, automatic day/night rearview mirror.

Option Group 1SC, GTP sedan	1650	1469
GTP coupe	1620	1442

Group 1SB plus leather upholstery, heated driver seat, power sunroof.

Security Pkg., SE	210	187

Remote keyless entry, theft-deterrent system w/alarm.

Powertrains

3.8-liter V6 engine, SE w/Group 1SC	415	369

Comfort and Convenience

6-way power driver seat, SE w/Group 1SB, GT	270	240
Driver seat 4-way power lumbar support	100	89

SE requires option Group 1SC. GT requires option group. Includes heat when ordered w/leather upholstery.

Leather upholstery	475	423

Requires option group.

AM/FM/CD player, SE, GT	140	125

SE requires option group.

AM/FM/CD player w/graphic equalizer, SE, GT	165	147

Requires option group. NA SE w/Group 1SB.

Bose AM/FM/cassette, GT	435	387
GTP	270	240

GT requires option group.

Bose AM/FM/CD player, GT	535	476
GTP	370	330

GT requires option pkg.

Power sunroof	570	507

SE requires Group 1SC. GT and GTP require option group. Deletes overhead console.

EyeCue head-up display, GT	275	245

Requires Group 1SC.

Appearance and Miscellaneous

Rear spoiler, SE	175	156

Requires Group 1SB.

Alloy wheels, SE	295	263

Requires option group and 225/60R16 tires.

5-spoke high-polished alloy wheels, GT, GTP	325	289

Requires option group.

225/60R16 tires, SE	160	142

Requires option group.

PONTIAC MONTANA

Pontiac Montana

Front-wheel-drive minivan; similar to Chevrolet Venture and Oldsmobile Silhouette

Base price range: $23,425-$24,535. Built in USA. **Also consider:** Dodge Caravan, Ford Windstar, Honda Odyssey

FOR • Ride • Passenger and cargo room **AGAINST** • Fuel economy

After last year's name change from Trans Sport to Montana, Pontiac's minivan enters 2000 with four sliding side doors standard on all models as its principal change.

Montana shares its underskin design with the Chevrolet Venture and Oldsmobile Silhouette and, like Venture, offers regular- and extended-length bodies. Montana's 3-door regular-length model is shelved, so all models now have dual sliding rear doors and seating for six or seven. A power sliding right-side door is optional on 7-seaters. The 7-passenger seating includes second- and third-row bench seats, while the 6-passenger setup uses all buckets. A second-row integrated child safety seat is available with the 7-passenger arrangement.

A 3.4-liter V6 with automatic transmission is the sole powertrain. Front side airbags, antilock brakes, and puncture-sealing tires are standard. Options include traction control, automatic load-leveling, an audio/video system with a dashboard-mounted VCR, and, for rear-seat passengers, a 5.5-inch TV monitor and headphone jacks.

For 2000, Montana gets a revised instrument cluster and child-seat tether anchors for all rear seats. Montana's performance and accommodations mirror those of similarly equipped Chevrolet Ventures.

The Chevrolet Venture report includes an evaluation of the Montana.

ENGINES

	ohv V6
Size, liters/cu. in.	3.4/207
Horsepower @ rpm	185 @ 5200
Torque (lbs./ft.) @ rpm	210 @ 4000
Availability	S

EPA city/highway mpg

4-speed OD automatic	19/26

PRICES

Pontiac Montana

	Retail Price	Dealer Invoice
Base regular length 4-door van, 7-passenger	$23425	$21200
Base regular length 4-door van, 6-passenger	23615	21372
Base extended 4-door van, 7-passenger	24535	22204
Destination charge	605	605

STANDARD EQUIPMENT:

Base: 3.4-liter V6 engine, 4-speed automatic transmission, driver- and passenger-side side airbags, front side-impact airbags, antilock brakes, daytime running lights, front air conditioning, interior air filter, power steering, tilt steering wheel, cruise control, dual sliding rear doors, cloth upholstery, front bucket seats w/manual lumbar adjustment, second row 2-passenger split folding bench seat and third row 3-passenger split folding bench seat (regular length 7-passenger, extended), second and third row bucket seats (regular length 6-passenger), front storage console, cupholders, heated power mirrors, power windows (6-passenger), power door locks, AM/FM/cassette, tachometer, visor mirrors, intermittent wipers, rear defogger, rear wiper/washer, auxiliary power outlets, front map lights, rear reading lights, automatic headlights, floormats, theft-deterrent system, roof rack (6-passenger), deep-tinted glass (6-passenger), fog lights, 215/70R15 self-sealing white-letter tires, wheel covers.

OPTIONAL EQUIPMENT:
Major Packages

Option Pkg. 1SB, 7-passenger	775	690

Remote keyless entry, power windows, deep-tinted glass.

Option Pkg. 1SC, regular length 7-passenger	1485	1322
extended	1935	1722

Group 1SB plus rear air conditioning, 6-way power driver seat, illuminated visor mirrors, overhead console, compass, outside temperature indicator, driver information center, roof rack.

Montana Vision, extended	2595	2310

Fold-down LCD color screen, videocassette player, video game input jack, remote control, six headphone jacks, videocassette storage. Requires Option Pkg., AM/FM/cassette/CD player, theft-deterrent system w/alarm, alloy wheels.

Sport Performance and Handling Pkg., 7-passenger w/Pkg. 1SB	1105	983
7-passenger w/Pkg. 1SC	930	828

Traction control, saddle-bag storage, automatic level control, roof rack, sport suspension, 215/70R15 performance self-sealing white-letter tires, alloy wheels.

Trailer Pkg., 7-passenger	165	147

Trailer wiring harness, heavy-duty engine and transmission cooling, heavy-duty flasher. Requires automatic level control or Sport Performance Handling Pkg., option pkg.

Prices are accurate at time of publication; subject to manufacturer's changes.

Powertrains

	Retail Price	Dealer Invoice
Traction control, 7-passenger...............................	$195	$174

Safety Features

Integrated child seat, 7-passenger.........................	125	111

NA w/7-passenger quad seating.

Comfort and Convenience

Power sliding passenger-side rear door, 7-passenger...	450	401

Requires power windows, remote keyless entry.

Rear air conditioning, extended	450	401

Requires Option Pkg. 1SB.

Power driver seat, 7-passenger	270	240

Requires Option Pkg. 1SB.

Power passenger seat, 7-passenger	305	271

Requires Option Pkg. 1SC.

7-passenger quad seating, 7-passenger.................	295	263

Includes quad captain chairs. Requires option pkg.

8-passenger seating, 7-passenger..........................	280	249

Includes five bucket seats, rear passenger split folding bench seat. Requires option pkg.

Leather upholstery..	1350	1202

Includes leather-wrapped steering wheel w/radio controls. Requires option pkg., power driver seat, 7-passenger quad seating.

Heated front seats, 7-passenger............................	195	174

Requires option pkg., leather upholstery, traction control.

Power windows	—	—
Overhead console, 7-passenger	175	156

Includes outside temperature indicator, driver information center, compass. Requires Option Pkg. 1SB.

AM/FM/CD player w/equalizer, 7-passenger...........	450	401
7-passenger ordered w/leather upholstery	265	236

Includes rear-seat audio controls and earphone jacks, leather-wrapped steering wheel w/radio controls, extended-range coaxial speakers. Requires option pkg.

AM/FM/cassette/CD player w/equalizer, 7-passenger..	550	490
7-passenger ordered w/leather upholstery	365	325

Includes rear-seat audio controls and earphone jacks, leather-wrapped steering wheel w/radio controls, extended-range coaxial speakers. Requires option pkg.

Leather-wrapped steering wheel, 7-passenger..	185	165

Includes radio controls.

Remote keyless entry, 7-passenger........................	175	156

Appearance and Miscellaneous

Theft-deterrent system w/alarm, 7-passenger..	60	53

Requires remote keyless entry.

Deep-tinted glass, 7-passenger.............................	275	245
Roof rack, 7-passenger	175	156
Automatic level control, 7-passenger.....................	200	178

Includes saddle-bag storage. Requires alloy wheels.

Alloy wheels	280	249

PONTIAC SUNFIRE

Pontiac Sunfire SE sedan

Front-wheel-drive subcompact car; similar to Chevrolet Cavalier

Base price range: $14,005-$21,745. Built in USA and Mexico. **Also consider:** Chevrolet Prizm, Ford Focus, Honda Civic

---

FOR • Fuel economy • Acceleration (2.4-liter engine) **AGAINST** • Rear visibility • Rear-seat comfort • Interior materials

Subtle cosmetic changes and some new interior features mark the 2000 Sunfire, which went on sale in summer 1999. Pontiac's smallest car comes as a 4-door SE sedan, 2-door SE and GT coupe, and a GT convertible. The convertible has a power top with glass rear window and defroster. Sunfire shares mechanical components with the Chevrolet Cavalier but has slightly different styling.

For 2000, Sunfire gets revised lower bodyside trim and a new rear fascia with round backup lamps. GTs have a reworked nose with integral foglamps, plus new-look alloy wheels. Inside is a revamped center console with two cupholders and a padded center armrest. GTs gain a leather-wrapped steering wheel, shift knob, and parking-brake handle. Automatic-transmission models now have a lighted console shift indicator. And a high-powered Monsoon audio system is a new option.

A 2.2-liter 4-cylinder is the SE's base engine. A 2.4-liter four is standard on GTs, optional on SEs. Manual transmission is standard and is now supplied by Getrag of Germany in an effort to improve shift feel. The 2.2 liter's optional automatic transmission is a 3-speed, the 2.4's is a 4-speed. Antilock brakes are standard, and traction control is included with the 4-speed automatic. Sunfire's performance and accommodations are similar to those of comparably equipped Cavaliers.

The Chevrolet Cavalier report includes an evaluation of the Sunfire.

ENGINES

	ohv I4	dohc I4
Size, liters/cu. in.	2.2/133	2.4/146
Horsepower @ rpm	115 @ 5000	150 @ 5600
Torque (lbs./ft.) @ rpm	135 @ 3600	155 @ 4400
Availability	S[1]	S[2]
EPA city/highway mpg		
5-speed OD manual	24/34	23/33
3-speed automatic..............................	23/29	
4-speed OD automatic	23/31	22/30

1. SE. 2. GT; optional, SE.

PRICES

Pontiac Sunfire	Retail Price	Dealer Invoice
SE 2-door coupe	$14005	$12955
SE 4-door sedan	14105	13047
GT 2-door coupe	16295	15073
GT 2-door convertible	21745	20114
Destination charge	510	510

STANDARD EQUIPMENT:

SE: 2.2-liter 4-cylinder engine, 5-speed manual transmission, driver- and passenger-side airbags, antilock brakes, daytime running lights, air conditioning, power steering, cloth reclining front bucket seats, center console with storage armrest, folding rear seat, AM/FM radio, intermittent wipers, tachometer, visor mirrors, rear defogger, floormats, left remote and remote outside mirrors, theft-deterrent system, rear spoiler (coupe), 195/70R14 tires, wheel covers.

GT adds to SE coupe: 2.4-liter dohc 4-cylinder engine, tilt leather-wrapped steering wheel, leather-wrapped shifter and handbrake, AM/FM/CD player, fog lights, sport suspension, 205/55R16 tires, alloy wheels.

GT convertible adds: 4-speed automatic transmission, traction control, cruise control, power mirrors, power windows, power door locks, remote keyless entry, power top, variable-intermittent wipers, map lights, cargo net, theft-deterrent system w/alarm, 195/65R15 tires.

OPTIONAL EQUIPMENT:

Major Packages

Option Group 1SB, SE coupe	1070	952
SE sedan	1220	1086

Tilt steering wheel, 3-speed automatic transmission, AM/FM/CD player, rear spoiler (sedan).

Option Group 1SC, SE coupe	1820	1620
SE sedan	2010	1789

Group 1SB plus cruise control, power door locks, remote keyless entry, variable intermittent wipers, overhead console w/storage, map lights, cargo net, theft-deterrent system w/alarm.

	Retail Price	Dealer Invoice
Sun and Sound Pkg. w/Group 1SB, SE coupe.......	$1800	$1602
Manufacturer's discount price	1375	1224
Group 1SB plus power sunroof, 195/65R15 tires.		
Sun and Sound Pkg. w/Group 1SC, SE coupe.......	2510	2234
Manufacturer's discount price	2085	1856
Group 1SC plus power sunroof, 195/65R15 tires.		
Special Edition Pkg. w/Group 1SB, SE sedan........	2210	1967
Manufacturer's discount price	1630	1451
Group 1SB plus power mirrors and windows, power door locks, remote keyless entry, theft-deterrent system w/alarm, 195/65R15 tires.		
Special Edition Pkg. w/Group 1SC, SE sedan........	2590	2305
Manufacturer's discount price	2010	1789
Group 1SC plus power mirrors and windows, 195/65R15 tires.		
Security Pkg., SE coupe	370	329
Power door locks, remote keyless entry, theft-deterrent system w/alarm. Requires Group 1SB.		
Option Group 1SB, GT coupe	1480	1317
4-speed automatic transmission, traction control, cruise control, power door locks, remote keyless entry, variable intermittent wipers, theft-deterrent system w/alarm.		
Option Group 1SC, GT coupe	2135	1900
Group 1SB plus power mirrors and windows, Monsoon sound system, over head console w/storage, cargo net.		
Power Pkg., SE coupe, GT coupe	380	338
Power mirrors and windows. SE requires Group 1SC. GT requires Group 1SB.		

Powertrains

2.4-liter dohc 4-cylinder engine, SE	450	401
Requires Group 1SC and 195/65R15 tires.		
3-speed automatic transmission, SE........................	600	534
NA with 2.4-liter engine.		
4-speed automatic transmission, GT coupe............	810	721
SE w/Group 1SB/1SC	210	187
Includes traction control.		
5-speed manual transmission,		
GT coupe w/Group 1SB/1SC, GT convertible (credit)		(810)
(721)		
SE w/Group 1SB/1SC (credit)	(600)	(534)
SE requires 2.2-liter 4-cylinder engine.		

Comfort and Convenience

Cruise control, SE w/Group 1SB...........................	235	209
AM/FM/cassette, SE..	165	147
AM/FM/CD player, SE..	320	285
AM/FM/cassette/CD player	100	89
SE requires Group 1SB or 1SC.		
Monsoon sound system, SE coupe, GT coupe.......	195	174
Requires AM/FM/CD player or AM/FM/cassette/CD player. SE requires Group 1SB or 1SC. GT coupe requires Group 1SB.		
Power sunroof, GT coupe w/Group 1SB................	595	530
GT w/Group 1SC	555	494
Replaces overhead console when ordered with Group 1SC.		
Alloy wheels, SE	295	263
Requires Option Group 1SC.		
195/65R15 tires, SE	135	120

PORSCHE BOXSTER

Porsche Boxster S

Rear-wheel-drive sports and GT car
Base price range: $41,430-$49,930. Built in Germany.
Also consider: BMW Z3 Series, Honda S2000, Mercedes-

Benz SLK230

FOR • Steering/handling • Acceleration • Braking **AGAINST** • Noise • Ride • Passenger room • Climate controls

A new high-performance model and more power for the base version are 2000 newsmakers for Porsche's mid-engine 2-seater. Boxster, the lowest-priced Porsche, is a rear-wheel-drive convertible with a horizontally opposed 6-cylinder engine mounted behind the cockpit. For 2000, the base model's 2.5-liter engine is enlarged to 2.7 liters and gains 16 horsepower, for 217. The new Boxster S has a 250-hp 3.2 liter. Manual transmission is standard; the base version has a 5-speed, the Boxster S a 6-speed. Both also offer Porsche's Tiptronic 5-speed automatic transmission with manual-shift buttons on the steering wheel. Antilock 4-wheel disc brakes and side airbags are standard. Boxster's rear tires are wider than the fronts, and the S comes with 17-inch wheels, a size that's optional on the base model in place of 16s; 18s are optional on both. The S also has larger brake discs, suspension upgrades, and dual exhaust outlets.

EVALUATION Boxster has excellent handling, but rides stiffly. Noise from wind, engine, and tires can be intrusive, too. Acceleration is lively; our test '99 5-speed did 0-60 mph in 7.5 seconds, slightly slower than Porsche's claim of 6.7. Porsche says the 2000 model does 0-60 in 6.4 seconds, and pegs the new S at 5.7 seconds. Our test Boxster averaged 21.7 mpg. Larger people may feel cramped in the Boxster, even with the top down. The audio and climate controls are confusing, and we'd prefer a tilt steering wheel to the standard telescopic adjustment. Front and rear compartments offer decent cargo room, and visibility is okay despite the low seating position. The plastic rear window is out of place at this price, however, and the optional wind deflector is effective but cumbersome to remove or install. It's not perfect, but Boxster is a genuine sports car and genuinely entertaining.

ENGINES

	dohc H6	dohc H6
Size, liters/cu. in.	2.7/164	3.2/194
Horsepower @ rpm	217 @ 6500	250 @ 6250
Torque (lbs./ft.) @ rpm	192 @ 4500	225 @ 4500
Availability	S[1]	S[2]
EPA city/highway mpg		
5-speed OD manual	20/28	
6-speed OD manual		18/26
5-speed OD automatic	17/25	17/24

1. Boxster. 2. Boxster S.

PRICES

Porsche Boxster	Retail Price	Dealer Invoice
Base 2-door convertible	$41430	$36261
S 2-door convertible	49930	—
Destination charge	765	765

S dealer invoice price not available at time of publication.

STANDARD EQUIPMENT:

Base: 2.7-liter dohc 6-cylinder engine, 5-speed manual transmission, driver- and passenger-side airbags, side-impact airbags, antilock 4-wheel disc brakes, integrated roll bars, air conditioning w/automatic climate control, interior air filter, variable-assist power steering, leather-wrapped telescoping steering wheel, leather-wrapped handbrake handle, partial leather upholstery, front bucket seats w/power recliners and driver-seat height adjustment, center console, heated power mirrors, power windows, power door locks, power convertible top, AM/FM/cassette, digital clock, tachometer, illuminated visor mirrors, heated washer nozzles, theft-deterrent system, rear spoiler, front and rear fog lights, 205/55ZR16 front tires, 225/50ZR16 rear tires, alloy wheels.

S adds: 3.2-liter dohc 6-cylinder engine, 6-speed manual transmission, remote keyless entry, variable intermittent wipers, sport suspension, 205/50ZR17 front tires, 255/40ZR17 rear tires.

OPTIONAL EQUIPMENT:
Major Packages

P09 Sport Pkg., Base	2110	1790
Cruise control, remote keyless entry, AM/FM/CD player, Hi-Fi sound system, wind deflector. Requires optional wheels.		

Prices are accurate at time of publication; subject to manufacturer's changes.

	Retail Price	Dealer Invoice
P10/P11 Sport Touring Pkg., Base	$5585	$4750

P09 Sport Pkg. plus trip computer, 6-disc CD player, aluminum instrument dials, silver-painted roll bar, aluminum/leather handbrake and shifter, stainless steel door sills, chrome exhaust. Deletes CD player. Requires optional wheels.

P25 Sport Pkg., S	2235	1899

AM/FM/CD player w/digital sound processing, cruise control, wind deflector. Requires optional wheels. NA with GPS Navigation System.

P26/27 Sport Touring Pkg., S w/manual transmission	5150	4377
S w/automatic transmission	5090	4236

P25 Sport Pkg. plus trip computer, CD storage shelf, aluminum and leather shift knob and hand brake, litronic headlights w/washers, body-colored roll bars. Requires optional wheels.

Powertrains

5-speed automatic trans. w/manual-shift capability	3210	—
Traction control	870	739

Comfort and Convenience

GPS Navigation System	3540	2986

Global positioning navigation system, cassette/CD player, on-board computer, climate control indicator.

Cruise control	560	477
Heated seats	400	341
Power seats w/memory	1520	1298
Full leather upholstery	1990	1699
AM/FM/CD player	345	293

NA with GPS Navigation System.

6-disc CD changer	831	707

Requires Hi-Fi sound system.

Hi-Fi sound system	600	512

Includes six speakers, amplifier.

Digital sound processing	1175	—
Remote keyless entry, Base	610	481

Includes theft-deterrent system w/alarm.

On-board computer	449	381

Appearance and Miscellaneous

Removable hardtop	2295	1960

Includes rear defogger.

Litronic headlights	1070	914

Requires headlight washers

Headlight washers	225	190
Sport chassis	690	589

Sport suspension, height adjustable shock absorbers.

Boxster-design alloy wheels, Base	1215	1033

Includes 205/50ZR17 front tires, 255/40ZR17 rear tires.

Turbo-Look alloy wheels, Base	2735	2335

Includes 225/40ZR18 front tires, 265/35ZR18 rear tires.

Dyno wheels, S	1110	943
Sport Design Wheels, S	2660	2260

Includes 225/40ZR18 front tires, 265/35ZR18 rear tires.

PORSCHE 911

Porche 911 Carrera Cabriolet

Rear- or all-wheel-drive sports and GT car

Base price range: $65,590-$83,820. Built in Germany.
Also consider: Acura NSX, BMW Z3 Series, Chevrolet Corvette

FOR • Acceleration • Build quality • Exterior finish • Steering/handling • Braking **AGAINST** • Control layout • Cargo room • Noise • Rear seat room/comfort

Porsche's "senior" sports car, the rear-engine 911, gains some power and an available antiskid system for 2000. The 911 continues in coupe and convertible form. Both are available with rear-wheel drive as the Carrera 2 or as the all-wheel-drive Carrera 4. For 2000, their 3.4 liter 6-cylinder with horizontally-opposed cylinders gains 4 horsepower, to 300. A 6-speed manual transmission is standard. Optional is Porsche's Tiptronic 5-speed automatic with manual-shift buttons on the steering wheel. Antilock 4-wheel disc brakes and side airbags are standard. Porsche's Stability Management antiskid system is standard on Carrera 4s, and this year is available as an option on Carrera 2s. It's designed to apply individual brakes to counteract skids in turns. A satellite navigation system also is optional on both models.

EVALUATION Any 911 is a high-performance sports car of the first rank. Acceleration is strong and smooth, ride very firm. Handling is confident and communicative, though the nose of the Carrera 2 convertible we tested went slightly wayward in hard acceleration and in crosswinds. That test car averaged 20.8 mpg, while a Carrera 4 coupe test car averaged 17.2; both had manual transmission. At highway speeds, engine and tire noise intrude on normal conversation, but that's true of most in this class. The interior is roomy for two, but front seatbacks can be uncomfortably narrow and the back seat has only enough room for small children. Cargo space is minimal, too, and the convertible's plastic rear window annoys at these prices. The 911 is relatively practical, as high-performance sports cars go. But BMW's Z3-based M-Roadster and Coupe and Porsche's own Boxster deliver similar thrills at a savings of $20,000 or more.

ENGINES

	dohc H6
Size, liters/cu. in.	3.4/207
Horsepower @ rpm	300 @ 6800
Torque (lbs./ft.) @ rpm	258 @ 4600
Availability	S

EPA city/highway mpg

6-speed OD manual	17/25[1]
5-speed OD automatic	16/25[2]

1. 17/24 w/Carrera 4.   2. 16/24 w/Carrera 4.

PRICES

Porsche 911	Retail Price	Dealer Invoice
Carrera 2-door coupe, 6-speed	$65590	$56736
Carrera 2-door coupe, automatic	69010	59610
Carrera 2-door convertible, 6-speed	74970	64855
Carrera 2-door convertible, automatic	78390	67729
Carrera 4 2-door coupe, 6-speed	71020	61437
Carrera 4 2-door coupe, automatic	74440	64311
Carrera 4 2-door convertible, 6-speed	80400	69546
Carrera 4 2-door convertible, automatic	83820	72420
Destination charge	765	765
Optional air transportation	4000	4000

STANDARD EQUIPMENT:

Carrera coupe: 3.4-liter dohc 6-cylinder engine, 6-speed manual or 5-speed automatic transmission w/manual-shift capablity, driver- and passenger-side airbags, front side-impact airbags, antilock 4-wheel disc brakes, air conditioning w/automatic climate control, interior air filter, variable-assist power steering, leather-wrapped telescoping steering wheel, cruise control, partial leather upholstery, front reclining bucket seats w/power back rests, front storage console, split folding rear seat, power sunroof, heated power mirrors, power windows, power door locks, remote keyless entry, AM/FM/cassette, digital clock, tachometer, rear defogger, intermittent wipers w/heated washer nozzles, illuminated visor mirrors, theft-deterrent system, rear spoiler, fog lights, 205/50ZR17 front and 255/40ZR17 rear tires, alloy wheels.

Carrera convertible adds: power folding convertible top.

Carrera 4 coupe adds to Carrera coupe: permanent all-wheel drive, antiskid system.

Carrera 4 convertible adds to Carrera convertible: permanent all-wheel drive, antiskid system, removable hardtop.

Ratings begin on page 213. Specifications begin on page 220.
CONSUMER GUIDE™

OPTIONAL EQUIPMENT:

	Retail Price	Dealer Invoice
Safety Features		
Antiskid system, Carrera 2	$1215	$1025

Comfort and Convenience

	Retail Price	Dealer Invoice
PCM Information/Navigation System	3540	2986
Global positioning navigation system w/separate CD-Rom drive, on-board computer, climate control indicator.		
Power front seats	1520	1298
Includes driver seat memory.		
Heated front seats	400	341
Hi-Fi Sound audio system	600	507
Includes amplifier system, 10 speakers (coupe), 8 speakers (convertible), multi-channel loud speaker system.		
AM/FM/CD player	345	293
NA with PCM Information/Navigation System.		
6-disc CD changer	705	594
Rear wiper, coupe	335	283
Trip computer	275	232

Appearance and Miscellaneous

	Retail Price	Dealer Invoice
Roof rack, coupe	390	329
Litronic headlights	1070	914
Requires headlight washers.		
Headlight washers	225	190
Sport Chassis, coupe	690	589
Sport suspension.		

SAAB 9-3

Saab 9-3 Viggen 2-door hatchback

Front-wheel-drive near-luxury car

Base price range: $25,900-$44,995. Built in Sweden and Finland. **Also consider:** Acura TL, Audi A4, Infiniti I30, Volvo 70 series

FOR • Acceleration • Braking • Cargo room (exc. convertible)
AGAINST • Rear-seat room/comfort (convertible) • Rear visibility

The OnStar satellite assistance system and more power highlight additions to Saab's compact-sized lineup. The 9-3 returns with 2- and 4-door hatchbacks and a 2-door convertible in base and uplevel SE form. For 2000, the high-performance Viggen 2-door is joined by convertible and 4-door versions. All 9-3s use turbocharged 4-cylinder engines. The base 2.0-liter again makes 185 horsepower. SE models now come with last year's optional 2.0 High Output engine, which gains 5 hp, to 205. Viggen's 2.3 liter has 230 hp, also a gain of 5. Manual transmission is mandatory for Viggens; base and SE models offer an optional 4-speed automatic. All have standard antilock brakes, front side airbags, and Saab's anti-whiplash front Active Head Restraints. Convertibles include a power top with glass rear window. New on SEs for 2000 are revised lower-body skirts, a special sports suspension for the 4-door, and a standard rear spoiler for the convertible. General Motors owns Saab's car-making division, and GM's OnStar communications system arrives as a first-time 9-3 option.

EVALUATION From the responsive but calm base model to the young-colt feel of the Viggen, the 9-3s offer sporting driving in a space-efficient—and somewhat quirky—package. Our base 5-speed test car ran 0-60 mph in a quick 7.5 seconds and averaged 19.4 mpg; High Output models are slightly faster, and our 4-door averaged 21.3 mpg. Neither delivers much power until 3000 rpm, and turbo lag—a delay in throttle response—makes

smooth driving tricky. Further, most rivals offer traction control, a feature unavailable on the 9-3. Handling is responsive, but SEs ride much stiffer than the notably compliant base models. Relatively narrow and tall, hatchbacks have fairly commodious seating for five and near-wagonlike cargo room. Convertibles seat four. Gauges and controls are well-located, though mounting the ignition key on the floor is a debatable bow to Saab tradition. Detail finish is good and materials classy, but our test convertible suffered noticeable body flex over bumps, plus a creaky top. For near-luxury Swedish-style, most buyers pick a Volvo S70 sedan or V70 wagon, leaving the 9-3 largely to Saab loyalists.

ENGINES

	Turbocharged dohc I4	Turbocharged dohc I4	Turbocharged dohc I4
Size, liters/cu. in.	2.0/121	2.0/121	2.3/140
Horsepower @ rpm	185 @ 5500	205 @ 5500	230 @ 5500
Torque (lbs./ft.) @ rpm	194 @ 2100	209 @ 2200	258 @ 2500
Availability	S[1]	S[2]	S[3]
EPA city/highway mpg			
5-speed OD manual	19/27	20/27	20/29
4-speed OD automatic	19/25	20/26	

1. Base; 184 lb-ft @ 1900 rpm with auto. trans. 2. SE; 184 lb-ft @ 1900 rpm with auto trans. 3. Viggen.

PRICES

Saab 9-3

	Retail Price	Dealer Invoice
Base 2-door hatchback	$25900	$24346
Base 4-door hatchback	26400	24578
Base 2-door convertible	39450	36491
SE 4-door hatchback	31895	29758
SE 2-door convertible	42995	39770
Viggen 2-door hatchback	37750	34353
Viggen 4-door hatchback	37750	34353
Viggen 2-door convertible	44995	40945
Destination charge	575	575

STANDARD EQUIPMENT:

Base: 2.0-liter turbocharged dohc 4-cylinder 185-horsepower engine, 5-speed manual transmission, driver- and passenger-side airbags, front side-impact airbags, front seat active head restraints, antilock 4-wheel disc brakes, daytime running lights, air conditioning, interior air filter, power steering, telescoping steering wheel, cruise control, cloth upholstery (hatchback), leather upholstery (convertible), front bucket seats, power driver seat (convertible), driver seat manual lumbar adjustment, folding rear seat w/trunk pass-through (convertible), split folding rear seat w/trunk pass-through (hatchback), cupholder, heated power mirrors, power windows, power door locks, remote keyless entry, AM/FM/cassette w/CD changer controls and six speakers, steering-wheel radio controls, power antenna, digital clock, tachometer, variable intermittent wipers, rear defogger, rear wiper/washer (hatchback), illuminated visor mirrors, power convertible top (convertible), automatic-off headlights, floormats, theft-deterrent system, headlight wiper/washer, front and rear fog lights, cornering lights, rear spoiler (hatchback), tool kit, 195/60VR15 tires, alloy wheels.

SE adds: 2.0-liter turbocharged dohc 4-cylinder 205-horsepower engine, automatic climate control, leather upholstery, 8-way power front seats w/driver seat memory, leather-wrapped steering wheel and shift knob, wood interior trim, power sunroof (hatchback), 8-speaker sound system w/Weather Band and subwoofer, trip computer, rear spoiler (convertible), sport suspension (hatchback), 205/50ZR16 tires.

Viggen adds: 2.3-liter turbocharged dohc 4-cylinder 230-horsepower engine, special interior trim, front sport seats, aerodynamic body cladding, sport suspension, 215/45ZR17 tires, deletes power antenna.

OPTIONAL EQUIPMENT:

Powertrains

	Retail Price	Dealer Invoice
4-speed automatic transmission, Base, SE	1200	1032

Safety Features

	Retail Price	Dealer Invoice
Integrated child seat, Base 4-door hatchback........	300	258
NA with leather upholstery.		

Prices are accurate at time of publication; subject to manufacturer's changes.

Comfort and Convenience

	Retail Price	Dealer Invoice
OnStar System	$895	$740
Includes Global Positioning System, roadside assistance, emergency services. Includes service fees for three months. Price may vary.		
Power sunroof, Base hatchback	1150	989
AM/FM/CD player	NC	NC
Leather upholstery, Base hatchbacks	1350	1161
Heated front seats,		
Base, SE convertible, Viggen	370	318
Heated front and rear seats, SE hatchback	520	447

SAAB 9-5

Saab 9-5 sedan

Front-wheel-drive luxury car

Base price range: $32,575-$39,775. Built in Sweden.
Also consider: Acura RL, Lincoln LS, Mercedes-Benz E-Class

FOR • Acceleration • Handling/roadholding • Passenger and cargo room • Build quality • Exterior finish **AGAINST** • Road noise • Climate controls

Saab's "senior" line gains a sporty new Aero sedan for 2000 to go along with base- and SE-model sedans and wagons. The new Aero has lower-body skirting, uprated chassis, and the 230-horsepower turbocharged 4-cylinder engine from Saab's 9-3 Viggen models. Base 9-5s retain a 170-hp turbo four. SEs now come with last year's optional turbo V6, which no longer is available for base models. All 9-5s have antilock brakes, front head/chest side airbags, and Saab's anti-whiplash front Active Head Restraints. SEs come with automatic transmission; the Aero and base 9-5s manual or automatic. A power sunroof and traction control are now standard on all models. Newly optional in place of 16-inch wheels and tires for base and SE models are 17-inchers—same size as those on the Aero. General Motors owns Saab's car division, and GM's OnStar communication system is a new 9-5 option.

EVALUATION We haven't yet driven the Aero, but other 9-5s are stable, relaxed high-speed cruisers that are also at home on twisty roads. Both the V6 and base 4-cylinder provide brisk takeoffs, good midrange punch, and reasonable mileage, but suffer minor, annoying "turbo lag," most particularly with automatic transmission. A base sedan averaged 22 mpg in our tests, a V6 19.7, both on regular fuel. Base and SE 9-5s have a little more cornering lean than we like; ditto tire noise except on smooth pavement. However, ride and braking are outstanding, interiors adult-size comfortable, and nicely appointed. Sedans boast great trunk space, wagons a large luggage bay that can be enhanced by an optional roll-out load floor. The automatic climate control is mounted too low, but the dashboard layout is otherwise good. Overall, the 9-5s are impressive European cars with a personality that appeals to both individualists and anyone interested in efficient design.

ENGINES

	Turbocharged dohc I4	Turbocharged dohc I4	Turbocharged dohc I4
Size, liters/cu. in.	2.3/140	3.0/180	2.3/140
Horsepower @ rpm	170 @ 5500	200 @ 5000	230 @ 5500
Torque (lbs./ft.) @ rpm	207 @ 1800	229 @ 2500	258 @ 1900
Availability	S[1]	S[2]	S[3]
EPA city/highway mpg			
5-speed OD manual	21/30		NA
4-speed OD automatic	19/26	18/26	NA

1. Base. 2. SE. 3. Aero; 243 lb-ft @ 1900 rpm with auto. trans.

PRICES

Saab 9-5

	Retail Price	Dealer Invoice
Base 4-door sedan	$32575	$30295
Base 4-door wagon	32575	30295
SE 4-door sedan	37750	34919
SE 4-door wagon	37750	34919
Aero 4-door sedan	39775	36792
Destination charge	575	575

STANDARD EQUIPMENT:

Base: 2.3-liter turbocharged dohc 4-cylinder 170-horsepower engine, 5-speed manual transmission, traction control, driver- and passenger-side airbags, front side-impact airbags, front seat active head restraints, antilock 4-wheel disc brakes, daytime running lights, air conditioning w/dual-zone automatic climate control, interior air filter, power steering, tilt and telescoping steering wheel, leather-wrapped steering wheel and shifter, cruise control, cloth upholstery, front bucket seats, power front seats, split folding rear seat w/trunk pass-through, wood interior trim, AM/FM/cassette/CD player, steering-wheel radio controls, digital clock, heated power mirrors, power windows, power door locks, remote keyless entry, power sunroof, tachometer, trip computer, cupholders, glove box refrigerator, illuminated visor mirrors, variable-intermittent wipers, rear defogger, remote decklid/fuel door release, automatic-off headlights, parcel shelf/cargo cover (wagon), floormats, theft-deterrent system, roof rails (wagon), front and rear fog lights, headlight wiper/washer, cornering lights, 215/55R16 tires, alloy wheels.

SE adds: 3.0-liter turbocharged dohc V6 engine, 4-speed automatic transmission, leather upholstery, memory driver seat and mirrors, tilt-down passenger-side mirror, Harman/Kardon sound system, automatic day/night rearview mirror.

Aero adds: 2.3-liter turbocharged dohc 4-cylinder 230-horsepower engine, 5-speed manual transmission, bodyside cladding, sport suspension, 225/45ZR17 tires.

OPTIONAL EQUIPMENT:

Major Packages

Premium Pkg., Base	1995	1716
Leather upholstery, driver seat memory, Harman/Kardon sound system.		

Powertrains

4-speed automatic transmission, Base, Aero	1200	1032

Comfort and Convenience

OnStar System	895	740
Includes Global Positioning System, roadside assistance, emergency services. Includes service fees for three months. Price may vary.		
Power-ventilated front seats	950	817
Base requires Premium Pkg.		
Heated front and rear seats	520	447
Wheel and Tire Pkg., Base, SE	1950	1615
One-piece alloy wheels, 225/45ZR17 tires.		
Wheel upgrade, Aero	1650	1370
Two-piece alloy wheels.		

SATURN L-SERIES

Saturn LS2

Front-wheel-drive midsize car

Base price range: $15,010-$21,360. Built in USA. **Also consider:** Honda Accord, Toyota Camry/Solara,

Volkswagen Passat

FOR • Acceleration (V6 models) • Steering/handling
AGAINST • Rear-seat comfort

After nearly a decade marketing 4-cylinder subcompacts, Saturn introduces midsize models with an available V6. The 2000 L-Series sedan and wagon are based on the German Opel Vectra; Saturn and Opel are part of General Motors.

The L-Series is assembled by Saturn in Delaware and uses Saturn's dent-and rust-resistant polymer panels for front fenders, doors, and bumper fascias; other body parts are steel. The L-Series is dimensionally similar to the Honda Accord and Toyota Camry, which Saturn used as benchmarks. Saturn's no-haggle, full-sticker-price policy applies.

Sedans come in LS, LS1, and LS2 form, wagons in LW1 and LW2 trim. LS, LS1, and LW1 use a new GM 4-cylinder engine. LS2 and LW2 borrow their V6 from the Saab 9-5, but without Saab's turbocharger (Saab is another GM holding). LS and LS1 get manual or automatic transmission; all other models are automatic. Antilock brakes are optional and include traction control. Side airbags are not offered, but Saturn says head-protecting "curtain" side airbags will be available in mid-2000. All models seat five and have split 60/40 folding rear seatbacks. LS2 and LW2 add 4-wheel disc brakes.

PERFORMANCE The L-Series is a reasonably accomplished performer distinguished by fine handling. Saturn pegs the volume-leading automatic-transmission LS1 at 9.8 seconds 0-60 mph, the V6/automatic LS2 at 8.2. That's roughly a second behind our test Accords, but in practice, both L-Series powertrains are up to most tasks. Some early V6 models we tested exhibited poor throttle response off the line and suffered slow downshifts in passing situations. Others felt spry, with automatics that furnished alert downshifts even in hilly terrain. The 5-speed adds a sporty flair, but provides no great leap in performance. We had no opportunity to measure fuel economy.

Suspension tuning copied from Opel pays off in impressive high-speed stability and confident cornering. Steering is linear and communicative, although it feels heavy at low speeds and, in the 4-cylinder/manual we tested, light at high speeds. Wagons and sedans handle nearly identically, although wagons ride marginally stiffer and neither absorbs bumps as well as a Camry. In short, L-Series buyers get a firm Eurostyle ride along with sporty road manners. The basic Opel braking system brings impressive stopping power and pedal feel.

It took years for Saturn to reduce intrusive noise levels in its subcompacts, but the L-Series starts out as quiet as most competitors, though it's not as isolating as a Camry.

ACCOMMODATIONS Four adults get as much room as in an Accord or Camry, though the L-Series doesn't match their interior refinement. The available leather-upholstered buckets come with seat heaters, but the cloth seats are more supportive. Rear head and leg room is ample, but the rear cushion is soft and low to the floor, the small fold-down armrest is useless, and there's no center shoulder belt.

Instrumentation is large and clear, but the cowl is rather tall, and vision directly aft is pinched by the high deck. There's independent control of air conditioning in any vent mode, but the crude fan-speed switch is in contrast to smooth rotary temperature and air-flow dials. Illuminated power-window switches are in the center console. So is the gear-position readout for the automatic transmission; unfortunately, it washes out in direct sunlight, and there's no redundant indicator in the instrument cluster. Cabin storage includes cupholders front and rear. The sedan's large, accessible trunk is a competitive advantage, as is the availability of the roomy wagon, a body style few rivals offer.

Our test cars were rattle-free, but L-Series interiors have a discount-bin feel in their details typified by the turn-signal lever's brittle movement, door handles of uninviting plated plastic, and small, plasticky audio controls.

VALUE FOR THE MONEY The long-awaited L-Series satisfies in most facets of performance, and while its cabin is roomy, it's furnished to meet modest expectations. L-Series base prices, however, undercut those of comparable Accord and Camry models. The volume LS1/automatic, for example, undercuts the rival Accord LX by about $1730 and the Camry LE by almost $2700.

ENGINES	dohc I4	dohc V6
Size, liters/cu. in.	2.2/134	3.0/183
Horsepower @ rpm	137 @ 5800	182 @ 5600
Torque (lbs./ft.) @ rpm	147 @ 4400	190 @ 3600
Availability	S[1]	S[2]
EPA city/highway mpg		
5-speed OD manual	24/32	
4-speed OD automatic	23/32	20/26

1. LS, LS1, LW1. 2. LS2, LW2.

PRICES

Saturn L-Series	Retail Price	Dealer Invoice
LS 4-door sedan, 5-speed	$15010	$13359
LS 4-door sedan, automatic	15870	14124
LS1 4-door sedan, 5-speed	16750	14908
LS1 4-door sedan, automatic	17610	15673
LW1 4-door wagon, automatic	18835	16763
LS2 4-door sedan, automatic	20135	17920
LW2 4-door wagon, automatic	21360	19010
Destination charge	440	440

STANDARD EQUIPMENT:

LS: 2.2-liter dohc 4-cylinder engine, 5-speed manual transmission, driver- and passenger-side airbags, daytime running lights, air conditioning, power steering, tilt steering wheel, cloth upholstery, front bucket seats, cupholders, split folding rear seat, AM/FM radio, digital clock, rear defogger, auxiliary power outlets, intermittent wipers, 195/65R15 tires.

LS1/LW1 adds: 4-speed automatic transmission (wagon), heated power mirrors, power windows, power door locks, remote keyless entry, cruise control, AM/FM/CD player, center console, map lights, rear wiper/washer (wagon), cargo cover (wagon), theft-deterrent system, roof rails (wagon).

LS2/LW2 adds: 3.0-liter dohc V6 engine, 4-speed automatic transmission, 4-wheel disc brakes, leather-wrapped steering wheel, AM/FM/cassette/CD player, floormats, fog lights, sport suspension, 205/65R15 tires, alloy wheels.

OPTIONAL EQUIPMENT:
Safety Features

Antilock brakes w/traction control	695	619

Comfort and Convenience

Power sunroof, LS1/LS2 sedan	725	645
6-way power driver seat, LS1/LW1, LS2/LW2	325	289
Leather upholstery, LS1/LW1, LS2/LW2	1095	975

Includes heated front seats, leather-wrapped steering wheel. Requires power driver seat.

AM/FM/CD player, LS	290	258
AM/FM/cassette, LS	390	347
LS1/LW1	100	89

Includes automatic tone control.

AM/FM/cassette/CD player, LS	510	454
LS1/LW1	220	196
Upgraded audio system, LS1/LW1, LS2/LW2	220	196

NA with AM/FM/cassette.

Appearance and Miscellaneous

Rear spoiler, LS1, LS2	225	200
Fog lights, LS1/LW1	170	151
Alloy wheels, LS1/LW1	350	312

SATURN S-SERIES

Front-wheel-drive subcompact car

Base price range: $10,685-$16,005. Built in USA. **Also consider:** Dodge/Plymouth Neon, Ford Focus, Honda Civic, Toyota Corolla

FOR • Cargo room (wagon) • Fuel economy • Acceleration (SC2, SL2, SW2) **AGAINST** • Acceleration (SL, SL1, SC1) • Rear-seat room • Brake performance

Saturn freshens its subcompacts for 2000 and gives them a

Prices are accurate at time of publication; subject to manufacturer's changes.

Saturn SL2

new family name: the S-Series. The revamped sedan and wagon bow first. The 2000 S-Series coupe gets their interior updates, but keeps last year's look until midyear, when a redesigned coupe appears as a 2001.

All retain Saturn's dent- and rust-resistant body panels. Sedan and wagon get new lower-body styling that adds 1.2 inches to their overall length. New inside is the instrument cluster, a console with redesigned cupholders, and audio and climate controls. The horn works via the steering-wheel hub rather than spoke buttons, and cruise control relocates from the side of the hub to the spokes. Front seats gain more travel and revised lumbar support, and sedan and wagon get top tether anchors for rear child safety seats.

Sedans return in SL, SL1, and SL2 form, coupes in SC1 and SC2 models. The wagon now comes in SW2 trim only. SL and "1" models retain a 100-horsepower 1.9-liter overhead-cam 4-cylinder, the "2" versions a 124-hp twincam variant of that engine. The twincam gets internal modifications and a new air-induction system aimed at a quieter, richer sound. Manual transmission is standard. An extra-cost 4-speed automatic is available on all but the SL. Antilock brakes are optional and include traction control. S-Series coupes retain their unique 3-door design, with a small rear-hinged left-side back door.

PERFORMANCE Saturn's efforts to quiet its smallest cars have finally paid off—at least in the "2" models: Their twincam engine now feels coarse and buzzy only at maximum rpm. Horsepower is unaffected, so acceleration with either transmission remains slightly better than the class norm, at about 8.7 seconds 0-60 mph in our tests. The 5-speed SL2 we tested averaged 22.4 mpg.

SL, SL1, and SC1 furnish adequate acceleration with manual transmission, but keeping up with traffic in automatic versions often requires flooring the throttle. Our 5-speed SL1 test car averaged a commendable 28.9 mpg. With any model, the automatic transmission tends to change gears frequently, which can help performance but makes for a jerky ride.

The "2" models lean least in turns, but all these Saturns corner with pleasing quickness and control. Their suspension absorbs minor bumps well, but rough roads cause abrupt, even harsh reactions. Simulated panic stops tended to prematurely lock the front wheels of non-ABS test models, while ABS models groaned loudly and swerved mildly from side to side.

ACCOMMODATIONS Interiors are simplified and refined for 2000. Gauges are easier to read, smooth-working climate dials replace awkward slide levers, radio buttons are closer to the driver, and stalk-mounted controls operate with more precision. Welcome surprises include an adjustable center armrest on "2" versions, and on all models, beverage holders in front-door map pockets. Interior materials also seem a step up in quality. Overall visibility is good in any body style, but the tail is too high in sedans and coupes to easily see straight back.

The increase in front-seat travel makes front leg room is adequate rather than marginal for those over 6 feet. Rear-seat space doesn't match that of the new subcompact champ, the Ford Focus, but grownups get sufficient knee room as long as the front seats are well forward. S-Series wagons provide lots of head clearance even for tall folk; sedans are a tighter fit. Coupes are tighter in back than sedans and wagons but aren't as confining as some other 2-door subcompacts. The coupe's rear door is useful for loading cargo but doesn't solve the difficult adult passenger ingress or egress.

Trunk space is adequate in coupes and sedans, and the split rear seatback folds. Few rivals offer a wagon body style, but

most that do have more space than the SW2.

VALUE FOR THE MONEY This General Motors division won its following selling reliable small cars with a one-price strategy. The S-Series shows its age, but is still reasonably fun to drive, and now, fairly refined.

ENGINES

	ohc I4	dohc I4
Size, liters/cu. in.	1.9/116	1.9/116
Horsepower @ rpm	100 @ 5000	124 @ 5600
Torque (lbs./ft.) @ rpm	114 @ 2400	122 @ 4800
Availability	S[1]	S[2]
EPA city/highway mpg		
5-speed OD manual	29/40	27/38
4-speed OD automatic	27/38	25/36

1. SL, SL1, SW1, SC1. 2. SC2, SL2, SW2.

PRICES

Saturn S-Series	Retail Price	Dealer Invoice
SL 4-door sedan, 5-speed	$10685	$9617
SL1 4-door sedan, 5-speed	11485	10337
SL1 4-door sedan, automatic	12345	11111
SC1 3-door coupe, 5-speed	12535	11282
SC1 3-door coupe, automatic	13395	12056
SL2 4-door sedan, 5-speed	12895	11606
SL2 4-door sedan, automatic	13755	12380
SW2 4-door wagon, 5-speed	14290	12861
SW2 4-door wagon, automatic	15150	13635
SC2 3-door coupe, 5-speed	15145	13631
SC2 3-door coupe, automatic	16005	14405
Destination charge	440	440

STANDARD EQUIPMENT:

SL: 1.9-liter 4-cylinder engine, 5-speed manual transmission, driver- and passenger-side airbags, daytime running lights, tilt steering wheel, cloth upholstery, front bucket seats, center console, cupholders, split folding rear seat, AM/FM radio, digital clock, tachometer, rear defogger, intermittent wipers, auxiliary power outlet, passenger-side visor mirror, remote fuel door and decklid release, theft-deterrent system, driver-side outside mirror, 185/65R14 tires, wheel covers.

SL1/SC1 adds: 5-speed manual or 4-speed automatic transmission, power steering, driver-side rear door (SC1), rear console (SC1), dual outside mirrors, 185/65R15 tires.

SL2/SC2 adds: 1.9-liter dohc 4-cylinder engine, air conditioning, variable-assist power steering, leather-wrapped steering wheel (SC2), driver-side rear door (SC2), driver-seat height and lumbar adjustment, center console armrest, fog lights (SC2), rear spoiler (SC2), sport suspension, 195/60R15 tires (SC2).

SW2 adds to SL2: rear wiper/washer, cargo cover, remote liftgate release.

OPTIONAL EQUIPMENT:

Major Packages

Option Pkg. 1, SL1	2090	1881
SC1	1965	1769
SW2	1130	1017

Air conditioning (SL1, SC1), cruise control, power mirrors, power windows and door locks, remote keyless entry, theft-deterrent system w/alarm.

Option Pkg. 2, SL2	1480	1332
SC2	1355	1220

Cruise control, power mirrors, power windows and door locks, remote keyless entry, theft-deterrent system w/alarm.

Safety Features

Antilock brakes	695	626

Includes traction control.

Comfort and Convenience

Air conditioning, SL, SL1, SC1	960	864
Power sunroof, SL1, SC1, SL2, SC2	725	653
AM/FM/cassette, SL	420	378
SL1, SC1, SL2, SC2, SW2	390	351

Includes automatic tone control, premium speakers.

	Retail Price	Dealer Invoice
AM/FM/CD player, SL	$320	$288
SL1, SC1, SL2, SC2, SW2	290	261
Includes premium speakers.		
AM/FM/cassette/CD player, SL	540	486
SL1, SC1, SL2, SC2, SW2	510	459
Includes automatic tone control, premium speakers.		
Remote keyless entry, SL1, SL2, SW2	370	333
Includes power door locks, theft-deterrent system w/alarm.		
Leather upholstery, SL2, SC2, SW2	700	630
Includes leather-wrapped steering wheel. Requires Option Group.		

Appearance and Miscellaneous

Rear spoiler, SC1	245	221
SL2	225	203
Fog lights, SL2, SW2	170	153
Alloy wheels, SC1	450	405
SL2, SC2	350	315

SUBARU FORESTER

✓ BEST BUY

Subaru Forester

4-wheel-drive compact sport-utility vehicle; similar to Subaru Impreza
Base price range: $20,095-$22,595. Built in Japan. Also consider: Chevrolet Tracker, Honda CR-V, Toyota RAV4

FOR • Visibility • Maneuverability • Cargo room **AGAINST** • Instruments/controls • Rear-seat room

A trimmed lineup is the main change to the 2000 Forester, a "hybrid" that blends attributes of passenger cars and sport-utility vehicles. Forester is based on Subaru's Impreza station wagon, but has a taller stance in the mode of a traditional SUV.

The base-trim model is dropped for 2000, leaving L and uplevel S models. Both retain a 2.5-liter horizontally-opposed 4-cylinder engine. Manual transmission is standard, automatic optional. Like all Subarus, Forester has standard all-wheel-drive designed to sense wheel slip and send power to the wheels with the most traction. Forester is not intended for serious off-road use, however, and its AWD system lacks low-range gearing.

Antilock brakes are standard on both models, but the S has 4-wheel discs, along with 16-inch alloy wheels instead of the L's 15-inch steel rims. The L gains standard cruise control for 2000, while the S adds a standard limited-slip differential.

PERFORMANCE Forester blends carlike manners and AWD utility, but it isn't as comfortable as a car, nor as off-road worthy as a true SUV.

Forester's single-cam 4-cylinder has good low-rpm power and feels livelier here than in the heavier Legacy. Still, acceleration is best with manual transmission but adequate with automatic. We tested a '99 Forester with automatic transmission and timed it at 9.3 seconds 0-60 mph. That's about par for a compact SUV. It averaged 22.1 mpg, also about the same as rival compact SUVs such as the Honda CR-V, but much better than a traditional sport-utility wagon.

Forester rides more stiffly than most subcompact cars but isn't uncomfortable. It is softer and less bouncy than truck-based SUVs, and far more agile, too. It responds quickly to steering inputs and has only moderate body lean in fast turns. Braking performance is adequate, but pedal action is spongy and there's a fair degree of nosedive in hard stops. There's also a lot of road and wind noise.

ACCOMMODATIONS Although it isn't "command-of-the-road" tall, Forester's driving position is higher than a traditional

car's and visibility is outstanding. Head room is generous all around, too. There's no step-up to speak of, though narrow lower back door openings hinder rear entry and exit. Forester's subcompact-class wheelbase also shows up in a shortage of knee clearance and foot space for rear-seat passengers.

The radio is mounted low and its controls are small, but the dashboard layout is otherwise good. Forester's cargo area is spacious and versatile. Split rear seatbacks fold fore and aft for a reclined seating position or a flat cargo floor. Some materials seem a bit flimsy compared to other SUVs.

VALUE FOR THE MONEY Forester delivers AWD capability and carlike economy with a dash of SUV image. For many buyers, it's a smarter choice than a truck-based SUV, and shares Best Buy honors in this class with the Honda CR-V.

ENGINES

	ohc H4
Size, liters/cu. in.	2.5/150
Horsepower @ rpm	165 @ 5600
Torque (lbs./ft.) @ rpm	166 @ 4000
Availability	S
EPA city/highway mpg	
5-speed OD manual	21/27
4-speed OD automatic	21/26

PRICES

Subaru Forester	Retail Price	Dealer Invoice
L 4-door wagon	$20095	$18324
S 4-door wagon	22595	20506
Destination charge	495	495

Prices are for vehicles distributed by Subaru of North America. Prices may be higher in areas serviced by independent distributors.

STANDARD EQUIPMENT:

L: 2.5-liter 4-cylinder engine, 5-speed manual transmission, permanent all-wheel drive, driver- and passenger-side airbags, antilock brakes, air conditioning, variable-assist power steering, tilt steering wheel, cruise control, reclining cloth bucket seats, reclining split folding rear seat, cupholders, power mirrors, power windows, power door locks, AM/FM/cassette, tachometer, overhead console (map lights, digital clock, and sunglasses storage), intermittent wipers, rear wiper/washer, rear defogger, auxiliary power outlets, automatic-off headlights, floormats, fog lights, roof rack, trailer harness connector, 205/70HR15 white-letter tires.

S adds: limited-slip differential, antilock 4-wheel disc brakes, heated front seats, heated mirrors, windshield wiper deicer, visor mirrors, 215/60HR16 tires, alloy wheels.

OPTIONAL EQUIPMENT:
Major Packages

Feature Group 3/4	596	369
Remote keyless entry, woodgrain trim kit, cargo cover, tail pipe cover.		
Feature Group 5	386	239
Remote keyless entry, cargo cover, tail pipe cover.		
Feature Group 6	221	137
Armrest extension, cargo net, interior air filter.		
Outdoor Pkg. 1	1208	863
Manufacturer's discount price	825	718
Brush guard, side under guard bar, differential protector, gauge pack (compass, altimeter, barometer, outside temperature indicator).		
Outdoor Pkg. 2	858	635
Manufacturer's discount price	625	544
Brush guard, differential protector, gauge pack (compass, altimeter, barometer, outside temperature indicator).		

Powertrains

4-speed automatic transmission	800	719

Comfort and Convenience

Leather upholstery	1295	975
CD player	350	264
Premium Sound Pkg. 1	905	625

Prices are accurate at time of publication; subject to manufacturer's changes.

	Retail Price	Dealer Invoice
Manufacturer's discount price	$695	$525
CD player with upgraded sound system.		
Security Group	365	225
Remote keyless entry, theft-deterrent system w/alarm.		

Special Purpose, Wheels and Tires

Trailer hitch	295	192
Alloy wheels, L	595	447

Post production options also available.

SUBARU IMPREZA

Subaru Impreza 2.5 RS sedan

All-wheel-drive subcompact car; similar to Subaru Forester

Base price range: $15,895-$19,295. Built in Japan.
Also consider: Honda Civic, Mazda Protege, Toyota Corolla

FOR • All-wheel drive • Cargo room (wagons) • Maneuverability **AGAINST** • Rear-seat room • Rear entry/exit • Engine noise

Impreza gets a sportier version of its sedan for 2000, and remains the only subcompact car with standard all-wheel drive. Imprezas come in workaday L coupe, sedan, and wagon; racy 2.5 RS coupe and new 2.5 RS sedan; and sport-utility-inspired Outback Sport wagon with raised roofline and extra ground clearance. All have manual or optional automatic transmission and horizontally opposed 4-cylinder engines. L models and the Outback use a 2.2-liter. The 2.5 RS models get the 2.5-liter used in Subaru's larger Forester, Legacy, and Outback models. Antilock brakes are standard for Outbacks and 2.5 RSs, but aren't available on L models.

EVALUATION Handy size and a balanced chassis make Impreza 2.5 RS models reasonably fun to drive in good weather, and the AWD makes all models reassuring in snow or rain. But take away the AWD and you have rather ordinary small cars, with tight interiors, a slightly choppy ride, and fairly gruff and growly engines. The 2.2-liter engine provides adequate acceleration, and the 2.5 makes for spritely performance, but both are rather loud and intrusive in hard use. Generally good workmanship is let down by tinny door closings and some cheap-feeling interior details. Still, if you're among those for whom AWD is a big plus, the smallest Subarus make sense as affordable all-weather transport.

ENGINES

	ohc H4	ohc H4
Size, liters/cu. in.	2.2/135	2.5/150
Horsepower @ rpm	142 @ 5600	165 @ 5600
Torque (lbs./ft.) @ rpm	149 @ 3600	166 @ 4000
Availability	S[1]	S[2]
EPA city/highway mpg		
5-speed OD manual	23/29	21/28
4-speed OD automatic	23/29	23/28

1. L, Outback Sport. 2. 2.5 RS.

PRICES

Subaru Impreza	Retail Price	Dealer Invoice
L 2-door coupe	$15895	$14604
L 4-door sedan	15895	14604
L 4-door wagon	16295	14967
Outback Sport 4-door wagon	18095	16592
2.5 RS 2-door coupe	19295	17686

	Retail Price	Dealer Invoice
2.5 RS 4-door sedan	$19295	$17686
Destination charge	495	495

Prices are for vehicles distributed by Subaru of America. Prices may be higher in areas served by independent distributors.

STANDARD EQUIPMENT:

L: 2.2-liter 4-cylinder engine, 5-speed manual transmission, permanent all-wheel drive, driver- and passenger-side airbags, air conditioning, variable-assist power steering, tilt steering wheel, cloth upholstery, reclining front bucket seats, split folding rear seat (wagon), front storage console, cupholder, AM/FM/cassette, digital clock, tachometer, power mirrors, power windows, power door locks, intermittent wipers, rear defogger, remote decklid release (sedan and coupe), auxiliary power outlet, cargo cover (wagon), rear wiper/washer (wagon), automatic headlights, passenger-side visor mirror, rear spoiler (coupe), 195/60H15 tires, wheel covers.

Outback Sport adds to L wagon: antilock brakes, cruise control, cargo tray, raised heavy-duty suspension, roof rack, mud guards, 2-tone paint, rear bumper cover, 205/60S15 white-letter tires.

2.5RS adds to L 2-door: 2.5-liter 4-cylinder engine, limited-slip differential, antilock 4-wheel disc brakes, leather-wrapped steering wheel, cruise control, sport bucket seats, reading lights, power sunroof, sport suspension, bodyside moldings, fog lights, 205/55VR16 tires, alloy wheels.

OPTIONAL EQUIPMENT:

Major Packages

	Retail	Dealer
Popular Equipment Group 1, L wagon	430	265
Floormats, roof rack, mud guards, tail pipe cover.		
Popular Equipment Group 2, L	189	116
Floormats, mud guards, tail pipe cover.		
Premium Sound Pkg. 1, wagons	905	625
Manufacturer's discount price	695	525
CD player, upgraded speakers, tweeter, subwoofer, amplifier.		
Premium Sound Pkg. 2, sedans, coupes	810	563
Manufacturer's discount price	625	470
CD player, upgraded speakers, tweeter, subwoofer, amplifier.		
Security Pkg. 1	365	225
Remote keyless entry, security upgrade kit.		

Powertrains

4-speed automatic transmission	800	725

Comfort and Convenience

CD player	350	264
Remote keyless entry	225	146
Gauge pack, L	395	296
Compass, altimeter, barometer, outside temperature indicator.		

Appearance and Miscellaneous

Fog lights, L, Outback Sport	245	160
Roof rack, L wagon	241	157
Alloy wheels, L, Outback Sport	550	413

Post production options also available.

SUBARU LEGACY

Subaru Legacy GT sedan

All-wheel-drive compact car; similar to Subaru Outback

Base price range: $18,395-$24,295. Built in USA.

Also consider: Mazda 626, Mitsubishi Galant, Oldsmobile Alero, Volkswagen Passat

FOR • Cargo room (wagon) • All-wheel drive

AGAINST • Automatic transmission performance • Seat comfort

Subaru's largest sedans and wagons are redesigned for 2000, with new styling that adds six inches to length and one inch to width on a wheelbase about one inch longer. The sport-utility-flavored Outback wagons become a separate model line but share Legacy's basic design.

Legacy sedans come in L, GT, and GT Limited versions. Wagons are offered in Brighton, L, and GT models. All retain Subaru's 2.5-liter horizontally-opposed 4-cylinder engine, which switches from double overhead camshafts to a less-expensive single-cam format and receives various internal changes to produce more torque at lower engine speeds. Horsepower is unchanged. All Legacys offer manual or optional automatic transmission. Subaru's all-wheel drive is standard and GTs this year get a limited-slip rear differential to enhance traction in very slippery conditions.

Front seatbelt pretensioners and antilock brakes are standard. Front side airbags are standard on the GT Limited sedan but are not available for other models.

PERFORMANCE Subaru wisely dropped Legacy's noisy, weak 2.2-liter 4-cylinder base engine, but should have fortified the 2.5 more than it did. Acceleration is adequate with manual transmission, but the car feels sluggish with automatic. The automatic shifts smoothly, but usually maintains too high a gear, then is reluctant to downshift for more power. The 5-speed GT Limited sedan we tested averaged a likeable 22.5 mpg; we haven't measured fuel economy with the automatic transmission.

Legacy soaks up pavement irregularities better than some larger, more-expensive cars. Steering feel and highway tracking are excellent, but there's body lean aplenty in turns, and tires used on the Brighton and L have modest grip, to the detriment of handling. With stiffer suspension settings and larger tires, GTs furnish genuinely sporty handling at the expense of some sharp reactions over bigger bumps and tar strips. The brakes are easily modulated and provide terrific stopping power. Wind and road noise are easily managed, while the engine's prominent snarl under hard throttle is considered sporty by some of our testers and unpleasant by others.

ACCOMMODATIONS More space and better materials highlight the new cabin. Front seats are set-and-forget comfortable for most drivers, though some of our testers found them lacking in long-distance support. All controls are within easy reach, and modern, intuitive dials replace the old climate system's mix of sliders and buttons. Undersized audio-system buttons are uninviting to use while driving, however. Outward visibility is very good.

Both body styles offer plenty of rear head, leg, and foot clearance for two adults on a nicely supportive seat. All rear passengers get headrests and 3-point seat belts. Tall doors make getting in and out a breeze.

The sedan's trunk is efficiently shaped and liftover is low, but volume is unimpressive, the lid's hinges dip into the luggage area, and Legacy makes due with a rear-seat pass-through opening while many rivals offer fold-down seatbacks. Split-folding rear seats expand the wagon's already useful cargo area.

VALUE FOR THE MONEY Legacy improves considerably over its predecessor, but except for all-wheel drive, it isn't an attractive value. A 5-speed GT is an intriguing sporty choice, but similar money buys a midsize Honda Accord, Saturn L-Series, or Mazda 626, all of which offer a V6 engine.

ENGINES

	ohc H4
Size, liters/cu. in.	2.5/150
Horsepower @ rpm	165 @ 5600
Torque (lbs./ft.) @ rpm	166 @ 4000
Availability	S
EPA city/highway mpg	
5-speed OD manual	NA
4-speed OD automatic	NA

PRICES

Subaru Legacy	Retail Price	Dealer Invoice
Brighton 4-door wagon	$18395	$17353
L 4-door sedan	19195	17470
L 4-door wagon	19895	18097
GT 4-door sedan	22795	20681
GT 4-door wagon	23695	21487
GT Limited 4-door sedan	24295	22019
Destination charge	495	495

STANDARD EQUIPMENT:

Brighton: 2.5-liter 4-cylinder engine, 5-speed manual transmission, permanent all-wheel drive, driver- and passenger-side airbags, antilock brakes, daytime running lights, air conditioning, power steering, tilt steering wheel, cloth upholstery, front bucket seats, cupholders, split folding rear seat, power windows, AM/FM/cassette w/two speakers, intermittent wipers, rear wiper/washer, 195/60R15 tires, wheel covers.

L adds: antilock 4-wheel disc brakes, power mirrors, power door locks, cruise control, tachometer, 4-speaker sound system, rear seat trunk pass-through (sedan), cargo cover (wagon), map lights, roof rails (wagon), sedan deletes split folding rear seat, rear wiper/washer.

GT adds: limited-slip differential, dual power sunroofs (wagon), single power sunroof (sedan), 6-way power driver seat, remote keyless entry, leather-wrapped steering wheel, variable intermittent wipers, illuminated visor mirrors, fog lights, sport suspension, 205/55R16 tires, alloy wheels.

GT Limited adds: front side-impact airbags, leather upholstery, AM/FM/weatherband/cassette/CD player.

OPTIONAL EQUIPMENT:
Powertrains

4-speed automatic transmission	800	722

Post production options also available.

SUBARU OUTBACK

Subaru Outback wagon

All-wheel-drive compact car; similar to Subaru Legacy

Base price range: $22,695-$26,095. Built in USA. **Also consider:** Audi A4, Saturn L-Series, Volkswagen Passat

FOR • All-wheel drive • Cargo room **AGAINST** • Automatic transmission performance

Recognizing that the Outback wagon accounted for 65 percent of Legacy sales, Subaru makes this quasi SUV a separate model line for 2000. Redesigned for 2000, the Outback wagon is accompanied by a sedan variant, which is but a small fraction of Outback sales.

Both share Legacy's chassis, engine, and all-wheel-drive powertrain. The wagon has a raised roofline, and both Outback models have an elevated suspension that provides 7.3 inches of ground clearance, an inch more than Legacy. Compared to last year's Outbacks, wheelbase grows about an inch, body lengths increase about 3 inches on the sedan and 1.6 on the wagon, and the cars are slightly wider and taller.

Outback's wagon comes in base and Limited models, the sedan in Limited only. Antilock 4-wheel disc brakes are standard, and Limiteds have front side airbags. Optional on the base wagon is an integrated rear child seat.

Prices are accurate at time of publication; subject to manufacturer's changes.

The only engine is Subaru's 2.5-liter 4-cylinder with horizontally opposed cylinders. A change from dual- to single-overhead camshafts provides slightly more torque. Wagons come with automatic or manual transmission; sedans get only the automatic.

PERFORMANCE Outback blends a little of the flavor of a sport-utility vehicle with the convenience of a compact car. It's not intended for off-road use, but makes up for that with a ride that's more civilized and better controlled than any truck-based SUV's. And despite copious body lean in turns, Outback handles far more competently than an SUV; it stops shorter, too.

This 4-cylinder still provides only adequate acceleration. Aggravating matters, the automatic transmission tends to settle in a gear higher than optimal for ready acceleration when cruising around town, then is reluctant to downshift. Acceleration is slightly better with manual transmission, and our long-term-test 5-speed Outback wagon averaged 19.9 mpg over its first 1100 miles. A '99 Outback wagon with this powertrain and automatic transmission averaged 20 mpg in an extended-use test. Our 2000 tester has been mechanically trouble-free.

Wind, road, and engine noise are subdued when cruising, but the wagon's roof rack roars on the highway, and the engine's somewhat coarse note grows prominent when accelerating hard.

ACCOMMODATIONS While it isn't as high-riding as a true SUV, Outback does have a slightly elevated driving position that provides a fine view down the road. Thin roof pillars and a large rear window help visibility to other quarters. New interior fabrics and plastics impart a notably upscale image, and controls for the climate and sound systems are now well within the driver's reach, though some of our testers still find the audio buttons too small to easily operate while driving.

Driver and front passenger have plenty of room. Rear-seater also get ample head room, especially with the wagon's taller roofline. Rear leg room is better than the compact-car norm, and so is entry/exit, thanks to tall doors. Outback is not wide enough for 3-across adult seating, however.

A revamped rear suspension improves cargo capacity and creates a wide and flat load floor. Outback sedans have a usefully shaped trunk, but only a rear-seat pass through instead of more versatile 60/40 split folding seatbacks of the wagon.

VALUE FOR THE MONEY If you need all-wheel drive but don't want the bulk of an SUV, Outback is a terrific choice. The deservedly popular wagon is clearly the star here.

ENGINES

	ohc H4
Size, liters/cu. in.	2.5/150
Horsepower @ rpm	165 @ 5600
Torque (lbs./ft.) @ rpm	166 @ 4000
Availability	S

EPA city/highway mpg

5-speed OD manual	NA
4-speed OD automatic	NA

PRICES

Subaru Outback	Retail Price	Dealer Invoice
Base 4-door wagon	$22695	$20588
Limited 4-door sedan	25895	23471
Limited 4-door wagon	26095	23635
Destination charge	495	495

STANDARD EQUIPMENT:

Base: 2.5-liter 4-cylinder engine, 5-speed manual transmission, permanent all-wheel drive, driver- and passenger-side air bags, antilock 4-wheel disc brakes, daytime running lights, air conditioning, power steering, tilt steering wheel, cruise control, cloth upholstery, front bucket seats, 6-way power driver seat, split folding rear seat, power mirrors, power windows, power door locks, remote keyless entry, AM/FM/weatherband/cassette, tachometer, overhead console, map lights, intermittent wipers, auxiliary power outlets, cargo cover, floormats, fog lights, roof rack, 225/60R16 white-letter tires, alloy wheels. **Limited** adds: 4-speed automatic transmission (sedan), limited-slip differential, front side-impact airbags, dual power sunroofs (wagon),

single power sunroof (sedan), leather upholstery, heated front seats, leather-wrapped steering wheel, heated power mirrors, AM/FM/weatherband/cassette/CD player, illuminated visor mirrors, variable intermittent wipers w/de-icer, rear seat trunk pass-through (sedan), sedan deletes split folding rear seat.

OPTIONAL EQUIPMENT:

Major Packages	Retail Price	Dealer Invoice
All-Weather Pkg., Base	$500	$451

Limited-slip rear differential, heated front seats and mirrors, front windshield wiper de-icer.

Powertrains		
4-speed automatic transmission, wagon	800	722

Safety Features		
Integrated child seat, Base	200	180

Post production options also available.

SUZUKI ESTEEM/SWIFT

Suzuki Esteem wagon

Front-wheel-drive subcompact car; similar to Chevrolet Metro

Base price range: $9,099-$16,399. Built in Japan and Canada. **Also consider:** Dodge/Plymouth Neon, Nissan Sentra

FOR • Fuel economy • Cargo room (wagon) • Maneuverability **AGAINST** • Rear visibility • Noise • Ride • Rear-seat room (Swift) • Build quality (Swift)

Esteem is Suzuki's 4-door sedan and wagon, Swift its 2-door hatchback. Both are front-wheel-drive subcompacts but Esteem rides a longer wheelbase and has a larger engine and outsells Swift 5-1. Esteem is built in Japan. It returns in GL and GLX models, as well as the GLX Plus, which is the only model with antilock brakes. New for 2000 is a GL Sport 4-door, which includes fog lamps and a rear spoiler. Esteems use a 1.8-liter 4-cylinder engine. Manual transmission is standard on all but the GLX Plus models. They come with a 4-speed automatic that's optional on other Esteems. Swift is built in Canada at a General Motors-Suzuki plant alongside the similar Chevrolet Metro. It uses a 1.3-liter 4-cylinder engine and manual or optional 3-speed automatic transmission. For 2000, the base Swift is renamed the GA, and a GL model with standard air conditioning and AM/FM cassette is added. Antilock brakes are unavailable on the Swift.

EVALUATION Compact dimensions give all these Suzukis nimble moves around town, but their skinny tires surrender grip easily in aggressive cornering. Esteem and Swift ride rougher than most competitors, and are noisy on the highway. Esteem has room for four adults, as long as those in back aren't over about 5-10, but the rear seat is thinly padded and the small rear doors hard to squeeze through. Swift is tighter still. Even if fuel economy and low price are your primary concerns, neither of these Suzukis strikes us as a great bargain. We'd look first at a larger, late-model used car.

ENGINES

	ohc I4	dohc I4
Size, liters/cu. in.	1.3/79	1.8/109
Horsepower @ rpm	79 @ 6000	122 @ 6300
Torque (lbs./ft.) @ rpm	75 @ 3000	117 @ 3500
Availability	S[1]	S[2]

EPA city/highway mpg

5-speed OD manual	39/43	28/35
3-speed automatic	30/34	
4-speed OD automatic		26/33

1. Swift. 2. Esteem.

PRICES

Suzuki Esteem/Swift

	Retail Price	Dealer Invoice
Swift GA 2-door hatchback, 5-speed	$9099	$8553
Swift GA 2-door hatchback, automatic	9749	9164
Swift GL 2-door hatchback, 5-speed	10099	9493
Swift GL 2-door hatchback, automatic	10749	10104
Esteem GL 4-door sedan, 5-speed	12899	12383
Esteem GL 4-door sedan, automatic	13899	13343
Esteem GL 4-door wagon, 5-speed	13399	12863
Esteem GL 4-door wagon, automatic	14399	13823
Esteem GLX 4-door sedan, 5-speed	13899	13343
Esteem GLX 4-door sedan, automatic	14899	14303
Esteem GLX 4-door wagon, 5-speed	14399	13823
Esteem GLX 4-door wagon, automatic	15399	14783
Esteem GLX Sport 4-door sedan, 5-speed	14499	13767
Esteem GLX Sport 4-door sedan, automatic	15499	14727
Esteem GLX Plus 4-door sedan, automatic	15699	15071
Esteem GLX Plus 4-door wagon, automatic	16399	15743
Destination charge: Swift	400	400
Destination charge: Esteem	450	450

STANDARD EQUIPMENT:

Swift GA: 1.3-liter 4-cylinder engine, 5-speed manual or 3-speed automatic transmission, driver- and passenger-side airbags, daytime running lights, cloth reclining front bucket seats, folding rear seat, front console, intermittent wipers, rear defogger, cargo cover, dual outside mirrors, 155/80R13 tires, wheel covers.

Swift GL adds: air conditioning, AM/FM/cassette.

Esteem GL adds: 1.8-liter 4-cylinder engine, 5-speed manual or 4-speed automatic transmission, power steering, cupholders, tachometer, variable intermittent wipers, split folding rear seat, rear wiper/washer (wagon), remote fuel-door and decklid releases, cargo cover (wagon), roof rails (wagon), 185/60R14 tires.

Esteem GLX adds: power mirrors, power windows, power door locks, remote keyless entry, passenger-side visor mirror, theft-deterrent system, rear spoiler (wagon), 195/55R15 tires, alloy wheels.

Esteem GLX Sport adds: fog lights, rear spoiler.

Esteem GLX Plus adds to Esteem GLX: 4-speed automatic transmission, antilock brakes, cruise control, power sunroof (wagon).

OPTIONAL EQUIPMENT:

Appearance and Miscellaneous

Two-tone paint, GLX Plus wagon............................	200	178

Other options are available as dealer-installed accessories.

SUZUKI VITARA

Suzuki Vitara 4-door

Rear- or 4-wheel-drive compact sport-utility vehicle; similar to Chevrolet Tracker

Base price range: $13,499-$22,699. Built in Japan. **Also consider:** Honda CR-V, Subaru Forester, Toyota RAV4

FOR • Maneuverability • Cargo room   **AGAINST** • Rear-seat room • Rear visibility • Acceleration

Vitara replaced the smaller Sidekick for 1999, and returns for 2000 with a new top-line model. Vitaras have 4-cylinder engines and are offered with four doors or as a 2-door convertible. Grand Vitara is a 4-door with a V6 engine and beefier body contours. It outsells Vitara models 5-1. All body styles use body-on-frame construction. Suzuki supplies versions of the Vitara to Chevrolet for sale as the Tracker, but Chevy does not get the V6 or a

Grand Vitara counterpart. The new top-line Grand Vitara Limited is the only model with leather upholstery, deep-tint glass, and fog lights. All models come with rear-wheel drive or 4WD that includes low-range gearing, but is not for use on dry pavement. Antilock brakes are standard on upper-trim Grand Vitaras but are unavailable on other models.

EVALUATION Four-cylinder Vitaras have mediocre acceleration and thrashy-sounding engines. Grand Vitara's quieter V6 provides only adequate acceleration, though an automatic 4x4 averaged 18.9 mpg in our tests—slightly less than a 4-cylinder Honda CR-V, but better than larger 6-cylinder 4x4s. No model rides harshly, but choppy pavement induces abrupt vertical motions. Vitaras are nimbler than larger SUVs, but still suffer lots of body lean and only moderate grip in fast turns. Suzuki's 4WD is less convenient than permanently engaged systems available on such unibody rivals as the CR-V and Toyota RAV4, but those competitors lack the Suzuki's 4-low range for off-road work. Wind and road noise are lower than in most compact SUVs. Front seats are comfortable and step-in height low, but rear leg room is tight, rear doorways narrow. Tiny, hard-to-decipher radio controls detract from a good dashboard layout. Cargo room is small for an SUV, and the one-piece rear hatch opens to the right, blocking curbside loading. These are reasonably refined wagons, with the Grand Vitara of most interest because of its V6. However, the Grand doesn't boast break-from-the-pack performance, and Vitara's strongest quality—off-road ability—is of no interest to most SUV buyers.

ENGINES

	ohc I4	dohc I4	dohc V6
Size, liters/cu. in.	1.6/97	2.0/122	2.5/152
Horsepower @ rpm	97 @ 5200	127 @ 6000	155 @ 6500
Torque (lbs./ft.) @ rpm	103 @ 4000	134 @ 3000	160 @ 4000
Availability	S[1]	S[2]	S[3]
EPA city/highway mpg			
5-speed OD manual	25/28[4]	22/24	19/22[6]
4-speed OD automatic	25/27[5]	23/25	19/21[7]

1. JS and JX 2-door. 2. Vitara JLS and JLX 2-door and Vitara 4-door. 3. Grand Vitara. 4. 25/27 w/4WD. 5. 24/27 w/4WD. 6. 19/21 w/4WD. 7. 18/20 w/4WD.

PRICES

Suzuki Vitara

	Retail Price	Dealer Invoice
JS 2WD 2-door convertible, 5-speed	$13499	$12959
JS 2WD 2-door convertible, automatic	14499	13919
JLS 2WD 2-door convertible, 5-speed	14999	14399
JLS 2WD 2-door convertible, automatic	15999	15359
JX 4WD 2-door convertible, 5-speed	15299	14381
JX 4WD 2-door convertible, automatic	16299	15321
JX 4WD 2-door convertible, 5-speed	16799	15791
JX 4WD 2.0-liter 2-door convertible, automatic	17799	16731
JS 2WD 4-door wagon, 5-speed	15499	14569
JS 2WD 4-door wagon, automatic	16499	15509
JLS 2WD 4-door wagon, 5-speed	16299	15321
JLS 2WD 4-door wagon, automatic	17299	16261
JLS 2WD 4-door wagon w/alloy wheels, 5-speed	16699	15697
JLS 2WD 4-door wagon w/alloy wheels, automatic	17699	16637
JX 4WD 4-door wagon, 5-speed	17099	15731
JX 4WD 4-door wagon, automatic	18099	16651
JLX 4WD 4-door wagon, 5-speed	17899	16467
JLX 4WD 4-door wagon, automatic	18899	17387
JLX 4WD 4-door wagon w/alloy wheels, 5-speed .	18299	16835
JLX 4WD 4-door wagon w/alloy wheels, automatic	19299	17755
Grand JLS 2WD 4-door wagon, 5-speed	18299	16835
Grand JLS 2WD 4-door wagon, automatic	19299	17755
Grand JLS Plus 2WD 4-door wagon, 5-speed	19499	17939
Grand JLS Plus 2WD 4-door wagon, automatic ...	20499	18859
Grand JLX 4WD 4-door wagon, 5-speed	19299	17755
Grand JLX 4WD 4-door wagon, automatic	20299	18675
Grand JLX Plus 4WD 4-door wagon, 5-speed	20499	18859
Grand JLX Plus 4WD 4-door wagon, automatic	21499	19779
Grand Limited 2WD 4-door wagon, automatic	21699	19963
Grand Limited 4WD 4-door wagon, automatic	22699	20883
Destination charge: convertibles	440	440

Prices are accurate at time of publication; subject to manufacturer's changes.

	Retail Price	Dealer Invoice
Destination charge: wagons	$450	$450

STANDARD EQUIPMENT:

JS/JX convertible: 1.6-liter 4-cylinder engine, 5-speed manual or 4-speed automatic transmission, driver- and passenger-side airbags, daytime running lights, power steering, tilt steering wheel, cloth/vinyl upholstery, front bucket seats, center console, cupholders, split folding rear seat, AM/FM/cassette, tachometer, passenger-side visor mirror, variable intermittent wipers, automatic headlights, folding convertible top, full-size spare tire, 195/75R15 tires. **4WD** models add: part-time 4-wheel drive, 2-speed transfer case, 205/75R15 tires.

JLS/JLX convertible adds: 2.0-liter dohc 4-cylinder engine, air conditioning, power mirrors, power windows, power door locks, cloth upholstery, map lights, 215/65R16 tires. **4WD** models add: part-time 4-wheel drive, 2-speed transfer case.

JS/JX wagon adds to JS/JX convertible: 2.0-liter dohc 4-cylinder engine, cloth upholstery, map lights, auxiliary power outlet, rear defogger, cargo cover, rear wiper/washer, roof rails, 215/65R16 tires, deletes folding convertible top. **4WD** models add: part-time 4-wheel drive, 2-speed transfer case.

JLS/JLX adds: air conditioning, cruise control, power mirrors, power windows, power door locks, remote keyless entry, steel or alloy wheels. **4WD** models add: part-time 4-wheel drive, 2-speed transfer case.

Grand JS/JLX adds: 2.5-liter dohc V6 engine, 235/60R16 tires, deletes alloy wheels. **4WD** models add: part-time 4-wheel drive, 2-speed transfer case.

Grand JLS Plus/JLX Plus adds: antilock brakes, CD changer, alloy wheels. **4WD** model adds: part-time 4-wheel drive, 2-speed transfer case.

Grand Limited adds: 4-speed automatic transmission, leather upholstery, deep-tinted glass, fog lights. **4WD** model adds: part-time 4-wheel drive, 2-speed transfer case.

Options are available as dealer-installed accessories.

TOYOTA AVALON

RECOMMENDED

Toyota Avalon

Front-wheel-drive full-size car
Base price range: $25,195-$29,755. Built in USA. **Also consider:** Buick LeSabre, Dodge Intrepid, Pontiac Bonneville

FOR • Build quality • Exterior finish • Acceleration • Automatic transmission performance • Quietness • Passenger room • Ride/handling **AGAINST** • Brake-pedal feel

America's only import-brand full-size sedan is redesigned for 2000. Avalon gains about an inch in body width and height, plus new styling. A 3.0-liter V6 and automatic transmission return, but variable valve timing helps add 10 horsepower, for 210. Antilock 4-wheel disc brakes and front side airbags remain standard. XL and uplevel XLS trim levels return. Newly optional for XLS is an antiskid system similar to that offered by Toyota's premium Lexus brand. It's designed to activate individual brakes to counteract skids in turns; it includes traction control, as well as a brake assist feature that automatically applies full braking force in emergency stops.

Avalon again offers front bucket seats or a split front bench. New standard features include a trunk pass-through and dual-zone temperature control. Leather upholstery, power seats, and power moonroof are among the options. New options include

memory power seats and a 115-volt AC outlet for household-type plugs.

PERFORMANCE Improved quietness was a major goal for Avalon's redesign, and Toyota has achieved that and more. Except for some mild tire rumble over very coarse pavement, this is one hushed car. Even pedal-to-metal acceleration produces only a distant, rich-sounding engine note. Acceleration itself seems a bit stronger in all situations, thanks to little-changed weight and the extra engine muscle. We haven't measured economy yet, but it shouldn't vary much from the 21 mpg we recorded with previous Avalons. The automatic transmission is responsive and glassy smooth.

Ride is comfortable, almost plush, yet improved body control and firmer, more communicative steering let the new Avalon hustle along twisty roads with almost sports-sedan poise. The only chinks in the dynamic armor are a bit more body drumming than we expected over rough patches and slightly unprogressive pedal action in routine braking.

ACCOMMODATIONS The old Avalon didn't want for room, but the reprofiled 2000 styling makes for a truly spacious interior. Even 6-footers ride in tandem with plenty of leg-stretch for both. Helping are higher-set seats that are matched by a raised roofline providing fine all-around head room. There's width enough for three adults front and back, though middle riders still straddle humps and won't have much foot room. Rear entry/exit isn't barn-door easy but is far from difficult, and all seats are comfortably supportive. Cargo volume increases slightly, and the trunk, though not as long as in the old Avalon, is taller and plenty spacious.

Avalon's new dashboard resembles some GM designs of yore, but it works far better, though the steering-wheel rim can obscure the tops of the main gauges. Climate and audio controls couldn't be better, and there's plenty of convenient small-items stowage, including a glovebox that will swallow a half-dozen Big Macs. Drivers have good visibility despite hard-to-see rear body corners, and door mirrors are usefully large.

VALUE FOR THE MONEY Toyota is loath to say this, but the new Avalon is a near-Lexus: roomier and quieter than before, just as comfortable ride-wise, yet more enjoyably roadable. If you want a spacious, posh sedan and can't quite stretch to a near-luxury model, the newest Avalon is the next best thing—and arguably the best of the full-size family 4-doors.

ENGINES

	dohc V6
Size, liters/cu. in.	3.0/181
Horsepower @ rpm	210 @ 5800
Torque (lbs./ft.) @ rpm	220 @ 4400
Availability	S

EPA city/highway mpg
4-speed OD automatic	21/29

PRICES

Toyota Avalon	Retail Price	Dealer Invoice
XL 4-door sedan, front bucket seats	$25195	$22058
XL 4-door sedan, front bench seat	26015	22776
XLS 4-door sedan, front bucket seats	29755	25742
XLS 4-door sedan, front bench seat	29655	25657
Destination charge	455	455

Prices are for vehicles distributed by Toyota Motor Sales, U.S.A., Inc. The dealer invoice and destination charge may be higher in areas served by independent distributors.

STANDARD EQUIPMENT:

XL: 3.0-liter dohc V6 engine, 4-speed automatic transmission, driver- and passenger-side airbags, front side-impact airbags, antilock 4-wheel disc brakes, daytime running lights, air conditioning w/dual-zone manual control, variable-assist power steering, tilt steering wheel, cruise control, cloth upholstery, manual front bucket seats w/center console or power split bench seat, cupholders, rear seat trunk pass-through, overhead console, power mirrors, power windows, power door locks, AM/FM/cassette/CD player, digital clock, tachometer, outside temperature indicator, rear defogger, auxiliary power outlet, illuminated visor mirrors, variable intermittent wipers, remote fuel door and decklid releases, automatic headlights, full-size spare tire, 205/65R15 tires, wheel covers.

XLS adds: dual-zone automatic climate control, interior air filter, leather-wrapped steering wheel, power front seats, heated power mirrors, JBL AM/FM/cassette/CD player, remote keyless entry, trip computer, compass, automatic day/night rearview mirror, universal garage door opener, theft-deterrent system, fog lights, alloy wheels.

OPTIONAL EQUIPMENT:
Major Packages

	Retail Price	Dealer Invoice
Pkg. 1, XL w/bucket seats	$1035	$828
Power front seats, remote keyless entry.		
Pkg. 2, XL w/bucket seats	1420	1136
Power front seats, remote keyless entry, 205/65HR15 tires, alloy wheels.		
Pkg. 2, XL w/bucket seats	2590	2072
Pkg. 2 plus leather upholstery, leather-wrapped steering wheel and shift knob.		
Pkg. 3, XL w/bench seat	670	536
Remote keyless entry, 205/65R15 tires, alloy wheels.		
Pkg. 4, XL w/bench seat	1820	1456
Leather upholstery, leather-wrapped steering wheel and shift knob, remote keyless entry, 205/65HR16 tires, alloy wheels.		
Pkg. 5, XLS	1375	1100
Leather upholstery, memory for driver seat and mirrors, A/C outlet, 205/60R16 tires.		
Pkg. 6, XLS	1625	1288
Pkg. 5 plus 6-disc CD changer.		
Pkg. 7, XLS	1940	1540
Pkg. 6 plus heated front seats.		
Pkg. 8, XLS	330	252
6-disc CD changer, 205/60R16 tires.		
Gold Pkg.	499	89

Safety Features

	Retail Price	Dealer Invoice
Antiskid system, XLS	850	680
Includes traction control and brake assist.		

Comfort and Convenience

	Retail Price	Dealer Invoice
Power sunroof	910	728
JBL sound system, XL	360	270
Security System, XL	249	155
Includes remote keyless entry and theft-deterrent system.		

Post production options also available.

TOYOTA CAMRY/SOLARA

✓ BEST BUY

Toyota Camry LE

Front-wheel-drive midsize car; similar to Lexus ES 300

Base price range: $17,418-$26,098. Built in USA, Japan, and Canada. **Also consider:** Ford Taurus, Honda Accord, Nissan Maxima

FOR • Acceleration (V6) • Ride • Quietness • Build quality • Exterior finish **AGAINST** • Rear visibility • Steering feel

Minor equipment revisions highlight year-2000 editions of the popular Camry sedan and its Solara coupe companion. Camrys also get some appearance changes.

Camrys continue in CE, LE, and top-shelf XLE models. CEs come only with a 4-cylinder engine, which gains 3 horsepower this year. A V6 is available on LE and XLE. CEs and LEs offer manual or optional automatic transmission; XLEs automatic only. Camrys get new grilles, bumpers and taillights, plus multi-reflector headlamps, and self-propping hoods. XLEs add imita-

tion wood interior trim and the XLE V6 goes to standard 16-inch wheels versus other models' 15s or 14s.

Solaras share Camry's sedan platform and are marketed as "Camrys," but have unique styling and chassis tuning. SE Solaras have a 4-cylinder or V6 and manual or optional automatic transmission. The upscale SLE is a V6/automatic.

Front side airbags are optional in both lines. Antilock brakes are optional with the 4-cylinder engine and standard with the V6, where they include rear discs. Other changes for both model lines include revised climate controls and upgraded audio systems, including a standard CD player.

PERFORMANCE Camry and Solara share chassis and power-trains with the posh Lexus ES 300 sedan, so they're smooth, polished performers, though a bit dull dynamically. Strong points include a supple, absorbent ride, outstanding quietness and strong acceleration with the V6 (under 8 seconds 0-60 mph), and low tire and wind noise. The 4-cylinder engine is also quite refined and decently peppy, if noticeably less muscular than the V6, especially with automatic transmission. A 4-cylinder Camry averaged 22.5 mpg in testing that included lots of urban driving, while V6 test models typically average in the low-20s; for example, a manual-transmission V6 Solara returned 23 mpg.

Though safe, predictable, and pleasant to drive, none of these Toyotas is truly sporty. Steering is quick and precise, but also a bit over-assisted and numb. Even the more firmly damped Solaras tend to "float" over dips and swells. There's also marked body lean in hard, tight turns, though it's far from alarming. Braking is strong, consistent, and easily modulated.

ACCOMMODATIONS Both body styles appeal for attractive cabins that easily carry four adults; insufficient rear shoulder width makes a fifth passenger feel cramped. Entry/exit is easy in sedans and not too bad in Solaras, though the coupes do suffer from low, narrowish rear passageways, no slide-forward feature on the driver's seat, and cumbersome front seat belts. Cargo space is competitive, but Solara's trunk opening is fairly high and not that deep. All models have split-fold rear seatbacks with in-trunk security locks.

Drivers get a wide range of seat/steering wheel adjustments, well-placed controls, and generally clear sightlines, although both body styles have nagging over-the-shoulder blind spots, Solaras particularly. Build quality is excellent regardless of model, though some interior decor borders on drab.

VALUE FOR THE MONEY Camry and Solara are exceptionally well-done mainstream midsizes with the attractions of Toyota reliability and high resale value. We might wish for more personality and lower prices, but these cars are hard to fault and tough to beat.

ENGINES

	dohc I4	dohc I4	dohc V6	dohc V6
Size, liters/cu. in.	2.2/132	2.2/132	3.0/183	3.0/183
Horsepower @ rpm	136 @ 5200	138 @ 5200	194 @ 5200	200 @ 5200
Torque (lbs./ft.) @ rpm	147 @ 4400	147 @ 4400	209 @ 4400	214 @ 4400
Availability	S[1]	S[2]	S[3]	S[4]
EPA city/highway mpg				
5-speed OD manual	23/32	23/32	21/28	21/28
4-speed OD automatic.....	23/30	23/30	20/28	20/28

1. Camry. 2. Solara. 3. Camry V6. 4. Solara V6.

PRICES

Toyota Camry/Solara	Retail Price	Dealer Invoice
Camry CE 4-cylinder 4-door sedan, 5-speed	$17418	$15427
Camry CE 4-cylinder 4-door sedan, automatic	18218	16136
Camry LE 4-cylinder 4-door sedan, automatic	20288	17761
Camry LE V6 4-door sedan, 5-speed	22258	19486
Camry LE V6 4-door sedan, automatic	23058	20185
Camry XLE 4-cylinder 4-door sedan, automatic	23968	20983
Camry XLE V6 4-door sedan, automatic	26098	22847
Solara SE 4-cylinder 2-door coupe, 5-speed	18938	16774
Solara SE 4-cylinder 2-door coupe, automatic	19738	17483
Solara SE V6 2-door coupe, 5-speed	21648	19175
Solara SE V6 2-door coupe, automatic	22448	19884

Prices are accurate at time of publication; subject to manufacturer's changes.

TOYOTA

	Retail Price	Dealer Invoice
Solara SLE 2-door coupe, automatic	$25838	$22887
Destination charge	455	455

Prices are for vehicles distributed by Toyota Motor Sales, U.S.A., Inc. The dealer invoice and destination charge may be higher in areas served by independent distributors.

STANDARD EQUIPMENT:

Camry CE: 2.2-liter dohc 4-cylinder, 5-speed manual or 4-speed automatic transmission, driver- and passenger-side airbags, variable-assist power steering, tilt steering column, cloth upholstery, front bucket seats, center console, cupholders, split folding rear seat, tachometer, automatic-off headlights, AM/FM/cassette/CD player, digital clock, intermittent wipers, remote fuel-door and trunk releases, outside temperature indicator, rear defogger, auxiliary power outlet, dual remote outside mirrors, 195/70R14 tires, wheel covers.

Camry LE adds: 2.2-liter dohc 4-cylinder or 3.0-liter dohc V6 engine, antilock 4-wheel disc brakes (V6), daytime running lights (V6), air conditioning, cruise control, height-adjustable driver seat, power mirrors, power windows, power door locks, variable intermittent wipers, 205/65R15 tires.

Camry XLE adds: 4-speed automatic transmission, antilock brakes, 4-wheel disc brakes (V6), daytime running lights, power front seats w/driver-seat manual lumbar support, remote keyless entry, automatic climate control, JBL sound system, illuminated visor mirrors, leather-wrapped steering wheel, automatic headlights, theft-deterrent system, 205/60R16 tires (V6), alloy wheels.

Solara SE adds to Camry LE: daytime running lights, illuminated visor mirrors, overhead console, theft-deterrent system, fog lights, full-size spare tire.

Solara SLE adds: 3.0-liter dohc V6 engine, 4-speed automatic transmission, antilock 4-wheel disc brakes, automatic climate control, leather-wrapped steering wheel, leather upholstery, 8-way power driver seat, remote keyless entry, heated power mirrors, JBL sound system, automatic day/night mirror, universal garage door opener, rear spoiler, 205/60R16 tires, alloy wheels.

OPTIONAL EQUIPMENT:
Major Packages

	Retail Price	Dealer Invoice
Value Pkg. 1, CE	1897	—
Manufacturer's discount price	897	807
Air conditioning, power mirrors and door locks, power windows, variable intermittent wipers, floormats.		
Value Pkg. 4, LE 4-cylinder	632	—
Manufacturer's discount price	NC	NC
Remote keyless entry, power driver seat, floormats.		
Value Pkg. 3, LE 4-cylinder	1242	—
Manufacturer's discount price	610	549
Antilock brakes, daytime running lights, remote keyless entry, power driver seat, floormats.		
Value Pkg. 5, LE 4-cylinder	2342	—
Manufacturer's discount price	1710	1429
Value Pkg. 3 plus leather upholstery, leather-wrapped steering wheel and shift knob.		
Value Pkg. 3, LE V6	632	—
Manufacturer's discount price	NC	NC
Antilock brakes, daytime running lights, remote keyless entry, power driver seat, floormats.		
Value Pkg. 5, LE V6	1732	—
Manufacturer's discount price	1100	880
Value Pkg. 3 plus leather upholstery, leather-wrapped steering wheel and shift knob.		
Value Pkg. 2, XLE	2604	—
Manufacturer's discount price,		
XLE 4-cylinder	1604	1444
XLE V6	1104	994
Front side-impact airbags, leather upholstery, power sunroof, JBL AM/FM/cassette w/6-disc CD changer, map lights, floormats.		
Sport Pkg., LE	1193	949
Fog lights, rear spoiler, badging, alloy wheels.		
Upgrade Pkg. 1, SE	775	620
8-way power driver seat, alloy wheels.		

	Retail Price	Dealer Invoice
Upgrade Pkg. 2, SE	$1675	$1340
Upgrade Pkg. 1 plus power sunroof, map lights.		
Sport Upgrade Pkg. 3, SE 4-cylinder	2810	2248
Leather upholstery, 8-way power driver seat, leather-wrapped steering wheel, power sunroof, map lights, alloy wheels.		
Sport Upgrade Pkg. 4, SE V6	1730	1368
Leather-wrapped steering wheel, 8-way power driver seat, JBL AM/FM/cassette/CD player, rear spoiler, rear spoiler, 205/60R16 tires, alloy wheels.		
Upgrade Pkg. 5, SE V6	2630	2088
Sport Upgrade Pkg. 4 plus power sunroof, map lights.		
Upgrade Pkg. 6, SE V6	3655	2908
Upgrade Pkg. 5 plus leather upholstery.		

Powertrains
Traction control, LE V6, XLE V6, SLE	300	240

Safety Features
Antilock brakes, CE, SE 4-cylinder	610	521
Camry includes daytime running lights.		
Front side-impact airbags	250	215
CE requires Value Pkg. 1.		

Comfort and Convenience
Cruise control, CE	250	200
Power sunroof, LE	1000	800
SE, SLE	900	720
JBL AM/FM/cassette/CD player, LE	290	218
JBL AM/FM/cassette w/6-disc CD changer, SLE	200	150
6-disc CD changer, Camry	550	385
Universal garage door opener, Camry	199	136
Security System, CE, LE	399	249
Remote keyless entry, theft-deterrent system.		

Appearance and Miscellaneous
Fog lights, Camry	399	249
Rear spoiler, Camry	539	329
Alloy wheels, CE	755	560
LE 4-cylinder	385	308
LE V6	592	440

Post production options also available.

TOYOTA CELICA

Toyota Celica GT-S

Front-wheel-drive sports coupe

Base price range: $16,695-$21,865. Built in Japan. **Also consider:** Acura Integra, Honda Prelude, Mitsubishi Eclipse

FOR • Acceleration (GT-S 6-speed) • Handling/roadholding
AGAINST • Acceleration (GT with automatic) • Noise
• Passenger room • Rear-seat entry/exit

Toyota's front-wheel-drive sporty coupe is redesigned for 2000 with styling inspired by Indy race cars. The only engine in this 2-door hatchback is a 1.8-liter 4-cylinder with 140 horsepower in the GT model and 180 in the GT-S. The GT gets a standard 5-speed manual transmission, the GT-S Celica's first 6-speed manual. Automatic is optional for both, and GT-S's includes manual gear selection via four steering-wheel buttons. Antilock brakes and front side airbags are optional. Air conditioning, power mirrors, tilt steering, and CD stereo are standard. The GT-S comes with rear disc brakes, fog lights, and aluminum foot pedals and offers optional 16-inch alloy wheels in place of

194   *Ratings begin on page 213. Specifications begin on page 220.*   CONSUMER GUIDE™

steel 15s. An external-sliding power moonroof is available for both models. No convertible is planned.

EVALUATION Toyota gave the new Celicas small engines to minimize weight. The payoff is agile handling and grippy cornering, abetted by sharp, responsive steering. The tradeoff is that both engines must rev like mad for best performance, and only the 6-speed GT-S is close to lively. The GT is expected to account for 70 percent of sales, and with automatic, it's sluggish. The high-rpm requirements combined with lots of wind rush and tire noise means any Celica is noisy except in gentle cruising. Both engines rate exemplary EPA fuel-economy figures, though the GT-S requires premium gas. As expected of sporty cars, ride is firm and rather busy on most surfaces. Our test cars had antilock brakes, and stopping performance was excellent, but ABS should be standard on cars like this. Even moderately tall front occupants have limited head and leg room—enough to cramp some drivers behind the wheel. The back seat is the usual token gesture, and entry/exit is sporty-car crouch-and-crawl. On the plus side, drivers enjoy racer-like positioning with simple, handy controls and fine shifter/wheel/pedal spacing. The hatchback design helps cargo carrying, but there's no inside hatch release, nor is the hatch lock linked to the power door locks. The 2000 Celica has a precision feel, but overall, an Acura Integra offers similar high-rpm kicks from smoother, better-sounding 4-cylinders, and Mitsubishi's 2000 Eclipse offers larger and quieter engines—including a V6.

ENGINES

	dohc I4	dohc I4
Size, liters/cu. in.	1.8/109	1.8/110
Horsepower @ rpm	140 @ 6400	180 @ 7600
Torque (lbs./ft.) @ rpm	125 @ 6400	133 @ 6800
Availability	S[1]	S[2]
EPA city/highway mpg		
5-speed OD manual	31/43	
6-speed OD manual		27/42
4-speed OD automatic	31/49	28/39

1. GT. 2. GT-S.

PRICES

Toyota Celica	Retail Price	Dealer Invoice
GT 2-door hatchback, 5-speed	$16695	$14873
GT 2-door hatchback, automatic	17495	15586
GT-S 2-door hatchback, 6-speed	21165	18748
GT-S 2-door hatchback, automatic	21865	19368
Destination charge	455	455

Prices are for vehicles distributed by Toyota Motor Sales, U.S.A., Inc. The dealer invoice and destination charge may be higher in areas served by independent distributors.

STANDARD EQUIPMENT:

GT: 1.8-liter dohc 4-cylinder 140-horsepower engine, 5-speed manual or 4-speed automatic transmission, driver- and passenger-side airbags, daytime running lights, air conditioning, variable-assist power steering, tilt steering wheel, cloth upholstery, front bucket seats, center console, cupholders, split folding rear seat, power mirrors, AM/FM/cassette/CD player, digital clock, tachometer, map lights, rear defogger, variable-intermittent wipers, visor mirrors, remote fuel door release, automatic headlights, 195/60R15 tires, wheel covers.
GT-S adds: 1.8-liter dohc 4-cylinder 180-horsepower engine, 6-speed manual or 4-speed automatic transmission w/manual-shift capability, 4-wheel disc brakes, leather-wrapped steering wheel, cruise control, power windows, power door locks, upgraded sound system, intermittent rear wiper/washer, fog lights, 205/55ZR15 tires, alloy wheels.

OPTIONAL EQUIPMENT:
Major Packages

Upgrade Pkg., GT	820	656
Cruise control, power windows and door locks.		
All Weather Guard Pkg., GT	270	223
Intermittent rear wiper/washer, heavy-duty battery and starter.		

Safety Features	Retail Price	Dealer Invoice
Antilock brakes	$550	$473
Front side-impact airbags	250	215

Comfort and Convenience

Power sunroof	880	704
GT requires Upgrade Pkg.		
Leather upholstery, GT-S	620	496
Requires power sunroof.		
Premium sound system, GT	330	248
6-disc CD changer	550	385
Security System	399	249
Remote keyless entry, theft-deterrent system. GT requires Upgrade Pkg.		

Appearance and Miscellaneous

Rear spoiler, GT	540	432
GT-S	435	348
GT includes fog lights.		
Alloy wheels, GT	385	368
205/50VR16 tires, GT-S	60	48

Post production options also available.

TOYOTA COROLLA

Toyota Corolla LE

Front-wheel-drive subcompact car; similar to Chevrolet Prizm
Base price range: $12,418-$15,868. Built in USA and Canada. **Also consider:** Honda Civic, Mazda Protege, Saturn S-Series

FOR • Fuel economy • Build quality • Exterior finish
AGAINST • Rear-seat room

Toyota's mainstay subcompact gets a bit more power for 2000. Corolla continues in VE, CE, and top-line LE sedans with a 1.8-liter 4-cylinder engine and manual or optional automatic transmission. The addition of Toyota's VVT-i variable-valve timing adds 5 horsepower, to 125, this year. And a tilt steering wheel is a new standard feature on CE and LE models. Antilock brakes and front side airbags are optional. A Touring Package option for CE and LE includes white-face gauges and gives the CE the same wider tires as the LE.

Corolla's design and powertrain originate with Toyota but are shared with the Chevrolet Prizm. Both vehicles are built at a General Motors-Toyota plant in California.

PERFORMANCE Corolla and Prizm are showing their age, but remain fine small cars. Manual-shift models feel frisky and average close to 30 mpg. Automatic versions return 26.5-29.3 mpg in our tests, and although they feel sleepy off the line, we timed one at a respectable 9.7 seconds 0-60 mph. The air conditioning saps some pep with either transmission, however.

The suspension on these cars favors ride comfort over handling. Bumps are absorbed well, and straight-line stability is good. Although a front stabilizer bar is standard on all models, body roll is still the rule in hard cornering, but steering response and tire grip improves noticeably with the 185/65R14 tires standard on Corolla LE and Prizm LSi and included in the Corolla SE Touring Package.

Corollas seem to be insulated better than Prizms against road and wind noise, but both are quieter than the subcompact-car norm. Engine thrash that's audible near full throttle goes away in moderate-speed cruising. The optional antilock brakes provide strong stopping power, though recent test Prizms suffered

Prices are accurate at time of publication; subject to manufacturer's changes.

mushy brake-pedal feel.

ACCOMMODATIONS These cars show their 1993-vintage design with a rear seat that's very tight for adults, with notably little toe and leg room. The more-modern, upright design of the new Ford Focus and Toyota's own Echo provide far roomier accommodations. At least the Corolla/Prizm rear doors are wide enough at the bottom for acceptable entry/exit by average-sized folks. Front seats are comfortable and spacious enough, and a low cowl and beltline make for great outward visibility. It's a slight stretch to radio and climate controls, but they're simple to use and clearly marked. The trunk is usefully sized, but the lid hinges dip into the load space, and base models don't offer the convenience of a split folding rear seatback. Corolla and Prizm are well built and have sturdy-feeling cabin materials. However, we've noticed irregular exterior panel gaps and minor steering-column rattles in recent examples of both versions.

VALUE FOR THE MONEY They're not the newest or cheapest subcompacts around, but both Corolla and Prizm are solid, safe choices that benefit from Toyota's great reliability record. Note that Corolla handily outsells its Chevy cousin and, being a Toyota, commands higher resale values.

ENGINES

	dohc I4
Size, liters/cu. in.	1.8/110
Horsepower @ rpm	125 @ 5600
Torque (lbs./ft.) @ rpm	122 @ 4400
Availability	S

EPA city/highway mpg

5-speed OD manual	31/38
3-speed automatic	28/33
4-speed OD automatic	28/36

PRICES

Toyota Corolla

	Retail Price	Dealer Invoice
VE 4-door sedan, 5-speed	$12418	$11318
VE 4-door sedan, automatic	12918	11774
CE 4-door sedan, 5-speed	13108	11610
CE 4-door sedan, automatic	13908	12319
LE 4-door sedan, 5-speed	15068	13346
LE 4-door sedan, automatic	15868	14054
Destination charge	455	455

Prices are for vehicles distributed by Toyota Motor Sales, U.S.A., Inc. The dealer invoice and destination charge may be higher in areas served by independent distributors.

STANDARD EQUIPMENT:

VE: 1.8-liter dohc 4-cylinder engine, 5-speed manual or 3-speed automatic transmission, driver- and passenger-side airbags, daytime running lights, power steering, cloth upholstery, front bucket seats, center console, cupholders, AM/FM radio, visor mirrors, intermittent wipers, automatic headlights, remote fuel door release, dual outside mirrors, 175/65R14 tires.

CE adds: 5-speed manual or 4-speed automatic transmission, tilt steering wheel, AM/FM/cassette, digital clock, rear defogger, split folding rear seat, remote trunk release, wheel covers.

LE adds: air conditioning, power mirrors, power windows, power door locks, tachometer, variable intermittent wipers, outside temperature display, 185/65R14 tires.

OPTIONAL EQUIPMENT:

Major Packages

	Retail	Dealer
All-Weather Guard Pkg., VE	275	223
CE, LE	80	67
Heavy-duty rear defogger, starter, and heater, rear heater ducts.		
Touring Pkg., CE	280	224
Mud guards, rocker panel extensions, white-faced gauges, tachometer, outside temperature indicator, 185/65SR14 tires, full wheel covers.		
Touring Pkg., LE	145	116
Mud guards, rocker panel extensions, white-faced gauges.		
Touring Pkg. w/alloy wheels, LE	510	408
Value Pkg., VE	1230	—
Manufacturer's discount price	730	657
Air conditioning, AM/FM/cassette, digital clock.		

	Retail Price	Dealer Invoice
Value Pkg., CE	$1590	—
Manufacturer's discount price	1090	981
Air conditioning, power windows and door locks.		
Value Pkg., LE	250	—
Manufacturer's discount price	NC	NC
Cruise control.		
Special Elite Pkg., CE, LE	899	429
Wood dashboard trim, trunk mat, floormats, rear spoiler, gold pkg.		

Safety Features

Antilock brakes	550	473
Side-impact airbags	250	215

Comfort and Convenience

Power sunroof, LE	735	588
Rear defogger, VE	195	156
Cruise control, CE	250	200
AM/FM/cassette, VE	231	162
CD player	335	235
6-disc CD changer	399	279

Appearance and Miscellaneous

Rear Spoiler	499	299
Alloy wheels	499	375

Post production options also available.

TOYOTA ECHO

Toyota Echo 4-door

Front-wheel-drive subcompact car

Base price range: $9,995-$11,095. Built in Japan. **Also consider:** Dodge/Plymouth Neon, Ford Focus, Honda Civic

FOR • Fuel economy • Maneuverability **AGAINST** • Acceleration (automatic transmission)

Echo, Toyota's new entry-level small car, is priced well below the company's subcompact Corolla, yet offers similar interior space within a shorter, taller body. Echo offers 2- and 4-door sedans with a new 1.5-liter 4-cylinder engine. Manual and optional automatic transmissions are available, the latter with "uphill shift logic" programming that Toyota claims minimizes "hunting" between gears on long or steep upgrades. Options include antilock brakes, air conditioning, power door locks (but not power mirrors), and split-fold rear seat. A tilt steering wheel is standard, but power steering is optional. Echo is among the few vehicles that does not offer power windows.

PERFORMANCE Mechanically, Echo is modern but ordinary. The engine is no powerhouse, but curb weights are around 2000 pounds—among the lightest in this class—so acceleration is adequate with automatic transmission and fairly lively with manual shift. Fuel economy awaits a full test, but lofty EPA ratings of up to 41 mpg highway seem realistic. Echo is more mechanically refined than the Tercel it replaces, and while noise suppression is nothing special, cross-country drives shouldn't be tiring.

Echo feels substantial for a low-bucks minicar, and also feels different to drive, thanks to its phone-booth body build. Fast corners are managed with good grip and stability, but both body styles feel a tad tippy if you rush, and front-end "plowing" sets in early. The upside is great close-quarters maneuverability despite slightly dull steering action. Ride comfort is better than the small-car norm, with only minor jiggle on washboard freeways and decent smothering of large bumps. The bluff-sided Echo reacts to stiff crosswinds even at moderate speeds, however, and we noticed minor tire-induced wander on grooved surfaces.

 Ratings begin on page 213. Specifications begin on page 220. CONSUMER GUIDE™

ACCOMMODATIONS Only Ford's new Focus rivals Echo for roominess among subcompacts. The tall cabin is too narrow for a center adult in back, but legroom is no problem anywhere, rear foot room good, and all-around headroom generous. The seats are comfortable if rather flat, and their high set lets legs rest comfortably. Entry/exit isn't that easy on the 2-door despite a standard slide-forward right front seat, and narrow rear-door bottoms are a minor nuisance on the 4-door.

The steering wheel is perched high and angled for a slight minivan position that may take getting used to. Visibility is commanding, compromised only a bit dead-astern. Less likable is the gimmicky central gauge pod atop the dash, which is angled toward the driver but may be too distant for some eyes. Other driving controls are simple and handy. The audio unit is flanked by open bins that will hold maybe 10 CDs each, and the cabin has plenty of other stash spaces. Cargo volume is ample for such a tidy exterior package, but the short tail leaves little fore-aft length without the optional split-fold rear seat. Our test Echoes were solid and well-finished. Interior materials are attractive but still entry-level in look and feel.

VALUE FOR THE MONEY Roomy and fresh-feeling, Echo's keenly priced and should maintain Toyota's strong quality and reliability record. Toyota hopes to sell as many as 60,000 annually (75 percent 4-doors), which should be easy—provided the young target buyers find the styling quirky-cool rather than quirky-nerdy.

ENGINES

	dohc I4
Size, liters/cu. in.	1.5/91
Horsepower @ rpm	108 @ 6000
Torque (lbs./ft.) @ rpm	105 @ 4200
Availability	S

EPA city/highway mpg	
5-speed OD manual................................	34/41
4-speed OD automatic................................	32/39

PRICES

Toyota Echo	Retail Price	Dealer Invoice
Base 2-door coupe, 5-speed	$9995	$9264
Base 2-door coupe, automatic	10795	10007
Base 4-door sedan, 5-speed	10295	9543
Base 4-door sedan, automatic	11095	10284
Destination charge	455	455

Prices are for vehicles distributed by Toyota Motor Sales, U.S.A., Inc. The dealer invoice and destination charge may be higher in areas served by independent distributors.

STANDARD EQUIPMENT:

Base: 1.5-liter dohc 4-cylinder engine, 5-speed manual or 4-speed automatic transmission, driver- and passenger-side airbags, tilt steering wheel, cloth upholstery, front bucket seats, center console, cupholders, AM/FM radio, driver-side visor mirror, dual outside mirrors, 175/65R14 tires, wheel covers.

OPTIONAL EQUIPMENT:
Major Packages

Upgrade Pkg. 1	1020	832

Power steering, intermittent wipers, split folding rear seat, digital clock, remote control outside mirrors, rocker panels, fender extensions.

Upgrade Pkg. 2, coupe	1420	1123
sedan	1465	1159

Air conditioning, power door locks, AM/FM/cassette/CD player. Requires Upgrade Pkg. 1.

All Weather Pkg................................	275	220

Rear defogger, heavy-duty battery, rear seat heater ducts.

Safety Features

Antilock brakes................................	590	505

Includes daytime running lights. Requires Upgrade Pkg. 2 or All Weather Pkg.

Comfort and Convenience

	Retail	Dealer
Power steering	270	231

	Price	Invoice
Air conditioning................................	$925	$740
AM/FM/cassette	170	128
AM/FM/cassette/CD player	270	203
6-disc CD changer	550	385
Power door locks, coupe...........................	225	180
sedan	270	216

Requires Upgrade Pkg. 1.

Security System	399	249

Remote keyless entry, theft-deterrent system. Requires power door locks or Upgrade Pkg. 2.

Appearance and Miscellaneous

Rear spoiler................................	100	80

Requires Upgrade Pkg. 1.

Alloy wheels	499	375

Post production options also available.

TOYOTA LAND CRUISER

Toyota Land Cruiser

4-wheel-drive full-size sport-utility vehicle; similar to Lexus LX 470

Base price: $50,828. Built in Japan. **Also consider:** Chevrolet Tahoe and Suburban, Ford Expedition, GMC Yukon and Yukon XL

FOR • Passenger and cargo room • Acceleration • Ride • Quietness • Build quality • Exterior finish • Interior materials
AGAINST • Fuel economy • Entry/exit

Added standard equipment, including an antiskid system, highlight Toyota's biggest SUV for 2000. Land Cruiser shares its design and powertrain with the luxury Lexus LX 470. It continues with V8 power, automatic transmission, and a permanent 4-wheel-drive system with a 2-speed transfer case providing separate low-range gears for off-roading. A manual locking center differential is standard. Maximum trailering weight is 6500 pounds.

Added for 2000 is Toyota's new Active TRAC traction control with integrated vehicle skid control. This uses data from the 4-wheel antilock brake sensors and other sources to direct power to the wheels with best traction. In addition, power sunroof and leather upholstery move from optional to standard status. Land Cruiser again comes with seating for five and offers an extra-cost 3-person third-row bench seat that now includes rear air conditioning, previously a stand-alone option. The rear A/C is independent of the regular system and features automatic temperature control.

PERFORMANCE Though too large and tall to drive like cars, the Land Cruiser and LX 470 are arguably the most refined big SUVs around. Fast turns induce predictable body lean and a slight tipsy feel, but the 4WD keeps grip secure, while the independent front suspension helps give the Toyota a surprisingly absorbent on-road ride. The Lexus includes driver-selected shock-absorber firmness via a console switch. We found it does little for handling and makes for a slightly wallowy ride in soft mode; the firmer settings just cause jitters over closely spaced bumps. With luxury-grade sound deadening and silken engines, both models are quieter than many passenger sedans, not to mention most all other truck-type SUVs. Still, some wind noise is noticed at highway speeds, inevitable with such bluff styling. The standard antilock brakes make "panic" stops stable and relatively short for heavyweight SUVs.

Despite that bulk, the 4.7-liter V8 delivers 0-60 mph in a brisk

Prices are accurate at time of publication; subject to manufacturer's changes.

9 seconds by our stopwatch. The transmission helps performance anywhere with prompt, smooth shifts up and down. Mileage is mediocre. Though an LX 470 gave us 15.4 mpg with lots of highway driving, the 13.6 mpg of our latest Land Cruiser is a more realistic overall average—and premium fuel is mandatory.

ACCOMMODATIONS Both these rigs have plenty of head room and good rear leg room, plus comfortable cabin width for three grownups on the second-row bench. The available third-row seat is cramped and inaccessible for all but children. Middle-row entry/exit is no picnic either, thanks to a tall step-up and narrow door bottoms. That high stance gives a commanding driving view, though headrests clutter things to the rear. The LX 470 slightly eases entry/exit with a suspension that automatically lowers the body a few inches when the ignition is switched off.

Lanky drivers enjoy generous rearward seat travel, and few vehicles of any type are more comfortable in front. The user-friendly dashboard, common to both versions, features simple rotary climate controls, though a few other switches aren't so easy to see. There's only grocery-bag space behind the third seat, but that seat folds up or removes fairly easily for generous cargo room. The drop-down tailgate means a long stretch to your cargo, though a plastic filler panel between the gate and the load floor makes sliding heavy items a little easier.

VALUE FOR THE MONEY Land Cruiser isn't cheap, and the lush Lexus version costs even more. Superior customer service and a longer warranty are the latter's only tangible advantages over the Toyota. Some SUVs offer more metal for less money, but Land Cruiser and LX 470 are highly capable off-road, as quick and comfortable as any rival on-road, and built better than most. Land Cruiser gets our Recommended nod.

ENGINES

	dohc V8
Size, liters/cu. in.	4.7/285
Horsepower @ rpm	230 @ 4800
Torque (lbs./ft.) @ rpm	320 @ 3400
Availability	S

EPA city/highway mpg

4-speed OD automatic	13/16

PRICES

Toyota Land Cruiser	Retail Price	Dealer Invoice
Base 4-door 4WD wagon	$50828	$43713
Destination charge	480	480

Prices are for vehicles distributed by Toyota Motor Sales, U.S.A., Inc. The dealer invoice and destination charge may be higher in areas served by independent distributors.

STANDARD EQUIPMENT:

Base: 4.7-liter dohc V8 engine, 4-speed automatic transmission, permanent 4-wheel drive, 2-speed transfer case, locking rear differential, traction control, driver- and passenger-side airbags, antilock 4-wheel disc brakes, antiskid system, daytime running lights, air conditioning w/automatic climate control, interior air filter, rear heater, power steering, tilt leather-wrapped steering wheel, cruise control, leather upholstery, heated power front bucket seats, center console, overhead console, cupholders, split folding rear seat, heated power mirrors, power windows, power door locks, remote keyless entry, AM/FM/cassette w/6-disc CD changer, power antenna, digital clock, tachometer, power sunroof, illuminated visor mirrors, remote fuel-door release, rear defogger, variable intermittent wipers, outside temperature indicator, rear intermittent wiper/washer, automatic headlights, auxiliary power outlets, theft-deterrent system, fog lights, rear privacy glass, front and rear tow hooks, skid plates, full-size spare tire, 275/70R16 tires, alloy wheels.

OPTIONAL EQUIPMENT:
Major Packages

Convenience Pkg.	1771	1109

Running boards, roof rack, rear wind deflector, towing hitch receiver.

Third Seat Pkg.	2265	1854

Leather split folding and reclining third row seat, additional cupholders, power swing-out rear quarter windows, rear air conditioning w/independent automatic climate control.

Appearance and Miscellaneous	Retail Price	Dealer Invoice
Roof rack	$449	$274
Towing hitch receiver	365	255

Post production options also available.

TOYOTA RAV4

RECOMMENDED

Toyota RAV4 4-door

Front- or all-wheel-drive compact sport-utility vehicle

Base price range: $16,668-$19,128. **Built in Japan. Also consider:** Honda CR-V, Jeep Wrangler, Kia Sportage, Nissan Xterra

FOR • Cargo room • Steering/handling • Visibility
AGAINST • Acceleration (automatic transmission) • Engine noise

After losing its 2-door "hardtop" body style last year, Toyota's pint-size sport-utility vehicle drops its 2-door semi-convertible due to sluggish sales. That trims the RAV4 line to a 4-door wagon, with redesigned cupholders and the addition of a standard full-size spare tire as the main year-2000 change.

RAV4's only engine is a 2.0-liter 4-cylinder teamed with manual transmission or extra-cost automatic. Antilock brakes are optional. Like the rival Honda CR-V, RAV4 is a car-based unibody design with all-independent suspension. Both are available with front-wheel or permanently engaged 4-wheel drive. Neither offers separate low-range gearing, although manual-shift RAV4s now have a standard center differential lock that's useful off-road; this feature had been an option.

PERFORMANCE RAV4 fills the role of daily commuter as well as any small SUV, but suffers more tire and wind noise than the average compact car, and its engine is loud when pushed. Ride is okay, but there's some choppiness on scalloped freeways and patchy pavement.

Performance also lags that of most small cars. We timed an automatic AWD wagon at about 13 seconds to 60 mph—marginal for the urban grind. And that's with just the driver aboard. At least that same RAV returned a solid 22 mpg. Fuel thrift and performance are a little better with manual shift, better still in the lighter front-drive versions. Toyota admits the RAV is not designed for severe off-roading; get a Jeep Wrangler if that's your bag.

ACCOMMODATIONS More front seat travel wouldn't go amiss for lanky types, but RAV4's interior feels as large as that of a subcompact car, albeit one with a really tall roof. Four adults fit pretty well, but back seaters don't get much leg room, and rear entry/exit is a squeeze for larger folk. Visibility is good overall.

Cargo space is decent for a small but tall wagon, though most users will likely resort to folding the 50/50 split rear seats for loads longer than about 2 feet. RAV4 is as soundly built as any Toyota, but it's still a relative lightweight, with lots of painted metal inside and economy-grade cabin materials.

VALUE FOR THE MONEY RAV4 has its points, but the CR-V is larger, roomier, and more practical. Shop both. And don't overlook the Subaru Forester.

ENGINES

	dohc i4
Size, liters/cu. in.	2.0/122
Horsepower @ rpm	127 @ 5400
Torque (lbs./ft.) @ rpm	132 @ 4600
Availability	S

EPA city/highway mpg
5-speed OD manual.................................... 22/25[1]
4-speed OD automatic............................... 22/26

1. 22/26 w/2-door.

PRICES

Toyota RAV4	Retail Price	Dealer Invoice
2WD 4-door wagon, 5-speed	$16668	$15193
2WD 4-door wagon, automatic	17718	16149
4WD 4-door wagon, 5-speed	18078	16199
4WD 4-door wagon, automatic	19128	17139
Destination charge	480	480

Prices are for vehicles distributed by Toyota Motor Sales, U.S.A., Inc. The dealer invoice and destination charge may be higher in areas served by independent distributors.

STANDARD EQUIPMENT:

Base: 2.0-liter dohc 4-cylinder engine, 5-speed manual or 4-speed automatic transmission, driver- and passenger-side airbags, power steering, tilt steering wheel, cloth upholstery, front bucket seats, split folding and reclining rear seat, cupholders, tachometer, digital clock, rear defogger, passenger-side visor mirror, intermittent wipers, auxiliary power outlet, intermittent rear wiper/washer, dual outside mirrors, front tow hook, full-size spare tire, 215/70R16 tires. **4WD** models add: permanent all-wheel drive, center differential lock (5-speed), skid plates.

OPTIONAL EQUIPMENT:
Major Packages

Value Pkg. 1	2797	2238
Manufacturer's discount price	1547	1392

Air conditioning, AM/FM/cassette, cruise control, power mirrors, power windows and door locks, cloth headrests, carpeted floormats, silver-painted bumpers and bodyside cladding.

Value Pkg. 2	3649	2919
Manufacturer's discount price	2399	2159

Value Pkg. 1 plus AM/FM/CD player, privacy glass, color-keyed bumpers and bodyside cladding, color-keyed mirrors and door handles, alloy wheels.

Special Edition Value Pkg. 3	4279	3423
Manufacturer's discount price	3029	2726

Value Pkg. 2 plus cruise control, leather upholstery.

Active Pkg.	450	315

Removable roof rack, rear mud guards, bodyside graphics, rear step bumper, tow hitch.

Convenience Pkg.	241	169

Removable rear door storage bags, center console, cargo mat.

Powertrains

Limited-slip rear differential, 4WD	390	322

Safety Features

Antilock brakes	630	539

Includes daytime running lights.

Comfort and Convenience

Power sunroof	815	652
CD player	335	235

Requires Value Pkg. 1.

6-disc CD player............................	399	279
Security System	399	249

Remote keyless entry, theft-deterrent system. Requires Value Pkg.

Appearance and Miscellaneous

Rear step bumper...............................	285	171

Includes tow hitch, rear mud guards.

Removable roof rack	155	95
Privacy glass	310	248

Special Purpose, Wheels and Tires

Alloy wheels	490	392

Post production options also available.

TOYOTA SIENNA

Toyota Sienna XLE

Front-wheel-drive minivan
Base price range: $21,968-$26,934. Built in USA. **Also consider:** Dodge Caravan, Ford Windstar, Honda Odyssey

FOR • Passenger and cargo room • Build quality • Exterior finish **AGAINST** • Fuel economy • Radio placement

Standard steering-wheel radio controls and an in-dash CD player top the brief list of additions to this Kentucky-built minivan for 2000. Based on Toyota's Camry car platform, Sienna comes in a single body length with a 3.0-liter V6 engine, automatic transmission, antilock brakes, and a low-tire-pressure warning system.

The base CE model is available with one or two sliding side doors; the LE and top-line XLE come with two. A right-side power sliding door is optional on LE and XLE. Sienna seats up to seven. The base arrangement is two front bucket seats, a 2-passenger second-row bench, and a 3-place third-row bench. A pair of second-row buckets is standard on the XLE and optional on the LE, and the XLE can be equipped with two third-row buckets for a 6-passenger setup. Rounding out the year-2000 changes is a new Sport option package for CE and LE models that includes running boards, a rear spoiler, and alloy wheels.

PERFORMANCE The 3.0-liter V6 that's so strong in Camry pulls much more weight here, but the automatic transmission is a prompt, smooth operator, so this minivan seldom feels underpowered. Our test model ran 0-60 mph in a brisk 8.9 seconds, though a full load and a running air conditioner slows things down. Premium fuel is recommended and our extended-use Sienna averaged 19.4 mpg over 9100 miles, including a substantial amount of highway driving.

Ride and handling are pleasant. Bumps are absorbed with little impact, and body lean in turns is moderate for a minivan, though there's some nose-heaviness on freeway on-ramps. Hard take-offs induce mild steering-wheel tug that highlights the lack of traction control, even as an option; that's a drawback in the snowbelt. Braking is swift and stable. Noise levels are subdued.

Our extended-use LE was trouble-free mechanically, but a severe instrument-panel rattle was cured after a dealer service department installed an underdash cushioning pad that had been omitted during the vehicle's manufacture. Another test Sienna suffered an irritating rattle from the mid-seat area.

ACCOMMODATIONS Sienna's well-designed cabin has a low floor for super-easy entry/exit. The driving position is commanding, though the middle roof pillars and rear headrests impede driver vision somewhat. Some on our staff find the cloth front seats too soft for long-distance comfort, but adults get plenty of room anywhere if no seats are fully aft. Second-row occupants lose valuable leg space with the seats ahead pushed back. Likewise the third row. A column-mount transmission lever allows full front-to-rear walk-through.

Most controls are convenient, but the radio is mounted too low for easy operation while driving, so the new steering-wheel controls should help. The available power rear-quarter windows operate together, not individually, which slightly limits their usefulness. Bins and drink holders of various sizes make for fine interior storage. There's room for a double row of grocery bags behind the third seat, which tumble-folds for more space. Removing the heavy middle or rear seats is a 2-person job.

VALUE FOR THE MONEY Sienna performs well in every area

Prices are accurate at time of publication; subject to manufacturer's changes.

required of a minivan while delivering better-than-expected power and economy. On the downside, the competitive base prices rise quickly if you add such desirable amenities as the power side door.

ENGINES

	dohc V6
Size, liters/cu. in.	3.0/183
Horsepower @ rpm	194 @ 5200
Torque (lbs./ft.) @ rpm	209 @ 4400
Availability	S

EPA city/highway mpg

4-speed OD automatic	19/24

PRICES

Toyota Sienna	Retail Price	Dealer Invoice
CE 3-door van	$21968	$19457
CE 4-door van	22858	20247
LE 4-door van	24898	21797
XLE 4-door van	26934	23579
Destination charge	480	480

Prices are for vehicles distributed by Toyota Motor Sales, U.S.A., Inc. The dealer invoice and destination charge may be higher in areas served by independent distributors.

STANDARD EQUIPMENT:

CE: 3.0-liter dohc V6 engine, 4-speed automatic transmission, driver- and passenger-side airbags, antilock brakes, low-tire-pressure-warning system, daytime running lights, front air conditioning (3-door), front and rear air conditioning (4-door), variable-assist power steering, tilt steering wheel w/radio controls, cloth reclining front bucket seats, console with storage, overhead console, 2-passenger second-row seat, 3-passenger split-folding third row seat, cupholders, AM/FM/cassette/CD player, digital clock, visor mirrors, auxiliary power outlets, variable intermittent wipers, rear intermittent wiper/washer, automatic headlights, dual outside mirrors, 205/70R15 tires, wheel covers.

LE adds: front and rear air conditioning, power mirrors, power windows, power door locks, cruise control, rear defogger, tachometer, illuminated visor mirrors, rear privacy glass, full-size spare tire.

XLE adds: 6-way power driver seat, heated power mirrors, upgraded sound system, quad captain's chairs, leather-wrapped steering wheel, remote keyless entry, floormats, roof rack, theft-deterrent system, 215/65R15 tires, alloy wheels.

OPTIONAL EQUIPMENT:

Major Packages

Extra Value Pkg., CE 3-door	2386	—
Manufacturer's discount price, CE 3-door	1386	1247
Extra Value Pkg., CE 4-door	1941	—
Manufacturer's discount price, CE 4-door	941	847

Front and rear air conditioning (3-door), cruise control, heated power mirrors, power windows and door locks, rear defogger, floormats, rear privacy glass, full-size spare tire. NA 3-door with Towing Pkg.

Extra Value Pkg., LE	1301	—
Manufacturer's discount price	301	271

Heated power mirrors, remote keyless entry, quad captain chairs, floormats, roof rack.

Upgrade Pkg. 1, LE	645	504

Upgraded sound system, power passenger-side rear door, rear privacy glass. Requires Extra Value Pkg.

Upgrade Pkg. 2, LE	1120	884

Upgrade Pkg. 1 plus alloy wheels. Requires Extra Value Pkg.

Upgrade Pkg. 1, XLE	1610	1278

Leather upholstery, third row captain chairs, CD changer.

Upgrade Pkg. 2, XLE	1275	1020

Power sunroof, power passenger-side rear door.

Upgrade Pkg. 3, XLE	2685	2148

Upgrade Pkg. 2 plus leather upholstery, third row captain chairs.

Luxury Pkg., XLE	2885	2298

Upgrade Pkg. 1 plus Upgrade Pkg. 2.

Sport Pkg., CE, LE	1199	749

Running boards, rear spoiler, alloy wheels.

Towing Pkg., CE 3-door	630	504

	Retail Price	Dealer Invoice
CE 4-door, LE, XLE	$160	$128

CE 3-door includes front and rear air conditioning.

Comfort and Convenience

Power passenger-side rear door, XLE	395	316
Universal garage door opener	199	136
Rear defogger, CE	205	164
Remote keyless entry, CE	220	176
Requires Extra Value Pkg.		
Security System, CE, LE	399	249

Remote keyless entry, theft-deterrent system. CE requires Extra Value Pkg.

Appearance and Miscellaneous

Running Boards, CE, LE	480	290
XLE	595	365
Towing receiver hitch	290	200
Alloy wheels, CE	592	440
LE	475	380

Post production options also available.

TOYOTA TACOMA

Toyota Tacoma extended cab 2WD

Rear- or 4-wheel-drive compact pickup truck
Base price range: $11,428-$25,178. Built in USA. **Also consider:** Dodge Dakota, Ford Ranger, Mazda B-Series

FOR • Acceleration (V6) • Build quality • Exterior finish
AGAINST • Rear-seat entry/exit • Ride (4WD models) • Step-in height (4WD models)

Minor technical updates are the only changes to Toyota's compact pickups for 2000. Tacoma comes in regular and extended Xtracab models, the latter with a pair of forward-facing rear jump seats.

Engine offerings are 4-cylinders of 2.4 and 2.7 liters and a 3.4-liter V6. All team with manual transmission or optional automatic. The specialty 2WD PreRunner sub-series comes in both cab styles with the larger 4-cylinder and as a V6 Xtracab. All PreRunners have automatic transmission and 4x4 appearance cues. An optional Off-Road Package for PreRunners and 4x4 Tacomas delivers higher-riding firm suspension, a locking rear differential, and sporty cosmetics.

Tacoma's 4WD system is not for use on dry pavement. Standard on the top-line Limited models and optional on other 4x4 Tacomas is Toyota's shift-on-the-fly 4WDemand system with automatic locking front hubs; the standard 4WD system has manual locking hubs. With Limited's optional One Touch Hi-4, 4WD is engaged via a button on the floor-mounted transfer case lever rather than by shifting the lever. Antilock brakes are optional on all models.

For 2000, intermittent windshield wipers are standard on all models, 4x4s get numerically higher axle ratios for quicker take-offs, and daytime running lamps are newly included on models with antilock brakes.

PERFORMANCE Four-cylinder Tacomas have more power and better performance than most 4-cylinder domestics, but the V6 is the best choice in the heavier 4x4s. It equals domestic V6s for standing-start snap, though it's not quite as strong at midrange passing speeds. Our test V6 Xtracabs averaged 16.1 mpg with manual transmission and 4WD and 19.4 with automatic and 2WD. Tacoma payload ratings are competitive, but towing limits fall short of domestic levels by at least 1000 pounds. And

Ratings begin on page 213. Specifications begin on page 220.

antilock brakes are optional; most rivals have standard rear-wheel ABS at least.

The 2WD Tacomas have a pleasant, fairly comfortable ride. Though 4x4s can get bouncy with their stiff damping and big tires, they're still more composed than most competitors. They also ride higher, yet feel stable in quick direction changes. The 2WD models can feel pretty sporty, although all Tacomas have slightly numb steering. Noise levels are relatively low across the board, except for the 4x4s' marked tire thrum.

ACCOMMODATIONS Regular cabs have good room for two adults, but middle riders are hemmed in on the base bench seat, making the optional buckets a better bet for comfort. Like most extended-cab compacts, Xtracab Tacomas are kid-size in back, though the rear bench will accommodate a child safety seat, something few rivals can. Unlike top competitors, however, Xtracab offers only two doors versus three on rival GM models and four on the Dodge Dakota, Ford Ranger, Mazda B-Series, and Nissan Frontier. Additionally, all Tacomas have a 6.2-foot cargo box; domestics come as long as 7.3. Interior step-in is steep on 4x4s. The dashboard is logical and convenient, but climate controls are obstructed by the pull-out cupholders. Toyota's exacting fit and finish are evident, although base-trim Tacomas look low-buck inside.

VALUE FOR THE MONEY Tacoma is way behind in the truck "door race," has higher base prices than most competitors, and gets quite costly with just a few extras. But a reputation for reliability, toughness, and high resale value help make Tacoma the best-selling import-brand pickup and a solid Recommended choice.

ENGINES

	dohc I4	dohc I4	dohc V6
Size, liters/cu. in.	2.4/144	2.7/163	3.4/181
Horsepower @ rpm	142 @ 5000	150 @ 4800	190 @ 4800
Torque (lbs./ft.) @ rpm	160 @ 4000	177 @ 4000	220 @ 3600
Availability	S[1]	S[2]	O
EPA city/highway mpg			
5-speed OD manual	22/27	17/21	19/24[3]
4-speed OD automatic	21/24	19/21	19/23[4]

1. 2WD. 2. 4WD. 3. 17/19 w/4WD. 4. 17/20 w/4WD.

PRICES

Toyota Tacoma

	Retail Price	Dealer Invoice
2WD 4-cylinder regular cab, 5-speed	$11428	$10417
2WD 4-cylinder regular cab, automatic	12148	11073
2WD 4-cylinder PreRunner regular cab, automatic	13518	12196
2WD 4-cylinder Xtracab, 5-speed	13978	12597
2WD 4-cylinder Xtracab, automatic	14698	13246
2WD 4-cylinder PreRunner Xtracab, automatic	16938	15282
2WD V6 Xtracab, 5-speed	15318	13805
2WD V6 Xtracab, automatic	16218	14615
2WD V6 PreRunner Xtracab, automatic	17868	16121
4WD 4-cylinder regular cab, 5-speed	15868	14137
4WD 4-cylinder regular cab, automatic	16768	14939
4WD 4-cylinder Xtracab, 5-speed	17748	15812
4WD 4-cylinder Xtracab, automatic	18648	16614
4WD V6 Xtracab, 5-speed	18838	16782
4WD V6 Xtracab, automatic	19738	17584
4WD Limited V6 Xtracab, 5-speed	24278	21630
4WD Limited V6 Xtracab, automatic	25178	22431
Destination charge	480	480

Prices are for vehicles distributed by Toyota Motor Sales, U.S.A., Inc. The dealer invoice and destination charge may be higher in areas served by independent distributors.

STANDARD EQUIPMENT:

2WD regular cab: 2.4-liter dohc 4-cylinder engine, 5-speed manual or 4-speed automatic transmission, driver- and passenger-side airbags, cloth bench seat, cupholders, auxiliary power outlets, intermittent wipers, carpeting, dual outside mirrors, painted front bumper, full-size spare tire, 195/75R14 tires, wheel covers.

2WD 4-cylinder Xtracab adds: split bench seat, split folding rear bench seat, swing-out rear quarter windows, painted rear bumper, 215/70R14 tires.
2WD V6 Xtracab adds: 3.4-liter dohc V6 engine, power steering.
2WD PreRunner regular cab adds to 2WD regular cab: 2.7-liter dohc 4-cylinder engine, 4-speed automatic transmission, power steering, power mirrors, painted rear bumper, skid plates, 225/75R15 tires, deletes wheel covers.
2WD PreRunner Xtracab adds: 3.4-liter dohc V6 engine (PreRunner V6), air conditioning, split bench seat, split folding rear bench seat, swing-out rear quarter windows.
4WD regular cab adds to 2WD regular cab: 2.7-liter dohc 4-cylinder engine, part-time 4-wheel drive, 2-speed transfer case, manually locking hubs, power steering, painted rear bumper, mud guards, front tow hooks, skid plates, 225/75R15 tires, deletes wheel covers.
4WD 4-cylinder Xtracab adds: split bench seat, split folding rear bench seat, swing-out rear quarter windows.
4WD V6 Xtracab adds: 3.4-liter dohc V6 engine, gas shock absorbers.
Limited adds: 4WDemand transfer case, automatic locking hubs, tilt steering wheel, cruise control, power mirrors, power windows, power door locks, front bucket seats, tachometer, AM/FM/cassette/CD player, power antenna, digital clock, variable intermittent wipers, passenger-side visor mirror, map lights, chrome bumpers, chrome grille and door handles, rear privacy glass, sliding rear window, 265/75R15 tires, alloy wheels.

OPTIONAL EQUIPMENT:
Major Packages

	Retail Price	Dealer Invoice
Value Edition Plus Pkg., 2WD regular cab	$2180	$1744
Manufacturer's discount price	1630	1467

Power steering, air conditioning, AM/FM/cassette, floormats, chrome front and rear bumpers, chrome grille and door handles.

Value Edition Plus Pkg., 4WD regular cab	3135	2508
Manufacturer's discount price	1485	1336

Air conditioning, front bucket seats, AM/FM/cassette, passenger-side visor mirror, floormats, sliding rear window, chrome front and rear bumpers, chrome grille and door handles, wheel lip moldings, 265/75R15 tires, alloy wheels.

Value Edition Plus Pkg., 2WD PreRunner regular cab	3145	2516
Manufacturer's discount price	2045	1840

Air conditioning, front bucket seats, AM/FM/cassette, passenger-side visor mirror, floormats, sliding rear window, chrome front and rear bumpers, chrome grille and door handles, wheel lip moldings, 265/75R15 tires, alloy wheels.

Value Edition Plus Pkg. with Color-Key Pkg., 2WD regular cab	2105	1684
Manufacturer's discount price	1605	1444

Value Edition Plus Pkg. with color-keyed front bumper and grille.

Value Pkg., PreRunner Xtracab	1175	940
Manufacturer's discount price	600	540

Chrome front and rear bumpers, chrome grille and door handles, AM/FM/cassette/CD player, passenger-side visor mirror, sliding rear window, privacy glass.

Value Pkg. with Color Key Pkg., PreRunner Xtracab	1100	880
Manufacturer's discount price	600	540

Value Pkg. with color-keyed front bumper and grille.

SR5 Pkg., 2WD 4-cylinder Xtracab	2475	1980
Manufacturer's discount price	1775	1597

Air conditioning, power steering, AM/FM/cassette/CD player, passenger-side visor mirror, sliding rear window, privacy glass, chrome front and rear bumpers, chrome grille and door handles. NA PreRunner, Limited.

SR5 Pkg., 2WD V6 Xtracab, 4WD Xtracab	2160	1728
Manufacturer's discount price,		
2WD V6 Xtracab	1610	1449
4WD Xtracab	1310	1179

Air conditioning, AM/FM/cassette/CD player, passenger-side visor mirror, sliding rear window, privacy glass, chrome front and bumpers, chrome grille, and door handles. NA PreRunner, Limited.

Prices are accurate at time of publication; subject to manufacturer's changes.

	Retail Price	Dealer Invoice
SR5 Pkg. with Color Key Pkg., 2WD 4-cylinder Xtracab	$2400	$1920
Manufacturer's discount price, 2WD 4-cylinder Xtracab	1750	1575
SR5 Pkg. with color-keyed front bumper and grille. NA PreRunner, Limited.		
SR5 Pkg. with Color Key Pkg., 2WD V6 Xtracab, 4WD Xtracab	2085	1668
Manufacturer's discount price, 2WD V6 Xtracab	1535	1381
4WD Xtracab	1235	1111
SR5 Pkg. with color-keyed front bumper and grille. NA PreRunner, Limited.		
Preferred Equipment Pkg. 1 or 2, PreRunner V6	770	576
Over or under rail bed liner, wheel lip moldings, 265/75R15 tires, styled steel wheels.		
Preferred Equipment Pkg. 3 or 4, PreRunner V6	1890	1481
TRD Off-Road Pkg. (off-road suspension, locking differential, tachometer, black overfenders, 31x10.5R15 tires, alloy wheels), over or under rail bed liner.		
Chrome Pkg., PreRunner, Xtracab	250	200
Chrome front bumper, rear step bumper, grille, door handles. Std. Limited.		
Color Key Pkg., 2WD regular cab	325	260
4WD regular cab, PreRunner, Xtracab	175	140
Color-keyed front bumper and grille, chrome rear bumper. NA Limited.		
Full Color-Key Pkg., 2WD regular cab	325	260
4WD, PreRunner	205	164
2WD Xtracab	175	140
Color-keyed front and rear bumpers, grille, door handles, and mirrors. NA Limited.		
TRD Off-Road Pkg., 4WD 4-cylinder Xtracab w/5-speed, 4WD V6	1660	1337
PreRunner 4-cylinder Xtracab	1320	1056
PreRunner V6	1590	1281
Limited	435	357
Off-road suspension, locking rear differential, black overfenders, tachometer, 31x10.5R15 tires, alloy wheels. 4WD V6 requires 4WDemand transfer case.		
Power Pkg., 4WD regular cab, PreRunner, Xtracab	470	376
Power windows and door locks. Requires cruise control. Std. Limited.		
Convenience Pkg.	440	365
Cruise control (4WD), tilt steering wheel, tachometer, dual trip odometers, digital clock, glove compartment light, ignition light, ashtray light. Std. Limited.		

Powertrains

	Retail Price	Dealer Invoice
Locking rear differential, 4WD, PreRunner V6, Limited	340	281
NA 4WD 4-cylinder w/automatic. Requires tachometer.		
4WDemand transfer case, 4WD (std. Limited)	240	198
4WD selector switch, Limited	135	111

Safety Features

	Retail Price	Dealer Invoice
Antilock brakes	630	539
Includes daytime running lights.		
Tilt steering wheel (std. Limited)	245	209
Cruise control (std. Limited)	250	200
Tachometer (std. Limited)	95	76
Manual sunroof, Xtracab	390	312
AM/FM/cassette, regular cab	430	323
Deluxe AM/FM/cassette, Xtracab	530	398
NA Limited.		
AM/FM/CD player	264	185
NA Limited.		
Bucket seats, 2WD regular cab	305	244
Xtracab	65	52
PreRunner Xtracab	75	60
Std. Limited.		
Security System	399	249
Remote keyless entry, theft-deterrent system. Requires Power Pkg. NA 2WD regular cab.		

Appearance and Miscellaneous

	Retail Price	Dealer Invoice
Tonneau Cover/Bedliner Pkg.	$623	$370
Sliding rear window, 4WD regular cab	160	128
Xtracab (std. Limited)	285	228
Xtracab includes privacy glass.		

Special Purpose, Wheels and Tires

	Retail Price	Dealer Invoice
Tow hitch	285	200
Alloy wheels, 2WD regular cab	550	440
2WD Xtracab	370	296
4WD (std. Limited)	405	324
Alloy wheels w/265/75R15 tires, PreRunner, 4WD	945	756
Includes wheel lip moldings.		
Styled steel wheels w/265/75R15 tires, PreRunner, 4WD	470	376
Includes wheel lip moldings.		

Post production options also available.

TOYOTA TUNDRA

RECOMMENDED

Toyota Tundra extended cab

Rear- or 4-wheel-drive full-size pickup truck

Base price range: $14,995-$27,830. Built in USA. **Also consider:** Chevrolet Silverado 1500, Dodge Ram 1500, Ford F-150, GMC Sierra 1500

FOR • Acceleration (V8) • Interior materials **AGAINST** • Rear-seat comfort (extended cab) • Fuel economy (V8)

The Indiana-built Tundra is the first import-brand challenger to American full-size pickup trucks. Unlike Toyota's discontinued "midsize" T-100, Tundra offers V8 power and a 4-door extended cab. Regular cabs have an 8-foot cargo bed, the Access Cab extended cab has a 6.5-foot bed. Other full-size pickups offer several wheelbases, but Tundra has just one, and it's about 10 inches shorter than a comparable Ford F-150's. Overall, Tundra is about 11 inches shorter than a comparable F-150.

Bucket or bench front seats are available, and the Access Cab has a 3-passenger, 60/40 split rear bench. As with extended-cab rivals, Access Cab's standard rear doors don't open or close independently of the front doors, though Ford is launching an F-150 with four regular side doors.

Base and SR5 Tundras use the 190-horsepower 3.4-liter dual-overhead-cam V6 available in Toyota's compact Tacoma pickup. SR5 V8 and Limited models use the 4.7-liter twincam V8 from Toyota's Land Cruiser, here with 245 hp, 15 more than in the Land Cruiser. Toyota recommends premium fuel for the V8; domestics use regular. The V6 comes with manual or automatic transmission; the V8 with automatic only. Tundra's 4-wheel drive transfer case is shifted with dashboard buttons on V8s, a floor lever on V6s. It's for slippery surfaces only; among full-size pickups, only the Chevrolet Silverado/GMC Sierra have 4WD that can be left engaged on dry pavement. Maximum payload and towing ratings are competitive with those of domestic rivals, at 2000 and 7500 pounds, respectively.

On full-size domestic pickups, rear antilock brakes are standard and 4-wheel ABS is optional. Ford and GM trucks with 4-wheel ABS also get 4-wheel disc brakes. Tundra does not have rear ABS, and its optional 4-wheel ABS retains the standard front-discs/rear-drums.

PERFORMANCE For really heavy work or towing, turn to three-quarter-ton Ford, GM, or Dodge pickups, with their huge gas and diesel engines and cargo beds up to 8 feet in length. But for the kind of refinement that's likely to appeal to light-duty or first-time full-size truck buyers, Tundra is a winner.

The V8 4WD Access Cab is the most-popular model, with just 10 percent of Tundras getting the V6. V8 models don't leap off the line, but power builds quickly and passing response is strong. Toyota claims a 0-60-mph time of about 8.0 seconds for the V8 Tundra, roughly equal to comparable domestic pickups with their largest V8s. The V8 4WD Access Cab we tested averaged 13.6 mpg. That's similar to comparable domestics in our tests, though the Toyota requires premium fuel. We have not tested a V6 model.

Tundra rides more comfortably than rivals with similar wheelbases, though it's still very much a truck, so the stiff suspension triggers abrupt vertical motions on uneven surfaces. Handling comes with a similar qualifier. Tundra takes corners with above-average balance, and its tail resists skipping in bumpy turns. But as with any full-size pickup, it suffers lots of body lean in corners, subpar maneuverability in close quarters, and slow, numb steering. We think rear ABS should be included in the base equipment, but stopping power and brake modulation with the optional ABS is top-notch by any standard. Similarly, noise levels are nearly carlike—particularly from the smooth-running V8.

ACCOMMODATIONS Front-seat room and comfort for two is the equal of any full-size pickup, although Tundra's cab doesn't feel quite as expansive as the domestics,' so a middle rider on the front bench gets scant knee, foot, and shoulder room. Positioning of the steering wheel, pedals, and the clear, simple controls is first-rate. However, the column-mounted automatic-transmission lever is close to the windshield-wiper stalk, so changing gears can trigger the wipers via an errant sleeve or wrist.

Two- and 4-wheel-drive Tundras have about the same ride height, and both demand a bit of a jump to get inside. Access Cabs have exterior rear door handles; competitors have handles only on the inside or in the doorjamb. Once aboard, the Access Cab's rear seatback is uncomfortably upright and there's little leg room without the front seats moved well forward. Overall, the Access Cab's rear seat is more cramped than any of the domestics,' and falls well short of the class-leading Silverado/Sierra's in comfort. Most cabin surfaces are covered in hard plastic, but it's richly grained, and no interior trim appears cut-rate.

VALUE FOR THE MONEY With an annual production capacity of around 100,000, Tundra isn't a threat to overtake Ford, GM, or Dodge rivals in sales. But it's a fine truck, priced competitively and executed with typical Toyota thoroughness. Except for rear-seat comfort, it's a match for any comparably equipped domestic.

ENGINES

	dohc V6	dohc V8
Size, liters/cu. in.	3.4/207	4.7/285
Horsepower @ rpm	190 @ 4800	245 @ 4800
Torque (lbs./ft.) @ rpm	220 @ 3600	315 @ 3400
Availability	S	S[1]

EPA city/highway mpg

5-speed OD manual	16/20[2]	
4-speed OD automatic	16/19[2]	15/19[3]

1. SR5 V8 and Limited. 2. 16/18 w/4WD. 3. 14/17 w/4WD.

PRICES

Toyota Tundra

	Retail Price	Dealer Invoice
2WD Base regular cab long bed, 5-speed	$14995	$13359
2WD Base regular cab long bed, automatic	15835	14106
4WD SR5 V6 regular cab long bed, 5-speed	20195	17992
4WD SR5 V6 regular cab long bed, automatic	21095	18793
4WD SR5 V8 regular cab long bed, automatic	22710	20232
2WD SR5 V6 Access Cab short bed, 5-speed	20175	17974
2WD SR5 V6 Access Cab short bed, automatic	20940	18656
2WD SR5 V8 Access Cab short bed, automatic	22250	19822
2WD Limited Access Cab short bed, automatic	24495	21822
4WD SR5 V6 Access Cab short bed, 5-speed	23375	20825
4WD SR5 V6 Access Cab short bed, automatic	24200	21560
4WD SR5 V8 Access Cab short bed, automatic	25585	22794
4WD Limited Access Cab short bed, automatic	27830	24794
Destination charge	480	480

Prices are for vehicles distributed by Toyota Motor Sales, U.S.A., Inc. The dealer invoice and destination charge may be higher in areas served by independent distributors.

STANDARD EQUIPMENT:

Base: 3.4-liter dohc V6 engine, 5-speed manual or 4-speed automatic transmission, driver- and passenger-side airbags, power steering, cloth bench seat, cupholders, AM/FM/cassette, digital clock, auxiliary power outlets, automatic-off headlights, carpeting, dual outside mirrors, painted front bumper, full-size spare tire, 245/70R16 tires.

SR5 V6 adds: air conditioning, four doors (Access Cab), tilt steering wheel, split bench seat (Access Cab w/automatic), captain chairs (Access Cab w/manual), split folding rear seat (Access Cab), tachometer, variable intermittent wipers, chrome front and rear bumpers. **4WD** models add part-time 4-wheel drive, 2-speed transfer case.

SR5 V8 adds: 4.7-liter dohc V8 engine, 4-speed automatic transmission, cruise control, cloth split bench seat. **4WD** models add part-time 4-wheel drive, electronic 2-speed transfer case.

Limited adds: power mirrors, power windows, power door locks, AM/FM/cassette/CD player, illuminated visor mirrors, rear privacy glass, sliding rear window, fog lights, color-keyed front and rear bumpers, 265/70R16 tires, alloy wheels. **4WD** models add part-time 4-wheel drive, electronic 2-speed transfer case.

OPTIONAL EQUIPMENT:

	Retail Price	Dealer Invoice
Major Packages		
Convenience Pkg., SR5 V6 Access Cab	$1310	$1048
SR5 V8	1060	848

Power mirrors, power windows and door locks, cruise control (SR5 V6 Access Cab), visor mirrors, lighting pkg., rear privacy glass, sliding rear window.

Leather Pkg., Limited	1420	1136

Leather upholstery, captain chairs, 8-way power driver seat, simulated wood trim.

All Weather Guard	70	59

Heavy-duty starter and battery, heavy-duty heater, anti-chip paint.

TRD Off-Road Pkg.,		
4WD SR5 V6/V8 Access Cab	925	740
4WD Limited	95	76

Fog lights (SR5), black overfenders (SR5), off-road suspension, Bilstein shock absorbers, 265/70R16 tires (SR5), cast alloy wheels.

Style Pkg., 2WD SR5 V8 Access Cab	455	364

Cloth captain chairs, stamped alloy wheels. NA with Convenience Pkg., AM/FM/cassette/CD player, antilock brakes, fog lights.

Safety Features

Antilock brakes	630	539

Includes daytime running lights.

Comfort and Convenience

Air conditioning, Base	985	788
Tilt steering wheel, Base	200	171
Universal garage door opener	199	136
AM/FM/cassette/CD player,		
SR5 V6/V8 regular cab	100	75
Deluxe AM/FM/cassette/CD player,		
SR5 V6/V8 Access Cab	250	188
Premium AM/FM/cassette/CD player, Limited	200	150

Includes 6-disc CD player.

Split bench seat,		
SR5 V6 regular cab automatic	230	184
Captain chairs, Limited	395	316
SR5 V6 regular cab automatic	305	244
SR5 V6 Access Cab automatic, SR5 V8	75	60

Limited includes 8-way power driver seat.

Security system,		
SR5 V6 Access Cab, SR5 V8, Limited	399	249

Remote keyless entry, theft-deterrent system. SR5 requires Convenience Pkg.

Appearance and Miscellaneous

Tonneau Cover/Bedliner Pkg., Access Cab	701	401
regular cab	744	427
Running boards, Access Cab	699	426

Prices are accurate at time of publication; subject to manufacturer's changes.

	Retail Price	Dealer Invoice
Fog lights, Base, SR5 V6, SR5 V8	$100	$80
Sliding rear window, Base	160	128
Painted rear bumper, Base	150	120

Special Purpose, Wheels and Tires

Towing receiver hitch, SR5 V8, Limited	379	259
Stamped alloy wheels, SR5 V6, SR5 V8	380	304
Cast alloy wheels, SR5 V6, SR5 V8	600	480
Includes 265/70R16 tires, chrome wheel lip moldings.		
Cast alloy wheels w/overfenders,		
SR5 V6/V8 Access Cab	730	584
Includes 265/70R16 tires, black overfenders.		
265/70R16 tires, SR5 V6, SR5 V8	220	176
Includes chrome wheel lip moldings.		
265/70R16 tires w/overfenders,		
SR5 V6/V8 Access Cab	350	280
Includes black over fenders.		

Post production options also available.

TOYOTA 4RUNNER

RECOMMENDED

Toyota 4Runner Limited

Rear- or 4-wheel-drive midsize sport-utility vehicle

Base price range: $21,938-$36,468. Built in Japan. **Also consider:** Ford Explorer, Lexus RX 300, Mercedes-Benz M-Class

FOR • Cargo room • Build quality • Exterior finish • Interior materials **AGAINST** • Entry/exit • Fuel economy

Toyota's midsize SUV sees only minor changes for 2000. 4Runner continues in 4-cylinder base and V6 SR5 and Limited models with 2-wheel or 4-wheel drive. The Limited's One-Touch Hi-4 system allows using 4WD on dry pavement. Other 4x4s come with Toyota's part-time 4WDemand usable only on slippery surfaces. Both setups provide low-range gears. Automatic transmission is standard on Limiteds and the 2WD SR5, optional elsewhere. Antilock brakes (ABS) are optional on base 4WD models, unavailable on base 2WD models, and standard on other 4Runner. Models with power windows also have power drop-down tailgate glass.

For 2000, daytime running lights are fitted to ABS-equipped 4Runners, while a new CD/cassette stereo is optional for base models and standard for SR5s and Limiteds. Also, body-colored fender flares are newly available for SR5s, replacing last year's black, and are included in an optional "Highlander" Sport option package along with hood scoop, foglamps, and color-keyed bumpers. Limiteds again count among their standard equipment leather upholstery, wood interior trim, and automatic climate control.

PERFORMANCE Avoid the 4-cylinder engine, which provides so-so performance at best. The smooth V6 delivers snappy takeoffs and good low-speed punch, though highway passing power is unexceptional in the heavier 4x4s with three or more people and their luggage aboard. The automatic transmission is a smooth, prompt shifter. Our test Limited averaged 17.2 mpg with lots of highway miles. The V6 is quieter than the 4-cylinder, but tire noise is well muffled in any model, leaving wind rush as the main noise source in this tall, boxy vehicle. 4Runner is engineered like a truck, so although its ride isn't bouncy stiff, it's not carlike either, especially on 4x4s. Steering is quick and precise for an SUV, and the 4Runner feels more stable in tight turns than some rivals. "Panic" braking is safe and undramatic with ABS.

ACCOMMODATIONS A tall build and big tires make for an unusually high step-in that's especially uncomfortable for shorter people. Once aboard, there's room enough for four adults, plus better-than-average comfort for a middle-rear passenger. Cargo space is generous even without folding the split rear seat, and the full-size spare mounts out of the way beneath the rear floor. 4Runner's available power tailgate window is an SUV exclusive and is a useful feature. A no-nonsense dashboard design and fine visibility ease driving, but the pop-out dual cupholders block the climate controls. Like most Toyotas, 4Runners we've tested have been impressively solid and trouble-free.

VALUE FOR THE MONEY 4Runner is among the pricier midsize SUVs, but a test drive might convince you that its top-notch quality, V6 refinement, and high resale value are worth the extra cost.

ENGINES

	dohc I4	dohc V6
Size, liters/cu. in.	2.7/164	3.4/207
Horsepower @ rpm	150 @ 4800	183 @ 4800
Torque (lbs./ft.) @ rpm	177 @ 4000	217 @ 3600
Availability	S[1]	S[2]
EPA city/highway mpg		
5-speed OD manual	17/21	17/19
4-speed OD automatic	18/21	17/20

1. Base. 2. SR5, Limited.

PRICES

Toyota 4Runner	Retail Price	Dealer Invoice
Base 2WD 4-door wagon, 5-speed	$21938	$19205
Base 2WD 4-door wagon, automatic	22838	19994
Base 4WD 4-door wagon, 5-speed	24098	21096
SR5 2WD 4-door wagon, automatic	25958	22725
SR5 4WD 4-door wagon, 5-speed	27108	23732
SR5 4WD 4-door wagon, automatic	28008	24521
Limited 2WD 4-door wagon, automatic	33968	29738
Limited 4WD 4-door wagon, automatic	36468	31926
Destination charge	480	480

Prices are for vehicles distributed by Toyota Motor Sales, U.S.A., Inc. The dealer invoice and destination charge may be higher in areas served by independent distributors.

STANDARD EQUIPMENT:

Base: 2.7-liter dohc 4-cylinder engine, 5-speed manual or 4-speed automatic transmission, driver- and passenger-side airbags, variable-assist power steering, cloth bucket seats, center console, split folding rear seat, cupholders, tachometer, AM/FM/cassette, digital clock, power tailgate window, intermittent wipers, passenger-side visor mirror, remote fuel-door release, automatic-off headlights, rear defogger, intermittent rear wiper/washer, dual outside mirrors, full-size spare tire, 225/75R15 tires. **4WD** models add: part-time 4-wheel drive, 2-speed transfer case, skid plates.

SR5 adds: 3.4-liter dohc V6 engine, antilock brakes, daytime running lights, tilt steering wheel, cruise control, heated power mirrors, power door locks, AM/FM/cassette/CD player, variable intermittent wipers, map lights, rear privacy glass. **4WD** models add: part-time 4-wheel drive, 2-speed transfer case, skid plates.

Limited adds: 4-speed automatic transmission, air conditioning w/automatic climate control, leather-wrapped steering wheel, leather upholstery, power front seats, power windows, remote keyless entry, power antenna, driver-side visor mirror, illuminated passenger-side visor mirror, wood interior trim, cargo cover, floormats, theft-deterrent system, fog lights, fender flares, running boards, 265/70R16 tires, alloy wheels. **4WD** adds: full-time 4-wheel drive, 2-speed transfer case, skid plates, heavy-duty battery, heavy-duty wiper motor and starter motor, large windshield washer reservoir.

OPTIONAL EQUIPMENT:
Major Packages

Upgrade Value Pkg. 1, Base	2568	2054
Manufacturer's discount price	1468	1321
Air conditioning w/automatic climate control, tilt steering wheel, cruise control, power mirrors and windows, power mirrors, variable-intermittent wipers, AM/FM/cassette/CD player, overhead console, passenger-side illuminated visor mirror, map lights, floormats.		

	Retail Price	Dealer Invoice
Upgrade Value Pkg. 2, SR5	$2198	$1758
Manufacturer's discount price	1298	1168
Air conditioning w/automatic climate control, power windows and door locks, remote keyless entry, AM/FM/cassette/CD player, power antenna, passenger-side illuminated visor mirror, cargo cover, floormats.		
Upgrade Value Pkg. 3, SR5 2WD	2978	2382
Manufacturer's discount price	2078	1870
Upgrade Value Pkg. 2 plus sport seats, leather-wrapped steering wheel, alloy wheels. NA with Leather Pkg. or Sport Pkg.		
Upgrade Value Pkg. 4, SR5	3593	2874
Manufacturer's discount price	2693	2424
Upgrade Value Pkg. 3 plus larger brakes, 265/70R16 tires, 16-inch alloy wheels. Requires chrome wheel lip moldings or fender flares. NA with Leather Pkg. or Sport Pkg.		
Upgrade Value Pkg. 5, SR5 4WD	3933	3146
Manufacturer's discount price	3033	2730
Upgrade Pkg. 4 plus limited-slip differential, special axle ratio. Requires chrome wheel lip moldings or fender flares. NA with Leather Pkg. or Sport Pkg.		
Sport Pkg. (Highlander), SR5	1625	1300
Leather-wrapped steering wheel, sport seats, color-keyed bumpers and grille, color-keyed fender flares, hood scoop, fog lights, larger brakes, special axle ratio, 265/70R16 tires, alloy wheels.		
Sport Pkg. w/Limited-Slip Differential, SR5 4WD automatic	1965	1581
Sport Pkg. plus limited-slip differential, special axle ratio.		
Convenience Pkg.	669	427
Roof rack, rear wind deflector, towing hitch receiver, cargo mat.		
Leather Trim Pkg., SR5	1250	1000
Leather sports seats, leather door trim, leather-wrapped steering wheel, leather-wrapped shift knob (4WD SR5 w/5-speed).		

Powertrains

Limited-slip differential, Limited	340	281

Safety Features

Antilock brakes, Base 4WD	630	539
Requires optional wheels.		

Comfort and Convenience

Rear heater	170	136
Includes rear storage console w/cupholders.		
Power sunroof, SR5, Limited	815	652
Cargo cover, Base, SR5	90	72
AM/FM/cassette/CD player, Base	264	185
6-disc CD changer	550	385
Deluxe Security System, Base, SR5	399	249
Includes remote keyless entry, theft-deterrent system. Requires Upgrade Pkg.		
Floormats, Base, SR5	84	51

Appearance and Miscellaneous

Rear privacy glass, Base	310	248
Roof rack	275	165
Running boards, Base, SR5	345	209
Fender flares	230	194
Chrome wheel lip moldings, SR5	70	56

Special Purpose, Wheels and Tires

Towing hitch receiver	305	215
Styled steel wheels, Base 4WD	600	480
Includes 265/70R16 tires, special axle ratio, wheel lip moldings. Requires antilock brakes.		
15-inch alloy wheels, Base, SR5 2WD	365	292
16-inch alloy wheels, Base 4WD	980	784
Includes 265/70R16 tires, larger brakes, special axle ratio, limited-slip differential. Requires fender flares or chrome wheel lip moldings.		
16-inch wheels w/limited-slip differential, SR5 4WD automatic	1250	1009
Includes 265/70R16 tires, larger brakes, special axle ratio, locking differential. Requires fender flares or chrome wheel lip moldings.		

Post production options also available.

VOLKSWAGEN CABRIO

Volkswagen Cabrio GLS

Front-wheel-drive sports coupe

Base price range: $19,990-$23,300. Built in Mexico.
Also consider: Chrysler Sebring, Ford Mustang

FOR • Steering/handling **AGAINST** • Cargo room • Rear visibility • Rear-seat comfort

Cabrio retains the platform of the 1994-98 Golf, and for 2000 gets an optional in-dash CD player, a revised alarm system, and a dashboard indicator light that illuminates when the brakes need servicing. Base GL and upscale GLS models are offered, both with a 4-cylinder engine and a 5-speed manual or optional 4-speed automatic transmission. Antilock brakes and front side airbags are standard. The folding top has a glass rear window and electric defroster; power operation is standard on the GLS.

EVALUATION Cabrio's 4-cylinder engine provides good acceleration with manual shift but struggles some with the automatic. Despite noticeable body lean in turns, handling is sporty and the ride absorbent, the latter aided by a structure that's stiffer than that of many convertibles. Drivers enjoy a high, comfortable driving position. But the rear seat is only wide enough for two, leg room disappears if the front seats are pushed back, and passengers have to duck under the roll bar to get in. Visibility suffers from wide rear "pillars" with the top up, and a tall top stack with it down. Cabrio is a solid convertible with good road manners, but it's pricey and sells in low volume.

ENGINES

	ohc I4
Size, liters/cu. in.	2.0/121
Horsepower @ rpm	115 @ 5400
Torque (lbs./ft.) @ rpm	122 @ 3200
Availability	S
EPA city/highway mpg	
5-speed OD manual	24/31
4-speed OD automatic	22/28

PRICES

Volkswagen Cabrio	Retail Price	Dealer Invoice
GL 2-door convertible	$19990	$18301
GLS 2-door convertible	23300	21309
Destination charge	525	525

STANDARD EQUIPMENT:

GL: 2.0-liter 4-cylinder engine, 5-speed manual transmission, driver- and passenger-side airbags, front side-impact airbags, antilock brakes, integral roll bar, daytime running lights, air conditioning, interior air filter, power steering, leather-wrapped tilt steering wheel, cloth upholstery, front bucket seats w/height adjustment, folding rear seat, center console, cupholders, heated manual mirrors, power door locks, tachometer, AM/FM/cassette w/CD changer controls, digital clock, rear defogger, intermittent wipers, heated washer nozzles, illuminated visor mirrors, auxiliary power outlet, floormats, manual folding vinyl top, theft-deterrent system, 195/60HR14 tires, wheel covers.

GLS adds: cruise control, leather upholstery, heated front seats, power folding cloth top, power windows, heated power mirrors, fog lights, alloy wheels.

Prices are accurate at time of publication; subject to manufacturer's changes.

OPTIONAL EQUIPMENT:
Major Packages

	Retail Price	Dealer Invoice
Power Pkg., GL	$625	$552
Cruise control, power windows, heated power mirrors.		

Powertrains

4-speed automatic transmission	875	864

Comfort and Convenience

Heated front seats, GL	150	133
CD player	295	—
In addition to AM/FM/cassette.		

VOLKSWAGEN EuroVan

Volkswagen EuroVan GLS

Front-wheel-drive minivan
Base price range: $31,300-$32,800. Built in Germany.
Also consider: Dodge Caravan, Honda Odyssey, Plymouth Voyager, Toyota Sienna

FOR • Passenger and cargo room **AGAINST** • Acceleration • Fuel economy • Noise

Available second-row bucket seats for the mainstream passenger model marks the primary EuroVan addition for 2000. EuroVan comes as the mainstream GLS passenger model and recreation-oriented MV (MultiVan), plus a Camper model on an extended wheelbase. All have a single right-side sliding door, V6 engine, automatic transmission, and antilock 4-wheel disc brakes. The GLS and MV seat seven, with the GLS using a second-row bench or, for 2000, a pair of optional buckets. The MV's second-row buckets face rearward. Both have a folding third-row bench; the MV's converts to a bed. Standard on the Camper and optional on MV is a "pop-top" roof incorporating a 2-person bed. The Camper adds refrigerator, sink, stove, and other gear. Other 2000 additions include rear-seat reading lights, tinted rear glass, and remote central locking.

EVALUATION EuroVan is a slow-lane device (12.2 seconds to 60 mph in our tests) and none too thrifty: Our test GLS averaged just 16.0 mpg even with lots of highway miles. EuroVan is stable at freeway speeds and highly maneuverable in tight spaces. But it feels somewhat "tippy" in tight turns and the front end is prone to plow severely in aggressive cornering. No minivan has more passenger or cargo room. Seats are firm and comfortable, and an adjustable rear luggage tray is a smart touch. Unfortunately, front entry/exit is tricky, and the lack of extras like power front seats and a left-side sliding door are omissions at EuroVan's price level. They betray a European design that's far from America's minivan mainstream.

ENGINES

	dohc V6
Size, liters/cu. in.	2.8/170
Horsepower @ rpm	140 @ 4500
Torque (lbs./ft.) @ rpm	177 @ 3000
Availability	S

EPA city/highway mpg

4-speed OD automatic..	15/20[1]
1. 14/19 mpg for Camper model.	

PRICES

Volkswagen EuroVan	Retail Price	Dealer Invoice
GLS 3-door van	$31300	$28417
MV 3-door van	32800	29772

	Retail Price	Dealer Invoice
Camper 3-door van, extended wheelbase	—	—
Destination charge	$590	$590

Camper prices not available at time of publication.

STANDARD EQUIPMENT:

GLS: 2.8-liter V6 engine, 4-speed automatic transmission, traction control, driver- and passenger-side airbags, antilock 4-wheel disc brakes, daytime running lights, air conditioning w/dual-zone automatic climate control, interior air filter, power steering, cruise control, cloth upholstery, front bucket seats, center 2-passenger folding bench seat, rear 3-passenger folding bench seat, front and rear carpeting, center console, cupholders, heated power mirrors, power windows, power door locks, remote keyless entry, AM/FM/cassette, tachometer, auxiliary power outlets, illuminated visor mirrors, variable intermittent wipers, heated washer nozzles, rear defogger, intermittent rear wiper/washer, cargo cover, floormats, rear privacy glass, full-size spare tire, 205/65R15 tires, alloy wheels.

MV adds: removable center-row rear facing bucket seats, 3-passenger rear bench/bed, side fold-up table, side curtains, deletes cargo cover.

Camper adds: swiveling front seats, 2-passenger rear bench/bed, Winnebago Pkg. (pop-up roof with two person bed, two tables, beverage tray, refrigerator, sink, LP gas stove, carbon monoxide detectors), window screens, front and rear curtains, closet, roof rack, deletes dual-zone automatic climate control, AM/FM/cassette, center row seats, rear privacy glass, alloy wheels.

OPTIONAL EQUIPMENT:
Major Packages

	Retail Price	Dealer Invoice
Weekender Pkg., MV	—	—
Pop-up roof with two person bed, rear facing seat with refrigerator in base, sliding window screens, curtains, heavy-duty alternator and auxiliary battery, deletes dual-zone automatic climate control.		

Comfort and Convenience

Power sunroof, GLS, MV	1000	883
NA w/Weekender Pkg.		
Heated front seats, GLS, MV	400	353
Center bucket seats, GLS.......................................	185	163
Center bench seat, Camper.....................................	—	—
Removable companion seat, Camper....................	—	—
AM/FM/CD player, Camper	—	—

VOLKSWAGEN JETTA/GOLF

RECOMMENDED

Volkswagen Jetta GLS

Front-wheel-drive subcompact car
Base price range: $14,900-$24,170. Built in Mexico.
Also consider: Honda Civic, Mazda Protege, Toyota Corolla

FOR • Cargo room (Golf) • Acceleration (V6) • Build quality • Fuel economy (TDI) • Quietness • Ride/handling • Visibility • Interior materials **AGAINST** • Acceleration (4-cylinder automatic) • Automatic transmission performance • Control layout

Jetta sedans and Golf hatchbacks are little changed for 2000 after debuting as redesigned models during 1999. Jetta outsells Golf and comes in GL, GLS, and GLX models. Golfs offer 2-door hatchback GL and GTI models and 4-door hatchback GLS models.

GL and GLS versions of both share a 4-cylinder gas engine. GL TDI and GLS TDI share a turbocharged diesel four. (Note that diesel models are not sold in California.) A V6 is available in

Ratings begin on page 213. Specifications begin on page 220.

CONSUMER GUIDE™

Golf GTI and Jetta GLS models and is standard on the Jetta GLX. All come with manual transmission, and all but the Golf GTI GLX offer optional automatic.

Front side airbags, tilt/telescope steering column, antilock 4-wheel-disc brakes, and a remote central locking/anti-theft system are standard on every Jetta and Golf. For 2000, they also gain anti-theft coded ignition keys and a dashboard light that illuminates when the brakes might need to be serviced. Newly standard on GLX models and optional other models is an 8-speaker Monsoon audio system. Also newly available is a dealer-installed in-dash CD player.

PERFORMANCE All Jettas and Golfs have sporty road manners. Ride is firm but comfortable, cornering stable, steering linear with fine on-center feel. V6 models handle best with only a modest sacrifice in ride comfort, though they have more body lean than expected. Braking is very good. Interior noise levels are among the lowest in the subcompact class. All engines are quiet, though the TDIs are somewhat noisier above 65 mph or so.

The 4-cylinder gas engine furnishes only modest acceleration with automatic transmission. Even with manual shift, our test Jetta GL needed a lengthy 10.8 seconds 0-60 mph, though keeping up with around-town traffic is less a problem than is passing power.

V6 models have authoritative acceleration and spirited passing response, though their automatic is reluctant to downshift at moderate speeds. Our test 5-speed GTI GLX did 0-60 in 7.6 seconds and averaged 23.5 mpg. Test V6/automatic Jettas averaged 18.9-21.6 mpg. A Golf GL 4-cylinder 5-speed returned a pleasing 25 mpg. TDI models are surprisingly spritely around town and get terrific mileage; our test 5-speed TDI Golf averaged 41.5 mpg.

ACCOMMODATIONS Golf and Jetta impress with high-class interior materials and workmanship, plus exceptional front head and leg room. The rear seats are more typically subcompact-tight. Modest leg room shrinks quickly as the front seats move back, though somehow, Golfs feel more spacious in back than Jettas. Neither has sufficient rear width for three adults.

All seats are comfortably firm, and the height-adjustable front buckets are supportive on long trips. A standard tilt/telescopic steering wheel—an unusual feature in this class—helps tailor the driving position. Gauges and switches are simple, logically arranged, and nicely backlit, but low-mounted audio and climate controls are tricky to adjust while driving.

Helped by smartly designed tip-slide front seats, rear access in 2-door Golfs far surpasses that of most coupes. Narrow doors make rear entry/exit a squeeze in Jettas and 4-door Golfs. Interior storage is plentiful, with cupholders front and rear. Jettas have large trunks and Golfs boast hatchback versatility. All have folding rear seatbacks.

VALUE FOR THE MONEY Jetta and Golf are priced at the top of the subcompact class, but even base versions are loaded with standard features, and no competitor offers a V6 engine. Solid build quality and fine warranty coverage are other pluses that earn these VWs our Recommended label.

ENGINES

	ohc I4	Turbodiesel ohc I4	ohc V6
Size, liters/cu. in.	2.0/121	1.9/116	2.8/170
Horsepower @ rpm	115 @ 5200	90 @ 3750	174 @ 5800
Torque (lbs./ft.) @ rpm	122 @ 2600	155 @ 1900	181 @ 3200
Availability	S[1]	S[2]	S[3]
EPA city/highway mpg			
5-speed OD manual	24/31	42/49	20/28
4-speed OD automatic	22/28	34/45	19/26

1. Jetta GL and GLS, Golf GL, GLS, and GTI GLS. 2. TDI. 3. Jetta GLS VR6 and GLX, Golf GTI GLX.

PRICES

Volkswagen Jetta/Golf

	Retail Price	Dealer Invoice
Golf GL 2-door hatchback	$14900	$13904
Golf GL TDI 2-door hatchback	16195	15101
Golf GLS 4-door hatchback	16350	15244
Golf GLS TDI 4-door hatchback	$17400	$16214
Golf GTI GLS 2-door hatchback	17675	16109
Golf GTI GLX 2-door hatchback	22620	20576
Jetta GL 4-door sedan	16700	15228
Jetta GL TDI 4-door sedan	17995	16764
Jetta GLS 4-door sedan	17650	16087
Jetta GLS TDI 4-door sedan	18700	17414
Jetta GLS VR6 4-door sedan	19950	18164
Jetta GLX 4-door sedan	24170	21976
Destination charge	525	525

TDI models not available in California.

STANDARD EQUIPMENT:

Golf/Jetta GL: 2.0-liter 4-cylinder engine, 5-speed manual transmission, driver- and passenger-side airbags, front side-impact airbags, antilock 4-wheel disc brakes, daytime running lights, air conditioning, interior air filter, power steering, tilt/telescoping steering wheel, cloth upholstery, height-adjustable front bucket seats, split folding rear seat, front storage console, cupholders, heated manual mirrors, power door locks, remote keyless entry, AM/FM/cassette w/CD changer controls, digital clock, tachometer, map lights, variable intermittent wipers, illuminated visor mirrors, rear defogger, rear intermittent wiper/washer (Golf), remote decklid and fuel door releases, cargo cover (Golf), auxiliary power outlets, floormats, theft-deterrent system, full-size spare tire, 195/65HR15 tires, wheel covers.

Golf/Jetta GLS add: cruise control, upgraded interior trim, heated power mirrors, power windows, upgraded sound system, front armrest.

Golf GTI GLS adds: power sunroof, front sport seats, fog lights, sport suspension, alloy wheels.

Golf/Jetta GL/GLS TDI add to Golf/Jetta GL or Jetta GLS: 1.9-liter turbodiesel 4-cylinder engine, cruise control.

Jetta GLS VR6 adds to Jetta GLS: 2.8-liter V6 engine, traction control, sport suspension.

Golf GTI GLX/Jetta GLX add: leather upholstery, leather-wrapped steering wheel, power front seats w/driver seat memory (Jetta), heated front sport seats, wood interior trim, automatic climate control, power sunroof, Monsoon Sound System, trip computer, automatic day/night mirror, rain-sensing wipers, rear window sunshade (Jetta), heated washer nozzles, fog lights, 205/55HR16 tires, alloy wheels.

OPTIONAL EQUIPMENT:
Major Packages

	Retail Price	Dealer Invoice
Luxury Pkg., GLS,		
GLS TDI	1175	1037
Jetta GLS VR6	1375	1214

Power sunroof, 205/55HR16 tires (GLS VR6), alloy wheels.

Partial leather,		
Golf GTI GLS, Jetta GLS,		
Jetta GLS TDI, GLS VR6	850	751

Leather upholstery, heated front seats and washer nozzels, leather-wrapped steering wheel and shifter.

Cold Weather Pkg.,		
GLS, GLS TDI, GLS VR6, GTI GLS	150	133

Heated front seats, heated washer jets.

Powertrains

4-speed automatic transmission	875	864

NA Golf GTI GLX, Jetta TDI.

4-speed automatic transmission,		
Jetta GL TDI, Jetta GLS TDI	1185	1137

Includes alloy wheels.

Comfort and Convenience

Power sunroof,		
Jetta GLS, Jetta GLS TDI, GLS VR6	865	764
Monsoon Sound System,		
GLS, GLS TDI, GLS VR6	295	261

Prices are accurate at time of publication; subject to manufacturer's changes.

VOLKSWAGEN NEW BEETLE

✓ BEST BUY

Volkswagen New Beetle

Front-wheel-drive sports coupe; similar to Volkswagen Jetta/Golf
Base price range: $15,900-$21,075. Built in Mexico.
Also consider: Acura CL, Chrysler Sebring, Honda Prelude

FOR • Handling/roadholding • Fuel economy • Build quality • Exterior finish • Interior materials **AGAINST** • Rear-seat head room • Visibility

A new option package with heated front seats is the main addition to Volkswagen's 2000 New Beetle. The New Beetle revives the general shape and character of the original Bug in a modern car that borrows its chassis and running gear from VW's Golf hatchback.

All New Beetles have 4-cylinder engines. GL and GLS models have 115 horsepower, the GLS Turbo and GLX add a turbocharger for 150 hp. The GLS TDI uses a 90-hp turbocharged diesel, and is not sold in California. Manual transmission is standard, automatic optional. Front side airbags, tilt/telescopic steering wheel, and antilock 4-wheel disc brakes are standard.

GLX comes with leather upholstery, heated front seats, alloy wheels, and a power sunroof. For other models, heated front seats and heated windshield washer nozzles make up the new $150 Cold Weather package. Those features were part of an $850 option group that also included leather upholstery. By contrast, alloy wheels, previously a $310 stand-alone option, are now part of a $1175 package that also includes a power sunroof. Rounding out the 2000 additions are anti-theft coded ignition keys and a dashboard light that illuminates when the brakes might need to be serviced.

PERFORMANCE The New Beetle is not only fun to look at, it's fun to drive. The smooth-running base gas engine feels peppy with manual transmission, though it's short on power at speeds above 60 mph with either gearbox. The turbodiesel has no problem keeping up with traffic, but its passing power doesn't match that of the gas engine, and it suffers more vibration and noise. The turbo gas four feels sleepy below 3000 rpm, but accelerates strongly after that; VW says 0-60-mph in 8 seconds, about 2 seconds faster than other gas New Beetles. In our tests, base models averaged 26.4 mpg with manual transmission and 21.1 with automatic, an automatic GLS Turbo got 22.7, and a manual-shift diesel averaged 42.1.

Teamed with large-for-this-class standard 16-inch wheels, New Beetle's firm-riding chassis comfortably soaks up most bumps. Steering and handling are a notch above the class norm, too. Braking is strong and sure. Above 70 mph, passengers must raise their voices to carry on a conversation, though automatic-transmission models are geared for lower rpm at highway speeds and so are somewhat quieter.

ACCOMMODATIONS The interior brims with high-grade materials and expensive-looking trim. Gauges and controls are attractive and functional, although it takes a few tries to become familiar with the unorthodox radio buttons. And power-accessory switches mounted flat on the door panels are awkward to reach.

Front seats are comfortable and supportive, and few cars offer as much front head and leg room. In back, leg room is tight with the front seats moved more than halfway back, and anyone over 5-foot-6 finds their head against the inner hatch lid. Doors open wide, and both front seatbacks tip far forward, so rear entry/exit is better than in most small coupes.

The front roof pillars have thick bases and the outside mirrors are mounted unusually high, cutting the driver's vision of some traffic. Interior storage space is skimpy and luggage room under the rear hatch is modest, but the rear seats fold nearly flat to conveniently expand the cargo area. Paint quality and fit-and-finish are excellent, the bodies solid and rattle-free.

VALUE FOR THE MONEY The New Beetle's driving and emotional appeal are strong enough to overcome its skimpy rear seat. Prices are reasonable, and, as sports coupes go, it's actually quite a practical car.

ENGINES

	ohc I4	Turbodiesel ohc I4	Turbocharged dohc I4
Size, liters/cu. in.	2.0/121	1.9/116	1.8/109
Horsepower @ rpm	115 @	90 @	150 @
	5200	3750	5700
Torque (lbs./ft.) @ rpm	122 @	155 @	155 @
	2600	1900	1750
Availability	S[1]	S[2]	S[3]
EPA city/highway mpg			
5-speed OD manual	24/31	42/49	25/31
4-speed OD automatic	22/28	NA	23/27

1. GL, GLS. 2. GLS TDI. 3. GLS Turbo, GLX.

PRICES

Volkswagen New Beetle	Retail Price	Dealer Invoice
GL 2-door hatchback	$15900	$15151
GLS 2-door hatchback	16850	15706
GLS TDI 2-door hatchback	17900	16675
GLS Turbo 2-door hatchback	19000	17691
GLX 2-door hatchback	21075	19608
Destination charge	525	525

GLS TDI not available in California.

STANDARD EQUIPMENT:

GL: 2.0-liter 4-cylinder engine, 5-speed manual transmission, driver- and passenger-side airbags, front side-impact airbags, antilock 4-wheel disc brakes, daytime running lights, air conditioning, interior air filter, power steering, tilt and telescoping steering wheel, cloth upholstery, reclining bucket seats w/height adjustment, folding rear seat, center console, cupholders, auxiliary power outlets, heated power mirrors, power door locks, remote keyless entry, AM/FM/cassette w/CD changer controls and six speakers, digital clock, illuminated visor mirrors, tachometer, rear defogger, remote fuel door and hatchback releases, variable intermittent wipers, floormats, theft-deterrent system, full-size spare tire, 205/55R16 tires, wheel covers.
GLS adds: cruise control, power windows, fog lights.
GLS TDI adds: 1.9-liter 4-cylinder turbodiesel engine.
GLS Turbo adds to GLS: 1.8-liter dohc turbocharged 4-cylinder engine, traction control, rear spoiler.
GLX adds: partial leather upholstery, heated front seats, leather-wrapped steering wheel, power sunroof, heated windshield washer nozzles, alloy wheels.

OPTIONAL EQUIPMENT:

Major Packages

Luxury Pkg., GLS, GLS TDI, GLS Turbo	1175	1037
Alloy wheels, power sunroof.		
Partial Leather Pkg., GLS, GLS TDI, GLS Turbo	850	751
Partial leather upholstery, heated front seats, leather-wrapped steering wheel, heated windshield washer nozzles. Requires Wheel Pkg. or Luxury Pkg.		
Cold Weather Pkg., GLS, GLS TDI, GLS Turbo	150	133
Heated front seats, heated washer jets.		

Powertrains

4-speed automatic transmission	875	864

VOLKSWAGEN PASSAT

Front-wheel-drive compact car; similar to Audi A6
Base price range: $21,200-$28,455. Built in Germany. **Also consider:** Mazda 626, Mitsubishi Galant, Nissan Altima

Volkswagen Passat GLS sedan

FOR • Ride • Passenger and cargo room • Build quality • Exterior finish • Interior materials **AGAINST** • Acceleration (GLS 1.8T w/automatic) • Tire noise

An available V6 engine for the Passat wagon highlights 2000 for Volkswagen's biggest car. Passat borrows pieces from sister-company Audi's A6 model to create a mid-priced family car with sporty ambitions. Four-door sedans and wagons are offered, all with front-wheel drive. VW says it plans later in the 2000 model year to introduce an optional all-wheel drive system.

GLS models offer a turbocharged 4-cylinder engine or extra-cost V6; the V6 was previously available only on the sedans. GLX sedans and wagons come standard the V6, plus leather upholstery, and wood interior trim. Exclusive to GLX models are 16-inch alloy wheels to the other models' 15-inch steel rims. The 16s had also been a GLS option.

Manual transmission is standard on all models and a 5-speed automatic with a manual shifting mode is optional. Antilock 4-wheel disc brakes, front side airbags, and traction control are standard.

Other additions for 2000 include a dealer-installed dashboard CD player, a wood shift knob for the GLX, and for all models, an anti-theft coded ignition key and a dashboard light that illuminates when the brakes might need servicing.

PERFORMANCE Passat has crisp handling, responsive steering, arrow-true highway stability, and a suspension that smothers all but the worst bumps. A solid structure adds to the sense of comfort. Braking is swift and undramatic.

The turbo 4-cylinder is quiet enough and generally free of turbo hesitation, but with automatic transmission, it doesn't deliver quick getaways or fuss-free passing. The automatic's manual-shift capability helps some, but the 4-cylinder models feel transformed with the real manual transmission, being lively, eager, and genuinely sporty. The smooth-running V6 provides more power at all speeds and is the engine we strongly recommend if you want automatic transmission. An automatic 4-cylinder sedan averaged 22.2 mpg in our tests; we haven't had an opportunity to measure fuel economy with a V6 Passat. VW recommends premium fuel for both engines. Wind rush at highway speeds is low, but the tires generate more noise than in many compact family cars.

ACCOMMODATIONS Passat beats most compacts for space and comfort; even three adults in the back seat isn't a problem on short hops. Six-footers have only about a half-inch head clearance beneath the available moonroof, but leg room is plentiful at all outboard positions. A comfortably tall driving stance is easily tailored with help from a standard tilt/telescopic steering wheel. The dashboard combines readable gauges and simple controls that move with a pleasing smoothness. Materials and workmanship rival those of more-expensive cars, and GLXs have real wood trim—though GLS V6 models no longer do. Entry/exit is easy all around. The sedan has a huge trunk, the wagon a cavernous cargo bay, and both have standard split/folding rear seats. Visibility is fine except to the rear, where the styling hides the car's exterior corners.

VALUE FOR THE MONEY Four-cylinder/automatic transmission Passats have barely acceptable acceleration for modern family cars, so try the different powertrain combinations to see which fits your needs. Otherwise, the sporty, spacious, solid Passat is strong on features per dollar, powertrain warranty, and European personality.

ENGINES

	Turbocharged dohc I4	dohc V6
Size, liters/cu. in.	1.8/109	2.8/169
Horsepower @ rpm	150 @ 5700	190 @ 6000
Torque (lbs./ft.) @ rpm	155 @ 1750	206 @ 3200
Availability	S[1]	S[2]
EPA city/highway mpg		
5-speed OD manual	23/32	20/29
5-speed OD automatic	21/31	18/29

1. GLS. 2. GLS V6, GLX.

PRICES

Volkswagen Passat	Retail Price	Dealer Invoice
GLS 4-door sedan	$21200	$19293
GLS 4-door wagon	22000	20016
GLS V6 4-door sedan	23800	21642
GLS V6 4-door wagon	24600	22365
GLX 4-door sedan	27655	25124
GLX 4-door wagon	28455	25847
Destination charge	525	525

STANDARD EQUIPMENT:

GLS: 1.8-liter dohc 4-cylinder turbocharged engine, 5-speed manual transmission, traction control, driver- and passenger-side airbags, front side-impact airbags, antilock 4-wheel disc brakes, daytime running lights, air conditioning, interior air filter, power steering, tilt/telescoping steering wheel, cruise control, cloth upholstery, height-adjustable front bucket seats w/lumbar adjustment, split folding rear seat, center console, cupholders, heated power mirrors, power windows, power door locks, remote keyless entry, map lights, tachometer, trip computer, outside temperature indicator, AM/FM/cassette w/CD controls, digital clock, rear defogger, remote fuel door/decklid release, variable intermittent wipers, auxiliary power outlet, illuminated visor mirrors, cargo cover (wagon), intermittent rear wiper/washer (wagon), floormats, theft-deterrent system, fog lights, full-size spare tire, 195/65HR15 tires, wheel covers. **GLS V6** adds: 2.8-liter dohc V6 engine. **GLX** adds: leather upholstery, leather-wrapped steering wheel, wood shift knob, heated 8-way power front seats w/driver seat memory, wood interior trim, automatic climate control, passenger-side mirror tilt-down parking aid, power sunroof, AM/FM/cassette/CD player w/Monsoon sound system, automatic day/night rearview mirror, rear window sun shade (sedan), rain-sensing wipers, heated windshield washer nozzles, 205/55R16 tires, alloy wheels.

OPTIONAL EQUIPMENT:
Major Packages
Partial Leather Pkg., GLS, GLS V6	1275	1126

Partial leather upholstery, heated front seats and windshield washer nozzles, leather-wrapped steering wheel and handbrake, wood shift knob.

Powertrains
5-speed automatic trans. w/manual-shift capability	1075	1063

Comfort and Convenience
CD player, GLS, GLS V6	295	—

In addition to AM/FM/cassette.

Monsoon sound system, GLS, GLS V6	295	261

VOLVO 40 SERIES

Front-wheel-drive near-luxury car

Base price range: $22,900-$23,900. Built in The Netherlands. **Also consider:** Acura TL, Audi A6, Infiniti I30, Lexus ES 300

FOR • Ride • Steering/handling • Brake performance • Cargo room (wagon) **AGAINST** • Rear-seat room

Volvo expands its lineup for 2000 with a compact sedan and wagon aimed at younger buyers than the automaker's traditional customers. The sedan is called S40, the wagon V40. With a 100.4-inch wheelbase, they're among the smallest cars in the near-luxury segment, and also among the least expensive, start-

Prices are accurate at time of publication; subject to manufacturer's changes.

Volvo S40

ing under $24,000.

They have front-wheel drive, a 160-horsepower turbocharged 4-cylinder engine, and a 4-speed automatic transmission. Standard safety features include front side airbags, antilock 4-wheel disc brakes, and front-seat active head restraints designed to minimize whiplash injury. Wagons get a split-fold rear seat, sedans a rear-seat pass-through. Traction control, leather upholstery, power moonroof, and integrated dual rear child booster-seats are options.

PERFORMANCE Most near-luxury cars have V6s and are a bit quicker than the 40 series, but this turbo 4-cylinder provides brisk takeoffs and good midrange punch. Aided by its optional traction control, our test V40 did 0-60 mph in 8.3 seconds and suffered little turbo-related throttle lag in the 45-70 mph range. The automatic transmission helps with prompt downshifts, but part-throttle upshifts are sometimes jerky. Fuel economy is only fair for a car of this weight and power, though our V40's 21-mpg average included gas-eating performance tests.

Despite a relatively short wheelbase, the 40 series has a supple, comfortable ride. Sharp bumps do register, but the suspension copes nicely with large ruts and humps, albeit with occasional "float." Handling and roadholding are good, and even the wagon corners with predictable front-drive grip and moderate body lean. Precise steering and powerful brakes also enhance driver confidence, but our wagon's tail tended to drift slightly left in simulated panic stops, which weren't super-short. Road and wind noise are well managed. The engine is quiet in top-gear cruising, but hard acceleration induces unwanted exhaust boom and intake growl, however.

ACCOMMODATIONS The interior caters well to hefty folk in front and provides sufficient room and comfort for two medium adults in back. Moving the front seats more than halfway aft, however, severely limits rear leg and foot room; it also complicates entry/exit, as do narrowish rear doors that should open wider.

Most drivers can get comfortably situated, helped by a standard tilt steering wheel and available power driver's seat. Visibility is hindered by the rear headrests. Gauges and controls are clear and handy, and the optional trip computer is user-friendly. Power window and mirror switches nestle inconveniently between the front seats, though there is a duplicate driver's window switch on the driver's door. Other lapses include small, rickety pop-out cupholders, though the console does have twin drink-box holders, and there's plenty of small-items storage. The sedan's roomy trunk has a small opening that could hinder loading bulky objects, while the wagon's cargo bay is fairly wide but not that long.

The 40 series has a generally solid feel, but some interior plastics feel brittle and cheap for a near-luxury car. Our test wagon arrived with slightly loose trim at the rear of the cargo bay.

VALUE FOR THE MONEY Optioned conservatively, a Volvo 40 can be an inviting alternative to, say, an Infiniti G20, and the wagon has little class competition. But a few options boost prices above $27,000; our fully loaded V40 cost a surprising $30,000-plus. For that, sedan buyers could have a Nissan Maxima or near-luxury Acura TL, both of which are roomier, quicker, and more refined.

ENGINES

	Turbocharged dohc I4
Size, liters/cu. in.	1.9/116
Horsepower @ rpm	160@ 5100
Torque (lbs./ft.) @ rpm	170@ 1800

	Turbocharged dohc I4
Availability	S
EPA city/highway mpg	
4-speed OD automatic	21/28

PRICES

Volvo 40 series	Retail Price	Dealer Invoice
S40 4-door sedan	$22900	$21329
V40 4-door wagon	23900	22339
Destination charge	575	575

STANDARD EQUIPMENT:

Base: 1.9-liter dohc turbocharged 4-cylinder engine, 4-speed automatic transmission, driver- and passenger-side airbags, front side-impact airbags, front seat active head restraints, antilock 4-wheel disc brakes, daytime running lights, air conditioning w/automatic climate control, interior air filter, variable-assist power steering, tilt steering wheel, cruise control, cloth upholstery, front bucket seats, center console, split folding rear seat, rear seat trunk pass-through (sedan), cupholders, heated power mirrors, power windows, power door locks, remote keyless entry, AM/FM/cassette w/CD changer controls, power antenna (sedan), digital clock, outside temperature display, tachometer, variable intermittent wipers, rear defogger, rear wiper/washer (wagon), map lights, illuminated visor mirrors, cargo cover (wagon), floormats, theft-deterrent system, tool kit, rear fog lights, 195/60VR15 tires, alloy wheels.

OPTIONAL EQUIPMENT:
Major Packages

Sport Pkg.	700	595
Manufacturer's discount price	550	470
Leather-wrapped steering wheel, front fog lights, rear spoiler.		
Touring Pkg.	1780	1513
Manufacturer's discount price	1500	1275
Leather-wrapped steering wheel, 8-way power driver seat, AM/FM/cassette/CD changer, premium speakers, trip computer.		
Sport Plus Pkg.	2330	1981
Manufacturer's discount price	1900	1615
Sport Pkg. plus Touring Pkg.		
Sunroof Pkg.	2585	2197
Manufacturer's discount price	2200	1870
Power sunroof, leather upholstery, simulated-wood dashboard trim and shift knob.		
Cold Weather Pkg.	935	795
Manufacturer's discount price	850	725
Traction control, heated front seats, headlight wiper/washer.		

Safety Features

Dual child booster seats	300	255

Comfort and Convenience

Leather upholstery	1200	1020
Power sunroof	1200	—

VOLVO 70 SERIES

Volvo S70 AWD

Front- or all-wheel-drive near-luxury car

Base price range: $27,500-$46,500. Built in Sweden and Belgium. **Also consider:** Acura TL, Audi A6, Infiniti I30, Lexus ES 300, Mercedes-Benz CLK, Toyota Camry/Solara

FOR • Acceleration (turbo models) • Steering/handling • Cargo room (sedans/wagons) • Build quality • Exterior finish

AGAINST • Road noise • Rear-seat entry/exit (coupes/convertibles) • Ride (16- and 17-inch wheel models)

Volvo trims the wagon models and revises some safety features in its best-selling line for 2000. S70 sedans and V70 wagons come with front-wheel drive or all-wheel drive (AWD), which automatically redirects power to the rear wheels when needed. The C70 coupes and convertibles are front-drive.

All models use a 5-cylinder engine. Base sedans and wagons have 162 horsepower. The GLT models, the S70 AWD, the V70 XC AWD, and the C70 2.4 are turbocharged and have 190 hp. The S70 T5 and the C70 2.3 also are turbocharged and have 236 hp. The turbo V70 R AWD has 261 hp.

Base models and C70 2.3s offer manual or automatic transmission. The S70 T5 comes only with manual transmission, all others only with automatic. Volvo labels the V70 XC AWD the "Cross Country" and gives it a raised suspension, roof rails, fog lamps, and other SUV cues.

For 2000, the base AWD wagon and the front-drive performance-oriented T5 wagon are dropped. Front side airbags and antilock brakes are again standard linewide, but the side air bags are new units designed to protect the head as well as the chest. Also newly standard is Volvo's WHIPS system, which is designed to move the front seatbacks and headrests rearward in a rear-end collision to minimize whiplash.

PERFORMANCE All 70 series models are good performers, with sedans and wagons proving more successful in their missions than the C70 coupe and convertible.

Acceleration is adequate with the base engine, satisfying with the 190-hp turbo, strong with the 236-hp turbo, and exciting in the V70 R AWD. Unfortunately, the turbos suffer frustrating lag at midrange speeds, and none of these 5-cylinder engines is as smooth as the V6s used by most rivals. Those shortfalls are most troubling in the coupes and convertibles, which come off as a touch crude compared to competitors such as the Mercedes-Benz CLK 320 or even a well-equipped Toyota Solara. Fuel economy is decent: 70 series cars averages 18.5-23 mpg in our tests, with our last S70 GLT AWD test car returning 19.8.

All handle well, too, but ride comfort varies from smooth on base models, to choppy on C70s, to jarring on sedans and wagons with 16- and 17-inch wheels. GLTs have the best ride/handling compromise. Braking is strong and sure, and Volvo's AWD provides terrific traction with no driver input needed.

ACCOMMODATIONS Sedans and wagons have adequate space for four adults, five in a pinch, and feature comfortable, supportive seating. The C70s are relatively practical. Two 6-footers can be comfortable in back on shorter trips, although the convertible's narrower rear seat is less accommodating, and rear access on either is frustrated by standard power-sliding front seats that move like snails—and only as long as a seatback lever is activated.

All these Volvos share an easily tailored driving position, though the tilt/telescope steering wheel hides some dashboard switches. Only the convertible with the top up has subpar visibility. Sedans and wagons have large, usefully shaped, and easily accessed cargo holds, and the C70's trunk easily holds a couple's weekend luggage. Minor interior rattles plagued our recent C70 and V70 XC AWD test cars, but workmanship is otherwise tight and solid, and materials are first-class.

VALUE FOR THE MONEY GLT versions are the best 70 series values, and the AWD wagons are sensible SUV alternatives, though our recent test GLT AWD listed for a steep $37,400. Similarly priced near-luxury rivals have smoother V6 engines and better handling. Volvo aims the C70s at empty-nesters ready for something with more sizzle than its sedans and wagons, but more-refined coupe and convertible rivals are available for less or similar money.

ENGINES

	dohc I5	Turbocharged dohc I5	Turbocharged dohc I5	Turbocharged dohc I5
Size, liters/cu. in.	2.4/149	2.4/149	2.3/141	2.3/141
Horsepower @ rpm	162 @ 6100	190 @ 5100	236 @ 5100	261 @ 5700
Torque (lbs./ft.) @ rpm	162 @ 4700	199 @ 1800	244 @ 2100	258 @ 2400
Availability	S[1]	S[2]	S[3]	S[4]

EPA city/highway mpg

5-speed OD manual	21/29		20/28
4-speed OD automatic.....	20/28	20/27	20/27

1. Base. 2. GLT, AWD, XC AWD, C70 2.4. 3. T5, C70 2.3. 4. R.

PRICES

Volvo 70 series	Retail Price	Dealer Invoice
S70 Base 4-door sedan, 5-speed	$27500	$25475
V70 Base 4-door wagon, 5-speed	28800	26788
S70 GLT 4-door sedan, automatic	31700	29517
V70 GLT 4-door wagon, automatic	33000	30830
S70 AWD 4-door sedan, automatic	33600	31136
V70 XC AWD 4-door wagon, automatic	36100	33411
S70 T5 4-door sedan, 5-speed	33300	30583
V70 R AWD 4-door wagon, automatic	41500	37615
C70 2.4-liter 2-door coupe, automatic	34000	31040
C70 2.4-liter 2-door convertible, automatic	43500	39635
C70 2.3-liter 2-door coupe, 5-speed	39000	35090
C70 2.3-liter 2-door coupe, automatic	40000	36100
C70 2.3-liter 2-door convertible, 5-speed	45500	41655
C70 2.3-liter 2-door convertible, automatic	46500	42665
Destination charge	575	575

STANDARD EQUIPMENT:

Base: 2.4-liter dohc 5-cylinder 168-horsepower engine, 5-speed manual transmission, driver- and passenger-side airbags, front side-impact airbags, antilock 4-wheel disc brakes, daytime running lights, air conditioning w/dual-zone manual climate control, variable-assist power steering, tilt/telescoping steering column, cruise control, intermittent wipers, cloth/vinyl upholstery, reclining front bucket seats, 8-way manually adjustable driver seat, split folding rear seat, rear-seat trunk pass-through (sedan), front armrest, cupholders, heated power mirrors, power windows, power door locks, remote keyless entry, remote decklid/tailgate and fuel door releases, tachometer, outside temperature indicator, 6-speaker AM/FM/cassette w/CD changer controls, power antenna (sedan), integrated window antenna (wagon), digital clock, rear defogger, rear wiper/washer (wagon), illuminated visor mirrors, front and rear reading lights, floormats, theft-deterrent system, rear fog lights, tool kit, 195/60VR15 tires, alloy wheels.

GLT adds: 2.4-liter dohc turbocharged 5-cylinder 190-horsepower engine, 4-speed automatic transmission, dual-zone automatic climate control, 8-way power driver's seat w/memory feature, premium AM/FM/cassette w/CD changer controls.

T5 adds: 2.3-liter dohc turbocharged 5-cylinder 236-horsepower engine, 5-speed manual transmission, 8-way power passenger seat, leather-wrapped steering wheel, AM/FM/cassette/CD player, trip computer, universal garage door opener, 205/55VR16 tires.

AWD adds to GLT: permanent all-wheel drive, traction control, heated front seats, headlight wipers/washers, 195/65R15 tires.

XC AWD adds: limited-slip rear differential, leather-wrapped steering wheel, trip computer, cargo mat, raised suspension, automatic load leveling suspension, roof rails, front fog lights, 205/65R15 tires.

R AWD adds: 2.3-liter dohc turbocharged 5-cylinder 261-horsepower engine, power sunroof, leather and suede upholstery, leather and suede-wrapped steering wheel, 8-way power passenger seat, 3-disc CD changer, universal garage door opener, alloy instrument panel inserts, deletes raised suspension, roof rails.

C 2.4 adds to GLT: rollover protection system (convertible), cloth and leather upholstery (coupe), leather upholstery (convertible), 8-way power passenger seat, leather-wrapped steering wheel, power convertible top (convertible), AM/FM/cassette/CD player, front fog lights, headlight wiper/washer, 225/50VR16 tires (coupe), 205/55VR16 tires (convertible), deletes outside temperature display, trip computer.

C 2.3-liter adds: 2.3-liter dohc turbocharged 5-cylinder 236-horsepower engine, 5-speed manual or 4-speed automatic transmission, leather upholstery, power sunroof (coupe), wood interior trim, automatic day/night rearview mirror, universal garage door opener, AM/FM/cassette w/3-disc CD changer, trip computer, outside temperature display, 225/45ZR17 tires (coupe), 225/50VR16 (convertible), deletes split folding rear seat.

Prices are accurate at time of publication; subject to manufacturer's changes.

OPTIONAL EQUIPMENT:
Major Packages

	Retail Price	Dealer Invoice
Touring Pkg., Base	$1505	—
Manufacturer's discount price	1250	1000

Leather-wrapped steering wheel, 8-way power driver seat w/memory, AM/FM/cassette/CD player, trip computer, universal garage door opener.

Touring Value Pkg., GLT, AWD....................	1460	—
Manufacturer's discount price	1200	960

Leather-wrapped steering wheel, 8-way power passenger seat, AM/FM/cassette/CD player, trip computer, universal garage door opener.

Touring Pkg., XC AWD	1060	—
Manufacturer's discount price	800	640

AM/FM/cassette/CD player, 8-way power passenger seat, universal garage door opener.

Sunroof Leather Pkg., Base, GLT, AWD, XC AWD, T5..........................	2625	—
Manufacturer's discount price	2200	1760

Power sunroof, leather upholstery, simulated-wood dashboard trim and shift knob.

SR Pkg., C 2.4-liter coupe	2400	1920
Manufacturer's discount price	1900	1520

Power sunroof, full leather upholstery.

Cold Weather Pkg., Base, GLT, T5	1000	—
Manufacturer's discount price	850	680

Traction control, heated front seats, headlight wiper/washer.

Sport Pkg., Base, GLT, AWD, T5	600	—
Manufacturer's discount price	450	360

Rear spoiler, front fog lights.

Outdoor Pkg., XC AWD	575	—
Manufacturer's discount price	475	380

Dirt protector, grey lower body and roof-rail cross bars.

Powertrains

4-speed automatic transmission, Base, T5	1000	1000
Traction control, C 2.4, C 2.3	550	440

Safety Features

Dual integrated child seats, wagons	300	240

Comfort and Convenience

Power sunroof, Base, GLT, AWD, XC AWD, T5......	1200	960
Leather upholstery, Base, GLT, AWD, XC AWD, T5..........................	1200	960
Premium leather upholstery, C 2.4 convertible, C 2.3........................	1600	1280
Heated front seats, C 2.4, C 2.3	250	200
Wood interior trim, C 2.4	600	480
Universal garage door opener, C 2.4 coupe	125	100
Automatic day/night rearview mirror, C 2.4	100	80
Trip computer, C 2.4..................................	250	200

Includes outside temperature display.

Dolby Pro Logic sound system, 2.4 convertible	1500	1200
C 2.4 coupe	1200	960
R AWD, C 2.3 coupe	600	480
5-spoke alloy wheels, C 2.4	400	320

Includes 225/45ZR17 tires.

Multi-spoke alloy wheels, C 2.4, C 2.3................	1500	1200

Includes 225/45ZR17 tires.

VOLVO S80

Front-wheel-drive luxury car

Base price range: $36,000-$40,500. Built in Sweden.
Also consider: Acura RL, BMW 5-Series, Lexus LS 400

FOR • Acceleration (T6) • Passenger and cargo room • Build quality • Exterior finish • Interior materials **AGAINST** • Radio and navigation system controls • Rear visibility

An option package with sun-blocking rear curtains is new for the 2000 version of Volvo's flagship. S80 uses inline 6-cylinder engines; the base model has 201 horsepower, the twin-turbocharged T6 has 268. Both team with a 4-speed automatic transmission, the T6's adding a separate gate for manual shift-

Volvo S80 T6

ing. Standard are antilock 4-wheel disc antilock brakes, traction control, and front side airbags. Also included is Volvo's Inflatable Curtain, air bags that drop down from above the side windows in a side impact, plus Volvo's WHIPS system, which moves the front seatbacks and headrests rearward to minimize whiplash in a rear-end collision. Called the Warm Weather package, the new option includes the rear curtains and a windshield with an infrared treatment designed to reflect the sun's heat.

EVALUATION The base S80 has only adequate power, while the turbocharged T6 is quick by most any standard. Fuel economy is good: our test base S80 averaged 19.2 mpg, a T6 20.7. Both have sure-footed handling, but some testers feel the steering is numb and overassisted. The base model easily absorbs bumps that register sharply in the stiffer T6. Stopping power is strong, but one test base model suffered numb pedal feel. Doors open wide for easy entry/exit, and there's generous room front and rear. The dashboard layout is clean and modern, but the radio's station-memory function uses a dial instead of buttons and is a chore to preset. When activated, the optional navigation system's map screen rises from the middle center of the dashboard. It's at eye level, and its controls are on the steering wheel, not the dashboard. But like many such systems, this one requires study and patience to program. A large trunk is tempered by a small opening. The S80 packs lots of safety and convenience features into a stylish, functional sedan. Both models are competitively priced, but we believe the quick T6 is worth the extra money.

ENGINES

	dohc I6	Turbocharged dohc I6
Size, liters/cu. in.	2.9/178	2.8/170
Horsepower @ rpm	201 @ 6000	268 @ 5400
Torque (lbs./ft.) @ rpm	243 @ 4200	280 @ 2000
Availability	S[1]	S[2]
EPA city/highway mpg		
4-speed OD automatic	19/27	18/27

1. S80 2.9. 2. S80 T6.

PRICES

Volvo S80	Retail Price	Dealer Invoice
2.9 4-door sedan	$36000	$33060
T6 4-door sedan	40500	37105
Destination charge	575	575

STANDARD EQUIPMENT:

2.9: 2.9-liter dohc 6-cylinder engine, 4-speed automatic transmission, traction control, driver- and passenger-side airbags, front side-impact airbags, front and rear side head protection, front seat active head restraints, antilock 4-wheel disc brakes, daytime running lights, dual-zone automatic air conditioning, variable-assist power steering, tilt/telescoping leather-wrapped steering wheel, cruise control, cloth upholstery, 8-way power front bucket seats w/driver seat memory, center console, split folding rear seat, cupholders, auxiliary power outlets, heated power mirrors, power windows, power door locks, remote keyless entry, AM/FM/cassette/CD player, steering-wheel-mounted radio and climate controls, tachometer, trip computer, intermittent wipers, illuminated visor mirrors, cargo net, floormats, theft-deterrent system, 215/55R16 tires, alloy wheels.

T6 adds: 2.8-liter dohc turbocharged 6-cylinder engine, 4-speed Geartronic automatic transmission, heated front seats, heated headlight wipers/washers, premium speakers, wood interior trim, automatic day/night rearview mirror, fog lights, 225/55R16 tires.

OPTIONAL EQUIPMENT:
Major Packages

	Retail Price	Dealer Invoice
Special Value Pkg., 2.9	$2400	$1920
Manufacturer's discount price	1200	960
Power sunroof, leather upholstery.		
Warm Weather Pkg.	700	560
Manufacturer's discount price	500	400
Infrared reflective windshield, rear and side curtains.		
Cold Weather Package, 2.9	450	360
Heated front seats, heated headlight wipers/washers.		
Ultra Security System	635	508
Manufacturer's discount price	600	480
Movement sensors, incline sensor, laminated security side glass, universal garage door opener.		

Powertrains

	Retail Price	Dealer Invoice
Dynamic Stability Traction Control	1100	880
Includes anti-skid system.		

Comfort and Convenience

Navigation System	2500	2140
4-disc CD changer	1000	800
Deletes cassette player.		

Appearance and Miscellaneous

Special alloy wheels	400	320
Includes 225/50R17 tires.		

SPECIFICATIONS

Dimensions and capacities are supplied by the vehicle manufacturers. **Body types:** 2-door coupe or 4-door sedan = a standard-body car with a separate trunk; hatchback = car with a rear liftgate; wagon = car or sport-utility vehicle with an enclosed cargo bay; regular-cab pickup truck = standard-length cab with room for one row of front seats; extended-cab pickup truck = lengthened cab with seating positions behind the front seats; crew cab pickup truck = extended-length cab with two forward-opening rear doors and rear seating. **Wheelbase:** distance between the front and rear wheels. **Curb weight:** weight of base models, not including optional equipment. **Height:** overall height of base models, not including optional equipment (on sport-utility vehicles, this is the overall height of the 4-wheel drive model). **Cargo volume** *(does not apply to pickup trucks)*: coupes and sedans = maximum cargo volume of the trunk; hatchbacks and station wagons = maximum volume with the rear seat folded; minivans and sport-utility vehicles = maximum volume with all rear seats folded or removed, when possible. **Standard payload** *(applies to pickup trucks)*: maximum weight the base-model can carry, including passengers.

SUBCOMPACT CARS	Wheelbase, in.	Overall length, in.	Overall width, in.	Overall height, in.	Curb weight, lbs.	Cargo volume, cu. ft.	Fuel capacity, gals.	Seating capacity	Front head room, in.	Max. front leg room, in.	Rear head room, in.	Min. rear leg room, in.
Chevrolet Cavalier 2-door coupe	104.1	180.9	68.7	53.0	2617	13.2	15.0	5	37.6	41.9	36.6	32.7
Chevrolet Cavalier 2-door convertible	104.1	180.9	68.7	54.1	2838	10.5	15.0	4	38.1	42.1	37.6	32.6
Chevrolet Cavalier 4-door sedan	104.1	180.9	67.9	54.7	2676	13.6	15.0	5	38.9	41.9	37.2	34.4
Chevrolet Metro 2-door hatchback	93.1	149.4	62.6	54.7	1895	22.5	10.3	4	39.1	42.5	36.0	32.8
Chevrolet Metro 4-door sedan	93.1	164.0	62.6	55.4	1984	10.3	10.3	4	39.3	42.5	37.3	32.2
Chevrolet Prizm 4-door sedan	97.1	174.2	66.7	53.7	2403	12.1	13.2	5	39.3	42.5	36.9	33.2
Daewoo Lanos 2-door hatchback	99.2	160.4	66.1	56.4	2447	31.3	12.7	5	38.9	42.8	37.8	34.6
Daewoo Lanos 4-door sedan	99.2	166.8	66.1	56.4	2522	8.8	12.7	5	38.9	42.8	37.8	34.6
Daewoo Nubira 4-door sedan	101.2	177.0	66.9	56.3	2800	13.1	13.7	5	39.0	42.0	38.1	34.7
Daewoo Nubira 4-door wagon	101.2	179.0	67.7	57.9	2888	65.0	13.7	5	39.0	42.0	39.5	34.7
Dodge/Plymouth Neon 4-door sedan	105.0	174.4	67.4	56.0	2559	13.1	12.5	5	39.1	42.4	36.8	34.8
Ford Escort 4-door sedan	98.4	174.5	67.0	53.3	2454	12.8	12.7	5	39.0	42.5	36.7	34.0
Ford ZX2 2-door coupe	98.4	175.2	67.4	52.3	2478	11.8	12.8	4	38.0	42.5	35.1	33.4
Ford Focus 2-door hatchback	103.0	168.1	66.9	56.3	2551	18.5	13.2	5	39.3	43.1	38.7	NA
Ford Focus 4-door sedan	103.0	174.9	66.9	56.3	2564	12.9	13.2	5	39.3	43.1	38.5	37.6
Ford Focus 4-door wagon	103.0	178.2	66.9	57.0	2707	55.3	13.2	5	39.3	43.1	40.0	37.6
Honda Civic 2-door coupe	103.2	175.1	67.1	54.1	2359	11.9	11.9	5	38.8	42.7	36.2	32.5
Honda Civic 2-door hatchback	103.2	164.2	67.1	54.1	2359	18.1	11.9	5	38.8	42.7	37.2	32.5
Honda Civic 4-door sedan	103.2	175.1	67.1	54.7	2339	11.9	11.9	5	39.8	42.7	37.6	34.1
Honda Insight 2-door hatchback	94.5	155.1	66.7	53.3	1856	6.5	10.6	2	38.8	42.9	—	—
Hyundai Accent 2-door hatchback	96.1	166.7	65.7	54.9	2280	16.1	11.9	5	38.9	42.6	38.0	32.8
Hyundai Accent 4-door sedan	96.1	166.7	65.7	54.9	2119	10.7	11.9	5	38.9	42.6	38.0	32.8
Hyundai Elantra 4-door sedan	100.4	174.0	66.9	54.9	2626	11.0	14.5	5	38.6	43.2	37.6	34.6
Hyundai Elantra 4-door wagon	100.4	175.2	66.9	58.7	2681	63.0	14.5	5	38.6	43.2	38.9	34.8
Kia Sephia 4-door sedan	100.8	174.4	66.9	55.5	2478	10.4	13.2	5	39.6	43.3	37.7	34.4
Mazda Protege 4-door sedan	102.8	174.0	67.1	55.5	2449	12.9	13.2	5	39.3	42.2	37.4	35.4
Mitsubishi Mirage 2-door coupe	95.1	168.1	66.5	52.4	2150	11.5	12.4	5	38.6	43.0	35.8	31.1
Mitsubishi Mirage 4-door sedan	98.4	173.6	66.5	53.5	2250	11.5	12.4	5	39.8	43.0	37.4	33.5
Pontiac Sunfire 2-door coupe	104.1	182.0	68.4	53.0	2606	12.4	14.3	5	37.6	42.1	36.6	32.6
Pontiac Sunfire 4-door sedan	104.1	181.8	67.9	54.7	2644	13.1	14.3	5	38.9	42.1	37.2	34.3
Pontiac Sunfire 2-door convertible	104.1	182.9	68.4	54.1	2906	9.9	14.3	4	38.1	42.1	37.6	32.6
Saturn S-Series 3-door coupe	102.4	180.5	67.3	53.0	2367	11.4	12.1	4	38.6	42.6	35.8	31.0
Saturn S-Series 4-door sedan	102.4	178.1	66.4	55.0	2331	12.1	12.1	5	39.3	42.5	38.0	32.8

Prices are accurate at time of publication; subject to manufacturer's changes.

SPECIFICATIONS

SUBCOMPACT CARS CONTINUED

	Wheelbase, in.	Overall length, in.	Overall width, in.	Overall height, in.	Curb weight, lbs.	Cargo volume, cu. ft.	Fuel capacity, gals.	Seating capacity	Front head room, in.	Max. front leg room, in.	Rear head room, in.	Min. rear leg room, in.
Saturn S-Series 4-door wagon	102.4	178.1	66.4	55.6	2452	58.2	12.1	5	39.3	42.5	39.2	30.7
Subaru Impreza 2-door coupe	99.2	172.2	67.1	55.5	2820	11.1	13.2	5	39.2	43.1	36.7	32.5
Subaru Impreza 4-door sedan	99.2	172.2	67.1	55.5	2730	11.1	13.2	5	39.2	43.1	36.7	32.5
Subaru Impreza 4-door wagon	99.2	172.2	67.1	55.5	2835	62.1	13.2	5	39.2	43.1	37.4	32.4
Subaru Impreza Outback 4-door wagon	99.2	172.2	67.1	60.0	2860	62.1	13.2	5	39.2	43.1	37.4	32.4
Suzuki Swift 2-door hatchback	93.1	149.4	62.6	54.7	1895	8.4	10.3	4	39.1	42.5	36.0	32.2
Suzuki Esteem 4-door sedan	97.6	166.3	66.1	53.9	2227	12.0	13.5	5	39.1	42.3	37.2	34.1
Suzuki Esteem 4-door wagon	97.6	172.2	66.5	55.9	2359	61.0	13.5	5	38.8	42.3	38.0	34.1
Toyota Corolla 4-door sedan	97.0	174.0	66.7	54.5	2403	12.1	13.2	5	39.3	42.5	36.9	33.2
Toyota Echo 2-door coupe	93.4	163.3	65.4	59.1	2020	13.6	11.9	5	39.9	41.1	37.6	35.2
Toyota Echo 4-door sedan	93.4	163.3	65.4	59.1	2030	13.6	11.9	5	39.9	41.1	37.6	35.2
Volkswagen Golf 2-door hatchback	98.9	163.3	68.3	56.7	2723	41.8	14.6	5	38.5	41.3	37.7	33.3
Volkswagen Golf 4-door hatchback	98.9	163.3	68.3	56.7	2875	41.8	14.6	5	38.5	41.3	37.7	33.3
Volkswagen Jetta 4-door sedan	98.9	172.3	68.3	56.9	2853	13.0	14.5	5	38.7	41.3	37.2	33.3

COMPACT CARS

	Wheelbase, in.	Overall length, in.	Overall width, in.	Overall height, in.	Curb weight, lbs.	Cargo volume, cu. ft.	Fuel capacity, gals.	Seating capacity	Front head room, in.	Max. front leg room, in.	Rear head room, in.	Min. rear leg room, in.
Daewoo Leganza 4-door sedan	105.1	183.9	70.0	56.6	3086	14.1	15.8	5	39.3	42.3	37.8	38.2
Ford Contour 4-door sedan	106.5	184.6	69.1	54.5	2769	13.9	15.0	5	39.0	42.4	36.7	34.4
Hyundai Sonata 4-door sedan	106.3	185.4	71.6	55.5	3072	13.2	17.2	5	39.3	43.3	37.6	36.2
Mazda 626 4-door sedan	105.1	186.8	69.3	55.1	2798	14.2	16.9	5	39.2	43.6	37.0	34.6
Mitsubishi Galant 4-door sedan	103.7	187.8	68.5	55.7	2835	14.0	16.3	5	39.9	43.5	37.7	36.3
Nissan Altima 4-door sedan	103.1	185.8	69.1	55.9	2859	13.8	15.9	5	39.4	42.0	37.7	33.9
Oldsmobile Alero 2-door coupe	107.0	186.7	70.1	54.5	3026	14.6	14.3	5	38.4	42.2	37.0	35.5
Oldsmobile Alero 4-door sedan	107.0	186.7	70.1	54.5	3077	14.6	15.0	5	38.4	42.2	37.0	35.5
Pontiac Grand Am 2-door coupe	107.0	186.3	70.4	55.1	3066	14.6	14.3	5	38.3	42.1	37.2	35.5
Pontiac Grand Am 4-door sedan	107.0	186.3	70.4	55.1	3116	14.6	14.3	5	38.3	42.1	37.6	35.5
Subaru Legacy 4-door sedan	104.3	184.4	68.7	55.7	3245	12.4	16.9	5	38.1	43.3	36.6	34.2
Subaru Legacy 4-door wagon	104.3	187.4	68.7	59.6	3265	68.6	16.9	5	38.5	43.3	37.2	34.3
Subaru Outback 4-door sedan	104.3	184.4	68.7	58.3	3485	12.4	16.9	5	38.1	43.3	36.6	34.2
Subaru Outback 4-door wagon	104.3	187.4	68.7	63.3	3415	68.6	16.9	5	38.5	43.3	37.2	34.3
Volkswagen Passat 4-door sedan	106.4	184.1	68.5	57.4	3245	15.0	16.4	5	39.7	41.5	37.8	35.3
Volkswagen Passat 4-door wagon	106.3	183.8	68.5	59.0	3201	78.7	16.4	5	39.7	41.5	39.7	35.3

MIDSIZE CARS

	Wheelbase, in.	Overall length, in.	Overall width, in.	Overall height, in.	Curb weight, lbs.	Cargo volume, cu. ft.	Fuel capacity, gals.	Seating capacity	Front head room, in.	Max. front leg room, in.	Rear head room, in.	Min. rear leg room, in.
Buick Century 4-door sedan	109.0	194.6	72.7	56.6	3368	16.7	17.5	6	39.4	42.4	37.4	36.9
Buick Regal 4-door sedan	109.0	196.2	72.7	56.6	3439	16.7	17.5	5	39.3	42.4	37.4	36.9
Chevrolet Impala 4-door sedan	110.5	200.0	73.0	57.5	3389	17.6	17.0	6	39.2	42.2	36.8	38.4
Chevrolet Lumina 4-door sedan	107.5	200.9	72.5	54.8	3330	15.5	16.6	6	38.4	42.4	37.4	36.6
Chevrolet Malibu 4-door sedan	107.0	190.4	69.4	56.7	3051	17.1	15.0	5	39.4	41.9	37.6	38.0
Chrysler Cirrus 4-door sedan	108.0	187.0	71.7	54.3	3197	15.7	16.0	5	38.1	42.3	36.8	38.1
Dodge Stratus 4-door sedan	108.0	186.0	71.7	54.2	2940	15.7	16.0	5	38.1	42.3	36.8	38.1
Ford Taurus 4-door sedan	108.5	197.6	73.0	56.1	3328	17.0	16.0	6	40.0	42.2	38.1	38.9
Ford Taurus 4-door wagon	108.5	197.6	73.0	58.0	3486	81.3	16.0	8	39.3	42.2	38.7	38.5
Honda Accord 2-door coupe	105.1	186.8	70.3	55.0	2948	13.6	17.1	5	39.7	42.6	36.5	32.4
Honda Accord 4-door sedan	106.9	188.8	70.3	56.9	2932	14.1	17.1	5	40.0	42.1	37.6	37.9
Mercury Sable 4-door sedan	108.5	200.5	73.0	55.5	3375	16.0	16.0	6	39.8	42.2	36.7	38.9
Mercury Sable 4-door wagon	108.5	197.7	73.0	58.0	3540	81.3	16.0	6	39.3	42.2	38.7	38.5
Nissan Maxima 4-door sedan	108.3	190.5	70.3	56.5	3186	15.1	18.5	5	40.4	44.8	37.2	35.4
Oldsmobile Intrigue 4-door sedan	109.0	195.9	73.6	56.6	3434	16.4	18.0	5	39.3	42.4	37.4	36.2

MIDSIZE CARS CONTINUED

	Wheelbase, in.	Overall length, in.	Overall width, in.	Overall height, in.	Curb weight, lbs.	Cargo volume, cu. ft.	Fuel capacity, gals.	Seating capacity	Front head room, in.	Max. front leg room, in.	Rear head room, in.	Min. rear leg room, in.
Plymouth Breeze 4-door sedan	108.0	186.7	71.7	54.3	2945	15.7	16.0	5	38.1	42.3	36.8	38.1
Pontiac Grand Prix 2-door coupe	110.5	196.5	72.7	54.7	3396	16.0	17.0	5	38.3	42.4	36.5	36.1
Pontiac Grand Prix 4-door sedan	110.5	196.5	72.7	54.7	3414	16.0	17.0	6	38.3	42.4	36.7	35.8
Saturn L-Series 4-door sedan	106.5	190.4	69.0	56.4	2910	17.5	13.1	5	39.3	42.2	38.0	34.4
Saturn L-Series 4-door wagon	106.5	190.4	69.0	57.3	3075	71.3	13.1	5	39.3	42.3	39.6	37.0
Toyota Solara 2-door coupe	105.1	190.0	71.1	55.1	3120	13.8	18.5	5	38.3	43.3	36.3	35.2
Toyota Camry 4-door sedan	105.2	188.5	70.1	55.4	2998	14.1	18.5	5	38.6	43.5	37.6	35.5

FULL-SIZE CARS

	Wheelbase, in.	Overall length, in.	Overall width, in.	Overall height, in.	Curb weight, lbs.	Cargo volume, cu. ft.	Fuel capacity, gals.	Seating capacity	Front head room, in.	Max. front leg room, in.	Rear head room, in.	Min. rear leg room, in.
Buick LeSabre 4-door sedan	112.2	200.0	73.5	57.0	3567	18.0	17.5	6	38.8	42.4	37.8	39.9
Chrysler Concorde 4-door sedan	113.0	209.1	74.6	55.9	3488	18.7	17.0	6	38.3	42.2	37.1	42.2
Dodge Intrepid 4-door sedan	113.0	203.7	74.7	55.9	3471	18.4	17.0	6	38.3	42.2	37.4	39.1
Ford Crown Victoria 4-door sedan	114.7	212.0	78.2	56.8	3917	20.6	19.0	6	39.4	42.5	38.0	39.6
Mercury Grand Marquis 4-door sedan	114.7	212.0	78.2	56.8	3917	20.6	19.0	6	39.4	42.5	38.1	38.4
Pontiac Bonneville 4-door sedan	112.2	202.6	74.2	56.6	3590	18.0	18.5	6	38.7	42.6	37.3	38.0
Toyota Avalon 4-door sedan	107.1	191.9	71.7	57.7	3330	15.9	18.5	6	38.7	41.7	37.9	40.1

NEAR-LUXURY CARS

	Wheelbase, in.	Overall length, in.	Overall width, in.	Overall height, in.	Curb weight, lbs.	Cargo volume, cu. ft.	Fuel capacity, gals.	Seating capacity	Front head room, in.	Max. front leg room, in.	Rear head room, in.	Min. rear leg room, in.
Acura TL 4-door sedan	108.1	192.9	70.3	56.7	3483	14.3	17.2	5	39.9	42.4	36.8	35.0
Audi A4 4-door sedan	103.0	178.0	68.2	55.8	3164	13.7	16.4	5	38.2	41.3	36.9	33.4
Audi A4 4-door wagon	102.6	176.7	68.2	56.7	3351	63.7	15.9	5	38.2	41.3	37.8	33.4
Audi A6 4-door sedan	108.7	192.0	71.3	57.2	3759	17.2	18.5	5	39.3	41.3	37.9	37.3
Audi A6 4-door wagon	108.6	192.0	71.3	58.2	3947	73.2	18.5	5	39.3	41.3	38.7	37.3
BMW 3-Series 2-door coupe	107.3	176.7	69.2	53.5	3020	9.5	16.6	4	37.5	41.7	36.5	33.2
BMW 3-Series 4-door sedan	107.3	176.0	68.5	55.7	3153	10.7	16.6	5	38.4	41.4	37.5	34.6
Buick Park Avenue 4-door sedan	113.8	206.8	74.7	57.4	3778	19.1	18.5	6	39.8	42.4	38.0	41.1
Cadillac Catera 4-door sedan	107.5	192.2	70.3	56.4	3770	14.5	16.0	5	38.7	42.2	38.4	37.5
Chrysler LHS 4-door sedan	113.0	207.7	74.4	56.0	3564	18.7	17.2	5	38.3	42.2	37.1	42.2
Chrysler 300M 4-door sedan	113.0	197.8	74.4	56.0	3567	16.8	17.2	5	38.3	42.2	37.2	39.1
Infiniti G20 4-door sedan	102.4	177.5	66.7	55.1	2923	13.5	15.9	5	39.2	41.5	36.8	34.6
Infiniti I30 4-door sedan	108.3	193.7	70.2	56.5	3342	14.9	18.5	5	40.5	43.9	37.4	36.2
Lexus ES 300 4-door sedan	105.1	190.2	70.5	54.9	3373	13.0	18.5	5	38.0	43.5	36.2	34.4
Lincoln LS 4-door sedan	114.5	193.9	73.2	57.2	3593	13.5	18.1	5	40.4	42.6	37.5	37.7
Mazda Millenia 4-door sedan	108.3	189.8	69.7	54.9	3241	13.3	18.0	5	39.3	43.3	37.0	34.1
Mercedes-Benz C-Class 4-door sedan	105.9	177.4	67.7	56.1	3250	12.9	16.4	5	37.2	41.5	37.0	32.8
Mitsubishi Diamante 4-door sedan	107.1	194.1	70.3	53.9	3440	14.2	19.0	5	39.4	43.6	37.5	36.6
Saab 9-3 2-door hatchback	102.6	182.3	67.4	56.2	2990	21.7	17.0	5	39.3	42.3	37.9	34.1
Saab 9-3 4-door hatchback	102.6	182.3	67.4	56.2	3160	21.7	17.0	5	39.3	42.3	37.9	34.1
Saab 9-3 2-door convertible	102.6	182.3	67.4	56.0	3130	12.5	17.0	4	38.9	42.3	37.9	33.0
Volvo 40 series 4-door sedan	100.4	176.5	67.7	55.6	2998	13.2	15.9	5	37.6	41.4	36.5	32.7
Volvo 40 series 4-door wagon	100.4	176.5	67.6	55.6	3042	61.3	15.9	5	37.6	41.4	36.5	32.7
Volvo 70 series 2-door coupe	104.9	185.7	71.5	55.7	3365	13.1	18.5	4	37.4	41.3	36.6	34.6
Volvo 70 series 2-door convertible	104.9	185.7	71.5	56.0	3601	7.9	17.9	4	39.0	41.3	36.6	34.6
Volvo 70 series 4-door sedan	104.9	185.9	69.3	55.2	3152	15.1	18.5	5	39.1	41.4	37.8	35.2
Volvo 70 series 4-door wagon	104.9	185.9	69.3	56.2	3259	70.0	17.9	5	39.1	41.4	37.9	35.2

LUXURY CARS

	Wheelbase, in.	Overall length, in.	Overall width, in.	Overall height, in.	Curb weight, lbs.	Cargo volume, cu. ft.	Fuel capacity, gals.	Seating capacity	Front head room, in.	Max. front leg room, in.	Rear head room, in.	Min. rear leg room, in.
Acura RL 4-door sedan	114.6	196.6	71.4	56.5	3858	14.0	18.0	5	38.8	42.1	36.8	35.4

SPECIFICATIONS

LUXURY CARS CONTINUED	Wheelbase, in.	Overall length, in.	Overall width, in.	Overall height, in.	Curb weight, lbs.	Cargo volume, cu. ft.	Fuel capacity, gals.	Seating capacity	Front head room, in.	Max. front leg room, in.	Rear head room, in.	Min. rear leg room, in.
Audi A8 4-door sedan	113.4	198.2	74.0	56.6	4068	17.6	23.0	5	38.9	41.3	38.2	38.4
BMW 5-Series 4-door sedan	111.4	188.0	70.9	56.5	3495	11.1	18.5	5	38.7	41.7	37.8	34.2
BMW 5-Series 4-door wagon	111.4	189.2	70.9	56.7	3726	65.2	18.5	5	38.7	41.7	38.5	34.2
BMW 7-Series 4-door sedan	115.4	196.2	73.3	56.5	4255	13.0	22.5	5	37.7	41.9	37.9	36.7
BMW 7-Series 4-door sedan	120.9	201.7	73.3	56.1	4288	13.0	25.1	5	37.7	41.9	38.1	41.9
Cadillac DeVille 4-door sedan	115.3	207.0	74.4	56.7	3978	19.1	18.5	6	39.1	43.2	38.3	43.2
Cadillac Eldorado 2-door coupe	108.0	200.6	75.5	53.6	3843	15.3	19.0	5	37.8	42.6	38.3	35.5
Cadillac Seville 4-door sedan	112.2	201.0	75.0	55.7	3970	15.7	18.5	5	38.2	42.5	38.0	38.2
Infiniti Q45 4-door sedan	111.4	199.6	71.7	56.9	4007	12.6	21.4	5	37.6	43.6	36.9	35.9
Jaguar S-Type 4-door sedan	114.5	191.3	71.6	55.7	3650	13.1	18.4	5	38.6	43.1	36.4	37.7
Jaguar XJ Sedan 4-door sedan	113.0	197.8	70.8	52.7	3938	12.7	23.1	5	37.2	41.2	36.3	34.3
Jaguar XJ Sedan 4-door sedan	117.9	202.7	70.8	53.2	3967	12.7	23.1	5	38.7	41.2	36.9	39.2
Jaguar XK8 2-door coupe	101.9	187.4	72.0	50.5	3709	11.1	19.9	4	37.4	43.0	33.3	NA
Jaguar XK8 2-door convertible	101.9	187.4	72.0	51.0	3943	9.5	19.9	4	37.0	43.0	33.2	NA
Lexus GS 300/400 4-door sedan	110.2	189.2	70.9	55.9	3638	14.8	19.8	5	39.0	44.5	37.4	34.3
Lexus LS 400 4-door sedan	112.2	196.7	72.0	56.5	3890	13.4	21.9	5	38.9	43.7	36.9	36.9
Lexus SC 300/400 2-door coupe	105.9	192.5	70.9	53.2	3560	9.3	20.6	4	38.3	44.1	36.1	27.2
Lincoln Continental 4-door sedan	109.0	208.5	73.6	56.0	3868	18.4	20.0	6	39.2	41.9	38.0	38.0
Lincoln Town Car 4-door sedan	117.7	215.3	78.2	58.0	4015	20.6	19.0	6	39.2	42.6	37.5	41.1
Mercedes-Benz CLK 2-door coupe	105.9	180.2	67.8	54.0	3213	11.0	16.4	4	36.9	41.9	35.8	31.2
Mercedes-Benz CLK 2-door convertible	105.9	180.2	67.8	54.3	3566	9.5	16.4	4	37.5	41.9	36.5	27.4
Mercedes-Benz CL500 2-door coupe	113.6	196.6	73.1	55.0	4115	12.3	23.3	4	36.9	41.7	36.8	30.8
Mercedes-Benz E-Class 4-door sedan	111.5	189.4	70.8	56.7	3691	15.3	21.1	5	37.6	41.3	37.2	36.1
Mercedes-Benz E-Class 4-door wagon	111.5	190.4	70.8	59.3	3757	82.6	18.5	7	38.6	41.3	37.0	36.1
Mercedes-Benz S-Class 4-door sedan	121.5	203.1	73.1	56.9	4133	15.4	23.2	5	37.6	41.3	38.4	40.3
Mercedes-Benz SL-Class 2-door convertible	99.0	177.1	71.3	51.3	4125	7.9	21.1	2	37.1	42.4	—	—
Saab 9-5 4-door sedan	106.4	189.2	70.5	57.0	3360	15.9	18.5	5	38.7	42.4	37.6	36.6
Saab 9-5 4-door wagon	106.4	189.3	70.5	58.9	3470	73.0	18.5	5	38.7	42.4	38.2	36.6
Volvo S80 4-door sedan	109.9	189.8	72.1	57.2	3602	14.2	20.1	5	38.9	42.2	37.6	35.9

SPORTS COUPES	Wheelbase, in.	Overall length, in.	Overall width, in.	Overall height, in.	Curb weight, lbs.	Cargo volume, cu. ft.	Fuel capacity, gals.	Seating capacity	Front head room, in.	Max. front leg room, in.	Rear head room, in.	Min. rear leg room, in.
Acura Integra 2-door hatchback	101.2	172.4	67.3	52.6	2643	13.3	13.2	4	38.6	42.7	35.0	28.1
Acura Integra 4-door sedan	103.1	178.1	67.3	53.9	2703	11.0	13.2	5	38.9	42.2	36.0	32.7
Chevrolet Monte Carlo 2-door coupe	110.5	197.9	72.7	55.2	3340	15.8	17.0	5	38.1	42.4	36.5	35.8
Chrysler Sebring 2-door coupe	103.7	190.9	69.7	53.0	3155	13.1	15.9	5	37.6	43.3	36.5	35.0
Chrysler Sebring 2-door convertible	106.0	192.6	70.1	54.8	3440	11.3	16.0	5	38.7	42.4	37.0	35.2
Dodge Avenger 2-door coupe	103.7	190.2	69.1	53.0	3137	13.1	15.9	5	39.1	43.3	36.5	35.0
Honda Prelude 2-door coupe	101.8	178.0	69.0	51.8	2954	8.7	15.9	5	37.9	43.0	35.3	28.1
Hyundai Tiburon 2-door hatchback	97.4	170.9	68.1	51.7	2633	12.8	14.5	4	38.0	43.1	34.4	29.9
Mercury Cougar 2-door hatchback	106.4	185.0	69.6	52.2	2892	14.5	15.5	4	37.8	42.5	34.6	33.2
Mitsubishi Eclipse 2-door hatchback	100.8	175.4	68.9	51.6	2822	16.9	16.4	4	37.9	42.3	34.9	30.0
Toyota Celica 2-door hatchback	102.3	170.4	68.3	51.4	2425	16.9	14.5	4	38.4	44.0	35.0	27.0
Volkswagen Cabrio 2-door convertible	97.4	160.4	66.7	56.0	3079	8.0	14.5	4	38.7	42.3	36.6	31.1
Volkswagen New Beetle 2-door hatchback	98.9	161.1	67.9	59.5	2769	12.0	14.5	4	41.3	39.4	36.7	33.0

SPORTS & GT CARS	Wheelbase, in.	Overall length, in.	Overall width, in.	Overall height, in.	Curb weight, lbs.	Cargo volume, cu. ft.	Fuel capacity, gals.	Seating capacity	Front head room, in.	Max. front leg room, in.	Rear head room, in.	Min. rear leg room, in.
Acura NSX 2-door coupe	99.6	174.2	71.3	46.1	3069	5.0	18.5	2	36.3	44.3	—	—
Audi TT 2-door hatchback	95.4	159.1	73.1	53.0	2910	24.2	14.5	4	37.8	41.2	32.6	20.2
BMW Z3 Series 2-door convertible	96.3	158.5	66.6	50.7	2701	5.0	13.5	2	37.6	41.8	—	—

SPORTS & GT CARS CONTINUED

	Wheelbase, in.	Overall length, in.	Overall width, in.	Overall height, in.	Curb weight, lbs.	Cargo volume, cu. ft.	Fuel capacity, gals.	Seating capacity	Front head room, in.	Max. front leg room, in.	Rear head room, in.	Min. rear leg room, in.
BMW Z3 Series 2-door hatchback	96.3	158.5	68.5	51.4	2943	9.0	13.5	2	36.7	41.8	—	—
Chevrolet Camaro 2-door hatchback	101.1	193.5	74.1	51.2	3306	12.9	16.8	4	37.2	43.0	35.3	26.8
Chevrolet Camaro 2-door convertible	101.1	193.5	74.1	51.8	3500	7.6	16.8	4	38.0	43.0	39.0	26.8
Chevrolet Corvette 2-door hatchback	104.5	179.7	73.6	47.7	3246	24.8	19.1	2	37.9	42.7	—	—
Chevrolet Corvette 2-door coupe	104.5	179.7	73.6	47.7	3173	13.3	19.1	2	37.8	42.7	—	—
Chevrolet Corvette 2-door convertible	104.5	179.7	73.6	47.8	3248	13.9	19.1	2	37.6	42.7	—	—
Dodge Viper 2-door hatchback	96.2	176.7	75.7	47.0	3460	9.2	18.5	2	36.8	42.6	—	—
Dodge Viper 2-door convertible	96.2	176.2	75.7	44.0	3440	6.8	18.0	2	NA	42.6	—	—
Ford Mustang 2-door coupe	101.3	183.2	73.1	53.1	3069	10.9	15.7	4	38.1	42.6	35.5	29.9
Ford Mustang 2-door convertible	101.3	183.2	73.1	53.2	3211	7.7	15.7	4	38.1	42.6	35.8	29.9
Honda S2000 2-door convertible	94.5	162.0	68.9	50.6	2809	5.0	13.2	2	34.6	44.3	—	—
Mazda Miata 2-door convertible	89.2	155.3	66.0	48.4	2299	5.1	12.7	2	37.1	42.8	—	—
Mercedes-Benz SLK230 2-door convertible	94.5	157.3	67.5	50.7	2992	9.5	14.0	2	37.4	42.7	—	—
Plymouth Prowler 2-door convertible	113.3	165.3	76.5	50.9	2838	1.8	12.2	2	37.4	42.9	—	—
Pontiac Firebird 2-door hatchback	101.1	193.3	74.4	51.2	3323	33.7	16.8	4	37.2	43.0	35.2	28.8
Pontiac Firebird 2-door convertible	101.1	193.3	74.4	51.8	3402	12.9	16.8	4	38.7	43.0	39.4	28.8
Porsche 911 2-door coupe	92.6	174.5	69.5	51.4	2910	11.7	16.9	4	38.0	41.6	NA	NA
Porsche 911 2-door convertible	92.6	174.5	69.5	51.4	3075	11.7	16.9	4	38.0	41.6	NA	NA
Porsche Boxster 2-door convertible	95.2	171.0	70.1	50.8	2778	9.1	16.9	2	38.4	41.6	—	—

MINIVANS

	Wheelbase, in.	Overall length, in.	Overall width, in.	Overall height, in.	Curb weight, lbs.	Cargo volume, cu. ft.	Fuel capacity, gals.	Seating capacity	Front head room, in.	Max. front leg room, in.	Rear head room, in.	Min. rear leg room, in.
Chevrolet Astro 3-door van	111.2	189.8	77.5	74.9	4186	170.4	27.0	8	39.2	41.6	37.9	36.5
Chevrolet Venture 4-door van	112.0	186.9	72.0	67.4	3699	133.0	20.0	7	39.9	39.9	39.3	36.9
Chevrolet Venture 4-door van	120.0	200.9	72.0	68.1	3838	155.9	25.0	7	39.9	39.9	39.3	39.0
Chrysler Town & Country 4-door van	119.3	199.7	76.8	68.7	4045	163.8	20.0	7	39.8	40.6	40.0	37.2
Dodge Caravan 3-door van	113.3	186.3	76.8	68.5	3536	142.9	20.0	7	39.8	40.6	40.1	36.6
Dodge Caravan 4-door van	119.3	199.6	76.8	68.5	3836	168.5	20.0	7	39.8	40.6	40.0	39.6
Ford Windstar 3-door van	120.7	200.9	76.6	66.1	3890	145.7	26.0	7	39.3	40.7	41.1	36.8
Ford Windstar 4-door van	120.7	200.9	76.6	65.8	4194	148.5	26.0	7	39.3	40.7	40.7	38.6
GMC Safari 3-door van	111.2	189.8	77.5	75.0	4323	170.4	27.0	8	39.2	41.6	37.9	36.5
Honda Odyssey 4-door van	118.1	201.2	76.3	66.1	4233	146.1	20.0	7	41.2	41.0	40.0	40.0
Mazda MPV 4-door van	111.8	187.0	72.1	68.7	3657	127.0	18.5	7	41.0	40.8	39.3	37.0
Mercury Villager 4-door van	112.2	194.7	74.9	70.1	3944	135.6	20.0	7	39.7	39.9	39.9	36.4
Nissan Quest 4-door van	112.2	194.8	74.9	64.2	3830	135.6	20.0	7	39.7	39.9	39.9	36.4
Oldsmobile Silhouette 4-door van	120.0	201.4	72.2	68.1	3948	155.9	25.0	7	39.9	39.9	39.3	39.0
Plymouth Voyager 3-door van	113.3	186.3	76.8	68.5	3516	142.9	20.0	7	39.8	40.6	40.1	36.6
Plymouth Voyager 4-door van	119.3	199.6	76.8	68.5	3683	168.5	20.0	7	39.8	40.6	40.0	39.6
Pontiac Montana 4-door van	112.0	187.3	72.7	67.4	3803	133.0	20.0	8	39.9	39.9	39.3	36.9
Pontiac Montana 4-door van	120.0	201.3	72.7	68.1	3942	155.9	25.0	8	39.9	39.9	39.3	39.0
Toyota Sienna 3-door van	114.2	193.5	73.4	67.3	3760	131.0	21.0	7	40.6	41.9	40.7	36.5
Toyota Sienna 4-door van	114.2	193.5	73.4	67.3	3881	143.0	21.0	7	40.6	41.9	40.7	36.5
Volkswagen EuroVan 3-door van	115.0	188.5	72.4	76.4	4220	190.7	21.1	7	39.3	37.8	41.3	28.3
Volkswagen EuroVan 3-door van	130.7	204.3	72.4	80.0	5235	NA	21.1	6	39.3	37.8	33.5	25.2

COMPACT SPORT-UTILITY VEHICLES

	Wheelbase, in.	Overall length, in.	Overall width, in.	Overall height, in.	Curb weight, lbs.	Cargo volume, cu. ft.	Fuel capacity, gals.	Seating capacity	Front head room, in.	Max. front leg room, in.	Rear head room, in.	Min. rear leg room, in.
Chevrolet Tracker 2-door convertible	86.6	151.8	67.3	66.5	2723	33.7	14.8	4	40.9	41.4	39.5	35.9
Chevrolet Tracker 4-door wagon	97.6	162.8	67.3	66.3	2987	44.7	17.4	5	39.9	41.4	39.6	35.9
Honda CR-V 4-door wagon	103.2	177.6	68.9	65.9	3126	67.2	15.3	5	40.5	41.5	39.2	36.7
Isuzu Amigo 2-door convertible	96.9	168.0	71.4	67.0	3329	62.4	17.7	5	38.9	42.1	37.3	33.3

COMPACT SPORT-UTILITY VEHICLES CONTINUED

	Wheelbase, in.	Overall length, in.	Overall width, in.	Overall height, in.	Curb weight, lbs.	Cargo volume, cu. ft.	Fuel capacity, gals.	Seating capacity	Front head room, in.	Max. front leg room, in.	Rear head room, in.	Min. rear leg room, in.
Isuzu VehiCross 2-door wagon	91.8	162.6	70.5	66.9	3955	50.4	22.5	4	38.2	43.1	35.4	29.5
Jeep Wrangler 2-door convertible	93.4	155.4	66.7	71.1	3094	55.2	19.0	4	42.3	41.1	40.6	34.9
Kia Sportage 2-door convertible	92.9	156.4	68.1	65.0	3108	39.4	14.0	4	39.6	41.3	38.2	31.0
Kia Sportage 4-door wagon	104.4	159.4	68.1	65.2	3280	55.4	15.8	5	39.6	44.5	37.8	31.1
Subaru Forester 4-door wagon	99.4	175.2	68.3	65.0	3125	64.6	15.9	5	40.6	43.0	39.6	33.4
Suzuki Vitara 2-door convertible	86.6	152.0	67.3	66.5	2756	44.7	14.8	4	40.9	41.4	39.5	35.9
Suzuki Vitara 4-door wagon	97.6	164.6	70.0	68.5	3197	44.6	17.4	5	39.3	41.4	39.6	35.9
Toyota RAV4 4-door wagon	94.9	163.8	66.7	65.4	2844	57.9	15.3	5	40.3	39.5	39.0	33.9

MIDSIZE SPORT-UTILITY VEHICLES

	Wheelbase, in.	Overall length, in.	Overall width, in.	Overall height, in.	Curb weight, lbs.	Cargo volume, cu. ft.	Fuel capacity, gals.	Seating capacity	Front head room, in.	Max. front leg room, in.	Rear head room, in.	Min. rear leg room, in.
BMW X5 4-door wagon	111.0	183.7	73.7	67.2	4828	54.8	24.3	5	38.9	39.3	38.5	35.4
Chevrolet Blazer 2-door wagon	100.5	176.8	67.8	64.9	3671	66.9	19.0	4	39.6	42.4	38.3	35.6
Chevrolet Blazer 4-door wagon	107.0	183.3	67.8	64.3	4049	74.1	18.0	6	39.6	42.4	38.3	36.3
Dodge Durango 4-door wagon	115.9	193.3	71.5	71.0	4360	88.0	25.0	8	39.8	41.9	40.4	37.3
Ford Explorer 2-door wagon	101.7	180.8	70.2	67.1	3898	69.4	17.5	4	39.9	42.4	39.3	34.5
Ford Explorer 4-door wagon	111.6	190.7	70.2	67.7	4128	81.6	21.0	6	39.9	42.4	39.3	36.8
GMC Jimmy 2-door wagon	100.5	177.3	67.8	64.9	3869	66.9	19.0	4	39.6	42.4	38.3	35.6
GMC Jimmy/Envoy 4-door wagon	107.0	183.8	67.8	64.2	4114	74.1	18.0	5	39.6	42.4	38.2	36.3
Honda Passport 4-door wagon	106.4	178.2	70.4	68.6	3774	81.1	21.1	5	38.9	42.1	38.3	35.0
Infiniti QX4 4-door wagon	106.3	183.9	72.4	70.7	4320	85.0	21.1	5	38.1	41.7	37.5	31.8
Isuzu Rodeo 4-door wagon	106.4	176.7	70.4	68.8	3651	81.1	21.1	5	38.9	42.1	38.3	35.0
Jeep Cherokee 2-door wagon	101.4	167.5	69.4	64.0	3181	66.0	20.0	5	37.7	41.4	38.0	35.0
Jeep Cherokee 4-door wagon	101.4	167.5	69.4	64.0	3226	66.0	20.0	5	37.8	41.4	38.0	35.0
Jeep Grand Cherokee 4-door wagon	105.9	181.5	72.3	69.4	3955	72.3	20.5	5	39.7	41.4	39.5	35.3
Land Rover Discovery 4-door wagon	100.0	185.2	74.4	76.4	4576	63.3	24.6	7	40.4	42.3	40.1	37.3
Lexus RX 300 4-door wagon	103.0	180.1	71.5	65.7	3900	75.0	17.2	5	39.5	40.7	39.2	36.4
Mercedes-Benz M-Class 4-door wagon	111.0	180.6	72.2	69.9	4586	85.4	19.0	7	39.8	40.3	39.7	38.0
Mercury Mountaineer 4-door wagon	111.6	190.7	70.2	70.5	4250	79.1	21.0	5	39.9	42.4	39.3	35.8
Mitsubishi Montero Sport 4-door wagon	107.3	178.3	66.7	65.6	3980	79.3	19.5	5	38.9	42.8	37.3	33.5
Nissan Pathfinder 4-door wagon	106.3	182.7	69.7	67.9	3886	85.0	21.1	5	39.5	41.7	37.5	31.8
Nissan Xterra 4-door wagon	104.3	178.0	70.4	69.4	3668	65.6	19.4	5	38.6	41.4	37.5	32.8
Oldsmobile Bravada 4-door wagon	107.0	183.7	67.8	64.2	4049	74.1	18.6	5	39.6	42.4	38.2	36.3
Toyota 4Runner 4-door wagon	105.3	183.3	66.5	67.5	3725	79.8	18.5	5	39.3	42.6	38.7	34.9

FULL-SIZE SPORT-UTILITY VEHICLES

	Wheelbase, in.	Overall length, in.	Overall width, in.	Overall height, in.	Curb weight, lbs.	Cargo volume, cu. ft.	Fuel capacity, gals.	Seating capacity	Front head room, in.	Max. front leg room, in.	Rear head room, in.	Min. rear leg room, in.
Cadillac Escalade 4-door wagon	117.5	201.2	77.0	74.3	5572	118.2	29.5		39.9	41.7	38.9	36.4
Chevrolet Tahoe 4-door wagon	116.0	198.9	78.9	74.0	5050	108.2	26.0	9	40.7	41.3	39.4	38.6
Chevrolet Suburban 4-door wagon	130.0	219.3	78.8	73.3	5123	138.4	33.0	9	40.7	41.3	39.0	39.1
Chevrolet Tahoe Limited and Z71 4-door wgn.	117.5	199.6	76.8	72.4	4419	118.2	30.0	5	43.3	41.7	38.9	36.4
Ford Excursion 4-door wagon	137.0	226.7	80.0	79.7	7087	146.4	44.0	9	41.0	42.3	41.1	40.5
Ford Expedition 4-door wagon	119.1	204.6	78.6	76.6	5198	118.3	26.0	9	39.8	40.9	39.8	38.9
GMC Yukon 4-door wagon	116.0	198.8	78.8	76.5	5050	104.6	26.0	9	40.7	41.3	39.4	38.6
GMC Yukon XL 4-door wagon	130.0	219.3	78.9	75.7	5123	138.4	32.5	9	40.7	41.3	39.0	39.1
GMC Yukon Denali 4-door wagon	117.5	201.4	78.8	74.3	5564	118.2	29.5	5	39.9	41.7	38.9	36.2
Isuzu Trooper 4-door wagon	108.7	187.8	69.5	72.2	4455	90.2	22.5	5	39.8	40.8	39.8	39.1
Land Rover Range Rover 4-door wagon	108.1	185.5	74.4	71.6	4960	58.0	24.6	5	38.1	42.6	38.2	36.5
Lexus LX 470 4-door wagon	112.2	192.5	76.4	72.8	5401	90.4	25.4	8	40.0	42.3	39.4	34.3

FULL-SIZE SPORT-UTILITY VEHICLES CONTINUED

	Wheelbase, in.	Overall length, in.	Overall width, in.	Overall height, in.	Curb weight, lbs.	Cargo volume, cu. ft.	Fuel capacity, gals.	Seating capacity	Front head room, in.	Max. front leg room, in.	Rear head room, in.	Min. rear leg room, in.
Lincoln Navigator 4-door wagon	119.0	204.8	82.5	75.4	5198	116.4	30.0	8	39.8	40.9	39.8	39.7
Mitsubishi Montero 4-door wagon	107.3	186.6	69.9	74.8	4431	67.1	24.3	7	40.9	40.3	40.0	37.6
Toyota Land Cruiser 4-door wagon	112.2	192.5	76.4	73.2	511597.590.8		25.4	8	40.6	42.3	39.8	34.3

COMPACT PICKUP TRUCKS

	Wheelbase, in.	Overall length, in.	Overall width, in.	Overall height, in.	Curb weight, lbs.	Standard payload, lbs.	Fuel capacity, gals.	Seating capacity	Front head room, in.	Max. front leg room, in.	Rear head room, in.	Min. rear leg room, in.
Chevrolet S-10 regular cab short bed	108.3	190.1	67.9	62.0	3031	1169	19.0	3	39.5	42.4	—	—
Chevrolet S-10 regular cab long bed	117.9	206.1	67.9	62.9	3102	1160	19.0	3	39.5	42.4	—	—
Chevrolet S-10 extended cab	122.9	204.8	67.9	62.7	3240	1086	19.0	5	39.6	42.4	39.6	NA
Dodge Dakota regular cab short bed	111.9	195.8	71.5	65.6	3378	1275	22.0	3	40.0	41.9	—	—
Dodge Dakota extended cab	131.0	214.8	71.5	65.6	3611	1275	22.0	6	40.0	41.9	38.0	22.1
Dodge Dakota crew cab	131.0	215.1	71.6	66.3	4124	1450	24.0	6	39.8	41.9	38.4	36
Ford Ranger regular cab short bed	111.6	187.5	69.4	64.9	3080	1260	16.5	3	39.2	42.2	—	—
Ford Ranger regular cab long bed	117.5	200.7	69.4	64.9	3100	1260	20.0	3	39.2	42.2	—	—
Ford Ranger extended cab	125.7	202.9	69.4	64.8	3280	1260	20.0	5	39.3	42.2	NA	NA
GMC Sonoma regular cab short bed	108.3	190.6	67.9	62.0	3112	1160	18.5	3	39.5	42.4	—	—
GMC Sonoma regular cab long bed	117.9	206.6	67.9	62.9	3367	1489	18.5	3	39.5	42.4	—	—
GMC Sonoma extended cab short bed	122.9	205.3	67.9	62.7	3274	1126	18.5	5	39.6	42.4	39.6	NA
Isuzu Hombre regular cab	108.3	187.1	67.9	63.9	3125	1138	18.5	3	39.5	42.4	—	—
Isuzu Hombre extended cab	122.9	201.7	67.9	63.9	3305	1154	18.5	5	39.6	42.4	NA	NA
Mazda B-Series regular cab	111.6	187.5	69.4	64.9	2998	1260	16.5	3	39.2	42.4	—	—
Mazda B-Series extended cab	125.7	202.9	70.3	64.7	3210	1260	19.5	5	39.2	42.2	35.6	40.3
Nissan Frontier regular cab	104.3	184.3	66.5	62.8	2911	1400	15.9	3	39.3	40.9	—	—
Nissan Frontier extended cab	116.1	196.1	71.9	65.9	3685	1400	15.9	5	39.3	41.4	NA	NA
Nissan Frontier crew cab	116.1	193.1	71.9	65.9	3742	1200	19.4	5	39.3	41.1	37.8	30.7
Toyota Tacoma regular cab	103.3	184.5	66.5	62.0	2580	1914	15.1	3	38.2	41.7	—	—
Toyota Tacoma extended cab	121.9	203.1	66.5	62.2	2760	1759	15.1	5	38.4	42.8	35.5	27.2

FULL-SIZE PICKUP TRUCKS

	Wheelbase, in.	Overall length, in.	Overall width, in.	Overall height, in.	Curb weight, lbs.	Standard payload, lbs.	Fuel capacity, gals.	Seating capacity	Front head room, in.	Max. front leg room, in.	Rear head room, in.	Min. rear leg room, in.
Chevrolet Silverado 1500 reg. cab short bed	119.0	203.3	78.5	71.2	3923	2177	26.0	3	41.0	41.3	—	—
Chevrolet Silverado 1500 reg. cab long bed	133.0	222.0	78.5	71.0	4032	2368	34.0	3	41.0	41.3	—	—
Chevrolet Silverado 1500 ext. cab short bed	143.5	227.5	78.5	71.2	4235	1965	26.0	6	41.0	41.3	38.4	33.7
Chevrolet Silverado 1500 ext. cab long bed	157.5	246.7	78.5	70.8	4442	1757	34.0	6	41.0	41.3	38.4	33.7
Dodge Ram 1500 regular cab short bed	119.0	204.1	79.4	71.9	4136	2264	26.0	3	40.2	41.0	—	—
Dodge Ram 1500 regular cab long bed	135.0	224.1	79.4	71.8	4298	2102	35.0	3	40.2	41.0	—	—
Dodge Ram 1500 extended cab short bed	139.0	224.1	79.3	71.6	4790	1610	26.0	6	40.2	41.0	39.4	31.6
Dodge Ram 1500 extended cab long bed	155.0	244.1	79.3	71.5	4946	1454	35.0	6	40.2	41.0	39.4	31.6
Ford F-150 regular cab short bed	119.9	205.6	78.4	72.7	4028	1675	25.0	3	40.8	40.9	—	—
Ford F-150 regular cab long bed	138.5	224.2	78.4	72.1	4339	1780	30.0	3	40.8	40.9	—	—
Ford F-150 extended cab short bed	138.5	222.9	79.3	72.8	4575	1765	25.0	6	42.5	40.9	37.8	32.2
Ford F-150 extended cab long bed	157.1	242.8	78.4	72.4	4658	1575	30.0	6	42.5	40.9	37.8	32.2
Ford F-150 crew cab short bed	139.0	225.9	79.8	74.6	4581	1765	25.0	6	39.8	41.0	39.8	36.8
GMC Sierra 1500 regular cab short bed	119.0	203.2	78.5	71.2	3956	2145	26.0	3	41.0	41.3	—	—
GMC Sierra 1500 regular cab long bed	133.0	222.1	78.5	71.0	4066	2334	34.0	3	41.0	41.3	—	—
GMC Sierra 1500 extended cab short bed	143.5	227.5	78.5	71.2	4289	1911	26.0	6	41.0	41.3	38.4	33.7
GMC Sierra 1500 extended cab long bed	157.5	246.6	78.5	70.8	4511	1689	34.0	6	41.0	41.3	38.4	33.7
Toyota Tundra regular cab long bed	128.3	217.5	75.2	70.5	3795	1705	26.4	3	40.3	41.5	NA	NA
Toyota Tundra extended cab short bed	128.3	217.5	75.2	70.7	4088	1612	26.4	6	40.3	41.5	37.0	29.6

RATINGS

The editors rate each model from a low of 1 to a high of 5 in 11 categories covering performance, room, comfort, and ergonomics. Each model also is rated for overall value based on its price. The ratings are derived from our road tests. Space allows only one version of a vehicle to be rated, usually the most popular model in the line. It's important to note that we rate cars, trucks, minivans, and sport-utility vehicles against the universe of vehicles, not against other models in their class. For example, a rating of 2 in Fuel Economy for a Chevrolet Blazer indicates below-average mileage compared to all vehicles, not just SUVs. **Note:** The cargo-room rating for pickup trucks refers to in-cab storage space and is not a measure of cargo-bed capacity. For all other vehicles, the cargo-room rating is based on the vehicle's maximum cargo volume, meaning with all rear seats folded or removed, when possible.

SUBCOMPACT CARS	Acceleration	Fuel Economy	Ride Quality	Steering/ Handling	Braking	Quietness	Driver Seating	Instruments Controls	Room and Comfort (front)	Room and Comfort (rear)	Cargo Room	Value for the Money	TOTAL
R **Chevrolet Cavalier base 2-door**	2	4	3	3	4	3	3	4	3	2	3	5	39
Chevrolet Metro LSi 4-door	2	4	1	2	2	2	3	3	2	2	3	2	28
R **Chevrolet Prizm base/LSi**	3	4	3	3	3	3	4	4	4	2	3	5	41
Daewoo Lanos SX 4-door	2	4	2	3	2	2	2	3	2	2	3	2	29
✓ **Dodge Neon 4-door, automatic**	3	4	3	4	3	3	4	4	4	3	3	4	42
Ford Escort 4-door	3	4	2	3	2	2	4	4	2	2	2	5	35
R **Honda Civic EX 4-door**	3	5	4	4	4	4	4	4	4	3	3	5	47
Honda Insight	2	5	3	4	4	2	4	5	2	—	1	2	34
Hyundai Accent GL, automatic	2	4	2	2	2	2	3	3	2	2	2	2	28
Hyundai Elantra 4-door, 5-speed	3	5	3	3	3	2	4	3	4	3	2	4	39
Kia Sephia LS w/Power Pkg.	3	4	2	3	2	2	4	3	2	2	1	2	30
R **Mazda Protege DX/LX, automatic**	2	4	4	3	3	2	4	4	3	3	2	4	38
Mitsubishi Mirage LS 4-door	3	4	2	4	2	2	3	3	2	2	2	3	32
Pontiac Sunfire GT 2-door	4	4	3	4	3	3	3	4	3	2	2	4	39
Subaru Impreza L 4-door	3	4	3	3	3	2	3	4	2	2	2	2	33
Suzuki Esteem 4-door	3	4	1	2	2	2	3	3	3	3	2	3	31
R **Toyota Corolla VE, CE, LE**	3	4	3	3	4	4	4	4	4	2	2	5	42
Toyota Echo 4-door, 5-speed	3	4	3	3	3	3	4	3	3	3	2	4	38
R **Volkswagen Jetta GL/GLS, 4-cyl.**	3	4	4	4	4	3	4	4	4	2	3	4	43

COMPACT CARS	Acceleration	Fuel Economy	Ride Quality	Steering/ Handling	Braking	Quietness	Driver Seating	Instruments Controls	Room and Comfort (front)	Room and Comfort (rear)	Cargo Room	Value for the Money	TOTAL
Daewoo Leganza CDX	2	3	4	3	4	3	3	3	3	3	3	3	37
Ford Contour Sport	4	3	3	4	4	3	3	4	3	2	2	4	39
Hyundai Sonata GLS	3	3	4	2	3	4	4	3	3	3	3	2	37
✓ **Mazda 626 LX/ES, 4-cylinder**	3	4	4	4	4	4	4	4	4	3	3	4	45
R **Mitsubishi Galant ES, 4-cylinder**	3	3	4	4	4	4	4	3	4	3	3	4	43
R **Nissan Altima XE/GXE**	3	3	4	3	4	4	3	3	4	3	3	4	41
R **Oldsmobile Alero GL 4-door, 4-cyl.**	3	3	3	3	4	4	3	4	3	3	3	4	40
Pontiac Grand Am SE2 2-door, V6	4	3	3	4	3	3	3	3	3	3	3	3	38
Subaru Legacy L 4-door	3	3	3	3	4	4	2	4	4	3	3	4	40
Subaru Outback Limited	3	3	3	3	3	4	2	4	4	3	5	4	41
R **Volkswagen Passat GLS 4-dr., 4-cyl.**	3	3	4	4	4	4	4	4	4	4	4	3	45

MIDSIZE CARS	Acceleration	Fuel Economy	Ride Quality	Steering/ Handling	Braking	Quietness	Driver Seating	Instruments Controls	Room and Comfort (front)	Room and Comfort (rear)	Cargo Room	Value for the Money	TOTAL
R **Buick Century Custom/Limited**	3	3	4	3	3	4	3	3	4	4	4	3	41
Buick Regal LS	4	3	4	3	4	3	3	4	4	4	4	4	44
Chevrolet Impala LS	4	3	4	4	3	4	3	4	4	3	4	4	44
Chevrolet Lumina	3	3	4	3	3	4	3	4	4	4	3	4	42
R **Chevrolet Malibu**	4	3	4	3	4	3	4	4	4	3	4	4	44
Chrysler Cirrus LXi	3	3	3	4	3	3	4	4	4	4	3	3	41

Rating Scale: ✓-Best Buy; R-Recommended; 5-Excellent; 4-Above average; 3-Average; 2-Below average; 1-Poor

MIDSIZE CARS CONT.

	Acceleration	Fuel Economy	Ride Quality	Steering/ Handling	Braking	Quietness	Driver Seating	Instruments Controls	Room and Comfort (front)	Room and Comfort (rear)	Cargo Room	Value for the Money	TOTAL
Dodge Stratus ES, V6	3	3	3	4	3	3	4	4	4	4	3	4	42
Ford Taurus SE sedan, dohc V6	3	2	3	4	3	4	4	3	3	4	4	4	41
✓ **Honda Accord LX/EX 4-door**	3	4	4	4	4	3	4	4	4	3	3	5	45
R **Nissan Maxima SE**	4	3	4	4	4	4	4	4	4	4	3	4	46
R **Oldsmobile Intrigue GX/GL/GLS**	4	3	4	4	4	4	4	4	4	4	4	4	47
Plymouth Breeze, 2.0-liter 4-cylinder	3	4	3	4	3	2	4	4	4	4	3	4	42
R **Pontiac Grand Prix GTP 2-door**	5	2	3	4	4	3	4	4	4	3	3	3	42
Saturn LS1	3	4	3	4	4	4	4	4	4	3	4	4	44
✓ **Toyota Camry LE/XLE, 4-cylinder**	3	3	5	3	4	4	4	4	4	3	2	5	44

FULL-SIZE CARS

	Acceleration	Fuel Economy	Ride Quality	Steering/ Handling	Braking	Quietness	Driver Seating	Instruments Controls	Room and Comfort (front)	Room and Comfort (rear)	Cargo Room	Value for the Money	TOTAL
R **Buick LeSabre Custom**	4	2	4	3	4	4	3	4	4	3	4	4	43
✓ **Chrysler Concorde LX, 2.7 V6**	3	3	4	4	3	4	4	4	4	4	4	4	45
✓ **Dodge Intrepid ES, 3.2 V6**	4	3	4	4	3	3	4	4	4	4	4	4	45
Ford Crown Victoria base/LX	4	2	4	3	3	4	3	3	5	4	4	4	43
Mercury Grand Marquis GS/LS	4	2	4	3	3	4	3	3	5	4	4	4	43
Pontiac Bonneville SE	4	2	4	3	4	4	4	4	4	4	4	4	45
R **Toyota Avalon XLS**	4	3	5	3	4	4	4	3	4	4	4	4	46

NEAR-LUXURY CARS

	Acceleration	Fuel Economy	Ride Quality	Steering/ Handling	Braking	Quietness	Driver Seating	Instruments Controls	Room and Comfort (front)	Room and Comfort (rear)	Cargo Room	Value for the Money	TOTAL
✓ **Acura TL**	4	4	3	4	4	4	4	3	4	3	3	5	45
Audi A4 2.8	4	3	4	4	4	3	4	3	4	3	3	3	42
R **Audi A6 4-door**	4	3	4	4	4	4	5	4	4	4	4	4	48
BMW 328i	5	3	5	4	5	4	3	4	4	3	2	3	45
R **Buick Park Avenue base**	4	3	4	3	4	4	3	4	4	4	4	4	45
Cadillac Catera	3	3	3	3	4	3	4	3	4	3	4	3	40
Chrysler LHS/300M	4	3	4	3	4	3	4	4	4	4	4	4	45
Infiniti G20/G20t	3	4	4	4	5	4	4	3	3	3	3	3	43
R **Infiniti I30**	4	3	4	4	4	4	4	5	4	4	3	4	47
R **Lexus ES 300**	4	3	5	3	4	5	5	5	4	3	3	5	49
Lincoln LS, V8	4	3	4	4	4	4	4	3	4	3	3	4	44
Mazda Millenia S	4	3	4	4	4	4	4	4	4	3	3	3	44
Mercedes-Benz C280	4	3	3	4	5	4	4	3	3	2	2	4	41
Mitsubishi Diamante	4	3	4	3	4	4	4	3	4	3	3	4	43
Saab 9-3 4-door hatchback	4	3	4	4	5	4	4	3	4	3	4	3	45
Volvo S40	3	3	4	4	4	3	4	3	4	3	3	3	41
Volvo S70 base	3	3	4	4	4	3	4	4	4	4	4	3	44

LUXURY CARS

	Acceleration	Fuel Economy	Ride Quality	Steering/ Handling	Braking	Quietness	Driver Seating	Instruments Controls	Room and Comfort (front)	Room and Comfort (rear)	Cargo Room	Value for the Money	TOTAL
✓ **Acura 3.5RL**	4	2	4	4	4	4	4	4	4	3	3	3	43
Audi A8	5	2	4	4	5	4	4	3	4	4	4	2	45
R **BMW 528i 4-door**	4	3	5	4	5	4	5	3	4	3	2	4	46
BMW 740iL	4	2	5	4	5	5	5	3	5	5	3	3	49
R **Cadillac DeVille Base/DHS**	5	2	4	3	4	4	4	3	5	5	4	4	47

Rating Scale: ✓-Best Buy; **R**-Recommended; 5-Excellent; 4-Above average; 3-Average; 2-Below average; 1-Poor

LUXURY CARS CONTINUED	Acceleration	Fuel Economy	Ride Quality	Steering/ Handling	Braking	Quietness	Driver Seating	Instruments Controls	Room and Comfort (front)	Room and Comfort (rear)	Cargo Room	Value for the Money	TOTAL
Cadillac Eldorado base	5	2	4	3	4	4	3	3	4	2	3	3	40
Cadillac Seville SLS	5	2	4	4	4	5	4	3	4	4	3	4	46
Infiniti Q45t	4	2	4	3	4	5	4	4	4	3	2	3	42
R **Jaguar S-Type, V6**	4	3	4	4	4	4	4	3	3	2	2	4	41
Jaguar XJ8L/Vanden Plas	4	2	5	4	5	5	3	3	4	4	2	3	44
Jaguar XK8 convertible	5	2	4	4	4	3	3	4	4	1	2	2	38
R **Lexus GS 300**	4	2	4	4	4	4	4	3	4	3	3	3	42
✓ **Lexus LS 400**	5	3	4	3	4	5	5	5	5	4	3	4	50
Lexus SC 400	5	3	4	4	4	4	3	4	3	1	1	4	40
Lincoln Continental	4	3	4	3	4	4	4	4	4	3	4	4	45
Lincoln Town Car	3	2	4	3	3	5	3	4	5	4	4	4	44
R **Mercedes-Benz CLK320 2-door**	4	3	3	4	5	4	4	3	3	2	1	3	39
✓ **Mercedes-Benz E320 4-door**	4	3	4	4	5	4	5	3	4	4	3	4	45
Mercedes-Benz S500	5	1	5	4	5	5	5	3	5	5	3	3	47
Mercedes-Benz SL500	5	2	3	4	5	4	5	3	4	—	2	2	37
Saab 9-5 4-door, 4-cylinder auto.	4	3	4	4	4	4	4	3	4	4	4	3	45
Volvo S80, 2.9	4	3	4	4	5	4	4	4	4	4	4	3	47

SPORTS COUPES	Acceleration	Fuel Economy	Ride Quality	Steering/ Handling	Braking	Quietness	Driver Seating	Instruments Controls	Room and Comfort (front)	Room and Comfort (rear)	Cargo Room	Value for the Money	TOTAL
Acura Integra GS-R 2-door	4	4	3	4	4	3	3	4	3	2	3	4	41
Chevrolet Monte Carlo SS	3	3	3	4	4	3	3	4	4	3	3	4	41
R **Chrysler Sebring JXi**	3	3	4	4	4	2	3	4	4	3	2	4	40
Dodge Avenger ES, V6	3	3	3	4	4	2	3	3	4	3	2	4	38
✓ **Honda Prelude base, automatic**	4	3	3	4	4	3	3	4	3	1	1	4	37
Hyundai Tiburon base, automatic	2	4	3	4	3	2	3	4	2	1	3	3	34
Mercury Cougar, V6 automatic	3	3	3	4	4	3	3	3	3	2	3	3	37
Mitsubishi Eclipse GS, 5-speed	4	3	3	4	4	3	4	3	3	1	4	4	40
Toyota Celica GT, automatic	3	4	3	4	4	2	3	3	3	1	3	3	36
Volkswagen Cabrio GL/GLS	3	4	3	4	4	3	4	4	3	2	1	3	38
✓ **Volkswagen New Beetle, 2.0 auto.**	3	4	3	4	4	3	4	4	4	2	3	4	42

SPORTS & GT CARS	Acceleration	Fuel Economy	Ride Quality	Steering/ Handling	Braking	Quietness	Driver Seating	Instruments Controls	Room and Comfort (front)	Room and Comfort (rear)	Cargo Room	Value for the Money	TOTAL
Acura NSX	5	3	2	5	5	2	3	4	3	—	1	2	35
Audi TT	4	4	2	4	4	2	4	4	3	1	3	2	37
R **BMW Z3 2.8 convertible**	5	3	3	5	5	2	3	3	3	—	1	3	36
Chevrolet Camaro hatchback, V6	4	3	3	4	4	2	3	4	3	2	2	3	37
✓ **Chevrolet Corvette hatchback**	5	3	3	5	5	2	3	4	3	—	4	4	41
Dodge Viper GTS	5	1	2	5	5	1	3	4	3	—	2	2	33
Ford Mustang base 2-door, auto.	3	3	3	4	3	2	3	4	3	2	2	4	36
Honda S2000	5	3	2	5	5	1	4	4	3	—	1	4	37
✓ **Mazda Miata**	4	4	3	5	4	2	3	4	3	—	1	4	37
R **Mercedes-Benz SLK**	4	3	3	5	5	3	4	4	4	—	2	2	39
Plymouth Prowler	5	2	2	4	3	2	2	2	3	—	1	2	28
Pontiac Firebird Formula/Trans Am	5	2	2	5	4	2	3	4	3	2	2	3	37
Porsche 911 2-door	5	3	2	5	5	2	3	2	3	1	1	2	34
Porsche Boxster	5	3	2	5	5	2	3	2	3	—	1	3	34

Rating Scale: ✓-Best Buy; **R**-Recommended; 5-Excellent; 4-Above average; 3-Average; 2-Below average; 1-Poor

MINIVANS

	MINIVANS	Acceleration	Fuel Economy	Ride Quality	Steering/ Handling	Braking	Quietness	Driver Seating	Instruments Controls	Room and Comfort (front)	Room and Comfort (rear)	Cargo Room	Value for the Money	TOTAL
	Chevrolet Astro 2WD	4	2	3	2	2	3	2	4	2	4	5	3	36
R	**Chevrolet Venture 4-dr. ext. length**	3	2	4	3	3	4	4	4	4	4	5	4	44
	Chrysler Town & Country LXi, 3.8 V6	4	2	4	3	3	3	4	4	4	5	5	4	45
✓	**Dodge Grand Caravan, 3.3 V6**	3	2	4	3	3	3	4	4	4	5	5	5	45
R	**Ford Windstar LX**	4	2	3	3	3	4	4	3	4	5	5	4	44
	GMC Safari SLX AWD	3	1	2	2	2	3	2	4	2	4	5	3	33
✓	**Honda Odyssey LX/EX**	3	3	4	3	4	4	4	3	4	4	5	5	46
	Mazda MPV LX	2	3	3	3	4	3	4	4	4	4	5	3	42
	Mercury Villager Sport	3	2	3	3	3	3	3	4	3	3	5	3	38
	Nissan Quest GXE	3	3	3	3	3	3	3	4	3	3	5	3	39
	Oldsmobile Silhouette	3	2	4	3	3	4	4	4	4	4	5	4	44
✓	**Plymouth Voyager base, 4-cylinder**	2	3	3	3	3	3	4	4	4	5	5	4	43
	Pontiac Montana 4-door ext. length	3	2	4	3	3	4	4	4	4	4	5	4	44
R	**Toyota Sienna CE, LE, XLE**	3	3	4	3	3	4	4	4	4	5	5	4	45
	Volkswagen Eurovan GLS	2	2	3	2	2	2	3	3	4	5	5	2	35

COMPACT SPORT-UTILITY VEHICLES

	COMPACT SPORT-UTILITY VEHICLES	Acceleration	Fuel Economy	Ride Quality	Steering/ Handling	Braking	Quietness	Driver Seating	Instruments Controls	Room and Comfort (front)	Room and Comfort (rear)	Cargo Room	Value for the Money	TOTAL
	Chevrolet Tracker 4-door 4WD	2	3	2	2	2	2	3	3	3	2	4	3	31
✓	**Honda CR-V**	2	3	3	3	3	3	4	4	3	3	5	4	40
	Isuzu Amigo, V6	4	2	2	2	3	2	3	3	3	2	4	3	33
	Isuzu VehiCross	4	2	2	3	3	2	4	3	3	2	2	1	31
	Jeep Wrangler SE, 4-cylinder	2	3	1	2	3	1	3	4	3	2	4	4	32
	Kia Sportage 4-door	2	3	2	2	3	2	4	4	3	3	4	3	35
✓	**Subaru Forester L**	3	3	3	3	4	3	4	3	3	2	5	4	40
	Suzuki Grand Vitara	3	3	2	2	2	3	3	3	3	2	4	3	33
R	**Toyota RAV4 4-door, automatic**	2	3	2	2	3	2	3	3	3	3	4	3	33

MIDSIZE SPORT-UTILITY VEHICLES

	MIDSIZE SPORT-UTILITY VEHICLES	Acceleration	Fuel Economy	Ride Quality	Steering/ Handling	Braking	Quietness	Driver Seating	Instruments Controls	Room and Comfort (front)	Room and Comfort (rear)	Cargo Room	Value for the Money	TOTAL
	Chevrolet Blazer 4-door 4WD	4	2	3	2	2	3	3	3	4	3	5	4	38
R	**Dodge Durango SLT 4WD, 4.7 V8**	3	1	3	2	2	3	4	4	4	3	5	4	38
✓	**Ford Explorer XLT 4-door, ohc V6**	4	2	2	2	3	2	4	4	4	3	5	4	39
	GMC Jimmy 4-door 4WD	4	2	3	2	2	3	3	3	4	3	5	4	38
	Honda Passport EX 4WD	3	2	2	2	3	2	4	3	4	3	5	2	35
	Infiniti QX4	3	2	3	2	4	3	4	4	4	3	5	3	40
	Isuzu Rodeo 4WD, V6	3	2	2	2	3	2	4	3	4	3	4	2	34
	Jeep Cherokee Sport 4-door	4	2	2	2	3	2	2	4	3	3	5	4	36
	Jeep Grand Cherokee Laredo, 6-cyl.	3	2	3	2	3	2	4	4	4	3	5	3	38
	Land Rover Discovery	3	2	3	2	3	3	3	3	4	4	5	3	38
✓	**Lexus RX 300 4WD**	4	2	4	3	4	4	4	3	4	4	5	4	45
✓	**Mercedes-Benz ML320**	3	2	3	3	4	4	4	4	4	4	5	4	44
R	**Mercury Mountaineer AWD, V8**	4	1	2	2	3	2	4	4	4	3	5	4	38
	Mitsubishi Montero Sport LS/XLS	3	2	2	2	3	2	2	3	3	3	4	3	32
	Nissan Pathfinder 4WD, automatic	2	2	2	2	4	3	4	4	4	3	5	3	38
R	**Nissan Xterra SE 4WD**	3	2	2	2	3	2	3	3	3	2	5	4	34
	Oldsmobile Bravada	4	2	3	2	2	3	3	3	4	3	5	3	37
R	**Toyota 4Runner 4WD, V6**	3	2	3	2	3	4	4	4	4	4	5	4	42

Rating Scale: ✓-Best Buy; **R**-Recommended; 5-Excellent; 4-Above average; 3-Average; 2-Below average; 1-Poor

FULL-SIZE SPORT-UTILITY VEHICLES	Acceleration	Fuel Economy	Ride Quality	Steering/ Handling	Braking	Quietness	Driver Seating	Instruments Controls	Room and Comfort (front)	Room and Comfort (rear)	Cargo Room	Value for the Money	TOTAL
Cadillac Escalade	3	1	2	2	2	3	4	4	5	5	5	2	38
Chevrolet Tahoe 4WD, 5.3-liter V8	3	2	3	3	3	3	4	4	5	5	5	3	43
Chevrolet Tahoe Limited	3	2	3	3	2	3	3	3	5	5	5	3	40
Ford Excursion XLT 4WD, V10	3	1	3	2	3	3	4	3	3	5	5	4	39
✓ **Ford Expedition 2WD, 4.6 V8**	3	2	3	2	3	3	4	4	5	5	5	4	43
GMC Yukon XL	3	2	4	2	3	3	4	4	5	5	5	3	43
GMC Yukon Denali	3	1	2	2	3	3	4	3	5	5	5	2	38
Isuzu Trooper S w/Luxury Pkg.	3	2	3	2	3	3	4	3	4	4	5	2	38
Land Rover Range Rover 4.0 SE	3	2	4	2	3	3	4	3	5	5	5	2	41
Lexus LX 470	4	1	4	2	3	4	5	3	5	5	5	2	41
Lincoln Navigator 4WD	3	1	3	2	3	3	4	4	5	5	5	3	41
Mitsubishi Montero	3	2	3	2	3	3	4	3	4	4	5	3	39
R **Toyota Land Cruiser**	4	1	4	2	4	3	5	3	5	5	5	3	44

COMPACT PICKUP TRUCKS	Acceleration	Fuel Economy	Ride Quality	Steering/ Handling	Braking	Quietness	Driver Seating	Instruments Controls	Room and Comfort (front)	Room and Comfort (rear)	Cargo Room	Value for the Money	TOTAL
R **Chevrolet S-10 ext. cab 4WD, V6**	3	2	2	2	2	2	3	3	4	1	2	3	29
✓ **Dodge Dakota ext. cab 4WD, V8**	4	2	3	2	3	3	4	3	4	2	3	4	37
✓ **Ford Ranger ext. cab 4WD, 4.0 V6**	3	2	2	2	3	2	3	4	3	1	2	4	31
R **GMC Sonoma ext. cab 4WD, V6**	3	2	2	2	2	2	3	3	4	1	2	3	29
Isuzu Hombre reg. cab 2WD, 4-cyl.	2	3	2	2	2	2	3	3	4	—	1	4	28
✓ **Mazda B2500 reg. cab**	2	3	2	2	3	2	3	4	3	—	1	4	29
R **Nissan Frontier ext. cab 4WD, V6**	3	2	2	2	3	2	4	3	3	1	2	3	30
R **Toyota Tacoma ext. cab 2WD, V6**	4	3	2	2	3	2	4	3	3	1	2	3	32

FULL-SIZE PICKUP TRUCKS	Acceleration	Fuel Economy	Ride Quality	Steering/ Handling	Braking	Quietness	Driver Seating	Instruments Controls	Room and Comfort (front)	Room and Comfort (rear)	Cargo Room	Value for the Money	TOTAL
✓ **Chev. Silverado reg.cab 2WD, 4.8**	3	2	3	2	3	3	4	4	5	—	1	4	34
R **Dodge Ram 1500 ext. cab, 5.2 V8**	3	1	2	2	2	2	4	4	5	2	3	4	34
✓ **Ford F-150 ext. cab 4WD, 4.6 V8**	3	1	2	2	2	3	4	4	5	2	3	4	35
✓ **GMC Sierra ext. cab 4WD, 5.3 V8**	4	2	3	2	3	3	4	4	5	3	3	4	40
R **Toyota Tundra ext. cab 4WD, V8**	4	1	2	2	3	3	4	4	5	2	3	4	37

Rating Scale: ✓-*Best Buy;* **R**-*Recommended; 5-Excellent; 4-Above average; 3-Average; 2-Below average; 1-Poor*